NEWS, NU
& NONSENSE

THE BEST OF VICE MAGAZINE
VOL. II 2003–2008

NEWS, NUDITY & NONSENSE
Edited by Jesse Pearson and Amy Kellner
Designed by Evil Twin Publications
Archivery by Thomas Morton and Sigurd Kongshøj Larsen

Copyright © 2009 Vice Books

Vice Books
97 North 10th Street, Suite 204, Brooklyn, NY 11211
www.viceland.com

DISTRIBUTED BY:
powerHouse Books
37 Main Street, Brooklyn, NY 11201
PHONE 212 604 9074 FAX 212 366 5247
powerHouseBooks.com

FIRST EDITION 2009 / 10 9 8 7 6 5 4 3 2 1

ISBN: 978-1-57687-502-5

Thank you Satan and no one else.

OK, OK. Thanks also to Erik Lavoie, Alen Zukanovich, Andy Capper,
Thomas Morton, Amie Barrodale, Rocco Castoro, Chris Cechin, Gabi Sifre,
Liz Armstrong, John Martin, Ryan McGinley, Tim Barber, Patrick O'Dell,
Sam Frank, Polly Watson, all our contributors, and the staff of every edition
of Vice all over the world.

And thanks to Suroosh Alvi and Shane Smith for starting this magazine
15 years ago and continuing to support and pay its staff in a timely manner.

Finally, much gratitude to Jacob Hoye at MTV Books.

CONTENTS

A CONVERSATION BETWEEN JESSE PEARSON, VICE EDITOR IN CHIEF, AND AMY KELLNER, VICE MANAGING EDITOR

Amy: Describe the *Vice* office for the readers of this book. Give them some visual context.
Jesse: It's a bustling newsroom with lots of young go-getters running around with press cards in their fedoras. There are teletype machines going off and it reeks of ink and sweat. No, I don't know. I stay in my little cave, physically and psychically.

Yeah, we're sitting in your little room here and it's like an isolation chamber. Why don't you have more stuff on your bulletin board? It's 90 percent empty.
Bulletin boards are kind of show-offy. I feel like it would tell people stuff about me. I don't want someone to be like, "Oh, Jesse's into *this* because it's on his board." But I do have a few things on there: a Born Against patch, a Johnny Ryan drawing called *69-11* of an airplane and one of the Twin Towers giving each other head, a sticker from Chris Nieratko's New Jersey skate shop that says "NJ All Day," our designer Alen's phone number—

So you can call him and yell at him with ease?
No, I would never yell at Alen. He's Bosnian. He'd fly down here and chop my head off with a scimitar. And then there's also a drawing that you did of me that says, "Where's Jesse? At home!" and it's me in a wheelchair with my cat and a bong between my knees, playing *Call of Duty*—because when I play video games I sit in an old wheelchair.

How has being the editor of *Vice* for six years affected your life?
It's destroyed my body completely. I have all kinds of weird intestinal issues now. I have a gray beard. My back hurts all the time. I have carpal tunnel syndrome. My teeth are damaged from grinding them in my sleep from stress. I see a shrink now—I never did before. Basically, it's ground me down to a nub, a raw nerve.

Ha ha ha! I'm sorry, I shouldn't be laughing.
It's fine. I think it's funny too. Physically it's destroyed me and emotionally it's made me defensive and paranoid. I have this weird feeling that I shoot the magazine out into a black hole—I always refer to it as jerking off into a sock—and whoever reads it comes back to me with hatred and misconceptions. I think that it's me against the world. It's made me feel kind of like Travis Bickle. It's made me misanthropic and it's also exacerbated my alcoholism a couple of times. That's some real talk right there.

What's the most violent thing you've ever done, at least in the office?
I don't get too violent in the office because I'm sober here. I punch walls and stuff. Throw books. I don't yell at the staff that much anymore.

So why do you do the magazine if it's crushing you

to death?
Inertia. Inertia and apathy.

Oh come on, that's not true. You're not apathetic or you wouldn't get so angry. We have to be more positive now.
You're talking to the wrong guy.

Dude.
OK, OK. I'm 95 percent fucking with you. Of course I love doing the magazine. Without it, I would be teaching poetry at a community college in Philly or something and be totally miserable. All other magazines are shit, so it's not like I could edit a different one.

What advice do you have for aspiring writers?
"Don't do it." Just kidding. Don't sit at a desk all day. You have to go places and meet people and put yourself inside the story. Too many wannabe journalists rely on Google and secondary sources. You have to be like George Orwell or John McPhee and go be there.

Is that why we did the Immersionism Issue?
Yeah, but we act like we invented the word *immersionism* and we didn't. We certainly didn't invent the concept of it. It's just good journalism.

Is that the same as "gonzo"?
Gonzo doesn't really exist. A couple of early, great Hunter S. Thompson books were gonzo, but anything else called that after him is bullshit. This whole thing where the writer is just as important as the topic and is kind of a hedonistic, decadent person who inserts a lot of their faults and foibles into their story has become a crutch for egomaniacal hacks.

So what's new in part two of *Vice*'s greatest hits?
Well, firstly, we haven't forgotten about the roots of *Vice*. Maybe the difference is that now when we talk about shit and piss and sex, the articles are a bit longer. In this book what you're seeing is the original *Vice* ethos being opened up and expanded.

Is that because of 9/11?
Absolutely. I watched the towers come down with my own eyes, and as I saw them fall, I thought, "We

have to get serious in *Vice*. We have to address these problems in the world."

I can't tell if you're being serious.
No. Nothing is because of 9/11.

OK, so why did *Vice* start doing longer articles and heavier topics in addition to boobs and butts?
It's because the magazine reflects what the people who are making it are into at the time that any particular issue is being made, duh. If we were going to be a magazine about sex, drugs, and rock 'n' roll exclusively, then I wouldn't be able to do it because I don't give a shit about just that stuff anymore. I would have to be a 34-year-old man pretending to be a kid, which is pathetic. What you're seeing is a magazine evolve as the people who make it evolve. We still have articles where we make interns shit their pants, but how could I only care about that for the rest of my life? That would be the real sellout—pandering to some aging-punk-dude idea of what the kids want.

What's your all-time favorite issue of *Vice*?
Come on.

You should say the one where you went to the Indian reservation.
I guess I could, but yeah, I don't know... It's probably the Appalachian Issue.

That's kind of similar to the Indian-reservation one.
They're both about disenfranchised groups of Americans. Native Americans and poor white Americans.

I can see that as a theme in the magazine. We like marginalized people.
Yep.

Are there any articles from *Vice* that you look back on and are totally embarrassed by?
Probably, yeah. I think we shouldn't have backed electroclash so hard. Then again, that wasn't me.

Ha ha ha.
That was ridiculous. But no, there's not much I'm ashamed of. Again, I see it as an evolution. If we see stuff that's embarrassing, we have to face the fact

that it was what we were into when that issue came out. It's like a diary. If you cringe when you go back and read it, it's nobody's fault but your own.

What's your favorite article in the book? What would you recommend people turn to first?
There are two sides, I guess. The Harold Bloom interview is my favorite thing in terms of brains, but then I also really like the articles that involve girls and that are kind of dirty. I love Tierney, the girl who sells her bodily fluids, and I love Peteuse, the girl who farts on the internet. I don't get off on farts in real life, but reading about her farting in the interview kind of turns me on. Is that weird?

Yeah.
I think a lot of guys felt the same way. It's just so... you know what, let's not intellectualize it too much. I like the fart and I like the pee.

What about the *Vice* guides? We're known for those.
Sure. My favorites are the guide to shit and the guide to cute stuff that you did.

Thank you!
I also like your "Hey DJ, Fuck You" article because it got people so angry. You wrote an article about how DJing is a scam and anyone can do it, which was partially a joke, but also sort of true, and then... Well, you tell it. What kind of reaction did it get?

It got more comments on viceland.com than any other article before it, a lot of which were death threats or just personal attacks on me in general. People wrote stuff like "If I see you, I'm going to make your face leak blood" or "I'm going to kill you and burn your fat for fuel," stuff like that.
Ha ha ha, all because you said DJing is easy!

Yeah, they were really mad.
I don't think I've ever gotten death threats. I got a couple of letters that were death threat-y, but nothing really sustained.

Well, you helped me write a lot of the DJ piece, and you added in a lot of the more vitriolic stuff, so you can claim credit for at least half of my death threats. So I almost got you killed, basically.

Yup!
Sorry. What are your favorite articles in the book?

Oh, so many. Let's see. I love the sex and drugs chapters, and all the guides. The Dash and Dan hamster nest is a classic. Hamilton's thing about druggy Hasidim, the test to see how pure street drugs really are, all the girly stuff like the bulimia experiment and Jaimie Warren trying to be a "normal" girl... The Kokie's oral history, which was my idea—just a little bit o' trivia there. What else? "Home Surgery Party" is fascinating and gross. Fred Armisen's thing about his favorite foods is so stupid I love it. Your interview with your dad is quite an eye-opener. "Stay Soft! Sexy Men Try to Take Back the Night" is definitely my favorite title. And my least favorite piece is the interview with the Hiroshima survivor because that gave me nightmares for like a week. How's that?
That's a lot.

It's 'cause I like my job soooo much! What will volume three of *Vice*'s greatest hits look like five years from now?
It's just going to be an encyclopedia. A liquid encyclopedia that you inject intravenously and then it appears in front of your eyes. And there will be lots of pop-up ads and irritating noises.

Wait. Do you think print is going to die?
Not at all. I would never use one of those portable digital book-reader things. They're stupid looking. I have a feeling they're going to be linked to eye cancer in a few years. Plus I just like to hold books.

I like to lie on my side and read in bed.
Reading on your side is terrible for your eyes—and your brain. To read in bed, you're supposed to sort of sit there propped up by pillows.

What? No way, I've been reading on my side my whole life.
All I'm saying is you're going to regret it.

So is that the optimal recommended position for people reading this book? Propped up with fluffy pillows?
Either that or sitting on the toilet, totally nude. ∎

I
THE VICE GUIDES

Photo by Maggie Lee, V15N7, July 2008

ABSINTHENYC

THE VICE GUIDE TO SHIT

Photo by Glynnis McDaris

How often have you found yourself at some horrible family event having mind-numbing conversations with 300-pound behemoths about the minutiae of pregnancy and babies? If you listen closely you'll realize all their talk of the runs, abdominal pain, and relaxed deep-breathing techniques is, in essence, all about shit. They are just repackaging the graphically scatological in Mommyspeak. As Freud brilliantly pointed out: Penises, infants, and poop are all solid bodies that stimulate membranous passages. Every conversation anyone has ever had always comes back to shit. Therefore, young urbanite, we provide you with the A to Z of poo.

ANAL RETENTIVE

Freud postulated that our adult psyche stems from the relationship we cultivate with our feces as toddlers. Those who grow up ashamed or traumatized by pooping retain their feces unnaturally and later in life prize cleanliness, order, and high blood pressure. Anal expulsive tendency is the flip side, wherein kids shit everywhere with huge grins on their faces and grow up to live in a studio apartment strewn with laundry where they type up A–Z guides three days after the deadline and have maggots in their Cheerios

box (although, when captured in a jar, these white caterpillars with black heads seem to spin webs, so I'm not sure what the fuck they are—moth larvae?).

More Shit: **Aloe Charmin actually aggravates the anus with long-term use and leads to a very itchy bum with raw skin.**

BUNNY SHITS

Girls don't really shit. Instead they drop these little pellets in the bowl and call it a bowel movement. That's like dumping a Lego set out and saying you made a castle. What comes out of girls' bums is the fecal equivalent of a miscarriage. See, what happens is, food leaves the stomach in a series of runny little wet balls called chyme, which eventually mush together in the colon and dry into a firm log. (Note: Your colon reclaims approx. 1.5 liters of water this way every day.) However, girls dehydrate their systems with coffee, diet pills, Midol, mimosas, you name it... and there's not enough wetness in the stool to bind a turd together. A mild version of the above affliction is the cluster poop that looks like a bunch of grapes squished together.

More Shit: **Biggest colon ever had 40 pounds of impacted feces and is currently on display in Philadelphia.**

CHILDREN'S BOOKS

What's funnier than Elmo pinching a loaf? Children's books are a trip because they explain the sordid facets of life in this Technicolor world where "*Even Dinosaurs Divorce*." The winner is *Everyone Poops* by Taro Gomi, which is done with that "too cool to actually draw well" mentality that *Vice* celebrates when kids who spray-paint bubble letters transition to being "artists." Ms. Gomi's book relaxes anal-retentive kids about shit, raising the Zen question "What does whale poop look like?" The final spread, showing a lion, gorilla, giraffe, goose, pig, and little Asian boy all shitting in solidarity, should be the next pictograph on interstellar satellites.

More Shit: *Cloaca* **was built by this guy from Belgium and it's a replica of the digestive system that is fed an actual meal, and 27 hours later, excretes a poop. It's 33 feet of tubes, pipes, glass jars, pumps, motors, and weird shit. Apparently someone figured out this is "Contemporary Art" and you can buy this shit at www.cloaca.be. Just don't tell the post office. Mailing feces is a felony.**

DIGESTING CORN

Yes, Dorothy, we do digest corn. If you root through your poo and pull out one of those so-called "undigested" pieces you'll notice that only the outer husk remains. The kernel inside is gone. This outer sheath is so fucking tough it inspired bulletproof Kevlar.

More Shit: **Dead bacteria makes up a third of your poop's weight. The rest is indigestible fiber, fats, intestinal mucus, cells sloughed off from your bowel's lining, dead blood cells, and a whole bunch of toxic compounds.**

ENEMAS AND COLONICS

These are very beneficial and important if you are a fucking idiot who doesn't know anything about science. Enemas are for show. All they do is make your inner ass look nicer for, say, a severe butt reaming later on (like straight people plan anal sex that far ahead). They make you shit because they put saline in your rectum which draws water in and helps lube out stool but they really only flush out the five-inch pouch of your rectum and can't reach the colon. Colonics, on the other hand, flush out your large intestine, where, according to wackos, five pounds of undigested red meat and ten pounds of hardened, impacted feces line your walls. The medical community (i.e., those who actually went to school) says this is nonsense.

More Shit: **Ebola liquefies your inner organs, which you then shit out as endless diarrhea.**

FLOATERS VS. SINKERS

You don't need to take a trip to the Russian baths to know that fat floats. Most vegetarian poops sink because they don't have the animal fat content, which lowers the specific gravity and allows for flotation. Some claim trapped gas leads to floaters, but that's not possible, as most gas formation is caused by bacteria nibbling on your already-formed stool. It's all about the fat content. Which is why floaters are soft as downy pillows.

More Shit: **Fiber isn't about creating more mass to push things along, but rather its function is to absorb water and therefore bring hydration to your colon. Not enough water is the real source of constipation.**

GAS

Farts are formed by friendly bacteria that live in your colon and eat the nutrients left in your stool that weren't absorbed by the small intestine. The bacteria give off the vitamins B and K, in addition to ten liters of gas. Your body absorbs the nutrients and expels the gas it doesn't want to the tune of one-to-three pints of flatulence a day. Anytime sugar makes it to the colon (sucrose, fructose, lactose) it's a bacteria feeding frenzy and therefore, fart city. Besides obvious shit like beans, you also get a lot of farts from cabbage, onions, cauliflower, dairy, bananas, and apples. Lactose intolerance is when your small intestine (which absorbs nutrients) fails to consume the sugar in milk, which the bacteria in your large intestine (aka colon) feast on. If you've ever heard Perry Caravello after a glass of milk you know how severe this ailment can be.

More Shit: **Gum that you swallow does not stay in your stomach for the next 40 years. It comes right out, because the gastrointestinal tract is constantly secreting mucus and shedding, leaving your gum nowhere to stick.**

HEROIN

Sick of having to go shit every day? Forget Kaopectate, heroin will dry out your gastrointestinal tract instantly because it tells the peristaltic propulsive momentum of your intestines to slow down from 12 waves a minute to "whenevs" (we're quoting your ass here). Drugs suppress the activity of the bowels, and this is why Elvis had a swollen colon. At five inches in diameter, it was twice the normal size and packed with feces so ancient they had turned ash white. Despite popular health-food propaganda, Elvis's fried banana/PB&J diet didn't have shit do to with it.

More Shit: **Highbrow insult of the month—Feculent (adj): To be full of shit.**

ITCHY ANUS

Do you have an itchy asshole? Well, if you've ruled out wiping material, there's a good chance pinworms and your subconscious are to blame. You see, the pinworm reproduces by laying eggs in your butt crack, which later hatch in your mouth. Amazingly, they figured out to irritate your ass every morning at around 5 AM (no joke) while you are sleeping, so that you unconsciously scratch your butthole and then your mouth. I know it's scary, but don't freak out. These little buggers live in your intestines and can be cured rather easily.

More Shit: **Interesting fact—the FDA allows for one piece of rat shit per 50 grams of food product. The guy who came up with this guideline is so gnarly and grody he ought to change his name to Gnarles Grodin.**

JAPANESE PERVERTS

And you thought Germans were bad. What do you say about a country with vending machines of soiled school-girl panties and automatic miniature bidet squirters inside high-tech toilets? This is the place where Hiroyuki Nishigaki's hipster coffee table book *How to Good-Bye Depression: If You Constrict Anus 100 Times Everyday. Malarkey? Or Effective Way* is already in its fifth reprint. Shit, there's even restaurants where you can order the freeze-dried feces of pretty girls pictured on the menu. Sort of like a formal, sit-down version of the Jack in the Box disaster (remember that? The E. coli outbreak that came from feces in the ground beef?).

More Shit: **Jif will get you excused from military conscription. To prove his mental unfitness for duty in Vietnam, Frank Zappa squeezed peanut butter up his ass prior to the draft physical. During the exam, he casually put a finger up his bum and then sucked off the brownness.**

KELLOGG, JOHN

The Corn Flakes guy is the biggest scat legend next to Mel Torme. Aside from the Cleveland Steamer, he basically pioneered every rectal phenomenon you've ever heard of. Surmising that all good health revolves around defecation, he invented breakfast cereal (i.e., daily bulk laxative), massive colonics, and warm bacteria-rich yogurt enemas. Nowadays the current alternative-medicine guru lunatic is the best-selling bearded pussy Andrew Weil, who claims fecal encrustation of the colon is a myth and that anyone into colonics does so for either sexual gratification or because they have the same "it's dirty" neurosis that makes women douche.

More Shit: **Keep your left hand for wiping and your right hand for eating, otherwise the locals will become irate and your pleasantly debauched sojourn as a heroin-addled bisexual expatriate in Northern Africa will end in bloodshed.**

LAXATIVES

Despite bulimics crossing their fingers and hoping the laxatives they just took are going to shoot that ice cream cake right through their system unabsorbed, they're probably just ejecting last night's dinner prematurely. Ex-Lax, Dulcolax, Senocot, and the like speed up intestinal contractions, but most of the stuff they shoot out is old,

digested shit that's already done its damage. If it's green and it burns like hell then congratulations, you managed to stop some food from being digested. If it's pooey then you're still going to get fat.

If you're not doing it to lose weight and you just want your poo to come out easier, you're better off with things that draw water to your colon, like milk of magnesia and saline. Stool-softener suppositories melt away your turd, true, but the glycerin burns your asshole worse than fire. If you really want it to slide out of there drink baby oil and you'll notice it travels through your system and coats your stool, enabling it to slip out like butter. As for bulk laxatives comprised of fiber, good luck—they take days to work.

More Shit: **Leaning forward and bearing down exerts the most abdominal force in pushing out a turd. Just imagine yourself squatting in a downhill-skiing position. This is why hovering over a public toilet results in the biggest shits.**

MODERN SEWAGE

Treatment involves primarily skimming off "floatables" and then secondarily oxygenating the liquid filth to promote bacteria growth and waste breakdown. The solid end result is termed "sludge," and for years has been polluting oceans (dumping), ground water (landfills), and the atmosphere (incineration). That was until Congress started banning some of this. Now the easiest way to get rid of all this human waste is by following Asia's lead. Since 1992 the EPA has renamed sludge "beneficial biosolids" and is campaigning for this new fertilizer in American farming. The fact that every worldwide disease epidemic is traced back to Chinese farms doesn't seem to be worrying people too much. Incidentally, you're not supposed to flush condoms because they don't break down during sewage treatment and often slip past the filters, right into Lake Michigan. However, if you pull out of her ass and it's so covered in shit it curls up like an elf shoe, then by all means turn that sucker inside out and flush it.

More Shit: **Magazines make shitting fun. That's why you can read the majority of *Vice* articles in the time it takes to have a poo. Ironically, this is one of the few articles that is too long for one sitting. You need to bookmark it with toilet paper. That's ironic too.**

NOT-FUNNY PLACES TO POOP

On the beach in Goa (locals squat in front of you and the tide carries it out—thanks!), semi-concealed in a phone booth, atop the plastic wrap someone placed over the rim and under the seat, in a condom that's sent floating down the lazy river of a water park, in the commode inside your holding cell, anywhere in Astor Place (you need a caged canary to safely enter the Barnes & Noble restroom, Starbucks is junkie central with vein-obscuring dim red lights, and Kmart's toilets are apparently a great place to hang out and menacingly sway back and forth if you're homeless).

More Shit: **Nitrate kills the bacteria responsible for spoilage and allows hot dogs, cold cuts, and beef jerky to sit around for months. Unfortunately, this same toxin poisons your bowels, so it's best allowed to form naturally, which happens anytime a food is smoked, BBQ'd, or cured.**

OH SHIT!

Whilst perusing for potty books, I came across a gem of young-adult reading material titled *Daddy's Roommate*. The cover shows some beefcake young lad wearing a tank top in a rowboat along with his middle-aged, pencil-mustached new BFF. Of course on page one Mommy and Daddy get divorced. Shortly thereafter we visit Daddy's new apartment and meet Daddy's new friend, who is anally vacuuming whilst wearing a "Le Theatre" T-shirt. Later that day Daddy gets in a big fight with his roommate after finding an ironing stain on his white dress shirt. However, don't fret, young reader, because Daddy and the new "roommate" cuddle and make up on the next page. I now understand the footnote in *Saga of the Volsungs*, where it explains that in medieval Norse culture the worst possible insult was to be called "passively homosexual."

More Shit: **"One that got away"— that regret right before we flush a mammoth bowl snake eating its own tail, where you wonder if the one-hour-photo guy will notice the photo you just snapped.**

PARISIAN SEWER FLOTILLA

Directly underneath the historic sidewalks of Paris, a war is raging. These guys cruise around the sewers in barges atop a foul brown river looking for accumulated "shit dams" that could clog the ancient system. When they find one, a dude hops into the deep effluent and goes to work shoveling mushy crap downriver. When not battling typhoid or sewer gators, these civil servants are available on call to look for and sometimes actually find wedding rings that slip down the drain.

More Shit: **Proctologists' top finds: vibrators, salt and pepper shakers, pens, candles, a tapered chandelier lightbulb, and a glass bottle, shattered by the patient's attempt to retrieve it themselves (try not to shudder when picturing that).**

QUIT PUSHING

Seriously, have you ever heard of rectal prolapse? It's when your ass muscles are super-Kegeled from straining with chronic constipation and you exert so much force that your rectum ejects out Uranus and turns inside out. This is most common during childbirth. Of note, 90-year-old gynecological manuals suggest manually prolapsing a patient's rectum by placing two fingers inside her vagina and pushing down and backwards against her... Suffice it to say, it sounds like some clinical celebration of womanhood that lesbians confuse with hot sex.

More Shit: **Questionnaire results: 1/4 of people stand to wipe, 3/4 of people check soilage on TP to determine if another wipe is warranted, and, by majority, women fold toilet paper whilst men crumple.**

RECTAL PYROMANIA

The fart stench is a combination of a few gases, chief among which are skatole, hydrogen sulfide, and methane. To deal with the environmental damage from 280 liters of methane-laced cow farts in America every day, some farm towns are going beyond Thunderdome and have harnessed "cow power" by fermenting their cattle dung to produce methane gas, which in turn fuels a power generator. When you light a match in the shitter, however, the methane is too dissipated to be burnt. Instead, the sulfur receptors in your nose get overloaded by the burning match head, deactivating the characteristic fart bouquet. That's why it doesn't work with lighters.

More Shit: **Roto-Rooter jobs usually involve recovering personal items lodged in the toilet (65 percent of the time). Recent top finds: vibrator, six-foot boa constrictor (alive), complete bedspread, seven-foot rattlesnake, piranha, and a working Timex watch.**

SIR THOMAS CRAPPER

Mistakenly credited with inventing the flush toilet, he was a mysterious figure in British toilet manufacturing who attained notoriety when American servicemen noticed his imprint on English toilets during WWI. Hence the birth of "the crapper." The "Sir" makes no sense as he was never knighted, but he did install plumbing for Queen Victoria.

More Shit: **Swollen Colon: name of the tuxedo-clad prom band comprised of the Walkmen and the French Kicks.**

TOILET SEAT DISEASES

Slut Alert! Slut Alert! You know Marcia who got mono from the loo on the Greyhound bus and missed junior prom? Total bullshit. Because according to microbiologists, it's impossible to get mono, AIDS, chlamydia, hepatitis B and C, genital herpes, gonorrhea, or anything from a toilet seat. These bugs just don't live on your thighs and buttocks. Actually, the transmission of disease in the bathroom comes from touching the faucet handle (people wipe and then... see?) or the aerosol mist from a flush that settles on your toothbrush. Yet toilet-seat protectors are a $2 billion worldwide industry, with the top-end model being the mountable Hygen-A-Seat, which comes in a shoulder bag. It's really just an eerie "personal yet shared" mindfuck, like hearing all about your girlfriend's "big slut" phase from five years ago.

More Shit: The water in the Southern Hemisphere doesn't flush in an opposite direction to the clockwise Northern Hemisphere flushes. Thanks to *Vice* Australia, we now know the Coriolis Effect is just bullshit invented for extra credit on geography tests.

URGE TO GO

It takes about 21 hours to graduate a poop (3 hours in the stomach + 6 hours in the small intestines + 12 hours in the large intestines). However, mass movements in the system happen 20 to 40 minutes after each meal (or coffee) to make room for the incoming. Solid, processed movements wind up in the pouch at the end of the colon, and when the rectum fills up to 25-percent capacity (200 grams), your inner butthole sphincter automatically relaxes. From this point on, you are consciously in charge of holding your outer brown eye shut. This semi-full trigger is also why a finger up the bum makes you wanna poo. In fact, doctors often refer to "digital stimulation," which is a natural laxative provided by slipping a lubricated finger into your bum, like an upside-down gag reflex.

More Shit: Urban Myths—that one about the guy who wrapped himself in plastic wrap and climbed underneath a rest-stop outhouse at the Grand Canyon? Not true. Montezuma cursing the water with his foul revenge? True.

VIOLENT RUNS

Stringy, watery stools are caused when your body senses there is something wrong with the food you ate, but it's too late to puke. Its reaction is to cut down on the time spent drying in the colon and just eject the crap before your body has a chance to reclaim its own water. This is why dehydration kills so many people with the runs in the Third World. However, if you're stressed, scared shitless, took stimulant laxatives, or have a viral, bacterial, or parasitic invader the transit time of your small intestine goes into overdrive. Meaning the excrement exits your system before the caustic bile has had a chance to break down. This results in burning, often-green squirts that scorch your sphincter. Foods known to trigger diarrhea: figs, prunes, chocolate, a thousand beers, shitty coke.

More Shit: Viz's Dr. Poolittle, who only talks to animals about constipation. Johnny Fartpants is good too.

WATER-FREE, NON-ELECTRIC, SELF-COMPOSTING TOILETS

Yeah, during the "freedom" of the Northeast blackout I was circle-drumming around a bonfire and scratching my dreadlocks thinking, "How can I be a bigger hippie douchebag?" Then I looked through *Dwell* magazine and

was like, "Yes!" No, but seriously, the next day some hippie rode by us on a bike and yelled, "It takes a blackout for you to see your freedom!" Then he pedaled one more block and turned around to look back.

More Shit: Wet Wipes were once considered the celebrity ass-wipe material, but the chronic dampness leads to an irritated bum rash in need of a wadded-up TP "manpon."

X

I always hated that band. They sounded so gay doing those perfect harmonies. Why did anyone call that punk? They sounded more like some Northern California cult chanting about the imminent apocalypse. Anyway, I wanted to find out what their shit was like because X is the ultimate test for an A–Z list, so I called up John Doe and he said, "What? Who is this?" and hung up.

More Shit: Xeri, Xane, Xevi, and any other Anglo names reworked with the Chinese letter for "Shh" are fucking cool as xit.

YELLOW TURDS

Why is shit brown? Basically food leaves the stomach and immediately mixes with green bile, thus forming gooey green chyme. From thereon the bile oxidizes to brown during its trip down the digestive pathway. After neon green it turns to gray, then mustard yellow, then finally light brown when it reaches your rectum. If it stays too long in the rectum, it will continue to oxidize to a dark brown. Tar black poop is a bad sign, as it signifies digested blood, meaning you have internal bleeding. But don't freak, because overdoing iron supplements is also a cause of black poop. Amazingly blood-red poop isn't that dire, because it means you're bleeding somewhere past digestion, namely your rectum. For a concise primer on the rectal rainbow, just attend childbirth. There every shade and consistency of poop will come flying out.

More Shit: Your body will always find a way. If your poop chute is chronically backed up, say due to a large impacted stool, new pathways will form going from your rectum to a freshly created hole in your butt crack. These additional anuses are very grossitating and go by the name "fistula-in-ano."

ZELNORM

A new prescription drug specifically for women who suffer from fake shits (see B). Basically it does the opposite of heroin and tells the wave-like propulsion of your intestines to "giddy up," but not as violently as a stimulant laxative.

More Shit: Z, the TV miniseries about aliens in human form eating rodents and looking all Berlin cool, was "the shit" and doesn't get enough props—it's like a watchable *Liquid Sky*. Oh wait, that was *V*. ∎

COUNT CHOCULA III

THE VICE GUIDE TO PARTYING

Party hosting isn't something one can just dive into headlong and willy-nilly. You don't throw a baby into the deep end of an Olympic pool with five-pound weights tied to its tiny legs (unless you want it to die), do you? As a *partymeister*, you have to be ready for any eventuality, such as running out of mixers or the token tranny slut not giving 100 percent on her blowjobs. You also need to have a clear schedule, divided into hourly increments, and you need to run that shit like a fucking drill sergeant. Don't believe me? Just try having a party without some rules. You'll have a bacchanalian free-for-all on your hands, and nobody wants that.

I am a party commando. I know the whys, hows, and whozits of every genus of shindig, soirée, and throwdown. You are a pathetic novice, so I'll start you off easy. Here's an idiot-proof recipe for party perfection. This is my formula for a Drug Pig, Shitty Coke, F-List House Party. I also have guides for an Unforgettable Babes—None Lower Than an 8—Cookout and All of Your Best Friends on the Beach in Aruba in Late Spring, but there's no way you're ready for those yet.

Photo by Vito Fun

First, you'll need an occasion. Don't be afraid—it can be anything. For the group of partygoers we'll be looking at today, the occasion was "Tuesday night." Location is equally important. For the sort of party taught here, the ideal apartment will have at least two asshole roommates who will come out from their bedrooms to harsh you out every ten minutes. They have "exams tomorrow" and don't like when drunk girls puke in their rooms. You will also need a miniscule living room, badly ventilated, and a kitchen with a working electric stove (more on that later).

Now to the guest list. Parties, just like life, thrive on variety. Write that down. I want you to think of your guests as little chess guys that you have to maneuver into what I call a "result encounter," which is a drink, any drug, a sex act, a fight, or barfing. Additionally, you'll need to think of your guests algebraically. Can Guest A suck Guest B's penis? And can Guest B, in turn, disgust Guest C so badly that she vomits? Can Guest D snort coke off Guest B's balls? The answers to these questions should all be a resounding YES.

Here are some of the types you'll need to invite.

TRANSSEXUAL: Pre-op is good, but post-breast implants, pre-gender reassignment is PERFECTION. All transsexuals are slutty, so don't worry about that. This guest is a very high priority and should be catered to accordingly. Put her first in the queue for cocaine and drinks. Tell her how pretty she is. Touch her a lot.

GUY WHO WILL FUCK TRANS-SEXUAL: He is your #2 guy, your party wingman. If the tranny doesn't feel loved, she will leave. Then you're fucked. If you don't have a tranny chaser in your six-degrees network, I have one word for you: craigslist.com. We posted there for this party ("Guy wanted to fuck tranny in ass") and had 20 respondents within an hour. I picked this particular man because he has the biggest ring through his cockhead that I have ever seen.

WANTON DRUNK SLUT: This is a surprisingly tough one to find. Once you get a reliable drunk slut in your life, someone who will shed her clothes and let a room full of people write on her with indelible markers at the drop of a hat, hold onto her like a dinghy in the perfect storm. She is a true party staple and will prove again and again the fact that nudity at a party is as contagious as the bird flu. Just as the night begins, give her (and only her) a handful of shrooms.

WACKY LONELY GUY: He sucked in seventh grade when he listened to They Might Be Giants and wore bright yellow sweatpants, but now he is grown-up and gagging for attention. This means that he will commit any repulsive act if you pat him on the head and tell him people like him.

CLASSIC ALCOHOLIC: The linchpin. Without someone

to pound "mixed" drinks that are 95-percent gin, talk ear-searing personal shit about everyone, rip off their shirt (in a nonsexual manner), and spray barf everywhere, your gathering is not legally allowed to be defined as a "party." She also serves as a human party clock.

THE CONCIERGE: This should be your best friend, but you must hold the power in the relationship. He will be required to function as butler, mediator, clean-up crew, and go-to guy for the duration of your event.

…And that, my sober friends, is the A-Team. Fill out the rest of the party with people whom you have seen so wasted they were unable to walk at least five times. And nobody too attractive—stick between 4s and 6s. They are usually fun enough to do whatever after a few drinks.

HOUR ONE

The event needs to start a bit quietly. A whimper, not a bang. Gather everyone in the main reception area (your living room). Pour the first drinks for your guests, as people tend to be shy with the booze when getting started. A good guideline for a plastic-cup drink is four fingers of liquor combined with enough mixers to mask the taste. After the initial drink, guests may be invited to serve themselves. They will already be little liquor-pigs by that point, and can be relied on to mix strong. Don't be afraid to deploy your concierge to help loosen things up either. Make him rub some feet, light cigarettes, and make introductions.

HOUR TWO

As the second hour of your party begins, some things need to be brought out and offered in turn to all your guests: heroin, Xanax, speed, meth, tranny tits, and most importantly, cocaine. The accepted rotation is counterclockwise, but it is also de rigueur to allow the person closest to the tranny to have first access to her tits. As for the coke, follow the standard social ladder, from the top down. Your priority is the tranny. Get her high first. Then comes the guy who is going to fuck her (though you have to moderate his intake if he's going to get it up). It's good to put a witty fag third in the coke line. Loosen his tongue up so the bon mots will start to flow.

HOUR THREE

Until 1975, it was generally thought gauche to allow sexual escapades to begin earlier than Hour Four. In these headier times, however, you won't have much luck getting your guests to wait past the three-hour mark. Therefore, expect some overlap between this and the previous phase. Although the tranny and her knight in shining armor are furiously necking while she jerks him off, the lower caste

of guests still haven't received their rations of cocaine. The best and most gracious way to solve this snafu is to have the remainder of the coke snorted off the tranny-chaser's balls. Many drunk sluts will feign horror when first offered cocaine au jus, but all will relent when they realize it is the custom of your house.

HOUR FOUR

By now, your party should have enough kinetic energy to be traveling smoothly without much interference. Sit back and enjoy the fruits of good hosting. Is the alcoholic taking her clothes off? Excellent. She should be throwing up into a bucket within 10 to 20 minutes of initial nudity. If so, you have done a better job than most experts did their first time around. Appoint the concierge to pat her head and keep her hair out of the puke.

HOUR FIVE

It's a good idea to present an unexpected victual to the revelers around this time. You are approaching the peak of the party, and the right incentive can push things irretrievably over the cliff into utter orgiastic abandon. We recommend hotknifing some opium in the kitchen. Your concierge should have arranged for the tar and should also be adept at smoking techniques. Obey the same preferential rotation as employed earlier with the cocaine.

HOUR SIX

You'll need to get back off the bench and take the reins again now, as the peak of the party is upon you. This is the wacky guy's time to shine. I suggest writing all over him and strapping a raw chicken to his waist so that his penis dangles inside it (he may piss inside it later on). It is also the hour to fully avail yourself of the drunk slut. A good icebreaker is to enlist the more normal girls at the gathering to suck one of her tits each. By now, she should be so high on mushrooms that her enthusiasm will lead half the party into a pasty white dog pile on your roommate's bed. Instruct the concierge to keep undesirable partygoers (i.e., wacky guy) away from the orgy room.

HOUR SEVEN

Not to be Sir Thomas Bringdown III, but every social function has a shelf life. Leave it on the boil for too long and it will start to stink. There is a surefire method to know when it is time to draw a curtain on the night. When the alcoholic barfs all over your roommate's little loveseat and her own arm, continue the party only at your own peril. Seriously, you can set your clock by the alcoholic's stomach. When the contents of it go, everyone else should too. Give the remaining coke to the concierge (he'll need it to stay up all night cleaning up puddles of alcoholic puke and tranny-chaser semen). ■

PIERRE BERTON

THE VICE GUIDE TO CANADA

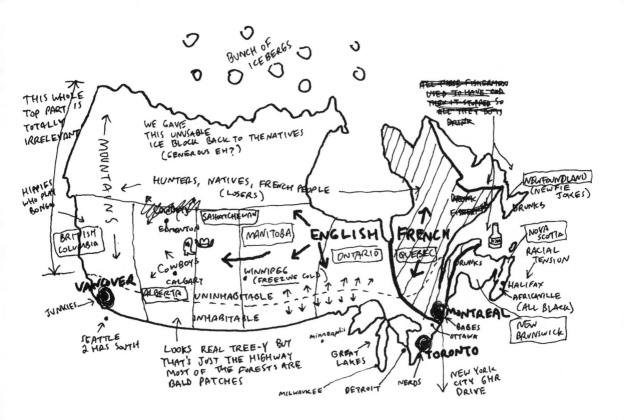

That's right America. Canada is not cool. It's bigger than you, correct. It's home to great things like *poutine* (fries, cheese curds, gravy, repeat), Chester Brown's *Louis Riel* comics, *SCTV*, Rush, Jack Black, Gordon Lightfoot, *Kids in the Hall*, hockey, David Cronenberg, The Dears, The Stills, *Ren & Stimpy*, French girls, basketball, and Nardwuar the Human Serviette, but the truth of the matter is, nobody lives there so there's just not that much to say about it. In fact, we can sum up Canada by focusing on the only three cities that live there: Vancouver, Toronto, and Montreal.

VANCOUVER—HIPPIE

Vancouver is on the very, very left-hand side. If you read about it online it sounds cool because pot and prostitution are basically legal. You'll even hear the board of tourism call it Vansterdam. However, if you ever end up going there, you'll see it's just a pile of junkies and potheads. The worst part is, the bars are only allowed to be open for 12 hours a day and, since all the drunk natives insist they get to start at 11:00 AM, there's nowhere to go after 11:00 PM. That means you can either wander around dark streets like Hastings and look at dead heroin addicts (one dies every day in Vancouver) or you can go home, smoke pot, and watch TV. The problem with the latter is, you're sitting around with 15 people sneering at how gay *America's Funniest Home Videos* is, like it's supposed to be good or something. It's for old people and kids, you assholes.

SO WHY SHOULD I GO THERE? This is the only place in Canada where there's so many natives that if you walk into an all-native bar by accident the music stops and everyone stares at you like that part in *Animal House* where dude accidentally walks into that black bar. Plus, the nude beaches are funny.

TORONTO—ENGLISH

One hundred-fifty hours of driving to the right brings you to Toronto. Jokingly referred to by Billy Bragg as "America's big thumb," Toronto contains both the lamest and the most patriotic Canadians there are. Though the population is about 5 million they all act like those small-town kids that tried to act big-city because Paris Hilton and Nicole Richie brought TV cameras and everyone's looking.

Here's why: In 1970, Quebec declared war on English Canada by blowing up some stuff and kidnapping some politicians. That scared the shit out of every English person in Quebec, so they all moved to Toronto. Almost overnight, Toronto went from a hick little lake village to New York City-size. That seems to have fucked with their heads, because all the males have regressed into this hillbilly, hoser mentality where they drink beer all day dressed as lumberjacks and call their friends by their surnames. The females, on the other hand, have decided to failingly grasp at big-city life by wearing tiny knapsacks and platform shoes and saying things like, "It's, like, ooooh kaaye." Both of them perfectly sum up how blindly liberal all Canadians are. They push the leftist agenda not because they believe it, but simply because it seems un-American. For example, Torontonians are so chuffed with themselves for living in the most culturally diverse city in the world (more than any American city) you can almost smell their balls. Of course, whenever you ask them why that's so great, they go on about being able to order Turkish food one night and Thai the next, so that means the merits of diversity are measured by how well they serve white people. What a bunch of fucking douchebags, eh?

SO WHY SHOULD I GO THERE? It's fun to dress up in bad outfits and go for a cornball vibe. You have dinner at the Hard Rock Café in the CN Tower and then go get drunk in the gigantic Rolling Stones-themed bar called the Stones Bar.

MONTREAL—FRENCH

French people, aka Peppers (so named due to their affinity for Pepsi-Cola), have the rest of Canada wrapped around their little fingers. Despite the fact that they are only 20 percent of the total population and all they do is sit around and drink wine in leather pants, most of Canada's prime ministers (presidents) are French. English Canada also insists everyone in every province (state) speak French, even if there are no Peppers to be seen for miles. They also funnel millions of dollars in grants into Quebec and plead for a "unified Canada," even though Quebec laughs in their face and has tried to secede about 80 times. You have to hand it to them, they have pulled in the most cash for the least work and still get away with calling themselves "the niggers of Canada." An ironic faux pas, considering most Quebecois blacks are bourgeois Haitians with blazers and $200 socks. Peppers get away with it because Canadians could give less of a shit about race. For them it's all about French vs. English and righting the wrongs of Britain's colonialist past.

The history of Quebec is about 400 years old, and it goes like this: 1) Missionaries from France tried to convince the natives that "Jesus saves," so the natives killed them; 2) French soldiers came next and killed all the natives; 3) England tried to take it from the French soldiers, but everyone was getting killed so they gave the province to the French church; 4) soldiers started fucking all the remaining female natives, so the French church sent in whores (France didn't want them).

The result is a province with the hottest women (half native, half whore) and the stupidest men (all soldier) the world has ever seen. If you don't believe us, try going there in the spring. There are more strip clubs than in any city in the world and there is less work to do than in Margaritaville. If every American spent a June in Montreal, they would be embarrassed they ever said anything bad about their neighbor to the north.

SO WHY SHOULD I GO THERE? I just told you, moron. The spring is dense with eye candy. The architecture is hundreds of years old. The *saumon au sel gris* at L'Express is mouth-shattering, Supersexe, jack shacks, the list goes on…

If you are American and you are still reading this, you are either not an American or you are taking the longest shit of your life. We already summed up the whole country, but here's some more stuff to read until your liar American bowels are totally drained.

9 THINGS ABOOT AMERICANS AND CANADIANS

1. Americans call round ham "Canadian bacon" even though such a thing does not exist in Canada.
2. Americans don't leave at the end of the movie, and will sit there watching all the credits, even the logos.

Canadians aren't into credits and will write articles that go on for pages and pages under a made-up name.

3. Lots of Americans have never used a condom. Also, American girls aren't into blowjobs until the third date and insist on getting down to full-on slamming right away. Canadians fit into two groups: the English, who never fuck, and the French, who like to have about three orgasms before any penetration happens.

4. Americans rarely finish college and make you feel like a pompous asshole if you use a word like *sycophantic*. They don't know anything about any other country but their own, they have never been overseas, and they think reading is for gaylords.

5. Americans hate French people with a passion. If you speak French at an American French restaurant, people will freak out on you. They even get mad if you pronounce "croissant" right.

6. Americans know the full name and entire history of every actor in America, even Jason Bateman. This is related to No. 2. They love celebrities. Even smart girls will buy a copy of *InStyle* for the train and happily read about Woody Harrelson's bathroom.

7. Americans are weird about confrontation and would rather get you back secretly. Like, if you had done something to piss a guy off he would bang into you on the way out of the cafeteria and say, "Oh, sorry," so you couldn't do anything about it.

8. Americans are really, really into Thanksgiving and every city shuts down that day. America used to have the same day as Canada, but Roosevelt moved the day to November to encourage Christmas shopping. Americans don't seem to mind, even though you're supposed to be celebrating the harvest and what's being harvested in late November? Snow pies?

9. Americans hate being criticized and even homeless natives get mad when you point out things like No. 4. Canadian identity is so wrapped up in American criticism, Canadians spend most of their time in high school trying to come up with something better than, "At least we're not a bunch of uneducated Americans."

Basically, the main difference is this: Americans are weird about having their picture taken, and they want their name on everything because they think you're going to get rich off of them. The American dream used to be "work really hard at something and don't let people walk all over you and you will prosper." Then that dude who invented Pet Rocks got rich because he was smart about copyrights. After that, everything changed. Now the American dream is "getting rich is a lottery and you never know what's going to catapult you into prosperity so make sure you copyright and get credit for every little thing you do, no matter how irrelevant, and you will become as rich as the Pet Rock guy." Canadians live in a communist country so even if they never get credit for anything, they're all looking at free Medicare and indexed pensions from here to eternity (no matter what that does to the dollar).

If you are still reading, you must be one of those weird Canadaphile Americans that rode the Trans-Canadian Railway and knows who Margaret Trudeau fucked. Let's just empty our whole load on your face so you never ask us about Canada ever again...

NORTHERN CANADA

The pioneers chased all the natives and frogs up to the top of the country, and now they span from coast to coast. The only thing to do up there is hunt, but the bugs are so insane it's almost impossible to hold onto your sanity. If you eat a sandwich, it's 30 percent black flies. If you take a shit in the woods, your ass will be covered in itchy freckles within about 20 seconds. It's hell on earth.

EASTERN CANADA

This used to be an okay place to live. It was mostly fishermen descended from the Irish, and there was some money to be made fishing cod. Then one day, for no particular reason, all the fish disappeared. Now all anybody there does is drink and do sad jobs like telemarketing and tech support.

HALIFAX

The Underground Railroad ended here, so it's about 50 percent black. There is a ton of racial tension, and one time it got so bad a bunch of black guys moved next door and started a town called Africaville that is 100 percent black.

CALGARY

There's a lot of oil and ranching here, and they have a big rodeo called the Calgary Stampede. It's weird to see full-on cowboys wearing the boots and the ten-gallon hats in the middle of Canada.

WINNIPEG

You have to give respect to anyone you meet from Winnipeg, because they live in the coldest place on earth. It's fucking -23°F (-31°C) for about six months of the year.

By the way, just so you know we're not another pile of ignorant Americans poking fun at this easy target, we'd like you to know that America sucks balls too. And so does Europe. In fact, the only bearable areas in the world are Montreal, New York City, Austin, Glasgow, Utrecht, Barcelona, Genoa, Languedoc, Paris, and Berlin. The rest of the world is filled with boring dipshits who like the Dixie Chicks and have fart in their hair. ∎

HEAVY METAL ALASTAIR, ANDY CAPPER, AND OMID FROM BATTLETORN

MOSH OR DIE

Who's the Best Thrash Mascot?

When he's not bawling about regret in $40,000-a-month therapy sessions like in *Some Kind of Monster*, Lars Ulrich likes nothing better than to bore people about how Iron Maiden and the New Wave of British Metal inspired the start of the thrash/speed metal revolution, changing music forever. The annoying millionaire is right. Not only did they influence the next ten years of riffs, solos, and lyrical themes, but Maiden's mascot, Eddie, ensured every imitator would have to have a mascot of its own.

Pre the boredom and bombast of death metal (early to-mid 90s), the goth pretentiousness of black metal (mid to late 90s), and the unbearable felch of nu-metal (now), thrash was the funnest form of metal, combining influences from punk, hardcore, and prog with lots of stuff to do with hell, spaceships, beer, futuristic disasters, and violence. Of course, none of that meant shit if they didn't have a mascot. Eddie went from a stupid skull head nicked from art school to an 80-foot giant that would lift Maiden's drummer into the sky and spin him around. If you want to follow in the footsteps of Maiden, you have to at least get Eddie's shoe size. Let's see who came closest.

RULES:

The mascot cannot have been confined to one album sleeve or one tour promotion. It has to have been a constant companion to the band and the fans, like Eddie. This is why Metallica's *And Justice for All* lady and Sodom's gas-mask guy from *Agent Orange* weren't allowed in the competition. Misfits, Samhain, and C.O.C. were also banned because, although they had their stickers on 90 percent of every thrash metal band's guitars, they weren't officially metal. If we'd have let them in, we'd have had to include the Descendents' Milo and fucking All's Allroy and that would lead to Marillion's jester guy. Motörhead was also banned because they are more rock and roll than metal. OK? No more fucking arguing. You have to have rules.

ANTHRAX (NYC, USA)

Invented by guitarist Scott Ian, the Anthrax "Not" guy would only appear occasionally throughout Anthrax's long and troubled career.

His main job was to signify the more light-hearted moments in the New York thrash kings' catalogue, such as the rap pastiche "I'm the Man" and the party thrash anthem "State of Euphoria." Looking a lot like one of those rubber-face puppets you'd buy from a toy store for $2 and get bored of in five minutes, he lacked any sort of menace at all. We hate him. For their more serious songs, Anthrax relied on Judge Dredd, from *2000 AD*.
1.4/10

ACCUSED (SEATTLE, USA)

Ah, Martha Splatterhead. The Accused used her up like the sleazy transvestite Eddie imposter she was. They ran her into the grave. She was on virtually every album cover and shirt they made from 1984 onward. While she did have the best tits of any thrash mascot, there's one little fact that we can't overlook—her name is Martha. So regardless of how many heads she could splatter, she still couldn't fuck with Eddie. We do give her credit for her longevity, though, and she's way tougher than Helloween's pumpkin (who we cut to put Martha in here).
8.84/10

Photos by Tim Barber

OVERKILL (NYC, USA)

Really badly animated in the video for "Hello From the Gutter" and not as far as I know named, a green flying skull was the mascot of Bobby "Blitz" Ellsworth's Overkill. He covered all the requisite thrash aesthetics in one lovingly created little package, i.e., aggression (scary sharp teeth), speed (wings), a sci-fi comic-book otherworldliness (the skull was green so obviously it didn't come from Planet Earth). Dude also had green eye lasers but his lack of hands would mean that he could carry no weapons so he would cause no threat to Eddie in a fight. Eddie would just duck and then plow him.

7.6/10

D.R.I. (HOUSTON, USA)

This is a design classic that deserves to be ranked alongside anything that Peter Saville did for Factory Records. D.R.I's chrome skankin' man told you all you needed to know about the band: They were punks who were also metal, and showed you the correct dance steps in the days before pit kung fu. Because he was so easy to draw on leather jacket/school books/venue walls, he had a slight advantage over Eddie. One thing, though—he never became an Egyptian God. Eddie did.

7.9/10

MEGADETH (LOS ANGELES, USA)

Vic Rattlehead was a skull with steel hooks embedded in his mouth and a steel plate bolted across his eyes in true metal style. In place from the start of the band's career, he was originally a photo on their *Killing Is My Business… and Business Is Good* album, then was painted by Thrash artist-in-residence Ed Repka for follow-up albums. He looked OK but was dropped in the 90s for some godawful sub-Hipgnosis nonsense. Though he's back now that metal nostalgia is filling venues once again, his deviance from the original path means he's just not in the same league as Eddie.

7.95/10

KREATOR (ESSEN, GERMANY)

This guy took a couple of albums to develop. He started on the band's *Pleasure to Kill* album as a scythe-wielding demon, courtesy metal artist Phil Lawverve. By *Terrible Certainty*—a fucking concept album about the AIDS crisis—he'd started to wear jeans and a leather jacket. Sadly, for *Extreme Aggression* he was dropped for a band shot. He would return periodically but they never even really gave him a name (they tried "Son of Evil" but later dropped it).

8.66/10

VOIVOD (CANADA)

Designed by drummer Away, the artwork centered around the concept of the Voivod and was a mix of sci-fi and an unhealthy obsession with insects, which perfectly summed up their odd mix of Tank, Motörhead, and Pink Floyd. As Away designed all the artwork for the band, they have retained a consistency throughout their 21 years. As they have become more prog over the years, the Voivod has kept pace. This is the only mascot that comes close to Eddie.

9.891/10

S.O.D. (NYC, USA)

The Skrewdriver factor is OK here because it's "funny" and they had a half-Eddie, half-G.I guy called Sergeant D who actually appeared in the horror movie *House*. He mainly existed to distract from the fact that the people in the band—pizza boy Billy Milano, *Muppet Show* reject Nuclear Assault guy Dan Lilker, and Anthrax's Scott Ian and Charlie Benante—were more like cartoons than the entire casts of *The Simpsons* and *Pokemon* combined. Total bullshit.

2.3/10

WINNER: VOIVOD (Sorry, it's nerdy but true.) ∎

Thanks to GenXGear.com.

MARY SECRET MYSTERYPANTS

STALKING FOR BEGINNERS

How to Ruin Someone's Life

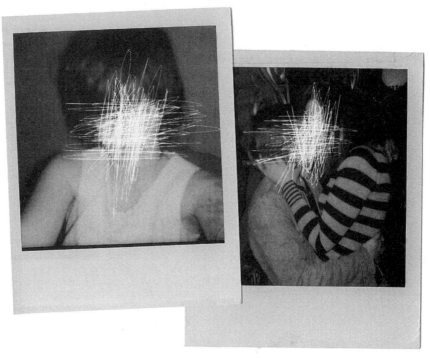

The author, and the author with her victim. She had to mutilate the Polaroids as part of the play.

I decided to pick a random stranger and stalk the shit out of him. Just for kicks. Here's what happened...

DAY ONE

I didn't want to stalk a friend of a friend. I needed to find some jock in a shitty bar. Me and my best friend headed out to the lame part of Montreal, to a bar you normally couldn't pay me to enter. There I saw my guy: blond-ish hair, ripped-up jeans, and a slick pair of shiny boots. Ew. My friend took off so I could be in complete control of the situation.

I pulled a chair up next to him, introduced myself, and bought him an incredible amount of drinks. Then I started telling him how wet he made me. He agreed to take me home with him. We had some pretty hardcore dark-alley oral sex, which actually ruled. You know when you take a piss in the shower? It felt THAT good. His tongue was as soft as a newborn lamb's coat.

Then we got to his place and he gave me the most pedestrian pounding I have ever had. Yawn.

After he fell asleep, I took down all the phone numbers in his cell while hiding in the bathroom. Mom, Dad, Susan, Rita, Jeff, and some guy named "Coke Delivery." Real subtle, dude.

I went back to bed with him and murmured, "I love you." He moved away from me. Everything was working as planned. He was getting stalked.

DAY TWO

I woke up fairly early, but he was already up and claiming

he had to go to work. I started hugging him and telling him that I had the best night of my life, and he just kind of stood there. I asked him for his phone number, and he said he didn't know what it was since he had just moved in. I knew it was a lie, but I said, "Fine, I'll just stop by sometime and we can hang out. I'd love to hang out with you, and I need more of this." Whereupon I tapped on his junk. He didn't say a word, but I could tell he was frightened. I also already had his phone number, stolen from his phone.

That night I showed up at his house piss-drunk at 4 AM with lipstick all over my face, and rang the doorbell six times. His roommate answered, and I ran in, jumped on my guy's bed, and started screaming, "TAKE ME, FUCK ME."

It was beautiful. He was almost crying from the stupefaction and he told me to leave. I begged him to come and sit on the porch with me to talk. I gave him a letter I wrote him along with several Polaroids. The letter is full of pyscho shit and it's half in French. That makes it even creepier somehow. Dude couldn't even speak. He was just like, "Please leave, you're fucking insane." I'm pretty proud, so this was the most awkward moment of my life, because I had to play it like a crazy whore with zero self-esteem. I kept telling him we were made for each other and that I wasn't able to take a shower since his scent was all over my body. He yelled at me, told me to leave again, and I ran into the house and hid under the covers in his bed, crying at top volume. His roommate came into the room and told me to leave. I could tell they felt awful for me. So I finally left, sobbing.

Once I got home, I laughed so hard I thought my head was going to fucking explode. I called him five more times (my number's blocked), leaving messages every time, that night. He doesn't know my full name, my address, or my phone number, so I don't think I can get in trouble. But I planned on fucking with him even more. Being a stalker is hard work, and I can't believe people can do this in earnest. It's exhausting. Every night during this experiment I slept like a log.

I decided that the next night, I would call his mom.

DAY THREE

Me: Hello, is this [name withheld, aka X]'s mom? I'm your son's new lover. How are you?

Mom [after 20 full seconds of complete silence]: I'm fine...

Listen, bitch, you're going to let him know that he better call me back or I'm gonna start with you for my new fireplace ornament. Get it?

Who are you?

A friend.

I thought I was going to puke for several hours after that call. I had never threatened anyone before that, and it felt awful. Now I know how Courtney Love feels.

DAY FOUR

I was sort of running out of ideas, so I decided to show up at his work wearing a T-shirt I had stolen from his house the first night we met. I actually looked kind of sexy in it, so I slapped myself in the face a few times to make sure I looked like I was on crack.

X's work was very close to my house, so I could actually take breaks from stalking him, come back home, have a coffee, watch the end of *Desperately Seeking Susan*, and get back on duty. I walked in front of the main window and waved for like an hour, then came in and waited for him to get off work.

His coworkers told me he didn't want to see me and that I had to leave. I started yelling, "I LOVE HIM, I'M PREGNANT WITH HIS BABY, PLEASE LET ME TOUCH HIM, PLEASE LET ME TALK TO HIM." Shit like that. He probably escaped through the back exit, because several minutes after they locked the front doors, my lover wasn't coming out.

I went home, cried, and tried to slash my wrists open. OK, no I didn't. Remember, I'm not really nuts. But I did take a shower and masturbate the fuck out of the shower pole.

DAY FIVE

I fell asleep after an intense night of drinking, only to be awoken by the ringing phone. It's X yelling at me, telling me he knows where I live and that if I don't stop harassing him, he'll call the cops. I just told him I loved him and hung up. Too tired to deal with him right now.

I wish I could have stalked him more, just for pure fun, but he called the cops. I was away for about three days, and once I got back to Montreal, my roommates announced to me that the cops had been to the house and asked to "discuss" something with me. I don't want to end up in jail or with a restraining order, so I called it quits.

Stalking is a real energy-sucker! I had no life for almost a week, spending all my time trying to get to this guy. You have to be completely insane to be a stalker. If anything, this experience has proven to me that I am not as crazy as I thought I was. Compared to the average stalker, I'm a pretty normal girl. Who knew? ■

[Handwritten letter:] You're pretty much messing with me And i'm convinced it's not your intention but you confuse me. I'm trying so hard to understand your views on things. Tes propos ne font parfois aucun sens et c'est presque comme si tu voulais en ajouter. a quelque chose de pourtant bien simple. you use million dollar sentences when you could just simply explain how you feel about me. you feel like drugs, i wonder what i'm doing. and i feel like an imbecile for trying constantly to understand. I'm tired. To me fatigue. I craved you so much, now i feel like this Situation is always going to be some sort of big cloud over my head. Following me around. I love to share thoughts with you i hope you enjoy my speaks. i speak in spanks mostly about nothing. I need some sort of goal, you're right. I now understand why the status has always been so important to me; because without it, i feel helpless, lonely. I hide behind a skull, every minute

BILLY BRAGG

THE VICE GUIDE TO BRITISH CUISINE

When people come to visit me from America, I often take them to a place where there are these amazing standing stones. It's like Stonehenge, but bigger. This stone circle is so enormous that there's a village in the middle of it. It's called Avebury. I always take American bands who came over to the UK there—everyone from Wilco to the Barenaked Ladies.

Once an American friend of mine, his parents, and I went to Avebury. We stepped into the local pub there for dinner, and written right up on the specials board they had listed "faggots stewed in their own juice." Then, under deserts, they had "spotted dick." Two English favorites. My American friends were more impressed with the menu than anything the druids made.

Maybe it will spoil it for all of you if I tell you what faggots really are, but I think it's best to clear this up now. So tell me—would it spoil the joke for you if I told you that faggots are just meatballs? And actually, I've never even eaten them.

I've had spotted dick though. It takes ages to clear up.

No, no—spotted dick is just a pudding. Do you know what suet is? It's kind of like a fatty pastry. Spotted dick is like that. One of the great things about living on this damp and cold island is that we have a real love of very stodgy puddings. They are a complete vice for us. The idea of a stodgy pudding with hot steaming custard on a winter's night? Mate, nothing can be finer than that. And spotted dick is one of the greats. If there were a place you could go and just have spotted dick, I would be binging on it all the time.

In Glasgow you can have a deep-fried pizza. They just fold it over and put it in the chip fryer. You can have a deep-fried haggis. Best of all, you can have a deep-fried Mars Bar. They just batter up a Mars Bar and fry it. Then you've got what they call "scrapes." It's a mess of leftover animal parts all fried up together.

I was on tour once, going up the Mississippi Valley. We were on the tour bus, which is like being on a submarine: You never know where it's going to surface. Whatever there is when you get out for a break, you've got to make the best of it. We ended up at a place in southern Illinois in the middle of the night. We walk in, there's a guy standing behind the counter, and I ask him, "Have you got any hot food?" He takes the lid off of a steam tray in front of him and there it is—scrapes! He just points at it and says, "Them's livers and them's gizzards." So to me there is a part of Illinois that is always Glasgow. ∎

ANSEL EGGLEFRANK

THE VICE DOS AND DON'TS OF PHOTOGRAPHY

A

Don't: Art school The only thing you will learn from four years of college photo classes is what not to do. You spend more time listening to anorexic rich girls talking about what a photo "means" than learning something practical like how to work a fucking camera.

Don'ts: Always taking photos, architectural photography, "advertorials," Ansel Adams calendars, alternative processes

Dos: Always taking photos, aerial photos, ambient light, automatic mode/auto-focus/aperture-priority

Photo by the author

B

Don't: Band photos What? Why are these four guys so mad at me? And why are they standing in front of a trash-strewn vacant lot? Who are you guys, a tough gang from the bad part of town?

Nope, you are every fucking band ever, and you are so boring to look at it makes me dizzy.

Don'ts: Black & white, blurry photos on purpose, photos in/of bathtubs, burning (and dodging), bums, Brooklyn, blinking

Dos: Blogs, breasts, bunny ears (when you hold up two fingers behind someone's head in a photo)

C

Don't: Cyanotypes and Cross-processing Both of these are alternative processes, which is a required course in most college photo programs. It's like forcing a painting class to forage for their pigments amid nuts and flowers. "Alternative" means experimenting with the flexibility of the print-film process or something. Cyanotypes are all blue and splotchy. Cross-processing is where the colors are supersaturated, like that movie *21 Grams*. Like using filters in Photoshop, it always looks bad.

Don'ts: Cell-phone cameras, Cindy Sherman, closeups, crooked framing, saying "cheese"

Dos: Color, cinematographers, collages, *cartes de visite* (small portraits, about the size of a business card, popular during the 1860s)

D

Do: Digital Shut the fuck up, you stupid Luddites. Digital cameras are great. It's free to take as many photos as you want; they don't take up any space; there are no stinky chemicals, negative binders, contact sheets, or lab fees; there's no dust, darkroom, or expensive paper; and you can easily send your pictures to all your friends. Go ahead and take a picture of everything you see, every second of every day, just don't show them all to me…

Don'ts: Developer (gives you cancer), dodging, dry-mounting, daguerreotypes

Dos: David Bailey, double exposures, dye-transfers, dust-off, David Hamilton

E

Do: Editing …because there is nothing worse than a bad edit. There are plenty of good picture-takers out there, but what makes a really good photographer is the ability to edit the million photos you took down to the 20 or 30 that make sense. They'll show the rest of it in a retrospective when you're old or dead and people give a shit about every little fart you ever mustered.

Don'ts: Enlargers, emulsion, ektachrome

Dos: The electromagnetic spectrum, Eadweard Muybridge, E. J. Bellocq

Photo found by Bobby Puleo

F

Do: Found photos Found photos prove that it's the photo,

not the photographer, that matters.
Don'ts: Fish-eye lenses, fashion, spelling it "foto"
Dos: Fill flash, film stills, fiber-based paper, fog

Photo of a German by Jake Gleeson

G

Don't: **Germans** The German canon of photography is rigid and boring. Why would a whole country share the same style and approach in a medium that has such endless possibility? What are you guys, Nazis?
Don'ts: Graininess, gallerists, gelatin (made from horse-hooves, in all film), gum-bichromate processing
Dos: German engineering, Gerhard Richter

H

Don't: **Homoeroticism** All these gays passing off their softcore porn as fine art has got to stop. If you want to look at naked boys, just fucking look at naked boys. Stop paying $8,000 a pop to do it.
Don'ts: Hand coloring, Holgas
Dos: Hasselblads, homemade porn, Henri Cartier Bresson, hidden cameras

I

Do: **Internet** Second-best to finding an amazing print in the garbage is stumbling across some lunatic's website. The Internet is the photo voyeur's Emerald City, and Google image search is like being God.
Don'ts: Interiors, calling photos "images," ink cartridges, infrared film
Dos: Interchangeable lenses, illuminance, infinity, inverse square law

J

Don't: **Jobs** Another thing they don't teach you in art school is that getting paid for taking pictures is super-fucking hard. Magazines just don't pay you. There are a million other dipshits like you out there who are willing to do it for free to get "tear sheets" for their "book." If you want to get paid you have to do ads or weddings.
Don'ts: Jockeying for position, Jeff Wall, *Juxtapoz*
Dos: Jpegs, jury-rigged cameras

Photo by Jerry Hsu

K

Do: **Kids** Have you looked at your yearbooks from high school lately? The awkwardness and self-consciousness, the toothy smiles and horrible hairdos—kids can't hide anything from a camera.
Don'ts: Kodak Instamatics, kitsch, Kodaliths
Dos: Kodachrome, Karlheinz Weinberger

L

Do: **Large format** With every douche on the planet swinging T4s over their heads, snapping away like Ron Galella every time someone breathes, it's refreshing to know that some people still lug gigantic, ridiculously expensive large-format cameras to remote locations just for the sake of grain density.
Don'ts: Long exposures, light leaks, live band photos, low resolution, Liquid Light
Dos: Leicas, Larry Clark, Lee Friedlander, lenticulars

Photo by the author

M

Don't: **The "Mundane"** This is one of those words that gets tossed around like a golden turd in art classes. Photographers love it because it makes things easy when they are floundering to explain a boring picture. But the fact is, if it's boring, it's boring, and there's no angle or filter or film that's gonna change that.
Don'ts: Models on the toilet (*Vice* has received this demystifying image at least a hundred times), montages, macro lenses, magazines, manuals
Dos: Medium format, mug shots, motor drives, megapixels, memories

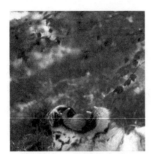

Photo by Jason Frank Rothenberg

N

Do: Nature photographers How could you ever hate a nature photographer? They're technically brilliant and brave. They sit around in a wet, mosquito-filled bush for days or weeks just to get the tiger yawning or the beetle mating. How serious is that?

Don'ts: Nan Goldin, scratched negatives, *Nylon*, night photography (as a genre)

Dos: Negative scanners, natural light, nudity, nostalgia

O

Don't: Overexposure Overexposure means two things in photoland. The first is the technical term for when too much light reaches the film. This is caused by an inappropriately long shutter speed or an overly dilated aperture, and the result is a washed-out image. The second is when one photographer's work and life is granted too much press and attention. This often leads to a succession of alcoholism and early death. (Ever heard of Robert Mapplethorpe or Diane Arbus?)

Don'ts: Objectification, oversaturated color, old black man's fingers as he plays the guitar (an image we've gotten almost more than the hot girl on the toilet)

Dos: Old magazines, optics

Photo by Angela Gaimari

P

Don't: Posing "OK! Everyone get in here! Come on, guys, squeeze in. Let's go, tallest to shortest! Mary, put your arm around Charley—just do it, don't argue! Jimmy, stop making that face. Come on now, guys, grow up. Let's do this together. Mark, stand a little closer to Jen, that's it.

Now, OK, hold still everyone. 'Wally World' on three. Ready? One, two, three…Wally World!"

Don'ts: Photoshop, panoramics, parallax, pushing and pulling, photograms, pinholes

Dos: Porn, postcards, Polaroid, photo albums, photo booths, point-and-shoot cameras, picture day at school

Photo by Mark Murray

Q

Do: Quick reflexes Good photographing is like a sport. You have to be fast, strong (cameras are heavy as shit), agile, and hyperaware. It's no coincidence that Spider-Man is such a good photographer.

Don'ts: Quick prints (expensive and look like shit)

Dos: Quick load (a godsend)

Photo by the author

R

Don't: Road trips Emo kids have sold this romantic ideal and ultimate picture-taking bonanza so far down the river that now, on its back in a jagged script the whip scars actually spell out: *Who cares?*

Don'ts: "Reportage," retouching, the rule of thirds, red-eye-reduction flash setting, reflections, roadkill

Dos: Rolleiflex, Robert Frank, rangefinders, Richard Prince, Roni Horn

S

Don't: Sports photos Just like live sports, sports photos are about watching the same people in the same places wearing the same clothes do the same thing over and over again.

Don'ts: Soft focus, stop bath (smells like eggs), sepia tone, self-portraiture, sprocket holes on prints, stock agencies

Dos: Snapshots, stealing souls, slide shows, self-timers, stereographs, starburst filters, slaves, Sally Mann

T

Don't: Text Please don't write on your prints, or scratch words into your negatives, or project text through the slide, or whatever. Has that ever been done well? Writers aren't illustrating their books with bad photos, are they? So don't illustrate your photos with bad writing. You can't just throw in some words to beef up a boring photo. Words are a whole other world that you and I know nothing about.
Don'ts: Tripods, thin negatives, timed exposures, tints, toning, tungsten
Dos: Telephoto lenses (for spying), terryrichardson.com, three-d, tintypes

Photo found by the author

U

Do: Us Weekly The photography in *Us Weekly* is like a cheap, super-hot whore who rubs your feet and swallows your load. It perfectly serves its purpose: to be entertaining, informative, and disposable.
Don'ts: Underexposure, used equipment, unipods
Dos: Underwater photos, ultraviolet light

V

Don't: Vacation photos Of all the sterling silver that is dug up in the world by underpaid, zombified miners, the largest percentage goes to making film (true). So, even though the swimming pool at the Chateau Shamrock was in the shape of a shamrock, no one needs to see the whole roll of film you went through on it. You just wasted what some poor Mexican lost three fingers digging up.
Don'ts: Variable contrast paper, vignetting
Dos: Vaseline on the lens, vistas

Photo by Balarama Heller

W

Do: War photographers All the way up to Vietnam, these motherfuckers were basically shooting guns and film at the same time. They were war heroes and artists and would inevitably end up getting shot in some hard-to-pronounce place and left to rot in a swamp.
Don'ts: Wide-angle, wedding photographers, white walls, web designers
Dos: William Eggleston, Wolfgang Tillmans, Walker Evans

X

Don't: X-treem anything No matter how wide-angle your lenses go, you fucking EXPN, tri-hawk-sporting, scar-bragging, tattooed "adrenaline junkies" can never see how extremely embarrassing you are to the rest of us. You combine every annoying aesthetic and then "Turn up the volume!" until we can't even see you against that fucking graffiti backdrop.
Dos: X-ray vision

Y

Don't: Photographing yourself The majority of self-portraits are annoying and bad because humans are far too self-aware to photograph themselves in any sort of candid, honest way. Everyone puts on their photo face (usually mopey, serious, or blank), squints their eyes, and tries to look sensitive, and/or tough. It's really gay.
Dos: Yearbooks

Photo by the author

Z

Don't: Zooming in You are not blowing anyone's mind with your vivid closeup of the intricate textures of that tree bark. Your photo of the *S* from the stop sign is not poetic. Yes, the ant looks big because you zoomed in, but no, that's not interesting. Don't tell us you were trying to broaden the viewer's perspective. If you think that is broadening *anything*, you are a simpleton, and you should get back to filling in all the spaces in the letters in your *Intro to Photo* guidebook.
Dos: The Zone system ■

KASANDRA MARIN

THE VICE GUIDE TO BEING A WHORE

Photo by Tod Seelie

OK, let's cut the shit here. Working in the "sex industry" fucking blows. Suicide Girls get to have hairy armpits, and it's fun to put your picture up on onlyundiesclub.com, but that's playacting. Real sex work is about showing up at a millionaire crackhead's house with a big box of Wet Ones, letting him bang the shit out of you for three days (even though he pulled a gun on you for sitting on the left-hand side of his bed), and then leaving with $1,900. No matter what the empowered academics in San Francisco pretend to believe, whoring—in any form—is hell, and the only reason women do it is to get money for coke NOW! If you want to try it out, be prepared to have nothing to show for years of suffering but a blown-out septum and some lumpy fake tits. It's like extreme waitressing. You make hundreds of dollars a night licking ass and then you immediately spend it on drugs just to feel normal again.

If you're really, truly still interested, please at least do us a kindness and read this A–Z before your first day on the job.

ANAL

A few years ago it might have been acceptable to be a whore who "doesn't do anal." Now you'd be lucky to get out of there without him making you cry on demand, gag on his dick to the point of puking, and THEN have anal sex while two dildos are simultaneously jammed into your pussy. I don't know why things have gotten so raunchy. Maybe guys have been corrupted by the internet and endless mpegs of Cambodian babies getting fucked by dogs. Point is, their idea of humiliating a woman (what sex work is all about) has been ramped up quite a bit, so don't think you're going to get away with smoking a cigarette in high heels while he takes pictures. The prices seem to have gone down too, but it's so hard to say in this business. The cheapest price I've ever heard a girl charging was simply "a place to stay," and the most I've ever heard a girl getting is $10,000 from a Japanese businessman who would fly her to Tokyo for one night. You'll probably make $100.

BACHELOR PARTIES

Bachelor parties are the cash cow of whoring, but they're fucking scary. Men have a tendency to try to outdo each other, so if you start the night with a blowjob and cum in your eye, your last trip to the hotel bathroom will involve something along the lines of getting fucked in the ass sans lube while the guy pours shampoo in your eyes. It's worth it, though, because they usually only last for one to five hours and you can make $6,000 pure profit.

COCAINE

Coke is what this whole industry is about. The majority of the clients are doing it in some capacity, and so are all the hos. Really high cokeheads are simultaneously the best and the worst johns you can have. The good part is the money, because they want you to stay over for a long time, but the bad part is the paranoia and the limp dick and how those two interact.

You have to make sure you look him in the eyes when you walk in and don't act too sketchy, because cokeheads are convinced everyone is trying to rip them off and if you contribute to that theory in even the slightest way, he's going to go nuts. When you finally convince him you're there to work and nothing else, he'll pull out his soft dick and get even more mad. Then he doesn't want to wear a condom for the blowjob because that's only going to make things worse. It sucks.

BTW, if the guy is giving you a hassle about having to use a condom for a blowjob, there's a way you can put it on his dick without him knowing. It takes some practice, but you start with it in your mouth and then kind of roll it on his penis as your head goes down. When you're done you can just leave it on him so he can see what an asshole he is.

DEODORANT

Strippers and prostitutes (and fags, for some reason) all know this secret way to prevent ingrown hairs after you shave your swimsuit area. It's simple and cheap and it never fails. Put deodorant on it. I think there's something about the alcohol in the deodorant that opens the pores wide enough that the hairs can't ingrow. It's the same principle behind that really expensive Tend Skin shit, but deodorant works about 80 times better.

ESCORT AGENCIES

You'll notice whores who work with an agency are a lot more patient than streetwalkers. Escorts are there for the full hour whether you get a boner or not. Streetwalkers, on the other hand, have a real live pimp, and he wants his money 15 minutes ago. If a john doesn't get it up with a streetwalker right away, he's dead.

FUCKED BY YOUR DAD

Second-wave feminists like Andrea Dworkin and Catherine MacKinnon made up this cruel stereotype that everyone in the sex industry got fucked by their dad. What do they know about it? Shit, that's not fair. I mean, I got fucked by my dad, and every single woman I've met in the industry (stripping, prostitution, internet, phone sex… everything) got fucked by her dad, but… oh shit, wait. It *is* true. I guess that's why we can lie underneath someone who has no business being on top of us and not give a shit. Statistics on incest are hard to gauge, but when you look at the number of women in the industry today and consider the fact that they ALL got fucked by their dad, it kind of makes your stomach turn.

PS: If your dad never fucked you and you're not a lesbian, quit now. Otherwise you will hate all men forever.

GANG BANGS

Whores never get asked to do gang bangs because most guys think it's too faggy. The only place you will ever see gang bangs is in porn. I don't know much about it because I'm a whore and we don't watch porn. It's like you watching a movie about sitting at your desk.

HATERS

You know you're in it for the long haul when you hate your coworkers. In this business EVERYONE hates everyone else. I'm here to make money, and anyone who is prettier than me (or cheaper) is the competition. I've even had nights at strip clubs where some bitch was all up in my face saying, "If you get one more dance tonight I'm going to kick your ass." That happens all the time, and you have to sit there and try to decide, "Do I go home now and know I won't get into a fight, or do I risk getting my ass kicked and make some more money?"

INTERNET PORN

Internet porn is the most tolerable type of sex work. If you can use a computer, you're in. Amateur websites with girls-next-door working out of their bedrooms still make millions, and even the chubby girl with the lazy eye is taking home $1,000 a month (though it's not worth it if you're making less than $4,000 a month). Most internet places have about 3,000 people working 24 hours a day, each charging about $3.50 a minute. That's over $15 million a day. And thus we come to the essential paradox of porn. It fucking sucks. It's depressing. It makes you hate men. But the money. Fuck.

To get started, all you need is a computer, a relatively fast connection, a webcam, and maybe a Hello Kitty pillow. Then you just click the "Become a chat host" button on your favorite porn site. After confirming your age they'll send you the software, and then whenever you feel like going online, horny guys will send you money. The good thing about working on the internet is, there are strict censorship rules on amateur sites that ban hardcore pornography, so you can say no to drinking pee and fisting and still not get fired. Don't get me wrong, you still get humiliated and bossed around, but it's easier on your knees and you can be fat. The internet is where old hos go to die.

JERKING OFF

Massage parlors will tell you in your interview that you don't have to do anything you don't want to and you can just jerk them off with a glove if you're grossed out. What they *don't* mention is, that means you'll go home penniless. The money you make is all about what you can negotiate for yourself after the massage. First, dude pays the agency around 40 dollars for the massage, which lasts 30 minutes to an hour. Then, after he's all "comfers cozers," you become a free agent and get to make your own money negotiating handjob and blowjob prices. The wage will be the average between how desperate you both are. Most places have a 3-2-1 plan, which means $300 for a fuck, $200 for a blowjob, and $100 for a handjob, but those prices all go down the tubes when some dumb cunt does anal for $80.

KLEPTOMANIA

The thing about whoring is, after being humiliated and spat on (literally) for an hour, you inevitably feel like you want to get back at the guy. That's why we steal. It's usually just frivolous shit like a size-12 sneaker or a little Buddha thing from the bathroom, but occasionally you'll get a really tenacious whore who will watch him use the ATM, memorize his PIN, steal his card when he's passed out or taking a piss, and eventually get away with thousands of dollars.

LUNCH

If you're a whore in 2004 you have two categories of food in your fridge: nonfood and cry-for-help food. The first category is things like protein bars and celery with a Crystal Light chaser: just enough food to kill the hunger pains but not enough to add any calories. Category two is about secretly trying to get fat and sabotage your career. Every few days a ho will break out of category one and make a jar of mayonnaise or an entire tub of ice cream disappear in seconds. Then it's back to energy drinks. The only consistent thing about what we eat is we all LOVE drinking pink cider. I don't know why.

MAMMARY GLANDS

Even though it meant having your nipples removed and placed next to you in a bowl of ice for a few hours, getting fake tits used to be a great way to make more money. Then, around two years ago, they became uncool, even with perverts. Now you can actually lose clients by having fake tits. I'm getting mine taken out because when you go out with nice civilian boys they are totally freaked out by them, and even if they look great, you have to replace them every five fucking years.

NATIVE AMERICANS

Agencies love anyone that looks remotely exotic because they can advertise you as the latest fetishized race, which changes about every four months. If you have dark hair and something minimally unusual about your face, you will make more money for everyone. If Mongolians are the hot new thing, you're Mongolian. If you have even a hint of Native in you, you're totally set because you can be advertised as anything from half-Asian to Fijian royalty.

ORGASMS

Whores cum on the job about once a career. Sorry, but if a clit gets pounded seriously and systematically enough, it may just send an orgasm to the brain. Also, about 25 percent of your clients are going to want to eat you out (I know, it's weird), and that can be a nice break that may lead to the dreaded "ho-gasm." The time it happened to me, the guy was so gross and I was so disgusted with the whole thing that I ended up cumming just out of how uncumworthy the whole thing was. You know?

PHONE SEX

A lot of single mothers do this as an easy way to make money. They think it won't make them feel repulsed, but that's bullshit. Like all whoring, phone sex makes you hate yourself and it puts you in a bad mood for about four hours after your last call. Plus, you'll be lucky to take home $300 a week.

QUITTING

The average sex worker's career is six months. If you work for an agency or (ugh) a real pimp, they will try everything from relentless nagging to kidnapping you with a bag over your head to keep you from quitting. Women aren't that great at saying no to begin with, and when you add getting fucked by your dad to the equation, cutting the cord ends up taking quite a few tries.

RETURNS

These are great. If the guy sends you back you make $40 without doing anything. All you have to do is pay the driver $10 to enforce the $50 minimum, and that's it. You're back in the car with your money and you didn't even take your jacket off.

SUICIDE GIRLS

Sorry hipsters, but this is not porn. It's not even sex work. It's more like a pretend tea party with your stuffed animals. I applied to it when it first came out and they actually expected me to do shit like explain why I'd be a good Suicide Girl. Excuse me? That's the first time a pimp ever wanted to see a résumé. The reason these girls can wax poetic about how it's the new porn and talk about empowerment is simple: They are not in the porn industry. Porn is about subordinating yourself for money. If it feels good, you're not doing it right.

TELLING PEOPLE (NOT)

You know you are doing real sex work when you can shut the fuck up. Bragging rights don't really exist unless you are looking for people to make a basset hound face at you and start crying. NEVER tell a civilian man you're trying to have sex with that you have ever taken money for sex. At first he will think it's kind of cool that he can have sex with a pro for free, but then he'll expect you to be Lil' Kim all the time and get all jock on you by telling you to "break out the toys!" when all you wanted was your sad, neglected pussy to be licked in silence for three to seven minutes. Or he will freak out and think his friend paid you to have sex with him on his birthday and then throw a beer through your bedroom window. He will never marry you. Read *The Rules to the Ring*.

UNDERWEAR

The second you get to the guy's house or hotel, it's a good rule of thumb to (after asking permission) get right down to just a thong. I do this right away because if you wait until he asks you, he might fuck you over by telling the agency that he's not going to pay because you kept your J. Lo tracksuit on for the first hour and smoked menthols while nursing a cider and didn't even look at his dick.

Every other kind of sex work is about drawing it out as long as possible. Especially the internet. The guy's credit card is being charged by the minute and he's in New Jersey, so keep milking him. What's he going to do, fax you a punch in the head?

VERBAL WHORES

Seventy-five percent of whoring is making small talk. Strippers and whores are really there because the guy is lonely and wants someone to complain to. I have a good system of smiling, nodding a lot, making eye contact, laughing, and speaking only to agree or say something charming after every five points he has made. After whoring for six months you will find you are better at guessing the answers on *Jeopardy!* and doing crossword puzzles because you have had to listen to hours and hours of men jerking their mouths off telling you pointless little facts to make them feel smarter. Just pretend you have been picked up hitchhiking and you have to stay awake and talk to the guy or he'll fall asleep driving and kill you both.

WET ONES

A Ho Bag is a wee sports purse you take with you on calls. Inside it you have: condoms (the free ones from the needle exchange), baby powder (helps putting on condoms), a driver price list (so you know what to pay him for what parts of the city), Band-Aids, Listerine (if you dare give a BJ unwrapped), Saran Wrap (so you don't get herpes when he eats you out), and the most important thing in the world: a pack of Wet Ones. If you don't carry Wet Ones with you at all times, you are not a whore. They make eating ass palatable, they help rid you of the "grossies" after a bad session, and they get jizz off your face in a way that makes it feel like it was never there.

X RATING

(*Vice* helped me with this one.) The MPAA instituted their ratings system in 1968, and X was the one that meant "no kids can come in here, no way, we don't care if your parents are with you." It was used for legit films like *Midnight Cowboy* (the first X-rated movie). Then porno makers, in a clever little marketing move, started using the made-up rating XXX (which was supposed to mean "so fucking dirty your eyes will burn," even though back then all you really saw was two hairy crotches mushing up against each other). Now in 2004, you have Max Hardcore fucking girls in the ass as they puke on each other with weird dental shit holding their mouths open, so the whole X thing has sort of gone out the window. That's why they made up NC-17 instead of X for "real" movies. NCCC-1777 isn't quite as catchy as XXX.

YOUTH

The younger you are, the better. You're stupider, you're easier to manipulate, and you have a tighter pussy, which means less ass fucking. I say fuck getting a tit job. Splurge for pussy-rejuvenation surgery and change that thing from a wet paper bag into a McDonald's straw.

ZZZZZZZZZ

Falling asleep. This skill, otherwise known as disassociation, comes in handy. It usually sets in around hour three of sucking a rich cokehead's limp cock. The old daddy-fucked-me thing means most whores are old friends with disassociation. You can get a lot done while you're disassociating, like deciding which movies you're going to put in your queue on Netflix.

Sometimes you can go so far with it that you actually fall asleep, and if that happens, you're fucked in every sense of the word. You're either going to get raped without a condom or have your face punched in. The only hos I know who survived falling asleep were the ones who were with those weirdo subservient guys who want you to laugh at their small dick and then let them eat you out for an hour. Those guys are fucking disgusting and depressing and they are about as good as whoring gets. Got it? ■

LESLEY ARFIN

THE VICE GUIDE TO REHAB

Photos courtesy of Alan Lewis, Photopress Belfast

A good rehab is essentially an anarchist socialist commune with one rule: Don't get high. There are no cops, no bureaucrats and no squares hassling you about riding your machine. The people there come from every class and social stratum. There're doctors (I actually referred my own dentist to a rehab), pathetic scumbags, best friends, police officers, drunk drivers that ran over babies—all sharing and caring like one big, happy, jonesing family.

A lot of people are grossed out by rehab. They can't handle the cultlike over-niceness and the part where you're supposed to talk about your feelings, but what's healthier: the cult of recovery or the cult of Coors with its whole "drink six of us a night and you can fuck twins" shtick?

Not everyone needs to go to rehab. A lot of addicts just stop and are able to stay sober forever. I'm not one of those people. If it weren't for rehab I'd be in a very, very, very, very bad place. Sound like you?

Here are the basics of getting sobes…

ADOLESCENT PROGRAMS

These are a waste of time. Teenagers are supposed to have fucked-up mentals. In fact, drugs will probably save them from committing suicide. Let them at it. My friend John got arrested for writing graffiti when he was in tenth grade, but he had never done any drugs whatsoever. His lawyers decided to tell the judge that he was "under the influence" when he was writing his nickname so that he'd get off easier. He ended up in South Oaks rehab for two months with a truckload of teenage junkies and trippers, all of whom described narcotics so romantically that when he

finally got out, he couldn't wait to get his hands on some PCP and methamphetamine. John never graduated high school. I have no idea where he is now.

BOREDOM

There is nothing to do in rehab. That's the way it goes, and it goes that way for a reason. Boredom will drive you to participation, and the more you engage, the more you learn about sobriety. Most addicts are socially fucked to the extreme and can barely have a conversation, much less a friendship or a relationship. Boredom helps you get out of your room and make some buds. It's either that or trying to stare a hole through your bedroom wall.

A typical rehab day consists of eating, AA/NA meetings, eating more, group therapy, smoking, more eating, more AA/NA, smoking and eating, and sleep. Getting crushes on ugly people is another activity (more on that later).

CAFFEINE

Coffee is not allowed in rehabs, but it's always available as contraband. It becomes a form of inpatient currency. If you get on bad terms with the girl who has the coffee, your other friends will dump you because they're addicts and really they have only known you for about a week, and, well, coffee has never really let them down, so… sorry.

DEATH

Contrary to public opinion, only two substances can cause death upon withdrawal: prescription pills and alcohol. Alcoholics get delirium tremens, or DTs. A lot of asshole doctors consider them a myth, but DTs are very fucking real, and they cause hallucinations (the bad kind), seizures, and can lead to stroke. That's the delirium part. The tremor part is because your hands shake when you're a drunk. DTs always make me think of Huck Finn's dad. I'm just saying.

Withdrawing from pills is the gnarliest, because they are synthetic and designed to chemically fuck up your brain, and the withdrawal treatment involves even more pills, so you have two gangs of chemicals trying to tear your arms off in different directions.

Rehabs can treat a pill addiction efficiently, but you'll suffer for a while from yeast infections and a poor immune system. And dear pillheads: It's not like you can't afford to go. You just had ten doctors all over the city writing you scripts, so I'm sure you can figure something out.

EATING DISORDERS

These go hand in hand with drug addiction, like two best friends who egg each other on. This is why they are often placed in the same facility (it's also way cheaper for insurance companies to lump diseases together). In rehab, we refer to them as "Double Winners," but in real life, we don't. Most likely because they are always fat losers. This leads me to...

FOOD

You've been replacing your meals with red wine for the past eight years and now that you've quit, guess what? You're fucking *starving*. You could eat a horse right now.

Junkies don't eat anything at first, because they're too sick, but once they can keep something down, they tend to develop yet ANOTHER disease, called chocoholism. (I am so glad that this is not a joke.) Maybe this is because chocolate creates endorphins that go to your brain and crank out pleasure.

Oh yeah, another "F" thing is Farts. Everyone farts all the time in rehab. People fart so much that the farts actually have their own conversations with each other. They have their own underground society and their own rules. Some farts even hate each other.

GAMBLING

Not allowed, in any form whatsoever. Even if you say something like, "I bet you it will rain tomorrow," you might get kicked out. Just kidding, but seriously, you can't gamble. Gambling is super-addictive. I once knew this kid who was addicted to gambling. He told me that he actually liked losing. Like, it made him feel really good when he lost. Weird, right? No gambling.

HAIRSPRAY

Not allowed in treatment centers. Hairspray contains 77 percent alcohol, and that would be enough to ease your delirium tremens.

ICE

One of my favorite rehab stories is about a guy who was addicted to "ice." He called it ice because he was about 50 years old and a total dork. (It's just speed, dude.)

He was an entertainment lawyer from LA and had never touched a drug in his entire life, not even during the 60s (because he was in law school). He represented a host of super famous people and felt really protected by all the powerful people who run LA. Then one night, he met his dream girl. "She was beautiful, an artist. Well, she called herself an artist, but most other people would call her a stripper..." Anyway, she introduced him to ice and before he knew it, he was ripping out drywall at the Four Seasons, convinced his room was wiretapped. He had moved all the furniture in front of the door, even the bed, and had taped garbage bags and aluminum foil over the windows. When his friends finally found him, he was ripping apart the minifridge, convinced that a bag of speed had been dropped behind it accidentally. He told this story on his second day of rehab. The next day he was gone.

JUICY COUTURE SWEATSUITS

Yes, that's right. Juicy. Bring more than one, because they were made for rehab days. Clueless JAPs wear them to the supermarket, women in their 50s buy them in cashmere, and Mafia wives get ones that say "New Jersey" on the butt. All of the above are completely inappropriate in the outside world. Even ghetto girls trying to look like J. Lo... no. You all look like fat, lazy slobs that are dying to get fucked in the ass. However, bring a suitcase full of these to rehab. You'll look and feel like a fucking queen.

KETAMINE

So many people are completely addicted to it, yet rehabs still don't know what it is or what to do with its users. There is seemingly no physical addiction or even long-term side effects, so counselors usually say, "Umm..." and then dismiss it as a disassociative. Most likely though, K-heads feel self-conch around people who use "real drugs" and never make it to treatment or AA/NA, which is sad. This drug is heavy shit and totally fucks your brain up.

LAZINESS

I knew a lady in rehab who was named Ingrid. She was an obese crackhead (I know, an oxymoron, but they exist) who had fully given up on life. When she entered rehab she was wheezing, smoking, sitting in a wheelchair, and eating a meatball sub. She was incapable of wiping her own ass, literally. I thanked God I was not a nurse, and prayed to sweet Jesus that she would NOT be my roommate. Her skin was gray. She beefed like a trumpet teacher, and you could hear her wheezing through the dormitory walls.

Once, during my methadone stint, I offered to wheel her around. I wasn't strong enough to move her one fucking inch. She was total deadweight. Then one day, after a meal, a nurse told Ingrid she could not smoke indoors. She got right up out of her wheelchair, walked outside, and lit up a Kool. The nurses were furious. Ingrid could walk. She was fully capable of getting around on her own, but chose to wheelchair it because she "didn't feel like walking." The bitch was that lazy! Seeing her waddle outside to smoke that cigarette was the first time I'd felt an emotion in almost a decade (it was a little thing called anger).

METHADONE

Is there a substitute for heroin? AA will tell you it's a "higher power of your choosing." Religion will say it's God. Your brain will tell you it's food, sex, and money. Every state hospital and social worker in the world will tell you it's METHADONE. It's an opiate that's taken orally, so you don't get the rush from shooting or sniffing it. Once you're high, though, it pretty much feels like smack.

And methadone totally does cure your dope habit—by giving you a whole new addiction that is way, way harder to kick! I have friends who did heroin for two years and methadone for the next 12. You know when you see junkies on the street with their hair and teeth falling out? It's mostly from methadone, not heroin. On heroin you'll pick at your face and such, but it certainly doesn't make your teeth fall out. Since doctors regulate the methadone high, you can stay hooked on it forever. Do heroin for too long, with its wildly varying quality from bag to bag, and eventually you're going to OD.

NICOTINE

If you aren't addicted to cigarettes upon entering rehab, you will be when you check out. Smoking is how you make friends. But I think this goes for real life too. It's perfect for self-conscious people who are used to stuffing all their feelings down in their guts and don't know where to put their hands when they're hanging out and everybody's riffing and they don't know what to say. [Or you could just get over it—Ed.]

OPIATE BLOCKERS

I've heard these can help withdrawal, but in most druggie communities they are known as something only pussy rich kids take. They lessen the actual pain, but definitely not the craving. Case in point: I once saw this kid spend $100 for ten bags of dope, shoot them all, and get no high whatsoever. He thought he could blast out the opiate blockers, but these fuckers are like a million microscopic Incredible Hulks designed to bar street dope from entering your brain. That kid was super-bummed!

PIT, THE

At my rehab this was the place where we would meet every night before lights-out to discuss concerns, problems, fears, and complaints. The first time I went into the Pit, it was "elections" night, and we voted on who did which chores that week (wake-up calls, sweeping, dishwashing, etc.). To vote you simply had to raise your hand ONCE. When I say that it took about five attempts for everyone to grasp this voting method, I am not joking. Drug addicts, known for their longing to fail, don't take direction very well. I couldn't help but laugh when we were asked if there were any complaints about roommates and this lady Stephanie said she wanted to switch because her roomie was "keeping chicken under her bed! It stinks!"

QUITTING

About 80 percent of inpatients do not make it through the full 28-day rehabilitation program. It's too hard and intense, so they quit. It's really funny when people "run away," like Luke Wilson's character does in *Bottle Rocket*, because unless you're under 18 or mandated to be there by law, you can just leave on your own. One day the entire rehab was freaking out about this guy who'd been missing for about five hours. He was really well liked and good-looking, so it was the day's hot topic—nobody wanted to see him go. Turns out he just jumped the fence and walked three miles to Starbucks.

ROOMMATES

Roommates always suck. I had this one lady who everyone called "Tomato on a Toothpick" because she was really skinny but had a huge red face (broken capillaries from drinking). She also talked like a robot and asked every day if she could wear my clothes (just inappropriate—she was 55). Then I had this other lady who would never fucking shut the fuck up, and when anyone else spoke, did that annoying thing that people who don't listen do—nodding her head real fast with her eyes closed, like "Yup, yup, I know what you mean." She farted constantly in her sleep, and showered and shat with the door open. I even walked in on her masturbating! Ew!

SEX

All the staff wants at rehab are two little things: 1) for at least one person to stay sober and 2) for no one to fuck. They really push the fraternizing rules at the nicer rehabs, which only makes inpatients want it more. You will find yourself drawn to the most mediocre-looking members of the opposite sex because beggars can't be choosers, especially while confined to a community as big as the Shire.

Your sex drive comes back with a vengeance, so don't

feel weird or guilty if you fantasize about doing it behind the laundry room with the 18-year-old pothead from Minnesota. If anything, revel in it! So you've always secretly wanted to eat out a skinny 60-year-old with flat boobs? Now you can do it, and you don't have to call her or anything, and ignoring her the next day is strongly encouraged! Most likely, she'll ignore you too!

THERAPEUTIC COMMUNITIES

TCs differ from rehabs because the people who usually enter these things don't need to be rehabilitated back into life, but habilitated, meaning that they are usually homeless people, Bloods and/or Crips, single mothers, and the rest of society's garbage who never knew how to live correctly in the first place. The system at these places often differs from the warm, cushy luxuries of regular-junkie rehab. For one, they use "tough love" tactics, which basically means you get yelled at and called names, like a tear-you-down, build-you-up approach. Sounds really fun while you're in the middle of withdrawal.

In upscale treatment centers, they have one counselor for every patient. In TCs there is one counselor for every 11 patients. (But just FYI, both places have the same recovery rate: 8 percent.)

URINE TESTING

People sneak drugs into rehabs. Doye. These are usually the people who are forced to be there by law and are just trying to dry up so they can lower their tolerance. These people have been to rehabs and detoxes 30 times or more and are another reason why insurance companies are cautious. If they suspect you've used, you'll get urine-tested. If your urine comes up dirty (and you're a mandated patient), you'll go to jail. If you're voluntary, you'll just get the boot. These tests are unannounced and a nurse actually stands there and watches you pee.

VANILLA EXTRACT

A woman told us a story about how she needed to drink so badly, and her husband had thrown away all the booze, so she drank an entire bottle of vanilla extract. It contains 35 percent alcohol. I thought that was a wives' tale, but I guess it really does happen.

WITHDRAWAL

They don't call it "cold turkey" for nothing. I'm serious. The phrase comes from heroin withdrawal symptoms. You get goosebumps like turkey skin, even if it's 90 degrees out. And "kicking" isn't just a cute way of saying it either, because your legs really do this involuntary kick due to muscle spasms. It gets so hurty that you turn into a child having a temper tantrum. Counselors in rehab describe it as "musical chairs" because after you sit in

one place and feel like you finally might be able to chill the fuck out, the kick starts creeping up and you move to another chair. After you've covered every chair in the room, you surrender to the toilet, the only chair that will open its jaws for the massive amounts of diarrhea you're gonna get. Be sure to shit with a bucket in your lap, because all those years of dopamine reactors blocking the pain that you're supposed to feel when, let's say, you get a paper cut, are now coming out ten times stronger. It's like there's a barf-filled firehose in your mouth, pointing out. This is your body reacting to you being a total asshole to it. But just wait until group therapy starts. That's when the real pain kicks in. Barfing and shitting are nothing compared with taking a personal inventory (a written list of all the ways you're a totally worthless turd). Physical opiate withdrawal only lasts five days. That's a cinch in comparison.

X-TRA SPECIAL REHABS

Strictly for celebs. Promises is the one that Ben Affleck went to, and the price isn't even listed on the website. I called and they said they would call me back and they never did. At Promises you get a personal chef, a room with a private porch or terrace, and specialized therapists who know how to deal with overinflated egos and superstars without kissing their asses too much. At Cirque Lodge, where Mary Kate Olsen went, you get a private Jacuzzi, a sauna, hair salons, and massage rooms. (Plus something about it may or may not be circus themed.)

There's also "equine therapy," which they had at the Mötley Crüe rehab (Sierra Tucson). I guess that means petting horses to make you feel better, which makes sense because horses have powerful vibes.

YAWNING

The first sign of heroin withdrawal is yawning a lot.

ZITS

When you detox, it happens out of every pore in your body. You sweat like David Dinkins giving a press conference, and sprout mountains of acne overnight.

Quitting drugs blows. You turn into a fat, sweaty, zit-faced pseudo cult member. Your friends dump you because you don't party anymore, and you realize you feel uncomfortable around most people, and most people feel uncomfortable around you.

But just walking around the real world after getting out of rehab is like a drug—it's way more intense than acid. Your new life is cooler than any trip you've ever had, but definitely not as good as your best high. Wait, does that make sense? I can't tell, I'm totally wasted right now. Just kidding. ∎

AMY KELLNER

FUCK BUTTONS

Vice's A–Z on Cute

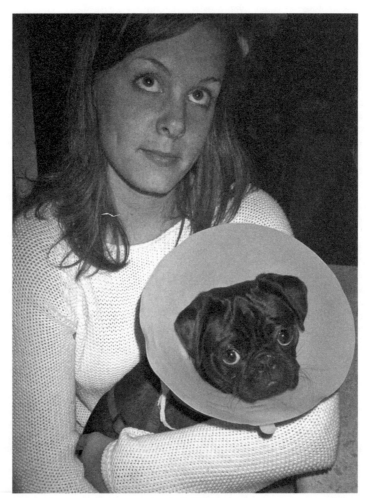

Photo by Todd Fisher

I know that Sanrio and pacifiers are raver garbage. I know that all the twee pop and lovecore bands of the mid-90s are counting spare change for ramen noodles now—doye—but there's something you should know.

Cute is eternally recurring. There will never be a time when people don't at least secretly want their hearts melted by doe-eyed naked babies with puppy whiskers and glitter wands in their big, white glove-paws.

Cute always wins. It's like in *Some Kind of Wonderful*, where Eric Stoltz keeps trying to get with untouchable prom queen Lea Thompson, while cutie-pants Mary Stuart Masterson, in her jean shorts and Doc Martens, is just pounding those fucking awesome drums with her fringed-leather glove and her insane dimples right in front of his stupid face the whole time. He finally realizes the drummer cutie is the way to go, then that cover of "Can't Help Falling in Love" comes on the soundtrack and you cry like a tiny (cute) baby. You can fight it all you want, but the truth is, in this country, cute is king. *WKRP*'s Bailey is better than the Loni Anderson chick. Betty is better than Veronica and Laci Peterson is better than Michelle Pfeiffer. Don't believe me? Let's let the alphabet decide! Here's 26 cute things that are, always have been, and always will be cuter than a button.

AMERICA'S FUNNIEST HOME VIDEOS

There's this one where this little girl gets a bicycle and it's all wrapped up in wrapping paper and bows. Her family must be poor because she starts unwrapping it and the bike is pink and all tricked out with a flower basket and streamers and everything and the girl just starts SCREAMING at the top of her lungs, and she just keeps fucking screaming like an insane person. It's really cute. Or there's another one with two little girls on Christmas and the dad is filming it and he gives them a dog bowl and the older one who's, like, six starts crying because she realizes what's going on, but the little one is all, "Why did you get us a dog bowl, Daddy?" And the dad says, "Gee, I don't know, why don't you go open the bedroom door?" And she does and the cutest little puppy comes bounding out wagging its tail so hard that its whole butt is moving so it can hardly get traction on the linoleum. And now both girls are totally WAILING and the little one is trying to hug the puppy, but between her sobs and the puppy's frantic wagging she can't get a grip. That clip won the award that episode.

See also: **Awkward teenagers, amateur kids night on *Showtime at the Apollo*, animal crackers, asking "Pretty please with a cherry on top?"**

BROKEN GLASSES

Or, more specifically, boys with broken glasses where they have masking tape on the corner or a weird safety pin. The perfect cute boy with broken glasses would be Harry Potter when he's 21 because his scarf would be all frayed at the edges with cigarette burns in it and he'd make bongs out of the beakers in chemistry class. You'd fall head over heels in love with him when he gives you a mini-baby pet unicorn that says, "Hello, Meghan."

See also: **Bunnies, babies, baby bunnies, barrettes, Björk, banana splits, the Banana Splits**

CHIPPED NAIL POLISH

Is way better than a fresh mani. Especially in black, red, or sparkly. Only short nails, though. You can't stick fingers with long nails up bumholes, so long nails basically tell the world, "I am a prude."

See also: **Candy hearts, clogs, Care Bears**

DRUNK KOALA BEARS

My friend told me that koala bears get drunk off the juice of eucalyptus leaves and then they fall off the tree they're clinging to and plop onto the ground. But they don't hurt themselves because they're so fluffy, round, and drunk. I think that's maybe the cutest thing yet and I really hope it's true.

See also: **Deer, Deerhoof, dancing kids at weddings**

ESL

Everything sounds better in Engrish. Just look at *Lost in Translation*. Without all the cuddly Japanese people talking in their funny-cry-happy syntax, that movie would've just been a two-hour-long Marc Jacobs ad. But beware: ESL is only cute when it's a Japanese person speaking it. Hearing a timid Mexican delivery guy mangle the English language is just frustrating.

See also: **Easter bunnies, epilepsy (just kidding)**

FREE GIFT WITH PURCHASE

My mom will buy anything if it has a free gift with purchase. The free gift is always a cute little miniature thing. Clinique is big on that. You buy one lipstick and they give you a free makeup bag stuffed with mini-samples of lipstick, eye shadow, blush, and useless little plastic eyebrow combs. My mom has a closet filled with free gifts. She doesn't even use them. She just keeps them there or gives them to me in a vain effort to get me to wear makeup. The only one I like is a cute little compact mirror I keep in my bag that was perfect for doing you-know-what on, when I used to do a lot of you-know-what. Mom also collects mini liquor bottles and silver miniatures of rocking chairs and tea sets. But that's mom-cute stuff, which is totally different. Like those horrific Hummels. Mom-cute is not always cute.

See also: **Funny answering-machine messages, Flossie & the Unicorns, flip-flops**

GAY PENGUINS

This wins the cute award, hands down. Roy and Silo are two male penguins that live at the Central Park Zoo and they have become the world's most famous gay penguin couple. They "shun female companionship," opting instead to entwine necks and "vocalize" to each other (i.e., fuck). They even tried to hatch a rock together by keeping it warm in the folds of their abdomens! The zookeeper

gave them a developing egg to care for and they hatched a little baby chick named Tango. I'm going to get a tattoo of them on my arm and whenever I am sad I will look at it and think, "Gay penguins, Amy... Gay. Penguins."
See also: Gummi bears, Gummi worms, Gummi brains, Gummi eyeballs, Gummi burgers

HOT VS. CUTE

Some people use the word *cute* when they really mean *hot*. Like someone will say, "Benicio Del Toro is so cute!" But no he isn't! You mean that he's hot. A dude who always plays bad boys and never smiles cannot be cute. The basic difference is that cute is happy and round while hot is sullen and pointy. Think apple cheeks vs. high cheekbones. Drew Barrymore vs. Faye Dunaway. Cute has a sense of humor while hot is all attitude and performance art.
See also: Harvey Milk High School, hearts, hats with pom-poms, Hamtaro

ICELANDIC PONIES

Iceland has special ponies that are really little and really fat and have big eyes and they totally look like My Little Pony for real. The only thing is that sometimes the weird Icelandic people make hot dogs out of them. I guess when you live in a land that's all rainbows and magical lagoons, you really have no choice but to eat enchanted forest creatures. Also, in Iceland there's no crime, so the prisons are basically really nice houses with picket fences. One time someone escaped, but he came back for dinner.
See also: Ice-cream cake, igloos

"JENNIFER JUNIPER" BY DONOVAN

"Jennifer Juniper rides a dappled mare/ Jennifer Juniper, lilacs in her hair/ Is she dreaming, yes, I think so/ Is she pretty, yes, ever so/ Whatcha doin', Jennifer, my love?" A very cute flute-y song by the very cute Scottish troubadour. When I saw the movie *Election*, I almost died of cuteness because they used this song in the scene where the little lesbian sister is swinging on a swing with her new girlfriend. And they're both wearing Catholic-school uniforms! Why don't you just trample me under a Pegasus and strangle me with a fluffy cloud while you're at it!?
See also: JonBenét Ramsey, Jonathan Richman, jumpers

KITTENS

No doye, right? Kittens playing pool. Kittens in a rock band. Kittens wearing sunglasses drinking Fanta through a straw. Cowboy kittens. A troupe of kittens touring comedy clubs. Kittens talking on the phone to other kittens. Kittens upside down. Kittens licking their buttholes with their leg sticking up in the air. *America's Funniest Kittens.* Teeny tiny little kittens. Kittens. Did you know that 90 percent of the kittens in those cute monthly calendars are taxidermy? That's not so cute.
See also: Kewpie dolls, Kimya Dawson, *Kids Incorporated*, "Kites Are Fun" by the Free Design

L-TRAIN DANCERS

There are these two brothers who break-dance on the L train. The big one does all the fancy moves, like swinging from the poles, while the little one holds the boom box as it plays "I've Got the Power." Then the big brother grabs the little brother and somersaults him with his legs, like a mama kangaroo might if they were any fun. Then they ask for money. That part isn't cute, it's depressing—but I like the rest of it.
See also: Ladybugs, Lynda Barry, Land of the Loops

MILO AND OTIS

This movie is to cute cinema what homemade anal rape videos from Chechnya are to porno. Undiluted 100-percent mainline cute.

It's from the land of pre-computer animation so there's no talking pigs, just Dudley Moore reading a story about an unlikely friendship between a puppy and a kitten while soft-focus images of fluffy barnyard animals frolic through the countryside. I actually bought this movie at a porn shop late one night with my friend Philip. We were stoned and wanted to rent a movie but everything was closed except the 24-hour porn shop on Bowery. Thanks to Giuliani, porn shops have to carry a certain percentage of non-porn movies, too. That's why when you go in there they have one corner filled with cast-off videos like *Yahoo Serious Is Young Einstein* and *Jo Jo Dancer, Your Life Is Calling.* We got *Milo and Otis* for $3.99, along with a bottle of Rush, and the clerk gave us the dirtiest look I've ever gotten in my life. Like he's thinking, what, we're gonna go home and sniff Rush and fuck to a children's movie about fuzzy baby animals? Duh, this movie is not good to fuck to. It is, however, the best thing to watch when you are coming down off a coke binge. For that, it's pure magic.
See also: Moon Pies, mooning people, making out

NARCOLEPSY

My friend's boyfriend has it. She says that sometimes it's really fucking annoying. But on those rare occasions when she's in the middle of showing him a dance routine and all of a sudden he's snoring, it's like, "Aww."
See also: Nermal (Garfield's nemesis), the Nutty Squirrels, New Edition

ORPHANS

Annie, Oliver—any fictional orphan is cute, especially on Broadway. They dance around and say cute phrases and

they dress like leprechaun crusty punks. Real ones are not so great. They get raped a lot and fight each other.
See also: Optimism, orangutans in motivational posters

DRUG BAGS WITH PICTURES OF HEARTS OR CHOCOLATE CHIPS ON THEM

When you get drugs in one of these, there's no way you're having a bad trip. Also it means that your dealer has an old soul and probably buys his bastard children pretty good toys and doesn't smuggle dope in their diapers.
See also: Pajamas, pigtails, pogo-ing punk chicks

QUEEFS

Pussy farts are totally cute because the girl gets all embarrassed and maybe blushes and giggles, but really it's the dick's fault for pushing all that air in there. If she knew how little the guy gives a shit, she'd laugh.
See also: Quilts, Quincy Jones (he looks like a baby lion!), quickies

ROUND THINGS

I don't really know why round things are cute, but when I asked other people, they just shrugged their shoulders and said, "Makes sense." Some cute round things include: Munchkins (the doughnuts and the race), cheeks, boobs, bunny tails, cupcakes, clementines, Tare Panda, marbles, pills, ball pits, snowballs, gumballs, and meatballs.
See also: Ralph Wiggum, riot grrrls, *Rushmore*

SCOTTISH ACCENTS

I have a Scottish fetish. Scottish accents kill me, they're so cute. With the "wee bonnie lasses" and the "two tae me, two tae you, that's eachy peachy, innit, ye daft fanny?" I even semi-stalked a clerk at my video store because he sounded Scottish. Turns out he was Welsh, shit. Jamaican accents are cute too. You know what would be the cutest? An old Jamaican woman arguing with her Scottish husband. You could put music to that.
See also: The Shaggs, strawberry lip gloss, Snoopy, Shrinky Dinks, sleepiness, silliness

TUSHIES

Er, duh. Tushies are the roundest, squeeziest things on your body besides boobs, and since they're closer to the private area, they win. Who cares if shit comes out of them?
See also: Tummies, "Take the Skinheads Bowling" by Camper Van Beethoven

UGLINESS

For example: that waiter at Veselka with the huge nose, or the teenager with acne at Hot Bagels. Ugly is so cute, it's way better than pretty. Pretty is for Republicans and people who made fun of you in high school.

See also: Underpants, Underoos, ünnecessary ümlauts

VANDALISM

When I was a kid in the suburbs I would write my nickname (Sandy) in bubble letters on my binder. Then we moved to the city and I saw all the cute boys writing their nicknames on brick walls in big HUGE bubble letters using a spray can. How cute is that? They love their nicknames so much they have to show the world AND THEY USE BUBBLE LETTERING! Sesk and Tets and Kask and whatever other weird names they gave themselves. The authorities call it vandalism but I call it nickname pride.
See also: Voles, valentines

WEEBLES

Have you ever tried to knock one of these over? Sure, they wobble. They wobble like a motherfucker. But good luck trying to knock one ever. They're too cute. You could hit one with a bazooka and it would just spring back up and be like, "Me so horny."
See also: "Windy" by the Association, *The Wind in the Willows*

XAVIER ROBERTS' SIGNATURE ON CABBAGE PATCH KIDS' BUTTS

When I was a kid this was the equivalent of a $5,000 Louis Vuitton/Takashi Murakami handbag, and the signature on the butt sealed the deal. I used to trace my finger along the embroidery of it like prayer beads. If your dad was a cheapskate and got you a knockoff, you were shunned.
See also: XOXO, *Xanadu*, xylophone players in grade-school bands

YOU!

Guess what, person? You're about as cute as they come. OK, maybe *I'm* not crazy about the smell and I'm not so into your tattoos, but remember the last time someone was really into you? They thought everything about you was cute. They thought that zit on the tip of your nose was funny. They loved the way you tried to sound all business-like on the phone. They even thought it was cute when you had stomach flu. No matter how bad things get, NEVER forget how cute you are.
See also: The Yummy Fur, youthful rebellion

ZOWIE BOWIE

That's what David and Angie Bowie named their kid, and he is probably about 37 times cuter than Ziggy Marley. His eyes are the size of dinner plates and his full name is Duncan "Joey" Zowie Heywood Jones. Zowie is, like, 33 now and goes by Joe Jones, which is pretty boring. Actually, fuck it. He's not cute anymore.
See also: Ziggy, Zoodles, zebra ponies ■

LESLEY ARFIN

THE VICE GUIDE TO FRIENDSHIP

Want to know about all the different kinds of friends? Welcome to the Friendship Forest. It can be a treacherous place, but its rewards are warmth, hugs, understanding, and chuckles. The ultimate goal is finding your BFF, but you'll really have to do some spelunking through thorns and brine to meet the magical unicorn that shits ice-cream cones and cries daffodils.

If you do find her, she will promise to be your best friend forever. If you ever betray her you will have to leave your whole scene and end up all *Sex and the City* with some cackling JAPs from your office that you hate (plus their assorted shitty dogs and moms) for the rest of eternity.

Here are some surefire guidelines to tell if the type of person you're hanging out with is a friend or just some douchebag using you for your car/other friends/money/couch.

Photo by Geoffrey Brown

FRIENDS MAKE YOU THINGS

Starting in ancient times, girls made each other friendship pins and stuck them to their shoelaces. These are just safety pins ornamented with plastic beads, sometimes sparkly! They mark your friend territory. Think of them as the platonic girl equivalent of tomcat pee. As we grow, friendship pins develop into mixtapes and then mix CDs (although iPod-sharing is now ruining this fine tradition by turning everyone into mix sluts). My friend Cindy makes dresses for a living for lots of money but she gives them to me for free. Not because I deserve it, but because I don't and she loves me anyway.

Friends like to exhibit friendship by returning from thrifting expeditions bearing gifts that pertain to your special obsessions. For me, that would be owls. Extra good friends will even make you a little book of photos of you guys together.

Friends will also give you clothes that maybe they got too fat to fit into but they fit you and your friend is actually happy to be able to have you wear them and she's not jealous at all.

FRIENDS ANSWER THE FUCKING PHONE

This is a friend prerequisite. I hate when people screen calls. Everyone thinks they're a drug dealer with their cell phone. Like my call isn't important enough to take while they're in the middle of checking Friendster? It's stoops in charge.* Either pick up the phone or call me back *that day*. You are not that busy, Donald Trump. What do you have to do, get ready for the Governor's Ball? We're all fucking occupied, but we make time for what counts. Like friendship.

Also, if they genuinely can't get the phone, a real friend will leave an outgoing voicemail message with a joke that only all their friends will get. Which leads me to...

FRIENDS ANNOY EVERYONE ELSE WITH THEIR STUPID PRIVATE JOKES

Would you know what I meant if you heard me say, "Dazzle, dazzle, scoop de jour, pride!" to my friend Derrick, or "Paint yourself a picture of an afternoon delight" to my friend Ben? No? Good, you shouldn't. Those jokes are private.

Secret languages can also form an ironclad friendship bond. For example, consider Hanna and Emily, two BFFs since high school. They communicate in their own magical tongue. It's called Swedish, and you can't learn it from a book! Together they use it to talk shit about people in front of their faces, and it brings them closer every day.

FRIENDS KEEP SECRETS

Well, the important ones anyway. Like Jennifer didn't

---

*Stoops in charge: adjectival phrase meaning "stupid." Comes from "Gnarls in Charge," an adjectival phrase meaning "gnarly" that is based on the title of the popular TV show Charles in Charge. *(See page 284 for the inevitable demise of this little trend.)*

want me to tell anyone she had an abortion, but we're not friends anymore because she stopped taking my phone calls. So I told everybody. To test out a new friend, tell them you used to have a weird little nubby tail, but make it a real sob story so they believe you. Then see how long it takes to ride the gossip express back to your station. If they don't tell anyone, they're a keeper.

Wait, they actually might just be boring. If it *does* get back to you that you had a tail, don't trust them, but keep them handy for spreading rumors about other people.

FRIENDS COPY EACH OTHER

This is another ancient ritual, dating back to the Egyptians, when Ramses II totally copied the way Ramses I tortured the Israelites (with sticks). Ally Sklover, my BFF from high school, copied my Adidas Sambas, but I got her back by rocking a pink tracksuit. We're BFFs, so it's all good. Friends also copy words and claim they started them, which led to a great war among my friends in 1999 over who started the word *fagét* (which means "an effeminate straight guy").

This is not to be confused with friends who claim they started trends that they clearly did not, like my friend Peter who said, "You know how everyone is moving to LA? I totally started that!" Er, what?

FRIENDS CALL POISON CONTROL WHEN YOU OVERDOSE ON RED BULL

Let's say you're at a party, and the only free drinks are vodka and Red Bull, and you are currently on the wagon. So you proceed to drink Red Bull after Red Bull. By your sixth Red Bull, you start to believe that you are in fact, a red bull, so you go home and repeatedly ram your head into the wall. You start to panic when you can taste your heart beating. So you call your BFF and she races over at 4 AM with Xanax in hand. When you don't calm down, she calls Poison Control, who tell her to take you to the hospital immediately. But you don't want to go, so instead she rubs your back until you fall asleep, and then she quietly leaves.

FRIENDS CUDDLE

Or make out. On rare occasions, they even fuck. It's true! Some friends can make love in the name of friendship and having orgasms, and it will still be cool. It does happen. Especially on road trips. In seedy motels. In Alabama. With a dildo you bought "as a joke."

The best thing, though, is making out with your friends "for practice." If you develop a crush on your friend after a steamy game of Seven Minutes in Heaven, you might get lucky and end up in a full-on Monica-Chandler love explosion. If not, get ready to cry 4-ever. Well not forever, but for a really long time (five days).

FRIENDS BEAT PEOPLE UP FOR YOU

I was at a show, standing on a chair, and I didn't know where to put the bottle cap from my beer. I thought it would be hilarious if I silently placed it on top of this random dude's head. And it was! Until the guy saw me laughing hysterically and realized what I'd done. Then he was like, "Stop laughing at my expense!" (He literally said that.) And he pushed me off my chair onto the floor. My friend Bob got right up in his grill and was like, "Dude!" and he pounded him, even though Bob just got out of jail. Now that guy and everyone around him know that shoving a girl is different.

FRIENDS ARE AT LEAST CORDIAL TO YOUR BOYFRIEND/GIRLFRIEND EVEN IF THEY THINK HE/SHE IS BORING, ANNOYING ON COKE, NOT ABLE TO PLAY "CELEBRITY," OR A FUCKING JUNKIE LIAR

That's all there is to say about that one.

FRIENDS TELL YOU WHEN YOU'RE BEING A DICK

For instance, just a minute ago my roommate, Christi Bradnox, made an AIDS-baby joke, and I was all, "Whoa, dude, not cool. In a different context, maybe, but not this time." Then she made another joke about cancer, but that one was actually pretty good.

Conversely, a real friend is not allowed to get mad at another friend's goofy and pointless jokes, like the time Amy stormed out of an otherwise fun Japanese dinner just because Kevin made a joke about not liking girls with asymmetrical labia. Come on, Amy. That doesn't even mean anything. Asymmetrical labia?

They were in a fight for a year after that.

FRIENDS GIVE YOU A SECOND CHANCE, MAYBE EVEN A THIRD

Like my friend Judi, who let me work at her store. My first day there I showed up an hour late wearing a ripped Van Halen t-shirt and cutoff jean shorts, my eyes basically sewn shut with crackhead crud. She looked at me like, "What the fuck?" and I slurred, "Dude, if you give me a bump of coke or a bong hit, I'll be fine." She looked at me sadly and said, "Lesley, go home." To this day, she is still my friend, and she even lets me work at the store sometimes. Also, I used to intern at *Vice* and do bumps of heroin in the bathroom every 15 minutes, and look, they still love me! I believe that true, true friendship is unconditional. Holding a grudge is pretty annoying, and it sucks to ignore your funniest friend. Think about all the good times you'd be missing out on and all the giggles you won't get to share.

Why are you crying? I'm being nice. ■

LESLEY ARFIN AND AMY KELLNER

OMIGAWD!

The Vice Guide to Girls

Illustration by Christy Karacas

I t's fun to be a girl. We get to giggle and cry and throw hissy fits and keep diaries and bleed out of our vaginas and care about stuff and we don't have to feel like a fag about it. We even get to vote, hooray! Sometimes we forget to though. Sorry, Susan B. Anthony!

Now before you go calling us dumb sluts (we know you love to do that), you should know that we also understand the problems with making essentialist assumptions about gender. We know that biology doesn't dictate who we are (society does!). We went to liberal arts colleges, thanks. So if you're a girl and you love fixing cars and playing football, that's aces. We can do whatever we wanna do, right ladies? And right now we wanna give you an A-to-Z list of some of the things we love (and hate) about being a girl. Girl Power! (Just kidding.)

ASSHOLES

Guys think we're attracted to assholes because that's their only defense for when we dump them. When girls are rejected we turn it inward and blame ourselves for not being prettier. That's our bad, we know. But when dudes are rejected they makes grand statements like, "Women love guys that are assholes, they don't care about us nice guys!" And then that grand statement spreads like the wave at a Yankees game and next thing you know it's written in fucking stone because dudes are able to write stuff in stone! Yes, they have that much power.

We don't want you to push our heads down to your crotch area when you want a blowjob, but we also don't want you to cry and write shitty emo poetry and paint our portrait in pastels. It's just that there's only a teeny wading pool in between the lake of total assholes and the bay of fucking pussies, so sometimes when we're horny we'll take what we can get. Ultimately we all want the same things: Good sex 'n' giggles. So learn how to eat pussy and start memorizing lines from Will Ferrell comedies like your sex life depends on it. Because it does.

Honorable mentions: Apple (the one that Eve ate), Andie from *Pretty in Pink*, Ally Sheedy

BLAHNIK, MANOLO

What's the big whoop with these things? We've never been able to justify spending half our rent on a pair of shoes so we have no idea and guess what? We don't care. Have you ever seen a foot come out of a high heel after several hours of wear? Not a pretty sight, no matter how expensive the shoe. It's like you crammed five sweaty, naked, fat people into a phone booth. They are red, puffy, and pissed off. Don't get us wrong, we like heels. Dress-up is fun. But we also like not having bunions and toes that will eventually look like Teen Wolf's fingers. So save the heels for museum galas and dancing naked for your boyfriend and rethink the penny loafer. They're sexier than you think!

Honorable mentions: Buffy, Babies, birth-control pills, brides, biological determinism, Betty & Veronica, baking, *Bring It On*

CHICK LIT

In case you've been living on *Lord of the Flies* island, "chick lit" is book-speak for literature written by women, for women who act like girls. We try to love it but we don't. Why? Because it's usually written about normal girls who have normal jobs and try to get ahead in their boring, normal careers and we can't understand why. They are filled with clichés and have stolen our

lingo, like "totes" and, even more embarrassing, ancient terms like "hottie" (so '96). Sometimes these books are about rich women who have nannies, and then maybe their nannies keep a diary and we're supposed to care about that too. This just in: We don't!

Honorable mentions: Cats, crafternoons, caring, cliques, Cookie Mueller, CeBe Barnes

DIET SODA

We know it's a cliché but goddammit, it just tastes better than regular soda. We swear. Isn't it lame how Pepsi made Pepsi One to trick macho dudes into drinking diet soda? Seriously, whose manhood is threatened by diet soda? Probably someone with a very tiny manhood. Ha ha ha! (Small-dick jokes. Classic.)

Honorable mentions: Dildos, Darlene from *Roseanne*

EATING DISORDER

Fun-fact time! Here are some statistics culled from NationalEatingDisorders.com: The average American woman is 5'4" tall and weighs 140 pounds. The average American model is 5'11" tall and weighs 117 pounds. Eighty percent of American women claim to be dissatisfied with their physical appearance, and 10 million women in the US have a full-on eating disorder. Depressed yet? Here, have some ice cream, it'll make you feel better.

But come on, do you really want to let TV and fashion magazines tell you that you're fat and worthless? You're smarter than that. If you act like you're awesome, people will think that you're awesome. And if you have to, fake it. Fake it till it's not fake anymore.

Honorable mentions: Emma Goldman, estrogen, Eileen Myles, essentialism vs. constructivism

FEMINISM

We get so mad when some nitwit says she's not a feminist. I guess if you're cool with being raped all the time and having no options in life other than being a baby machine or a prostitute, then yeah, you're probably not a feminist. But if you enjoy birth-control pills and not being beaten up by your owner—I mean, husband—then you pretty much are one so you may as well stop shaving your legs right now. Just kidding. Somewhere along the way feminism got a bad rep, but it doesn't mean you have to be a sourpuss or that you can't write tongue-in-cheek articles riddled with silly gender stereotypes. All it means is that you don't hate yourself.

Honorable mentions: Feelings, face cream, flirting, *Foxes*

G-SPOT

Ooh, the G-spot. How do I find the G-spot? Where can I buy 500 books about finding the G-spot? Listen, for the millionth time: If you put your fingers in a lady's vagina and tap up in a "come here" motion right behind the area that feels kinda spongy, that's it. It usually feels pretty awesome for the lady and she might even cum on your face if you're lucky. The end.

Honorable mentions: *Ghost World, Grey Gardens, Golden Girls*, getting fingered, gossiping

HITACHI MAGIC WAND

This machine, aka the Cadillac of vibrators, is the answer to your orgasm prayers. If you don't have one, buy one. Now. And stop writing to *Glamour* about how to achieve an orgasm through intercourse because who are you kidding? Clits need vibes like diamond rings need fingers.

Honorable mentions: H&M, *Heathers*, horses

ICE SKATING

The delicate twirling. The death-defying leaps. The sparkly outfits. Pitting preteen girls against each other and making them cry. Ice skating is as girly as it gets. It's the only Olympic event we really care about. Well, and gymnastics, which is basically ice skating without the ice. Oh, and men's swimming, which is just sexy.

Honorable mentions: Intimacy, *I'm With the Band* by Pamela Des Barres

JENNY LEWIS

Dear Jesus,

Thank you for giving us Jenny Lewis. She sings real purdy and has nice hair.

Love,
Girls

Honorable mentions: Judy Blume, Jerri Blank, Joni Mitchell, jumping up and down when we're happy

KATHLEEN HANNA

Dear Satan,

Thank you for giving us Kathleen Hanna. She doesn't care what you think, and we don't either.

Love,
Grrls

Honorable mentions: Knickknacks, Kate Bush, Kimya Dawson, Kim Kelly from *Freaks and Geeks*

LUGS

If you went to a liberal arts college you already know that LUG stands for Lesbian Until Graduation. Real lesbians get annoyed that straight girls experiment with lesbianism in college just to hopefully scare their parents when they mention it at Thanksgiving. And we can't really blame the lesbos—LUGs are the leading number-one cause of lesbian heartbreak in America. Every dyke we know has been used then chucked by at least one "bi-curious" girl.

Honorable mentions: Lita Ford, Lynda Barry, leotards, *Little Darlings*, *Ladies and Gentlemen: The Fabulous Stains*, Laurie Alpert (author of *Growing Up Underground*—read it)

MEAN GIRLS (THE MOVIE)

"I don't hate you because you're fat, you're fat because I hate you." And there you have the best line from the best movie about teenage girls to come out since John Hughes dumped Molly for Macaulay (bad move, man). You would think that by starring in a movie about exactly how not to be a stupid teenage bitch, Lindsay Lohan would have learned a thing or two. Oh well. Tina Fey is the real hero of this one. We watch the DVD over and over and wish that we were the ones to have written the screenplay.

Honorable mentions: Maternal instincts, Mama Cass, Margaret Cho, Mo'Nique, Maureen Dowd, marriage, manipulating, martyrdom, Miss Hannigan

NICE TITS

Everyone loves boobs. Boobs are the best. Except for our own. They're way too small/big/pointy/droopy/lopsided/ whatever. Girls never ever like their boobs. It's like a curse. But here's the thing to consider: Real men love real boobs. We mean, real ones—squishy tits that flop over when you lie on your back. No one likes hard, fake boob jobs except for porn fetishists and hair-gel frat jocks and do you really want those creeps touching your special areas anyway?

Honorable mentions: Nancy Drew, Nikki Corvette, Nomi Malone, not wanting to have butt sex

OMG

OMG, can you believe that girls invented slang and no one gives us props for it? In fact, we totally invented the following things: Saying "like" every two seconds, reducing "totally" to "totes," "stupid" to "stoops," and expanding "stoops" to "stoops du jour." We changed "gnarly" to "gnarls" and then upped the ante with "Gnarly Lama," "Gnarls in Charge," and yes, even "Gnarls Barkley." That one got stolen big-time! We put the "grody" in "Grodo Baggins" and the "jealousy" in "peanut butter and jelz" (we know you're jelz of that one!).

OK, maybe inventing slang like this isn't something to be proud of. It doesn't make us sound particularly smart (unless you come up with a 'licious [delicious] word combo such as "God, this party is so Gnarlito's Way!") but boys around the globe have been ripping us off for years. We heard them use "douche chills" on a syndicated sitcom and we invented that! We know we're just getting territorial and making it seem like girls invented all plays on words. But we did! We just wanted you to know. It's

not like we don't want dudes to say stuff like, "OMG, it's so chilly con carne out tonight!" We do, we just want you to admit that WE invented the way you talk, OK?
Honorable mentions: Orphan Annie, overthinking stuff

PAULA BEGOUN, THE COSMETICS COP

We heart Paula because she calls bullshit on fancy make-up and skin-/hair-care products. But she's not anti-make-up—you can tell from her picture that she wears more than her share. She just calmly explains what the ingredients in the products actually mean (plant extracts are bullshit—thanks, Clarins), alerts you to the insane amount of irritants contained in most skin creams (screw you, Origins), and then rates the best and worst ones for you. And it's all online for free.

PS: You know that Crème de la Mer stuff that is supposedly the best moisturizer ever and costs $160 for a teaspoonful? Well, according to Paula, it is "almost exclusively water, thickening agents, and some algae." Suckers!
Honorable mentions: Pink, pink, PMS, Patti Smith, Poly Styrene, Pammy and Nicky from *Times Square*, people-pleasing, processing, Punky Brewster

QUIZZES ON MYSPACE

Girls only do those stupid MySpace quizzes to send secret, subliminal messages to boys they have crushes on. Now you know.
Honorable mentions: Queen Latifah, quilting (we do that, right?), Queen Elizabeth, questioning everything!

ROM-COMS

Rom-coms are romantic comedies (*When Harry Met Sally* is the mother of all rom-coms), and oddly enough we know more boys who are into these movies than girls. Just ask our editor. Rom-coms are pretty good for a Sunday afternoon. Flip on 11-Alive (that's what channel 11 was called in the 80s) and fold your laundry to *You've Got Mail, Serendipity, Just Like Heaven,* and *The Truth About Cats and Dogs.* It's actually one of the only guilty pleasures we can honestly say we feel a little guilty about. It seems like these movies were made specifically for us single women to feel hopeful about finding our soulmate and it's OK because all nice guys and chubby girls finish last and don't worry, you will too, and damn you Hollywood big-wigs for making us fall into your devilish trap!
Honorable mentions: Rainbows, Regina Spektor, the Runaways, Rizzo, Ramona Quimby, *Rollerderby* magazine

SASSY MAGAZINE

If the cassingle of "Betty Boo: Doin' the Do," randomly showed up at your house, then you were a subscriber to *Sassy* magazine! Congratulations! You've just been awarded 25 cool points. Add an extra 1,000 if your riot-grrl band was ever featured in the "Cute Band Alert," and, if you're a boy, add 10 for being the boy of the month in "Dear Boy." If you interned at the magazine, wore overalls, cut your hair short, had a pair of Chinese slippers or John Fluevog Mary Janes, made your own skirt out of neckties, submitted to "It Happened to Me" or that weird little poetry page, still own the issue with Kurt and Courtney on the cover AND the 7" single by Chia Pet on bubblegum-pink vinyl then you are the winner of being one of the coolest girls ever to exist on this planet. Yay!

PS: There's a book about *Sassy* coming out in April. We'll be buying our copies at the stroke of midnight.
Honorable mentions: Slutty Halloween costumes, self-help books, Sarah Silverman, *The Sweetest Thing*, strap-ons, saying yes when we really mean no, the Sundays, the Shangri-las

THONGS

One question: Why? I own one thong and the only time I wear it is on laundry day. And typical me, every laundry day I forget how fucking annoying they are and I find myself picking at invisible wedgies the whole time. But you can't pick thong wedgies because a thong IS a wedgie. You are choosing to give yourself a wedgie. And why, because it looks hot to dudes when you lean over and they see the little stringy triangle sticking out? Where were you born, Asbury Park? Do your kids go to preschool in a casino? Thongs are fucking cheesy! If you don't want your panty lines to show (reconsider, however, panty lines can be really hot) then why not just wear... nothing? What a shocker. And don't be scared that people will be able to see your woo-woo like Paris and Lindsay. Those girls want to show off their vaginas. And why shouldn't they? Vaginas are way prettier than thongs.
Honorable mentions: Tina Fey, *Three Women*, tomboys, thrifting, talking about other people, talking about relationships, talking on the phone

UNICORNS

All girls love unicorns. And we all love the movie *The Last Unicorn.* And the theme song to that movie by the band America is our favorite song and we all have the lyrics written in calligraphy next to our poster of a bouquet of roses that have been strewn over a piano. And when we hear this song, we all put on our pointe shoes and one of those masquerade-type masks and dance around our bedrooms singing, "When the last eagle flies over the last crumbling mountain/ And the last lion roars at the last dusty fountain/ In the shadow of the forest/ Though she may be old and worn/ They will stare unbe-

lieving/ At the last unicorn... I'm alive! I'm alii-iiive!"
Honorable mentions: "Uptown Top Ranking" by Althea & Donna, Ugly Betty, Uggs (why won't they die???)

VIAGRA

Who wants to be pounded for five hours? What modern woman has the time? Hey, ever wonder what would happen if a girl took Viagra? We know a lesbian who took some with her girlfriend and here's what she said: "It was the worst sex we ever had. Clits are sort of like little penises, so they got all swollen and hard and it took FOREVER for us to come. But I guess technically that's what Viagra's supposed to do so I don't know what we were expecting." Fascinating!
Honorable mentions: Viola Swamp (the mean teacher from *Miss Nelson is Missing!*), vaginas (doye), *Valerie*, V. C. Andrews

WAXING

Waxing hurts. It hurts a lot. God forbid you should choke on a pubic hair while you're eating us out. Thank you, Larry David. What's with girls waxing everything though? We can understand a bikini wax, and even a betweeny wax (only Jewish and Italian girls need apply), but getting a Brazilian and having absolutely no hair down there is a little weird. Looking like a five-year-old when you get naked is just gross. If men like it, if they're the ones that specifically request it, you might want to take into consideration that they're pedophiles. Sorry but it's true. We understand that not everyone wants to embrace their inner Andrea Dworkin, and we agree that personal grooming is important. But it doesn't mean you have to look like a porn star. No one looks like that. Sex is supposed to be awkward and weird and dirty, with stray hairs and stinky pits. Those are the things that sometimes make it the sexiest.
Honorable mentions: Witchcraft, women's studies, Wendy Williams, Wendy O. Williams, Wanda Sykes, wanting more than he's willing to give, Weetzie Bat

X-PENSIVE PURSES

Are we the only ones who find the popularity of $10,000 handbags with WASPy names like "The Clive" or "The Eliza" disturbing? Seriously, it's a place to put your tampons. I mean, true, girls love a cute purse. It's because a purse is a metaphor for a vagina—it's small and velvety and pretty and you want to put things in it again and again and again. Still, our criteria for a good bag are: a) lots of zippered pockets, and b) big enough to fit all our crap inside because, like Alison in *The Breakfast Club* says, "You never know when you may have to jam." If it happens to have a cute heart pattern on it and lots of shiny things hanging off it, then yay, bonus. But really, like they always say, it's what's inside that counts—carry useful things in your purse and lend them freely. People will be impressed by your generosity and resourcefulness! Much more so than they would be by a price tag anyway.
Honorable mentions: *Xanadu*, *Xena: Warrior Princess* (we miss that show every day)

YOU

You are a girl! You are a gift, a rainbow, a ray of sunlight and a fresh summer breeze. You give life and eat forbidden apples with pride and determination. You are beautiful and don't ever let anyone tell you otherwise. As a girl there are a few simple commandments. One of them is that jealousy kills girl-love, so the next time you and a bunch of your girlfriends gang up against another girl and make her cry because she hooked up with your ex, just remember that it's really not cool to do that! You don't even care about Kevin anyway, YOU dumped HIM! Another thing to remember is, "Beer before liquor, never been sicker. Liquor before beer, you're in the clear." Sitting on the sidewalk while Mandy holds your hair back while you puke is not a good look!

In all seriousness though, you are a girl so you should be siked. Give your man a great idea and don't be surprised when he turns to his friends and says, "Hey man, why don't you listen to my great idea?" Since you're a girl you won't mind because that's how we roll. Do you think Yoko cared when she told John Lennon about peace and he acted like he invented the damn thing? No, she didn't. You're smart. You don't need to prove yourself to anyone. You know the truth, so stop acting like you don't already. It's giving the rest of us a bad rep.
Honorable mentions: Yoko Ono, yeast infections, yogurt

ZODIAC

"Oh my gosh, you are SUCH a Libra!" Sandra said after she showed me where the frozen-yogurt machine was in the caf. It was my first day working for Mr. Spencer, the top dog at the law firm were I had landed my first real secretarial job. Oops, I mean "executive assistant." Gosh, I'm so forgetful, I guess I truly am a Libra after all! Sandra was so sweet. After she offered me a Diet Coke she told me where I could hide my Reeboks. "Mr. Spencer makes sure all his girls wear pumps but I know it's only natch to wear 'boks, just don't let him see you." Thank gosh Sandra was a Gemini. We were compatible as lifelong friends. I just knew I was going to make it in Big Apple city!
Honorable mentions: Zines, zero (the number of girls who think *Fletch* is funny). ■

JAMES FLUCK

———

PICKPOCKET POINTERS

12 Methods to Do the Dip

Wise up, cholly! Pickpockets are all around you. You think these guys stopped working in the 1940s? Come on! Why do you think we still have those announcements on city buses about watching out for them?

In 2001, $8,665,446 worth of property was stolen by pickpocketing in New York State. In 2004, larcenies in the NYC subway went up 4.9 percent. Care to hazard a guess why? Because everyone has an iPod on them, complete with the telltale white headphones. You guys are sitting ducks out there!

Randy Stoever was the head of the NYPD's pickpocket squad for nine years. He's seen every lushworker, dip, cannon, stall, and vic in the city (we have no idea what the fuck that means either).

"Pickpockets are some of the smartest uneducated people around," says Stoever. "Their techniques can be inventive and daring, but you still see guys arrested four or five times—career pickpockets. They're usually about 40 years old and a lot of them have been doing it since they were 12. Most of the people I busted that worked the buses in Queens were South American but I have arrested every kind—all races, creeds, and ages.

"When we would see a known pickpocket who was on parole, we'd bring him to the attention of his PO and get stipulations added to his parole that would stop him from going on subways or buses.

"We were a really aggressive squad, so we were very effective. I personally debriefed all the pickpockets we arrested. Perps always told me that they knew about us and lived in fear of being caught by my unit."

1. STANDARD PICKPOCKET

This is the guy who reaches his hand into your front or rear pocket to take your wallet. Most of his vics are male. A good way to foil this jerkoff is by wrapping a rubber band around your wallet, making it impossible for him to just slip it out.

2. BAG OPENER

He mostly preys on women with purses, but can also target anyone with a backpack. Most of the time, he's shielding his working hand with a coat or newspaper in his free hand, providing a screen to work behind.

3. BUMP AND STALL

This is a team. The stall stands in front of the vic and drops something, like money or a Metrocard. He bends down and stops the vic in his tracks. The vic bumps into the stall and falls into a forward-leaning position. The cannon comes in from behind and removes the vic's wallet from his pocket. This happens a lot at the tops of escalators.

4. THE CUTTER

He uses a straight razor to slice the side of a bag that he wants into, then reaches into the slit. This one is big during the holidays, when women are riding the subways with a lot of packages in addition to their purses. Some cutters even use scissors to cut the straps right off a bag and take the whole thing. How about the balls on these guys?!

5. THE LUSHWORKER

He walks along the outside of trains looking for sleepers, then comes in and nudges them to see if they wake up. If they do, he acts like a Good Samaritan. If the vic doesn't wake, he goes into their pocket. If he can't get into a pocket, he'll cut their pants, taking the pocket right off.

A PICKPOCKET'S DICTIONARY

Fanning: lightly touching a pocket to see if there's money or a wallet in it

Cannon, Hitter: a pickpocket

Stall: a partner who distracts a victim

Vic, Mark: the victim of a pickpocket

Jostling Squad, Po-Po: the police

Players: fellow pickpockets.

Hide: a wallet

Looping: when a pickpocket goes from one end of a train line to another, transferring back and forth for hours

---

6. THE SQUIRTER

The classic ketchup or mustard pickpockets. Sometimes these guys even squirt their vic with pigeon shit. Often the squirter will be an elderly woman or man. They'll squirt you from afar, then come over and offer to help clean you up with napkins. While they're scrubbing away, either they or an accomplice robs you.

7. DISTRACTERS

These guys work in teams. A couple of them will start a fake fight. While the vic is watching this, the cannon will make the dip.

8. THE EATERY WORKER

He targets restaurants, hitting purses that are hanging on chairs. Randy Stoever says, "I once saw a team at a Krispy Kreme on 86th Street. He had his back to a couple of old ladies. His partner was signaling to him when it was all clear. He went behind his back, reached into her purse, and removed her wallet."

9. THE PRATFALL

One of the perps walks up to a train door that's about to close and pretends to get his foot stuck. When the well-meaning vic comes forward to help, another pickpocket swoops in and robs him. After they get the wallet, the first perp will get up and walk away. Again: Balls.

10. THE OLD MAN ON THE BUS

He takes his left arm out of its sleeve and reaches all the way behind his body and into his neighbor's bag or pocket. "We saw this guy contorting himself so bad the vic thought he was having a seizure," says Randy. "He said, 'You need the whole seat, sir?' and the perp snapped at him, 'Don't move! Just stay there!'"

11. LADIES' ROOMERS

These female pickpockets snatch purses from right off the coat hook on the inside of a stall door while a female vic is using the john. Often, the perp will have a partner in the stall next to the vic who will create a distraction like dropping something on the floor near their shoes.

12. THE CREEPER

He will pick pockets with no crowd around, coming right up behind you, opening your bag, and removing your wallet. This fucker is what is known as deft. Most vics won't even recall being bumped.

If you can rob a guy coming the opposite way you are basically a Thetan level 8 of pickpocketing. ∎

HOWARD C. ADELMAN WITH JESSE PEARSON

HOW REAL IS HORROR?

The Vice Guide to Gore

Dr. Howard C. Adelman is a pathologist who does consultations for police, private investigators, and local morticians. To a horror-movie fan and true-crime fan, the guy is also a living legend. He was the deputy chief medical inspector at the original Amityville murders on Long Island in 1977. The story that was bastardized again and again for books and movies, the six people shot in one night by a family member? This is the first guy who walked around that crime scene with the cops checking stuff out.

We showed him clips of kill scenes from some iconic slasher flicks and then asked him, "Is this bullshit or what?"

FRIDAY THE 13TH

Method: Ax to the head

Dr. Adelman: "This is certainly possible. With one swipe, you can get an ax right into the head. It usually does take more than one swing, and we'll get defensive wounds on the victim's arms from trying to ward off the attack. But if somebody takes you by surprise and gets a full-force swing going, this could happen. The skin is relatively elastic, which makes it almost as hard to penetrate as bone. So this wound, which looks almost unrealistically clean, is actually entirely feasible. The scalp and the forehead are very rich in blood vessels. It bleeds profusely even on the slightest injury. The amount of blood here, for the initial blow, is adequate. This death wouldn't be instantaneous. The frontal part of the brain is not vital, so if left untreated she would have bled to death. Also, she could have remained conscious for some time with this ax in her head."

Bullshit factor: Low. It could happen to you or someone you love.

HOLLYWOOD CHAINSAW HOOKERS

Method: Chainsaw to the stomach/chest area

"If it hit her stomach, the victim's intestinal contents would come spewing out, and the murderess would be splashed with hydrochloric acid. She would get acid burns. It didn't seem like that was happening here, but that could depend on when the victim had her last meal. If she hadn't eaten in a while, there would be less acid. The killer would certainly be spewed with fecal material and partially digested food. This could be an accurate portrayal."

Bullshit factor: Shockingly low. This is realism.

PHANTASM

Method: Spiked metal ball with drill between the eyes

"That's an awful lot of blood. I doubt that there is a weapon like this. I would say that this is total hokum. If something were to drill through your eye, it would simply liquefy the eye. You would not see that amount of blood spurting out. You would see both liquid and viscous fluids from the eye. They are clear and colorless."

Bullshit factor: You lie, Phantasm.

BRIDE OF CHUCKY

Method: Jennifer Tilly gets electrocuted with a TV in the bathtub

"The main effect of electrocution is that it stops your heart from beating. It's instant. You also get third-degree burns at the electricity's site of entry. People do spasm like this when they are electrocuted. They thrash about because of all the muscle contractions. It depends on the voltage, but death can occur within seconds or it can take a bit. The only thing that strikes me as unreal here is that she wouldn't be screaming. She would be unconscious."

Bullshit factor: Half and half.

FRIDAY THE 13TH

Method: Poker through throat

"Hey, that's Kevin Bacon. So the killer was supposed to have gotten a fireplace poker through the back of his neck and out the front. Going through the back of the neck, you would encounter the vertebral column, which is hard as stone. Getting on either side of that would make life easier for the murderer. If they managed to make it through a gap in the vertebrae, severing the spinal cord, it would preclude any movement of the victim's extremities. There would not be as much blood as we see here. The main arteries are off to the side of the neck. The poker would have punctured the pharynx and the trachea, or larynx, but there would be no blood spurts. This blood was only a dramatic device. Any muscle of the neck is easy to get through. You go through muscle every time you cut a steak."

Bullshit factor: Too much blood, but totes possible.

HELLRAISER

Method: Hammer to the head and face

"Once again, we would be likely to see defensive wounds in a hammer attack. The blood is in the wrong place here. If she hit him in the face, she would likely get him in the nose, which protrudes. She would break it, and it would bleed. Usually when you are struck in the face, you bite your tongue off, which also causes a lot of blood. Often, a blow to the face will rupture a little membrane in your upper and lower lip called the frenulum. But it wouldn't cause this much blood. As for the blow to the back of the head, we would probably see the imprint of the hammer on the skull. It would leave a pattern that would be consistent with an actual hammer's head."

Bullshit factor: More like Hell-Exaggerator.

HAPPY BIRTHDAY TO ME

Method: Weight dropped on crotch, leading to fully loaded barbell dropped on neck

"In this case, you wouldn't see blood, although there is a large spurt here. In the autopsy you would see internal lacerations, especially of the liver because of the weight being dropped on the abdomen. As for the weight falling on the neck, it is unlikely it would have broken the skin. There would have been severe trauma to the throat. So the death would likely be of asphyxiation, which takes up to one or two minutes. It is also possible that the internal damage to his abdomen could lead to death by way of internal bleeding. The spurt of blood we see in this scene, however, is completely unrealistic."

Bullshit factor: Real, real high.

SILENT NIGHT, DEADLY NIGHT

Method: Impaled on antlers

"She dies instantly, but death would certainly not be instantaneous in this case. It rarely is with impalement. Look at the most infamous impaler of all time, Vlad Teppes, who was the inspiration for the character Dracula. He took great pleasure in the days it took for impalement victims to die. I had a case of someone who was impaled in an accident in which a large piece of fence went through his chest. It missed his heart but went through his lungs. He was alive for at least a half hour after that. The only way that death by impalement can be immediate is if the heart or the aorta is penetrated. Also, the killer would have to be inhumanly strong to lift a person over his head and calmly lower her onto a pair of trophy antlers."

Bullshit factor: High. This ain't happening.

A NIGHTMARE ON ELM STREET

Method: Hanged with a bedsheet

"With hanging, there are two major ways of death. The first is strangulation, which does not occur instantly. That's why people can dangle and struggle for quite a while before they die. The other way of death via hanging is an internal decapitation. This is where a great height is used, and their body weight separates their vertebral column. So the skin doesn't break, but the spinal column is pulled apart. The height here is not nearly enough for the neck to break, yet he dies quite quickly, which is not concurrent with a strangulation via hanging."

Bullshit factor: No way, guy.

THE AMITYVILLE HORROR

Method: Shotgun blasts to the head

"Six people were killed in this case. Each bedroom was a separate crime scene. The real mystery here, which to my mind has never been solved, is that they were all—except one girl who was shot in the face—murdered in very similar positions. They were all facedown. There was supposedly only one perpetrator. Our ballistics expert told me that when the type of gun that was used here is fired, it sounds like a howitzer. Yet nobody seemed to awaken or become alarmed as the killer went from room to room. Very strange. There was a theory that they had been drugged, but our toxicological results disproved that. I have difficulty with the accepted conclusion in this case, which is that Ronald DeFeo acted alone. I could see no signs of a struggle on the scene either. In one of the bedrooms, there was even a partially fixed puzzle on one of the tables, which even a mild struggle would have disturbed."

Bullshit factor: It really happened, dude. He saw it himself. ∎

MINO JIBILLA

THE VICE GUIDE TO IRAQ FROM ٱ TO ى

Photo by Kevin Smith

Iraq is more than just exploding bodies, bloodthirsty zealots, and confused American soldiers. It's also got spicy meat soups and raisin-juice, verdant rosebushes, and centuries of culture and tradition. Here's our guide to Iraq from Alif to Yaa'.

ALIF IS FOR AHWAR

Ahwar is the name of the marshlands in the southern part of Iraq. The people there have lived the same way for thousands of years and are among the few remaining ancient cultures on earth. To this day they live in huts made of braided reeds surrounded by water buffalo. Saddam made life hell for them by building a dam that dried up their territory. Now that Saddam's gone and the water's back they have sectarian death squads, cancer, and jumpy military folk to keep them busy.

BAA' IS FOR BAGHDAD HIGH SCHOOL FOR GIRLS

If you are a teenager, have a car, and are looking for a girl to go out with on a date,

Baghdad High School for Girls is the place to go. Placed in a very fancy neighborhood, this school teaches the daughters of some of the richest families in Baghdad. This should be obvious from the luxury cars with drivers waiting in the parking lot outside the front door at any time of the school day. Unfortunately, there are policemen protecting the girls from being harassed. You have to be very charming and have a very fancy car to outsmart the police—pretend to be a sibling and pick up the girl as quickly as you can before they notice, or you'll be in trouble.

TAA' IS FOR TEA TIME

Undecided about where to go out for the weekend with friends? There is always the old standby Tea Time. Established in the mid-90s in the rich Harthiya neighborhood, this fast-food restaurant serves enormous sandwiches. Their burgers are so huge that they make the Big Mac look like a White Castle slider. Tea Time has been slowly extending its property for the past few years and now owns the entire two-story building in which it was once-upon-a-time renting a small shop. Iraq is still free from all the American junk-food restaurants at this point—most Iraqis believe that if a Burger King were to open in Baghdad, it'd still lose business against the local fast-food chains.

THAA' IS FOR THIREED

Thireed was originally a Bedouin meal but flourished and became very popular in Iraq. It consists mainly of bread dipped in meat soup and huge chunks of meat. Iraqis are so into meat they even eat kebabs at breakfast, and this is like the Iraqi rib-eye steak dish.

JEEM IS FOR JADIRIYA CLUB (NADI AL-JADIRIYA)

Jadiriya Club is the top social club of high-aristocratic families in Iraq. Uday Hussein originally founded it in the early 90s as a horseback-riding club for his fellow equestrians, but the beautiful gardens, brilliant scenery, and nice settings began to attract all the rich families in Iraq. These families tend to have a very Westernized lifestyle, and it became normal to see daughters and sons of different families dating, partying, or going on boat rides in the river Dijlah. After the war, the Jadiriya Club was taken over and now serves as a military base.

HAA' IS FOR HAJJI ZBALA (OLD MAN GARBAGE)

A small cafeteria in Baghdad that opened in 1901 and is named for its owner, Mr. Zbala (that's the Arabic word for "garbage"). His parents named him "Garbage" at a time when some superstitious Iraqis would also give their kids names like "Donkey" or "Piss" to ward off the evil eye. This obviously worked for little Zbala, as it sealed his destiny as the most popular raisin-juice-shop owner in Iraq. It was the photo-op place of choice for Iraqi political figures over the past century.

KHAA' IS FOR KHANDAQ

A *khandaq* is what you dig to hide in to save your life during bombing. It's a shelter. When the war was close, people started to prepare themselves and their houses. They stored food, first aid, and all sorts of fuel and money for emergencies. A lot of people dug wells in their houses, but some people dug a khandaq too. A lot of stories of the older men that participated in the Iran-Iraq war are about things they did in their khandaq during the war. Iraqis, living through long years and having experienced many wars, consider the khandaq an essential part of their lives.

DAAL IS FOR DIJLAH

Dijlah, or what you know as the Tigris, is the river that runs through Iraq, north to south coming from Turkey. It meets up with the Euphrates River right by Basra. Iraqis have romanticized this river in poems, songs, paintings, and books for its beauty. Nowadays it's just a good place to dump dead bodies.

HAAL IS FOR THIBEEHA

Iraq is well known for the hospitality of its people. When an important guest visits, you have to give them a *thibeeha*, or an offering. You slaughter some of the sheep you have if you are in a tribal area or a village, or just get them from a restaurant if you are in a city. Thibeeha is also given at weddings and funerals. If an important figure dies, like a head of a tribe, literally hundreds and even thousands of sheep are slaughtered to make food for the visitors coming from all over the country to pay their respects and express their condolences.

RAA' IS FOR RASHEED STREET

This posh street is located in one of the affluent areas of Baghdad. It used to be frequented by young college students who would hang out at famous restaurants serving different types of food. Rasheed was also teeming with fashion shops, which drew a considerable number of women shoppers. No one goes here anymore. There's no point.

ZAAI IS FOR ZARQAWI

The name that has literally shaken the streets of Iraq with car bombs and drenched it with innocent blood. He was to blame for terrorizing the whole country, driving a wedge between Iraqi countrymen, and turning the people's lives into waking nightmares. Though he's officially dead, the scars he caused are still fresh and painful. A lot of people believe that he isn't responsible for attacks against civilians and was only attacking the American army. A lot of people believe that his role was overexaggerated by the media and used as a political card by many sides. Just like with a lot of other things in Iraq today, nobody knows for sure what the truth is.

SEEN IS FOR SA'AH RESTAURANT

Sa'ah is a very famous Iraqi restaurant. A lot of foreigners even know it because it was in the news many times during the war. Saddam was believed to be hiding in a house behind it, so the American army dropped a ton of bombs on it, which turned the house into a big hole in the ground and damaged the crap out of all the surrounding buildings. It was rebuilt later. The restaurant is in the Mansour neighborhood and is still running although many car bombs have exploded near it since the start of the war. Like all Iraqis, this restaurant is a survivor.

SHEEN IS FOR SHAY

In Iraqi it's pronounced *chay*, (the "ch" sound is common in the Iraqi dialect but has no equivalent in the Arabic alphabet). This tea is so mean it makes black coffee look gay. It's brewed for hours with a ton of cardamom, it's dark as death, and it is consumed with piles of sugar. This is the drink of choice for all Iraqis. They drink it all day long at home, at work, and in public. Today if you see an Iraqi in the street who isn't nursing a cup of shay, he's probably about to reach for an RPG.

Photo by Reuters

SAAD IS FOR SAYD CLUB (NADI IL SAYD)

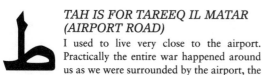

Sayd Club is one of the most famous social clubs in Baghdad. It's the place where families would get together to spend an evening and have dinner, or children would go during the day to swim or play basketball or tennis. Uday, Saddam's son, used to go there a lot too, but as long as you stayed away from him and minded your own business, you'd generally be fine.

DHAAD IS FOR DHARBA (ATTACK)

The 1991 war on Iraq is often referred to by local Iraqis as "the Bush's Dharba." After a number of attacks ensued people started tagging on numbers to distinguish them: the First Dharba and the Second Dharba, and so on. There were smaller dharbas in between too, during the 90s. People used to use "the Dharba" as a reference for time, like: "I started working two years after the Dharba." Now when you say "the Dharba" everyone's like, "Which one?"

TAH IS FOR TAREEQ IL MATAR (AIRPORT ROAD)

I used to live very close to the airport. Practically the entire war happened around us as we were surrounded by the airport, the national security college, and the presidential warehouses. I can't possibly count how many thousands of rockets and missiles went over our heads. The airport road, which we used to take every day to go home, was one of the most

beautiful in Baghdad. It's very wide and was decorated with flowers, bushes, and tall palm trees. Since the American army used the airport as a base, they were being targeted daily on that road with roadside bombs, car bombs, and RPG attacks—all of which left the street full of holes. Eventually the American army had to remove and burn all the trees and bushes to make sure nobody was hiding among them to attack them.

DHA IS FOR DHILAL

Al-Dhilal is a bus company that was once one of the most important means of transportation between Iraq and Jordan. Before the current war, as part of the sanctions, no airplanes were allowed to fly over Iraq. People had to use the desert highway to go to Jordan. It was a 1,000-kilometer trip, and it could take as much as a good 24 hours on the road to make it due to delays at the border. Also, because of the bad security situation, people sometimes prefer to use buses instead of the charter SUVs that started to operate on that road a couple of years before the war. It's safer to be with 40 people because you're less likely to be hijacked or attacked on your way out of Iraq.

AIN IS FOR 'ASHURAA

This is a Shia religious festival that was banned under Saddam Hussein's reign. Shia get together once a year and put on a blood-soaked parade where men and boys chant and cut and beat themselves with chains as a reminder of their atrocious past. The Sunni/Shia split originated in southern Iraq a few hundred years after the prophet Mohammed died. At the time, the people of Karbala murdered and mutilated the prophet's grandson Hussein. 'Ashuraa shows that the Shia are still not over it. It's also practiced in Bahrain, Iran, and Lebanon.

GHAIN IS FOR KING GHAZI

The gay (and only) son of Iraq's first king, Faisal I, this little prince was crowned at age 21 when his dad kicked the bucket in 1933. He took his hatred of the British (who had pulled the strings throughout his father's rule) to its natural conclusion by buddying up with the Nazis, and helped support the Arab world's first military coup d'état—against his own government. Much to the nation's relief, he died in a suspicious sports-car crash only six years into his reign.

FAA' IS FOR FERIDA

Ferida is a girl's name. For some reason the names of the three brands of Iraqi beer are all girls' names. *Ferida* means "unique" in Arabic, and she meets the requirement of a lot of Iraqi men: Available, strong, and cheap.

QAAF IS FOR QOOZI

Qoozi is a badass traditional Iraqi dish. It's basically a mountain of rice prepared with a mix of spices that give it a funky taste and brownish color and is usually served with a whole roasted lamb on top. It's the mother of all indigestion-causing meals. Qoozi is what people make for weddings and other important occasions. When my family used to invite people over and make qoozi, we planned it assuming that each guest would eat a good pound of meat and some two heaping plates of rice.

KAAF IS FOR KATHUM AL-SAHIR

Al-Sahir is a famous contemporary Iraqi crooner and sex symbol known for his trademark wailing-style singing. Kathum fled Baghdad after getting sick and tired of having to write songs about Saddam. He's one of the biggest celebrities in the Middle East. He cut a track with Lenny Kravitz in 2003, but it bombed. He loves Baghdad and sings about it all the time.

LAAM IS FOR LAHAM

Laham is Arabic for "meat." Iraqi lamb is the best of the lot. That's why sheep smuggling has become a lucrative business for some people in neighboring Iran and Saudi Arabia. The fact that most Iraqis cannot live without meat has allowed greedy butchers to keep making their products' prices higher and higher. Iraqis eat meat at two or even sometimes three of the daily meals. All meat in Iraq is organic and thus incredibly tasty. Sheep and cow are very popular, but some people also like camel's meat. And you can forget about pork.

MEEM IS FOR MUTHAFAR AL-NAWWAB

This guy's a legendary communist rebel poet, famous across the Middle East for his dramatic

Nothing beats an ice cold Ferida!

Photo by Reuters

and political writing. In the early 70s he was invited to recite his poetry at an Arab League meeting, at which he proceeded to curse and swear at every head of state present in the room. His comrades had to quickly smuggle him out of the country and he now lives in Syria. He's also a renowned drunk.

NOON IS FOR NABUG

The dictionary says the English equivalent for this round-shaped fruit is "Christ's thorn." To Iraqis, it's all kids' favorite fruit. If you see a bunch of little Iraqis gathering around a tree and hurling stones, sticks, and sometimes shoes, you know it's a *nabug* tree. Though it stinks like smelly socks, it's delicious. A spooky myth is linked to this tree—they say if a house has one in its yard and the owners intentionally chop it down, a family member will croak soon.

HAA' IS FOR HUMMER

These boxy US military vehicles have become an inbuilt part of post-invasion Iraqi culture. When a fleet of Hummers passes by any Iraqi street, people tend to keep a distance, lest they are shot at by the jumpy American soldiers inside. The sight of a Hummer in any neighborhood means trouble. If Americans are attacked, all hell breaks loose in the shape of detentions and random gunfire. To Iraqi children in more rundown areas, Hummers means US-made candy bars from less aggressive soldiers.

WAW IS FOR WARD JOORI

These bright-colored Iraqi roses look as nice as they smell. Iraqis are fond of gardening and ward joori really brighten the landscape. In springtime, schoolgirls like to pick red, pink, and white flowers to give to their teachers as a token of respect.

YAA' IS FOR YEZIDIS

The Yezidis are an ancient Iraqi devil-worshipping sect. Originally from northern Iraq, they bow down to Melek Ta'us (the Peacock Angel), whom they also call Shaytan (Satan). Melek Ta'us is basically Lucifer except the Yezidi side of the story of creation says that God gave Lucifer props and a camp peacock outfit for defying his orders. ■

II
SEX

Photo by Jaimie Warren, V14N4, April 2007

QUENTIN GONZABLE

GAYS OR GIRLS?

Slobbing the Knob for Science

Men have simple sexual needs. They want to cum. That's about it. They might sometimes cum in ways that they think are inventive, like on your face or your tits, but it all comes down to the same end: a squirt of some white ropy stuff followed by a brief Xanax-y stupor. After about 20,000 orgasms, most men start to wonder, "Is that all there is to this cumming thing?" They get bored with orgasms.

Men in Middle America are suffering uninspired blowjobs from girlfriends on a daily basis. Is it any wonder a growing number of guys are thinking that maybe the best way to wrestle themselves out of their carnal torpor would be to try a blowjob from a bona fide homosexual? After all, every gay man they've ever met has told them a queer blowjob is so much more exciting and enjoyable than a boring woman blowjob. "Nobody knows how to make a penis happy like a person who *owns* a penis of their own!" (That's what gay guys say to get straight penises in their mouths.)

But remember this: Most "bi-curious" men aren't thinking about how delicious it might feel to have another man's dick buried in their ass. They're just thinking about how the inside of a dude's

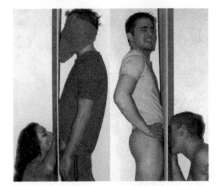

Photos by James Stafford

mouth is technically the same as a woman's, especially if you're drunk. *Especially* especially if you're drunk, ugly, and lonely. Bisexuality, quite simply, doubles your chances. It's the refuge of the pathetically horny.

New statistics from Italy say that, weekly, one gay man sucks more dicks than 12.7 women. Can you say, "Man alive!"? Who's receiving all these BJs from gay men? Not just other gay men—there aren't enough of those around for 13 (I rounded up) times more head sessions than girls perform a week. Especially in Italy—those sluts suck dick as casually as our women choke down apple martinis. There is only one answer: Straight guys are getting their joints coughed by benders with reckless abandon.

The only question left to ask is, "Who's better at it?" Do we have to go gay to get the best head? To find out, we got a gay man and a straight man to get blowjobs from a gay man and a straight woman. We blindfolded both of our suckees and built a glory hole. Then we sat back and basked in the heady milieu of the most erotic and revealing experiment ever conducted in the name of sensual truth.

THE RULES

Safeguards were made to prevent giving the suckees a clue to the sucker's gender.

Our female sucker was given orders not to make any erotic moaning noises and to keep her expensively painted and lengthy fingernails away from the shafts. Ewww.

Our male sucker had his face freshly shaved and was not allowed to whimper things like, "Ooh, your cock is divine" in his manly French baritone. Again: Ewww.

ROUND ONE

First up was Rick in his stained gray shell-suit trousers. As soon as he popped through the hole, Daniel moved in for the kill, lapping away excitedly at Rick's trunk as if the reputation of every gay man in the world depended on it.

After 10 floppy minutes of Daniel's best efforts, Rick's dick was still quite shy of the promised eight-and-a-half inches.

Just before he pulled out, he told us, "To be completely truthful, it's not the best I've ever had. But it wasn't the worst either."

It was obvious to all present that these were just words of kindness and encouragement for poor Daniel, who seemed genuinely confused by his inability to stir the snake.

Time to move on to mouth two.

Suckee One

Rick is a 24-year-old Londoner with an eight-and-a-half-inch cock. He works as a gay male escort. "The greatest blowjob I ever had was from a client a few weeks ago," he told us nervously. "It lasted for about 15 minutes, and it was mind-blowing. I've not taken part in anything involving a so-called glory hole before, but I'm looking forward to it immensely."

Suckee Two

Sam is a 20-year-old model from London. He's straight. This will be the first time ever that another man will touch Sam's thing.

Sucker One

Avalon is a 26-year-old who's worked in the adult film industry since she moved to London from Malaysia in her teens. She prepared to give head by sucking on a menthol lozenge, which she always brings to blowjob shoots because they numb the throat *and* the menthol tickles the recipient's *glans*, thus enhancing his pleasure. (Oooh-kaye.)

Sucker Two

Daniel is a poet from France who was extremely confident that he'd win the challenge. He even invoked the old "men know what other men want" chestnut. We pointed out that with that reasoning, there would be no war, politics, or conflict, and no babies born ever again, but Daniel maintained his sangfroid.

After Rick struggled to get the condom on his flaccid member, we encouraged him to just put it through the hole *au naturel*. Avalon sprang into action with a condom ready to roll on with her mouth. She made his dick disappear and within a minute, it was growing in her mouth at an alarming rate. Her effortless glide-and-lick technique impressed all present, most importantly Rick, who, in between murmuring and closing his eyes, told the judges: "Can I just say something? I think this is the male. This one's a lot better than the first one."

A minute later, he filled his condom with jets of hot gay spunk and Avalon leaped to her feet and punched the air like a lottery winner.
RESULT: Womankind 1, Gay Men 0.

ROUND TWO

Sam prepped by jerking off behind the glory booth to a copy of *Maxim*. "It can take me up to an hour to cum sometimes, but I can always get my dick hard in a matter of minutes," he told us.

Daniel sank to his knees while blindfolded Sam shuffled his wobbling sword into the glory hole. Our disheartened gay friend got to work immediately, this time using teeth, spit, face rubbing, and the "licking down the side" technique that he learned in the "nightclub toilets of Brighton."

It soon became apparent that this rough lick-and-tickle technique wasn't doing the business, as Sam started to become droopy. He looked around the room as if desperately seeking a way out.

"I think I'll give No. 2 a go, please," he pleaded. "This one is very rough."

Fearing that the contest was already over, we decided to tip the scales and add a handicap—we told Avalon to give Sam the worst blowjob she could. She dallied around with his cock like an Iraqi prisoner of war forced to suck his best friend off for the pleasure of American troops. Still, though, Sam's member responded immediately. This was turning into a bloodbath.

Drunk on her success and given the nod to go in for the kill, Avalon sank to her knees and showed off the smooth yet firm deep-throat technique that had wowed Rick so much. Within a couple of minutes, Sam's features had relaxed and he gazed up at the ceiling while telling us, "This one is a lot more sensual. Umm, uh, that's important when you're, uh, doing a thing like this."

Just to be totally sure, we gave Daniel a last chance to uphold his reputation. Sam still wasn't feeling his efforts.

"No," he sighed. "I like the vigor of this, but I definitely prefer the other." With that, Avalon took over and brought the young man to an intense, shuddering climax.
RESULT: Womankind 2, Gay Men 0.

So that's that—girls suck better cock than gays. It's a good thing, too, because if men had continued to waste their precious seed inside other men, the human race could have ended up extinct within, say, 2,000 years. ■

KIKI MOOLER

FUCK FOOD

Screw What You Eat

Photo by Skip McGee

When I was in junior high, I stuck a hot dog up my vagina. It broke in half while it was up there. I almost had a heart attack until it just dropped out when I squatted. You should have seen it hit the bathroom floor. Anyway, I vowed never to stick anything up there again. But that was years ago and like they say, once you stick a hot dog in your vagina, you never go back. To play it safe, though, I've graduated on to safer foods. Here are the results of some recent test-driving I did. These are listed from best to worst.

CARROT

Quite simply the most underrated vegetable in the sex industry. Carrots are like the Jean Naté of getting raunchy: The preteen dildo, good for girls who have just graduated from maxi pad to superslim tampon. Peel carrot and run under warm water for a little while until it's nice and gentle and sweet and warm and, after you've fucked it, you can kiss it and snuggle with it and ask it if it likes rainbows and/or dolphins.

CUCUMBER

Cucumber, zucchini, aka the biggest cock you will ever have inside you. If the carrot is the ultraslim tampon, the cucumber is the jumbo size for heavy-flow days. It's the Samantha from *Sex and the City* of sex veggies.

I accidentally cut off the narrowest part before I started, so the entry was a bit hardcore. For newbies I suggest the most petite cucumber you can find. It will still be really big, don't worry. For extra credit, try sticking this baby up your boyfriend's butt! (If he lets you do it that means he's a gay.)

CORN ON THE COB

Nature's own ribbed condom. Washing all of these veggies before you use them should go without saying, but don't be dim and not shuck the corn or peel off any of those hairy things. Make this clean and glistening. Keep it room temp and obviously, narrow end first. This fucker totally gashed me out.

GINGER

"Holy shit, what the fuck is coming out of your vagina!?!" This is what a person will say when they accidentally walk in on you trying to masturbate with ginger. This is NOT for amateurs! With all the knobs, bells, and whistles, it might make your G-spot start to drool. If you don't know where your G-spot is, just ignore this spicy root altogether.

EGGPLANT

I realize that our vaginas are big enough for babies to get through, but I don't think you can actually put babies back in the same way. There is no fucking way this thing is going to fit inside my pussy. I greased it up like crazy and made a valiant effort, but this thing is a fucking football. The eggplant gets an F-. ∎

INTERVIEWS BY MELISSA BURGOS & PEGAH FARAHMAND

LANDING A MAN: WHAT DO YOU DO?

DEBORAH: "I'm friendly and consistent and loyal. I stick to my word or I don't give it. It's worked. I've had trusting relationships."

JILLIAN: "I drink four vodka on the rocks and start dancing on the bar. It works every time. I'm just naturally magnetic."

MIHO: "I can't explain. I am stylish. Drinking. I came here three days ago."

HALEY: "I act nice and make myself look like a slut. They seem to like that."

SHORTY: "I bat my eyelids and I razzle bedazzle with my personality. I basically prick-tease them and flirt. I don't have problems picking up men."

NICOLE: "I ignore them. The cat-and-mouse chase never fails. Everyone likes a challenge."

ASHLEY: "I tell them they have a nice ass. I grab their butt and then pretend nothing happened. It works for me. Guys like having their ass grabbed."

SAMANTHA: "Just treat them terribly. I'm going out with someone now and I treat him so bad. He never gets sick of it."

VERI-ANN: "I tell 'em I like 'em. Straight up. It works. I know it works, trust me."

CATHY: "I talk in a cute voice. It's girly and squeaky, a bit like Mickey Mouse. It gets guys to like me if they're into that whole girlish, dopey thing."

IRINA: "I give them presents. I make them things, like trinkets."

KASANDRA: "I guess I make fun of them, make them feel a little vulnerable."

Photos by Tim Barber

ANN HIGGINS

EW, I SAW MY PARENTS DOING IT

ANGELA
I had the hots for all of Mom's boyfriends. She was good-looking and brought home lots of hunky men. There was rampaging at our house every week, and I loved it. They always brought presents for me and I didn't mind them groping Mom in the kitchen.

ERIK
The worst thing I ever saw was parental make-up sex. My family was out camping, there was a fight over something, and suddenly they were having sex in the back of the van. I couldn't see, but there was clearly something going on. My sisters got embarrassed and it felt weird sleeping in the van later.

KATARINA
When I got my first job I rushed home to tell my parents all about my first day at work. I had never thought of them as sexual beings and was surprised to see them in action. It seemed kind of violent, but I guess I was just stunned. I remember the smell of their bedroom.

NINA KRISTINE
I used to spy on my parents doing it in the garden. My room was on the second floor and I was sleeping out on the balcony. I'm sure they knew where I used to sleep. They probably didn't think I was there, but I was watching everything from there. I didn't mind at all, and I thought it was something really special and beautiful. They were very quiet.

MAREIKE
I went to the bathroom one day when I was nine or ten and ran into my parents. My mother was bent over the sink, doggy-style.

SISSEL
My mom died when I was very young and I don't think my father started dating again. I have never seen him with another woman but I surprised him jerking off in the bathroom. It was totally weird and I considered running away from home. It taught me to knock. I think he was masturbating in front of the computer one time, but I'm not sure.

MARGRETHE
My father rented a sailboat. At night, you could hear everything, and me and my sister heard it all. Every night, sometimes for hours, boobs flapping. My sister didn't understand what was going on and was all curious and wanted to see for herself. I hated it so much. I hated both of them.

INGEBORG
There was a lot of noise and I think there was a special smell too. I was very afraid, and thinking about it still makes me sad. But I know it was a good thing for them 'cause they're still married.

CARMEN
I have eight sisters and brothers, and I am the oldest, so you can imagine things were happening at our house. Mom and Dad could be doing it in the living room when I got home from school. I've seen his dick a million times. They're from Finland and they don't care at all.

THERESE
On Christmas Eve my mother got really drunk and did it with her boyfriend at the time. They went for it in the bathroom, with the door open and everything. He was this cool Swedish guy and I really liked him, but seeing him with my mom on top made me hate his guts.

LARS ERIK
Seeing my parents going at it scared the living shit out of me. I was very young and my mother had to comfort me for hours. I cried and was afraid of Dad for months. I think he yelled at me when I opened the door to their room and that was probably what freaked me out, not the humping. ∎

GABI SIFRE

CONVERSATIONS WITH PEOPLE WHO JUST HAD SEX WITH EACH OTHER A COUPLE OF MINUTES AGO

The rules here were simple. We waited downstairs while these couples fucked, then we came in and got the play-by-play after they were done.

TINA & BUCHANAN

Vice: How was the fucking?

Buchanan: We haven't seen each other in a month, first of all. And that was the first time we met, and we had sex in the woods a lot then, so a couch was great.

Tina: And I told her, "Imagine what we could do in a fucking bed!" Anyway, first we drank whiskey. Then we took each other's shirts off.

Buchanan: Then we drank more whiskey.

Tina: And then we put on Bob Dylan. I think he's sexy.

Buchanan: Then we were making out. It was hot.

Tina: We were playing with each other's titties.

Photos by Ed Zipco

Were the pants still on?

Buchanan: Yeah, but then I went to the bathroom and came back with them unbuttoned.

Tina: She was wearing boxer briefs. I'm wearing panties.

Buchanan: We kept making out, then we started touching each other's "special areas." Her pants were really hard to get off.

Tina: It rained last night, so they're like suctioned on there! It took a lot of tugging.

Buchanan: She got on top of me. She was wearing pink panties. The kissing was perfect.

Tina: I made her take off her underpants as well. And then she fucked the shit out of me.

Whoa, slow down there. Let's go back.

Tina: She definitely fucked me first.

Buchanan: She was on top and I started off touching her with my hand. First it was just rubbing, then I slipped a finger inside. She laid down and I started kissing all over her chest and then proceeded to kiss her thighs and then kissed her other parts. I sucked on her clit for a while, with my fingers inside of her. It was two fingers at this point.

Tina: I was moving my ass up and down. There was lots of moaning.

Are you usually loud?

Tina: Not unless I like someone. If it's just happening to happen, then no moaning. But if it's someone special, I express it. That's why we put on the Bob Dylan.

Buchanan: His frequencies can cover anything. I was also saying her pussy was hot.

Tina: There was definitely expression.

OK, what next?

Buchanan: She came, and we slowed it down for a bit. I kept my fingers in her, but I started kissing her mouth and stuff.

Tina: I came the first time within two minutes. The second, third, and fourth time were all consecutive. Then I was like, "This is stupid, you can't just give to me, reciprocation is important." So I went down on her.

Buchanan: I don't usually let girls do that to me. It's just my preference. I was sitting on the couch and she was on the floor, and I was grabbing onto her hair and she had fingers in me. She has nice hands.

Tina: I don't go in that far, though. I have long fingers.

Did you come?
Buchanan: Yes, which is a new thing to me. It's only been happening the past couple of years.
Tina: Yeah, we fucked the shit out of each other. First she fucked the shit out of me, then I fucked the shit out of her. She finally let me touch her shit.

How'd you finish up?
Buchanan: We had a smoke, had a little more whiskey, listened to the Mamas and the Papas. We drew happy faces on each other, around our moles.

Cute.

ANDY & ALANA

Vice: OK. Take it from the top.
Andy: We had some beers and we smoked some cigarettes, and we talked about doing it in a different variety of places.
Alana: And then he said, "Let's go have sex."

How did you get started?
Andy: We made out a little bit, then I took her tights off, and I took my shirt off because it was hot in here. And then I asked her to take her dress off but then I ended up taking it off for her. And then we had to lay down a blanket, because she has her period and we didn't want to make a mess.
Alana: It's natural and beautiful!

If you say so. What else?
Andy: She had matching bra and panties on today, which was exciting.
Alana: That never happens, I'm disorganized.
Andy: So we laid down the blanket, got a little cozy. Then we spooned a bit and kept making out. I started grabbing and kissing and suckling her boobs.
Alana: That felt good.
Andy: Then I started fingering her.
Alana: I was starting to get wet, from the fingering.
Andy: Then she played with my cock.

Played with it how?
Alana: I was touching it, rubbing it through his boxers.
Andy: She was using both hands though. That was pretty hot. Her panties came off and I threw them, and then we

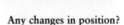

kept jerking each other off. I was still kissing her tits and her belly. We were taking our time. Eventually, I got on top of her, straight missionary.
Alana: He lifted my legs up in the air, and that felt good.
Andy: Alana's very flexible, and she's got these long legs too.
Alana: I teach yoga.

Any oral at all?
Alana: I need to know a guy well before we go there, and we haven't known each other very long.

So at this point were you just fucking, or was there any touching too?
Alana: I would say we were just fucking, but it didn't seem like just fucking at the time.
Andy: We made out a little in the beginning, when we were working into it. It started out slow. We were easing into it at first.
Alana: But not for long. I wanted it harder and faster, and it happened, which was awesome.
Andy: I was enjoying it because she was holding on to the bars of the bed, and girls grabbing on to things is always a turn-on. It's kind of like when girls squeeze the pillow, but better.

Any changes in position?
Andy: I was still on top, and I bent her legs more toward her stomach. And I was really pounding.
Alana: I was pretty close to coming, but only when he bent my legs. It hit a different spot then.
Andy: Then I came inside her, since she had her period, and that was really nice.
Alana: Yeah, it was really nice that he didn't have to pull out and do that whole thing.
Andy: We should that do more often.

Why are you both so touched by this cream-pie business?
Andy: We didn't have to go through the whole jerking off at the end.
Alana: He could stay inside me and there was no stress about it.

Did the period change anything else?
Alana: Well, we laid the blanket out, but it didn't end up being that messy.

Andy: My shit was all bloodied up when were done. But, listen, I'm not going to take away sex days because of her period. None of that "the woman has to go out into the woods for a week." Fuck that.

CAITLIN & ANDY

Vice: Hey, you're the same guy as the last interview. Are you a man-whore?
Andy: Um, I'm just a really nice guy?

OK, stud. This was a bit of an afternoon delight, huh? Walk me through it.
Caitlin: We did it this morning when we were waking up, and then again an hour ago. In the morning, I was going to leave, but I realized he had a hard-on, so I was like, "Hrm, maybe not, if that's saying hello right now."
Andy: We started with the closed-eyed groping, the kind you don't really remember.
Caitlin: We were spooning, and I was like, "Oh, that's a hard penis, that's what that is."
Andy: It was sort of like blind people grabbing each other in the morning. Then we went straight into the fucking. I was on top, and we were very close, right on top of each other, holding on. I came very quickly.

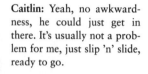

Like, five, ten minutes?
Caitlin: Maybe like three minutes.

What does that say about you?
Caitlin: That I'm super hot and my pussy's hella tight! [*laughs all around*]

How'd you get into it the second time?
Andy: We were just wearing underwear, and started making out. Then she got on top—
Caitlin: That's how I do.
Andy: Then I kind of slipped her boobs out of her bra.
Caitlin: I don't wear bras with clasps anymore, so it's always a hassle getting them off. So sometimes it's easier breastfeeding-style.

What was happening with the boobs?
Andy: Kissing, suckling, and squeezing. She was doing a little clit grinding, little bit of dry humping.

Caitlin: We did that for a little while, but I wanted to make sure he still had condoms.
Andy: I dug one out and came back to the bed. Underwear came off, condom went on. Silly condom.
Caitlin: Well, me no likey no babies. I had these fancy Swedish and Japanese condoms.
Andy: There's definitely a difference. They're very thin and they don't seem to be just like, tubular. They're more cock-shaped, I guess?

Who was on top?
Caitlin: Andy, 'cause he had left and come back, so I was sort of lying there.

Were you wet yet?
Caitlin: Yeah, no awkwardness, he could just get in there. It's usually not a problem for me, just slip 'n' slide, ready to go.

How was the missionary going?
Andy: It was nice. Then we got more into it.
Caitlin: It was pretty fast, and then I was grabbing his ass to get him to slow down because it felt really good.
Andy: She wrapped her legs around me, which was hot. Then we intertwined legs.
Caitlin: It was a good missionary, a good take on an old classic.

Any coming?
Caitlin: I did. It was a great orgasm. I usually come from just penetration. It tends to be the easiest way for me to get off. I found out in college that a lot of my friends are not like that.

Lucky you. Anyway, did you stay in missionary the whole time?
Andy: We stayed in it for a little bit, then we went into doggy style.
Caitlin: I was on my elbows, because it was more comfortable.
Andy: It was great, but then I got tired, and we just stopped.

You just stopped? That's it? You didn't come?
Andy: I came earlier this morning. And I'm hungover.
Caitlin: I didn't come that first time, so we evened it out. ■

TOMOKAZU KOSUGA

A 74-YEAR-OLD
JAPANESE PORN STAR

Video still from Tit-lover Old Man Kameichi and His Horny Pranks *(Glory Quest)*

How long into his life can a man keep fucking? Here in Japan, there is one brave grandpa who is using his own body to answer that question. His name is Shigeo Tokuda and he is a 74-year-old porn performer. He often stars in movies staged in old-age homes—like, as in "gramps fucks his hot little nurse"—which frankly we have no clue who would want to watch, save for the morbid chuckles factor.

Regardless, we headed over to meet this geriatric pussy master and ask him questions about his ancient cock.

Vice: Please tell us how long you've been working as a porn star and how many films you've been in.
Shigeo Tokuda: I've been doing this for 14 and a half years, and I've been in around 250 films so far. That said, there's only been a handful, maybe 10 percent, where I've starred one-on-one with an actress. Usually I'm in a supporting role. But all of them are adult films. I've never acted in any other genre.

What sort of roles do you play?
I'm over 70 years old, so I don't necessarily have sex in all of my films. I often don't do anything sexual myself at all, like for example if I'm playing an authority figure like a father forcing his child to have sex with some other guy. Lately I'm also starring as the main actor in a porn series set in a senior-care home. The girl that I'm costarring with might play my son's wife, a daughter of a relative that I happen to be looking after, or a helper at one of the care homes. I shoot about one episode of this series per month. The other day I played a ceramic artist. He was very strange, totally obsessed with women. He's a professional craftsman, but all he thinks about is girls.

And how often do you shoot?
Some months I go without a single shoot, and other times I have as many as nine. It's pretty erratic, as the production companies usually come to me when they have a project, rather than vice versa.

What started you off in the industry?

About 20 years ago, I wanted to buy a porn film that specialized in kissing. It was full of kissing scenes. What drew me to it even more, though, was the fact that it was structured like a real TV series, with a story and everything. Back then, I couldn't face buying something like that in a huge video store, so I actually went directly to the production company that distributes the software and bought it there. As I began to frequent the place, I eventually became friends with a director there. One day he asked me to star in a film because the demand for "old-people porn" was increasing. I had never dreamed of actually being in one myself, though, so I initially refused. But as I got to know the director more, I gradually began to understand his ideas and intentions. After two or three years, I said yes. That's how my career started.

Are there many elderly actors in this industry?

When I began working as an actor, there was one other man who was around 12 years older than myself. We often starred alongside each other. I've never met any other performer apart from him who is in his senior years. In that sense, I believe that I am a rare breed in the industry, and I guess there is value in that.

Does your family know about your job?

I have told my family that I work as an extra in videos and on TV, and I occasionally get called in for adult movies. Neither my wife nor my daughter pursues the subject any further. So I guess my family thinks that the fact that I am healthy and am continuing to work is a good thing in itself.

Didn't you get into trouble with your family when you first brought up the subject?

No, not really. It's great that I can continue to work at my age, and I think that both my wife and I agree that our relationship will last longer if we keep a certain distance, seeing as we have different interests and hobbies and so on.

Have any of your family members seen your films?

No. They're all porn, so I highly doubt that they'll ever come across any. And there's no way I'm going to show them myself, that would just be digging my own grave.

Are the actresses that star alongside you usually younger or older?

I'm guessing that from the production companies' perspective, it looks better and is more commercially salable if they couple an elderly person with someone very young. So most of them are young actresses. But frankly, I don't have much in common with the girls in their teens and 20s, and I am more relaxed and can find more to talk about with people in their 30s and 40s. I prefer the

sexual charm of mature, middle-aged women, so I'm especially enthusiastic when I shoot with those kinds of actresses. Such occasions are rare in reality, though, which I find quite sad.

Is there anything in particular that you do in order to get your penis ready to go on cue during shoots?

Personally, a big factor is whether or not the age, appearance, and physical attributes of the actress suit my taste. In other words, it basically comes down to what kind of girls turn me on, so my performance is often affected by my costar. Depending on who they are, I'll instinctually think, "Yes, this one's going to be good" or "I might have a little trouble today."

Do you penetrate for real on set?

In general, all penetration shots are real and unsheathed. Just before they cut to the next shot, we wear condoms. Of course, the genitals are blurred out in the entire sequence so theoretically you shouldn't be able to tell if we're already wearing one or not, but actually the rubberiness and texture of the condom shows through the blur, which is why we penetrate unprotected first. I guess in this sense they're trying to make it look as realistic as possible.

No rubber? Won't you catch STDs that way?

I'm not sure if I can say this for every single person, but most actors and actresses are regularly tested. On some shoots you even have to show proof that you're clean. It may only be a formality, but I get the impression that most sets are sensitive to these issues. Personally, I've never caught any diseases through sex.

Do you ever use Viagra during shoots?

I have tried it before when a director offered me some. I only had half or a quarter of one though, as I had to consider my age. And even that was six years ago. It was indeed effective, but in my case I completely lost interest mentally. I could keep it up for a long time, though, so even if I wasn't into it, I had a great erection. So I can say that I have experienced the effect of the drug, although again, I would say that the effects totally depend on who I'm costarring with.

What's your favorite position?

I like having the girl on top and letting them take the initiative. I actually don't like taking the lead myself, which might be surprising since it's the complete opposite to the roles I play.

What motivates you to keep starring in porn even at your old age?

I mentioned before that I like films that are set up like TV dramas. This is partly because I've always had the desire to turn into all sorts of different people. So personally, I don't get off just having sex with somebody. I continue working in this industry not because I like starring in adult films, but because I am given the opportunity to act in various roles. The appeal for me is in the fact that I can play different people, not that I can boast about my acting skills. Consequently, most of the films that I'm in have a proper plot and narrative.

What's the most important thing that you keep in mind when working in this industry?
I think the most important thing is to stay healthy. There are times when I have to walk around with a light summer kimono in the freezing winter or wear many layers in the summer heat. The seasonal setting of a shoot might be completely different from the actual season, so I find that it's very important to take care of my health on a daily basis. I've always liked outdoor activities as well, so in that sense I think I'm more physically fit than other people my age. Also, this might be because of my days of mountain-climbing, but I can adapt very easily to different climates. I don't sweat all that much in the summer and don't feel very cold in winter—I walk around barefoot. I'm not sure if my body learned to adapt or if I'm just not very susceptible to these things. Maybe it's an innate ability I have. Another thing that I keep in mind on set is to always communicate with the staff and other actors, because in the end it's all about people socializing and connecting.

Photo by Tomokazu Kosuga

Do you have any interesting stories about experiences that you had on set?
About five years ago, I was in this TV-drama-like porn film called *Japan During the Greater East Asian War*. I was the head of the municipal community, telling everyone in the neighborhood to evacuate because we were being bombed. Then I find this sick girl who has been left behind, so I carry her over my shoulder to a shelter where we have sex. This was a very memorable shoot because I'm familiar with what it was like during the war and I was given the opportunity to reenact that.

What are your views on the sex climate in Japan?
I first learned about sex in the postwar period, when we didn't have anything. Everybody was so focused on living, studying, graduating, and working that neither my class-

mates nor myself were all that interested in sex. So for my generation, it's all about getting back those lost dreams of our youth. Society is more open about porn now, which I guess is a good thing. But personally, I think that sex should be regarded as something more austere. I mean, it's the physical communion of two people. I know it sounds rich from somebody doing the work I do, but I sincerely believe that. I would like to make a deeper human-to-human connection with the people that I sleep with.

Do you have any ambitions in terms of working in porn in the future?
I turned 74 this August, and obviously it's difficult for me to continue working in this field for decades to come. I would perhaps like to produce my own film one day, though, something that might stand as a memorial piece of work in my career. It will be based on my own sexual preferences, so I don't think it will be very popular commercially. Everybody has their own sexual tastes, and I would like to express my personal preferences in my own film, even though maybe only a handful of people will appreciate it.

What exactly do you have in mind?
I don't have the details laid out yet. But it will be based on my idea that with videos, everybody relies on the movements within the picture to give meaning. But I don't necessarily think that the creator's intentions are always expressed adequately through movement. That said, it would be boring for the audience if they were made to watch a still image where the people in the videos never moved. So there needs to be some movement for the video to say something to the audience. In my case, though, I get more out of seeing still images, rather like photography, but in a video format. My dream is to create emotionally moving still-video porn. But this is only a personal project and I don't necessarily need an audience. I'll make it so that I can watch it myself and I'll be satisfied. I still need to figure out the details, so it probably won't happen for another couple of years.

You're going to continue starring in porn until you die, right?
Sure. Right now I don't have any illnesses, so I guess I'll keep watching my health and at least try to go on until I'm 80. [*laughs*] ∎

Translated by Lena Oishi

GABI SIFRE

MY BABYSITTER WAS A GAY PORN STAR

Here's His Best Flicks

Uncle Chad and Gabi, 1987

When I was a kid, my babysitter was Chad Douglas. I called him Uncle Chad. He used to sing me to sleep and organize my Barbie clothes for me. When I was 6, he died of AIDS, and my mom let slip that he had once been a famous gay porn star. She'd known it when she hired him, but it was news to my dad.

It should go without saying that I saw Uncle Chad as an uncle figure. He was sweet and cool and wonderful. But ever since my mom spilled the beans, I always wondered what his movies were like. Last week, I finally went ahead and ordered them: *Below the Belt* and *Spring Break*.

BELOW THE BELT (1986)
Uncle Chad plays "Greg," the sensei at Ginko Dojo. In the first scene, one of the karate students confesses that he has been dreaming of Greg, and we are taken to a stylized dream sequence in which Greg rescues the young student from an evil samurai. The student wants to thank Greg, so he morphs into a young Asian guy named Sum Youngh Man, whom my uncle Chad proceeds to ream. When he's done, my uncle leaves Sum Youngh Man to the mercy of the seven other students.

In the next scene, Uncle Chad turns to his pal Robert and says, "Hey, why don't you limber up and then we'll work it out?" Then he kicks Robert to the floor a few times, Robert licks Uncle Chad's crotch through his karate robe, and my uncle reams Robert and then falls asleep on a mat. When he wakes up, there's an orgy going on. Everyone jizzes on a practice mat. This was from 1986, when I still had to make sure Uncle Chad left the door open a crack so I wouldn't be left in the dark.

SPRING BREAK (1988)
Uncle Chad plays a character called, um, "UNCLE Chad," and teaches his nephew how to suck his cock. He pulls his nephew's hair, hits his nephew's face with his dick, and demands to be called "sir." This was shot in 1988, so around the time that Uncle Chad was my cool babysitter who gave me rad colored tights, he was also shooting the scene in which he cums inside his nephew, then inserts a butt plug so the cum won't dribble out.

I was sitting there in the dark after it ended—relieved, not too traumatized—when the screen lit back up and the word "WARNING!" flashed multiple times, followed by the message: "MASTER'S DELIGHT is presented in the MAIL ORDER VERSION only and is presented as a SEXUAL FANTASY." I lunged for the remote. The only thing I saw was a shot of an old office chair surrounded by a ring of dildos and a sling, but I still can't get that chair out of my head. ∎

TRACIE EGAN

ONE RAPE, PLEASE (TO GO)

I Paid a Male Whore to Rape Me Because I Wanted To

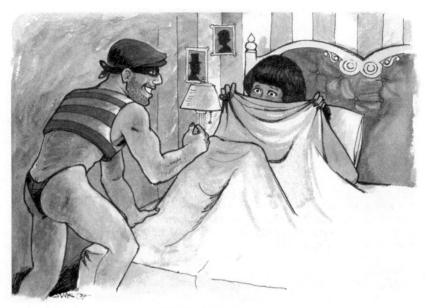

Illustration by Jim Krewson

I blame my recurring rape fantasy on the fact that I'm a feminist. I've never made any bones about getting boned in exactly the fashion that I want. But as a girl, my equipment can be trickier to manage, therefore I need to be a boss in the bedroom to ensure I get worked the right way. It gets really tiresome always being the one in charge, and don't shrinks say that people usually fantasize about the opposite of their reality? I guess that's why I find myself wishing that my typically sugary-sweet sexual encounters were sometimes peppered with assault. I decided that the best way to forfeit that control—while still holding on to a modicum of it for safekeeping— would be to hire someone for the job. Not to put too fine a point on it, I wanted a male whore to rape me.

My first thoughts were of New York artist Brock Enright, who founded Video Games Adventure Services in 2002. It's a company that provides a rather violent "designer kidnapping" for a price that actually rapes a wallet more than it does the customer, but I'd heard tell that some escort services provide similarly realistic rape and abduction scenarios for a fraction of the cost. I didn't want mine to be crazy violent, with, like, punching and stuff. (I wouldn't mind some fingerprint bruises on my wrists, but my face needs to stay pretty so I can keep getting sex for free on other occasions.) I also didn't want any duct tape involved, and I didn't want to be gagged (unless, you know, it's with a cock).

And so began my quest to hire a rapist. I started by reviewing hustlers' profiles through escort websites, but I was totally turned off. Even when they said they only serviced women, they all looked like total homos. Don't get me wrong, I have nothing against gay dudes. I just don't want to get raped by one. I knew they wouldn't be "up" for the job, har har har. I actually had a lot more luck in the "erotic services" section of Craigslist. I didn't have to go through a middleman, and all the dudes I corresponded with were more than happy to send me cock shots, free of charge.

The pictures were really important to me. One of my main concerns about hiring a hooker was that he might be ugly. I'm not one of those girls who needs an emotional connection to fuck a guy. Shit, I don't even need to know his last name. But he needs to be attractive. Swagger and wit can only get one so far. I'm into faces. And I wasn't sure I could get into it if he had an ugly one. I decided he would need to wear a ski mask, because then I wouldn't know if he was ugly, and because it would also be extra scary and thrilling and hot. Of the dudes on my short list, only one of them had a ski mask. But he also mentioned in the same sentence that he had a gun we could use, and thus ended his brief tenure on my short list.

I ended up making a date with a 21-year-old guy (let's call him Dick), who said that he exclusively services women. I liked him because in the picture he sent to my phone, he wasn't ugly. He looked half-Guido, half-frat-boy, and that seemed like a pretty rape-y combo. He assured me he could handle the rape fantasy, as role playing was his specialty. Dick said he would perform the whole fantasy, with no time limit, for $300.

Even though he wasn't heinous looking, I still wanted him to wear a ski mask. Because of my preconceived notions about hookers regarding their reliability and character in general, I decided that I'd take the reins on procuring the mask. I made the trek to a large sporting-goods store only to find out that ski masks weren't in season. Oh well. As I left the store, sans ski mask, I was gripped with just how real this was. I was going to be face-to-face with my rapist in a few short hours. I called Dick up and told him that there was a change of plans. Instead of accosting me outside of my apartment building, we decided that the best way to go would be date rape. We agreed to meet at a bar in my neighborhood, and get a few drinks first.

I went to the drugstore and picked up some condoms and some Tucks. I was so nervous that I was like borderline diarrhea. I knew he was just some whore, but I still didn't want to have a dirty butt in front of him. I also stopped at the liquor store, bought two bottles of wine, and began drinking as soon as I got home, to help me relax.

About an hour before our date, I got a text from Dick: "Yo, I don't want to charge for this."

I texted back, "If it's all the same, I'd rather just keep the arrangement as we have it." He responded with, "Are you a cop?"

Oh God, I thought. I called Dick up and explained to him that I didn't want to get raped for free, because I felt that the exchange of money was the only way I'd be able to maintain the small amount of power I needed to feel comfortable. Besides, at this point, a large part of the allure of this whole thing was that I was actually going to fuck a hooker. Giving me a freebie would've robbed me of that opportunity. I set him straight and an hour later, I got a text letting me know he was at the bar. It said: "I'm here babe."

As I walked up the street toward the bar, I could see him having a smoke outside. He was cute enough, but skinnier than his picture, and he looked younger than 21. I'm 28. Christ, I thought, who's raping who here?

We hugged briefly, then went inside and began pounding vodka sodas to cut the tension. I was pleasantly surprised that Dick immediately took control. He decided that our safe word would be *surprise*, and he told me that he was just going to keep coming on as strong as possible, until he heard me say the word. We played a few rounds of Erotic Photo Hunt on the bar's Megatouch. I was taking the game sort of seriously, but he wasn't really paying attention to it. He kept pushing his face into my neck, and saying stupid yet appropriate things, like, "Oh, you're such a dirty girl," and, "Yeah, I like when you touched her titty," referring to the naked girl in the game. He put on the full-court press, groping my boobs and reaching his hand down between my legs, beneath my minidress.

By this point, I was sufficiently drunk and getting turned on by his dirtbag display. My tights were soaking wet (which he, of course, pointed out). I began to think I wasn't really cut out to play the victim, because I was fighting my inner slut, which ached to push my crotch toward his hand, instead of pulling away like my fantasy required. I knew it was time to get the show on the road, before I ended up ruining the whole thing by dragging him into the bar bathroom to fuck him in one of the stalls.

We got back to my building and climbed the four floors to my apartment, with him trailing behind, goosing me the whole way. As soon as we got inside, he started in with a DFK (that's hooker for "deep French kiss") on my couch.

"Let's go to your room," he breathed in my ear. I was about to be like, "Fuck yeah," but then I remembered why we were here, so instead I said, "Oh, I don't know."

"Yeah, come on," he insisted, as he got up from the couch and pulled me toward my bedroom.

We sat on the bed and he started kissing me again. He pushed me down and I tried to politely nudge him away and sit back up, but he wouldn't let me. Whoa, I thought, this is really happening! Holy fucking shit! He grabbed my wrists and held them down with one hand as he started frantically undoing his pants with the other. I tried to wriggle free, but I was pinned.

"Don't act like you don't fucking want it, you little bitch," he sneered.

That's actually when I began really fighting him, because I wanted to be sure that he put a condom on before anything else happened. The last thing I need in my life is a trick baby. Or HPV. I reached toward my night-stand and grabbed the strip of condoms I'd carefully laid out earlier in the evening.

He lifted my dress up over my head, so I couldn't see what he was doing, and we began a tug of war with my tights, with me trying to keep them on, and him trying to rip them off. The struggle went on for maybe 90 seconds before my tights gave way. He jammed it in.

One Mississippi, two Mississippi, and he came. Literally, two fucking seconds, and it was over. Hmm, I thought, I wonder if this is what it's like with real rape. It makes sense. Rapists are probably not too worried about premature ejaculation. It behooves them to get it over with fast.

Dick immediately began apologizing, saying, "It's just that you're so sexy. Give me a minute. I'll get hard again. Let me just collect myself." But I drowned out the sound of his voice with the sound of my vibrator. There was no fucking way I wasn't coming after all of that. He tried to make amends by putting his fingers in me, but I swatted his hand away, saying only, "Surprise."

Within a few minutes I came twice, then tossed the vibe on the floor. Dick just stared at me the whole time. Again, he tried touching my pussy, now tender from having been properly massaged. "Surprise!" I hissed it this time, before shooting up off my bed and stumbling into my living room.

I poured myself a glass of wine, plopped down on my couch, grabbed the remote, and scanned the TV. Dick emerged from my room, wearing only his boxers. He sat down next to me and rubbed my thigh. "I want to make you come again," he whispered in my ear. I laughed in his face.

"You're so cute, how you always giggle at what I say," and then he started in with another DFK. This time, when I closed my eyes, my head began spinning and I realized just how drunk I was. I thought I might puke in his mouth, so I pushed him away.

"Why don't you get your clothes on," I said.

"No, I want to go one more time. C'mon. You know you want it."

He wouldn't let up. So finally I was forced to yet again yell out, "Surprise! Get dressed. It's time for you to leave."

He got his clothes on and as he was tying his shoes, I reached into my bag and pulled out an envelope filled with the cash he was owed, plus an extra $50 as a tip. I handed it to him, and he said, "I still feel bad that it ended so quickly."

"Yeah," I said, "you're right." So I reached in the envelope and removed two of the 20s. "This is for the drinks I bought." I thought for a minute, reached back in, and grabbed another, saying, "And this is for coming too fast." I put his $60 docked pay in my wallet.

He hung his head and said, "Yeah, that's only fair."

I called him a cab and literally had to push him out of my place. He kept trying to hug me and gently kiss me all over my face. I grimaced as I ducked and dodged his attempts at intimacy or cuddling, or whatever the hell he was trying to do. As soon as he was gone, I sank back into my couch. About five minutes later I received a text from him: "You sure? I just wanna make u come again and that's it."

Ugh! What the hell made him think he did it the first time? I ignored him. Six minutes later I received another text: "Oh great. Story of my life ha ha. I'll talk with you soon I hope."

I ignored that one as well. Eight minutes later I received another text: "But hey seriously you were amazing. Def give me a call some time soon."

I hadn't answered the first two, so I didn't bother answering this one either. I drank my wine and eventually passed out on my couch. My phone woke me up several hours later, at around 1 AM. It was him! I pressed "ignore" with more purpose than I ever have in my life. I saw that there were two new text messages as well. One was at 11:54 PM, about two and a half hours after Dick left my place. It said, "You still up? I bet u are... call me."

The other message was a picture that Dick took of himself—naked and wearing only a bow tie. The text said, "I really like you."

Oh my God. I ordered a rape and was served a stalker. A little after 3 AM I received one last text for the night: "You still awake? I miss u."

In the morning, I checked my email, and what do you know? It's Dick in my box! He wrote, "Hey little lady, sorry for calling you so much last night. I guess I was a lot drunker than I thought. LOL! But really, you are great, and I'd love to see you again. We should really hang out again."

I wrote him back, saying only, "Yeah, I was really drunk, too. Take care." That seemed like a sufficient kiss-off to me.

Two days later, guess who called me? Hi, Mr. Clingy Prostitute. I never took any of his calls ever again, or returned his texts or emails.

You know what really pisses me off? People are always quick to accuse girls of too easily becoming emotionally attached after they sleep with a guy. But I've *never* heard of any call girl who tried to hang out with a john for free because she liked him so much. It just wouldn't happen. Women are far more capable of compartmentalizing issues of love and sex and work and play than people (dudes) give us credit for.

So, considering the way we each handled ourselves after our business transaction, it turns out that *I'm* the dick—and he's a pussy. ∎

MARIE-ELAINE GUAY

FUCK THE POLICE

No, I Mean Really Fuck Them

Photo by Brenda Staudenmeier

This month I fucked three Montreal cops just for the what-the-heck of it. It was kind of like an experiment in hate-fucking, since I am not really fond of the police. I discovered that two out of three of the police officers that I fucked in the past month were molested during their childhood, and that the rest (all one of them) are just sexually deviant.

COP FUCK NUMBER ONE

We meet at a bar where he's hanging out with coworkers. I'm dressed like a perfect bourgeois office girl. Square heels and all.

He's divorced with three kids. One of his daughters is my age. Hello, creepy! Still, aside from his escalator-shaped forehead, he's a pretty good-looking man.

He says that he has "never done this before" ("this" meaning slept with a random jailbait female stranger), but he reeks of pedophilia and therefore I don't believe it for a second. Also, I can tell he's a quick fuck—the kind of sex where I'll have to go to the bathroom to finish myself off.

Men like him get turned on by silly little girls, so I just laugh at everything he says. I pretend to be impressed when he tells me that he kicked the shit out of some insubordinate punk less than a week ago. He rants about the dumbest crap: "Kids these days have no respect for authority, or even for their parents." A minute with him feels like a year, so I end up getting blind drunk. By the time he asks me to go back home with him, I don't even know my name anymore.

We hop into a cab and he starts caressing my leg like it's a puppy. At his house, I drag him into what I assume is his bedroom. It turns out to be the bathroom. Fine—works for me. I lift up my skirt and he slides his smelly hands in between my legs. For some odd reason, I've never been this wet. He fingers me really hard, and I reach for his cock. He doesn't even have a hard on? Great! I pull down his pants, and whoops—he does have a boner, it just consists of the smallest penis I have ever seen. I could jerk him off with my pinky, which I end up doing. He suddenly flips me around and starts mounting me. (At least I think he does, but I'm not really sure since I can't feel him inside me. It's like getting fucked by air.)

He's moaning and saying, "I'm about to cum" every two seconds. Finally, he pulls out and the most ridiculous drop fizzles out while he yells really loud. It looks like a Q-tip taking a piss.

This cop gets a 4 out of 10 because he at least got me inexplicably wet.

COP FUCK NUMBER TWO

A couple days after my trip to Snoresville, it's time for me to get back on duty. And boy, do I—Agent Jones is quite the catch. Tall, with dark brown hair and an ass that would make a whore skip an entire night of work just for a glance. He's also surprisingly nice, knows what punk rock is, and just turned 27 years young.

It takes four dates before he lets me come over. I had to sit through *The Hills Have Eyes*, a Mexican dinner that gave us both food poisoning, and a walk at the mall (What's up, 1987!). I actually start to fall for him when he takes me to his Batmobile one night and we access my file through his police computer. He laughs when he discovers I got in several fights and got arrested for possession of narcotics when I was 19. Hanging out with him is so much fun.

I think that maybe if you can snag a cop when he's young and fresh out of the academy, you'll be OK. It's

the years on the job that turn these guys into lousy lays. Just a theory.

On our fifth date, we watch a movie at his house and start making out. I try the aggressive, "We've been wanting each other for so long now—let's fuck" approach, but he won't budge. We talk for another hour or so, but I finally get too impatient, so I just unzip him and go to work giving him a blowjob. He just sits there and plays with my hair. He's huge and I gag on every bite, but he seems to enjoy it. He moves between my legs and rips my panties free. Hurray! It's on.

We run to his bedroom and have the cutest lovey-dovey sex. He comes all over my back and we kiss goodnight. I sleep over because his condo smells like warm bread. Breaking my own self-prescribed "no sleepovers" law with a cop seems kind of ironic. I sneak out in the morning and think to myself that it's too bad I'll never see him again.

This guy gets an 8 out of 10. One point off for taking so long to get down to it, and another point off for kind of fucking like a wimp.

COP FUCK NUMBER THREE

The next week, a friend calls me up and invites me to her DJ night at this gay bar near my house. I decide to go. Lesbians are really fun.

I get introduced to a million girls and they're all pretty cute, but I'm not in the mood for muff diving, so I just get sauced on vodka-cran and chat with my friend. She points at a girl on the dance floor and mentions that she's a cop. Immediately, there's a fucking halo of white light shining around her. I run to the dance floor and shake my ass against hers. Right away, we start making out. It's fucking unreal—she's so cute! She's tall and a bit chubby, probably 30 to 32, and her tits are huge. I ask her to come home with me, and she refuses! I keep asking and drinking and asking. No dice.

I am about ready to drop some GHB in her drink when she finally agrees and we walk back to my house. We then proceed to have the BEST SEX EVER. There's lots of sex toys and porn watching. Her fingers taste like Aunt Jemima's syrup; I suck on them like they're the last things I'll ever have in my mouth. She eats me out like I paid her to do it.

After I tie her up with yellow rope, then lie on top of her and dildo-rape her while she pinches my tits and fingers me, we drift off to slumberland. This woman was a revelation. When we finished, there was so much saliva, pussy juice, and poop stains on my bed that we could have baked a cake with the residue. We both felt concussed. I kissed her goodbye and it tasted like candy. I want to see her again.

This lady cop gets a solid, unequivocal 10 out of 10. I think she might have made me into a dyke. ■

III

DRUGS

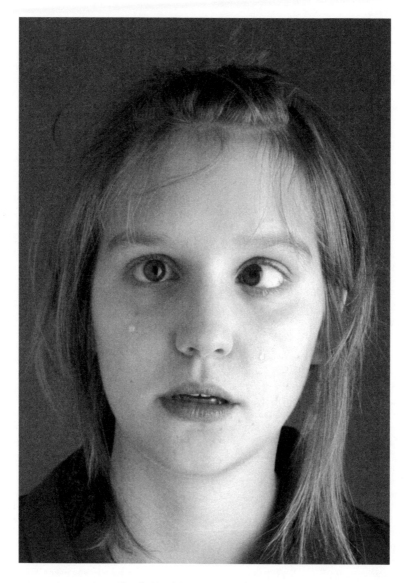

Photo by Maciek Pozoga, V16N2, February 2009

ANN HIGGINS

CUT THE SHIT

How Pure Are Street Drugs?

I bought cocaine, heroin, crack, weed, and ecstasy and had them forensically analyzed by a chemist at MIT because I thought they would all turn out to be poison. Guess what? Drug dealers don't cut drugs with cement and ground glass. They barely even cut drugs at all, because they don't need to. Relax, I'll explain later.

The samples were analyzed by a PhD chemist at MIT (we can't say his name or he'll get fired) using acid/base extraction, proton nuclear magnetic resonance, and thin-layer chromatography. Acid-base extraction is the method used to isolate the chemicals. Once they're isolated, the nuclear magnetic resonance machine is what you use to analyze and identify stuff. Basically, the kind of NMR done here tells you about the hydrogen atoms in the molecules in the drugs. So it's like, the spectrum of heroin has 20 lines in it, all at different positions and heights, and you basically look for that particular set of lines. If you see another set of lines, you go,

Here are all the drugs we bought.

"Oops, there's something else besides heroin in here." Finally, thin-layer chromatography is a quick method that tells you how many components there are in a mixture. MIT guy says it's "like that experiment you did when you were a kid (if you were a geek) where you put ink on a paper towel and, when the water diffused up the paper towel, all the colors separated." It tells you how many components are in a mixture but not what they are. That's what the NMR is for. Still confused? Show this to a smart guy and have him explain it more.

COCAINE

The cocaine was the first sample to come back from the lab. It was 98 percent pure. When everyone was done high-fiving, we started to wonder what was going on. According to the movies and *NYPD Blue*, you can only get cocaine like that from pharmacies. Street cocaine is basically poison, right? It's all strychnine and gasoline and nail polish remover or something.

I was not going to go buy 50 more samples of coke, because that would be a waste of money and drugs, but there's this guy named Peter Cohen who did his thesis on just that. Actually, his work is even better than that, because he not only analyzed 50 samples of cocaine, he also interviewed the 50 cokeheads who had bought the samples. So he got the perception and the reality, see. He asked the cokeheads whether they thought their coke was pure, and 80 percent of them said no. Of those, 75 percent thought their stuff was adulterated with speed. They also commonly figured their drugs were diluted with ground glass, Drano, laxatives, and dirt. Cohen took samples from these cokeheads to the lab. The average purity was 65.1 percent. The samples were cut with speed, Daro, vitamin C, caffeine, sugar, nicotinamide, lidocaine, mannitol, and sodium bicarbonate. Daro is an anti-headache powder. Nicotinamide is vitamin B. Lidocaine is a topical anaesthetic. Mannitol is the sugar they put in diabetic candy. Sodium bicarbonate is baking soda. These are all innocuous things that bulk the drug out—most evidence of dangerous cutting agents is anecdotal. There's no glass in your coke, you fucking psycho.

I guess that doesn't mean that drugs are never cut with poison. The Drug Prevention Network of the Americas reports on a gang in Dublin that cuts coke with Phenacetin, a carcinogen that causes cancerous tumors in urinary tracts and nasal passages. Of male rats. There are a hundred million stories like that, and they get picked up eagerly by anti-drug sites, druggies, and editors who want sensational copy because that is the world we live in.

Findings: Most coke is way over 60 percent pure, and our coke is especially good. Thank you, Rico.

HEROIN

Our sample was 60 percent heroin, 20 percent acetaminophen, 10 percent caffeine, and 10 percent unidentifiable chemicals. Even though that sounds like a lot of additives, it's about right. New York heroin is 63.3 percent pure on average. Oh, forget the whole idea about heroin being cut with Drano. Heroin is most often cut with acetaminophen, caffeine, malitol, diazepam, methaqualone, or phenobarbital. Diazepam is a sedative hypnotic. Methaqualone is Quaaludes. Phenobarbital is a sedative used to stop seizures and treat insomnia. See, they just cut it with stuff that makes you sleepy but doesn't cost as much or cause as much hassle to get as dope. That's all. If you want some better shit, move to that shithole London. Ross Coomber of the University of Greenwich, London, analyzed 228 samples of heroin and found that 44 percent of them weren't cut with anything at all. The rest were cut with the same stuff as above. Coomber did another study where he gathered information from 17 heroin dealers at varying points in the chain of distribution. He asked them if they adulterated (that is the word for adding other drugs to) or diluted (that is the word for adding inert substances to) the drugs they sold. Eleven said that they never adulterated/diluted at all, four adulterated/diluted only sometimes, and only one (dealing four to five ounces a month) said he always diluted the heroin (with glucose, by around 10 to 20 percent). *Asshole.*

Findings: Heroin is a little more cut than coke, but ours is average. And dealers don't want to poison their customers. It's bad business, and if you're dead you can't buy any more smack from them. The most important finding to us in this section was this great new dealer who got us a bundle of smack delivered to our door in 20 minutes in the middle of the workday. Too bad we're in recovery.

CRACK

Our crack, purchased from some human garbage in Bushwick, was about 95 percent pure, and the impurities were likely by-products of the synthesis, not contaminants. That means they weren't added after the crack became crack. Rather, they were a part of how the crack came to be. Crack is actually one of the purest drugs you can buy, usually about 85 to 95 percent, because it gets washed with solvent before or after heating. Just because of the way it's made (by "freebasing" it—or removing the active chemicals from cocaine from their base), you can get high-purity crack from only moderately pure coke.

Findings: Crack is a good bet. If you think your coke guy is stomping on your shit at all, cook it up and you'll take out all the dirt.

WEED

So according to an article published in the *New York Times* in April 2004, "Law enforcement officials said they are also seeing more examples of marijuana laced with other drugs, like cocaine, a narcotic; LSD, a hallucinogen; and PCP, a hallucinogen also known as angel dust." Our sample didn't have coke or heroin or PCP or anything in it. It was just normal. Sucks.

Now read that *New York Times* quote again. "Law enforcement officials"? I like cops and I trust them to protect me from getting raped. Journalists are liars though. Why would police give quotes about drugs and not give their names? Is this a top secret thing that the "law enforcement officials" are afraid to go on record about? Seriously, there are a million alarmist accounts of PCP-dipped weed being sold as regular weed, but not one systematic analysis to back up the claim. Just look at the slang terms for weed laced with other drugs and the whole thing starts to seem like a priest dreamed it up: "Boat, Loveboat, Chips, Donk, Lovelies, Love Leaf, Woolies, Zoom, Caviar, Cocoa Puff, Gremmies." What?

Findings: PCP-soaked marijuana that is sold as PCP-soaked marijuana doesn't actually have PCP in it most of the time. There is no evidence at all I can find that marijuana sold as marijuana is soaked in PCP. However, if you want to deck your weed out, sprinkle some coke on it. It's called a snowcap and it gets you laced.

ECSTASY

Our sample was pure MDMA. Once again, that's because we have good dealers. We all know that E is often cut with dope, because we've all seen those little brown freckles in pills that we've taken. That's heroin, stupid. So while E can be dirty, it is not as dirty as a 1993 *Time Out* magazine article, "Bitter Pills," made it out to be. In that article, it was reported that E dealers spike tablets and capsules with heroin, LSD, rat poison, and crushed glass. That story was repeated all over. Stephen Beard of the Newham Drugs Advice Project was the source for all this, and he said he got his info from a single dealer. This single supposed dealer said he made fake ecstasy by crushing lightbulbs. The word for that is *hearsay.* There was no supporting evidence such as lab tests or reports from doctors who had treated users. Oh, but again, it does happen that there is poison. In London, in 2000, there was an unmarked, half-scored, yellow-flecked tablet that was 8 mg of strychnine. The lethal dose of strychnine is 10 mg.

The verdict: It's not hard to get good shit. Drug dealers think, I can sit here trying to figure out how to dilute this shit or I can get it on the street and paid for as soon as possible. If my shit is too pure—great. All that means is I'll have a reputation as Bobby PurePants and more people will want to buy from me. ∎

Additional reporting by Gideon Yago

JERRY McPHEERSON

HIGH PARK

Acid vs. Shrooms

In the past two years, the tides have turned drastically in the world of recreational drugs. Boredom and unemployment have brought on a massive resurgence of acid and mushrooms.

The late 90s belonged to coke, and it made perfect sense. Dot-com brats on $10,000 mountain bikes were the most natural demographic for coke since hair-rocker brats got way too laid in the mid-80s. Then the bubble burst and everyone's confidence was flushed down the financial toilet like poo. One month, you thought nothing of dropping $120 on an eightball of "Mt. Everest" every fucking night. The next, you were lucky if you could afford a nickel bag of the world's worst pot. What happened?

The unemployment rate among the college-educated went up 7 percent last year, and thanks to the $87 billion funneled into Iraq, it shows no signs of improving. This "lost generation" is more lost than

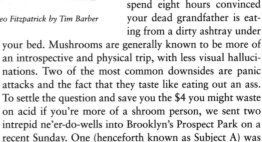

Polaroids of Will Lemon and Leo Fitzpatrick by Tim Barber

ever. After all, you can only drink so much cheap coffee before a stronger buzz is in order, and idle hands do the devil's drugs. Shit, have you seen daytime TV lately? It's all court shows and infomercials and blah blah. Watching it makes you hate yourself and turns blasting your brains into the stratosphere for twelve hours at a time with high-powered drugs into an almost irresistible option. It's not like you have to be at work—or even vaguely functional—tomorrow. The hippies, pampered kids who were afforded the luxury of rebellion, took sheet upon sheet of acid because they were rich and boring. We're taking it because we're poor and bored.

The demand for mindbending trips has mushroom picking and acid production at staggering volumes. Vancouver and northern Florida, two of the biggest centers for psychedelic fungi, are becoming centers of culture in response to their sudden relevance to the rest of the US and Canada. This is evidenced by a sharp rise in art-college enrollment in Vancouver and a fresh crop of ever-stranger death metal bands from the Florida panhandle. San Francisco, still the acid capital of the world, is lumbering back awake like a gigantic sleeping hippie bum. The truth is undeniable: From sea to shining sea, everyone is hallucinating shining seas.

That is why, as we watch our previously square friends start turning on, it becomes ever more important to offer a helping hand and some cogent advice about swallowing drugs. What's the answer when your back's against the wall and the oblivion of hallucinogens seems like your only option? Or, to put the question more succinctly, which is more fun—acid or mushrooms?

The conventional wisdom about acid is that you go on a heavy trip of life-changing proportions and you see and hear beautiful and nonexistent things. The classic pitfalls: You might freak the fuck out and spend eight hours convinced your dead grandfather is eating from a dirty ashtray under your bed. Mushrooms are generally known to be more of an introspective and physical trip, with less visual hallucinations. Two of the most common downsides are panic attacks and the fact that they taste like eating out an ass. To settle the question and save you the $4 you might waste on acid if you're more of a shroom person, we sent two intrepid ne'er-do-wells into Brooklyn's Prospect Park on a recent Sunday. One (henceforth known as Subject A) was on a hit of high-quality blotter acid. The other (Subject B) ate about an eighth of the best shrooms we've ever seen.

HOUR ONE

Subject A (yes, that's the acid guy) first started exhibiting signs of tripping one half hour after swallowing the tab. He became shifty-eyed and a little apprehensive—a common state when one feels the onset of the drug and isn't sure what to expect from the coming trip. "I just tripped out on some guy's pants. They were a weird plaid but I couldn't tell if it was the drug or not. People's faces are starting to look really pink. But I feel good."

Subject B was already getting off a mere 15 minutes after eating the mushrooms. He projected an air of quiet serenity. "I wish we'd eaten some breakfast first. It's happening a lot faster than I thought, which is nice because it's been a long time since it was like in the daytime, in the park…" [trails off and stares at the sun]

HOUR THREE

The subjects move deeper into the park at this point, and soon encounter a quintessential hallucinogen dilemma: Is something weird because we're high, or is it actually weird? Nobody seems to know if those creepy dudes we just saw in that fucked-up part of the park wanted to kill Subjects A and B or if everyone was just being paranoid.

Subject A is agitated and seems to have a surplus of confused physical energy. "I feel so good now that we're out of the basketball jungle. There were some really weird things going around. It didn't sound like nature. It sounded like cars and fucked-up shit. We could have been walking into an ambush. Those guys in there made it a point not to look at my face because they were about to slit my throat."

Subject B is on a bench calmly sipping Gatorade. "I think we just went into the part of the park you aren't supposed to see. The sketchy dudes, like, plotting our demise. They were ready to mug us in broad daylight. But I don't know—the shrooms have been on forever now. It's, like, everything. Just walking in the grass, and the sounds… It's, like, sensory."

HOUR FIVE

It's decided that even completely sober, Prospect Park would be a bum trip. At this point we adjourn to a nearby diner, thereby making one of the larger mistakes in relation to LSD: looking at food.

Subject A is visibly uncomfortable and muttering nonsensical half phrases like how he is glad he had his own entrance into the diner (something that nobody else can understand). He gradually kneads a cloth napkin into a tightly wound knot sculpture, which gets tinted gray by his sweaty hands. "There's some kind of metal in my tea here. I think it's magnesium. I feel like I can taste everything. Maybe I'm just paying all the attention."

Subject B manages to order food (chicken fingers and cream of chicken soup). He eats two bites before giving up. "God, this soup looks gnarly. It's like a mental hospital in here. [looks at Subject A] I feel like we're hanging out with Ponce de Leon."

HOUR SEVEN

Back at home base (the Vice office), both subjects have reached the peaks of their trips. Subject A is almost com-

pletely incoherent, alternately pacing and laughing maniacally. "I can still see stuff moving. Like the table and all, it's shifting like an ocean. But it's OK. The best part of today has been talking. Like, we had the best crew. Everyone was talking, and just, the laughter, man…"

Subject B started to come down, and has just eaten another handful of shrooms. "I'm in it for the long haul… just hanging out with everything." [closes eyes and stops talking]

HOUR NINE

Subject B is completely high again, and Subject A seems to still be peaking. Subject A's trip has taken on an edge of anger. At this point, we decide to take each of them out to the hallway one at a time and ask them what their favorite thing about nature is.

Subject A is nervous about being questioned, and doesn't want to be apart from Subject B for too long. "Oh, man. Fuck. Nature is the best possible thing. Nature is the everything that is not a human being, you know? We could all die—every fucking person on the planet could collapse and die, and you know what? I don't know what's gonna happen. Compared with nature, humans are the worst. Mother Nature keeps on giving good things and we keep giving them shit. I mean, I smoke too, but cigarettes are like the most horrible thing that comes from nature. But I don't know. Fuck it. Nobody should be around to destroy it. But also, imagine if it was just a bunch of naked dudes playing with balls."

Subject B has a magnanimous glow and is unfazable. As a result, he also seems a bit distant during his private interview. "I like that nature is there at my disposal. For a guy who likes to do mushrooms, it's weird but I like it to be distant, like in parks and shit. I'm pro-nature, I guess. There's no answer to this puzzle. It's like, who's better, the Smiths or the Cure? There's no answer."

CONCLUSIONS

Subject A exhibited the quintessential characteristics of a person in the grips of LSD. He was wary, fragile, and difficult to speak with. According to his reports, he experienced mild visual hallucinations, a sense of utter detachment from the world, and uncontrollable laughter. He also reported feeling "fucking weird."

We recommend LSD for users 18–24, people who watch more TV than they read books, and "dog people."

Subject B exhibited the classic symptoms of psychedelic mushroom intoxication. He was introspective but kind of endearing and, like Subject A, distant. Subject B reported feeling wise, physically warm, and "like, everything."

We recommend mushrooms for people 25 and older, those who are erudite, and, obviously, "cat people." ∎

DICK SNIFFER

HAMSTER PARTY THROWDOWN

Two Men Enter, One Man Leaves

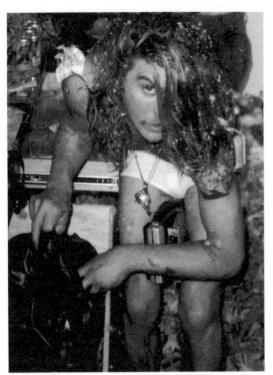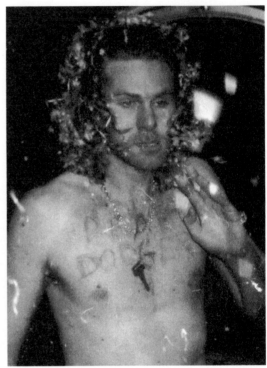

Dash and Dan. Photos by Ryan McGinley.

In the interest of putting an end to drinking contests forever (they kill tens of people a year, you know), we decided to stage the ultimate throwdown of all fucking time so that anybody who ever thought about doing one again would be like, "Oops, can't hack it. I'm a total pussy compared to those two guys who ingested 50 beers, two bottles of Wild Turkey, and six grams of coke in five hours in a tiny hotel room full of 28 shredded Yellow Pages and six live parakeets. Guess I'll just have a virgin mimosa please." As my friend Steve Harvey would say, "You got ser-rrrvvvved, faggot!"

So, as I was saying, who can handle their shit better in the Party Thunderdome: a total degenerate dirtbag or a total degenerate dirtbag? We conned the Maritime Hotel in New York out of a free room with the steely-eyed intention of finding out, or going to the hospital trying. Let's get ready to rumble:

IN THIS CORNER (OF THE HAMSTER CAGE) — DAN

Aka Gargantuan Dan, Danimal, Liquor Face, El Cheapo
Height: 6'6" / Weight: 200 lbs.
Age: 24 / Occupation: Artist / Years Drinking: 11
Father: Moderate drinker but "only drinks Manischevitz wine"
Mother: Nondrinker

...AND IN THIS CORNER — DASH

Aka Tropical Fantasy, Shaniqua, Gutter King, Fuck Face
Height: 5'11" / Weight: 140 lbs.
Age: 22 / Occupation: "Scumbag" / Years Drinking: 10
Father: "Heavy drinker of piss"
Mother: "Drinks piss and also drinks shampoo with piss"

To prepare the arena, 28 New York City Yellow Pages were ripped to tiny pieces (both by hand and in a professional document shredder) and spread about, filling the room. The debris became four feet deep in places. Fifty cans of Pabst Blue Ribbon were put on ice in the bathtub. Six live parakeets ($9 each) were deployed across the shower-curtain bar to, as the combatants put it, "guard the beer." The first beers were cracked at 8 PM, and all things imbibed from that point forth were tallied, with regular check-ins on the hour.

ROUND 1 (9 PM)

DAN: 5 BEERS, 4 SHOTS OF WILD TURKEY, 3 LINES
DASH: 4 BEERS, 4 SHOTS OF WILD TURKEY, 2 LINES

At the one-hour mark, both subjects are clearly intoxicated, with Dash being way drunker than Dan. This is because Dash hasn't touched booze or drugs for 16 days prior to the contest. He's been sober because, until two days ago, his entire body (face included) was covered in a vicious rash. Apparently, Dash has given himself a chronic case of eczema. His doctor told him it was from his "lifestyle," but they always say that.

FIGHTERS' COMMENTS

Dan: "I just want to get naked in here. I wish I could get naked, man."
Dash: "I can't lie. I was already drunk before we made the hamster nest. I invented this hamster thing in Mexico. It's a work of art. We've done it already in L.A., South Carolina, Georgia, and Miami. If anyone tries to steal my idea, I'll fucking kill them."

STANDINGS THUS FAR: Although Dan is technically ahead in quantity; Dash's medical condition must be taken into account. He is going to look like a burn victim tomorrow, and that kind of dedication earns him points. So far, it's a tie.

ROUND 2 (10 PM)

DAN: 12 BEERS, 9 SHOTS OF WILD TURKEY, UNQUANTIFIABLE LINES
DASH: 12 BEERS, 9 SHOTS OF WILD TURKEY, UNQUANTIFIABLE LINES

At the start of the second hour of competition, the phrase "Draft Dodgers Rule" is spelled out in coke on the dresser. Both subjects have worked more than halfway through the huge letters of blow, each starting at separate ends. Dash's skin is already starting to look weird, and Dan has been gurgling mostly unintelligible nonsense since he got to the letter f in "Draft."

FIGHTERS' COMMENTS

Dan: "Our crew is the draft dodgers because we're like... draft dodgers. That's what we'd be if there was a draft. We'd fuckin' dodge it."
Dash (to Dan): "I'll sniff coke off your dick if you'll sniff coke off mine."

The tally is exactly tied now because, starting at 9:50 PM, Dash pounded three beers and two shots to catch up because he didn't want "that faggot to win another round." When it's pointed out that the last check-in actually resulted in a draw, Dash looks puzzled. The offer of dick-coke sniffing (which doesn't actually begin until much later in the night) ushers in a homosexual undertone to the proceedings, which seeps into the contest from that point on in.

STANDINGS THUS FAR: Still a tie, doye.

ROUND 3 (11 PM)

DAN: 19 BEERS, UNQUANTIFIABLE WILD TURKEY AND LINES
DASH: 17 BEERS, UNQUANTIFIABLE WILD TURKEY AND LINES

As the third hour draws to a close, both parties are recovering from a sudden and shocking burst of violence, which began when Dash threw a huge armful of shredded paper in Dan's face. Dan, in a semi-nude rage, flipped Dash across the bed and into the nearby nightstand, which collided directly with the healing tattoo that Dash had gotten the day before. In retaliation, Dash swallowed a slug of whiskey and sprayed it in Dan's eyes. Dan, blinded, managed to spray his own mouthful of whiskey directly into Dash's eyes. Thus, hour four is greeted with both combatants shrieking as if they've just been maced.

FIGHTERS' COMMENTS
Dan: "Ohhh, it fucking stings! What the fuck?!?"
Dash: "Fuck! Was I bad?"

The room is now a quagmire of beer-soaked paper, making maneuvering almost impossible, which leads to much crashing and falling. When a hotel employee comes in to check on the room, Dash streaks out of the door behind her and disappears for 30 minutes.

STANDINGS THUS FAR: Dan is now in the lead, not only in quantity, but also by virtue of the fact that he didn't just run away like a little girl.

ROUND 4 (MIDNIGHT)

DAN: 23 BEERS, A HALF BOTTLE OF WILD TURKEY, THE REST OF HIS COKE
DASH: 20 BEERS, A FUCKING LOT OF WILD TURKEY, THE REST OF HIS COKE

Dash slips back into the room and mumbles a perplexing explanation about having to "make a phone call." Dan responds with a groggy mumble, thus beginning an hour during which he won't speak aloud, but only whisper mysteriously into Dash's ear. They slip into the bathroom together, scaring the parakeets enough that one falls into the icy beer-filled tub. Dan makes it his mission to nurse it.

FIGHTERS' COMMENTS
Dan: "We named these birds Saddam. They're all named that. Saddam 1 through 6."
Dash: "Here, dude, check it out." (Forming his testicles into one turgid ball mass). "Smash balls with me. Let's do it."

Despite repeated admonishments from Dash to "put the fucking bird away," Dan is carrying around the soaked parakeet as if he's Rutger Hauer at the end of *Blade Runner*. The two combatants are becoming secretive, and at one point ten empty cans are found in the bathroom. Were these drunk? If so, who drank them? Dash explains

that "the hamster nest breeds brotherhood. I don't even care about winning this shit. Fuck it." When *Vice* explains that it paid for the beer, coke, and parakeets, Dan adds, "All time and objects get lost in the hamster nest. I gotta bring this fucking bird back to life."

STANDINGS THUS FAR: Dan is still ahead, although Dash's willingness to get his balls out and do fucked-up shit with them earns him some extra credit.

ROUND 5 (1 AM)

DAN: 25 BEERS, 3/4 BOTTLE OF WILD TURKEY, PLUS HE JUST CALLED HIS COKE DEALER
DASH: 22 BEERS, 1/2 BOTTLE OF WILD TURKEY, PLUS HE MADE DAN CALL HIS COKE DEALER

As the finish line approaches, the combatants become philosophical. Dan has successfully resuscitated Saddam 3 and sees this as confirmation of the essential goodness of the world. Dash has changed into a pair of hot-pink jeans.

FIGHTERS' COMMENTS
Dan: "I said to myself, 'You just have to let the birds fly, Danny. Just let them fly.'" [His eyes tear up.]
Dash: "These are my favorite bubblegum pants. I won them in a Double Dutch contest."

Dash is now firmly locked into the persona of a little black girl, while Dan is grinding his jaw furiously enough to generate the electricity needed to power a small city. Also, they have become cagey about who drank what and when. Those ten beers in the bathroom, whose were they? "Saddam's," cackles Dash. They seem equally hammered, and are acting suspiciously gay, sitting side by side on the edge of the paper- and feather-covered bed. It is clear that *Vice* is expected to leave now. It seems it's bedtime. The last thing we see as we shut the door is Dan discovering an uneaten room-service steak. Dash makes a dive for it.

And the winner is... nobody. Though it is reasonably certain that Dan drank more and sniffed more coke than Dash, it is impossible to gauge with 100 percent accuracy. It was fucking fun, though. ∎

JESSE PEARSON

IN THE BLOOD

Dealing With Dad's Junk

After this interview I went and got the same tattoo as my biological dad. It's the Zig Zag man.

My father liked heroin. A lot. He liked it so much that I guess one day he went out for a pack of smokes or something and never came back. I swore I would never get into heroin. Until I got into it. A lot.

I'm better now and I'm pretty sure he's better too, but then again, he lives in Yellville (I didn't make that up), Arkansas, and we've barely spoken in ten years. So I called him up.

Vice: Hi, it's your son. Listen, I was wondering, who do you love more—me or heroin?
Dad: Well, I've got to be honest with you. A lot of the times the drugs took precedence. Let's just say that at times I loved the drugs more.

How did you start using?
With marijuana, when my brother came back from Vietnam. Then, from the first time I got high, I was constantly smoking pot. I didn't use heroin until I was 16, but I did a lot of LSD and diet pills. Dexedrine, double-scored X's, Christmas trees, Apexes... you know.

Not really. I only ever heard of Dexedrine.
You'd really get a good high off of them. So I did them, and I did acid, and I smoked a lot of pot. But yeah, I started snorting heroin at 16, moved onto shooting, and before I knew it, I had a $200-a-day habit.

How did you support that?
Armed robberies. I got busted for robbing a dry cleaner. I had done other places, but that's when I went to jail the first time. It was my dad's gun. I broke into his gun cabinet—took the screws out of the hinges. I was doing stick-ups like that. I was even sticking dealers up.

I did dope the first time totally by accident, thinking it was coke. Four years later I was holed up in a room with sheets over the windows, shooting up all day.
I had really nice reusable glass works for a long time. In a case and everything—real fancy.

That sounds great. Does it bum you out that I was getting high?
You know, I'm actually kind of glad that we have that common ground now. ■

JEFF RUGGLES

MY COKE DEALER

We've all got dealers we like to call "our guys," but aside from their numbers, general delivery hours, and where they usually are at 1:30 AM Saturday morning, how much do we really know about them? I was introduced to my current guy through a mutual friend. I've been calling him for over a year and he's always been reliable as well as super friendly, so I figured maybe he would actually let me sit down with him and get acquainted. It probably helped that I told him I'd double my usual purchase.

Vice: How's it going?
Coke Guy: It's going all right, taking it easy.

What did you want to be when you were a kid?
I wanted to be an astronaut or a pilot. I like the sky. I was always into space movies and sci-fi.

Do you like what you do now?
Yeah. I enjoy it, you know? I know guys who got into it and don't like it. They just need the money, and they're always stressed out thinking about the consequences. But me, I really like doing it.

What's the secret to dealing drugs but not becoming a paranoid lunatic?
Just keep a tight, tight group. I don't associate myself with a lot of people. You only ever see people get into trouble because of someone else opening their mouth. Cops never know what's going on until somebody talks.

Do you ever have deliveries where you're like, I have a bad feeling about this?
Yeah, I get that feeling once in a while. And sometimes you can start to feel like you're invincible. It's easy to forget that you're doing something illegal. It becomes as normal as getting up and drinking a glass of water.

Are your parents around? Do they know?
My dad was never around. My mother has suspicions, but she doesn't ask. I just make sure to not make it obvious that I make a certain amount of money. I take off my jewelry when I'm at home and if someone needs a ride I tell them I don't have a car.

Photo by Jeff Ruggles

So what do you tell her is going on?
Oh, well, I work. I went to school and have had a real job for about ten years.

You were legitimately working before you started dealing?
Yeah, it's good to have something else going on. The person that brought me into this grew up in the middle of it, all the way uptown where it was drug infested. But I didn't grow up around it. I was going to school, but then I started hanging out with him more and the rest is history.

Have you ever had a customer you had to cut off because he was spinning out of control?
Yeah, there was one guy who got to the point where he would try to give me stuff from his apartment. He'd offer his TV, anything he could to get some. And look, we're here to make money, not to fuck up people's lives. I didn't want this dude to be out on the street. He must have also been getting stuff from other people too 'cause it got to the point where you'd go to his apartment and it was just a futon on the floor. I stopped dealing with him. I heard from someone that he eventually went to rehab and moved in with his parents.

What about weirdo customers, have you got a lot of those?
There's one who stands out. He's this gay guy I deal to and he has this thing with suits and tuxes. I come over one night at three in the morning and he's fully dressed up, and he has a suit laid out for me to wear. And, like, to fuck in. He's usually a cool dude, but I think he'd probably been drinking before he called. I was like, "It's cool, dude, but that's just not my thing." He still calls me.

Do you go back?
Yeah, yeah. He's cool, but once he gets in those moods he turns into suit man.

OK, one last question: Just to quash the myth once and for all, are there baby laxatives cut into our coke?
Look, they put a bunch of shit in there depending on where you get it from, but I never heard about fucking baby laxatives. ∎

EMMANUEL COBOS & MARCO TULIO VALENCIA

A COKE DEALER IN MEXICO, WHO IS WAY BADDER THAN THE ONE IN NEW YORK WHO YOU JUST READ ABOUT

Julián is a coke dealer. He's 44. He's been working Mexico City for two decades. He agreed to take us on a ride-along as he worked. The phone never stopped ringing, not for a minute.

Vice: Do you have contacts with the police or politicians?
Julián: Of course. I take care of the heavyweights from the AFI [Mexican FBI]. They send their bodyguards to me in armored cars.

Do you work all over the city?
Yeah, but I don't get near downtown. More cops. More probabilities. If a guy calls me from down there, asks me for only one bag, and tells me he's paying by check, I say, "Buddy, go fuck yourself."

Have you ever been in a gun-fight?
Sure, years ago when I was powerful and moved a lot of kilos. But I've never been to jail. The thing is, you get caught and you get fucking kidnapped. It's not like in the US, where you get arrested and go to jail. Here, they grab you with the intention of taking your money. They take you in a car and do all sort of things to you so that you shit your pants.

Anyway, I used to carry weapons, but not anymore. They only get you in trouble. That was in the 90s when I made 10, 15k daily. But so much dough goes to your head. The cops fucked me up three times in two years.

So you don't want to be the next Tony Montana?
Not anymore. There's an old saying: "It's better to be the president's brother than the president." I don't want anyone looking at me.

Do you sell to anyone?
Not to rapists and kidnappers. Not to assholes.

Photo by Marco Tulio Valencia

How about 13-year-old kids?
No, not at all. It would look like pedophilia. You don't sell to a kid. No kids or pregnant women. But the thing is, generations change. You have to adapt to your times. Sometimes, someone kind of young calls me, and they get the vibe, so they never call me again. It's better that way. And where do they get the money? They steal it from their parents. I mean, you make your money, you buy your drugs, it's your own problem. But if you're stealing from your parents, that's when problems come. I have a lot of clients my own age, and I don't give a shit about them. It's like, when I tell them, "Take care," it's like, yeah, take care because you're the source of my income.

Do you get a lot of new clients?
No, not anymore. I have my client base. I've got some really strong ones who spend between 5,000 and 8,000 pesos a week. Even I have to tell them, "Man, what do you do with so much shit? You should invite me sometime, you fucking asshole, you're going to have a heart attack." I don't like selling to crack users. I hate it. They're a pain in the ass. They're on my case all night, and it's business, sure, but I also need to get my rest.

Do you take any vacations?
That's the problem. I could go to Cuba or the States or wherever the fuck I want to go but the only thing in my mind right now is my kid, Fatty. He has autism. He was deaf, but now the little fucker can hear thanks to a cochlear implant. I'm sending the little asshole to China for some really expensive therapy and then I'm buying a house with a pool, because the fucker loves water. My motivation, my goal, and my project is my kid. That's it. ■

GRAHAM JOHNSON

THE (EX) BIGGEST HEROIN DEALER IN THE WHOLE WIDE WORLD

By the time Suleyman Ergun was 21 years old, he was the world's most prolific and powerful seller of smack. Known throughout the junkie and police communities as the North London Turk, Ergun and his gang flooded Britain and Europe with heroin for five years.

For his pains, the former factory worker got mansions filled with cash and unlimited underworld cachet. At the height of his powers he was a multimillionaire and his favorite tipple was a bottle of champagne with eight grams of cocaine dumped into it. Today, he is almost penniless and lives with his mum. He's 39. What happened?

Vice: Tell me a fond memory of your drug-dealing days.
Suleyman Ergun: There's nothing like the feeling you get when you've got 100 kilos of heroin in the trunk of your car. Just to be near it, to smell it. Driving along at 120 mph in France somewhere and think-

Photo by Stuart Griffiths

ing: "I know what I've got in the car." Police stopping beside you. A gun under my seat. Wouldn't think twice about shooting them. Taking the risk. At the end of the day that's why I became a drug dealer. Not the money or the power, but the buzz.

Did you serve an underworld apprenticeship?
At 15 I was an errand boy working in the Turkish rag trade in North London. I was earning £70 a week. At 17, I started selling coke, E, and pot, and I was earning £1,000 a week. Then I muled a couple of kilos of coke direct from Colombia and sold it in the clubs, along with tablets. Someone tried to rob me in the toilets of the Camden Palace once—I shot him in the leg.

How does one go from selling coke in a bathroom in Camden to being the king of all heroin in Europe?
Me, my former brother-in-law Yilmaz Kaya, and an Istanbul *babas* [godfather] named the Vulcan founded the Turkish Connection—that's a network that smuggles heroin from Afghanistan across Turkey into Europe. Up until the early 90s, Turks had been bringing it in piecemeal. An immigrant would bring in ten keys, sell it, buy a shop in Green Lane, and pack it in. We were the first to start bringing it in 100-kilo loads. Stack 'em high, sell 'em cheap....

It's that simple, eh?
No, that's only the supply. On the demand side, we bypassed all the usual gangsters and crime families in London. We fucked the Adams family off when they asked us to serve up to them. Instead, we sent it all to one distributor in Liverpool who sold the lot.

What was your role?
I was hands-on. The gear was driven from Istanbul to Paris in, say, a coach load of Turkish folk dancers. I coordinated the handover to the scousers in France.

Then I'd drive up to Liverpool a few days later and come back with black bin bags full of cash—£140,000 one week, £100,000 the next, £68,000 the next, £150,000 the next, and so on. Then I'd count it, stack it, and box it in cereal packets and send it back to Turkey using a former Turkish Army colonel disguised as a bone-china collector as a courier.

After a while, we rolled out the same system across Europe—Spain, Italy, Holland, and Germany. We dealt with the Mafia, all of that. At one point we could afford to buy our own oil tanker.

Where did it all go wrong?
One of our workers was having an affair with a woman who was a police informant. He got nicked. Customs put us under surveillance for a year, and then bingo. The whole thing got walloped in July '93.

What was the upshot?
Fourteen years, nine months. The gang got 123 years between them.

Did that teach you a lesson?
Did it fuck. I started dealing in prison within two days, trading heroin and coke for phone cards, food, tobacco. In September 1995 I used heroin for the first time, out of boredom and curiosity. It felt lovely and warm, like somebody putting an electric blanket over you. But the best thing about it, and this is why the jails are full of heroin, is that it makes time go by very quick. Twenty hours on heroin is like two hours normal. I got out ten years later and I didn't know I done the bird [prison time].

How did you get your heroin in jail?
Before I got nicked, I had five kilos of pure heroin straight from Turkey buried along with two Berettas, an Uzi, and four shotguns at St. Pancras graveyard in North London. Every week I'd phone a girl up and use the word *brandy*, which was code for brown—heroin—and she would go and get it. She dug up the stash and shaved off some, and then it was given to a second girl who had a boyfriend in my prison. It was wrapped in a condom and nylon sheeting, shaped up proper like a dildo. She stuck it up her cunt. On the visit, they'd snuggle up close, and her boyfriend would put his hand slyly down her knickers, get it, and then stick it up his arse. Back in my cell, he'd get 60 grams and I'd get 60 grams.

Didn't the prison wardens ever find out?
I had the DST—Dedicated Search Team—permanently on my case. They even used to take apart my batteries in the radio. But they never found gear in my cell because I used to hide it in my vegetable plot. I hollowed out an onion and put the gear inside and buried it. When the stalk wilted, I just taped a fresh one on. Take three grams out a day. Sell half a gram for my phone cards and that, and smoke the rest. Sometimes I would put it up my arse wrapped in tape so if the screws made me squat during a search, it wouldn't fall out.

Couldn't anyone smell you smoking it?
As long as you're not causing trouble, cutting people over deals, and fighting, then the screws turn a blind eye. They know you're on it because your pupils are like tiny pinholes and you start scratching and go red and raw. But the authorities let it go because if you stop the heroin it causes murders and they can't handle that. Withdrawal symptoms. Kicking doors. Drugs will never be stamped out in jail.

How many bent screws did you know?
About six all over. They approached me because I was rich. I never ate prison food. They brought me in Marks and Spencer salads. In one prison the screw brought me in four ounces of weed, half a carrier bag full of phone cards, half a bag of tobacco, a TV, a phone, and two bottles of brandy, every week, for £500 a week, plus the bill for the food. He'd wink and say: "Your box is under your bed." Then I'd pay another inmate to look after it. If you don't have money, you have nothing.

I suppose when you got out of prison in 2003 you gave up drugs?
No, it got much worse. I discovered crack cocaine. The world had changed so much. I couldn't cross the road—it was too fast. I used to see people talking to themselves on their hands-free and think they were off their heads.

What's crack like?
It's great. It blew my fucking head off. Over the next four years I blew half a million pounds on it. Sold my flat. My jewelry. Spent the few hundred grand I had stashed away.

What was the lowest point?
My mate robbed a rock off my table. I dragged him into the kitchen and chopped his little finger off with a knife on a chopping board. Then I flushed it down the toilet.

Some people would say that it was natural justice—that you were being punished for selling heroin by becoming a drug addict.
An eye for an eye. I'd created thousands and thousands of addicts. My past had caught up with me. I got depressed and then I took more crack and heroin to stop thinking.

How did you finally get off drugs?
I went for treatment in Turkey twice. A detox where they put you to sleep through withdrawal. It cost £20,000. My family paid. But when I got back onto the streets here in London, I kept slipping. Finally, I fell in love. It's as simple as that. I haven't touched a stone since.

Would you ever go back to being a heroin baron?
Not in a million fucking years. I've been offered a million pounds in cash to start up again. I could fly to Turkey now and get 100 keys and be away—£100,000 in cash by tomorrow. Mine. I get approached every week by someone or other, some of the country's biggest gangsters, to go into business. But I can't do it.

Why? Are you scared?
Fuck off. D'you want a smack? ■

CHRISTOPH REUTER

HEROIN'S HOMETOWN
Peering Down the Brown Rabbit Hole

Our friend Christoph, a reporter in Afghanistan, tells us what it's like at the source of those little baggies full of brown death that we used to buy from a hole in a brick wall in a building that now houses a Japanese-French fusion bistro...

The story was that villagers had informed the local drug-eradication unit of a heroin lab in the village of Adam Khor in Badakshan, northeastern Afghanistan. An extremely mountainous area where fertile land is scarce, Badakshan is a place where poppy is cultivated in every valley. It is then harvested and the raw opium, or *teryak*, is smuggled across the borders with homemade mini-planes, or simply by bribing policemen.

A raid was staged based on the villagers' information, and several people died when it was carried out. Western officials claimed it was a success. They said that the fact that villagers had informed them of the area's heroin lab showed that the local resentment over heroin production was growing. But some of us began to wonder... Nearly everyone grows poppy in Badakshan. Why would the villagers want a heroin lab destroyed? A bit of asking around yielded the truth: The warlord who had installed the lab only allowed farmers from his villages to use it. Farmers from the neighboring villages pleaded for access, were repeatedly denied, and finally grew so angry that they burned down the lab and informed the authorities of its existence. Now that the playing field is level, no one smuggles heroin across the border. They all smuggle raw opium instead.

Where smack grows on trees...
Poppy field photo by Paul Kooi, dope bag scans courtesy of Pedro Mateu-Gelabert and Liza Vadnai

I have spent several months in Afghanistan over the last few years, talking to poppy farmers, dealers, policemen, Taliban, and foreign diplomats, and they have all told me that the current opium-eradication program is a joke. Opium is Afghanistan's big business. Last year's crop of 6,100 tons, enough to produce 610 tons of heroin, was the largest ever in Afghani history. It provided 90 percent of the world's supply. While US officials claim that opium funds the Taliban, the reality is far more complicated. Opium profits are shared among government officials, affiliated warlords, and, yes, the Taliban. Most poppy farmers I talked to paid bribes to the local police to escape the regular eradication campaigns. This is the case not only in Badakshan in the north, but as well in Kunar in the east and Helmand down south. Sometimes, however, police begin to ask for more than farmers can afford. A farmer in the Balagh district close to Mazar-i-Sharif told me, "Local officials get about 2,000 afghanis [$40] per *jerib* [approximately half a square meter] of land as a bribe. Those who can't pay have their crops destroyed. We are gathering the harvest as fast as we can so that they don't hold us up for money again."

"The richer farmers can pay bribes to avoid eradication, while the poorer ones can't," said Abdul Manan, head of the government's counter-narcotics department in Helmand.

The poppy farmers who can't afford to bribe the police often call on the Taliban for protection. These farmers fight side by side with the Taliban against the police and the Afghan National Army (ANA). A farmer in Helmand said to me of the collaboration, "I am happy about it—if everyone is busy fighting, I can grow my poppy in peace."

And a Taliban spokesman in the Nadali district said, "This is a good opportunity for us to win local support. We can continue our jihad, and local people can keep their lands. Our Taliban are ready to go anywhere in Helmand to help people fight the eradication campaign."

Though the Taliban help protect the fields by fighting against the police, they also do so by eliciting their tacit cooperation. In the mountain town of Cinar on the Kandahar-Helmand border, 20 yards away from the mud-brick compound housing the district police heardquarters, a large field of poppies flourishes. Captain Said Farad, an Afghani army commander based just outside the town, said that the district chief in the region has no choice but to cooperate with the Taliban: The last three chiefs sent there by the governor were killed.

"The police definitely have a hand in the poppies. Those two vehicles near the compound help with the drug smuggling and run supplies for the Taliban," Farad says. "Nobody will kill the current chief because he had a deal with the Taliban."

Since the Taliban were ousted in 2001, the old mujahideen warlords and drug lords have taken positions in Afghanistan's new democracy, and poppy cultivation and drug production have skyrocketed. None of this is a secret. According to a recent report by the UN Office on Drugs and Crime, "This emerging underworld is connected through payment and patronage to senior political figures who provide the required protection."

Qayoum Babak, a political analyst in Balkh Province, says, "Many of the ministries involved in poppy-eradication plans are the main cultivators of the crop. These officials will never get rid of poppy, since they are the main beneficiaries. They are just trying to defraud the world community." The drug trade has corrupted virtually every level of Afghan society, notably law enforcement and the judicial system.

And the corruption reaches the highest echelons of the Afghan government. Last year, the DEA compiled a list of the 14 most important drug smugglers in Afghanistan. In cooperation with US authorities in Kabul, president Hamid Karzai managed to have two names removed from the DEA list: Mohammed Daud, the assistant interior minister personally in charge of drug eradication, and Wali Karzai, the brother of the president himself.

Chris Alexander, deputy special representative of the UN Secretary General, even joked about it during a press conference in Kabul last November. Speaking of the Afghani narco-trade, he quipped, "It is important to realize that not everyone [in the government] is involved." When the laughter died down, he added, "But it is an absolute imperative to remove those who are."

At present, the reverse seems to be happening. On the top floor of a Soviet-built apartment building at the edge of Kabul lives General Aminullah Anarkhil. He used to be in charge of security and customs at Kabul International Airport. We sat on pillows on the floor of his living room, surrounded by pictures of arrested drug mules and their contraband, hidden in body packs, capsules, and elsewhere. Anarkhil helped create a secure international airport from little more than an airstrip adjoined by some wooden shacks and damaged buildings. Undaunted by the paltry facilities, he began to intercept and arrest drug couriers. But the smugglers mysteriously kept being released once they were out of Anarkhil's direct custody. After a month of these arrests, people from Attorney General Abdul Jabbar Sabit's office showed up to investigate unspecified corruption charges. Then Anarkhil was fired. He is convinced it was because he was interfering with the drug-trafficking business. "I received many death threats, telling me that I should stop, I would be killed, and so on," he says.

Anarkhil fears for the safety of his family. The government took away his bodyguards when he was fired. "It is a very powerful and dangerous mafia," he says. "They are very well connected in the government." Since Anarkhil was fired, no drug couriers have been arrested at the Kabul airport.

All that said, though, things may finally be looking up for the current antipoppy campaign. It's starting to gain some powerful supporters, namely, the big drug traders. It's the same situation as it was with the Taliban's 2000 opium ban. Last season there was overproduction of 30 percent. "I'll be very happy if the eradicators are successful," said one trafficker in Lashkar Gah, the capital of Helmand Province, early this spring. "I have lots of poppy stored. If they don't destroy poppy, I'm afraid the price will come down." Which has actually started to happen already. In Balagh, the price for one kilo of teryak has suddenly plunged from $100 to $30. Most local farmers have given up on planting poppies for this season: "We live in a flat, accessible area and cannot hide our fields. There are no Taliban around here. The policemen would still demand the same bribes as last year, therefore we have ceased cultivation this year."

Officials from the office of the governor in Mazar-i-Sharif laud this decline in poppy cultivation as a great success in their antipoppy campaign. In reality, it is no more than a market correction.

As the poppy farmer in Balagh said: "I still have half a dozen oil barrels full at home and so do all my neighbors. If we would sell now, we would lose—so we win by waiting for better prices!" ■

Christoph is a reporter for Germany's Stern *magazine and the author of* My Body Is a Weapon.

D. H. TICKLISH

A GIANT CHINESE FINGER TRAP MADE OF RAINBOWS TRIED TO SUCK ME INTO THE SKY

My Many Trips Into the World of Chemical Psychedelics

Illustrations by Tara Sinn

I have spent the last year of my life on an exhausting psychedelic journey. I managed to get my hands on some of the most potent and rare hallucinogenic drugs ever made, drugs that are mainly illegal. The ones that are not illegal are only approved for analytic studies on things like MP range, GC-MS, and receptor binding affinity. If you have no idea what I'm talking about, it might be better to stick with mushrooms.

But if you know a naughty chemist, you might be able to get your hands on a few of these compounds. How did I get them? For simplicity's sake, let's just say that I pretend to be a doctor. It isn't easy and I don't want to risk arrest or competition by divulging anything about my methods.

These drugs are as rare as they come. They are super potent and not recreational by most people's definition. People have died from taking these drugs for reasons nobody yet understands because there is no research being done on their toxicity. It is quite possible that I could wake up ten years from now with irreversible brain damage, or I could screw up a dose by a few milligrams and end up dead—and from what I gather, tripping to death is not a lot of fun.

It might seem odd that I would spend so much time experimenting with substances that have no guarantee of being safe or enjoyable, but to me that's the entire point of psychedelic exploration—to dive into the unknown. Why drink alcohol every night when you can drink gamma-Butyrolactone? Why snort coke when you can eat N-ethylcathinone? The psychedelic revolution has come cloaked in drug names that are difficult to pronounce, and it's time to wake up and smell the 4-fluoroamphetamine.

A quick note on dosage: These are the doses I take. Don't take the same as me and then get mad when you die. All of these drugs are dose sensitive, so 1 milligram can be the difference between a good time and a permanent psychotic break.

Also, they almost always come as powdered white crystals, usually with the characteristic taste of their chemical precursor, which is called indole and which is present in human shit. It is wise to keep track of which white crystals are which, to avoid a potentially lethal trip cocktail. In other words, if you are going anywhere near this stuff please be really, really careful.

DPT

Dose: oral 140 mg, nasal 100 mg
My proposed street name: Christ
There is a cult/church on the Lower East Side of New York called the Temple of the True Inner Light that has been taking this drug as the Eucharist for the last 30 years. Apparently it's tough to join because they already have enough people willing to participate in Holy Communions where they smoke Christ's psychedelic flesh out of a communal pipe instead of eating a flavorless wafer. Understandable.

The first time I snorted DPT it terrified me so much I felt like I had just railed a line of haunted houses. Eyeballs were peeping out of everything around me and when I looked up I saw a giant Chinese finger trap made of rainbows try to suck me into the sky. Also, snorting it was so painful it made me cry. I would rather snort a handful of sand.

2C-T-21

Dose: oral 12 mg
My proposed street name: Heat Stroke
This drug had a brief stint about five years ago as a legal ecstasy alternative, but it was taken off the market when a quadriplegic from Florida tried to lick an unknown amount of a vial he bought online, gave himself a massive overdose, and literally fried his brain. That paralyzed man was the infamous party pooper of this entire drug scene, and it was his overdose that got most of these unknown drugs scheduled by the DEA.

I tried 2C-T-21 about a week ago. While walking around my neighborhood, I got so hot that I had to take off my shirt. My body was actually steaming. I decided to go swimming in a nearby urban river but instead threw my house keys into the water just to see what it looked like when they splashed.

4-ACO-DMT

Dose: oral 24 mg
My proposed street name: The Greatest Drug in the World (Some people call it Aurora but that'll never catch on.)
Some wayward chemists figured out a way to twist around the structure of psychedelic mushrooms to fit them into a legal loophole so they could be sold from gray-market laboratories. Thus, 4-AcO-DMT was born. The second it touches your gut it gets converted into the active ingredient of mushrooms. But one big difference is if you eat too many mushrooms you vomit, which prevents many overdoses. With 4-AcO-DMT it's easy to accidentally swallow what would be equivalent to a trash bag of shrooms. My friend took too much in the middle of Times Square, went nuts, and ended up strapped down in a hospital. As soon as he got out he attacked his mom for lying to him about Santa Claus as a child.

DOC

Dose: oral 3 mg
My proposed street name: DOC Feelgood
Since a scale that is accurate down to the microgram would cost more than all of these drugs combined, I measure DOC in a liquid solution. I dissolve 10 milligrams of DOC in 10 milliliters of vodka and then use a syringe to measure doses. 1 ml = 1 mg. Easy!

DOC is a psychedelic amphetamine that is unrivaled in potency. A lot of the acid that people think has angel dust in it is actually adulterated with DOC. The big difference between DOC and acid is that DOC lasts about 24 hours, and since it's an amphetamine, you're looking at 24 sweaty hours. This is the kind of drug you really want to have some Valium around for. Any food I put in my mouth tasted like polyester. By the end of the trip I'd eaten a potted plant and the dirt it was growing in.

5-MEO-DMT

Dose: smoked 5 mg, nasal 15 mg
My proposed street name: Crystal Death
This one actually occurs in nature. A rare variety of desert toad squirts it on predators in order to render them defenseless in a psychedelicized stupor. The dose is about the size of one grain of salt and when smoked it sends the user into a death trance. It is not uncommon for people high on this stuff to pee their pants.

"Psychedelic" does not quite describe the 5-MeO-DMT experience. If there's a chemical way to shoot yourself in the face and survive, this is it. Once I gave it to a drunk guy who didn't believe there was such a thing as psychedelic toad venom. Within moments his eyes rolled back in his head and he fell to the floor motionless. When he regained consciousness (after vomiting on me while passed out), he said he had touched God.

2C-T-7

Dose: oral 22 mg
My proposed street name: 7-Up

Another chemical in the same family as mescaline that is totally synthetic and never gained any significant level of popularity in the United States. Around 2001 a couple of suburban teens overdosed on it and the DEA immediately put it in the same legal schedule as heroin. Last time I took 2C-T-7, the moment I began to hallucinate I decided to get on the $15 Fung Wah bus to Boston, five hours away from where I live, for no reason. I closed myself in the bathroom and pretended I was time-traveling in a septic tank, and when we arrived at our destination the driver had to pry open the bathroom door.

AMT

Dose: oral 40 mg
My proposed street name: Jaw Clench Vomit Powder

This drug was born in Russia 50 years ago. Pharmaceutical companies marketed it as an antidepressant called Indopan. I think the problem was that it worked too well and it didn't take long before people realized it was capable of sending them into an insane vibrating notionscape if they simply took twice the dosage.

During my first trip on AMT, I was supposed to stop briefly at a party before going to a friend's house. I foolishly took the pill beforehand and ended up staying at the party the entire night exchanging pleasantries with strangers while watching them melt into the carpet. I was actually having the time of my life until I had to pee and realized that it was a psychological impossibility.

2C-E

Dose: oral 17 mg
My proposed street name: C-Esspool

This one is somewhat related to mescaline but about 20 times stronger. It made me so violently nauseous that I vomited out of my nose. Later that night I collapsed on a bench and watched the trees lining the roads slowly grow genitalia—splintery leafed penises and big sappy vaginas. I sat watching this in awe with two friends while taking an occasional whippit, but after a while a passing woman suddenly started beating the shit out of her boyfriend ten feet in front of me. It was more of a downer than a thousand Chris Farley overdoses. When the cops showed up I was climbing one of the vagina trees to get a better view.

DIPT

Dose: oral 70 mg
My proposed street name: Dipthong

Whenever people ask me what DIPT is like, I have trouble explaining it. It is vaguely related to mushrooms, but at the same time not really. It's totally synthetic—a lab-made psychedelic anomaly that only affects the regions of your brain dedicated to auditory perception. DIPT gives you ultra-sensitive canine hearing and drops the pitch of all sounds down a couple of octaves. Sound waves that fall below the human range of hearing are called infrasound and are associated with earthquakes, exploding volcanoes, and screaming whales. On DIPT, I was listening to a steady infrasonic thrum being generated by a parking meter. Everything sounds like you're underwater, in a broken transistor radio, talking to a bullfrog. I could hear people having conversations inside their apartments as I walked down the street. I also learned to translate the language birds speak. I still have the notebook I was carrying, which has about 40 pages of phonetically transcribed bird chirps that read like this: "percheap twererp cherwerp."

DIPT is like a fun version of being schizophrenic, but I stopped taking it after a high-dose trip where I had an epiphany and figured out that fire-engine and ambulance sirens are a city-wide conspiracy to give people headaches. Also (and in retrospect I should never have done this), riding a crowded city train through a not-so-great neighborhood while on this drug was comparable to listening to a thousand howler monkeys being burned alive—through a stethoscope.

DMT

Dose: smoked 50 mg
My proposed street name: Demetri

This one is a classic but still a lot of people have never tried it. You can inject it, snort it, smoke it, or eat it—and have a totally different experience each time. Once I smoked 50 mg after taking a special type of antidepressant that makes it impossible for your body to break down the drug. I began having a vicious argument with my left hand, speaking from both sides—my hand's point of view and my face's. I said, "I'm sorry. I will never do drugs again," and my hand replied, "It's too late!" I thought I was every crazy person that had ever lived in the past, present, and future simultaneously. A lot of people report having sexual encounters with aliens while on this drug but I think before experimenting with DMT, those people experimented with being molested. ∎

HAMILTON MORRIS

THE MAGIC JEWS
From Manischewitz to Mescaline

Photo by Jess Williamson

When I first walked into the apartment on Ridge Street on the Lower East Side of Manhattan, I didn't see much because the lights were off. It was a long empty room with couches lining the walls. Empty cans and bottles everywhere. At four in the morning all that was left were the remnants of a party. Nothing unusual. A Hasidic Jew was passed out on his back, yarmulke resting on the cushion next to his head. His cell phone was wildly ringing digitized klezmer music from within his wool pants. He lay totally still. I walked toward him, wondering if he was alive. The phone cycled through four more rings before he swiped at his pocket, at which point I let out a sigh of relief.

I could hear muffled singing coming from behind a closed door down the hall. I stepped over the passed-out Hasid, making my way into the next room. Inside, it was completely dark. The air was warm with the smell of bodies. Ten, maybe fifteen, naked Jews were perched, chanting in flawless harmony with one another. They stopped briefly to greet me and then resumed. I watched them speechlessly for a moment before posing the question "What's going on?" A voice in the dark made an incomprehensible remark about LSD, and everybody broke out in bouts of electrified laughter. And then the chanting began again. I only stayed for a few minutes, watching them in awe before I felt for the doorknob and got up to leave. Back in the other room, a Hasid I had not noticed before informed me that the party was over, the acid was gone, and I should come back the next day. I asked him when and how frequently this sort of thing happened. He responded: "Constantly."

For many, religion is tedious work. A chore handed down from generation to generation, rewarding only by virtue of its being unpleasant. Few have had a genuine religious experience, something that warrants worship, reverence, time, and faith. I know I haven't. In Jewish mysticism, God is partially defined by his lack of definition. He is infinite and unknowable, the eternal question mark. I had my first psychedelic experience smoking salvia in a friend's station wagon when I was 16. I lay screaming with laughter, soaking myself with tears, snot, and drool. I knew that something significant had happened, something that would definitely fit under the "infinite and unknowable" heading. But to say that it was a religious experience would be wrong. It was better.

Two days after the party I received a phone call from one of the Jews. I expected it to be along the lines of another party invitation, but to my chagrin it was a request to attend the funeral of one of their friends. He had overdosed on cocaine the previous night. I got on the F to Parkville, Brooklyn, and then walked toward 39th Street nervously. Attending the funeral of a Hasidic Jew I had never met, without a yarmulke, wearing a purple leather puff-coat, made me generally uneasy. Outside the Shomrei Hadas Chapel, Hasids paced nervously while smoking cigarettes. I walked through the door and took a seat in the back, trying to remain unnoticed. At the front of the synagogue a wall of black-clad Jews blocked any view of what was going on. I listened to the Hebrew prayers drone on and found my social discomfort slowly melt into sadness. When the service ended I filed out to watch the pine box heaved into a Ford Excursion as mobs of family and friends cried and smoked and talked on cell phones. It was here that I met Aaron, one of the few in attendance who was without religiously sanctioned clothing. He began to explain things a bit.

The previous night one of his ex-Hasidic friends had been on a drug binge, taking massive doses of coke, ecstasy, and an assortment of benzos. He was fine, if extremely inebriated, when he retired to bed, falling asleep next to his girlfriend. The following morning she woke up next to a corpse. Aaron explained, "It's a nonstop drug binge without drug education. These Hasids have all lived incredibly sheltered lives. You really can't even imagine unless you've been there. When they stray from their families nobody has told them not to mix this with that, speed and ecstasy, alcohol and Xanax. It gets seriously dangerous." "Who's selling them this stuff?" I asked. "There are drug dealers who get a kick out of the whole thing like, 'Let's get the Hasids fucked up,' you know? Which is fine, but they don't realize that's exactly what's going to happen—they are going to get really, really fucked up."

As he told me this I felt overcome by frustration. Maybe it was selfish, but the thought that I would only have one tantalizing taste of this renegade Hasid drug world was incredibly disappointing. It was already over, everybody would be scared straight, and the scene would disintegrate into obscurity before I got a chance to learn exactly what

was going on. "So I guess this is the end of it all?" I asked. Aaron paused and said, "No, no, no. Definitely not." And on that note I was invited to a party the following night.

To take a moment and clarify my religious background: I am a Jew. I was bar-mitzvahed (at Masada no less) but I never went to Hebrew school. I never went to temple. I learned a CliffsNotes version of Hebrew and memorized my Torah portion from a recording on a MiniDisc. In short, I know nothing about Judaism. I am also not religious or "spiritual" in any way. I feel awkward even saying the word *prayer*. The Jews I met at Ridge Street come from Hasidic and Orthodox Brooklyn neighborhoods. Most speak Yiddish as their first language. Aside from a love of psychedelics and maybe some shared genetics from way back when, we have nothing in common. I was introduced to all of them by a friend of a friend of a friend. A psychedelic mushroom is called a magic mushroom, and by that logic these Jews could be called Magic Jews. So that's how I started to think of them.

The doorbell at the Ridge Street apartment had a placard labeling it a photographer's studio, which may or may not have been true. Inside there was an array of Jewish fauna, ranging from those in full Hasidic costume to others looking like they had just arrived from a Rainbow Gathering in Vermont, all originating from an environment of extreme religious oppression. Some were old. Most were young. There were almost no women, and those who were there seemed to have minor if not nonexistent ties to Hasidism. They were spectators like me.

After the funeral, Aaron and I had discussed working with an uncommon spiritual catalyst called 2C-E. At the party that night, we opened a bag, cut the white powder into small lines, and offered it around. Somebody asked what it was, and I said it was a synthetic psychedelic in the same chemical family as mescaline. A guy with long curly hair shouted from across the room, "2C-E is not mescaline!" I was stunned at his psychedelic bravado but rushed to agree with him and point out a second time that this chemical was not mescaline, just related to it. Jews began to crowd around the lines of powder. Aaron stepped forward, volunteering his nostril and a rolled-up dollar bill. He bent over the book, snorted a line, winced, and then sneezed the crystals into a cloud around the table—the most Jewish drug blooper imaginable. Literally a Woody Allen joke. Everyone else rushed to rescue what was left with credit cards while Aaron stumbled into the bedroom followed by a girl with frizzy red hair. I began gnawing on a piece of kugel with jittery anticipation.

Aaron is obscenely charismatic and one of the few Magic Jews who can pass for a gentile. He speaks without an accent, wears normal clothes, and flirts ruthlessly with any woman around him. Upon leaving the bedroom, he turned to a friend and declared, "I broke my vow of celibacy after one day!" The friend cried back, "You're an animal!" Despite all this, Aaron comes from a family he calls "hardcore Orthodox" and has gone through the same sort of religious trials as everyone else in the room. He told me, "I had two circumcisions because my mom is a convert and Judaism goes by the mother. I lived in California until I was 13, then we moved to New York where it was much more religious and they said, 'Oh, the California rabbis are not legitimate. You have to convert again.' I was 14 years old and it was bad timing for a circumcision, but they took a knife and went to work on my penis. I was just starting to go through puberty and these three 80-year-old rabbis were cradling my balls. I was like, 'Do I have to do this?' They said, 'Don't you want to be Jewish?' and I was like, 'No!'" Aaron's parents think he's a degenerate drug user and they wait patiently for him to return to a life of Orthodoxy in Monsey, New York. He assured me this is not going to happen.

At Ridge Street, another Jew, this one in his 30s and named Hershel, consumed a line of 2C-E. Hershel has a light brown beard and a round body. His voice is hypnotically buttery and his general aura is like being wrapped in a warm towel. Hershel was married by force at 18. He has a wife and two kids in Williamsburg, Brooklyn, from whom he escaped in order to explore psychedelics. He has no home and drifts from place to place, praying and eating LSD. He is thought of as the leader of the Magic Jews but is too modest to accept the title. He explained to me, "I have one agenda, and that's more Hasidim doing psychedelics. I grew up Hasid, but I didn't know God at all. Then I was an atheist, and then psychedelics came to me and I understood. Psychedelics allowed me to rediscover God. Before LSD, I hated God."

Amid all the debauchery I wove my way out the door and began walking toward the Manhattan Bridge. It all would have been strange enough if I wasn't tripping. A few days later I received a call from Aaron, who told me they had all been evicted from Ridge Street and had already moved into a cabin in the Catskills, a place without electricity or running water. He gave me a list of phone numbers and told me to catch a ride up as soon as possible. I met my ride at his home in Brooklyn, where I was greeted with an eye-wateringly large gravity-bong hit that made me more or less comatose for the entire trip into the woods.

I came to in the dark as the car slurped into a muddy clearing. Aaron emerged from the trees with a giant flaming torch in hand. I followed the flame through the trees, unsticking my feet from the mud with each step. In front of me was a corrugated-tin two-story A-frame monstrosity. Beyond it was a moonlit lake with a waterfall and hundreds of acres of Eden-esque land. The property and house were paid for by a group of mysterious Jewish elders who were sympathetic to the cause. Their only stipulation? That nobody uses the land to grow weed.

Inside the cabin it was candlelit, filled with singing, and extremely hot from a blazing fire set inside an oil-drum furnace, which was right in the middle of the room. Sweaty, half-naked Jews were festooned about, lying on dark couches, sleeping in beds, in corners, on the floor, in the rafters. A picnic bench at one end of the room was crowded with boxes of matzo, glass prayer candles with depictions of Jesus and the Virgin Mary, and bottles of Manischewitz wine. I took a seat and swallowed a tab of LSD, then handed one to Hershel, who laughed uproariously as he placed it in his mouth. He proceeded to heat pans of water on the stove so he could draw himself a mikvah in a kiddie pool outside. Then it started to rain. It was too dark to write so I just lay on my back and listened to April showers pelt the tin roof. I was in total ecstasy. It felt as if each raindrop was falling from the sky to give my eardrums a handjob. Hershel emerged from the rain and I commented on how beautiful it sounded, to which he responded, "What rain?" I was totally confident that I had discovered some impossibly strange version of paradise.

I woke up harshly the next morning to a screaming argument between two Jews. "You behave this way, you won't get anywhere. You want to have women, don't you, Yoni? You want to fuck a woman in her vagina?!" Yoni wore a yarmulke and was still in the gray area between Magic and Hasidic, like some sort of deeply uncomfortable psychedelic puberty, doubtful of the old way but afraid of the new one. Offended by the Christian icons, he had scratched the faces of Jesus and Mary off their respective candles the previous night. A Jew named Lavvy screamed at Yoni, "Jesus loves you even if you scratch off his face." Yoni screamed, "NO! NO! NO! Fuck Jesus!" while he covered his ears in agony. This sort of scene was not uncommon and was done for Yoni's own good. A seemingly insignificant lesson turned into a painful, paradigm-shattering, reality-crumbling theological crisis. Lavvy, who comes from the same part of Brooklyn as Yoni, adjusted with more ease. He has made a name for himself as a burgeoning fashion designer, causing an uproar in the Orthodox blogosphere for sending models down the runway wearing outfits made from deconstructed prayer shawls, yarmulkes, and other traditional Jewish attire.

Lavvy got tired of reeducating Yoni, wrapped himself in an American flag, put on a motorcycle helmet, and pranced out the door looking like an Israeli version of Evel Knievel. He walked through the woods toward an automobile graveyard, stripping off his clothes with each step. Lavvy straddled the cab of a half-disintegrated bus, wearing nothing but his helmet. It was around this point that I started to wonder when and if I would ever be able to get a ride back home. I went looking for the Jew that had driven me up, but much to my dismay I found him passed out in an unexplained Clifford the Big Red Dog costume. I made sure he was breathing and then nudged him a few times in a futile effort to wake him up. By the time it had gotten dark again, I realized that nobody beside myself had any intention of leaving. I poured a glass of Manischewitz and lay down. I hadn't eaten anything except matzo and LSD for over 24 hours.

Around the time I had totally given up hope, I was approached by a couple returning to the city who I had not met or noticed the previous night. I got into their car and we began driving home listening to a scratched Ricky Martin CD. The girl began to question me about what I was doing upstate since I looked a bit different from the rest. I told her I was writing an article about drug use in the Hasidic community, which had become my stock answer. Nobody responded for a few moments, then she cleared her throat and said, "Yes, it's quite a problem." She paused, turning down the volume on the stereo, and then went on. "My boyfriend died two weeks ago from a cocaine overdose." My heart skipped a beat. "I was at the funeral, it was terribly sad," I said. "Yes," she responded, her voice strained. Her new boyfriend shifted in his seat and said, "It was terribly sad, but you know you have to move on." I jumped in with a quick "Yes, yes, of course. You cannot dwell on these things." Her boyfriend put his hand on her shoulder and cranked up "Livin' La Vida Loca." Nobody spoke for the rest of the ride. Back in the city, I got out on Canal Street feeling as if I had just overdosed on confusion.

The next call that I received from the Magic Jews informed me that they had been kicked out of the house upstate. It turned out that the elders didn't really own it after all. They all reconvened at a synagogue on the Lower East Side one evening. I arrived around midnight to find Jews spilling onto the street smoking cigarettes, drinking, and flirting with shiksas. A Hasid I had never met before took my hand and said, "Welcome home." Inside, I saw the word *rabbi* scrawled across a wall with an anarchy symbol replacing the *a*. In the corner, a Jew sat at a piano picking out "Stairway to Heaven." I took a seat and before long was approached by Aaron, who suggested we smoke some DMT on the back stoop. A bag containing a yellow powder the color and consistency of dried earwax was produced and the powder carefully poured into a pipe. We both inhaled, sitting side by side on the unlit steps, shrouded by low-hanging tree branches. My brain started to divide into two, then four, then eight brains. I exhaled and was suddenly aware of a flip-flop-wearing jock scowling at us from across the street. I started to wonder once again: What was the significance of any of this?

In the 60s, Reform Jewish rabbis started to use psyche-delic drugs for the pursuit of God. Some came to the conclusion that the psychedelic experience was in every way more real and important than the religious experience, even going so far as to say that any comparison between the two would only serve to desecrate the sanctity of psychedelics. In 2000, a group of Orthodox Jews living in Queens was found to be selling more than 100,000 MDMA tablets a week. Police seized a million tablets from their apartment. Some papers reported it to be the largest drug bust in New York history. But why is any of this surprising? Everybody gets high. At this moment somewhere there is a nun robo-tripping and a monk inhaling computer duster. What matters is how it's done. While some of their contemporaries quibble about whether or not it is permissible to smoke weed on the Sabbath or if LSD is kosher, the Magic Jews have completely rid themselves of religious bureaucracy and distilled what they know of Judaism to its tastiest essences, shamelessly consuming it and hoping others will follow by example. In that way, it is psychedelic religion at its purest.

I made one last trip to the Catskills, where a sheet of LSD was acquired and then greedily consumed in a matter of minutes. Magic Jews were frothing at the mouth with psychedelic lust. Hershel took my arm and said he would like to speak with me alone. We walked down an unlit road and looked at each other's silhouettes. "You know, Hamilton, some people want to do this for the wrong reasons," Hershel said. I nodded as he went on. "Sometimes they only want orgies, and sometimes we have orgies, but you must understand your intentions." I nodded again, wondering what he was suggesting. He continued, "These are powerful places. When you bring light back into the picture, it automatically takes care of a lot of darkness, but I don't think it's inherently good. I think it destroys everything you've got. If you're focused, you can rebuild. But not everybody is." By that point both of us were tripping pretty hard. Hershel was branching into a celestial tree-human chimera, but his point still came across: We are all on drugs, and these drugs are the essence of God. Enjoy yourself, but don't ignore their infinite power.

A few hours later one of the Magic Jews railed a line of ketamine while navigating the lake in a rowboat. He staggered onto the shore, then collapsed on the ground, spewing vomit all over himself and dropping into a deep and unresponsive K-hole while everyone watched in horror. Eventually they got distracted, turned him onto his side, and returned to a bonfire to snort more ketamine. As the sun rose and the alien chirps of what I can now only identify as glass harmonica birds lulled me into a trance, I saw Hershel emerge from the woods. He was alone with a prayer book in his hands, grinning. We both listened to the birds sing for a minute while I accepted the weirdest thing of all—the real possibility that it all made sense. ∎

PATTON OSWALT

SPIKIN'

Sideways, But With Smack

Photo by Jake Michaels

I'm never going to try heroin. I hate needles. I hate feeling sleepy and smug at the same time. And finally, I've never seen it depicted well in movies.

Heroin addicts always end up unwittingly killing a friend or having a gangrenous limb hacked off or being raped in prison while simultaneously jonesing or dying or becoming shitty poets.

According to the movies, other drugs are much better. Pot smokers are giggly and fun. No one takes ecstasy unless by accident, and usually right before a big holiday family dinner. Cocaine usually leads to jail, but it leads to *cool* jail. The journey to cocaine incarceration involves trim, tense torsos, car chases, wild sex, and then an attractive, brooding stance of regret as you look back on it all and smile ruefully.

And drunks! Where do I start? There's a bar somewhere with Arthur Bach, Hawkeye and Trapper John, Foster Brooks, and Otis the Town Drunk all singing "Working for the Weekend" while Nick and Nora Charles make out in a booth.

But heroin is dimly lit hotel rooms, haggard girlfriends, and an atonal soundtrack. Before getting hooked, or even shooting it once, I'd need to see it depicted in a movie like *Sideways*, where two lovable, cuddly heroin addicts—middle-aged in that sitcom-y kinda sheepish smile way that middle age is depicted in movies—do a jaunty tour of Alphabet City, sampling a weekend's

worth of dope before one of them gets married.

"Oh, this is hitting me just right. I feel—there's some strychnine, but underneath there's a loamy bass note of autumnal Afghanistan poppy fields, and... and... *there* it is!... a flutter of tangy stomach acid from where they cut the baggie out of the mule's belly after they chloroformed her in a Super 8 Motel in Hoboken."

Then our two heroes get mistaken for extras in a zombie movie shooting nearby and end up at the director's penthouse, where one of them steals a reel of dailies and sells it for another fix. Soon they're being chased through the city by a born-again Christian P.A. from the movie. And to add to the hassle, they pick up a teenage runaway whom one of the dudes lusts after, while the other one is gently reminded of his daughter who no longer speaks to him because he offered to blow her prom date to get $75 for a skin popper.

But that's just the beginning of the shenanigans! Twenty-nine wrecked cop cars, a musical dream sequence set to Billy Squier's "In the Dark," a return-from-the-dead OD jump-up-and-gasp scene, and one love-crazed moose later, our two heroes have got to somehow buy back the reel of dailies, jury-rig a wedding between the runaway and the Christian P.A., and win a Transcendental Meditation contest.

It's called *Spikin'*. I've already sold it to New Line, so hands off. ∎

COMPILED BY VICE STAFF

PLEASE SNORT ME

An Oral History of Brooklyn's Most Notorious Bar

Photo by Sharky Favorite

hy hello there, sonny. You too, little miss. So you're the young whippersnappers that're living in good old Williamsburg, Brooklyn, now, huh? Well let me tell you kids, I may not look like much more than an old fogey, but I was here in the WB back when the likes of you were sucking on your mammy's teat. Why, I was there at the first Fischerspooner show. I have a copy of Andrew WK's home-recorded demos—he gave them to me himself. We used to sit around and spin yarns at the Stinger Club on Grand Street all night long, and then Peaches and Larry Tee would come in trailing Adult. records, Nike Dunks in black and yellow, and steaming

fresh copies of *index* magazine. After that we'd go over to P.S.1 on Saturdays and listen to Chicks on Speed play a show while we all tried to recover from the night before at Kokie's...

Wait, "What's Kokie's," you said? These old ears ain't what they used to be but I could swear you just asked me that. You did! Well, sit down here on this stack of back issues of *Purple*, and let me tell you about a time long past... a hazy era known as 1999...

Just before the turn of the millennium, on the soon-to-be gentrified corner of Berry and North 3rd in Williamsburg, Brooklyn, there was a bar called Kokie's Place. It was the stuff of legend. Or, to put it more bluntly, it was a dingy Puerto Rican coke bar. But really, it was so much more! 1999-2001 was a pivotal era in Williamsburg history—it's when the neighborhood finally went from kind of depressing because it wasn't Manhattan to really depressing because it's full of assholes fresh out of art school—and Kokie's was at the center of that transformation.

So this is a tale of gentrification. It's a tale of people from different cultures coming together in really weird ways. And of course, it's a tale of wrecking your life and wasting your 20s doing tons of the worst cocaine that a Spanish-speaking New York drug dealer has ever stepped on.

We've compiled a history of Kokie's, straight from the mouths of the locals, the regulars, and the people whose lives were touched and/or destroyed by this very special place... a coke bar called Kokie's.

ANCIENT HISTORY

JEFF JENSEN: I first noticed the Kokie's sign in 1991. It wasn't open to the public at the time but we knew there were people doing coke inside. You have no idea how blown-out and desolate the neighborhood was back then. The token booth dude at the Bedford stop of the L train was narcoleptic and you could just push the crappy old wooden turnstiles open. No one cared. I tried to wake him up once to pay for my ride and people laughed at me.

TOM C: In the early 90s, the cops called South 2nd Street between Berry and Bedford, right around the corner from Kokie's, "The Drugs and Death Corridor." You could buy drugs right out on the street. It was all Puerto Rican and they loved to beat up white guys. I got jumped at least three times.

GARY J: The Southside was no joke. And those Kokie's guys were not the kind of people you'd want as friends or enemies. They were all criminals, in and out of prison.

JEFF JENSEN: So it took real balls for me to finally knock on the door in 1995. I convinced the doorman to let me in. I said, "I want to become a member of this club." He wouldn't let me in at first but I know how to hustle. Plus I had a pretty serious cocaine habit at the time. At first I would just buy coke from them and leave, but then I started hanging out with the Overlords guys. There was a biker bar called Road Sores on South 6th Street. This gang called the Overlords would always hang out there or at Kokie's. I became really good friends with one of them, a Puerto Rican biker who changed his name to Muskrat after his wife died in a chain fight. They had both really loved the song "Muskrat Love." I used to do

immense quantities of cocaine off the end of Muskrat's knife. He would just dip it into a Folgers can full of coke right there in Kokie's.

GARY J: If you want a little bit of history, the landlord told me that the bar started off in the early 1900s as an Italian social club. Then in the 50s it got taken over by a Puerto Rican gentleman and he turned it into a Spanish social club—they had cockfighting and gambling there. That went on for about 20 years and then he passed it on to his godson or someone like that. The bar wasn't making any money because its clientele was all old-timers paying something like a dollar for a beer. So the godson had the bright idea to turn it into a coke den.

BRIAN F: Word spread fast. Everyone heard about Kokie's the same way: "Hey, have you been to Kokie's? It's a COKE bar called KOKIE'S!"

GARY J: Oh, by the way, the name of the bar comes from a little green tree frog from Puerto Rico called a coquí (pronounced "kokie"). It's called that because when it chirps it makes a sound like, "Ko-kee! Ko-kee!" That's where the name comes from, not from cocaine.

THE SNOWY HEYDAY

JERRY P: Kokie's went through a series of changes after I started going there in '98. You could tell how long somebody had been a regular based on whether or not they were familiar with certain milestones. When I first started going, they had a live salsa band in the corner on certain nights.

BRIAN F: Wednesday night, I think, was salsa night. Man, it was decked out. They had a huge band in there—vibes, percussion, everything. It filled up the entire back room. An old man in brown pants would be dancing with some hot mama with a flower in her hair. It felt like being in Cuba in the 50s or something. I felt like Henry Miller.

JUDY W: They had karaoke nights there too, but they started at 6 PM and ended by 10 so we never got there in time to do it. The karaoke setup looked like an AV unit that was stolen from a high school or something.

JERRY P: Eventually they phased out the band and got a jukebox. But it was still pretty decrepit. Just dark, dingy walls and little yellow lightbulbs. It was all empty and weird on weeknights. I loved the shittiness of it.

SHARKY FAVORITE: One night in 1999 I was at Kokie's

and I was wearing this scarf that my girlfriend had spent two months knitting and had just given to me that day. Well, of course, within a couple of hours of running around Kokie's like an idiot, the scarf was gone. I spent the whole night looking for it and complaining about how she was gonna kill me for losing the thing. When it finally came time to face the music, sure enough, she was pissed. I followed her around the apartment, apologizing over and over again. She looked at me and said, "You just don't get it," and left. I glanced at the clock. It was 2 PM. I had no idea I'd just spent 13 hours at Kokie's. It was a time vacuum and it made me a bad boyfriend.

MEG SNEED: The windows were blacked out in the front and there were no windows at all in the back—you had no sense of time or reality.

LORI A: Nothing good ever happened to me at Kokie's. I'd only go there when I was already too drunk and it was 3:30 AM and someone would inevitably shout, "I know! Let's go to Kokie's!" The next thing I knew I'd be back in that curtained booth doing the worst coke in the world until well past dawn.

JERRY P: The coke was stepped on like crazy. I think it was cut with meth, because it lasted so fucking long. I personally didn't mind it.

BRIAN F: It was convenient living nearby because the coke was so awful. As soon as I did a bump I would run home, shit my brains out, and then come back refreshed and ready for more.

MEG SNEED: The coke there was pretty bad, true, but it was such a pleasant place to be. A real positive atmosphere and community feeling. I even thought about hanging out there without drugs once or twice. Of course I never did.

LUCY P: I don't know if I ever talked to anybody there who I didn't know, but I felt as though I could've. And it wasn't just the drugs. There was a sense that everybody was there to enjoy some sort of desperate eked-out freedom. As though a line had been crossed into comity. You know, the purity of purpose people shared.

STEVE L: The first time I walked in there, I could see that all the action was in the disco room, where a crowd of mostly middle-aged Puerto Rican mamis were dancing around to what sounded like electro-merengue. One of them, in a hot-peach tube top, bleached cutoffs, and espadrilles, dragged me out on the floor to get down with her. I must have pranced with every orange-haired lady in the place.

STUART McCLENNAN: Kokie's usually came alive around 3 AM. It always looked so dead from the outside but then inside it was packed with people partying like extras in an 80s party movie. The crowd was about 75 percent Puerto Ricans dancing the mamba or whatever with perfect precision and 25 percent college kids grinding their jaws and doing a jittery hip-hop version of the mamba in a futile attempt to blend in.

VALENTINA A: I'd never heard of Kokie's until early 2000. I was walking with my boyfriend who had just moved to Williamsburg. It was late, maybe 2 AM, and as we walked by Kokie's I heard a psychedelic 70s Colombian salsa song that I love—not the kind of song that you normally hear coming from some dive bar in Brooklyn. I had no idea what kind of place Kokie's was. The door was locked, so we waited for a minute and when this hipster girl went in, we scooted in with her. I was hoping to find a crazy dance party, but instead there were a bunch of very white kids sitting at tables and not doing much of anything. We ordered beers and I soon realized that everyone serving at the bar was Colombian. I started talking to them about Colombia, one thing led to another, and this bartender named Nora ended up giving me a bunch of coke for free!

STUART McCLENNAN: You bought coke from this guy who stood in a fucking closet in the back room. It was $20 a bag, right? If you had a mustache he would say, "I have no idea what you're talking about," at which point you'd have to give your $20 to a girl and have her do it.

JERRY P: I remember they wouldn't serve [singer of a then-popular band] because he had this big, goofy mustache and he looked like a policeman. He asked me if I would cop for him, and I said no. I didn't want them to see me getting drugs for the guy they didn't want to serve. I was like, "Sorry dude, serves you right for looking like that."

MEG SNEED: In the early Kokie's stages, you couldn't just walk in and buy the coke right away. You had to sit in the bar area in the front and buy a drink. The drinks were tiny. They had these mini Budweisers that looked like baby bottles. One time I ordered a vodka with orange juice and they gave it to me in a Dixie cup.

LESLIE R: It wasn't so hard to figure out how to buy the coke. I just went up to some college kid who seemed high and asked, "How is it done here?" He pointed to a booth in the corner. It was like a little closet. I walked over there with a $20 and stuck out my hand. The guy took the $20 and handed me a bag. Boom. Finished.

STUART McCLENNAN: The first time I went there I had no idea how to go about scoring the coke. I noticed a curtained-off booth in the corner. That was where people go to do their bumps after buying it. But I didn't know that and after watching about a dozen people go into the closet and come out sniffing, I was sure that was where to go buy the coke. I ducked in behind the curtain and there was nobody there. Doye. There was, however, a big hole in the wall that had pipes running through it. I figured the dealer was behind that hole so I stuck my hand in with $20 and waved it around. "Just a twenty-bag, thanks," I said. Nothing. Maybe he was taking a break or something. So I wedged my head in the hole and said, "Psst. Hey... you there?" How *Mr. Bean Goes to Kokie's* is that?

STEVE L: I'd heard about the infamous tooting area and headed over expecting to see a dimly lit gauntlet of art hipsters (this was just before the swarms hit Williamsburg), gangbangers, and mamis all giggling and snorting together. Instead, I threw back the curtain and saw an orange-haired older lady, bent over like Betty Boop, enthusiastically blowing a British painter of my remote acquaintance. I said howdy, did three bumps, and went back to join the dance party.

THE COMEDOWN

JERRY P: Eventually they refurbished the coke closet. When we first started going it was the size of a phone booth, but then they put up some drywall to double the size. And they had a bouncer stand outside the booth to regulate how many people were in there at a time. There would be a line around the side of the room waiting to go into the coke closet, and if they caught you doing coke outside of the coke closet they'd kick you out immediately.

ANN G: One night I was in the booth and this Dominican guy was giving me bumps off his key. People were usually pretty nice about sharing. We were chatting and he said that he was the brother-in-law of the owner. I tend to be a real lighter klepto, like I'm always pocketing people's

lighters and whatnot just absentmindedly, and I guess I pocketed his key ring. I got home that night (or morning, technically) and when I dumped out my pockets there was this huge ring with like 20 keys and a million dangling key-chain doodads. I was scared. That guy was scary! I shame-spiraled into a total coke depression. Those keys symbolized everything that was wrong in my life and I wanted to keep them as a reminder. I never returned the keys and I never went back to Kokie's again.

MARIA S: My friend and I met this group of greasy leather-and-chains-clad biker dudes one night at Kokie's and they invited us back to their clubhouse someplace in bumblefuck Brooklyn. Their place was a garage in the front and a rec room with a bar in the back. It was decked out in pink balloons and streamers for a baby shower that was happening the next day. One of the dudes kept going around with a paper plate and a switchblade, giving us bumps off the tip. The sun was starting to come up and we were about to call a car and the guy asked if we wanted one for the road. Sure! Why not? So he cuts up a new batch and comes around with the knife, bump bump. I began to sweat. I mean, profusely, like I needed a towel. As I headed toward the door to get some fresh air I saw one of my friends hunched over the toilet barfing. I could barely walk. I found a stoop in the sun and plopped down. I remember this incredible, warm, peaceful wave go through me as if all was right in the world and I didn't care about anything. We cabbed home during morning rush hour. Traffic was backed up on the Williamsburg Bridge and every time the cab stopped we would open the car door to puke. We spent the rest of the day tag-team vomiting into my friend's toilet. We were so out of our heads that it took us hours before we realized that the biker dudes had slipped us heroin.

LUCY P: One time we were all kicked out in the morning and it was very bright and no one wanted to go home. Some people said there was a party at their apartment. So everybody (20 or so people at least, mostly total strangers) tromped over to an industrial building through this maze-like series of corridors to find the apartment with the

January 12, 2001

Polaroid courtesy of Lindsay R.

party. Well, a party it sure as hell wasn't. No booze. Just some lame band practicing. Not playing. Not a show. Band practice. And a whole bunch of really disappointed, hopped-up goofballs watching them. No one knew how to get out but it was clear within minutes that it had to be done. I found a door down some corridor and went back and led the people out. The thing here was the total abuse of goodwill. Man, you just don't abuse that trust. If there's no party at your apartment, that's fine, but don't tell people your idiot roommate and his idiot bandmates are a goddamned party.

JERRY P: My roommate and I started talking to these two people one night: Tony, a 35-year-old Latino man, and Adrian, a 38-year-old black woman. Adrian was a dental technician and Tony was a marine who was on leave. It got late and I invited them back to my house. And it was far, all the way out in Greenpoint. We got to our tiny, railroad apartment and my roommate immediately freaked out and went to bed, but of course he couldn't sleep because he was all coked up. He told me that he sat on his bed listening to us all night. Tony and I argued about who the best rapper of all time was for about an hour. He thought it was KRS-One and I thought it was Biggie. Adrian didn't really say much. Toward the end of it, when I started to get really weirded out, Tony was telling me that he could see my aura. He was like, "Man, it's all about auras, man," so I finally kicked them out around dawn. We were standing on the front steps, squinting in the sun, like, "Yeah, great meeting you guys, bye!" Stuff like that happened all the time. I shiver just thinking about it.

S
718•486-6187
KoKie's Place
"Dress Casual but in good taste"
212 Berry Street—Corner North 3 & Berry
Brooklyn, NY 11211

THE BUBBLE BURSTS

BRIAN F: In 2001 Kokie's became the official hipster cocaine vending machine. They started to pander to the crowd. The place closed down for a week and reopened up with, like, mod Ikea gear and neon lightning bolts everywhere.

JERRY P: Yeah, the final milestone before it died was that they painted these lame tropical murals on the walls. You'd walk in and be like, "What the fuck?" It was so weird, they wanted to jack it up and make it nice, but it was so out of touch with their new clientele.

JUDY W: Sometime toward the end of the era, a guy who worked there invited me to a party at a new place that the Kokie's owners were opening up. I think it was on Broadway and it had Trinidadian dance vibes. He gave us cards for it. They were glossy and had color photo of chicks in bikinis on them.

GARY J: Around this time, someone went on the internet and wrote, "Oh man, it's like Amsterdam in Williamsburg! It's awesome!" And that was the beginning of the end.

RICK P: The final nail in the coffin came when the local precinct got a new police captain who had come straight from doing narcotics and vice work. She wasn't having a coke bar in her precinct. They busted the place a few times and that's pretty much the end of the story. They went out of business. They couldn't conduct their trade anymore.

GARY J: I worked at the Antique Lounge, which is what Kokie's became after it went out of business. The owner told me that he found bullets in the walls when he gutted it out.

SUSAN S: I own the Levee, the bar that opened after the Antique Lounge closed. I think business was pretty bad for the Antique Lounge. People thought it was still the same owners as Kokie's so they had a hard time drawing a new crowd. People still come in to this day and talk about how they miss Kokie's. There are so many different stories about Kokie's that at this point it's kind of a local legend. A few of the door guys who had worked there come in and play pool sometimes. They're really sweet. One of them brought his dad in to show him where he used to work. We've really had to work hard to shake off the coke stigma.

JEFF JENSEN: Kokie's has a huge place in Brooklyn's history. I would also like to submit that the genre of electroclash was officially started at Kokie's. I can prove it because I was there. In the early days, there was a janitor who worked at Kokie's who was from Saskatoon and claimed that he had seen Bigfoot. Me and Casey Spooner used to laugh like crazy over his Bigfoot stories. That's what gave Casey the idea to start Sasquatch, his Bigfoot-themed band that eventually became Fischerspooner.

MEG SNEED: Kokie's and electroclash. That's all I remember about 2001. ∎

IV
SWEET JAMS

Photo by Jamie Lee Curtis Taete, V15N12, December 2008

AMY KELLNER

HEY DJ, FUCK YOU!

Anyone Can Rock the Party

You know that thing called DJing? Playing records in bars or at stupid art openings for money? Guess what DJing is? The biggest fucking bullshit con of all time! People who get over as DJs are making the easiest money ever, because they've convinced every PR person and club owner in the world that they're doing something only a few natural-born geniuses can do. It's laughable. A 70-year-old blind Ethiopian leper with 10 broken fingers can "spin" just as well as any B-list celebrity at any in-store party for some gay snowboarding jeans company. I promise.

And those other guys who do all the little flick-flick, crabby moves on records that are covered with spots of adhesive tape that are supposed to mean something? Those aren't DJs! I don't know what to call them. Nerds, maybe? They called themselves "turntablists" five years ago, but I think that got embarrassing. One thing is for sure, though: Those guys don't DJ on the actual paying gig circuit that I'm on, because no hammered jock chicks or guidos from West Orange, NJ, will dance to an hour-long abstract scratch frenzy over a P-Funk B-side.

Photo by Tim Barber

I've been making loads of supplementary income by DJing for a few years now, and I can barely even scratch my own back. All you really need is a CD burner, Kazaa, and passably cool taste in music. Here, I'll tell you all about my life as a party DJ:

TECHNIQUE

FLOW: The only slightly ephemeral skill to learn is flow. Have you ever made a mixtape for someone you had a crush on? Then you already know what flow is—the ability to maintain a mood. I was at a party once where the DJ kept playing one danceable hip-hop track, then one

undanceable slow classic-rock track, one hip-hop, one slow rock, on and on like that for an hour! We would get up and dance, and then sit down, and then we finally just stayed down and shot him really dirty looks. It was the opposite of flow. To master flow, you just need to not be a fucking moron. Can you handle that?

Segueing from one genre to a totally different one is easy. You just build tiny little bridges instead of taking one big leap. For example, let's go from a hip-hop set to a punk-rock set. You play your last rap song, then a Prince track. Then maybe some ESG. Then the Slits. Boom! You're into the punk before they know what hit 'em.

LCD: This is your audience. It stands for Lowest Common Denominator. You are DJing for drunks and cokeheads, and they need the aural equivalent of safety blankets. What would you rather hear when you're high as fuck in a bar: Journey or some obscure acid-house? (If you're a geek, don't answer that.)

I used to spend all my time collecting the rarest tracks, stuff that when I heard it at home it would totally blow my mind. Guess what? No one cared. In fact, they stopped dancing. Now I stick to playing stuff that I liked when I was a teenager (the Misfits, "O.P.P.," and songs from John Hughes movies) and I'm golden. When in doubt, go nostalgic.

CUEING: This is where you enact the flow thing I just told you about. You have two sides, right and left. When something's playing on the right, think of a song that would sound good after it. Cue that song up on the left by pressing the same buttons on a CD player that you've pressed 1,000 times before (or putting a needle down in the appropriate groove on a record). When the song on the right side is about to end, slide the little thingy in the box between the decks to the left. When you're a little less than halfway over, press "play" on the CD or "start" on the turntable. Congratulations, you're DJing. Can I get a "That was easy"?

PERKS

LINES: A huge guilty pleasure is cutting the line and marching right up to the velvet rope all casual, going, "Hi, I'm the DJ." I like to go to a gig dressed like a total slob. The nicer the club, the shittier I look. Then I can stroll past all the people who used to spit on me in high school and make a big huge deal about going through the door first.

MONEY: Depending on who you are, a DJ's salary for one night can range from a few free drinks to obscene amounts (for the big shots) that make you hate capitalism. I heard Paul Sevigny got fucking $15,000 to DJ at Sundance. I hope that is DJ urban legend. Most DJs I know are pretty psyched if they get a couple hundred. Art openings should pay more, like $350. And remember: Always get paid in cash on the night of. Within 24 hours all money magically transforms into cocaine blown up some model's ass.

COMPLIMENTS: One of the best things about DJing is when you play a really kickass song and people come up to you dancing, going "I love this song!" You get all proud and pretend you wrote it. You're like, "Thanks!" Yeah, I downloaded "Youth Gone Wild," I rule. It's like being told your air-guitar skills are fucking SICK.

GEAR

NEEDLES: Those sleek, aerodynamic, $500 fancy-pants needles are the second biggest scam in DJing besides convincing people that DJing is hard. For totally serviceable needles, go to one of those electronics stores on Canal Street and get the cheapest set possible. You can talk them down on the price, too. I got a pair plus some shitty headphones for $90 after I sweet-talked the sales guy for a minute. (BTW, the cheap needles are called hip-hop needles and that's mean against blacks.)

MIXERS: There are a few brands of mixers, but who cares. DJs would like for you to think mixers are all complicated, but they're really about as hard to figure out as a home stereo. I once spun at this lesbian party where I ended up giving girls DJ lessons all night. They were lined up across the room, and it only took me a few seconds to show each of them the basics. As Garfield would say, "Big fat hairy deal." Once I showed them how simple it really is, they were shocked at the big deal that people make about the whole thing. Yeah, there are cute little tricks you can do. If you're playing a hip-hop song, it's fun to cut out the bass after the second verse and then kick it back in full force on the chorus. It's a nifty party trick and it makes girls lose their shit. But you can also just say, "Fuck it," set them all in the middle, and read a book in between tracks.

WHEELS OF STEEL: Please don't call them that. Don't call them "the ones and the twos" either. It sounds like your mom saying, "Homie don't play that."

ETIQUETTE

OOPS: You're going to fuck up. The record will skip or you'll be distracted by some drunk kid telling you how much "Bizarre Love Triangle" means to him or you'll let two Wire songs play in a row. No big whup. Everyone's too wasted to care. You should be too. Just take the opportunity to make announcements. I usually shout out important information such as, "Don't stop the rock, motherfuckers!" or "I need to pee!"

REQUESTS: Try not to cry when people request Missy Elliott, again. Or "Hey Ya!" or "Milkshake." Or Cher when you are spinning Minor Threat. Or simply "hip-hop." Or any genre of music, in fact. You wouldn't believe how often people request an entirely different genre of music than what the DJ is playing. It's infuriatingly rude. You're telling the DJ that you hate his or her music. If you don't like what I'm playing, wait 10 fucking minutes and I'll be onto a new thing anyway.

If you simply *must* request a song, it better be within the scope of what I'm playing at that very second AND it better be such an insane song that it'll make me go, "Oh shit, yeah, why didn't I think of that?"

True fact: That's only happened to me once out of hundreds and hundreds of requests. The song was "Sweet Emotion" by Aerosmith, believe it or not.

SAVING YOUR BEST STUFF: This is tricky. You don't want to blow your load before the night hits maximum party time, so you squirrel away your guaranteed crowd-pleasing monster jams and you wait, thinking, "Now? Now? Do I drop it?" And finally you're like, "It's time, I'm gonna hit it." And boom! It's a fuckin' nuclear-bomb explosion. A roomful of people you would barely be able to look at in the daytime are freaking out like they just won the lottery, all because you pressed a button. That's why you do this shit. That, and the fact that you are a total fucking spaz. ∎

DAVE ONE AND ERIK LAVOIE

STILL DIRTY

Dirt McGirt Rises From the Flames of Ol' Dirty Bastard

Every conversation about Ol' Dirty Bastard brings up the same five things: the original rah-rah rap style, the twenty-odd babies, the picking up welfare checks in a limo, the drug addictions, and the manic police pursuits. But for the last couple of years, we've had nothing else to talk about. He got locked up in 2000 for everything from weed to carrying a gun on parole, and only got out a few months ago under strict supervision. Shit, his parole officer won't even let him be near any place that sells booze. What the fuck? What's going to happen to Ol' Dirty Bastard or, as he now refers to himself, Dirt McGirt?

We're keeping the faith. And we're not the only ones. In a power move of Suge Knight proportions, Roc-a-Fella's Dame Dash signed ODB the minute he got released, promising him his own Dirt McGirt clothing line and a VH1 reality TV show. The result is hype of 50 Cent proportions, a testament to the overwhelming love the world has for our hero Dirt Dog. Nobody's heard the album or seen the clothing line, but we have a sneaking suspicion they are both going to fucking rule.

Photo by Terry Richardson

We talked to VH1 about their new show *ODB on Parole*, and they told us about all the crazy shit they've filmed since he got out ten days ago. The show is going to put Ozzy and Anna Nicole to shame. Wait, what's all this ten days shit? He got out months ago. I guess VH1 doesn't want to get into the two months he spent in a mental institution. Besides, *ODB on Parole After a Brief Purgatory at the Mental Hospital* doesn't have the same ring to it.

We don't blame them for blacking out months of the past. Do you know what kind of shit rappers go through in prison? Whether they're a so-called badass like Beanie Siegel or just some guy from Van Full of Pakistanis, every inmate piece of shit feels obligated to pound anyone famous in the face again and again until every last bit of popularity and pride is bashed out of them. There's no Courvoisier and hos in prison. Just fights, fights, and more fights. In the April 2002 *Vibe*, Dirty confirmed all this, basically saying, "Get me the fuck out of here. I am going to die behind bars." If you ask Dirt about it now, though, he goes off on a huge, long tangent about how Bush and Clinton are conspiring to kill him and how they have meetings about it all the time.

The rough-time-inside rumors seemed confirmed again when we met up with Dirt and noticed his neck was quite swollen and he had considerably fewer teeth than a man his age should. Speculation on our part, but that sounds kind of like a broken jaw, right? What the fuck happened in there?

Anyway, all this shit is bad for Dirty and a bummer to get into, but it is kind of great for his fans. Can you imagine the kind of weirdo, fucked-up shit he is on now? He's like a phoenix rising from the flames. "The government is after me!" is going to sound trite when this next album comes out. Come on—he even showed up to the photo shoot with "Dirt McD" spelled out on the hood of his car in hockey tape.

Erik Lavoie: What do you think of me?
Dirty: You're cool, man, just laid-back, you know what I'm saying? Just loosen out and be sharp, be witty, and it'll all come to you.

I'd like to ask you something here, um, where did you get your new name?
Dirt McGirt comes from Dirt McGirt Island. It's a place that's right off the block from the next island off of Batman Island. I can't let you know exactly where it is—it's a secret, you know? Wonder Woman told me not to say nothing.

Why have you changed your name so much?
It's like Picasso making a new picture. It feels good.

And what can you tell us about your style, about who influenced you?
My influences come from China; my style comes from Africa, Egypt, Tokyo, and Russia, with love; and the rest comes from Neptune.

You're the international rapper.
Yes, exactly.

But you're also deeply rooted in New York.
Yeah, Seneca, the one that sold Manhattan to the white man, that's my great-great-great-grandfather. [*Yelling over to Poppa Wu*] Yo, Freedom, how old our granddaddy go back? I'm talking about Seneca, my war clout. [*Poppa Wu answers: He was born in 1774. He owned Manhattan*] See, Seneca Indians owned Manhattan.

So you're the original King of NY.
Yes, definitely, no other. I'm the original New Yorker. A toast to it.

What do you think about the stuff we hear on the radio today? It seems that a lot of it comes from you.
I hear that. I think it's real hip-hop, I think it's something smashing, lovely, radiant, you know, and gospel. I'm liking the groove that I'm hearing, but I think I set the trend. I'm the one that came with the "fuck you" and shit, I'm the one that taught rappers how to be themselves. Because before Ol' Dirty came, they was too tight, they wouldn't allow you to be yourself. And when Dirty came, I put the cramp in your leg in rap. I'm the wildest nigga on Earth, man, period. When Wu Tang started out, they was humble, afraid to get up on stage. I was wild. And I just said, "No, we're doing it wild, crazy, we bug the fuck out." So we just started going crazy on niggas, letting our anger out, emotions and shit. We came with the beauty of music. Like Jesus for example, he's beautiful, you feel me? So this is what Wu Tang do, come with something beautiful for you, like high science. Einstein has a formula, Wu Tang has a formula. A part equals a square and all that stuff, you know what I'm saying? We have a formula, too.

You guys dropped the bomb.
Yeah, the formula is to attack everything at any given time. Just attack and shit like a waterfall, or like water in rapids or more like a fucking whirlpool, "Fuck you."

And you also got something for the ladies.
Definitely. I'm like Marvin. He got a way of words with the ladies and I have a way of words with the ladies, too. Shit like: "Girls with honey dripping from your ass/ Arms with the funk of smoking grass/ You notice me down the block, I'm that good/ So do your people in your neighborhood/ The way you walk, your period is yummy/ The diamonds in my mouth I eat are gummy." Shit like that, you know what I'm saying?

But don't lie, you're a family man, too. How does that manifest itself?
Being there for them, taking care of them. Being a father, you know, living fat, living lovely, plentiful, and healthy.

How's the new record coming along? You've got the Roc behind you now, but RZA is still making beats for you, too. Are there too many chefs in the kitchen?
Nah. It's just fun doing it. I'm really into it and I'm just trying to make it as hot as possible. Cuz you got flavor out there and I want to contribute to the flavor out there, you know what I'm saying? Cuz I'm liking the groove that I'm hearing. I'm just trying to come and be like the eagle over the other birds.

Yeah, but what does it sound like?
I'm coming with new shit, futuristic 2005-2006 shit. And that's it. Cuz RZA got some shit that's dangerous, you know what I'm saying? He's definitely the Abbot. And Roc-a-Fella's coming tight as hell. So it's just going to be something for the ear to hear. I got something for the ladies also. I got one with the Neptunes called "Operator." That shit is hot. Future shit.

Do you see things? Like visions and stuff? I think I do sometimes.
I guess so. I don't know. We only got two eyes so I guess everything else is limited. You got two eyes, and you got two people, that makes four eyes. So when you're trying to use four eyes, it makes it difficult to have one eye, you feel me? It limits things. I see things from a one-eye perspective and the four-eye perspective. The one-eye perspective is being able to see everything, as clear as my eye can see it.

I know exactly what you're saying. It's like sometimes I feel like I have eyes in the back of my head, and on the sides. It's like, if you think you're psychic, then maybe you are. Like the Five Percenters?
You mean the "black man is God" ones? If you keep it a secret, we'll keep it like that.

As an artist, do you feel the need to comment on the political situation of the last couple of years? Do you follow that stuff at all? Because I think artists who feel like they have to say something about it are pussies.
I don't follow shit. I just come and I leave. I come and I go. I'm Ol' Dirty, man. You forgot? ∎

BUSTA NUT

FISH AND GRITS

Ghostface Chows Down

Photo by Chris Glancy

What more could be said about Ghostface at this point? The guy epitomizes every single thing this magazine stands for. His musical contributions are unsung, yet unmatched. He's single-handedly responsible for the soul sampling that made Kanye famous, the emo raps that became Jay-Z's blueprint, and the Clarks Wallabees that got you through life without wearing a pair of square shoes. His retrofuturistic slang is inimitable. He gave truck jewels a new cultural significance. He's the only reason you own a bathrobe.

That said, his relevance within rap's current climate seems to be in jeopardy. Indeed, for a hip-hop audience of inner-city reggaeton-bred *borinqueñas* and wiggered-out suburban G-Unit soldiers, what does this middle-aged eccentric have to offer? The answer is: a cryptic, experimental, and decidedly left-field classic album. Let's go over the Tony Starks discography for a second. *Ironman* came out at the height of the Wu era, when RZA's awkward percussions and lo-fi Gregorian chants could do no wrong. Four years later, *Supreme Clientele* drops, and it's absolutely flawless. Effortlessly conjuring up Wu nostalgia, it solidifies Ghost's rep as the Clan's only remaining star. However, Deini attempted to replicate the formula the following year with *Bulletproof Wallets* and it flopped. And let's face it, aside from an amazing first single, 2004's *Pretty Toney Album* wasn't much of anything either.

So how does this year's upcoming *Fishscale* manage to recapture and even transcend *Supreme Clientele*'s magic? Well, for one, RZA's out of the picture. Oddly enough, the Wally Champ replaced him with backpack superlegend MF Doom. And the results are spectacular. Instead of shying away from Ghostface's oddities, as did his previous efforts, *Fishscale* emphasizes them. What you get is the spontaneity of *Clientele* mixed with the off-the-wall lyricism of *Ironman*. Once again, it's time to eat fish, toss salads, and make rap ballads. Perhaps Ghost's been rejuvenated by the equally food-obsessed Doom. To find out, we caught the gargantuan MC at the catering table on the set of his latest video. As Jay once put it, this is food for thought, so get a plate.

Vice: What was the food rider like today, Ghost?
Ghostface: I didn't even make this rider, G. I came in this morning and there was pork. I didn't ask for that shit, the pork was already in the kitchen, you know? So I said what I had to say and shit, I barked a little bit, like "cut that shit," and they went and got me some other shit. Like three hours later. Somebody went to the store for me and got me a little something something.

You had a mixtape a couple of years ago that was called *No Pork on My Fork*.
Yeah, Kay Slay named the mixtape that. It's really just a

name. But that CD was righteous right there, so there's definitely no pork on my fork, period.

So being that today's rider was a bust, what would be on your ideal, perfect craft table?
I'd just put like some soul food, man, you know? Macaroni and cheese, cornbread, you know what I mean, like I said in the song. Fish. There could also be some turkey wings or even meatloaf. Let's see, what else? You know, some pasta, give me some stuffed shells or some lasagna or some ziti or something. That's really it, you know what I mean? We can eat a steak, too.

What did you mean when you said "My raps is like ziti"?
That's just how I come across, how I put my words together in my flow and my thinking. Since I might go left-field, that's exactly what it is: My raps is like a bangin' pot of ziti, you know what I mean?

So you wouldn't put anything fancy in the rider. Like, no caviar or none of that bougie shit.
None of that. Caviar? I haven't tasted that in my life, B.

How about drinks?
The best shit is right here: Water. That's what I drink the most in my day. I like that Vitamin Water too, cuz it don't got that much sugar in it, so that's good for you. I like that. [*pointing to the faucet*] That's the best water right there, G. [*to his manager*] He don't know nothing about that, [*back to Vice*] you don't know about tap water, man. Before bottled water was out, man, tap water was all you got. It's in the hood, man, you run in the bathroom and that shit be cold as shit. Drink it right out the shit, fuck a cup, you know what I mean? But that's how it is, G. The hood is different now, now you got bottled water, there wasn't that shit back in the days. Now you can pay for water, you know?

You also said "Sugar water was our thing." I bet you some people still drink it out of habit.
They probably do, yeah, but I haven't tried that since back then. Sugar water was when we was poor, coming up. I might fall the fuck out if I drink me some sugar water.

How do you prepare it?
Just put it in water, G, sugar and water. But it's not good for the teeth, it's not even good for your body, really, you know what I mean? You know, that's when you poor, coming up in the hood and you ain't got no Kool-Aid or nothing like that. And as a kid, you love sugar. It wasn't like your mother told you to go make that, you know, you just made it on your own.

OK, so just water on the rider, no juice?
I mean it's whatever your tongue tastes like. If your tongue tastes like an orange or a grape, you know what I mean, then you get some juice or something. Whatever your tongue tastes like, then that's what it is, you know what I mean? Orange juice, apple juice, lemonade, iced tea—I like a lot of iced tea. I like iced tea, the regular ones, you know, Nestea iced teas and all that.

How about fine wine? It seems that you were really into that in the *Cuban Linx* era.
One of my chicks used to drink wine and shit. I don't be knowing names though, all I know is Opus One, that's the smooth one. I'm not into all that Cabernets and shit.

Chardonnays?
Oh there's a Chardonnay and a Cabernet? See, I didn't know that, you know what I mean? I just thought it was Cabernets and Merlots. Wine is wine, but the smoothest wine is Opus.

Now on to the dessert section of the rider. What do you need?
I don't have a favorite dessert, you know, but I love ice cream. I'm a diabetic, man, but I still love carrot cakes and chocolate cakes and pound cakes and shit like that. You know what I mean? Cookies here and there, it depends on the cookies and how your tongue feel. I'm not too big on the desserts. I just sent my grandma a carrot cake though.

You had a song called "Mighty Healthy." You were never a vegetarian, right?
Nah man, I'm not vegetarian, G. I eat my vegetables and all that shit but you know, I get my little meats in here and there. You know what I mean, poultry and all that shit.

You do seem to have lost a little weight. Is it safe to say you watch what you eat?
Here and there. Those was just carbs I was eating just now. So you know, as long as I take my insulin, man, I'm all right. Do a little exercise here and there and I'm good. But I don't watch everything and shit, I'm a regular person, I run around and shit. Sometimes it don't be the correct shit that you should be eating on the road when you're moving around, you know what I mean? I don't have nobody to cook for me every day, so I eat what I can eat. I could cook for myself, but I don't be doing the shit too often, you know what I mean? But if I do it, then of course it's gonna be right. You know my moms and them, I been around all that shit. I know what I gotta do. It's just that you be too lazy to really get down like that. But I got pots and pans, G. ■

JESSE PEARSON

HELLO, WHITE PEOPLE!

Prussian Blue Look to the Future

Is there anything cuter than two identical twin 12-year-old girls who have a band together? How about if they dress in matching plaid skirts—that ups the cuteness quotient, right? And what if they perform folky versions of classic racist songs by bands like Skrewdriver and Rahowa? Whoa! Now we are heading into the cute danger zone.

And the best part of it all? These girls have the talent to back it all up. They sing like angels, harmonize like only siblings can, and are more adept at their chosen instruments than most one-hit-wonder crap. Prussian Blue are doing nothing short of trying to change the course of humanity. Ladies and gentlemen, we give you Lynx and Lamb, the girls of Prussian Blue.

Vice: Hi girls. So, who plays what?
Lynx: I play violin and sing.
Lamb: And I play the guitar and sing. We've been playing for two years now.

Your set is a mix of covers by white-power bands, some traditional fare, and some originals. How do you determine a song that you would like to cover?
Usually our friends suggest songs that they'd like to hear us sing. We choose ones that we like and that can easily be changed to acoustic. And they have to be songs that have meaning to us and our listeners and have a good message for white youngsters.

What sort of gigs do you generally play? I know that you played the Folk the System 2004 festival, which was sponsored by the National Alliance, but do you also play in any local establishments or at county fairs?
Sure, we just finished playing at a local county fair. We also play at open mic nights and Renaissance fairs. We play a lot of National Alliance events, like meetings and conferences, as well as other events like a recent IHR [Institute of Historical Review] conference.

If you play to a crowd that's mixed in terms of political views, are there certain songs that might not make it

Photo by Kelly Parsell

into the set?
We do play a different set when we play a mainstream venue than we do when we play in front of racially conscious people.

Do you feel the need to tone down your politics when playing for certain crowds?
It's not that we're embarrassed about our message or our songs that are more obviously pro-white, it's that we know that if certain people complained about the content of our songs (like if we use the term "Aryan"), we might not be allowed to play again at that venue.

What do you think is the most important social issue facing the white race right now?
Not having enough white babies born and generally not having good-quality white people being born. It seems like smart white girls who have good eugenics are more interested in making money in a career or partying than getting married and having a family. We are working on some new songs about this issue.

Please tell me the significance of the name Prussian Blue.
Part of our heritage is Prussian German. Also our eyes are blue, and Prussian Blue is a really pretty color. There is also the discussion of the lack of "Prussian Blue" coloring (Zyklon B residue) in the so-called gas chambers in the concentration camps. We think it might make people question some of the inaccuracies of the "Holocaust" myth.

What are some of your favorite groups of all time?
We really like Avril Lavigne, Evanescence, Three Days Grace, Green Day, AC/DC, and Alison Krauss. For racial groups we like Final War, CutThroat, Saga, Max Resist, Youngland, Brutal Attack, and of course Skrewdriver. But our all-time favorite is Barney the purple dinosaur! ∎

See resistance.com for more info. No, we did not make this up.

JIMMY KIMMEL

HOLY CHALICE

How I Got My First Pimp Cup

I don't normally hang out with celebrities after the show (their choice, not mine), but it happens once in a while. Recently, my childhood friend Tommy was in town with his father, who is also named Tommy and looks exactly like his son. There was a knock at the door. Someone said our musical guest that night, the rapper Lil Jon, wanted to bring me a gift. He is black, so naturally I welcomed him with open arms.

Lil Jon gallantly walked in wearing what I think may have been a mink pirate costume. Here was one of hip-hop's leading Lils, with a mouth full of gold teeth and an attractive, nearly nude girl of undetermined ethnicity on each arm. He gave me a "Here I am" kind of look.

I immediately began to worry that this was my "gift"—that I was being presented with a young lady of my own, with whom, because of my eagerness to show I am not racist, I would have had no choice but to have unprotected sex. I knew that I would do this just to please Lil Jon—even if it meant fucking in front of 63-year-old Tommy Sr.—and I also knew that that this woman (or, possibly, these *women*) would almost certainly become pregnant, possibly with twins.

Jon (as I now call him) handed me a big black velvet bag. Inside was a collection of porn DVDs. I thanked him for these and politely noted that the women on the packaging were indeed the same women in the room. I did this by pointing at them and saying, "Oh, hey— that's you guys! Wow! That's really great!" And then Jon gave me the real gift: The best blow job I ever had in my life. Just kidding. It was my very own chalice. A gold (plastic, painted gold) chalice—encrusted with diamonds (fake plastic diamonds) that spelled out my name: "JIMMY."

I've never had my own chalice before. I was delighted both by the gift and by the (albeit slight) possibility that Lil Jon himself sat at home gluing little plastic letters onto this thing to spell my name.

I thanked him for the chalice and didn't even have to pretend to be excited. I was.

And then Lil Jon commanded the women to get naked and plop down on my friend Tommy's dad's lap. I know this sounds like a great thing, but we were all really embarrassed and anxious because we are old white people and that kind of stuff makes us uncomfortable.

Anyway, all I know is I own a fucking chalice. Do you own a fucking chalice? No, you do not. ■

PENNY RIMBAUD

FUCK PUNK

By Penny Rimbaud, Legend Of Punk

Photo by David Titlow

I've got no allegiance whatsoever to punk as a form of music. Never really did. Punk as I knew it has a political purpose. What is classified as "punk" music these days is absolutely empty and gutless.

I genuinely believe that if it hadn't been for Crass and the movement which grew out of it, punk would now only be remembered as another old dame in the rock and roll pantomime; just the same old attitudes dressed up in a different costume. The Pistols certainly didn't do anything more radical than Elvis Presley—the only difference was that Elvis could handle his drugs better than they could.

Crass wanted to change the world, and in some respects we did, but nowhere to the degree that we set out to. We wanted to undermine the prime institutions of the State and everything that it represented. We went to great lengths to do that. The rock and roll swank of performing in a band was simply the platform we used.

What we did as activists was much more important to

us than the music. We were always looking for some way of moving beyond being just a band. In our history we had dealings and run-ins with all sorts: Baader Meinhoff, the KGB, the CIA, the IRA, MI6, Margaret Thatcher. You name them, they all tried it on. When you compare that to bashing away onstage, you can see where we were at. I guess our interest in performance was secondary.

Punk in the hands of the showbiz world is an absolutely pointless farce. It means nothing. Fine, rock and roll can be fun, you can have a good night out, but what's that got to do with punk? All these reformed punk bands and major label acts who like to think of themselves as punk are okay if you want a laugh and a good old jump around, but it's nonsense to imagine that it's anything to do with what punk was really about. Punk was a way of life, not a pop fad.

If you're a band there's a degree to which you have to make a commitment to put forward a public image, and the only way you can do that is to keep up a personal front. In the end we found it impossible to keep up that front, which is one of the reasons we stopped—1984. Very Orwellian.

The lyrics, music, and imagery of Crass were involved with global politics, but ultimately I think the effect we had on people was more on their personal politics. Punk used to be a massive cry against inequality and injustice, but then it became incorporated into the mainstream. I detest people who allow that incorporation to happen. It makes me angry. Time and time and time again you hear youth expressing its voice. Time and time and time again you see that voice destroyed by drugs, self-indulgence, stupidity, and sell-outs. It's sad.

But for all that, you have to go on believing in possibilities, believing that people want something better in life, looking for something outside of ugliness, vulgarity, cruelty, and exploitation; something that has a meaning, that's got connection. But every time there seems to be a possibility of that happening, it gets knocked down. It was like that with the Clash. Everyone was so excited because finally there was someone talking politics and saying things like "I'm so bored with the USA," and then the next month what are they doing? They're snorting coke and doing big gigs in the USA: big deal, guys.

People are so endlessly let down by their heroes, but I guess that's their fault. They shouldn't have heroes, but that's the society we live in: big heroes, little people. Sure, I acknowledge that there are people who might see us as heroes, but those are the people who completely missed our central message—"There is no authority but yourself." However, I know from the letters we continue to get from all over the world that many people were deeply and properly moved, not toward their pockets, but in their souls. That's because it wasn't a matter of us saying,

"Come on, buy our latest fucking album"; no, we were trying to let people know that their life was important, that it was the only one they'd ever have, and that they should try to live it their way, whatever that way was.

We offered information, and I do believe that a lot of that information was real and correct. When I say correct I mean actually presenting something of value that people could take hold of and say, "Yeah, maybe I could make something of my life." The thing we wanted to help people understand was a sense of autonomy and authenticity of the individual human soul. Just as soul is constantly demeaned in the media, so it is undermined by drugs, inside or outside, but in the end it's the only thing we've truly got. As personalities we're just a series of remarks picked up on our journey through life, and, sadly, this becomes what we think we are. But beneath all that we've got something we were born with, something we die with, something that exists beyond time, and that's our deepest inner soul. I guess I'm talking about a kind of immortality. To me the purpose of life is to connect with that inner soul, because by doing so we actually become part of life's continuum. If we exist as separate entities, as individual personalities, there's no reality to life and no continuity beyond it.

There's a connectedness between everybody, and we all breathe, we all eat, we all sleep, and we all have an inner soul that enables us to do that. It's all so obvious and natural. That's a starting point, and that's what we were actually (well, I was) attempting to promote through Crass. Yes, the lyrics of Crass were a lot to do with "the bomb" or "the State," but what I was saying was "Look beneath all that, look beyond it, and where do you find yourself?" If you can do that, if you can find your soul, you connect with all humankind, with all of life.

We all exist in a day-to-day reality of lies and deceit, and nobody will ever make any sense of it. That's why we need to allow for tenderness, for silence, for contemplation. We need to find our own soul within all this mess. We've let ourselves become commodities, pawns in the marketplace. The only way we can get out of that is to realize that our personality, the very thing we think we are, is no more than a costume of ideas. We all like to think we're someone special, so we mouth the right words and dress up in the right gear, but it's all projection, all so fucking irrelevant.

But for all that, I believe people want to connect. Deep down they're tired of being no more than an idea of themselves. That's why people look for more, that's why they have sex, why they smoke dope, why they go on binges. They probably won't find the answer that way, but all the same, they want to connect. People want to know that they're alive, but let's face it, in a consumer society, that's no easy job. ∎

ANDY CAPPER

MALCOLM McLAREN INVENTED EVERYTHING

Illustration by Milano Chow

Malcolm McLaren began to design clothes in the early 70s, after he quit art school. In 1971, along with his then girlfriend Vivienne Westwood, he opened a boutique called Let It Rock. They sold gear for teddy boys, rockers, and greasers. Boring.

But then Malcolm met the New York Dolls, saw a little glimpse of the future of music, and convinced them to hire him as their manager. He designed a whole new look for them featuring red leather and Soviet symbols, and it totally failed and the band went down in flames. It's become the popular punk party line to blame the Dolls' demise on McLaren, but we think the real reason is because they only had a few good songs and were almost all worthless fucking junkies.

On a trip to New York in the mid-70s, McLaren met Richard Hell. He tried to become his manager too, but Hell said no. So McLaren did the next best thing: Returned to London, changed his shop's name to SEX, and started selling Hell-inspired ripped t-shirts and bondage gear. Then came the Sex Pistols, blah blah blah, you should already know that part a thousand times over.

After the Pistols, McLaren founded Bow Wow Wow. Not only did he get the ball rolling on world-music-influenced pop, but he also invented a look for 15-year-old Annabella Lwin (he called it pirate punk) that is still giving men titanium boners to this day. Adam and the Ants used the pirate-punk look too, of course, but they aren't giving anybody boners anymore.

Then McLaren got into rap, virtually introducing it to the UK with his Duck Rock album. He invented the buffalo gals look, which basically involved looking like an overlayered bag lady. Oh and he also stole the whole voguing thing from drag queens before Madonna did.

What this all amounts to is that Malcolm McLaren is at least partially responsible for every good idea from about 1970 onward. The trickle-down from the fashion and music trends that he Svengali'ed is a part of almost everything that you like.

Vice met up with McLaren in Paris last month and he is one charming fucker—sweet as can be and hyperintelligent. He was dressed in blue jeans, a white shirt, an orange scarf, and a light brown overcoat. We ate at Au Bascou on rue Réaumur in the 3me. McLaren had sparkling Badoit water and a pork and cabbage stew.

Vice: Why did you get into the whole teddy-boy thing in the 70s?
Malcolm McLaren: I did it as an act of revolt against the hippies. I made myself a blue suit, copying the cover of an old Elvis Presley record, and I walked down the Kings Road to try and do something with my life. I wanted to be exploited but no cunt would even look at me! I was brought up in a family that worked in fashion and I had my art school hooligan imagination. The two came together and I set out to create antifashion.

So eventually, after weeks, I was stopped by an American guy dressed completely in black who pointed to a little hole in the road and invited me in there to sell clothes. It was 430 Kings Road and that's where I began to create the "art school look" for the street. My girlfriend at the time, Vivienne Westwood, had a kid by me. She was a schoolteacher and I had to look after the kid. I convinced her to leave her job and I bought a couple of sewing machines.

So what was your first shop like, exactly?
It was called Let It Rock, which I later changed to Too Fast to Live Too Young to Die. That part of the Kings Road was known internationally as the tastemaking, rock and roll capital of the world, so people like the New York Dolls were drawn to it, along with people like Iggy. It was in the era of caftans and beads so I put a jukebox in there that blared out rock and roll constantly.

But when the shop got successful I couldn't bear it. I only liked it when it sold to the young and dangerous. When we sold to just anybody it became a commercial exercise. Whenever it started making money I closed it down. This would make Vivienne mad.

Can you explain your concept for the Dolls a little bit?
The idea behind the Dolls was to dress them in red patent leather and to debate the politics of boredom. I wrote a manifesto that was titled "Better Red Than Dead." It was

at the close of the Vietnam War and the Watergate scandal was soon to arise. The idea was to put a certain social and political commentary back into pop culture. That was the start of the stage that the Sex Pistols would later perform on.

It wasn't a very successful look for them, was it?
It was successful in the sense that it was a magnificent failure. I recall a journalist at the time, Lisa Robinson, rushing backstage, looking at the darlings of this demimonde of rock and roll and asking the question, pointedly, to Johnny Thunders, "Are you a communist?" His answer was simple and poignant. He said, "Yeah. You want to make anything of it?"

What made you want to open the store SEX?
I wanted to sell things that were normally sold in brown paper bags under the table. I tracked down manufacturers all over the UK… black rubber t-shirts, black rubber raincoats, tit clamps, and cock rings. We sold it all.

And the place looked like a sex shop?
People were terrified to come in. It was fantastic. At the very beginning, our clientele included the dirty-old-man brigade and a lot of them turned out to be famous politicians. One of them used to host the News at Ten and he would say to the girl in the shop, "Watch the news tonight because I'm going to be wearing rubber knickers!"

Then the kids started to come shop there.
Of course. They loved it because it was a new look and it was outlaw.

One of our main items were the erotic t-shirts. I used to bring them back from Christopher Street in New York. There was one shirt with a big black man with his huge penis drooping down. They were very, very tight, so you'd be wearing it and his wonger would be dropping down below your belly button. It was perfectly placed. Some of the kids, by the time they'd walk down the length of Kings Road to Sloane Square, would be arrested. We were raided twice by the police and went to court, but I didn't give a damn. Everything got confiscated but we replaced it and all the kids thought, "This is the coolest place on earth."

Well, then why did you close it down?
It was at the peak of the Sex Pistols' popularity. At the start, they appealed to the intellectually curious and the emotionally connected but then they became a fucking household name.

And that's no good.
So I opened up another shop called Seditionary. I went to the war museum and got copies of photographs of the

ruins of Dresden and blew them up and used them as wallpaper. Then I smashed a hole through the ceiling of the shop because I wanted it to look slightly derelict. I also had rats underneath the cash register, running back and forth. It was really fun.

And you had people like Boy George, Adam and the Ants, and Bow Wow Wow hanging out there asking you to make them a look, right?
They were there, yes. What happened was, I was involved in a French independent record company called Barclay. On the side they used to make porno movies and they wanted to get me to put some music to it. They said, "Don't fucking give us a hard time with any music that's copyrighted. Use African music or something."

I went up to the library at the Centre Pompidou in Paris and they had a big music collection. I fancied the girl there so I would go every day and look at her and listen to ethnic music. She played me one of these records, mistakenly, at the wrong speed and it fucking blew my ear off. I thought, "What the fuck is that? It's a hell of a beat." So I took the idea back to London and I gave it to these kids who were called Adam and the Ants.

At the same time, Vivienne was diving into 18th-century fashion with these cheesy ball gowns and I said, "If you're going to do that, Vivienne, you're going to have to give it a label that kids will understand." Vivienne was like, "Fuck the kids! I want to sell to elegant women."

But we didn't have a shop like that. We had to stay in the pop culture. We had to label it somehow, so I came up with this idea of taking images of pirates from the 18th century so the kids could key into it. I needed a group that looked like pirates. I told the kids in the shop: "You've got to look like a pirate! You're not from this corny back alley of London anymore. You're from Zanzibar and that's going to give you license to play these drums that I'm now going to play to you that have this ethnic beat and you're going to look like pirates!" That's how Bow Wow Wow came about.

But why pirates?
At the time, a big news story was cassette players and the ghetto blaster and kids copying music off the radio. The record industry was trying to put a license on blank cassettes because kids were taping their own music. So it was all about piracy and my kids looked like pirates.

It was a perfect success so I said to Vivienne, "Let's take this fucking pirate look to the catwalk!"

So was this around the time you started to fall out with Vivienne Westwood?
She wanted to be recognized as a designer and I wanted the exact opposite. Plus I'd learned to fuck some other

girls when I was on my hiatus in Paris. Anyway, I knew that she was going to continue to push to create these 18th-century ball gowns and I just didn't get it. I couldn't see a rock and roll bone in its body.

I decided that I didn't want to be a commercial success in fashion. I thought it would cost us a fortune and then we'd no longer be outside the culture, we'd be in it. I knew we'd end up pissing each other off really badly, which eventually we did. So I left and she said, "Well it doesn't have to fuckin' be like that."

I said, "I thought that's what you wanted to do. You can sign up with some Italian company and become completely engrossed in fashion and this whole heritage that you've had with me can stand you in good stead. And you'll be able to live off that legacy and it'll give you all the credibility you need."

And that's what she did. I went off to make an album of my own, called Duck Rock. The main single was "Buffalo Gals" and that's what I based my last ever collection on.

How did that pan out?
I thought, "What does a buffalo gal look like?" And I came up with the idea that it would be like a big, fat girl that wanders around like a buffalo all over the planet. It was like a bag lady, basically.

The look included big sheepskin coats, giant hairy skirts, and a hat five sizes too big for you. We would throw a few ethnic patterns on it here and there. It was a scramble. I wanted the shoes to look like the polythene bags that bag ladies wear on their feet. So I did that with chamois leather.

How did the buffalo-gal thing go over with the fashion world?
I'll never forget this moment when, after a show in Paris, this woman from Italian *Vogue* came backstage and convinced me that I'd better do something else.

How did she manage that?
She said, "Malcolm, Malcolm, the music is bellissimo, BELLISSIMO, but the clothes, they look so poor. Why you make everybody look so poor?"

Nice.
I didn't know what to say, so I said, "Well have you heard of Robin Hood? He's a very big, famous character in English literature. I'm trying to make the rich look poor, so the poor can look rich! That's the idea."

She didn't buy it?
She said, "Malcolm, you'll never get away with this. The music is bellissimo, but forget the clothing." ∎

TREVOR SILMSER

BLOODCLOT!

John Joseph of the Cro-Mags Makes the Rest of Us Look Like Pussies

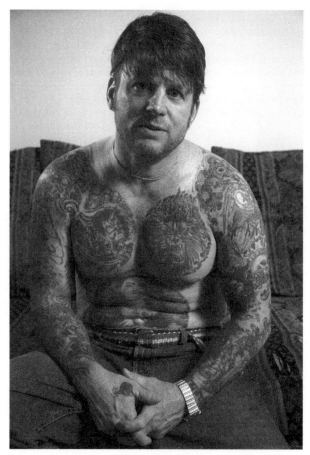

Photo by Richard Kern

One morning on my way to work, hungover and feeling sorry for myself, I ran into John Joseph, who I knew a little bit through our mutual friends in the hardcore scene in New York. John was the lead singer of the Cro-Mags, who are responsible for *Age of Quarrel*, the best hardcore record of all time. Through the years I've always heard these insane stories about

him but never had the balls to ask him what's for real and what's not. Now that I've read his autobiography though, I know that all the shit I'd heard about John—and way more—was indeed true. Yes, he was a 14-year-old runaway on the streets of Rockaway in Queens. Yes, he sold fake acid at Madison Square Garden, joined the navy and then went AWOL, rolled with Bad Brains, and hustled with Hare Krishnas in New York City and Hawaii.

But anyway, I digress. So I ran into John and I was feeling like shit. I said hello and he said, "What's up, man? You don't look so good." I said I was feeling ill. He grabbed me by the shoulder, walked me into a nearby juice joint, ordered me a combination of stuff that I had never even heard of before, then handed me a bottle of all-natural liquid medicine and said, "That should set you straight." He was carrying all these deli bags with him, and I asked why. He said they were meals and that he was on his way to feed the homeless. What the fuck!? That moment had such an impact on me. I felt like I was fucking up—that I had lost the plot. I mean John Joseph is out there helping hungover dudes on their way to work and feeding the homeless all at the same time. What? Plus he was in the Cro-Mags and just wrote one of the most intense memoirs I've ever read. What the fuck have you done?

Vice: This is not a thin book you've written here. It's hefty.
John Joseph: Ha, that's what my uncle said. He goes, "Jesus Christ, I could use it for a fuckin' weapon." I was at the restaurant Caravan of Dreams with Googie from the Misfits recently and some dude came up telling me he got the book and that it's fucking insane. These girls we were sitting with were like, "Oh, you wrote a book?" So I started telling them stories about the Lower East Side—some crazy shit. They asked Googie if he read the book and he was like, "I don't have to. I heard these fuckin' stories a million times already."

He's in the book, right?
Yeah, because when I was a kid he saw me riding on one of these junkies' bicycles in Rockaway. He was like, "What the hell is this kid doing?" Rockaway was like the Irish Riviera then. All the poor Irish people had their summer bungalows out there, and his family had one.

You were like 14, living on the streets.
Yeah, I was a heroin mule for addicts.

How were you involved with so many drugs without doing them all?
I did do drugs. I tried heroin one time. I fuckin' skin-popped it, vomited, and I was like, "Fuck that." I was more into hallucinogens like mescaline, microdots, and acid. Weed, too—I was a huffhead and I was fuckin' smoking dust.

Union Square was a big place to score drugs in the late 70s, right?
Fourteenth Street and Union Square Park, people don't know this now, but that place was a drug supermarket. You could buy anything there. There were hookers there, too. Once, me and my crazy friend Dave Dolan, we bought Placidyls there and then we went to Max's Kansas City. That was my first time going to that club.

What were Placidyls like?
They called them "jellybeans." They were horse tranquilizers and they were the size of a fuckin' 50-caliber machine-gun round.

What would they do to you?
Just lay you the fuck out. There were also Tuinals and Seconals—they're all barbiturates. I must have good genetics, because with all the shit I've done to myself, I'm still running marathons and triathlons. I can pop off a 20-mile run in a clip.

But anyway, we got the shit stomped out of us that night at Max's. I was passed out in the doorway outside, but my friend Dave went in there and stole all these dudes' money off the bar. I was outside, 14 years old, fucking drooling all over myself, and next thing I know the door comes flying open. I see this guy getting the shit stomped out of him. All the punk rockers back then used to wear those pointed shoes and the dudes in Max's back in the day were ass-kickers. It wasn't like these punk-rock motherfuckers right now. Like I said in the book, they would stab you in the face 20 times with a bottle because they just didn't give a fuck. Plus you could get away with it back then. So I'm looking and this dude is getting fucked up. He crawls over and looks up and was like, "Yo, John, help," and they're all like, "Oh, you're with him?" Boom!

Did you consider yourself a punk at that time?
I don't know. I wasn't like, "Yo, I'm a punk rocker." I didn't call myself nothing. I called myself a mess, you know what I'm saying? But then I hooked up with this girl Nancy and she turned me on to a lot of stuff. She took me to CB's and Stickballs and these crazy after-hours punk-rock clubs. I liked the energy and the craziness of it.

Were you on the streets back then or were you in a group home?
I was already on the streets. I had been in the Saint John's Home for Boys but I just wasn't feeling it.

How did you get involved in spirituality? From what I got out of the book, you were intrigued by the higher power that HR from Bad Brains was tapping into.
There are two dudes that I credit a lot of my spiritual development to and one is undoubtedly HR. He's such a brother to me. He put a mic in my hand and was like, "Get the fuck out there and sing." I was trying to be a drummer.

But yeah, it was HR and Jerry Williams, who was a really instrumental person behind the Bad Brains' first album. He produced it, recorded it in his studio, and even put the Bad Brains up there. If it wasn't for Jerry Williams that album never would have happened. He also got me into raw foods. Then one time HR took me for vegetarian food and ordered me a dragon bowl. I was like, "OK, where's the dragon meat, motherfuckers?" It was seaweed, and I was like, "What the fuck?" I loved HR but I ran around the corner and got a burger. Then he started taking me to Vegetarian Paradise and this place on Sixth Street called the Cauldron; I thought that this shit could taste pretty good. Then I got me a job at Prana Foods and, shit, the state didn't raise no fool. I was like, "All right, I'm eating this shit for free now."

Were you hooking up all the Bad Brains dudes with free food too?
Oh yeah, they were coming by. They rolled up every day and I was loading bags of sandwiches—$100 worth of groceries—for them.

I'm just trying to picture you working at Prana and all the dreads showing up.
It was like the window for the juice bar—it was a to-go window [*laughs*]. All of a sudden five dreads would pop up in the window and I would be like, "All right, what do you guys need?"

Going back a bit, I like how you describe the first time you ever heard of the Bad Brains from some guy at a club in Virginia.
I was like the wildest squid then, man. I fuckin' did drugs, I sold drugs, I just did whatever the fuck I wanted.

You were a squid—you were still in the navy at this point?
Yeah. I would sneak off base to go to happy hour. I'd get out of my uniform, put my leather on, and go see all the bands. I saw the Teen Idles and the Untouchables at the Taj Majal. So I was going there for happy hour one day and Doug, the owner, comes running out and he was like, "Dude, you got to fuckin' see this band." I was like, "Cool, all right, I'll go check it out." He was like, "No, no—you don't understand." He looked like he'd just seen 20 people get gunned down by a fuckin' terrorist or something. He was blown the fuck away. So I went upstairs and the motherfuckers clicked off a song and I was just like—get the fuck out of here.

It must have been insane to see them that early on.
And you couldn't praise HR. He would give all praises to the most high. You know, I don't care what the fuck that man is into now or whatever. I owe him a lot of shit and

I can't ever disrespect him. He's a genius and an amazing human being. All of us have our problems and you can't knock anybody for it. Bad Brains changed the whole fuckin' game, you know.

That's why when I ask these kids today if they ever heard of the Bad Brains and they're like, "Nah," I'm like, "Go buy the fuckin' ROIR CD today. Go get the *Live at CBGB 1982* DVD today. Do your fuckin' homework and know where this shit comes from."

I don't see any current punk-rock bands trying to go anywhere near as hard as the Bad Brains now. Nobody is going for a revolutionary thing.
They don't. They are just a bunch of whiny douchebags with eye makeup and it's disgusting.

And with shit being so fucked up now... George W. Bush, the Iraq war, the coming recession... This could be debated but there is not a lot of great music addressing that shit.
I ain't gonna debate you on that. I will pat you on the back for saying that. I don't even listen to 90 percent of the shit that's out there now. I like shit where there is some soul pouring out of it. If motherfuckers ain't going through something, how are they going to say anything about anything? You're singing about how tough you had it in the suburbs of Connecticut because you didn't get your fuckin' Gameboy on time. I mean, give me a fuckin' break. If you don't go through some adversity in life, you don't have shit to say as far as I am concerned. That is why the Cro-Mags put out *Age of Quarrel*. I was living in a motherfucking squat—and it wasn't like we were summer squatters going to Western Union to get money from Mommy and Daddy. We lived that shit and that is why the album was the way it was.

Are you the type of person who gets bummed about New York City now compared to the way it once was? Do you miss the crazier days?
Well, my mom can walk down the street now and not get mugged. But I think you would see a lot less of these fuckin' jerk-offs around here if it was still dangerous. Back then you didn't go to Alphabet City. Avenue A was adventurous, B was bold, C was crazy, and D was dead. And like, I'm paying all this rent now. But what goes up must come down. I wrote a song called "Seeds of Destruction." We have been planting these seeds for a while. No great empire lasts forever, and you know America is next. ∎

We've barely scratched the surface here. If you ever cared about punk rock or "underdogs beating the odds," you need to read John's book The Evolution of a Cro-Magnon. *It's available at punkhouse.org.*

ANDY CAPPER

POGUE MAHONE MEANS KISS MY ARSE

An Interview With Shane MacGowan

We won't go too much into who Shane MacGowan is here because, for God's sake, you should know. He's got our vote for best lyricist of the 20th century, and he's a singer who can bring grown men to tears with just one well-turned phrase. Is he a drunk and a now-and-then junkie? Sure. But the fans that find amusement in that, the ones who hold him up as some kind of mascot of Irish debauchery, are missing the point entirely. That's a simpleton's way of looking at Shane. That's how fucking Walt Disney probably saw the Irish. The only thing we want to say about his boozing is that it's a shame it will probably kill him before his time. Or who knows, maybe it will kill him right at his time. Who are we to guess how long Shane MacGowan will live? He turns 51 this year. We hope he lives forever.

We interviewed Shane on March 1st in his kitchen in Dublin's Donnybrook area. Donnybrook is historically one of the unruliest parts of Ireland thanks to the reputation of the Donnybrook Fair, which was notorious for its drinking, fighting, carousing, and banshee-like shrieking. It was banned in 1855, and Donnybrook is now one of the city's most respectable areas, but the legend remains.

During our time in his kitchen, Shane was projecting images from a DVD of traditional Irish folk music from the 60s and 70s onto the wall of his living room while singing along to the music. He drank white wine and gin from a mug with "Morphine" written on the side and chain-smoked hash. He punctuated almost every sentence with "Know what I mean, yeah," and then made his trademark laugh, which is indescribable but can best be transcribed as, "Eeeeshshshsh."

Vice: Hi, Shane. We came to take your photo and maybe talk a bit about history.
Shane MacGowan: OK, you better sit down then. Some people would say that these cameras were worse than

Photo by Ben Rayner

guns because they could steal your souls. Know what I mean, yeah? Eeeeshshshsh.

Which Irish historical figure do you most admire?
Gerry O'Boyle.

But he's your friend, so let's say anyone apart from Gerry.
Eamon de Valera. He was the Irish prime minster, president, and, like, the main author of the Constitution of Ireland. He had an American passport because his mother was an immigrant who went over to America, right? She got married to a Hispanic American. So they got their American passports and they came back.

He was president of Ireland all through the 60s, right?
Yeah. He was a politician but he was a crack shot as well. He was tasty. He took it up with the Brits in the civil war.

What else was special about him?
He did what Stalin did, but without killing all the people, know what I mean, yeah? He was a great figurehead for Ireland. When World War II came around, the English asked him for their support and he said, "Fuck you, Churchill, you bastard!"

Excellent.
Churchill kept saying, "We want to use your ports," but Valera pointed out that he already had the main ports across the world. Eeeeshshshsh.

What do you think about Churchill?
A lot of people nowadays complain about Mad Bomber Harris and what he did, but really all he was doing was carrying out the orders of Churchill, who was a mad, fascist, racist nutter. And the fucking Americans were as well. They completely destroyed Dresden and they had to rebuild it, stone by stone, over 15 or 20 years. The

Germans were keeping all their most valuable treasures underground, know what I mean?

You've been a big supporter of Irish independence your whole life. How do you think the cease-fire and the withdrawal of troops from Northern Ireland have changed the country?
Well, there have been less bank robberies, you know what I mean, yeah? Eeeeshshshsh. There's generally been less paramilitary activity.

Right. What else has changed?
Well there have been a few things like girl-napping and child-napping and child killing and girl killing and girl and boy abuse and that's led to a lot of people getting kicked out of their jobs in the priesthood. Eeeeshshshsh. That was a joke, that was a joke. I didn't mean that.

It's funny because it's true. But what have been the actual benefits of the cease-fire?
For a start, we got rid of the Brits. And now Ireland's, like, the biggest growing economy in the world. Ireland was like a child at school that was bullied. Then one day it says, "No fucking more, right?" This country's been growing at something like 3.7 percent per year. Ireland leads the way in education in the world. This didn't happen overnight but it's happened and it's growing all the time.

So Ireland is in a good place now, in your opinion.
Look, when you get to the point where people are complaining about the price of a pint you know that you're out of the real shit, yeah?

How much is a pint here anyway?
I couldn't tell you. Thirty years ago I could have told you what a pint cost. It was about ten pence.

When the British were in Ireland, what were the darkest times?
Things like Bloody Sunday and when they were bringing in the SAS. Know what I mean? It wasn't looking good.

And now in Belfast, the ex-loyalist paramilitaries are entrenched in criminal activity because there's nothing else for them to do.
When you've been in full-time active service for years and then suddenly it's done, you've got to do something, right? Whenever there's change in society there's criminality, you know what I mean? The English had their highwaymen. They would rob from everybody.

Is there a time during the Troubles that you remember fondly?

There was a cease-fire in '64, and then in '66 there was a celebration of the Easter Rising, which was the rebellion attempted by the Republicans to win independence from the Brits. The celebration wasn't in any way threatening to the English. It was just a year of people getting pissed and it started at Easter with Nelson getting his first blowjob. Know what I mean, yeah?

Right, when the IRA blew up Nelson's Pillar. That was an unpopular monument to the British admiral Lord Nelson that was on O'Connell Street in Dublin.
Ireland is like Vietnam, right? The forces had to leave. They were flushed out of Vietnam, just like here.

Wasn't Irish hero John F. Kennedy president of the United States when Vietnam began, though?
Yeah, but Kennedy was going to pull out. He probably would have pulled out and that's probably why they shot him. He was sick of getting shafted by the army and the navy telling him what to do all the time. Then Bobby Kennedy was carrying it on and he got plugged before he even got time to do anything. Bobby also got shot because he was an Irish Catholic immigrant.

History hasn't been kind to the Irish.
On the whole, history has been absolutely, stupendously stupid. But the thing is that Ireland has got faith and hope. We have that more in abundance than any other country. We live in the moment.

I guess we should talk a bit about music too. How've you seen the music industry change?
I remember times when I first started dealing with labels and things, there were people like Chris Blackwell at Island who were good. When I was first around there was like a huge musical and cultural revival going on. There was no generation gap really in music and now there is. And I remember MTV starting as well, and that was meant to stir things up and be good but then it just turned into Dire Straits and Van Halen and then Michael Jackson and then all the rest. You know what I mean, yeah?

Are you still making music?
Of course. But I don't really write music. I just play and the song comes out, you know what I mean? And I still listen to the old Irish music because it's incredibly powerful, you know?

Are there moments in your life that you don't care to remember?
No! I remember all of it. And I liked all of it—even all the bad stuff that happened. That was all OK as well. Eeeeshshshsh. ∎

JAKE AUSTEN

SAMMY DEVIL JR.

The Candy Man Was a Satanist

I f nobody else is willing to say this out loud, I'll step up to the plate. Barack Obama is totally ripping off Sammy Davis Jr. I'm willing to overlook their general similarities (cross-racial appeal, Amazon brides, chain smoking), but the senator's appropriation of Sammy's mantra is what really gets my goat. What's worse, this alleged master orator is actually guilty of motto misquoting.

Quite frankly, Obama's "Yes, We Can" is a hackish catchphrase that invokes the empty sloganeering of the old politics he decries, and its bland meaninglessness makes a glut of unwatchable celebrity YouTube videos inevitable. But Sammy's sublime 'Yes, I Can" is a pledge that genuinely means something. "I Can" represents Davis' refusal to recognize barriers, be they Jim Crow policies, societal norms, or sodomy laws. And "Yes" is basically what Sammy would say if anyone offered him anything.

All that Mr. Entertainment needed to partake in a new vice was an invitation. From clichéd descents into drug addiction to rebellious embraces of Republican politicians, he took everything to an obsessive extreme. Sure, everyone wacks off to porn, but after the nanosecond-long "porno-chic" trend of the 1970s (when *Deep Throat* had celebrities lined up to appreciate Linda Lovelace's big-screen talents and it was cool for couples to go to porn theaters on dates), Sammy spent years in shame-free indulgence, screening 35 mm porn prints at parties, visiting adult-movie sets where he treated the actresses like Hollywood royalty, and, according to her biography, taking fellatio lessons from Ms. Lovelace herself. As Sammy explained in his 1989 memoir, *Why Me?*, "I wanted to have every human experience."

Sammy with Temple of Set founder Michael Aquino and the Church of Satan's founder and high priest, Anton LaVey, in San Carlos, California, after he had become a Warlock II° in the church. Photo courtesy of Dr. Michael A. Aquino. Says Aquino: "I remember Sammy as a very gentle and good-hearted man who was habitually curious and adventurous—which explains much of his career as well as his somewhat daring (for a professional performer) dalliance with Satanism. He stood up for his own integrity and stood by his friends throughout his life."

There's no better example of this than Sammy's dabblings in satanism. Christian by birth, Jewish by choice, Sammy started his personal relationship with Satan during a 1968 visit to the Factory, a nightclub he partially owned. He was invited to a party by a group of young actors sporting red fingernails, signifying their allegiance to the Church of Satan. Founded in 1966 by Anton LaVey, a horror fan with a background in carnival work, ghost-busting, and nightclub organ, the San Francisco-based ministry combined LaVey's interests in ancient paganism, a media-savvy flair for publicity, and a philosophy of indulgence over abstinence.

When Sammy arrived at the party (whose theme he summarized as "dungeons and dragons and debauchery"), all attendees were wearing hoods or masks. The centerpiece of the "coven" was a naked woman chained spread-eagle on a red-velvet-covered alter. Davis was confident though that human sacrifice was not on the menu that evening. "That chick was happy," he wrote, "and wasn't really going to get anything sharper than a dildo stuck in her."

Not all the satanists at that orgy would be so lucky. As Sammy was getting stoned and serviced, one of the ritual's leaders tilted back his hood, revealing himself as Jay Sebring, the singer's barber. Hollywood's all-time greatest hetero hairdresser, Sebring was responsible for the shaggy style sported by Jim Morrison, helped get Bruce Lee on TV, and was engaged to actress Sharon Tate. During the Manson Family's infamous 1969 massacre, Sebring would be bound to Tate, shot, then stabbed seven times. His bio on the website for Sebring International (his still-active haircare company) fails to mention his satanism, though until recently the company's logo was an ankh, a symbol frequently used by occultists.

Sammy continued to attend satanic orgies and eventually joined the Church of Satan, though the chronology of his association presented in *Why Me?* deviates from the one offered by estranged LaVey associate Michael Aquino in his 1983 history of the church. Aquino's account is supported by numerous satanic interoffice memos, though it should be noted that the one-time fourth-degree satanic priest was known for creating documents he claimed to have transcribed from conversations with high-profile supernatural demons (his 1970 *Diabolicon* quotes Satan, Asmodeus, and Leviathan).

In 1972, after several years of partying with hooded hedonists, Sammy decided to put all his eggs in Beelzebub's basket by reinventing himself as the star of the first satanic sitcom. Though far worse ideas have made it onto network schedules, it is fair to say that the feature-length NBC pilot for *Poor Devil* (aired Valentine's Day 1973) is genuinely fucked. Inverting the story of Clarence the angel from *It's a Wonderful Life*, it features Davis as a bumbling coal-shoveling demon who is offered a chance to move up in hell (and to finally fuck Satan's fine black secretary) if he can successfully procure the soul of a San Francisco accountant played by Jack Klugman. After 73 minutes of Sammy's bumbling attempts to fulfill Klugman's bitter revenge fantasies, the one-eyed devil with a heart of gold takes pity and lets his client out of his contract, returning to his sulfuric furnace with a comedic shrug.

Even without the satanic overtones, this is a profoundly disturbing film, with Sammy employing that creepy "innocent" voice he utilizes in the talk-sing opening of "Candy Man," and the soulless sitcom non-funniness rendered even more sinister by the lack of a laugh track. But what makes this show stand out is the "realism" of hell. There have been plenty of comical pop-culture devils (Hot Stuff, the comic-book devil of mudflap and tattoo fame, *Bedazzled*), but never with this detail. Not only is Lucifer played by the genuinely evil Christopher Lee (who opted not to notch down the Hammer horror vibe), but his imposing office features a gigantic inverse pentagram behind his desk, framed by walls of lurid, glittering flames. Each devil wears a pentagram pendant, and Lee casually gestures to his minions using a devil horn salute. And just in case there was any ambiguity that this show was turning a sympathetic horn to satanism, at one point Klugman, in search of Sammy, lunges for the phone book declaring, "I'll call the Church of Satan downtown, they'll know how to contact him."

Upon seeing *Poor Devil*, an excited Aquino drafted a letter to LaVey, calling the show a "magnificent commercial for the church." It was decided to offer Davis an honorary second-degree Church of Satan membership. LaVey's sorceress wife, Dianne, pondered, "Wonder what Mr. Davis would think about being a black, Jewish, satanic warlock?"

He apparently thought pretty well of it. Davis extended an invitation to a Bay Area concert, where he gleefully accepted a membership certificate, card, and a II° Baphomet medallion, which he wore during his performance. After the show, Davis invited Aquino and LaVey's daughter Karla to dinner, where he discussed his interest in the occult, and assured them that the *Poor Devil* shout-out was no coincidence. Soon after, LaVey himself struck up a friendship with Davis, who began appearing in public with a painted fingernail. When Sammy was in the Bay he would reserve front-row seats for LaVey's entourage and flashed them the Sign of the Horns during the show. In private conversations, Davis revealed a deep, passionate interest in the satanic philosophies and LaVey reportedly considered making him a senior official of the Church.

But it was not to be. The first blow to the ascension of Satanic Sammy was *Poor Devil* not being picked up as a series because, in addition to sucking, the pilot reportedly received a good deal of protest from religious groups. One can only wonder what the series would have been like. Would Klugman continuously vacillate between heaven and hell, ultimately accepting Sammy as his satanic slave every week? Or would it be a series of celebrity soul-sellers, a Love Boat on the River Styx?

The world will never know, nor shall this mortal realm know what a Sammy-led Church of Satan might have wrought. Early on, LaVey decided to keep Davis's entourage at arm's length, branding Samala's PR chief David Steinberg "a professional Jew" bent on separating Sammy from the Dark One. And by 1974, probably without Steinberg's influence, Davis decided to move on. In *Why Me?* he offers that "one morning after a 'coven' that wasn't all fun and games… I got some nail polish remover and I took off the red fingernail."

In a *New York Post* advance excerpt from his 1980 memoir *Hollywood in a Suitcase* (subsequently edited out of the final edition) Sammy placed his devilish experiences in the context of his "Yes, I Can" philosophy. "It was a short-lived interest, but I still have many friends in the Church of Satan… I say this to only show that however bizarre the subject I don't pass judgment until I have found out everything I can about it. People who can put up an interesting case will often find that I'm a willing convert."

And he often was. And until a certain politician gets the pronouns in his buzz phrase right, I'm voting for Sammy. ■

IAN SVENONIUS

REFLECTIONS ON IKE TURNER

Drawing by Jim Krewson

Ike Turner, one of the principal innovators in American music, died recently after a brilliant career. His records from three decades are classics, and his live revue with then-wife Tina was a spectacularly kinetic and hypersexualized showbiz explosion.

His composition "Rocket 88," about a particular make of luxury automobile, was declared by the Rock and Roll Hall of Fame in 1991 to be the "first rock 'n' roll song." Though this is a nice accolade, it should be viewed with a certain amount of circumspection. When an institution like the Hall of Fame draws seemingly arbitrary magic demarcations around particular cultural events or forms, it is plain suspicious. After all, jazz, blues, R&B, rock 'n' roll, et al., were once fairly interchangeable terms, used to

denote black or "race" music, until "rock 'n' roll" became specifically the purview of whites, in the late 50s. So why the citation? Is "Rocket 88" the first rock 'n' roll song because Sam Phillips recorded it? Because it sounds like something the Hall of Fame thinks constitutes later rock 'n' roll? Perhaps, to the Hall of Fame's mind, "Rocket 88" sounds like what rock 'n' roll became by the middle 60s, a Europeanized variant of African-American R&B.

To name a particular tune the singular genesis of the genre seems artificial. After all, rock 'n' roll as we know it is a famously broad musical form, not dependent on a particular beat, arrangement, or set of instruments to be classified as such. It is the musical counterpart to the anti-ideological liberal market system that spawned it. A rock section in a record store includes Kraftwerk, Elton John, Bobby Day, and Motörhead. However, regardless of whether Ike Turner "invented rock 'n' roll," he was indisputably a maverick in the exciting and fecund world of R&B music, the music that was eventually chosen by mainstream America to replace big-band jazz as the official soundtrack and expression of the postwar world, a universe in which the USA, having emerged from the conflagration as nuclear conquistador, was lord of all it surveyed.

Anyway, whether or not he invented rock 'n' roll, Ike Turner had an influence far beyond his own chart hits. In the 50s, he was a talent scout, "discovering" and signing blues singers like Elmore James, B.B. King, and Howlin' Wolf. He also worked as a session player for people like Fontella Bass, Dee Clark, and Buddy Guy. Eventually he had his own bands, for which he wrote, arranged, and produced music, like the Ike & Tina Revue, the Ikettes, and the Mirettes. In 1971, he built his own studio in LA called Bolic. This was where Ike and Tina recorded some of the most exciting soul/rock crossover records ever: "Workin' Together," "Her Man, His Woman," "Feel Good," "Nuff Said," "Nutbush City Limits," and "Let Me Feel Your Mind." Ike and Tina were musically omnivorous, trying out anything they liked in the blues/rock paradigm. Black Sabbath's "Evil Woman" is performed effectively as "Evil Man," for example.

Making music as prolifically as he did, however, doesn't come cheap. Ike was a taskmaster, was considered difficult and paranoid by some, and had developed strange habits. He kept an AK-47 spring-loaded beneath his mixing board, for example. He abused drugs and made illegal long-distance telephone calls, for which he was investigated by the FBI. Eventually, his string of hits in collaboration with Tina and sundry other feats were overshadowed by their divorce and the subsequent release of her book, *I, Tina*. This became the 1993 blockbuster biopic *What's Love Got to Do With It* and outlined, in Hollywood style, Tina's grievances against Ike as a physically and mentally abusive spouse. Thereafter, "Ike Turner" became a synonym for "wife beater," symbol to a benighted mass audience oblivious to his achievements and influence. Ironically, Ike and Tina's marketing of themselves through their career had been very much based not just on their relationship but also on the dysfunction of it.

Ike and Tina's love affair began in 1959, a short time after the start of their musical collaboration. Though their union apparently had all the earmarks of a modern-style romance, with its prioritizing of emotions above practical concerns (*"amour fou"*), as evidenced by the abuse, it also had the attributes of an ancient idea of love, that of the political union, since it was a tool for Ike and Tina's mutual advancement, musically and economically. The modern idea of love, the irrational model, the blinding force that demands submission from its victims, is a relatively recent invention, coinciding with the rise of the bourgeois or "middle" class and the inevitable displacement of their superstitious and illogical royal nemesis. After the bourgeois ascension, love, in fact, became the only irrational aspect of life to be tolerated in an otherwise martial, logical, and self-policing social system. It simultaneously became the inversion of what it had once been, the sensibly considered stewardship of strategizing matchmakers who joined spouses for the mutual benefit of the families involved. Indeed, conjugal partnership had always been determined logically through considerations of status, dowry, property, and hierarchy. Before love's reinvention by the "middle class," love was ephemeral (*"eros"*) and was kept separate from marriage, which was a political transaction. Though the bourgeois era replaced much of the ancient world's arbitrary brutality with order and law—necessary since capitalist aggression and subjugation are largely legalistic—love was strangely exempt from the stringent codes of the new age.

Under feudalism, marital partnership was akin to buying a cow. Under bourgeois rule, it was an alluring and mystical illness, an irrational transgression, even cautioned against as a possible threat to the existing social order that might lead to folly, death, and idiocy (as dramatized in *Romeo and Juliet*, written by William Shakespeare, the great bard of the burghers). Love was now allowed to survive as the singular form of rebellion in the face of institutionalized, insidious, and crushing class oppression, a liberating specter of the savage and sensual life of the prebourgeois age.

To understand a prebourgeois mindset, one must look to colonial countries or to nations that sidestepped the Masonic-Napoleonic upheavals of the 19th century, such as Russia. Since Russia never experienced a true middle class and went from feudalism straight to communism and then to CIA-sponsored mafiocracy, the Russian's consciousness is as yet unaffected by sensible ("middle-class") concerns about health care and savings accounts, while alcoholism and thuggery are the orders of the day. Love as we know it is also something a Russian would find quite foreign unless it were as an affectation, like an American practicing sitar. Though often quite refined and impressive in his or her job as ballerina or chess master, the Russian stumbles through life much as a fish glides through the ocean or a bird swims through the sky, soaring in pure, unaffected, eternal consciousness. The insanity, irrationality, and confusion we equate with love are a Russian's entire life. For those trapped in the Western middle-class paradigm, though, things are not so simple. There is a love/life dualism that the "Westerner" dances around, an elaborate tango that is invisible to all but them and confusing to the uninitiated onlooker (foreign cabbies, for example).

Because love was sanctioned as the sole freedom/transgression in this most repressive and conformist society known to history, it is sung about at a rate that people in older eras would have found baffling. Indeed, old story songs about canals, murderers, gray geese, moles, and mountains have been almost entirely replaced in the postindustrial "rock 'n' roll" genre with songs about love. In fact, songs that aren't about love are typically considered inauthentic, dishonest, or even—the worst crime of all—intellectual. Since love's role as official transgression survived the various permutations of bourgeois society through to the industrial era, it would be the domain particularly of black Americans—that caste specifically exempted through systemic racism from the benefits of the "Land of Opportunity"—to express it, particularly through their music, one name for which was rock 'n' roll.

Since love/sex was the sole allowed transgression in bourgeois society and everything else was regulated "work," those who were disallowed from the wealth system became unconsciously appointed the guardians and priests of sexuality. Black Americans had created much of the wealth for what would be the USA (by 1776 already among the world's largest economies) without recompense through slave labor, and after emancipation were still largely barred from education and economic opportunity, so they inevitably became the keepers of carnality and love, since these were the inversions of the bourgeois obsession with logic and order. Therefore black music, or "blues/rock 'n' roll," became the music of sex and *amour*. Rock 'n' roll—like love—was similarly a rebuttal to bourgeois order, an expression of irrationality, nihilism, lust, romantic love, and animalism. Rock 'n' roll was resolutely antibourgeois, the romanticized and semisanctioned sound of proletarian discontent, controlled, harnessed, and distilled through capitalism to eventually help subjugate recalcitrant elements in the rest of the world.

Just as Ike Turner was a seminal figure for rock 'n' roll and arguably invented the form, Ike and Tina Turner were the embodiment of both rock 'n' roll and love's irrationality, marketing themselves as the volatile adult supersexual duo, involved in a highly passionate and even abusive relationship.

Most of Ike and Tina's material through their prolific 60s period dealt in direct terms with their dysfunctional relationship. The song titles speak for themselves: "The Argument," "Please Don't Hurt Me," "You're a Jive Playboy," "Hurt Is All You Gave Me," "I'm Yours (Use Me Anyway You Want To)," "Cussin,' Cryin,' and Carryin' On," "Don't Play Me Cheap," "Tell Her I'm Not Home," "I'm Going Back Home," "Tina's Dilemma," and the list goes on. Part of the mythology of love was that it held an irrational and mystical power over those affected, that a person "in love" was unable to resist the object of their desire, no matter how abusive, savage, or uncaring. Imbalanced power relationships therefore are central to the very appeal of the love affair to prospective lovers. The Ike & Tina Turner Revue capitalized on the sexuality and the power dynamics evident in their relationship, elements that charged the imagination of the onlookers at their shows, making them a consistently hot ticket throughout the 60s and early 70s.

Whether their torrid affair was initially a construct to motivate buyers or whether it was real can only be conjectured, since historical memory is untrustworthy, but it was certainly an effective marketing tool. Any member of any group can also attest to the fact that resentment, competition, and even hatred within a group can fuel creative prolificacy. Certainly this was the case for the Ike & Tina Turner Revue who were, by the late 60s, a crossover phenomenon that scored on the R&B and pop charts, put out 21 full-length LPs between 1969 and 1974(!), and toured, sometimes 270 nights a year, on and off the R&B "chitlin' circuit." By the mid-70s, though, despite the continued dynamism of their recorded work together, Tina left Ike and wrote her autobiography, which outlined Ike's abuse and was eventually turned into a major motion picture.

When *What's Love Got to Do With It*, starring Laurence Fishburne as Ike and Angela Bassett as Tina, came out in 1993, it was released to critical and public acclaim, to a mass audience who for the most part had never heard of Ike and Tina Turner and, even if they'd heard their music, were oblivious to what they were listening to. The indignation toward Ike as an abuser was instantaneous, though, as he became the patron saint of wife abuse, while Tina became an inspirational survivor and feminist icon. Though Ike decried his celluloid portrayal, Tina's move, besides being smart, was an economic inevitability. No longer was marital dysfunction considered to be sexy, hot, or attractive as it once was. Women's roles had drastically changed along with the insidious class oppression of the postindustrial world, a place where women were forced from stifling relationships with dictatorial spouses en masse into the totalitarian workplace. The sadomasochist excitement that had previously been expected from a relationship was now dispensed by the boss class to worker women. Therefore, in the new slave state, rock 'n' roll and love were both discharged from their roles as official rebellions against the ruling class. No dissent, however ineffectual and ritualistic, would be tolerated anymore.

What's Love Got to Do With It is an apt title for a film that declares that love, the last refuge of irrationality from capitalist numerological subjugation, is dead. The title song itself, an awful Streisand-esque MOR anthem, is a telling sonic declaration that rock 'n' roll is also dead. Now Ike, the man who maybe invented rock 'n' roll, the final stand of the id, has passed away as well. May he rest in peace. ∎

V12N3, MARCH 2005

STEVE McDONALD

BLACK FLAG B-DAY

Photo by Al Flipside

In 1978, my older brother Jeff and I started our band Redd Kross. I was 11 and he was 14. Our first public performance was at an eighth-grade graduation party, opening for Black Flag—and we got them the gig! We had met Black Flag only a few months earlier at probably one of their first shows ever. It was at a Moose Lodge in Redondo Beach. I remember they were incredibly loud, really muddy sounding, and the lead singer, Keith Morris, was particularly obnoxious. Although that night I much preferred the headlining band, Rhino 39 (one classic single on Dangerhouse Records), we still made sure to buy the opening band's self released 7-inch at the merch booth. It turned out to be the now-classic "Nervous Breakdown" EP.

We were all disillusioned by surf culture, Led Zep, and mainstream teens. All the assholes at school and on the beach could go fuck themselves. We were proud to be outside of their bullshit. Our drummer at the time, John Steilow, was a slightly different story. He was popular at school. He was even a surfer, and he got us our first show. It was at Lisa Stangles's graduation party. John was in Lisa's eighth grade class, and since he was a popular dude, known for his drumming prowess in the school orchestra, she asked if his band would play her party. We jumped at the chance, and offered to get our friend's band to play as well. There you go: Lisa Stangle had just booked the first Redd Kross show ever, and a headlining set from an extremely vintage version of the best Black Flag lineup.

I had just turned 12. We set up in the living room. We only got through a couple songs before they started booing, "Punk shit, you suck, faggots." Some dude with a pubescent cheecho shouted, "Play some Zep," and without hesitation Jeff announced that we would do some "unreleased Led Zeppelin." John clicked off a four-count, and we dove into the gnarliest noise jam, so fierce it would've made Thurston Moore green with envy. For the first 30 seconds or so, the kids really got into it, then they started questioning the new sound we were laying on them, and eventually they began to boo and berate us once again.

Black Flag's set included all the early classics: "Nervous Breakdown," "Wasted," "Fix Me." I think the kids were way too intimidated by these older dudes to give them any hassle. Most of them evacuated the living-room area, leaving our small group of friends to enjoy a private show by one of the most ferocious and innovative punk bands of all time. Keith Morris recently told me that he remembered a teenage girl being carried away from the party. Apparently she drank an entire pot of coffee, leading to caffeine overdose.

That still stands out as one of the best shows I've ever seen. ∎

JUNE SPRIG

SILVER FOX

Dave Berman Went and Got Shit On

Dave Berman and Harmony Korine harassing local talk-show host Johnny B. at a Nashville anti-immigration rally. Photos by Robyn Daniel

Dave Berman, aka the Silver Jews, is the best lyricist in rock today. That might be because he is also at the top of the heap of the best published poets in America today. His new record, *Tanglewood Numbers*, features his wife, Cassie, and his friends Stephen Malkmus and Mike Fellows laying down solid rock-country backgrounds for his heartbreakingly funny and weary songs.

We asked him about being scared and dressing up.

Vice: What is the most scared you can remember being in your life?
Dave Berman: When I was 19 I was working as an orderly at the State Hospital in Virginia. There were a lot of morbidly obese people, cut out of their houses in the mountains, lying ill on these massive hospital beds. A lot of the job was rolling these completely immobile behemoths over on their side, then rolling them 180 degrees to their other side while the nurses changed the sheets and stuffed these eight-inch-deep holes in them (which were longtime-forming bedsores) with fresh cotton.

One night they brought in a guy from death row. He was a big black killer paralyzed from the neck down, and we were called to roll him over. He's lying there in a gown, looking at me with full-on hate when I come in. It was four in the morning, and even knowing he was helpless they had him handcuffed to the bed. The dopey officer undid the handcuffs. With the help of my partner, I pulled him first toward me, fairly terrified but ready to do the job and get out of there. I stared at the wall and kept my hands away from his mouth.

Here comes the horror part: When I rolled him back the other way, I was shoving his huge ass up and over, and roughly a quart of dark green liquid shit squirted out all over my hands and forearms. To this day I wonder if he somehow retained control of his sphincter until that moment and let me have it.

What is the scariest nightmare you can remember having?
I was a kid. My parents are dressed up like they're going out somewhere. They are looking for me to come along, walking out the front door. Leaving me behind. I can see their shoes from where I am trapped underneath the coffee table with a burning man covered in fire who is holding me down so I can't crawl out. The whole underneath of the coffee table is like a cage of flames.

What was the best Halloween costume you had as a child?
Casper the Friendly Ghost. ■

STEVIE NICKS AS TOLD TO ANDY CAPPER

LONG-DISTANCE WINNER

Surviving the 70s

Photo by Paul Canty

I'm 56 now, but music still has the same effect on me as when I was 15. Every so often, I'll hear a couple of songs that will just kill me and make me go instantly to my desk to write, and then straight to the piano to compose. That feeling is something that's never gone away and I feel really blessed by that.

I know some people say they used to write better when they were younger, but I feel the greatest writing for me is yet to come. I'm always working on new material and I'm always inspired. At the moment, I'm going between preparing for a short residency at Caesar's Palace in Las Vegas and composing a series of songs based on the books of Rhiannon, these Welsh legends that I really love. They're such beautiful stories. It's what the old Welsh people left behind to teach future generations about how

to raise their children and how to deal with relationships—how to run their lives, basically.

Another thing that inspires me in my music at the moment is my niece Jesse. She's 13 but she's an inch taller than me, with black hair and blue eyes. Sometimes when I'm running on my treadmill and listening to music on my CD player, I'll be singing and howling along while Jesse's in the same room and I'll make her listen to how the singer is singing. Jesse was with me when I wrote four songs for the last Fleetwood Mac album, and she even got to sing on the title track, "Say You Will." That was fun.

It's not that I want to push her into music. I would never do that. The arts are not something that you can push on anybody. People either have it or they don't. I really believe that. I would say to girls who are thinking about getting into making music that the most important thing to do is to learn how to play an instrument well. If you're a girl who can play, you can always get a job. You can play keyboards or guitar in a band no problem. Since you're a girl, you're even more special.

But making it all last, you know, having longevity, is another story. The thing that's kept me going all these years is absolutely "the music." It sounds like a cliché, but the music is way more personally motivating than being in a band. Yes, I was in a band, but it's not like Lindsey Buckingham and I wrote songs together. We never did. We were very, very separate in that. He was a very good producer for my music but that was that.

I was very selfish and was not willing to give up my art for a family and a husband. Now, at this point in my life, I am really glad, because I see so many of the people that did get married and did have relationships—they're all divorced, they're all miserable, their children are miserable, and it's like I'm thinking to myself: "You made the right decision."

I guess for me, as a woman, there was nobody who would tolerate my lifestyle. Even the richest of rock stars had reason to be jealous of me. The poorest of people, the waiter, the great men in my life, it hit them all very hard.

There was the waiter. There were the doormats and the security guards with some other famous bands. There were all these really beautiful and sweet men who have been in my life and then there's the rich, famous men, but at some point or another, my life was too much for ALL of them. They started to make demands. Like, "Where are you going? And what do you mean you're coming home from your tour but you're stopping over in England for a month?"

That kind of thing doesn't go over well. The long black limousine drives up the long path to your house to pick you up and your boyfriend is waving goodbye to you. It's never fun to be left. It wouldn't be for me.

I had my chances but I would never marry a rock star either. Because you can never trust them. I know, I have watched them while I was out there. There was an unspoken society, which Christine McVie and I always stayed completely away from. We didn't really ever know what the rest of the boys in our band did, but we knew what boys in other bands did because that gossip got to us. Whatever went on in Fleetwood Mac was kept from us. We didn't wanna know anyway. As a woman who lived in that world of groupies and rock and roll excess, I can understand why the men do what they do. But I don't have to like it.

I swear on my mom's grave (and she's not even dead yet) that Christine and I didn't go out and have one-night stands while we were on tour. We never met someone in a coffee shop and then went back and slept with them, ever.

But the guys would. And in the rest of the world it happens all the time and it's not a big deal. It still happens now with all the new rock and roll bands.

Whatever went on—and plenty of things did—I'm just grateful that I've had so many beautiful memories in this life of music. I would say the most memorable day I ever had was when I was 29 and we played the first ever "Day on the Green" concert in San Francisco. It was Peter Frampton headlining. We were on before him. The concert was a tribute to the success of Peter's *Frampton Comes Alive* album, so the promoter Bill Graham had built a huge fairytale castle on top of this massive stadium stage. The castle was so gorgeous. It was sparkling and glittering, and it had turrets and stairs that went up on both sides. The turrets had seats, so it had this Rapunzel kind of feeling. This was the beginning of 1976, and at that point Lindsey and I had only done a small tour with Fleetwood Mac, where there were like 5,000 people per show. This audience was 75,000 people!

We had no idea what to expect. When I got there, I saw each of our dressing rooms had personalized, carved-wood signs in beautiful calligraphy with our names written on them. Of course they were just trailers, but oh what trailers they were!

The first performer was this guy named Lee Michaels. I'd lived in San Francisco, where he's from, so I was a fan of his already. I went out and hid on the side of the stage and watched the show, and then I went back and got dressed during the last half of the next act's set. When we finally got onstage to do our set, I just thought to myself: "Where would I ever want to be in the world except for this sparkling castle in front of 75,000 people?"

I was standing in the middle of the stage thinking, "This is the big time!"

Even better than that was that my best friend and I got to go up the stairs on the side of the castle and sit in those little princess chairs and watch Peter Frampton play live. Peter's an amazing guitarist and back then he had that shoulder-length golden hair. He was so gorgeous. He looked like a king. So to sit up there and watch him from that vantage point was just wonderful. When the show was over there was a huge party in Frampton's hotel suite. It was just a magnificent rock and roll moment.

At the party, everybody was drunk. But I can remember it like it was yesterday, so that means it was fun. Everybody was drinking wine, and there were wine spritzers there because of all the English people. It was a beautiful thing. At that point the serious drugs hadn't kicked in yet.

So yes, some bad days came later, but there's always been good days too. All of it, the good and the bad, is what allows me to sit now in a house that overlooks the ocean and have complete freedom in my life. I'm just really grateful to music every day. ■

V

BOOKS 'N' SUCH

Photo by Roe Ethridge, V15N12, December 2008

JESSE PEARSON

HAROLD BLOOM

Harold Bloom is the preeminent literary critic in the world, and as such he is perhaps the last of a dying breed. Bloom adheres, passionately and single-mindedly, to the true and first tenet of lit crit—to take a book and judge it on its own merit, to see it as a thing in and of itself. The aesthetic value of the prose, the mastery of metaphor, strength and conviction of theme—these are the sorts of things that a critic like Bloom pays attention to.

Much of contemporary criticism takes a novel and holds it up to a series of incongruous and irrelevant sociological magnifying glasses—gender theory, feminism, Marxist analysis, and all sorts of postmodern muck. These critics, whom Bloom has memorably called the School of Resentment, have gained such strength that they have colored, even infected, writers whose careers have started since the Resentment began. So what we are seeing is criticism that changes literature for the worse and, as Bloom laments, contributes to the idiot-ization of the entire world. It's a mess, and it may be irreversible.

And so we return to Harold Bloom, the old voice crying out in the wilderness, who, besides writing one of the most important and useful books on Shakespeare (*The Invention of the Human*) and coining the term "the anxiety of influence"—an extremely useful theory of literary evolution—in the book of the same name, took on the whole of academia (for that is now just another name for the School of Resentment) in the towering 1994 work *The Western Canon*. It is in this book that Bloom first and most comprehensively did his part to preserve what's im-

portant—essential, really—to humans from all the great works of writing that have been produced from the Bible and *Gilgamesh* all the way up to, well, right now. The professors and critics of the world will only get their hands on my copy of this book when they pry it from my cold, dead fingers.

Portrait by Tara Sinn, with photo by Michael Marsland/Yale University

Vice recently spoke with Bloom over the phone. He was in his office at Yale, where he teaches two classes a week.

Vice: I was hoping to talk first about *The Western Canon*.
Harold Bloom: Do you mean the whole category, or what I wrote about it?

I mean your book.
But can we make an agreement? Let's forget that damned list.

Ha. Do you mean the appendix in the back of the book that lists all the canonical works?
The list was not my idea. It was the idea of the publisher, the editor, and my agents. I fought it. I finally gave up. I hated it. I did it off the top of my head. I left out a lot of things that should be there and I probably put in a couple of things that I now would like to kick out. I kept it out of the Italian and the Swedish translations, but it's in all the other translations—about 15 or 18 of them. I'm sick of the whole thing. All over the world, including here, people reviewed and attacked the list and didn't read the book. So let's agree right now, my dear. We will not mention the list.

It's a deal.
I wish I had nothing to do with it. I literally did it off the

top of my head, since I have a pretty considerable memory, in about three hours one afternoon.

It does seem like the sort of thing that a publisher would ask for to make the book more palatable to a casual reader.
It doesn't exist. Let's go on.

I started college in the same year that this book was published—1994.
Yes, 1994. That's a long time ago now. That's 14 years. I am now 78 and I've come off a terrible year. I nearly died. But I'm all right now and I'm back teaching.

What happened?
A whole series of mishaps and illnesses, but the big one that knocked me out for six months and nearly killed me was that I quite literally broke my back in a fall. But let's forget about it. It's over now.

Looking at the book, and thinking about it being available right when I was starting college—
Where were you at college?

Well, that's part of the problem. I went to a very small liberal-arts college with no grades and no majors. Let's not speak its name. Or OK, let's. It's called Hampshire.
Oh yes, I know it very well. It was supposed to be very elite. I remember they once wanted me to talk there and I sort of dodged it because I felt it wasn't going to work.

It wouldn't have worked. And I feel like I should have just read your book instead of going to school there. But can you tell me, do you think that things have become better or worse in terms of the School of Resentment since the book was published?
Obviously they've gotten much worse. Just look at the enormous international as well as domestic dumbing down and decline in serious reading and indeed the falling apart, inevitably, of standards.

Yet you're still soldiering on, teaching undergraduates.
But I've turned my back on the academy even though I still teach at Yale. I am part of no department—I became a department, or nondepartment, of one when I walked out on the English department back in, my God, way back there in 1976. That's a long time ago now. Thirty-two years. But I started to write books pretty early on—certainly from about the late 1980s on to the present, so for about 20 years now, addressed to the general reader all over the world. And it has worked because I now have an enormous general readership, mostly in an incredible number of translations. So there is always a saving remnant of read-

ers out there, as I have discovered. On the other hand, every single one of those countries, like our own, does suffer from a kind of dumbing down.

It's in all sorts of culture and media, but it's mostly in books.
It has something to do with, though not everything to do with, technological change—the fact that most kids grow up not reading deeply or going to a museum and staring at a picture or going to a concert and really listening to authentic music—including authentic jazz. People are trapped in the age of what you might call the triple screen: the motion-picture screen—and this is in ascending order of evil in terms of what it does to their minds throughout the world—the television screen, and finally the computer screen, which is the real villain.

It's disappointing because the internet could have been such a good thing. It could have been like an indestructible Library of Alexandria, but with porn.
This goes back to what I said about the saving remnant. You're part of that saving remnant. As I've been saying for years: If, in fact, you have an impulse to become and maintain yourself as a deep reader, then the internet is very good for you. It gives you an endless resource. But if, in fact, you don't have standards and you don't know how to read, then the internet is a disaster for you because it's a great gray ocean of text in which you simply drown.

I started school, ostensibly at least, as a poetry major. But I couldn't find a class there that wasn't "Transgendered Chicano Poets of the Latter Half of 1982" or something. Not that I don't like transgendered Chicano poets of 1982—they're great, I'm sure. But I wanted to learn more than that. Or rather, I wanted to start from the very beginning and work my way up to transgendered Chicanos. I wanted the context of history, and I couldn't get it at college.
Oh my dear, let's not get into that. I'm so weary now of being called a racist or a sexist. I can't take that anymore.

But where does this fear of reading the works of what some critics derisively call "dead white men" come from?
Well, we're about to crash on the scale of 1837, the Great Panic, or 1929, and now we're going to have the Panic of either 2008 or 2009. That is a consequence—it's one of many consequences including a lot of innocent dead everywhere—of the way in which the counterculture ultimately, by its enormous recoil, helped give us George W. Bush and Sarah Palin. They are both semiliterate at best. They both exude self-confidence. And they both claim a direct relationship with God.

Hopefully she'll disappear now, or just start a talk show or something.

She is a very, very dangerous person.

Agreed. But moving on... If a person wants to seriously approach literature on their own, outside of academia, it's very difficult.

Without a real teacher, an authentic teacher, a real mentor, it's very difficult for anyone to get started.

Can you explain to me your concept of the solitary reader? That's who you say you address your books to.

It's not a concept. It's just a fact. There are solitary readers all over the world. I don't have any special insight into this. I do not know why it is that certain young people, from the beginning, are loners—perfectly sane—who want to go and be alone with a very good book. Again, it's the saving remnant. It's a sort of strange grace and of course I'm profoundly thankful for it. So you don't have to ask me what I mean by the solitary reader. I mean you—on the basis of what you've told me. All you need to know about the solitary reader is Pearson.

Nice! Can we talk about the School of Resentment?

Their name is Legion. I have wasted my breath on them. Doctor Samuel Johnson, my hero, told us to clear our minds of cant. But my friend John Hollander keeps warning me to stop ranting against cant, which is what I do. By the time you've spent a certain amount of energy ranting against cant, it becomes a kind of cant in itself. So let's not bother with it.

But it's been a struggle of yours for so long.

Phrases that you formulate come back and haunt you. I shouldn't have formulated "the School of Resentment." I once called them a "rabblement of lemmings," and I run into that phrase everywhere. And I now wish that I hadn't formulated the single phrase that I seem to have given to the language: "the anxiety of influence." Of course everybody misunderstands it.

How do they get it wrong?

They interpret it as an affect in the later writer. But it isn't an affect in the later writer. It doesn't matter whether the later writer does or does not feel an anxiety, conscious or otherwise, with regard to a precursor figure. It's actually the relationship between one poem and another poem, one novel and another novel, and so on and so forth.

It's an inescapable thing, and an ancient thing. It's simply what happens from being part of the lineage of writers and writing.

The current paperback of *The Anxiety of Influence* has a

long introduction by me on Shakespeare and Marlowe, which makes very clear that I don't think of it as a post-Enlightenment phenomenon anymore. In fact it exists in Pindar in relation to Homer and obviously in Plato in relation to Homer. It's universal. It's in ancient Chinese. It's even in the Hebrew Bible. Think of the relationship between Ben Sira and the Apocrypha, so-called, the ecclesiastical, so-called, the wisdom of the fathers, in relation to Coheleth or Ecclesiastes. But go on.

Yeah, I'd better because I'm getting way out of my league there. In the introduction to *The Western Canon* you say that you agree with this idea that "there is a god, and his name is Aristophanes." What's so great about him? He was sort of the first literary critic, right?

Yes, the great point about Aristophanes as I see him is that he is the real beginning of Western literary criticism, particularly when he savages Euripides in favor of Aeschylus. In fact, he really talks about a kind of anxiety of influence on the part of Euripides in relation to Aeschylus. What I can recognize as Western literary criticism really began more in Aristophanes than in Aristotle. His formalism tells me that criticism always has a close relationship to the origins of parody, of satire, of a kind of desperate irony. And of course we don't have literary critics anymore. It's an archaic notion.

Oh, but hey, what about James Wood? I'm sort of kidding, of course.

Oh, don't even mention him. He doesn't exist. He just does not exist at all.

I thought his last book was fun to read because he gets so enthusiastic about things, but yeah, I don't really understand the phenomenon of him on the whole.

My dear, phenomena are always being bubbled up. There are period pieces in criticism as there are period pieces in the novel and in poetry. The wind blows and they will go away.

His last book seemed to be a period piece at least in terms of its cover design. It looked like a textbook from the 30s or 40s. It was kind of cute.

A publisher wanted to send me the book and I said, "Please don't." I think it was my own publisher, of the huge book I'm working on called *Living Labyrinth: Literature and Influence*, in which I've been bogged for five years now. It's meant to be a grand summa and may be my undoing. Anyway, I told them, "Please don't bother to send it." I didn't want to have to throw it out. There's nothing to the man. He also has—and I haven't ever read him on me—but I'm told he wrote a vicious review of me in the *New Republic*, which I never look at anyway, in which he clearly evidenced, as one of my old friends put it, a certain anxiety of influence. I don't want to talk about him.

OK. Maybe this next one is a silly question.
Ask what you will, dear.

How do we read Shakespeare?
Well, I of course teach Shakespeare. I'm back to teaching again after a year off, and I always teach a class on Shakespeare that goes through the year and a class on how to read poems that goes through the year. But this is a very hard thing to answer. Critical books on Shakespeare usually don't help much.

Is going to see productions of his plays valuable while reading him?
If it's the right production. I won't go to almost anything because I know it's going to be hacked up and smashed by some stupid, pigheaded, politically correct, high-concept person who thinks his or her concepts are higher than Shakespeare's, which is ridiculous. So I don't even go once a year. I doubt that I'll ever go to one again.

So are there no useful guides besides your own?
I also like Harold Goddard's book. It's called *The Meaning of Shakespeare*. It's now in two paperback volumes and I really urge you to read it and get other people to read it—as well as to read my admittedly rather ramshackle book on Shakespeare.

I'll do what I can. How many of his plays do you get through in your course on him?
I manage in the course of a year to cram in 24 of the 38 or so plays because two dozen of them really are of the highest quality.

You have a particular affection for the character of Falstaff, who appears in the two *Henry IV*s and *The Merry Wives of Windsor.*
Oh yes, yes. In this I follow [literary scholar] A. C. Bradley, who was there before me. In fact, that's still a good book. His work on Shakespearean tragedy is far preferable to most modern books on the same thing. Bradley said that the four Shakespearean characters most inexhaustible to meditation are Falstaff, Hamlet, Iago, and Cleopatra—which might at first seem an eccentric choice, but you brood on it and you see that he is right. Lear is beyond you so you can't really keep meditating on him past a certain point. Macbeth is too uncomfortably close—you can't meditate on him. Rosalind is too free of you, is too sane and normal.

What makes those four characters so rich?
They're so powerfully, elliptically presented, and I guess in-creasingly that's the clue to my Shakespearean teaching. From the first moment on, I try to show the students that even though he is the richest of writers, he is also paradoxically the most elliptical. You always have to follow what it is that he's leaving out on purpose to make your mind's work harder. With Falstaff, Hamlet, Iago, and Cleopatra, an enormous amount is left out.

Does teaching young people give you any hope for the future of literature and criticism?
It gives me personal exhilaration at the moment because I was awful tired of lying on my back and being cut off. And I refuse to teach graduate students. I have for a number of years now for obvious reasons.

Is it because they are ruined by contemporary academia at that point?
Look, I've become the pariah of the profession. You have to write letters for graduate students and I found that I was giving them the kiss of death. I'm not going to put that on my head in my old age. So I gave it up maybe eight or ten years ago, when I was already old. The only thing that I think is a little awkward is going into my Shakespeare class every Wednesday and my poetry class every Thursday and finding that my students are, after all, since these are Yale undergraduates, very good and highly selected ones. They're all quite wonderful, I think. But they are between roughly 19 and at most 22 years of age and I'm 78. There is an age gap there and I can't always be sure that I'm able to bridge it.

And which era of poetry are you teaching?
Oh, I did a huge anthology called *The Best Poems of the English Language: From Chaucer Through Robert Frost*, though it actually goes beyond Frost. He's simply the last person to be alive and to write poems. I wanted to end it with the close of the 19th century in terms of the poet's birth, with Hart Crane, who is still my favorite poet, born in 1899. I follow that book out for the first semester, and in the second semester I go back to the four poets who after all this time are the ones I most care for among the 20th-century poets: William Butler Yeats and Wallace Stevens, upon whom I've written very large books, Hart Crane, on whom I've written a couple of essays, including the centennial introduction to the current best paperback of Crane's poetry, and D. H. Lawrence, whom I've written only a couple of essays on through the years, but who is a marvelous poet.

And now my voice is failing. We'll have to stop.

Thanks for talking to us.
And thank you, Mr. Pearson. Before I go into the Great, perhaps we will meet. ∎

JAMES KNIGHT

MARTIN AMIS

Martin Amis is one of the great writers of contemporary fiction. Even if he'd given up putting pen to paper after his third novel, *Money*, this would be an irrefutable fact. Period. Sorry. He writes grippingly of ugly characters consuming for the sake of consumption, blind to their own greed. His hideous, and occasionally hilarious, creations have always been both of their own time and chillingly in line with whatever is going on outside your window on any given day.

Amis gives interviews rarely and has a reputation for being spiky and guarded. Having read all of his work and been more than a little bit into it, actually picking up the phone to talk to him had me shaking like a wee little leaf on a tree. Luckily, Amis ("Marty" to his buddies) was kind, willing, and open. He also has the most mesmerizing way of emphasizing words midsentence. Go watch him talk about his book *House of Meetings* on *Charlie Rose* on YouTube right now and you'll hear what I mean.

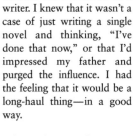

Portrait by Tara Sinn, with a photo by Alex Sturrock

Vice: Having grown up with the towering novelist Kingsley Amis for a father, was there a point where you made a conscious decision to be "a writer," or was it always sort of a given?
Martin Amis: At around 13, a certain self-awareness came over me as I was writing prose and poems in notebooks and diaries. What you are doing at that age is communing with yourself in a new way and becoming articulate within yourself. I think that everyone goes through that state and the people who end up becoming writers are simply those who never grow out of it. I never did. I also have to admit my father as an early influence. I read his stuff, but I also felt like it was an independent decision that I made to be a writer. I knew that it wasn't a case of just writing a single novel and thinking, "I've done that now," or that I'd impressed my father and purged the influence. I had the feeling that it would be a long-haul thing—in a good way.

What other novelists were early influences on your writing?
Well, I'd not read Bellow by the time I had written my first novel. I read a lot of Austen early on but I fail to see how anybody could be influenced by her, she's simply too *lucid*. I'd read some Nabokov too, but I suppose the biggest early influence was Dickens. His stuff was just nuts and wild, which is beguiling at that age. It's impossible to imitate Austen, as it is all understatement, whereas with Dickens the prose is so hairy and muscle-y; you can really gorge on it.

Early on you seemed preoccupied with the present—its excess and its vacuity—both in the rampant consumerism of *Money* and the Thatcherite capitalism of *London Fields*.
Certainly during the early period, yes, but there comes a point where you're not really *in* the culture any more. You become removed from it. My father put it well to me once. He said: "At a certain age you think it's not like that

anymore—it's like *this*. But you are not quite sure what *this* is." I think it would be insane to harbor the idea that you can remain plugged-in forever.

You've also spoken of being "addicted to the 20th century." Has the 21st proved not quite as compelling so far?
Possibly that was the point where, for me, *that* became *this*. The novel I am coming to the end of now is set in 1970, so perhaps I am clinging to the 20th century.

London has always had a looming presence in your novels. What was it about the city that fascinated you?
I always felt grateful to be in one of the world's great cities. It would have been completely impossible to write anything like the novels I wrote if I were living somewhere like Cambridge. It was very much a case of being in it again—living, breathing, and swimming in it. And as we all know, the fish doesn't ask about the water. You just sit there, run your nerve endings up against it, and it all comes out of the other end of your pen.

At times you have written in forms outside of fiction to reflect on society in the same way you have within your novels.
Fiction utilizes a different part of the mind and you can see it in action and see the difference when you produce nonfiction. I studied Stalinism and Russian history extensively when working on *Koba the Dread* [nonfiction] and then *House of Meetings* [fiction], and due to the formal differences, similar feelings were expressed in different ways. Fiction acts like a slow zoom lens, it allows you to go deeper in and say something else. It took three years to get from the brain to the back of my spine, and then I felt ready to say something.

Even when not dealing directly with politics, your novels exist in an atmosphere of political threat. Over time the threat has shifted from Soviet Cold War to the axis of evil, but always with a sense of potential Armageddon.
I was very apolitical as a young man. I was left of center, but being surrounded by Trotskyites like Christopher Hitchens made me seem moderate in comparison. I was unattractively proud of not knowing a great deal about politics. Literature was what I had and it was my thing. Despite writing about nuclear weapons in *Einstein's Monsters* and the Holocaust in *Time's Arrow*, I only really gave myself a political education when I began to study Russia. Suddenly I could see the categories and the precedents. It all came alive to me. When September 11 came along, I wasn't prepared for anything as interesting as that to happen in my lifetime. If I had to explain what my novels were about in one word it would be masculinity, and here was masculinity in a whole new form.

It takes the essence of what it is to be a man straight back to violence, and really the political history of man is the history of violence. The social history of man is simply sex. Those have always been the most interesting questions to me: What is it that makes man put himself about in such a way and what is it that makes him treat women in the way he does? When I have chosen to speak out about topics in nonfictional form it is with these concerns in mind.

Are you talking about *The Second Plane*, your collection of pieces about Islam?
Yes. I felt I had something to say and nonfiction was a very immediate way of saying it. So I did.

The plot devices that you became infamous for using came to be classified as postmodern. Were they conscious, formal decisions or were they subconsciously demanded by the story?
Postmodernism wasn't really this grand bandwagon that it may have seemed at the time. It was in the air and if you were of your time you saw the point of it. In the end it proved not the rich vein some had hoped and something of a dead end, but it was very predictive in terms of life itself becoming very postmodern, what with buildings having their piping on the outside and politicians talking openly about "the plumbing." There was a whole new level of self-consciousness that developed, as well as an interest in one's own age that would have been unknown in, say, the 18th century. History is still speeding up and I want to reflect that, so when I sit down to write I want to push the form of the novel and play so that there is a conscious and deliberate sense of pushing the form. If anything, though, I am now returning to realism with a modernist sensibility without that tricksiness of postmodernism.

How do you feel about the current state of fiction?
It will always be produced; I worry more about it being read. Poetry is already dead in those terms. Poetry requires that you stop the clock. When you read a poem the writer is saying, "Let's stop and examine this writing." People don't like solitary reflection anymore, so poetry no longer has a place in the culture. This will eventually seep out to include the novel. The day of the long, reflective, discursive novel, such as the great Saul Bellow novels, which were eight-month best sellers in their time, are over. The novel now is streamlined and sped up. It is a reflection of the age.

Are there any young novelists working now who you admire?
The truth is that I don't read my youngers. It seems a

terribly uneconomical way to organize your reading, by studying those unproved by time. I read my friends, so I take in Will Self and Zadie Smith with great interest. It all seems healthy out there but I can't make any broad statements about "where" the novel is now. Sorry.

In conversation with Self you have said that "the middle classes are underrepresented in my novels." You also seem to have a recurring preoccupation with the lower classes.
I like extremes. There is a certain latitude necessary to be a character, often in a repulsive way in the case of the upper classes, but it gives you the freedom to be a little more extreme and extravagant at either end of the social scale. The pressures at the lower end of the spectrum are very intense and that leads to characters becoming interestingly twisted into strange shapes. The middle classes are written about by everyone. They shan't whimper with neglect because I am not writing about them. All fiction is essentially kitchen-sink. It is just that some kitchen sinks are more expensive than others.

You mentioned a novel that you are working on now. Can you tell us any more about that or will you get in trouble?
I hope not. It is a novel set in the social revolution, and the main character is 20 years old. Its title is *The Pregnant Widow*, which comes from a remark by the wonderful Russian thinker Alexander Herzen. He said that when political or social orders change by revolution one should be pleased that the old is giving way to the new, but the trouble is that you get the death of the new order and no heir apparent. You are left not with a child but a pregnant widow, and much grief and tribulation will take place between the death and the birth. I would say that even now the baby of the social revolution is yet to be born 30 years on.

Like London, America figures often in your novels. In *Money* you portray the country as the unbridled consumerist paradigm that London strived to be, but lacking that British inhibition.
America is a wild place, an awesome place, and like Henry James I very much believe it to be a world rather than a country. As a place it is very difficult to generalize. Having watched the last eight years with horror I am of course thrilled about the election because the potential to go wrong in America is so huge and here at last is someone genuinely impressive as well as someone who can help heal that great wound in American life. I think we could be entering a great era.

Perhaps an era in which we see the baby of the social revolution born?
Perhaps.

There was talk at one point of David Cronenberg making a film of *London Fields*. Was there any truth to that?
There was. I met him a couple of times and he rewrote the script a little but he would only have got a sliver of the novel and not the whole book, so it was left. The project is still alive, though. They did *The Rachel Papers*, which was fun, and *Dead Babies*, which was sort of fun. They are making my novels in order—just at 20-year intervals. I have never had a great time with writing for cinema, though. I did a terrific script for an adaptation of *Northanger Abbey*, which was picked up by Miramax and then sat on. I'm not sure what happened to it. I should probably check on that, actually. Cinema is a wonderful form, though, and a young form. As Bellow said: Film is about exteriors whereas the novel is concerned with interiors. So there are many possibilities yet to explore.

What caused you to move to Uruguay for two years?
My wife is half Uruguayan and half New York Jew—a heady mixture. She has about 25 first cousins out there. We visited it for a winter and liked it very much so we stayed. We eventually left as our girls outgrew it and needed better schools. The landscape is fantastic but it was too quiet politically to have any impact on my writing. It is a real anomaly in terms of how gentle and sane it is in the context of South America.

Recently you began teaching at Manchester University. Why, of all places, Manchester?
Quite simply: They asked me. My father taught and by all accounts was fairly good at it and I felt that I might do all right at it as well. I enjoy it very much and I like my colleagues, which is rare for a job. All I do is teach novels. What could be more agreeable than that? I don't guide my students' elbows while they write. In fact I don't even see what they write. We talk about it a little and I talk a lot about Nabokov, Kafka, and Dostoyevsky, all of whom are the people I like to talk about anyway. So I'm rather happy with myself.

Is it true that you were a mod and then a hippie during the 60s and 70s?
I was a mod but that all ended after my fifth scooter crash. And then, yes, I was a rather opportunistic hippie. All that free love and music sounded fun, but I was never particularly pious. Mod was more about having the right pink socks on the right day anyway. The hippie thing was a coherent idea, but there was a very dark side to it. Like John Updike said, it was a "fascinating dark carnival." All this optimism with a dark underbelly where, if you rooted around in it long enough, you'd find Charles Manson. ∎

JESSE PEARSON

HARRY CREWS

Portrait by Tara Sinn, with a photo by John Zeuli Photography

Harry Crews is one of the most original and important living American novelists there is. He was born the son of sharecroppers in Georgia in 1935. He served as a marine during the Korean War and since then he's had just about every job a man might have to take in his lifetime—from working in a cigar factory all the way up (or maybe down) to teaching creative writing.

His books are bitterly funny and expertly observed shots of fiction taken straight out of his own life. He can outfight, outfuck, outwrite, and outthink anyone from the entire generation of little boys that came after him, and he's still kicking today. Harry is down there right now in his secret hideout in Florida as you read this, and he's working away on a new novel. He says it might be his last because he's sick. But we don't know. There might never have been a human being who combines smart and tough as perfectly as Harry Crews does, and we wouldn't be surprised if he's still cranking out his amazing books when we're all old and gray too.

Vice: Hey Harry. Is this still a good time to talk?
Harry Crews: We're supposed to do this now?

I think we said that I would just give you a try on the phone today and see what happened.
Morphine will fuck up whatever memory you may have left. I take it every four hours around the goddamned clock. So I know we said Friday afternoon but I thought we said one or two and, hell, it's after three now. It doesn't matter except, I don't know if I told you or not, but I'm trying to finish one last novel. If God will give me this one, I'll quit. But I didn't leave it alone. I started working very early today and—listen, are you sure this is worth your fucking time?

Definitely. I just don't want to climb up your ass.
You aren't climbing up my ass, man. If you were bothering me I'd tell you. Last time we talked you said something like, "If I were where you are, last thing in the world I'd be worrying about was whether or not to give a fucking interview."

Right.
Well, I am worried about it and the reason I am is because I told you I would. You'll find this out—when you get as old as I am, about the only goddamned thing you'll have left is your word. If I tell somebody I'm gonna do something, by God I do it if I possibly can. And I don't mind doing it. Truth is, I've probably given more fuckin' interviews than I should have. Do you know a book called *Getting Naked With Harry Crews*?

I've looked at it. That's the compilation of interviews with you, right?
What some dipshit college professor did was call me and ask me if it would be all right for him to find all the interviews I'd given and publish them. I said, "I don't give a shit, man. Do it if you want to." It's a hardback book and it's about four inches thick or something.

And it's every interview you'd ever given up to that point.
Yeah, and some of them aren't too shabby. I didn't read the book but I looked in it. And then some of them I was drunk as a skunk or fucked up on dope or otherwise non-copacetic. And they aren't worth a damn and they certainly shouldn't be in a book—but they are.

But I don't know, I like to talk about writing and I like to talk about books and I like to talk about all that stuff. I mean, such as it's been, it's been my life.

Your enthusiasm for all that hasn't diminished as you've gotten older?
No. Hell no. I'm so fucking in love with it. I thank God I got this book to work on. That, and a girl named Melissa who not long ago was a gymnast at Auburn University in Alabama. She is an Alabama girl. And, well, you know what a gymnast looks like. Goddamn, she is just extravagantly beautiful with a body that will stop your fucking heart.

And she's hanging out with you down there?
Oh, she'll be here in about an hour and a half and spend the weekend with me.

That's good news.
You're telling me? It's wonderful. And she's gonna cook lobster tonight and it's gonna be a good thing. She's a great lady, man. Like I say, she's real nice to look at. And she's enthusiastic about all things good. I dig her a lot.

Did she know your books before she met you?
Yeah, she knew, but it was kind of strange how we got hooked up. After I'd been around her for like four or five hours, she looked at me and said, "You're not the guy that writes the books, are you?" I said, "Well, yes, I've written some shit." As soon as she put it together, she read some of my stuff. But thank God that ain't why she likes me.

You probably have some scary fans.
My phone number is in the book but my address is not in there because strange assholes show up at your door. A lot of them are young people who don't quite know what they're looking for, but they want to talk. Most of them want to talk to me or see me for all the wrong reasons. They think if they rub against me or something they'll be able to write.

And you taught writing for some time, right?
Well, thank God the University of Florida gave me this deal that every writer needs. I worked with 10 or 12 graduate students a year. They were just young people who thought they wanted to be fiction writers. By and large, they fell in love with the idea of being a fiction writer and then they were introduced to the slave labor of it and they pretty soon decided, "No, I don't want to do this."

It takes a lot of time, doesn't it?
If you're going to write a book, you don't know what you're looking at. You have to disabuse them of all these ideas they have that they are sure are right but which are almost exclusively, always, all of them, wrong. It's all very boring. But I love my students—the few that turned out to

be writers. There's a boy named Jay Atkinson in Massachusetts. He's now written four books. My students are all around the country. All that shit that's on the, whatever you call it, the internet or something? Google or something? I don't have it on my computer.

That's probably a blessing.
Well, I do have it, but I just don't pull it up. But there's a ton of shit about me on there. There's a boy named Damon Sauve in San Francisco. He's a fine writer. He put all that shit on, I guess it's called a website? I know very little about computers. I just do the best I can and leave all that shit alone. I write in longhand, I write on a typewriter, I write on a computer, I'd write with charcoal if it would make me write better. I don't care what it is as long as it gets the words down. I only want about 500 words a day. Five hundred words a day is just wonderful if you can get that many, but you usually can't—not that you can keep anyway.

Do you write for a certain amount of hours every day?
I don't do the hour thing. I've got a time when I start and I try to get 500 words. That's only two manuscript pages, double spaced. If I can get two pages that'll do it. You'd be surprised what that will turn out if you do it every day of your life.

What can you tell me about the book that you're working on now?
It's called *The Wrong Affair*. I'm fairly confident that I'll be able to finish this before I die. And that'll be just wonderful. It will cap off the work I've done nicely. I like the book an awful lot. But it's out of my life of course.

You mean it's based on real experiences.
Everything I've ever written is. I got a book called *Karate Is a Thing of the Spirit*. I studied karate for 27 years or so. A long, long time. I got a book called *The Hawk Is Dying*. I trapped, trained, and flew hawks. If I haven't done it, I can't write about it. If I haven't been involved in it, smelled it, tasted it, floundered around in it—the subject, that is—I can't write about it. I know there are some guys that can, and do it well. But I'm not one of them.

The memoir you wrote of your childhood was amazing.
I come from a tenant farm in southern Georgia. If the crop failed—tobacco was the money crop—you just about couldn't farm the next year either.

Tenant farming is a sickening system.
Yeah, it means you farm on someone else's land—you're a sharecropper. Then we had to move down to Jacksonville, Florida. My daddy died when I was 21

months old. He died of a heart attack—I never knew him. Ma raised us. She worked at the King Edward Cigar factory. Largest cigar factory under one roof in the world. Huge fuckin' thing. Before I went in the marine corps I worked there for one summer. What a brutal fuckin' job. How my dear old ma stood that all those years I'll never know. She did it because she had to do it. That's why she did it.

Anyway, man, look here. Can you stand the notion of us trying to start this at another time?

Sure, I've got a little time. But we're kind of already doing the interview now.
Hey, I've got a little time too. I'm always here. We've got to work it out so that I haven't just taken the fuckin' dope or I haven't been working all day or some fuckin' thing.

Is there a time of day that's better than another?
I hate to act like it's something special. It's not. It's just a matter of the way my life runs and the things I have to do. I went to the damn doctor yesterday. He's a good guy and I like him but when we got through I said, "This has been a waste of my time and a waste of your time and I'll not be back again, but I love you and wish you well, so take care of yourself." Then I left because, you know, I don't know what he wanted. I guess he wanted to make sure I don't do myself in. He wanted to talk about suicide and shit. I said, "Well, we can talk about suicide if you want to."

Last time we talked on the phone, you told me that you're very ill.
Yeah, I'm really ill. But I don't want to talk about it much. I'm all right.

I guess a lot of great writers have worked while seriously ill.
Flannery O'Connor was dying the whole time she was writing, and I can name a number of other writers who were dying the whole time they were writing. Look, Flannery got to this place where she could only write three hours a day. The doctors told her: You can write three hours a day. You can't write any more. What a shit thing to tell somebody. Goddamn. Anyway, the worst thing for me now is the pain. Pain will humiliate you and humble you and I'm not used to being humiliated and humbled and I don't like it. It offends my notion of who the fuck I am and what I am and everything else. I'd rather do just about anything, up to and including cutting my fuckin' throat.

Speaking of which, you told me about a recent fight you got in. You got sliced up the belly and it left a massive scar.
It's really a beautiful scar. It starts right in my pubes and it goes up through my navel to my sternum, where it is

equidistant between my nipples. I was gutted, man. I had my guts in my hands.

And it happened at a fish camp, you said?
It did indeed.

Kind of ironic, getting gutted at a fish camp.
Well, yes and no. This is a fish camp that's more a sort of drinking and fighting bar that just happens to be on a nice lake where a lot of fish swim. You can get a boat there and you can go out and fish or you can drink beer and shoot pool and fight and fuck and whatever else you can find to do. But it is a great fishing place. Marjorie Kinnan Rawlings's old house, Cross Creek, is not far from where I live. On one side of the road is Orange Lake—10,000 acres of water—and on the other side is Lake Lochloosa, which is 18,000 acres of water. And then there's the creek which runs from Orange to Lochloosa, right across the road near where her house is.

What's in there, catfish?
There's catfish in there, but there's catfish in every body of water around here. These lakes have got great bass, great brim, speck... You got a bunch of good panfish in there. Good bass lake, if you like to fish bass. But the bass get too big. The ones that are good to catch are not very good to eat. A bass that gets very big, it's too gamey. Too fishy. Not very tasty. Little bass are the ones you want to eat, but they aren't very fun to catch because they don't put up a fight. Anyway, whatever.

Yeah, but can you tell me how you ended up getting split open?
I've known this guy for a very long time and there's been bad blood between us. This was not the first fight we've been in with each other. There have been times when he went to the hospital and times when I went to the hospital and this time both of us went to the hospital. And I told about a million lies to keep him out of jail. I don't want the son of a bitch in jail.

What is it with this guy and you?
We're like a couple of fuckin' dogs. I drove up to the fish camp and I thought I could smell the son of a bitch. I said, "Goddamn, I oughta turn right around and go home. That son of a bitch is out here just as sure as I'm alive." And he was. When we lay eyes on each other it's like two goddamn pit-bull dogs looking at each other from their corners, you know? They scratch and go. And there it is.

How long ago was this?
Oh, I haven't been out of the hospital very long. I was in there over a month. I was in ICU. I couldn't talk. I had

a trach tube in and I had to get food and water through a tube too. My son teaches at a university for a bunch of Yankee kids up north, and he came home and that was good. I don't see him as much I'd like to and he's just a great fuckin' kid. He's about six-three, 220, all lean and righteous. Good athlete. He's very bright—writes plays, and they're produced. He's a good writer. I don't know how he got started with plays, but he did. His wife is the head of the drama department at that university. She directs the plays he writes, at least initially, to get the kinks out of them. So they got a thing going and it gives them a life they tell me they love, and I don't doubt it. But he rarely gets home.

But he came back when you got hurt.
He stayed by my bed forever. I was in there over a month. I was in the ICU for 16 days and then I went to rehab. The surgeon had to sew me up and all that good shit. Now I've been out for about four and a half months. It's a short enough time that the goddamn scar is sore. When you get a really big, wide one... I've never had a scar like this. Now, I've got scars on me all over and I've broken damn near everything you can think of at one time or another, including my neck. At my age, whatever you broke growing up, however you nicked yourself, in that place of course, you're arthritic. And arthritis ain't a fuckin' joke.

It's an evil, evil thing.
It really is. I broke my neck diving off the Main Street bridge in Jacksonville, Florida. It's a really high bridge that boats go under and shit. Nobody had a gun to my head saying I had to dive off that son of a bitch. And the water is deep enough that I shouldn't have been hurt.

Were you drinking or something?
No, no. I was just young. I was with a bunch of other guys and somebody went off it and so I went off it. I just did it wrong. I broke a vertebra in my neck and I had to wear one of those halos. Had to sleep in the son of a bitch.

So now you've got an arthritic neck. That's the kind of stuff that makes me feel terrified of growing old.
You oughta be terrified of growing old! It's a motherfucker. What you've got to do is to just have no respect for it whatsoever. Cuss it a lot and kick and raise hell. Spit and scratch your ass and do all the things you can do when you're an old guy. And don't suck up and suck around when you're an old guy. Fuck it. So you're old, so what else is new?

So don't behave like a senior citizen, basically.
Anger has gotten me through a lot of things in my life. I have to confess—and I don't recommend it really to any-

body else—but hell, I stay mad. Mad as a motherfucker.

And that's just the way you've always been?
Yeah, for one reason or another. If I can't finish a book, I'm mad. If I'm not writing a book, I'm mad. If I am writing a book, I'm mad. It don't matter. I just got a very short fuse. I try to be polite and civil and decent and whatever, but I'm not very good at it. I'm just not.

Did you ever think that anger would go away if you reached some kind of a brass ring, like finishing a certain amount of novels or finding the right woman?
No. All the males in my family are like this. They're like a bunch of goddamn sore-tailed cats. They just walk around looking for pussy and a fight. I was the light heavyweight champion of the first marine division. My nose has been broken I think six times. For a long time I never knew which side of my face it was gonna be on from year to year. But I liked boxing for a long, long time and I like karate and I like blood sports. I like a lot of things that are really not fashionable and really not very nice and which finally, if you've got any sense at all, you know, are totally indefensible. Anybody who is going to defend much of the way I've spent my life is mad. Crazy. It's just that there's so much horseshit in the world. How can you live through it without being madder than hell?

You can set yourself aside from it.
Well, yeah, you can, but getting away from the world means getting away from bars, getting away from women, getting away from all the stuff that's been good in my life. I, curiously, don't drink at all anymore. I haven't had a drink in ten years. Not a drop of anything. But goddamn, I drank my share in my life and I'm not a bit ashamed of it.

I wish I could say the same.
Well, do you regret much of it?

Some, but I also know that it would have gotten way worse if I'd kept going.
Alcohol was good to me and good for me. I swear to God. But I swear on my dead mother's eyes, man—and my dead son's eyes—I ain't had a drop in ten years. I put it down for the very reason you said. I thought, Well man, this is gonna get really sloppy and really bad if you go on with it. You're just not strong enough to do this anymore so you've got to put it down. I was thinking yesterday about Hemingway killing himself. Did you know the things that were wrong with Hemingway when he shot himself?

I read a biography of him, but it was a long time ago.
You know how he drank all his life. He drank like a

European drinks. Sometimes he drank wine for fuckin' breakfast, and usually at lunch and dinner he drank a bottle of fuckin' wine. He drank, period. A lot, his whole life.

Right.
And then he went down there to that clinic, that psychiatric clinic, and they told him he could have one eight-ounce glass of wine a day, all right. He weighed about 220, 225, his whole fuckin' life, and they told him he had to go down to 180 pounds. So he couldn't eat the way he did. There was something wrong with his ejaculatory duct, whatever the fuck that is, so he couldn't have conjugal relations with Miss Mary anymore. So check that one off—he couldn't fuck anymore. So now we got a guy that can't eat, can't drink, can't fuck... and whether or not he could write then, he thought he couldn't. He tried and it made him sick—he just couldn't stand what came out of his pen. Sixty-two fuckin' years old and he puts what was called an English bulldog—it's a short double-barreled shotgun—in his friggin' mouth and that was the end of him.

Because he had too much taken away from him.
Well, I don't know, man. He just got mad enough with it. But there's a number of things you can do. Something with your ejaculatory duct and you can't fuck? Well, who says I can't fuck? I'll find another way to get off. Damn, do something. You say I can't drink anymore—the hell I can't. I might die, but I can drink. Listen, if I can't have but one glass of wine, I don't want any at all.

There's no point in getting part of the way there.
And it was the Mayo Clinic, that's where it was. And while he was up there those fucking shrinks would take him home on the weekend and have a cookout in the backyard and invite all their shrink friends over and show him off. "Look who we've got as a houseguest—Hemingway. Look at this." And he was just old—well, not old, 62—but he was hurt and confused. It was terrible. Just awful.

Maybe he did the right thing at the end then.
Maybe so, man. I don't know.

Why do so many writers end up being drunks?
I've thought about it a lot, and I don't know.

People seem to think it goes hand in hand with the solitary life a writer needs to lead to get their work done.
Well, that may be true. I don't know what it is, but it would seem to be a true thing. Alcohol is the writer's friend or enemy or something, and they do a lot of it. ■

AMY KELLNER

LYNDA BARRY

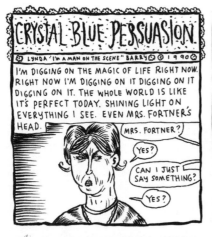

From My Perfect Life *(HarperCollins, 1992)*

If you were ever a weird kid or a sad kid, you have to read Lynda Barry's comics and novels immediately because they will freak you out with how much you'll relate. It's embarrassing how many of her comics have made us get all emotional, even the funny ones. They're like repressed memories of childhood coming to the surface in cartoon form and going "Holy shit."

And then there's *Cruddy*. *Cruddy* is the novel where you're either with us or against us. It is the dark, and we mean daaaaark, tale of a teenage girl who meets a bunch of freaky kids, does acid with them, and then recounts her experience of going on a crime and murder spree with her insane dad when she was 11. It's gory and nightmarish but also unexpectedly kooky. And it's beautifully written in this signature language that Barry has that is so perfect, it kills us. Oh, and she wrote the whole novel by hand! Man.

So basically Lynda is our #1 hero. We're excited because Drawn & Quarterly is putting out a gorgeous five-volume hardcover reprint collection of all her *Ernie Pook's Comeek* strips. Yay! And if she ever brings her Writing the Unthinkable workshop to New York (please!), we are very there. We're sorry to hear about her turbine problems though. We officially hate turbines now. Down with turbines!

Vice: You. Are. Amazing.
Lynda Barry: Thanks, but I'm not feeling very amazing at all. Ever since I found out an industrial wind farm is being planned for right beside our place—67 turbines, each standing 40 stories tall, 1,000 feet from our door. We're looking at losing everything we've worked for—maybe having to move and start over. I'll try not to mention it again, but if you would like to know more about a whole other side of "wind energy" you can visit the website I run for our community. It's at betterplan.squarespace.com. I do want people to know these machines are not benign. They bring a lot of misery to those who are forced to live among them.

I'm sorry to hear that. But you're still amazing. Which of your characters do you most identify with? Are you Marlys or Maybonne or Arna or Freddy or bits and pieces of all of them? Do you have a favorite?
I dig them all, completely! Even Arnold, the very straight brother of Arna. They all appeared at once in one comic strip called "The Night We All Got Sick" in the mid-1980s. I had no idea they would stay with me for so long. I relate to all of them and I'm always glad to have them come out of my brush or my pen because it's the only way I get to see them. I never know what they are going to do or say because I don't plan anything out before I start a strip. It's kind of the way kids don't have to plan everything out before they start playing with hand puppets. You just start wiggling the puppets and the story comes. I wiggle a pen or a brush but it's the same thing.

Can you tell me what a typical day in your life is like? Do you write and draw every day?
Well, there was life before the turbines and life after the turbines. My life now is nonstop work on helping our community and other communities in Wisconsin get the word out that 1,000 feet from a home is just too close for these machines. I'm working to get setbacks of at least 2,640 feet. The wind developers are livid about this because it cuts into their profits, but it gives people some chance to stay in their homes. The main problem with the turbines is the noise they make at night. But enough about turbines.

Before the turbines I had a very happy, hardworking life that actually makes me cry when I remember it. I liked getting up at dawn or just a little before dawn, and going to my studio, which is an old grain barn about 500 feet from our house. I did work every single day, but to me it was a joy. It's like asking a kid if they really played every single day. I did. I painted and read and wrote every day. It was my job, the beautiful job I always dreamed of. I can hardly stand to think about it. I don't get to do any of that now. I try to find some time to make a few pictures or write a bit but my head is too worried about our future to work very well. We put all our savings into our farm. My husband, Kevin, has a small native-plant nursery and he does prairie-restoration work. We heat with wood and cook with wood and grow a lot of our own food. We don't have a dryer and we hang our clothes outside all year round on our covered porch. I can't believe we're going to lose it all but it's looking that way.

I'm really sorry. Writing in a barn sounds great.
It's a small barn with a wraparound porch my husband and my neighbor built. It has a tin roof and a lot of windows and a wooden ceiling and it's filled with books and art supplies. Before I start to write I always read something—I'm still trying to keep that up every day before I start my AT (After Turbines) work. I either read poems—Emily Dickinson is a favorite—or philosophy—Zhuang-zhi, who is considered to be the kind of far-out Lao Tsu—or one of Shunryu Suzuki's wonderful Zen talks. I like to read something that shifts my mind from the hamster wheel that it can become otherwise. BT (Before Turbines), I would grind my ink on my inkstone and paint out the alphabet slowly on legal paper. Sometime during that painting of the alphabet I'd get a feeling about something to make. If it felt like writing then I'd work on my novel—writing it with a paintbrush. Slower writing is better for me. Better for my ideas. The novel is in an overflowing laundry basket on the floor of my studio right now. I miss it so much. If the feeling I had while writing the alphabet was more toward drawings or collage I would work on those. If there was no particular feeling I'd keep on writing the alphabet and moving my brush around the page in an unplanned way. Something always came up to meet me from this activity. There weren't many bad days.

What is the best thing about living on a dairy farm in rural Wisconsin? What is the worst thing?
We have an old oak grove behind the barn—with trees dating from before the Civil War. We have a lot of birds. I love birds. I can't believe how many kinds there are. The barn swallows build their nests in the barn. Kevin has done a lot of restoration to the land here so the plants that support the native populations of insects and animals are here, and the birds seem especially happy.

I love my community too. It's good having friends who farm. It's good to know the names of their cows and the calves that come in the spring. It's fun to see the new ones when I head up to get eggs from my neighbor. It's good knowing they would be here in a minute for us anytime day or night, and it's good knowing they can count on us the same way. We have a 1958 Ford tractor that I love. We have silos and a barn that has been here 100 years. The original house burned down years before we got here. Our house is a little tract house—nothing much at all. But we put on a tin roof and a covered porch and built a masonry bread oven. We have a big garden—man, I'm starting to cry here. It's not the prettiest farm at all, but it's the best place I've ever lived in my life.

Wow. Do you bother watching TV at all? What do you like to do for fun?

I love TV. When we moved to our farm Kevin asked that we not get a satellite dish and that we make do with local reception. At first I couldn't even consider it. But it's been very good for me to have an actual limit on what I can watch. Our reception is horrible. We hardly get a channel clearly. And pretty soon when the analog signal is gone we'll get nothing at all, and I'm ready for that step. But I love TV! My favorite shows are *Wife Swap* and *Super Nanny*. I'll miss those the most. When I travel I have a hard time leaving a hotel room that has cable.

What I like to do for fun is draw, write, garden, and visit the historical society in Footville—the closest town. It's packed with scrapbooks and diaries from people in our area. It's in a tiny old bank and smells like the best library. I call it the time machine. The woman in charge of it, Kay Demrow, is 72. I love her. She has devoted her life to organizing and transcribing thousands and thousands of handwritten documents.

Can you tell us about how your most recent book, *What It Is*, came about?

What It Is is based on a writing class I teach called Writing the Unthinkable. I'd been wanting to make a book version of the class for a while but couldn't figure out how to do it. I didn't want it to be just text instructions or texts of ideas about how to write. I wanted handwriting to be a big part of it and I wanted to make people just itch to make something. To me, writing or painting or collage are not different at all. They are like different hand puppets—but the living part of them is something I call "the image" because my teacher, Marilyn Frasca, called it that when I studied with her in college in the 70s. I was able to work with her for two years straight and everything I've done since is connected to what she taught me. My class is based on it, and the book is dedicated to her, and in a way all of my work is dedi-

cated to her. She gave me something that has shaped my entire life and made me want to find a way to show it to other people.

I love teaching my class. Actually it's been the one thing untouched by the turbines. When I leave here to go teach a workshop in Chicago or San Francisco I am free of worry and I am always elated by being in a room with students who are working hard. When I was little I wanted to be a teacher but never thought I could do it because I'm a terrible speller. I'm so happy to have found a way to manage it anyway.

Did you know that *Cruddy* is in our top five all-time desert island books? What would yours be?

I'm so glad to hear that! I adored writing *Cruddy*. It was the best time. I was having just as good of a time writing the novel I'm working on too—I could really feel it moving. I miss it as badly as I miss a person I love. But anyway, my desert island books are: a complete anthology of Dr. Seuss, D. W. Winnicott's *Playing and Reality*, the complete poems of Emily Dickinson, the whole George Smiley series by John le Carré, and an anthology of talks given by Shunryu Suzuki.

Is it true you wrote *Cruddy* entirely by hand, in cursive?

I wrote it with a paintbrush on legal paper. I don't think it would have happened any other way. I came to that way of working because I had been trying to write a novel on my computer but the problem was that dang delete button. You can get rid of something before you even know what it is. Also there is all the difference in the world between tapping a finger to make an "a" and drawing the letter "a." For me at least, it's the movement of my hand that makes a story come to me. After ten years of trying to write a novel on a computer in the way I thought novels were written, I gave up. I remember walking around my workspace saying "OK! OK! If I were doing this, how would I do it?" And I realized that all I needed to do was do what I did when I made a painting or a comic strip. That meant slowly and by hand. It seems like writing a novel with a paintbrush would take a long time but I finished the first draft in nine months. I had the best time working on it. The story was so alive and unexpected. It seems like slowing way down is no way to write a story but it made *Cruddy* the way it is.

The weirdest thing about that book is the day I finished it, the book really ended. I never saw Roberta or any of the other characters again. I think of them, but they don't think back to me the way they did when I was working on it. I was really lonely for them until the new book showed up. Now I think to the characters in it and they think back. It's been especially hard not to work on it. I believe I will again after this turbine stuff is settled. I feel a real longing to be with the characters inside of it. To see what they are up to, and what happens. I love the not-knowing part, and at the same time having the feeling that they know, the characters know, they just have to move my hand on the page like a Ouija board for a while to tell me.

You have such a cool way of writing dialogue for your characters, especially for kids. The weird phrasings and grammatical strangeness is like a whole other language.
The language comes from handwriting. It really comes from the motion of the hand. Like a hand puppet—you start moving its mouth with your fingers and you look into its eyes and you get the feeling it is saying something and the it that is doing the saying is a little bit different than you. Different puppets have different ways of talking. My characters are like that. I crack up when I hear the next sentence they say. They make me laugh really hard sometimes. I know it's me! But it's also not me. The best part of this is there is nothing magical about it at all. Human beings have been doing it for a very long time and we all seem to be able to do it. Once I saw two guys do a scene from *Romeo and Juliet* using garbage they had just found in the street. It was at one of those freaky Renaissance fairs and I was not finding the groove of the situation at all until these two young men picked up a bottle cap and cigarette butt and did Romeo and Juliet's balcony scene with them, and I stared at that cigarette butt and bottle cap like they were actually talking. It was mind opening.

In your book, one of the writing exercises you describe is using specific words or phrases like "car" or "other people's mothers" to bring up memories that can then be described in detail and begin to tell a story. So, can you tell us a quick, short story about, I don't know… "haircut" or "mosquitoes"?
I could if I had more time. I'd have to do it by hand and I know that my head won't go there today with all the turbine stuff hanging over me. But you should come to my class and I'll show you how to do it. It's a lot of fun! You can find out information about the class on MySpace—do a search on "writingtheunthinkable."

OK, well, at least please tell us about some of your upcoming projects so that we can have something in life to look forward to.
My novel! I want to say the name of it but I can't until it's done. And the great singer Kelly Hogan and I are working together to get the writing workshops going in different areas. And I really, really want to write a musical with her because she is a genius and hilarious and also serious and deep. I don't want to die before I do that. And more paintings and more comics. But for now I'm in the army, fighting irresponsibly sited turbines. I've been drafted and I have to give it my best.

Do you like teaching?
I adore it!

What kind of stuff happens in the workshop?
Spontaneous and surprising story writing. It's a hard class to describe but it's pretty intense and also very anonymous. We don't introduce ourselves, and we don't discuss the work at all. It's not a social situation, but it's pretty fun anyway. I try to make it so that any student can be as involved or as uninvolved as they want. The writing method I teach is really specific so we're basically just working on learning the method part of it so that people will be able to do it when they get home. A lot of what we do is in the activity section of *What It Is*.

Do you think people can really be taught how to write?
I don't think anyone needs to be taught how to write. They just need to be reminded that they already know how to tell stories in the same way they know how to use their thumbs and fingers. The class is about what people already know how to do but most have abandoned, kind of like the way I abandoned my best ways of working to try to write a book on a computer.

What is your favorite animal?
I love dogs. Also birds. Also cephalopods. And fungus.

Have you ever had a vision or seen a ghost?
I have a vivid memory of seeing a ghost when I was about five. I can still see it. It was at the top of the stairs of a house we just moved to. It was just a shape that moved kind of like the northern lights move. A weird glow-in-the-dark ripple. I remember backing down the stairs and going back to bed and freaking out. Luckily I was sleeping in a bedroom with about 15 of my cousins and my grandma so I wasn't alone. I still don't know what it was or even if it was. It's just an odd vivid memory. I also met a drag-queen psychic in the Philippines who told me my boyfriend and my best friend were in bed together at that very moment. He turned out to be right. I think he was a slightly mean drag-queen psychic because he was laughing when he told me. He was kind of a catty psychic. I'm not sure about psychics.

Can you tell me the key to eternal happiness? I have a feeling you know it.
I do! The key to eternal happiness is low overhead and no debt. The key to temporary happiness for me at least is no turbines. Solar power and manure digesters will be mentioned in my next letter to Santa. ∎

KATIA JARJOURA

OUR HERO

Robert Fisk Is a Journalistic God

Photo by Katia Jarjoura

Best-selling author and British journalist Robert Fisk has lived in Beirut for the past three decades. He is the Middle East correspondent for *The Independent* and holds more British and international journalism awards than any other foreign correspondent. He has covered every major event in the region including the Algerian civil war, the Iranian Revolution, the American hostage crisis in Beirut, the Iran-Iraq war, the Russian invasion of Afghanistan, and the American invasion of Iraq.

His most recent book, *The Great War for Civilization*, is a 1,300-page epic eyewitness account of Middle Eastern history, and a best seller in the UK. It's been translated into eight languages.

In short, there aren't many better guys than Robert Fisk to talk to at a time like, oh, right fucking now.

Vice: Has reporting changed a lot since you started 30 years ago?
Robert Fisk: Oh yes! Hugely. Technologically, we had no mobiles, no satellite dishes; we had to write on telex machines. I still have one at home. I even did a two-year course in Dublin on how to repair telex machines. Later, I was in Kabul in 1980 during the Soviet invasion of Afghanistan and my type machine wouldn't print the letter *a*. I could repair it and I was still able to send my report on time. Years later, in 1993, I went to Bosnia and I was trying to send a piece by satellite but a signal on my computer just kept saying: "Total disk failure." I didn't know how to repair that!

And how has this change affected journalism?
In my sense, the bigger and more sophisticated the machine became, the weaker journalism became politically. Journalists are no longer independent. They have the technical abilities to do their work, but they are bound to the multinational corporations who back them financially. They also have to deal with local institutions in order to be able to broadcast on foreign grounds. For example, during the Balkans conflict, TV crews had to make a deal with the Serbian government in order to bring their communication systems into the area. Ultimately, this type of agreement influences the truth. If you agree to "cooperate," you lose your freedom to report both sides of the story accurately. Reporting has become garbage because there is no more street-reporting like what a few of us did the first day we went up to Tripoli: watch a real gun street

battle in the heart of the city, without being bothered by the security forces.

Have you mostly been welcomed by the local people in the countries you've covered?
Yes, I've been welcomed because people in the Middle East have an open view of foreigners. It's a Muslim tradition. I have been in the poorest part of Pakistan where they've never seen a Westerner before and their first reaction was to bring me into their house and offer me coffee. People there today are less trusting of foreigners and more frightened because of the "war on terror"—a phrase that I hate—but not with me, especially if they know my name. They treat me really carefully and with great courtesy. I went to Tripoli recently and people recognized me because their children read my articles on the internet and they trusted my views.

Has the Middle East become a more dangerous place for reporters?
Absolutely, 120 percent. You cannot travel freely anymore as a reporter in Afghanistan, Iraq, Pakistan, the Palestinian occupied territories, and many other places. I can recall when, according to my own experience, journalists lost their immunity. It was in Lebanon, in 1983, during the civil war. American warships were shelling the Chouf Mountains. I was with Terry Anderson in a car and we were stopped at a Palestinian checkpoint. When Terry showed his press card, the gunman threw it on the ground. He didn't care that we were journalists. I remember picking it up and looking at Terry. His eyes were saying: "We lost our protection." Within 12 months, Terry was taken hostage by the Shia militias and kept for seven years.

Today, reporting in the Middle East is all about racial differences and the war against the West. When I go to Afghanistan, with my fair skin and blue eyes, it's impossible to hide who I am and where I come from. But if you never take risks, you'll get nowhere. One day, during the first Gulf War, I said to a young Irish reporter who was asking me if she should go or not, "You are not going to die! You are going to report." Of course, some journalists do die, but so few of them. The people who live in war-torn countries, they are in danger. They die by the thousands.

You were badly wounded in Afghanistan. How did it happen?
It was in November 2001. I was on my way to Kandahar and my car broke down in a village near the Pakistani border. There happened to be a bunch of people there who had just fled Kandahar the night before because of a B-52 air strike. Many of them had lost family members in the shelling. They were bitterly furious. When they saw this Westerner—me—a little boy said, "Is this George Bush?" and a group of children started throwing small stones at me. I was with a colleague. On the other side of the road, we saw a bus. The driver signaled us to get in, which my colleague did. But before I could get on, the kids grabbed my satchel and pulled me out. They started banging my face and head with stones. I really thought I was about to die. I remember thinking, "How long does it take to die?" When I recall the smell of my blood falling down my face, I think about that quote from Lady Macbeth: "Who would have thought the old man had so much blood in him." I came close to fainting, but then I remembered what a Lebanese man had told me during their civil war: "If you're in danger, the worst thing you can do is nothing!" So I defended myself. I started punching. Finally, an imam pulled me from the crowd, took me by the arm, and led me to safety.

You've been to Iraq may times after the fall of Saddam. Haven't you ever been afraid of being kidnapped?
Of course. We all have the nightmare of seeing ourselves on TV wearing an orange jumpsuit, with a knife held to our throat. But when you're doing a story, you can't sit at the hotel and use a mobile phone. You have to get out on the streets and see it with your own eyes. Another *Independent* correspondent, Patrick Cockburn, is in Iraq now. He takes the risks needed to cover the story. I should be going back to Iraq soon.

So the fear is there, but you still get out in the field.
Yes, but sometimes I imagine Tony Blair watching a videotape of me begging him to withdraw the British troops from Iraq or else I will be beheaded. What would he say? "Hum... poor old boy." After all I wrote about him, I guess he wouldn't move a finger to save me!

You're probably quite lucky to still be alive.
When my second book came out, my editor bought me champagne—not to celebrate the book launch, but to celebrate that I survived. And I have been lucky. I remember the Battle of Fish Lake during the Iran-Iraq war in the 1980s. I was on the Iranian side. The Iraqis were shelling heavily. I remember a British journalist who was there saying, "I don't think I could take more than a day of this." When we got to the end of the dike, a revolutionary guard took me up to the front line and I could see the lights of the Sheraton hotel in Basra on the other side. The bullets were flying like wasps, but at a time like that I find you lose your fear of death because you're too close to it.

So why is it so important to take such risks and to report from war zones?
For the sake of history but also so that people in the

future will never be able to say, as they did with the Holocaust, "We didn't know. No one told us." We write about the Middle East simply so that people will know what happens here.

In your view, what is the biggest threat in the area today?
Pakistan.

Wow, you didn't even hesitate for a second there.
We are told that the biggest threat is Iran, but it's rubbish. The story of Iran's nuclear crisis isn't what you'd expect. Originally the Shah of Iran, who was like our policeman in the Gulf—our friend—wanted nuclear facilities. We practically gave them to him. The nuclear facility at Busher was built by Siemens, a German company. The Shah even went to New York and gave an interview to CBS or ABC, I can't remember, where he said, "I want a bomb because the Americans and the Soviets have one." President Jimmy Carter welcomed him. There was no problem. Then later on, during the Islamic Revolution, I was in Tehran when the Ayatollah Khomeini said, "Nuclear facilities are the work of the devil." He used the word *sheitan*, meaning "devil," and he said, "We are closing them down." And he did. In 1985, when Saddam was swamping Iran with chemical weapons that had been given to him by the U.S., the Iranians said that they would have to reopen the nuclear facilities because they were afraid that next time, Saddam would use atomic bombs against them.

Anyway, I think that Pakistan is a much greater threat to the West than any other country in this region.

I'm almost afraid to ask this, but why?
Because it's a Muslim country packed with Taliban and al-Qaeda supporters, because it has a nuclear bomb and a dictatorship which could be overthrown at any time, and because it has security services which I believe substantially support the Taliban and al-Qaeda. At the moment, Pakistan's dictator, General Pervez Musharaf, is our friend, so there's no problem with Pakistan. It's on our side. Iran is the bad guy. This is what my colleagues in journalism would say. But I say that Pakistan is the danger.

Be sure of one thing though: We will not bomb Pakistan, because it has the bomb. It's the same reason we will not bomb North Korea.

What do you think of as the greatest scoop of your career?
It was in 1996, when Israel bombed the UN compound in Cana, South Lebanon. One hundred and six people were killed, half of whom were children. Israel immediately said it didn't know it was targeting a UN compound, but I proved the opposite. I got a UN video showing an Israeli drone over the camp. The UN officer who gave it to me said, "I give it to you because the children who died in the compound were the same age as my own children." The next day, I flew to London and I asked all the senior editors of my newspaper to watch the videotape of the drone flying over the camp as it was being bombarded. We could even hear a UN officer shouting, "Help! Help! We are being bombarded!" The story made the three front pages of the Monday edition. It was titled "Video Puts Israel in the Dock." I gave dozens of interviews after it went out and we sent the video to all major media outlets.

Does a story stand out for you that was particularly life-changing? Something that transformed you personally?
The Massacre of Sabra and Shatila in September 1982. I spent the whole day, September 18th, climbing over the dead bodies of children, women, men... even horses. My hands smelled like death. That day, I said to myself, "I'm not afraid anymore of being abused or categorized as anti-Semitic or racist or whatever." It didn't matter anymore what people would say. I would face up to anyone who would dare to lie and say that I was anti-Semitic. The Israelis watched the whole massacre and let it happen.

How do you cope with the pressure of your job?
[*Laughing*] I hate the word *cope* and I hate when journalists are asked, "How do you cope? Do you need counseling?" It's rubbish.

Sorry.
The people here who suffer and are killed in air raids— they need help. We don't. We are quite well paid. We can go home in business class if we want.

Let's rephrase it. How do you relax?
I listen to music. I have the entire works of Bach. I read a lot of poetry. I read Shakespeare. I always remember an extraordinary poem that W. H. Auden wrote. I think it was called "Epitaph on a Tyrant." It was obviously written about Stalin but I always thought it applied quite well to Saddam. It reads, "Perfection of a kind is what he was after, / And the poetry he invented was easy to understand; / He knew human folly like the back of his hand, / And was greatly interested in armies and fleets; / When he laughed, respectable senators burst with laughter, / And when he cried the little children died in the streets."

I think you've got to transfer history into art to truly understand it.

Does your job affect your personal life?
I'm afraid that my personal life is called journalism. It doesn't give much room for anything else. ∎

VI
OTHER CULTURAL CONCERNS

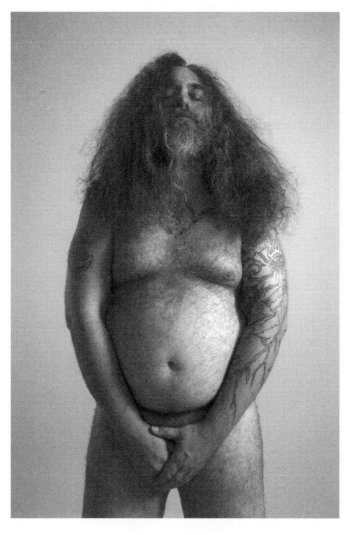

Photo by Richard Kern, V15N10 October 2008

LETTERS GATHERED BY JEFF JOHNSON

WHAT DO YOU HATE?

A Special Letters Extra

Drawing by Jimmy Kimmel

Hello *Vice*,

I detest smoking. I smoked for more than 50 years and finally quit when I had my car accident a few years ago. I was then shocked at how awful everyone smelled when they smoked. In fact, I stopped performing in places that allow smoking and even when I play outdoor concerts, I make sure that no one sitting in the front row is a smoker. It's funny how it never bothered me for so many years and that I insisted on smoking wherever I went. In fact, when the airlines banned smoking, I went to private Lear jets.

GEORGE

George Jones is one of country music's most legendary rabble-rousers.

Dear *Vice*,

I hate it when people throw their cigarette butts in the street. That asinine sense of entitlement is some selfish bullshit and is symbolic of thinking that someone else is respon-

sible for keeping this place a beautiful one to live in. Same goes for gum. Chew it and smoke it all you want, but own your trash. And I hate it when people aren't nice to each other. I shouldn't even say that's what I hate, because I don't hate it. I just really like it when people are nice to each other. And the thing I really love is when people who you expect to be hateful toward each other do the opposite.

Yours,

ANTHONY

Anthony Kiedis is the lead singer for the Chili Peps. His dad first blew weed smoke in his face when he was four.

Vice,

I hate the sun. It is too bright. I hate what it brings out in people. Playing Frisbee, wearing shorts. Terrible.

Best,

FRED

Fred Armisen appears weekly on *Saturday Night Live*.

Dear *Vice*,

I hate sugar, bad food, and rap music with bad lyrics.
Best wishes,
BRIAN

Brian Wilson is the visionary leader of the Beach Boys.

Vice,

I hate people waking me up to ask me what I hate most!
Ahhhhh, fuck it. I hate haters, man. Hatin' ass punks that
wanna be me. Fuckin' bitches.
CHINGY

Chingy's albums provide the soundtrack to many high-school kids' sexual mishaps.

Hi *Vice*,

I hate the color brown. I fucking hate wet socks. I hate
people when they sneeze sitting next to me on airplanes. I
hate the amount of time that I piss away doing nothing. I
hate almost every movie that I have ever made. I hate that
in America the right to vote is taken for granted. And I hate
that having an opinion that might differ from the fucksticks
on Capitol Hill is considered unpatriotic. It's the new
McCarthyism (which I would have hated had I lived in that
time). I hate people who use the words *organic* and *indeed*
in a sentence. I hate shaved poontang (don't get me wrong,
I will tolerate it, but I just hate it). I hate pleated pants. I hate
puking when I'm drunk. I hate when I'm hungover and my
tongue feels furry. I hate clever bumper stickers on cars. I
hate crowds. I hate intolerant people, and I hate people with
too much tolerance. One is full of ignorance, the other is full
of shit. Oh hell, I almost forgot, I really hate pantyhose. And
with the exception of Vladimir Nabokov and Iceberg Slim,
I hate authors who use hundred-dollar words to complete
their two-dollar thoughts. I hate the Santa Ana winds. I
fucking despise West L.A. I hate people who think their religion is the only real truth. I hate anyone who picks a fight
with someone they know they can whip. I hate when people
think by fucking someone smart and talented that they
themselves miraculously become smart and talented as well.
And I hate people who think they are so goddamn smart.
Best,
JOHNNY

Johnny Knoxville is the inventor of *Jackass* and he is in movies.

Dear *Vice*,

I hate mushrooms. They are too slimy.
Sincerely,
DONNA

Donna Shalala was Secretary of Health and Human Services under President Bill Clinton.

Vice,

I hate kids today. When I was young, you'd get a
peanut butter and jelly sandwich and you'd be happy.
Now you've got kids fucking dying because they're aller-
gic to peanuts! Nothing like that existed back then.
PAUL

Paul Bearer sang for Sheer Terror. Now he sings for Joe Coffee.

Dear *Vice*,

I hate Mondays because Mondays mean I can't sleep as
much as I can on Sundays. I love to sleep. Monday is the
start of the working week and I've never been busier. I'm
working on my solo album, which is out next year.
Where's my favorite place to sleep? In my bed in my beautiful house in the South of France.
Love,
SIOUXSIE

Siouxsie Sioux was the first goth chick. She made that whole thing happen.

Hello *Vice*,

I hate dumbness. People have lost their jobs over the
past four years voting for Bush, but they're still going to
vote for him. He's an asshole. Voting against your own
interest is dumb. He's a fuck-up. I got a lot of friends who
are fuck-ups, doesn't mean I want them to be President.
HUNTER

Hunter S. Thompson is the author of many books that you like. He died in 2005.

Dear *Vice*,

I hate when people drag their feet. Walk with a purpose,
that's what my mother always said. Also when people exit
at the front of the bus—that really annoys me. And when
people don't practice umbrella etiquette.
Yours truly,
CHLOË

Chloë Sevigny is an Academy Award-nominated actress and also a professional cool person.

Dear *Vice*,

I hate unctuous Hollywood agents with nuclear families and Blackberry cell phones who screw artists from
their lounge chairs by the pool whilst drinking Sapphires,
reading *Blender,* and fondling their soon-to-be amputated
twin cancer-landing sites.
Truly,
DIAMANDA

Diamanda Galas is a scary singer who influenced everyone from Marilyn Manson to Will Oldham. ■

ALASDAIR HALLY

PILE OF SHIT

Interior Decorating the Garbage

Photos by Shawn Scallen

I fucking hate that magazine *Wallpaper**. Sad yuppies beating off to the impossibility that one day, they too may be rich enough to build a giant chrome sphere on top of a Spanish mountain. It's just like the *Vogue* magazine syndrome, where a bunch of homosexual men decided what women should look like even though nobody wants anyone to look like that, ever. Or the Wire song that goes, "You're a waste of space/ No natural grace…No style no heart/ You don't even start/ To interest me."

What about Blake and Josh's house? They don't buy any magazines or make any money and their place looks like a magical blowjob made of shit.

Vice: Nobody cares about you or your house. You live in Shitsville, Canada, right?
Josh: I like Ottawa. It's close to the woods. You can get out of the city in ten minutes, so it's good for outdoors stuff. Plus, everybody knows each other here and not too many big bands come to play, so it's a really tight community. There's lots of drinking and parties and stupid stuff.

Your house is literally full of shit? What's that cost?
It's kind of impossible to quantify. I've been a pack rat ever since I was a kid. I have never thrown shit out—maybe when it's broken, but sometimes not even then. My parents never had a problem with it either. I used to go to the city dump and scavenge for shit all the time. Once I found two huge bags of those little trophy men. I dragged them home and tried to make a huge trophy man out of all of them.

It seems like there's some kind of method to your madness. Albeit a shitty one.
Thanks, the bathroom is the shark-themed room. I've got the *Jaws* poster and tons of plastic sharks. In the kitchen I have this McDonald's playset where I set up this huge massacre scene. All the McDonald's characters have their hands up and there's this Indian dude killing everyone. Then there's a SWAT team on the roof and all kinds of camera crews. It's like 9/11 at McDonald's. That takes up an entire shelf in the kitchen. Then I've got a rock band scene set up on another shelf in the kitchen there. We also

have a whole display of weird foods—things like cans of peeled lamb tongue and seal meat.

And where'd you get all this shit?
Well, I've lived here for seven years now and a lot of this stuff is from when eBay first started. The rest is from secondhand stores and garage sales. Then whenever my friends are going to throw a bunch of shit out, they just give it to me instead. And, as I said earlier, I've been collecting stuff since I was a kid. You heard me say that, right?

Shit, I didn't. When's all this collecting going to stop?
I think I might be at the point now where I need to take it easy. I just have boxes and boxes of crap that isn't even on display anymore. I've got three or four boxes of *Star Wars* stuff alone. I had to get a roommate when my girlfriend and I broke up recently, so I cleared out a whole room for Blake. It sucked because I'd had a scene set up in there with about 3,000 action figures all fighting each other glued down on some shelves. That's all boxed up now too.

You glue shit down?
I had to start gluing everything down because my dogs were always chewing on stuff and pulling it over. Plus every time I'd get up at night to take a piss or something, I'd bump into a display and have to spend three hours putting it back together.

What other shit do you get up to?
I do effects for movies—like gore and makeup for horror movies. Our last film was called *Jesus Christ Vampire Hunter*. I use latex mostly, but then also a lot of garbage I find on the street, so it's kind of related to the whole house thing. Like I can't walk by and not collect an old vacuum hose that's out in a pile of trash on the sidewalk.

A lot of guitarists are like that, Joe Strummer, B.B. King…There's something about being a musician that makes you want to collect shit.
That's a stupid theory. You based that on what, two guys? ∎

JESSE PEARSON

JUERGEN TELLER DOES WHATEVER HE WANTS

Illustration by Milano Chow

Juergen Teller is, in large part, responsible for everything that you like about photography. He is a member of the holy trinity (along with Terry Richardson and Wolfgang Tillmans) that saved fashion photography from shittiness in the 1990s. Teller, totally unafraid to show humanity, ugliness, harshness, and humor in his photos, leavened the fashion-magazine standard of overblown sets and jacked-up, theatrical prom photos. His commercial work was, when it first appeared, a revelation.

But Teller blazed a trail which, unfortunately, was soon overrun by an unruly mob of jokers with battered Yashica T4 cameras and very little talent, and the mood and look that he and his contemporaries defined started to become a fashion- and portrait-photography cliché. Bright, bright flash? Check. Simple and "real" setting? Check. A general vibe of casual degradation or something like that? Check, check, check.

Teller, along with Richardson and Tillmans, avoided being overrun by their imitators with a novel and hard-to-duplicate strategy: They entered the gallery and museum worlds and became really successful artists. At first, Teller made art out of the weird things he witnessed in the fashion world. His 1999 book *Go-Sees* was a photo parade of casual model castings, taken at his studio's front door in London. On the surface, it was just a bunch of girls. But what it really amounted to was one big portrait of all the different faces of pretty young women thrust into the fucking weird psychological space of making a living off their looks. Some were fun, some were awkward, some were creepy, and some were sublime. As Juergen Teller's

artwork progressed, he started going back into his German heritage and made photos out of it, as attested to by his brilliant recent book *Nürnberg*.

In a seemingly inexhaustible stream of new books, new exhibitions, and good ideas, Teller has become one of the most recognizable art photographers in the world now. And he still does fashion photography when he feels like it. He just makes it into weird and beautiful art at the same time.

Vice: Do you like the fashion industry? I know that's a stupidly broad question, but I really want to know.
Juergen Teller: I do. For me it's very light and fun and exciting. Like, I'm excited about these boots I'm wearing. I can't wear the white, low-top Converse that I wore for 30 years anymore because they were hurting my feet and my lower back as I got older. So I'm wearing heels now. And I'm, like, really excited about it. These boots are transforming me. Suddenly I'm wearing a scarf and a Rolex watch and a jacket.

You're a changed man.
I'm just getting lighter about fashion. It's quite funny. But fashion, you know, it's a huge business. If you have the right attitude and don't take it too seriously, and if you can push the levels of commercialism, it can be fun.

What's the right attitude?
Well, I just want to do what I want to do.

That's pretty good. What kind of clothes do you like to

wear the most? I've seen you a few times and you always have the most perfect worn-in old t-shirts on.

Actually, right now I'm smartening up a bit in my old age. [*laughs*] I'm really into these scarves from this old-fashioned British company called Turnbull and Asser. I have a cashmere scarf on right now. In orange!

Orange. That takes guts.

And I'm also getting into these Martin Margiela boots.

What are they, like motorcycle boots?

No, they're Chelsea boots.

Beatle boots. Those are so British. What did you dress like when you were a teenager?

It hasn't changed much. Back then it was still the washed-out t-shirts. I also wore quite a lot of pajama trousers.

That was like, a look that you wore out into the world?

Yeah. For years. I wore them to New York and everywhere. It sort of made sense at the time! [*laughs*]

As you got more involved in the fashion industry, did you start to appreciate design more? Did you start to pay attention to, I don't know, silhouettes and who was doing what kind of stitching this season or whatever?

I was never interested in that stuff. But I would notice a girl who would be wearing a certain specific thing, and then that would make me interested in watching the girl. You know?

For sure. You would notice the way someone wore something not so much as what they were wearing.

Right.

It seems like there was kind of a radical turn in your artwork around the early 2000s. All of a sudden, you were all over your own photos and you were often naked. And not just naked, but like NAKED... Naked at your father's grave, naked taking a shit in a snowy forest, and so on. These photos are pretty ballsy and people thought they were all kinds of things: Brave, funny...

Stupid!

Yes, stupid too. Why did you start making these photos?

I got mentally—and maybe also physically—tired of photographing all these people, whether it was models or actors or musicians. It's quite draining to get involved in their psyches and work with them. I just thought, "Fucking hell, I can't do it anymore. I should just photograph myself."

Simple as that.

Yes. I think I also wanted to feel what it's like to be photographed—to look at myself the way I'd looked at other people. So I worked myself really hard.

What is it about taking someone's portrait that's draining?

You need to listen to them and analyze them and deal with each person. It can be done in a very short time or it can take a long time, but it's really quite draining to be involved with another human being and to get things out of them. It's also hard when there's vanity involved or when the photograph is really just going to be used to promote their product, like a film or a record.

Right, like a portrait for a magazine of a new band or a young actor...

And they just want to look young and airbrushed. It's not about how they might really look. That can be the most draining thing. But I more or less gave that up.

You're at a level where you can choose and reject assignments with no problem.

Now, when people ask to have their portrait done by me, they pretty much know what they're running into. But if it's a certain type of Hollywood actress asking me to photograph them, I say no. Or they know not to ask me anymore.

Maybe my favorite portrait you've taken is that one of Yves Saint Laurent where he looks really demonic.

He's very fragile looking though. I did a campaign for them ten years ago or so when he was still involved in the company, and I still work for them.

You must get offered a scary amount of commercial and editorial work.

A lot, yeah. Most of it I turn down. Sometimes there is something interesting in an offer, and then I might take it. Like I did Patti Smith for the *Observer*, and I'm traveling to L.A. soon to photograph David Lynch. I'm quite keen to do that.

That's a good one.

Yeah. So I don't really see it as commercial work when I do commercial work. I see it more like... Let's say somebody wants to do an independent film, right? They have to cast actresses and choose locations and all that. So I'm just using this stuff to create my own fantasies and dreams.

As if it were a movie you were putting together.

Like, for the new Marc Jacobs campaigns, I used William Eggleston. He's in his late 60s and he's a friend of mine. He's such a stylish man. I wanted to photograph him for these ads as much as I just wanted to hang out with him.

And he wanted to meet the actress Charlotte Rampling, who was already in the ads I'd been shooting, so we all got together in Paris and she ended up being in the pictures too. So that's what I want to do. I just want to have a nice time, an interesting time.

The new women's campaign is starring...
Dakota Fanning.

What a crazy choice.
She was Marc's choice. I thought it was a really good idea. They had to shrink the clothes down to fit her.

When you're hired by Marc Jacobs to do a campaign, how does the creative process work?
There are always a couple of people we're thinking about who we'd like to use as models. I had wanted to use Charlotte, for example, for quite a while because I know her quite well.

And then the right time came and you did it. But how did it move on from being an ad campaign to being art?
I finished the campaign and then I was like, "Hang on a minute. I don't really have to wear these silver underpants from Marc Jacobs just to shoot her." The campaign I did for Marc with Cindy Sherman was similar. We kept on taking photos after the ads were done.

What's the backstory for the Charlotte Rampling photos?
I thought it would be interesting to do self-portraits with Charlotte. I had no idea what it would be like, but I wanted to try it. And when I first talked to Charlotte about it, she said that she would normally never do any kind of advertising for any fashion client, but because it was me she was really pleased. She found it exciting.

It was more than just a fashion campaign though.
Right. It wasn't just a photo of her wearing some of the clothes and a caption underneath that said, "Marc Jacobs, thank you very much." We went on a journey together instead. I wanted to explore the idea of an intimate relationship between an older woman and me, a 40-year-old guy.

Was it sort of like acting?
Yeah. There were ideas set up, and then we tried them out on Polaroids and then moved on from there. For the book that we did after the campaign, there was a six-month period where I went to Paris on random weekends to shoot more pictures. Then I would go back to London, develop them, and have more ideas for things to do with her. Plus, she was losing weight and I was putting on weight, and I had a beard and then shaved it off.

You both physically changed a lot during it.
We had like five or six sessions. They were all shot in the same hotel, too.

So, to recap: You get to do whatever you want, and the people whose campaigns you do are always happy with the results. It's pretty much utopia.
Nobody else does it. There's no fashion designer who would do what Marc does with me. It's a collaboration all the way through. For instance, it was Marc's idea to use Winona Ryder and I was like, "That's a great idea." It was right when she was busted in an L.A. department store shoplifting Marc Jacobs clothing. That was the perfect moment to use her.

Was it hard to convince William Eggleston to be in a series of fashion ads?
Well, it took me a few days to make that phone call. I was too scared! But when I finally did, he said, "I'll do anything for you."

He's an older photographer who inspired you. Are you aware of your influence on younger photographers?
I can see it, yeah. If it's close to the bone, it's really annoying. When it's like a total rip-off...

You kind of get ripped off a lot.
Yeah. And then you think, "Oh God." But the more it happens, the less you care.

What does a person have to do technically to copy you? How should one go about ripping off Juergen Teller?
[*laughs*] I don't know. It's just the surface of the photo that they're copying anyway. Years ago, I was a bit concerned about it but now I'm kind of over it. I'm so excited about living in my own world that I don't think about getting ripped off.

Right. I mean for your latest book, *Nürnberg*, you went back to Germany, where you're from, and photographed all around a pretty notorious Nazi site. It's so personal but still tells a universal story.
See? Nobody can rip that off. It's my past, my present, and my future. It's very specific to me. Someone can easily rip off a girl lying on the floor naked with a bright flash. Lots of people can do that with no problem.

Are you working on any new books now?
I'm going to do one that's a collection of all the Marc Jacobs ads I've shot. It's been a long time. There are a lot of things people forgot about... Jarvis Cocker, Thurston Moore, Meg White, Lisa Marie. It will be great to see them all together. ∎

ANDY CAPPER

CHRIS CUNNINGHAM

Chris Cunningham is a dark, reclusive genius who lives in an underground cave beneath the Thames. He spends his days rocking back and forth in a creaky old chair while projecting binary code onto the wall and reading the Russian translation of Dante's *Inferno* while Squarepusher records play backward at 78 rpm through speakers made out of space-shuttle rockets. And all the while, he's frowning and sighing.

Pretty much every article I'd ever read about Chris led me to believe that the above would be true. So I was quite relieved when I met him a few years ago that it wasn't. At all.

Instead, the reclusive-ish genius who made the darkest music videos and short films ever is actually one of the giggliest people I know. It's a giggle that reminds you of when you would sit at the back of class and be pissing yourself with laughter at the teacher's speech impediment or at the giant dicks you were drawing in your geography textbook.

For this issue we spoke to Chris about the new photography and films he's been working on and how they relate to two of his favorite topics: British soft porn from the late 1980s and videos of dogs wanking themselves off.

Vice: The main thing we had in common when we met was our appreciation of classic British "top-shelf jazz mags," aka softcore wank books.
Chris Cunningham: Ha ha, yeah. My favorites were always *Razzle* and *Men Only*.

Me too. What is it about them you liked?
I've often tried to figure it out. I think it's the photographic style. It was really unlit and plain. My photographic style is starting to get more and more overtaken by that look. I've just shot Grace Jones for a magazine and the way I shot her is kind of like the way they would shoot the girls in *Razzle*.

Chris made a photo montage/self-portrait to go along with this article. It was influenced by the aesthetics of the Readers' Wives section of Razzle *magazine. This is the only corner of it that isn't horrifying. You can see the rest on viceland.com, though we don't recommend it.*

How? The girls in *Razzle* were usually flashing their tits while eating baked beans by the side of the road.
Ha ha ha, no, I mean I just shot her in a really plain way. I don't think sex should be lit in a complicated way. It should be really plain. The other mags of the time had a lot of expensive lighting but *Razzle* was the opposite.

A lot of other British soft porn was like big-production lighting with girls wearing elaborate silk robes in four-star hotel rooms.
Yeah, I didn't like those ones.

Playboy and Penthouse would have girls shot through soft focus lenses on long exposure with log fires in the background.
The *Razzle* stuff was meat-and-two-veg porn. It was girls next door and secretaries, shot really simply.

And that style of porn is what's come back around again. You have Sasha Grey wearing no makeup and being shot with Contax cameras. And that's how *Penthouse* is doing things now.
Yeah, well, something must have happened to me in the last seven years because it's not something I pay much attention to anymore. And seven years ago I would have felt a lot more comfortable talking to you about it!

There's no thrill in acquiring porno anymore. The days of going to the newsagent, really nervous, aged 14, and pleading with the guy in there to sell it to you are gone.
Absolutely. When I think about it I reckon the things that shocked me most when I was a teenager are the things that were most important in influencing my work.

Like what?
I remember the Readers' Wives section of *Razzle* and it was so shocking to see these horrible-looking women,

with their bodies all mashed up, shot in this plain style. And I took that style of photography to shoot unusual things that you wouldn't ever see in real life. I'm talking about stuff like the *Rubber Johnny* book or the shots I just did of Grace Jones, for example. Actually, I guess that style of photography is like what *Vice* has sometimes. Most of the imagery for my photography book is of that style.

What's the book?
It's a book of my own photography and stills from films, all taken by me over the last ten years really.

Wow. When's it coming out?
I think I've got to get a couple of feature films finished first. There's one I'm working on now that you could loosely describe as a horror. Actually, talking about this reminds me of that scene in *American Werewolf in London* when he changes into the werewolf in the front room. That really shocked me. I think it was because it was shot in a brightly lit, stark front room and he's naked and although there's something really shocking happening in it there's a sexual element to it.

I can definitely remember sexual experiences that have involved brightly lit English front rooms and something really shocking happening in them.
Ha ha ha. I mean it's usually quite shocking for me, the whole experience. I don't know about you. That's just reminded me about one of the most shocking things I saw in my teenage years. It was finding a copy of *Whitehouse* magazine behind the scout hut.

Yeah. *Whitehouse* was really gynecological. It was the first hardcore porn you could get in Britain. I remember walking across a park near my home and finding a bunch of issues somebody had thrown away in a fit of guilt or something. The images were made more shocking by the way they were all drenched by the rain in this public place. They had slugs and stuff crawling in between the pages.
When I first moved to London my front room flooded and it drenched my stack of old *Razzle*s. Ha ha, that reminds me—an old flatmate of mine had a huge stack of porn mags and his tastes were a lot more gynecological than mine. They were almost like snuff. I mean, I didn't like to look at them. Anyway, one day he asked me if I could look after them for him because his girlfriend was coming around. He had a pile of 100 or so and I didn't know where to hide them so I had to spread them out in piles of around 15 all around my room. Well, my own girlfriend came around later but I went out to the shops for a while and when I was gone she

accidentally found a stack underneath the phone table or something.

What happened?
When I got back from the shops she was gone.

No way.
Ha ha ha. She'd totally left. I couldn't get hold of her for days and then when I did I found out what had happened. She'd dropped something on the floor, then gone to pick it up and her hand brushed against a big wodge of these magazines.

Whoops.
I picture her being there and finding them like that scene in *The Shining* where she's going through his papers.

And she's walking out of your front door with terror in her eyes, bawling.
And I'm walking the other way back from the shop, all nonchalant with no idea of what's happening.

Amazing.
Yeah, well, I got dumped over that. I got chucked for a couple of weeks at least but we got back together.

I suppose it's harder and harder to be shocked by anything you could label as "porn" these days because of the way it's so omnipresent. What was the last thing you saw that made an impression on you? Is it that film of the dog wanking itself off that you're always showing people on your phone?
That dog wanking itself off is literally my favorite thing I've seen in the last decade. You wouldn't believe how many times I've watched it. To me, it's like when the monkey throws the bone up in the air in *2001*. In that movie, it symbolizes the monkey moving onto the next stage of evolution or something. I feel the same way about the dog wanking itself off.

What do you like about it so much?
I love the fact that the person filming it is having the same reaction as I do when I watch it.

Which is what?
Ha ha ha. "I can't believe this is happening." I love the way animals have absolutely no dignity about things. The wanking dog is an organism that's completely out of control.

When did you last watch it?
I watched it again last week. I'm hoping people will forget about it actually because I've based a scene in my new film on it. ■

V14N9, SEPTEMBER 2007

JESSE PEARSON

THE FOLLIES OF DOCUMENTARY FILMMAKING

Frederick Wiseman's 20-Year Fight

Photo by Jennifer Smith-Mayo

Frederick Wiseman is probably the best documentary filmmaker there is. He's definitely the purest. But it's very likely you haven't heard of him yet, much less seen his films, even though he's been working at a relentless pace since 1967.

Wiseman's work, until this fall, has been unavailable on DVD or VHS. It has had zero commercial distribution. Your only chance of spotting one of his films would be if you followed your local PBS affiliate's schedule very carefully, and we both know you don't do that. You might have also been able to see one at a museum or film fest, but that would have been rare, like spotting a unicorn walking through the MoMA. So why hasn't Wiseman let his films out to video-rental shops, Netflix, and the like until now? Because he doesn't compromise on anything,

and it took him this long to work out a system through which he could get his films available on a large scale without taking it up the ass financially. Simple as that.

Now that you can see his movies, you should start doing so immediately. A Frederick Wiseman documentary is the most perfect form of immersive reporting. He goes to a place (anything from a mental hospital, to a high school, to an army basic-training camp, to an upscale New York modeling agency, to Central Park) and stays there for anywhere from four to 12 weeks and shoots, and shoots, and shoots. He never interviews anybody. He never appears on camera. The people and the place tell their own stories, and they do it better than anyone else could. These films are the closest you can come to having been somewhere yourself.

Any conversation with Wiseman will almost inevitably

return to *Titicut Follies*, the 1967 documentary he made at Bridgewater, a state mental institution in Massachusetts. It is an incredibly harrowing, moving, and—most surprisingly—entertaining portrait of the inside of a place that nobody was supposed to see. Prisoners are kept naked and abused. Heartless psychiatrists decide the fate of men during blithe staff meetings. An inmate stands on his head in the courtyard and calmly sings, and another one is force-fed—through a tube that goes into his nose and down to his stomach—by a staff member who is pouring liquid mush into the funnel with one hand and smoking a cigarette with the other. You really sometimes cannot believe what you're seeing as you watch *Titicut Follies*.

We recently talked to Frederick Wiseman on the phone from his home base in remotest Maine. He told us, mostly, about the decades-long war of attrition he went through to get his first movie seen.

Vice: Can you tell me how you got interested in documenting institutions?
Frederick Wiseman: When I was doing *Titicut Follies*, which is the first one, it occurred to me that while I was doing it at Bridgewater, I could have done it at a number of other institutions. Out of that came the idea of doing a so-called institutional series. At that point—and I think it's still true to some extent—the kind of subjects I'd been choosing were not subjects that were being picked for documentary films. But the idea of making a movie about one place, from my point of view, was useful because it provided a boundary.

Having clear borders that framed what the film could and couldn't be about was helpful.
The place serves the same function as the lines and net of a tennis court. Whatever happens within the place is suitable for the film and whatever happens outside is for another film. So I tried to pick places that existed for a while, that were up and running, that were thought to be good examples of their kind, and that affected the lives of a lot of people.

That way they would be more rich in things to cover. Were places like hospitals, high schools, and police beats not being covered in documentaries before you did them because filmmakers weren't thinking in broad-enough terms?
I could speculate, but it would be completely hypothetical.

Please, speculate away.
Well, I got started 40 years ago. The first movie I made was in 1966. It was only about 1958 when the technology that allowed you to shoot handheld sync-sound movies was developed. So when I got started, there weren't that

many films where people were using that technique. And because the technique was new, there were many different aspects of contemporary life that weren't explored with it yet. There still are today.

But early on, after 1958, people who were making sync documentaries were mostly following people, either politicians or criminals or both. The idea I had was to make the place the star rather than one person. So the film is about the people at the place.

What do you say to someone before you start rolling film on them?
I'm pretty straightforward. Ethically, that's the only way to be, but it's also the best thing to do tactically. I don't want to put myself in a position where after a film is made, someone can say, "You lied to me about what you were going to do." So, in the beginning, I say some version of this: "I'm going to make a documentary film. Nothing in the film will be staged. I want to be around for four to eight weeks. During that time, 80 to 110 hours of film will be shot. I don't know what the themes of the film will be until I edit it. All I am doing now is collecting material. If anybody doesn't want to be photographed, all they have to do is indicate that and there will be no debate about it. I discover the film in the course of the editing. The final film will be shown on PBS and distributed in different formats."

It must be hard to do that in the midst of some of the chaotic scenes you're shooting.
Often it's not possible to ask permission before the sequence is shot. You can't say, "Hey, doc, wait a second before you fix that man's broken leg. I want to tell you what I'm doing." I shoot till it's over and then I say, if the people don't already know, what I just said to you. I ask if it's all right to use the material, and I tape record my explanation and their response. In my experience, it's extremely rare that anybody ever says no.

Why do you think that is?
Again, I would only be able to speculate. But I think that people are pleased that you're interested in them and that their picture is being taken and their voice is being recorded. You can't underestimate vanity as a reason.

Even when their activities are unsavory?
That's a complicated question. I think most of us feel that what we do is OK. We don't necessarily see what we do in the same way that somebody else does. That's often the case. If we thought we were being cruel or hypocritical or sadistic or whatever, presumably we wouldn't do it. All of us are unconscious of the impact or the effect or the ambiguity of what we're saying and doing.

Do you feel like you've gotten a lot of insight into human psychology and human nature while making your films?
I wouldn't reduce it to lessons, but anybody—not just a documentary filmmaker—whose experience brings them in contact with a lot of people learns a lot about human nature. Or maybe they just deceive themselves into thinking they've learned a lot about human nature.

What do you do when somebody starts getting too performative or unnatural when you're shooting them?
If I actually think they're performing for me, I stop.

You just walk away?
Yes. It happens sufficiently rarely as to not be a problem. Again, that's something that's rooted in nonfilm experience. As a journalist, if you think someone is bullshitting you, you make some adjustment to that in your reaction to whoever you're talking to.

The presence of a filmmaker is unusual, but not as unusual as the presence of an interviewer or someone who's intervening in the situation. That's more artificial. I think it's true that the events you see in my movies would have taken place if the movie had not been made. That's not true of an interview movie or a print interview. Those things are done specifically for a particular event.

Do you never feel the urge to ask questions?
Well, I sometimes do, but I don't do it—at least not on film. In order to try and inform myself about what's going on in a place, I'll often ask questions, but not about a specific event. I might want to know when the weekly staff meeting is or who sets the agenda, who are the people at the place who are thought to exercise the most power. I spend a lot of time on those sorts of questions.

Watching your films takes me through a huge range of reactions, from amusement to disgust and back again. But at some point in all of them, I have to wonder about you and what it was like to be there. For instance, the scene where they put a feeding tube down an inmate's nose and feed him through it in *Titicut Follies*. What's it like for you when things get that intense?
There's a variety of things going on. I'm probably thinking it's a good scene and I want to do whatever I can to make sure I have it. Second of all, there's a corner of my mind that's amazed that people can treat other people this way. It's hard to reconstruct the way it feels now. When you're in the midst of it, it's hard to go beyond thinking, well, this is a great scene. And that's just because you're busy. It's different when you're in the editing room and you have the opportunity to try and reflect on it. The editing is a much more analytical situation. You have to identify to yourself what you think is going on, and you can

run it backward and forward and upside down and sideways as many times as you want.

Titicut Follies is legendary. It was banned and suppressed in various ways. Can you tell me about that?
The movie was completely banned for about six or seven years. It came out in the fall of '67, and almost immediately after it appeared there was an injunction, and then a trial.

I made the film with the permission of all the relevant authorities. You can't make a film in a maximum-security prison without being accompanied. When the film was finished, I showed it to the superintendent and to a man named Elliot Richardson who, when I got permission to make the film, had been lieutenant governor supervising Bridgewater and the other prisons. When the film was finished, he was attorney general of Massachusetts.

That name sounds familiar...
He went on to great fame when he was both attorney general and secretary of state under Nixon for a short period of time. He quit over Watergate. Anyway, I showed it to the superintendent and he liked it. I showed it to Richardson and he liked it.

That's really surprising.
It amazed me that they let me in to shoot there in the first place.

Did they really think that the conditions there were presentable to the outside world?
Well, the superintendent was my buddy—in a professional sense. I had known him because I had taught law for a few years and I used to take students on field trips to mental hospitals and prisons. It was out of that experience that I had the idea to do *Titicut Follies*. So I had met the superintendent when I was making arrangements to bring the students to Bridgewater, and when I thought of making a movie there, I approached him. He became my advocate within the penal system. He guided me around the politics of getting permission. Even with his help, it took around a year and a half to get the OK.

Why could he possibly have wanted the movie made?
At that point he'd been superintendent for something like nine years. He wasn't getting any money out of the state legislature. He wasn't getting any additional funds, and he needed money for new programs.

He wanted to show that money was needed.
Right. And Richardson helped just because he thought it was a good idea! They both initially liked the film. They knew that Bridgewater was like that, in part because of the absence of money to attract and train competent

guards, psychiatrists, and social workers. That was one of the points. The film was then scheduled to show at the New York Film Festival. It got some prefestival reviews, which were very good. They both praised the film and condemned the state of Massachusetts. Then some social worker from Minnesota wrote the governor of Massachusetts, a man named John A. Volpe, a letter saying, "How could you allow a movie to be made that shows naked men?" She hadn't even seen the movie—she had just read the reviews. Volpe, not having heard of the movie before this letter, felt that his political career was going to be jeopardized by the movie. He proceeded to get what's called an ex parte injunction, which means that he got an injunction without having me represented at the hearing. It was against the film being shown at the New York Film Festival.

Just at that festival?
Well, that was the only public place that he knew it was going to be shown. But they showed it anyway, and then it opened in New York and he got a permanent injunction against it. Then there was a committee of the Massachusetts state legislature, which was controlled by the Democrats, that had it out for Richardson. They convened hearings to find out how I had gotten permission to make the film. They wanted to use that information against Richardson.

The movie became a tool for so many different people's agendas.
That's exactly right. So then there was a 19-day trial, where they made three principal allegations...

First, that the film was an invasion of privacy of the inmate named Jim, the man who's shown naked in his cell. Second, that I had breached an oral contract giving the state editorial control over the film.

Was there anything like that?
There was no document whatsoever that in any way supported that view. But still, the superintendent testified to there having been an oral contract.

So he perjured himself?
Yes. Richardson, a very clever lawyer, cooked up that theory as a way of asserting that I had contracted away my First Amendment rights. He was afraid that I would get the case removed to federal court.

Because federal courts are really by the book on constitutional law.
Yes. And it is possible to contract away your First Amendment rights, so they were trying to prove that I had.

The third assertion they were making was that all the receipts of the film should be held in trust for the benefit of the inmates.

They really wanted to nail you.
The judge found in this case a right of privacy for the first time in the history of Massachusetts.

Wow. I'm surprised they'd made it to the late 60s without having set a privacy precedent.
On the contract issue, the judge simply believed the state over me. I said X, they said Y, and the judge—who was specially appointed to deal with the case and who had absolutely no sympathy for the film at all—decided in their favor. He also decided that all the receipts would be held in trust for the inmates.

So it was a resounding state victory. But I'll bet there wasn't any money there to hold in trust anyway.
Yes. At that point there were no receipts! He also declared that the negative should be burned.

Jesus Christ!
He described the film as a "nightmare of ghoulish obscenities."

It's more like a documentation of ghoulish obscenities.
The next thing I did was appeal to the Massachusetts Supreme Court. They decided that the film had value but could only be seen by limited audiences: doctors, lawyers, judges, health-care professionals, social workers, and students in these and related fields, but not the "merely curious general public." And this was on condition that I give the attorney general's office a week's notice before any screening and that I file an affidavit after that everyone who attended was, of my personal knowledge, a member of the class of people allowed to see the film. Those were the conditions under which I could screen *Titicut Follies*.

In other words, effectively impossible.
Effectively impossible! What was I going to do? Interview everybody who wanted to see the film? Five years later, a new attorney general was appointed in Massachusetts. My lawyers went to see him and he agreed to modify the injunction so that I could show the film if I could rely on someone's representation to me that the audience was going to consist of the accepted class. If a teacher at, say, the University of Illinois, wanted to show the film, he had to sign a form saying that the audience was going to be within the class of people allowed to see the film, send the form to me, and I would have to file with the attorney general's office and the clerk of the supreme court. And then, within a week of

the screening, I would have to file another piece of paper verifying that the people seeing it were within the class that were allowed to have seen it.

It's too many hoops to jump through. Did anyone go through all this to screen it?
Well, yes. There were a lot of people that wanted to see the film so they went through that, you know, charade.

Were film students allowed to see it?
No. Nor were journalists.

So it would have been illegal for a journalist to view *Titicut Follies*.
Yes. But it's a question of who is a student in "these or related fields." I think that sometimes the film was able to be screened in journalism schools because the argument was made that journalists were within the class.

The censors focused on the sequence of the film with Jim, where we see an inmate, totally nude, walked from his cell to a bathroom where he is shaved—he even starts to bleed from a nick—and then washed, and then walked back to his cell, where he loses control and starts to pound his feet and scream. This is, of course, after a guard has been baiting him mercilessly with the same question again and again: "Is that cell gonna be clean tomorrow, Jim? You gonna clean that cell, Jim?" It's total psychological abuse...
Also, as Jim is walking up the stairs, one of the guards slaps him. You hear the noise but you don't see it because it's shot from behind.

What were you hoping to show about this situation when you edited the sequence?
I wanted to show the way he was treated because this was no way to treat a human being, obviously, no matter what crime he committed. Also, I didn't understand why some inmates had to be kept naked. The announced rationale was that they were suicidal. But they could have been given paper suits. In fact, for six months after the film came out, they were given paper suits—until the budget for it ran out. The real reason for the nudity was just that it was easier to keep them that way. Some of the men were incontinent, and the guards didn't like the idea of having to strip smelly clothes off them.

How long did the ban on the film last?
It lasted until 1990. In the mid-80s, I started another action. The original judge in the case had died. There was a headline in the Boston Globe saying "*Titicut Follies* Judge Dead." So I brought another case, saying that circumstances had changed. The new judge appointed a spe-

cial master, which means someone to assist him, and tasked him to investigate whether the showing of the film would damage the surviving inmates. The first job was to figure out who was still alive. The judge appointed a lawyer to inquire about the status of the surviving inmates. The lawyer wrote a report saying that, in his view, the film could be publicly shown without damaging the surviving inmates. The judge then said I could show the film if I blacked out the faces of the inmates.

All of them? That's impossible.
Yes. I refused to do that, and I also said that while it was possible to do that on videotape, it really wouldn't be possible to do that successfully on film. But I would not do it even if it were doable. So we asked him to reconsider. He did, and then he wrote a decision saying that the film is fully protected by the First Amendment, and it could be freely shown. And then it was shown on PBS.

Wow, and it only took 23 years. When you're shooting, you relocate to wherever the film takes you and then what? Shoot till you drop, get some sleep, and then get back to it?
Exactly. Sometimes the place is open day and night, like a hospital, or sometimes it's open from seven in the morning until seven at night. It varies. If a place is open 24 hours a day, I'm probably there for 15. If it's open 12, I'm there all 12. Then at night I watch rushes. It's a long day. You don't get much sleep. But it's very intense. It's fun.

It must be physically taxing.
Documentary filmmaking is a sport in that sense. You have to be in reasonably good shape because you're running around all day with the equipment, and you have to have to be able to get along with very little sleep.

And you're still shooting at the same pace today as you always were?
Yeah. I do sound and I direct, then there's a cameraman and a third person to carry the extra mags and do whatever odd jobs are required. During shooting, I basically lead the cameraman with the mic. I pick out what gets shot. We have signals that we use during the shooting.

There's a lot of responsibility in editing a documentary— in making a documentary in general, really—because you can be suggestive and manipulative if you choose to be.
Well, there's the danger that it can be manipulative in the bad sense of the word. But it has to be manipulative in the good sense of the word! Choices have to be made, and the choices have meaning and consequences. I feel that I have an enormous responsibility to the people who have let me shoot them. ■

STEVE LAFRENIERE

MIKE LEIGH

Photo by Leo Leigh

I've been watching Mike Leigh's movies for almost 20 years and every time I see a new one I have a fantasy conversation with him afterward, which generally consists of me trying to worm crucial personal info out of him. Because his characters can be so hyperreal—the kind of people who are so interesting or honest or insanely, baroquely fucked up they make you curious about living another day yourself—I usually feel like I've just met them offscreen. Like, in *Abigail's Party* has anyone considered that Angela might be retarded? In *Naked*, for which of several reasons would Johnny be faking his cough? Does Gary Oldman's skinhead have some kind of schoolgirl crush on Tim Roth's nerd in *Meantime*? Not many other directors could even get me to wonder this sort of stuff.

When *Vice* asked me to actually talk with Mike Leigh for this issue, I gulped. For one, he's got a reputation as a hairy interview. Legend has him cutting off journalists he thinks haven't done their homework and being hostile to anyone he even slightly perceives as having an agenda. Good for him, but erm... Then I saw his new movie, *Happy-Go-Lucky*, which is about a woman so cheerful she makes Amelie look like Diamanda Galás. I didn't like it that much at first. It seemed kind of weak for a Mike Leigh film. But sure enough over the next few days I found myself mentally rerunning almost every scene, amazed yet again at the densely woven characters and what made each one tick. Now I love it. So yeah, I looked forward to getting him on the phone.

It turns out Mike Leigh is nothing like they say. It's just that he doesn't cotton to the idea of being misunderstood, period. He'll vigorously argue any mistaken notions about his work that you put across, no matter how slight, and calibrate every opinion of his own to a precise click. He's also mordantly funny about people and things he doesn't like. He's basically just like half my friends. Except that he's one of the best living filmmakers in the world.

Vice: *Happy-Go-Lucky* **looks different from your other films. It's jammed with bright, saturated color and it's shot in wide-screen.**
Mike Leigh: When it got to the stage where I had a clear conception of what the film was going to be, I talked to Dick Pope, my cinematographer, about the central character, Poppy, and what she's like. How positive she is, what a great sense of life she's got. Just as we were about to shoot tests we discovered that Fuji had brought out a new stock called Vivid. It's great with primary colors. We used that, so then it seemed a natural thing to go wide-screen.

A first for you.
Yeah, it was. We'd thought about it for earlier films but this was the first time it was absolutely the right thing for the feel of the picture.

Poppy is almost obnoxiously chirpy, but that's just one of an ensemble of qualities. Her stubbornness not to be afraid of life is great to watch. What made you want to present this particular character now?
In a way it's a kind of anti-miserabilist film. The fact is, we're knocking lumps off each other and we're destroying the planet. Things are looking quite tough, bleak, and indeed we have good reason to be gloomy. But while all that is going on, there are people out in the real world who are just getting on with it. Not least among those are teachers. If you teach kids, you are by definition being optimistic. You are cherishing the future. So, yes, I wanted to make a film that was motivated by and carried by a generous, open-spirited, funny, optimistic, positive person. Now, that wouldn't be interesting if it was just a sim-

ulation of those things on a surface level. But as you said, Poppy is actually a rounded and proper person. Now, on another level it's due to Sally Hawkins, the actress who plays Poppy.

She had interesting parts in your two previous movies, ***All or Nothing*** **and** ***Vera Drake.*** **But I'd never have guessed she could carry a lead like this.**
Sally has this great energy and sense of humor and that obviously played its part in the chemistry of the proceedings. If you're familiar with my films you know that I make them by collaborating with actors to create characters. And although the characters that we get in the films are never the actors themselves, I do tap into their various energies. Having worked with Sally Hawkins, I got to know her and I did absolutely think it was time to put her at the center of things.

There's an encounter between Poppy and a homeless guy she meets late one night. He's talking gibberish but she looks him in the eye and seems to get exactly what he's going on about. Given your extemporaneous method, did Sally Hawkins know how that scene was going to play?
Everything you see in any of my films comes out of improvisation work from when I first set these things up, in which none of the actors ever know what's going to happen. But of course we then draw from that and build and distill and construct scenes, and *then* we shoot them.

So when you improvised at the start of your process, had it even been explained to her who this person was that she was going to encounter?
No, no, no. That would run counter to the whole principle of how I work. I simply set up a thing where she's moving around and suddenly this guy's there. When actors agree to take part in one of my films I won't say anything about it. They will never know anything about the film or the other characters or anything other than what their character would know at any stage of the game. Obviously the more the actors get to know each other through their characters the more they find out. But it's still only from that perspective. In fact, given how we shot the scene, even if she watches the film now she doesn't really know any more about him than you do.

You start the process with only a vague idea of who the characters are, who even Poppy is.
Yes. In a way I discovered who I was making the film about through the journey of making the film.

Well, all this has an interesting effect. More than once after seeing one of your movies I've found myself thinking about a character as if they were someone I'd actually

met. They seemed to enter the part of my brain reserved for new, possible friends. Or enemies.

That's the objective. That's the job.

When did that first become the objective?

I'm a movie watcher and I have been since an early age. And I used to sit, as a kid, thinking, why can't we have movies where people are like how people actually are? To me that's what it's about still—trying to put on the screen people like we actually are. Now, there are a million things I try and do to make that happen and what we've been talking about is the key to it: being completely spontaneous and organic. But it's not only that. It's hard to know how to express it, but there are hidden elements that have to do with the unpredictability of creative exploration and a certain kind of telepathy, so that the characters function and operate the way that we do in real life. Hopefully what I don't put on the screen are characters who are only a function of the plot, or this moment in the story, or who are in other ways two-dimensional. Or indeed characters who are behaving, rather curiously, like actors.

An ongoing problem in the cinema.

[*laughs*] Especially when such a character wouldn't know any actors.

You've been making plays and films for over 40 years. What was the atmosphere in 1960s London for accepting your ideas when you started out?

There was a lot going on. And you shouldn't underestimate the degree of transatlantic exchange of ideas. For example, when I hit London in 1960, the very first breach, *Shadows*—Cassavetes's first film—was playing. One also knew about the Living Theatre. In fact, I saw the Living Theatre in London. And by the mid-60s, when I started doing this stuff, one of the major things in theater was the work of Peter Brook. A lot of other barriers were coming down, and then happenings began. Do you know about happenings?

Like Claes Oldenburg and Yayoi Kusama.

Yes. There was also the documentary-play movement, where one went out and talked to people in various industries and made that into plays.

How did you fit into all this?

I started up writing in hidden corners. I put on plays with actors in fairly remote, fringe places and for very few performances. A lot of people didn't understand what I was doing because my work was, and this remains the case, not concerned with displaying in an obvious way the manifest signs of experiment. I was concerned more with creating work where you actually did suspend your dis-

belief because it was so real. Or because of a sense of heightened realism that took you through the barrier. This was fairly unfashionable. Experimental theater at that time was very much about displaying its experimentation. You had action going sort of sideways, people walking on their hands, all kinds of linguistic tricks and surrealist things, and all the rest of it. It wasn't until I got into my stride with what is in fact my natural habitat—movies—that I started to be taken more seriously. Then, of course, the plays started to be taken seriously too. By the time you get to *Abigail's Party*, which started as a stage play, people were right on the case.

One of my favorites is your first film, *Bleak Moments*. It also started as a play.

Yes. We made it into my first film simply because I was desperate to make a film. It's not really a dramatization, but more a reinvestigation of the play. A large portion of what happens in *Bleak Moments* is never in the play at all. *Nuts in May* is also a reinvestigation of a play.

How were the original plays received?

It wasn't understood what people were looking at. There was a review in the London *Times* of the play *Bleak Moments*. The play was like a clock, meticulously structured with silences. In the audience you could hear a pin drop. Yet the heading of the piece in the *Times* was "Embarrassed Actors." He'd got hold of the fact that it was an improvised play and thought the actors were improvising before your very eyes, which they were not. If you've seen the film version, the atmosphere, the moods, the tensions, the silences, the embarrassments were all in the original play. The whole review was predicated on the premise that because they were improvising, the actors were tongue-tied and didn't know what to say.

The reason I ask you about the early responses is because you seem to still encounter confusion from audiences and critics now.

People try and decode my films. For example, there have been reviews of *Happy-Go-Lucky* that say the problem is it's got no plot. Well, by the most extreme and crude Hollywood criteria, sure it has no plot. But there are two kinds of plots. There are causal plots and there are cumulative plots. A causal plot it certainly hasn't got—A happens and therefore B happens and therefore C happens and that makes D happen, et cetera. *Happy-Go-Lucky* has a cumulative plot.

Critics can be rough on your actors, too.

There are responses to *Happy-Go-Lucky* that say "Sally Hawkins's acting is dreadful because she's just improvising and she's self-indulgent and it's all hanging out all over the place and it doesn't add up to a real person." Apart from anything else, that is someone coming to it so marinated in preoccupations with form that their natural ability just to respond to a human being as a human being seems to be cauterized in some way.

Another standard detraction is that you're sneering at the working-class characters in your films. I know you don't agree with this.
What drives it is cynicism. There's a certain amount of cynicism out there that makes people perceive it in that way. OK, to tell you the truth, that's me trying to come up with an answer, because to a considerable extent I don't get it. It's dreadful. Certainly there's nothing serious to say about it. Large numbers of people find my work compassionate, as I hope it is.

I showed *Abigail's Party* to someone recently and they had that knee-jerk reaction. A real lefty, I might add.
The fact is, *Abigail's Party* is a passionate lamentation on the way people become seduced and indoctrinated by all kinds of received behavior and materialistic preoccupations. It's obvious.

Do you use actors with the same background or class as the characters they're going to play?
It's no big deal. There are a hundred examples. Say Imelda Staunton, who plays Vera Drake, comes from a London working-class background. It's a bonus, but that isn't to say much. Or Leslie Manville, for example, who I've worked with a lot, has played characters from all sorts of class backgrounds, from posh people to the kind of working-class woman she did in *Grown Ups* or indeed *All or Nothing*. Sometimes it's useful, but it's not the only criterion. We're talking about versatile, intelligent, sensitive, sophisticated, imaginative actors who can pitch tent in all kinds of different territories and explore with me. Sometimes it is a territory they're familiar with, sometimes it isn't.

And I guess you could say that, being as it's set in the 1880s, *Topsy Turvy* would be a good example of unfamiliar territory.
Exactly. We had to go and pitch tent in a whole other century. Actually, *Topsy Turvy* is my film about filmmaking. It's the one time I dealt with the real fundamental issues of filmmaking. I thought it was a liberated way to explore those preoccupations.

Would you be interested in making a film about actual filmmaking?
I don't think I would find out any more about the subject than I know. Each film is an exploration anyway and there are other things to explore.

I wonder if your films operate as psychoanalysis?
No. I'm not concerned with that one bit. I'm a storyteller. What I'm concerned with is storytelling and audiences. I'm also an artist, hence I'm concerned with the synthesis of the craft of film with the substance of it. So far we've talked mostly about actors, but in the end the real investigation is the shooting of the film and the postproduction. It's about the coming together of the performance and what the camera does and the design and the rhythm and the tempo and the music. So when I'm working with the actors I'm working to create fictitious characters and I'm working toward making a movie. I assume they should be enjoying themselves and they should be feeling very positive and creative. Obviously part of my responsibility is the pastoral care of the actors. But I'm not concerned with their psychotherapy.

Sally Hawkins and Mike Leigh on the set of Happy-Go-Lucky.
Photo by Simon Mein/Courtesy of Miramax Films

Actually, I meant your own psychoanalysis.
The same answer applies, except that these films are very personal and very much a part of my life and they come out of me, if you like. Therefore they move me on and they form how I look at the world. In that case, yes. But it's not something I think about consciously.

I'm talking about watching one of your own films years later and understanding something different about not only the film, but yourself. If any director would be interested in that I thought it might be you.
Well, yeah, that may be true. But I think we directors fall into two categories. To put it very crudely, there are hired hands who come in and do a movie and they're not really concerned with its provenance and its meaning in a personal way. They only execute the job of getting a movie

made. The rest of us make films very much from our hearts. So you ask that question of us.

You're known for casting the same actor again in different films, sometimes many years later. Is this partly because you wanted to investigate something else about them? Phil Davis comes to mind. Anthony O'Donnell. For those familiar with your films, it adds another layer as well.
You're barking up the wrong tree. Look, if I work with somebody and they're really good, I want to work with them again. Occasionally I work with people who it turns out I don't particularly like. That's very rare. But on the whole it's about getting on with people and us liking each other. If there's somebody I really like they become a friend of mine. It's great to be able to come back to someone you know and like and you stimulate each other both personally and creatively and then you go on another journey and explore somebody else. But it's all about the job. To tell you the truth, the idea that I come back to an actor to investigate something about them in a personal way actually has never occurred to me until you suggested it. The first time I work with an actor, whatever we do goes in whatever direction. The second time I always say, whatever we do we're not going to repeat ourselves. But that's an artistic thing. It's not to do with our relationship.

Although it's one of your most brutal films, I noticed a new audience for your work after *Naked*.
It's true. But don't forget it's also true that it's the first film that I made that went to Cannes. And it also won prizes at Cannes. So apart from anything else, we went wider with that one. But in terms of the film itself and its spirit, it certainly spoke to people who would not previously have been concerned about *Life Is Sweet* or *High Hopes*. If there's a previous film with which it's a younger sibling, it's *Meantime*, which enjoyed cult underground status for years with unemployed people before it came out on commercial DVD or video. Although *Naked* doesn't have that kind of specific constituency, nevertheless it's enjoyed a similar kind of cult.

***Naked* is a great example of this: Your films can be harsh in their depiction of people's lives, but they've all got this seductive entertainment factor too.**
Hitchcock once famously said that a woman who spends all day washing and cleaning and ironing doesn't want to go the movies at night to see a film about a woman who spends all day washing and cleaning and ironing. In my experience Hitchcock in this particular instance is talking a load of crap. Because people get a real buzz out of being able to relate to what they see. At the same time a film must be entertaining. A film that's just a bland, surface record of reality would be extremely tedious and alienating. And pointless, in my view. My job is to make films that resonate with people's lives, in all ways. I haven't invented that. It was going on when Shakespeare wrote *King Lear*.

Give me a Hollywood movie that you've seen lately. And approved of.
I don't know whether you'd count *There Will Be Blood* as a Hollywood movie, but it's a great piece of work. I'm a sucker for cinema, you know. It's about movies to me. A painter can be into all kinds of paintings but it doesn't mean to say that he or she is going to paint like all kinds of painters. My passion for cinema of all kinds feeds in on a conscious or a subliminal level to what I do.

What about younger audiences? Do you think it's true that they're too ADD to focus on anything but the mythical, served up with big-budget effects?
Younger audiences are ready for anything and everything. They're extremely sophisticated, they're extremely open, and the more you chuck at them the more interested they are. People now understand film not just in part because the means to explore film is readily available to them. The only ones who are saying that people only want big-budget films are the studios.

Are you thinking about the next generation?
I am. As a matter of fact I am the chairman of the London Film School. It's been going since the mid-50s and it's a great international house. I put a lot of time and energy and effort into young filmmakers. It's something I'm very concerned with and passionate about.

But in regard to your way of creating a film, can that be taught to a new generation in the same way as, say, method acting?
It can't. Perhaps one could teach the surface mechanics, but what I'm actually able to do each time can't really be, as it were, quantified and turned into a set of instructions for a manual. Does that make sense?

Sure, I figured as much. Not that you're about to leave anytime soon anyway, but what about critics who say that with *Happy-Go-Lucky* Mike Leigh has mellowed?
First of all, and you know this perfectly well, every movie I make is in some way different. Of course it's also true, as Jean Renoir said, that we all make the same film over and over again. So, following *Vera Drake* I got around to making this one. It's a question of choices. No doubt in some ways I am mellowing. In any case I'm 65 and was somewhat younger when I made my first film. But it's simplistic to review *Happy-Go-Lucky* as merely a function of a person going soft. Anyway, they haven't seen the next film yet. ∎

JESSE PEARSON

DAVID THEWLIS

Even if he hadn't been the star of maybe our favorite movie of all time, Mike Leigh's *Naked*, David Thewlis would still be one of our favorite actors. Not only that, but he's a great writer. Thewlis deals in funny, observant rhyming poems and hilarious-but-harsh fiction. Then, every once in a while, he goes and portrays Professor Lupin (clearly the best teacher at Hogwarts) in a Harry Potter movie, just to pay the rent.

This month, Thewlis's debut novel is being released. It's called *The Late Hector Kipling*, and it features one of the most misanthropic, hopeless pricks of a protagonist that's ever been wrought by a Man With a Typewriter. As Thewlis's (non)hero makes his way through the London art world, he systematically lays waste to everything good in his life, from friendship to family to love. And just when you think it can't get darker, it does. But all along, the book is garnished with Thewlis's ruthless wit and stop-you-in-your-tracks insights, which are like little life buoys in a sea of violence and betrayal.

Vice: Your novel alternates its location between London, where the British art world lives, and Blackpool, where you grew up and which us Americans don't really know about. What's it like there? It's a resort town, right?
David Thewlis: Yeah. From speaking to other Americans, I understand that it mostly resembles Atlantic City or Coney Island. In Britain it's a very famous resort. As mentioned in the book, there's a tower there...

Blackpool Tower...
Right, which was built and designed with inspiration from the Eiffel Tower—although it's not nearly as graceful and elegant as that. [*laughs*] It's much more industrial-looking. But it's very famous in England, the Blackpool Tower.

What sort of people come to Blackpool?
It's a working-class resort. A lot of people from Glasgow, Manchester, Liverpool, and the Yorkshire towns go there on holiday. In recent years it's become more of a stag-night place. Do you say that?

Yeah, sure, stag night. Like a bachelor party.
Right. But when I was growing up in Blackpool, there was a great circus in the base of the tower. There were literally clowns walking the streets. It was kind of like living in Disneyland. There was a huge theme park there called the Pleasure Beach. In fact, I grew up in a toy shop next door to a candy store.

Jesus. The perfect boyhood.
I've got this really romantic image of my growing up, but it's true. I really did grow up in a toy shop next to a candy store in the shadow of a huge theme park in a resort town...

With clowns roaming the streets.
Right! And then I became an actor, so now I've got no sense of reality at all. Anyway, I sentimentalize Blackpool, but it's quite a unique town.

So you decided to make your novel's protagonist a native of Blackpool.
I just thought there was some fun to be had from saying that his childhood was in Blackpool and his parents were still there. Actually, the parents are the closest thing to anything to do with my life in the book. They aren't a million miles away from my parents.

The mother especially is such a strong character. She has this really endearing naïveté about art, but her son is an artist. Does that have a parallel in your life with your mother?
It does, in terms of my own mother's attitude toward the film world and some of the more independent films that I

Photo by Dan Monick

might have acted in or been friends with the people involved in. I remember taking her to see *Edward Scissorhands* and her being totally baffled. She was like, "What's all that about?" I said, "It's Tim Burton," and she was like, "But he's got scissors on his hands. It makes no sense." [*laughs*] So she's not exactly experimental in her way of thinking.

Has she read the book?
She hasn't, not yet. My father has, and he liked it a lot apparently, even though he's not read much in his life. He said to me, "It's a long time since I've read a book." I was like, "You've never read a book, Dad!" I've never seen my dad with a book in his hands. But I actually feel a lot closer to him since he's read it. He's more affectionate with me and a lot more outgoing now.

A lot of writers can reveal things about themselves emotionally in their work that they might have trouble getting out in their real life.
Yeah, exactly. Even if their characters stray further and further from their real selves as the book goes on, and they start behaving more irrationally.

So are there incidents in the book that are based on real events?
The whole story in the book of my mother buying an ugly, expensive sofa and then my father being so upset about it that he gets ill is true. He didn't become quite as ill as he does in the book. He wasn't hospitalized. But he was in bed for a few days.

Because of a hideous sofa that your mother bought?
Yeah! My mother really did buy it. I remember, I had the idea that I could pay a friend to go and buy it based on an ad I could put in the newspaper, and that might have taken all my parents' stress away. Then when I was starting to write the book, I thought that story might fit quite nicely into it, so I started to thread it all the way through.

The book is also set amid the Young British Artists scene. People like Tracey Emin and Damien Hirst are mentioned.
It was an alternative to setting it in the film world. I didn't want to be an actor writing about acting and films, but there were still some things I wanted to talk about in terms of celebrity and rivalry—some of the things I've experienced in my own career. I also thought it would be much more visual and entertaining to set it in the art world, of which I am a fan. I'm usually to be found at the openings of most things back in Britain, or wherever I am. I'm in Los Angeles now and I always try to see all the exhibitions and go to the galleries.

So I figured it would be sort of expected of me to write a book that had to do with acting, but I found it more interesting to investigate the art world. I'd like to get away from being perceived as an actor who's written a novel and get the book judged more on its own merit.

You've written a lot of poetry, but fiction writing is a real bitch. Was it difficult to get this done?
The hardest thing, which is what I'm going through now as I try to write my second book, is structure. Having a solid plot and knowing where you're going with it, rather than writing in a void and painting yourself into a corner. To know what you're saying from the beginning helps, and I always pretty much knew how this book would end. I knew it was going to end in violence because that was something that interested me.

What sort of violence interested you?
People who find their lives at such a dead end that they commit a crime like a random shooting—that's always fascinated me. Whenever that pops up in the news, it's very intriguing. How can someone have lost it so much to not only kill themselves or one other person but actually kill strangers at random?

When you set out to write the novel did you have a philosophy or a theme in mind, or was it more about having a narrative and letting the morality take care of itself?
It was more about the narrative. I didn't necessarily want to say anything thematic apart from exploring the nature of envy, jealousy, rivalry, and the theft of creative work. Morally...

It isn't a hugely moral book!
Yeah, I don't think there's a strong moral at the end of the book. It's about an amoral character—a selfish, self-involved character. A monster in the end.

But the book is so funny too.
I always wanted it to be comedic, but a very black comedy. I would have bored myself if I wrote such a thing in a serious tone. I also didn't want it to be just a farcical series of escapades. I wanted to use comedy to investigate something very dark and psychologically disturbing.

I think the most effective part of the book for me is the dialogue, especially Hector's inner monologues. Is it your acting experience that taught you to write such great speeches?
Yeah, I think so. Obviously, I'm used to not only speaking dialogue all the time but also reading scripts—often with very, very bad dialogue. It happens so often that you'll get a script with a good story but the dialogue is found wanting. So I'm forever on the set trying to change the dia-

logue. A lot of writers of film scripts, I think, don't actually read their work back to themselves. They don't see how it can't be spoken very well and it doesn't sound like the way real people speak.

You've got experience not only with writing, but with a lot of improvisation as well.
Well for me, the dialogue tends to be some of the easiest stuff to write because it's like improvising, really—improvisation with myself. I'd take a conversation between Hector and his mother that had to do with A, B, and C and let it ramble on for like 20 pages of longhand in a notebook and then I'd return to it and cut out whole pages of what wasn't interesting or funny or relevant.

Most of your dialogue in *Naked* was improvised...
Yeah.

Is that character, in a way, a piece of fiction that you wrote?
I mean, I see this book as a kind of relative of *Naked*, much more than anything else I've done acting-wise. I certainly don't think I would ever have written this book if I hadn't done *Naked*. Doing that movie was when I realized that I could write something substantial. Mike Leigh gave me the opportunity and the wherewithal to channel a lot of ideas I may have had in my head for many years and to put them into a form to which he gave a structure and characters to bounce it all off.

The book does have a real kinship with the film.
Mike was the first person who suggested to me that I should write a novel. He thought that was where my future lay. And I always did want to be a writer of stories and novels. Even before I wanted to be an actor, that was my ambition. So Mike certainly helped me gain confidence in thinking I was capable of doing such a thing.

There's a common thread of misanthropy that runs through your book and your character in *Naked*.
There's a natural progression there. I think the book is probably funnier than *Naked*—although *Naked* is quite funny. A lot of people don't think so. They'll say, "What do you mean? It's not funny at all." But I'm like, "There are some good gags in *Naked*!" It was meant to be a black comedy, of course—maybe more black than comedy.

I liked how as I read the novel my feelings for Hector, the main character, shifted. At first I felt empathy for him, but I started to realize that he was transforming into an awful person. Where did the inspiration for this guy come from?
He's a mixture of some people I know. He's partly me,

obviously. But only partly. In some ways, you could say I'm more like his best friend, Lenny. Their relationship is somewhat based on my experiences with a few friends who resented my success. When I did *Naked*, for example, I started getting calls from Hollywood and ended up kind of where I am right now, driving around meeting anyone who's anyone in this town, then coming back to England and telling a few stories of this kind of adventure I'd had out in Los Angeles. A lot of people were like, "Wow, that's fucking great, how exciting, what a great novelty, that must be interesting." But then a handful of people were very resentful of it. So in the book, in a way, I'm more like the character Lenny, who's just come back from America with his name-dropping and his success and everybody wanting to photograph him and getting recognized in public. That's more what happened to me. I had the bitter friend at my side, and that's the sort of person Hector is based on.

There are real-life precedents for these guys.
Yeah. Again, when you work with Mike Leigh you base your characters on a real, living person who is in your acquaintance. And I really enjoyed creating such a sort of sad guy as Hector. [*laughs*] At the same time, I struggled to keep him likable, to not turn the reader off too much. I didn't people to be like, "God, I don't even want to know what happens to this guy because he's such a pain in the ass." I wanted him to have something so pathetic about him that you're going to follow him because you want to see this loser fall, but also keep him nice enough to maintain that interest. Even though he's diabolical at times, there's his love for his mother and father and his love for his girlfriend.

But he's such a mess. You want to grab him and slap him and go, "Snap the fuck out of it!"
He's always making the wrong decisions. I thought it would be interesting to create a character that is just constantly making the wrong decision. I wanted to have him do that again and again and again, and see where that landed him.

The pace of his descent, and even the pace of the actual writing, really accelerates as you get toward the end of the book. The climax is quite shocking.
I wanted it to be a sudden rush at the end. I didn't want people to anticipate it once it started going. As I was writing it, once it got very dark, once the first two deaths occurred, I started to think it was maybe too much. But then I thought, well, maybe I should just kill everyone! I thought, look at Shakespeare. He did that all the time and nobody complained. Look at the end of *Hamlet*. There are like 15 bodies on the floor! ∎

RYAN McGINLEY

DICK FACE

Why Is Jack Walls the Coolest Motherfucker on Earth?

Jack Walls and Ryan McGinley at Patti Smith's house, Michigan, 1999

I spent two weeks making 500 hand-drawn balloons for Jack Walls's 50th birthday party. It was my present to him. With a black Sharpie, I drew all of his classic expressions on 500 silver balloons. He's well known for these sayings and everyone who knows him has their own Jack Walls imitation.

Jack is an artist, writer, muse, and infamous man-about-town. He was Robert Mapplethorpe's boyfriend for many years, up until his death. Jack grew up as a gangbanger in the ghetto of Chicago. He joined the navy for a few years and then moved to New York and met Robert in the early 80s. Jack is in many of Robert's most famous photographs.

I met Jack in the late 90s, right around the time I started making my own photographs. He's been like a big brother to me. After his birthday party was over I couldn't part with the balloons. I deflated them all and took them back to my studio and made a book out of them. Jack claims he didn't say half the things we say he did, but if you've ever heard him talk, you know that everything he says is instantly quotable.

Vice: You have these sayings that all your friends know you for. Everyone tries to imitate you.
Jack Walls: Some of this stuff I never said. People tell me I said stuff and I know I didn't say it and they argue with me! Like I never said, "Spaghetti is straight until you boil it." What is that? Dash Snow made that one up. He is the main culprit. I'm not even lying. Look, out of all the shit I say, do I ever make reference to food? That's a dead giveaway. I cannot equate food with talking shit. I don't operate like that.

I'm calling this article, "Why Is Jack Walls the Coolest Motherfucker on Earth?" and that's my question for you. Why does everyone want to be your friend?
Bad judgment.

Come on, you're a celebrity in certain circles.
Yeah, a very limited circle. The circle's about an inch.

People want to know you. You've lived like ten exciting lives. You've been in the navy and in a gang, you've been a notorious downtown New York junkie, you've been the boyfriend to basically the most famous photographer of the later part of the 20th century…
I don't know, I don't think that's nothing. I think I'm a late bloomer and for the first time in my life I've decided to really pay attention to art and writing, so I really do believe that I'm just starting out.

Shit, I guess that gives hope to all of us.
Hey, it ain't over till it's over.

"Trade Alarm"
That's when you look at someone and you just know they have a huge cock. Instinctively, bells go off. That's also what you call a "dick face." When you see somebody and you go, "Oh, they got a big one."

"Basket Picnic"
Ha ha ha, that means you see somebody with a big package—it's a basket picnic! You get it, don't you? Listen, I'm drunk half the time. These things I say, I don't even know I say. I can't think about it, I just talk.

"Clock the Basket"
Again, look at the basket. There's a lot of basket sayings. And packages. Every day is like Christmas for me, darling!

"What Did My Pussy Ever Do to You?"
That's from a Bobby Garcia porno. A marine is fucking him and the guy is screaming, "Oh my pussy, you're destroying my pussy! What did my pussy ever do to you, you treat it so bad!"

"Motherfucker I Will Slap the Shit Out of You Right Now"
Because sometimes you have to represent. Because before I slap the shit out of a person I'm gonna let them know that that's what I'm about to do. I don't like to get physical but I can.

Where are you from?
I was born in Chicago, 1957. I lived there until I went into the navy in 1978.

You were a gangbanger, right?
I participated in gang activities, yes. I'll tell you one thing, being in a gang is like being gay. Anything that's all guys is gay, that's why I knew the navy would be perfect for me. Psychologically, I already knew, even at a young age, that being in a gang or the military or being an athlete, it's all homoerotic. Plus I was a big Jean Genet fan. Being in a gang was romantic. Everything I do has a sense of romance to it, everything.

Tell me about your gang.
The gang I was in was called the Morgan Deuces, in the Chicago area called Pilsen, and I was in the gang from the age of 14 to 17. I got arrested all the time. My brother was killed from gangbanging. He was shot and killed.

Me and you both have two sisters and six brothers, one of whom died. It's such a weird coincidence, isn't it? What was it like growing up with such a big family? What were you like?
I don't know, I'm pretty much the same. People don't change. I've known you for ten years and you're exactly the same, except maybe you got a little bit worse.

I thought I got better.
Well, think again.

Do you remember how we met?
I can tell you exactly. We met in June 1998. I had just come back from LA and the day I got back the actor Dwight Ewell said, "You have to meet these kids, they're the best." And I told him, "Look, I don't want to meet anyone, I just want to go to Cherry Tavern." Somehow he tricked me into going to this party and the first time I saw you, you were sitting there getting your hair cut. I was so pissed off that Dwight had set me up, I went out and sat in the hallway. Later that night some people were hanging out at my place on 29th Street and you showed up at 4 AM. We talked about photography.

That was our initial bond. You had Mapplethorpe prints and Patti Smith drawings, and it was a clutter of art books and weird art objects and postcards everywhere. It was 20 years of collecting stuff. All I could think was, this was the coolest place I'd ever been to. I've styled my own place based on how yours was. You knew so much and you taught me so much.
But at that point in my life I had turned my back on the art world. I definitely didn't think of you in terms of being an artist. I remember one night, you were about to drop out of college, and you said, "Jack, I don't know what I'm going to do now. I'm not gonna get a job and I'm not gonna bartend." And I remember thinking, OK, he's on the right track, because that's exactly how anyone I've ever known who ever did anything with themselves did it—they never developed another skill. That's the trick. I'm gonna be an artist and nothing else. And that's when I decided I would help you. And I helped get you that show at 420 West Broadway.

That was my first photo show. You also helped me get my first internship. You always helped me out. Yet I never took

your advice, and you were always right. You're always like, "You're so stupid. I told you two years ago not to do that!" So tell me about this new art project of yours.

Well, last winter I started making collages and I'm going to have a show of them at Fuse Gallery this February.

What inspired the collages?

Last year around this time I quit smoking. And every time I wanted to smoke a cigarette I did a collage instead. And the next thing you know I had 66 of them! That's the truth. I'm not gonna make it seem like Robert came to me in a dream and said I should make collages from one of his images.

The image in your collages is a Mapplethorpe photo of a girl named Ada. Tell me about her.

I met Ada in the summer of 1982. She was walking down 8th Street with an old friend of mine from Chicago, this Puerto Rican girl named Margie. She yelled out, "Hi-Fi!" which was my old nickname from back home, and I turned around and said, "Margie!" And she said, "Oh, it's Cita now, as in *mamacita*." She had a blond mohawk and Ada was bald and rail thin. I thought, "What a look!" I was headed over to Robert's and I invited them to come along. He photographed both of them that day. Later that summer, the girls were living in Queens and I heard that both of them got pregnant at the same time. They disappeared. That day is a special memory for me and I've always loved that image. Robert did too.

How did you meet Robert Mapplethorpe?

Oh, everyone knows that story. It's old and gray and dusty.

I love that story and I want to hear it again.

Fine, we met in 1982 because I had just gotten out of the navy and was living in the West Village, the hub of gay activity. Christopher Street was the center of the universe if you were a fag. I would see Robert around and check him out because he was a good-looking cat.

Who cruised who first?

We cruised each other. We would look at each other and finally one day he gave me his number. I called him up that night and he invited me out for dinner. We met at the Pink Teacup and then we never stopped seeing each other.

Wait, I thought you told me that you met in an ice-cream parlor.

Well, I saw him around for a while before we actually met. Eventually he came up to me and handed me his business card, which just said "Robert Mapplethorpe, photographer."

I love that story because you told me that it was the middle of summer and he was wearing full leather and getting ice cream.

Yeah, it was 99 degrees out and he had on those motorcycle boots that go all the way up your leg. Eating a big waffle cone. I'll tell you he had a great look. He was the most amazing-looking fucking beautiful boyfriend I've ever had. The best boyfriend ever. Let me tell you something, I loved Robert. Still to this very day.

When I look at pictures of Robert, I think, oh my God, if I saw that guy on the street I would have sex with him in a minute.

He was something else, darling. Who would have thought when I met him in 1981 that he would be dead by 1989?

Tell me about the early days of AIDS.

There's nothing to talk about. It was just sad.

Well, I like talking about it because it's been a big part of both our lives. Robert and my older brother Michael both got HIV at around the same time. For all we know they could have fucked each other.

Probably not… Maybe they both fucked the same person.

Yeah, my brother was into black guys too, so it is possible. How come Robert never did heroin?

He did it once. But, you know, Robert was bourgeois. Robert was piss-elegant. He didn't want to hang out with a bunch of junkies.

In 1985 Basquiat painted your portrait for a series he was doing of all the downtown black kids on the scene at the time. What was it like being painted by him? Was it interesting seeing his process?

Nah, we were just smashed on heroin. But I tell you one thing, I had done so much heroin that day that when I left there I got amnesia. It's the only time that's ever happened in my life. I was walking around Manhattan and it was snowing and for about four hours I could not remember who or where I was.

Can I ask you about your sex life?

You know what? Honestly, I don't have a sex life.

You are such a liar.

But see, if I talked about my sex life I would incriminate people.

Well, you don't have to use their names.

Yeah, but it's not even that important. I mean, you suck a dick, you suck a dick. ■

TOMOKAZU KOSUGA

NOBUYOSHI ARAKI

There lives in Japan a relentless monster who has released 450 photo books—and still continues to take photographs every day. His name is Nobuyoshi Araki. Those of you who don't know much about him might, after a cursory glance, see nothing more than a horny old man. And yes, sure, at times his themes are super-erotic, and that's not only when he shoots women. He can make anything look sexy. Who else can make a photo of the ground look so much like a vagina that you start to seriously consider jerking off to it? Nobody but Araki. There are a quintillion photographers in the world, but none have lived and breathed photography like Araki, who is constantly producing work and at times releases as many as 20 books a year—an accomplishment that can be achieved because of his perpetual focus on everyday life. Not only that, he writes books on photography. His magic words render his images all the more potent. Unfortunately, most of his books have only been published in Japanese, and we can't read Japanese. That's why we sent Tomo from Vice Japan to talk to Araki. Sick of being interviewed countless times throughout his career, Araki tried to demolish him from the very beginning. But Tomo hadn't cut classes in university to read the entire collection of Araki's books in the school library for nothing. And so an unprecedented battle of wills over photography began...

Photo by Tomokazu Kosuga

Vice: Today I want to ask you about your photographs.
Nobuyoshi Araki: Look, if you want to know about my photos just read a book or something. You writers all end up asking the same damn questions over and over. What exactly is it that you want to know?

OK, well, why don't you start by telling me about the first time you picked up a camera...

No, no, no, forget it! Let's just forget about this whole thing. I'm leaving. Why don't you just go and watch some TV or something—don't bother me. I'm not fucking doing this anymore. You should know all about this crap. It's so boring. You don't even ask about my current projects. Don't fucking ask me about the first time I took a photograph or whatever—it's pathetic. And I don't need you to go writing this up in an article for other ignorant people who don't know me to read either, OK? I don't give a shit. I'm not interested in money or fame. I'm not looking for that anymore.

Well then, can I ask about all the photo books that you've published?
That's such a stupid question, man. Which one do you want to talk about? I have 450 books, for God's sake.

In *EROTOS*, you made ordinary flowers and cracks in the ground look like male and female genitalia. Why do you think your photos come across as being so erotic?
Why do they come across as erotic? Because I shot them. That's what my photos are. You're wondering why they look erotic? It is what it is, you know? You're going to keep asking me these dumb questions and write it up in your little article? Oh, come on, you can do better than that. I've been asked the same question a million times, dude.

Well, let's talk about your book *Kofuku Shashin* ["Happiness Photographs"]. Compared to your old photographs, these were more reminiscent of keepsake portrait pictures that fathers take of their families. It seemed to me like they are crossing a line that was almost taboo in your former photographs. What made you shift your perception so drastically?
So you noticed that, eh? You're not so clueless after all. [*laughs*] It's probably because right now, I believe that

"happiness is the best state." That's all. Rather than shooting something that looks like a professional photograph, I want my work to feel intimate, like someone in the subject's inner circle shot them. Now that I'm older, I can finally say that happiness is truly the best state to be in. It's so cheesy, right? When you're young you try to keep a distance from your subject and be really cool about everything, but eventually this is what you come to feel. I also noticed that both professional and amateur photographers have stopped shooting these kinds of photos. So I tried doing it myself, and guess what? It's way more difficult than shooting stuff like *EROTOS*. With *EROTOS* you just try to be as horny as possible and it works, but with *Kofuku Shashin* it's all about creating a relationship with your subject. It's just not the same.

Right. There's the danger of the images ending up like professional portraits, but you didn't want that.
Exactly. Everyone thinks that "art" means taking a step back from something familiar or precious to you. But my stance is "Don't make a work of art, don't 'do' photography." That said, with *EROTOS* the initial concept was to create a book of ultimate photographs, where the audience is forced to understand the photos without any text whatsoever. I'm not saying that it was bad or that it was a mistake. It's not about one being better than the other, it's just that in terms of where I'm at now, the notion of *Kofuku Shashin* appeals to me more. I guess I've aged or wised up or something. [*laughs*] Not that I'm ever giving up my eroticism. Once you give that up, you lose the strength to live. Anyway, when you compare the two books it's hard to believe that it's the same person behind the camera, the same photographer, right? There's, like, five Arakis inside of me.

Kofuku Shashin consists mostly of snapshots. Do you ask for permission from each person before taking a photo of them in the street?
In the past, no one knew me, so I could secretly take snapshots of random people. I can't do that anymore because they spot me first. That means that I have to communicate with them before taking each photo. But in the end, I think it's best for both parties, because we both acknowledge one another's existence. I'd make them laugh and forget about the mundane troubles of yesterday or whatever and try to create our own little time together. And I shoot that moment. That's far more profound. Of course the spatial relationship that we create for ourselves at that moment is also important, but the time that we share together is far more appealing and precious to me. So to be pedantic, it's like I frame "time" rather than "space." That's what differentiates my photos from the rest of them. And that's where happiness lies, you know? In the "time" that we spend together.

But you once said that "a camera is a penis," and you were all about unleashing that tool onto your subjects.
Sure. But now it's become a cunt, the exact opposite. Now I'm the one that accepts and embraces, just like a vagina.

I see. With your Nihonjin no kao ["Faces of Japan"] project, you've been traveling to various prefectures in Japan and shooting the citizens there. I hear that you shoot anyone and everyone who sees the ad and comes along.
That's nothing to be surprised about, though, because the world around us is so magnificent that you can't help but shoot it all. There's the phrase "artistic expression," but I believe that the people truly expressing themselves are the subjects, you know? It's not about the photographer trying to express stuff. It doesn't work like that.

So you're saying that you need to embrace the subjects?
Yes, because the people in front of you, the subjects, they're far more extraordinary than you. They all have their own charms. But often they themselves aren't even aware of their charms, so you have to discover it and present it to them, like, "This is it!" They're radiating all this aura, so your job is to pump up that aura even more and give it back to them by capturing it on film. That's how I approach my work.

You don't just want to shoot beautiful people then.
No. I don't discriminate in terms of my subjects. You have to always be able to accept and embrace them. They're all amazing, but each person has that extra-special unique something in them. Usually photographers have their preferences, and some might really want to shoot a particular actress or something, but I don't have that. Anything and anybody who I have the privilege of encountering is significant in themselves. Some people may seem like assholes, but you have to be accepting enough to think that maybe you're projecting a preconceived idea onto them, and they're not really assholes. That way, you might be able to discover something nice about them. Now, it's easy to say that, but I must admit, there sure are a lot of bitches out there! [*laughs*]

Like many of your works, this series suggests that you are particularly intent on shooting Japan. Why is that?
You have to shoot what's around you, what's familiar. I'm often invited to go overseas, but when I get there I always think, "Shit, I have to take more photographs of Japan." So I focus on my neighborhood and things around me in daily life, like my girlfriend. I mean, we're Japanese, so you shouldn't even have to consciously tell yourself to shoot Japan. It should just come naturally to you. So in my case, I was like, "OK, I should shoot a bunch of Japanese people," which led to, "Well, why don't I shoot

the entire country," and that eventually resulted in this "Faces of Japan" series.

You must have so much energy to even conceive of shooting the whole of Japan.
I know! I mean, I shoot about 500 to 1,000 people in each prefecture. I've only been to six prefectures so far and I don't think I'll be able to finish the project. I can't do this forever! I'll die! [*laughs*] I've only got so many years left to live. But usually I tend to run with an idea and just go for it even if it's only very vague. Once I start working and encountering more and more faces, I learn something new from them all the time.

For example, a lot of people come when I call for volunteers, and obviously they're from all walks of life. I've had elderly couples who say, "Please take a picture of us because we've been together for 60 years but don't have a single photo of our wedding," and so on. Or, "We have a new grandchild, please take our family portrait." In the past, my stance was to focus on the sentiments that emerge through the relationship between myself and the subject, but when people come up to me these days or a married couple say, "Please take a photo of us," I find that the sentiments or emotions that they have toward one another are much stronger than mine. I came to realize that I can get much more out of the shoot if I focus on the relationship that my subjects have among themselves, rather than the relationship between them and me. Shooting all those people taught me so much about the essence of human beings. *Kofuku Shashin* was the endpoint of that realization. You can't do that kind of photography when you're young—it's way too embarrassing. But really, it's the best thing. Like you'd go to the park during the cherry blossom season, and you'd see two children climbing on top of the father who's lying down on a picnic mat, and the mother would be sitting demurely by their side. You just can't beat that, you know? There's nothing like it. I guess I'm at a point now where I have enough room in my heart to finally be able to say, "Wow, that's so awesome." Listen to me, I sound like I'm going to die soon or something!

Funny. So, any interesting things happen to you lately? What else is new?
Everything is always interesting to me. One thing that comes to mind is that I'm currently doing an exhibition in Berlin called *Kinbaku* ["Bondage"], consisting of 101 black-and-white photographs. We held an opening party and everybody went crazy. People overseas are so fascinating—there are so many weirdos. Even TV interviews are different. They'd be like, "I brought a rope, please tie me up," and they'd conduct the rest of the interview tied up in rope. The camera's still going and everything, you know? There was another incident—

obviously I can't speak the language so I don't exactly know what was going on—where this huge fan of mine suddenly took all her clothes off in the middle of the venue and began grinding her hips. I was like, "What the fuck?" and then she suddenly pulled out a tampon from her slit and came toward me swinging the damn thing above her head!

Whoa.
She was utterly crazy. It was unreal! [*laughs*] So yeah, those kinds of things are interesting to me, little incidents like that.

Your portrayal of bondage makes it seem somewhat different from the typical image that we have of it.
A lot of people say that to me, and when they do, I tell them that "I free their souls by tying up their bodies." Sounds like nonsense, huh? Up until recently I used to say, "I don't tie up their souls, only their bodies." But now I say the opposite because I asked this girl which is better and she said that she liked the idea of "freeing the soul" more. So I stuck with it.

You brought *EROTOS* along today, huh? Wow, it's amazing you even have this. When I go overseas, a lot of female critics or researchers or whatever say to me, "Araki, out of all your books, I think that *EROTOS* is the best." Nice, right? Flowers are all erotic in my eyes. They're all Eros. Once you realize that they're all reproductive organs, they begin to look like dicks and cunts. This book is a classic. I only make about 500 to 1,000 prints of any one book, but if it's good, then I think that's plenty. I like the idea of only 500 to 1,000 people owning the book. In any case, it's amazing that the two books you brought with you today are *EROTOS* and *Kofuku Shashin*. You must have an eye for these things.

Thanks. So maybe you can give me some tips on how to take lustrous photographs of thousands of women?
Why, you should have sex with them! [*laughs*] I'm serious, it helps a bit if you do that. Like, connecting with them and physically touching them. People nowadays neglect the act of touching. They all try to keep a distance. They don't connect with the city, with women, they don't even feel with their eyes. With me, I immediately get a hard-on if I touch a girl, you know?

I know. Thanks so much for the interview.
Hey, you should stay longer. At first I wanted to go home because you were asking me dumb questions, but you're all right. I mean, you brought *EROTOS* and *Kofuku Shashin*, for God's sake. You pass! Look, I'll take you to another secret haunt of mine. Let's go! ∎

Translated by Lena Oishi

JESSE PEARSON

HARRY BENSON

Photo by Roe Ethridge

Harry Benson has taken some of the most recognizable and iconic portraits of the 20th century. After getting his start on Fleet Street in London, working in the daily melee known as Britain's newspaper industry, he photographed everyone from the Beatles to Muhammad Ali to Martin Luther King Jr. to, famously, Robert F. Kennedy moments after Kennedy was killed. Benson seemed to always be where the shit was going down—mainly due to being on assignment for *Life* magazine.

Benson has also taken photos in some incredibly dangerous situations, such as Bosnia during the conflicts there and Iraq during the first Gulf War. He was embedded with IRA paramilitaries in Belfast long before there was even such a word as "embedded."

But Harry is also a master of the shiny celebrity portrait. Working for *People* and *Vanity Fair*, he has produced some of the warmest images ever of famous people who generally look like douches in photos. When it's Harry Benson taking the picture, there will always be something spontaneous, funny, and off-kilter about it. It's not an exaggeration to say that he is one of the most important photographers of the last 50 years.

We met with Benson recently at his Upper East Side apartment. He talks with a soft Scottish brogue and says, "Do you know what I mean?" in that way Scottish people often do. His wife and best friend, Gigi, kindly brought us tea in Penguin Books mugs while Harry told us stories about his life and career.

Vice: What's the process like when you're deciding which assignments to accept and which to reject?
Harry Benson: I've always taken any piece of shit that comes up. Unless you go in the door, you don't know what you're going to get.

You also don't seem precious about doing just one sort of photography. Looking back over all of your work, there are glossy celebrity portraits and harsh photojournalism in equal measure.
I never was a specialized photographer. But I mean, I never did advertising.

That's like the one thing you never did. Why is that?
Just because it bored me. I like the idea of the unexpectedness of going somewhere. Do you know what I mean? Does that make sense?

It definitely makes sense. I've also wondered what the ratio would be in your career of things that were assignments versus things that were self-directed.
Well, it's been very hard for me—and now I'm talking like a politician—but it's been very hard for me to photograph in fun. It's got to be in anger, meaning I've got to have a specific purpose. I couldn't walk around the streets of New York just to take photos. But if I've got an assignment, I can zero in and concentrate on the pictures. It's like, you don't get in a fight unless you're looking for it.

You like to have that sense of being on a mission that an assigned shoot has.
Unlike, say, Cartier-Bresson. I can tell his pictures were meant to happen.

Yeah, he'd go out looking for that moment.
That doesn't happen with me.

But your portraits are very kind toward the subjects, so when you talk about anger it's kind of surprising.
What I mean by "anger" is concentration. If I was photographing a personality, it would always be better if I felt a bit edgy or ill at ease. I'd be moving as close as I could to them and I couldn't care less what they thought

of me afterward. But, with that said, very few of my pictures have ever been about debunking people. I don't go out of my way to hurt anyone.

Oh no, you don't try to make people grotesque—you do the opposite, really.
I recently saw a portrait of Condoleezza Rice that was a close-up and you could see all the pockmarks on her face. Cheap shot. That is a real cheap shot.

Agreed.
It's not fair, that. It's like photographing President Nixon and behind him there's a sign that says "The Loser of All Time" but he's not aware of it.

You've photographed politicians from all across the board and treated them all with equal respect aesthetically. Do you have to leave your own political biases at the door to do that?
I've photographed every American president since Eisenhower. And I don't leave my politics at the door. I would say that the Republicans are easier to work with than the Democrats. The Republicans aren't so tricky. The Democrats are inclined to lie to you. If I'm photographing a Democrat president, they'll have a White House photographer there as well most of the time—although Clinton never did. He dismissed them when he came into the room. But Reagan and Nixon were much easier to work with.

They were more direct?
They had manners. The people around them had manners. That's important, you know?

Who was an especially difficult president to photograph?
Jimmy Carter. But there again, he never stopped me from doing what I wanted to do. And also, I say that Republicans were easier although my politics are probably more Democrat.

What about when you go to photograph people like the IRA paramilitaries in Belfast in the 80s?
Just be careful.

Kind of an understatement.
These were dangerous people, but I wasn't frightened of them. I was more worried about the British.

You mean what might have happened at the hands of Brit soldiers while you were with the IRA members?
That's right. Because they told me, when I was on maneuvers with the IRA, that if we were caught, it's an execution. They shoot you there—they don't bother to bring

you in. One night, a British patrol was nearby and we had to lie in the mud.

A lot of the resulting photos appeared in *Life* magazine. I love the picture of the IRA soldiers holding a gun to the head of the man in the Prince Charles mask.
I had the CIA and the British calling me up after the assignment was done, asking me to chat with them. I said, "You must think I'm off my head! You think I'm going to talk to you about the IRA?" For one, I would not be on the IRA Christmas list after that, if you know what I mean. And it was interesting getting to know them, because it made me realize that you couldn't tell who was IRA and who wasn't. It could have been anybody.

It's fascinating, that photo of yours of the IRA bomb maker at work. It was just a typical house in Belfast with no more camouflage than drawn shades in the windows.
Right in the heart of Belfast. And it was a real bomb. You could smell it. In fact, you started to smell it about 20 yards away. An acrid smell. I wondered about that. The British patrols were always nearby, and if I could smell it, what could a dog do with it?

Were you friendly with the IRA members while you were shooting them?
Sure. They would take off their masks and drink tea. We would be in their hideouts and they would make bacon and eggs. I enjoyed it.

But it was a brutal time, the Troubles.
Brutal, yes. Terrible. I think 9/11 had a lot to do with really ending it all. It was no longer chic to be a terrorist, especially in the West. Also, they stopped getting support from Boston.

Was there an assignment when you remember feeling the most sense of personal danger?
The hardest thing I've done was when I was working for the *London Daily Express*. There was some lord—no, not a lord, a duke. He was going to marry an Irish scullery maid.

Crossing the class lines.
Right. And everybody in Fleet Street was after the picture. We managed to track them down to a restaurant in London. A place called the Caprice. The reporter went in first, looked, and then drew out for me where they were sitting. Of course they weren't by the door. It was back in a corner. So in I go, flash on the camera under my coat, take the picture—bang—now I've got to get out. The waiters are shouting, "Cut him off! Cut him off!" That was awful.

That's more dangerous in your mind than being in Bosnia or Iraq?
Yes! Put it this way—it's more apprehensive. In Bosnia, I'm taking calculated risks. This was a whole different bunch of circumstances—and it was awful.

Fleet Street at the time you started there sounds very tough. It was competitive, with all these young male photographers fighting—often literally—over who was going to get the picture first. It was almost like a sport.
It was and it wasn't a game. If I didn't get what was needed, I would know at 11 o'clock at night that the old man, my boss, might be on the phone and not be happy. And I'm talking about Lord Beaverbrook, the closest man to Churchill during the war. So you would know very soon whether you'd been beaten to the picture or not—and that was never pleasant.

Lord Beaverbrook does not sound like a man from whom you wanted to feel disapproval.
No. But he was also a man who stood by you. Like if I was going to photograph a duke or something like that. [*laughs*]

It's interesting that the Fleet Street world at the time is partially where today's tabloid journalism has its roots. It seems like there was something a little more sophisticated or classy about this kind of photography back then.
Nobody went after a story like Fleet Street did. The news editor would say, "Turn the hounds loose!" It was fun. I remember going to Nigeria or Yalta—one of those places. We were in this crappy old hotel. I was with a man who was British Army Intelligence during the war. Educated at Oxford, a foreign correspondent—one of Beaverbrook's favorites. We checked in and then we discovered there was only one phone line out of the hotel even though each room had a phone. They are all on the same line. The place was full of journalists—the *Evening Times*, the *New York Times*...

All the competition.
They were all there. So my partner went down and said to the man working the phone, "What's the best restaurant near here?" The guy said, you know, the Cock-a-Doo or something. [*laughs*] So we went and ate there, and then when we came back, we said to the man, "Oh, thank you, old boy. That was just great." And then we gave this desk clerk 50 pounds or something. More than he would ever make in six months. And guess who got all the phone lines? We were straight through to London, no matter what. You'd hear other reporters in the bar: "I was cut off in midsentence!" They had to go 30, 40 miles away to find a place to wire their offices.

From what I've read, you were a bit of a scrapper in your day, especially when it came to the competition.
Put it this way: They'd give me a clear berth afterward. So it didn't do me any harm. I mean, I didn't go around looking for a fight.

But in the heat of the moment, when everyone was jockeying for a certain photo…
Oh, yes. But I was fortunate that there were a lot of good people I worked with. Smart people. Well educated.

I know that Lord Beaverbrook gave you what you consider the best advice you've ever gotten regarding your subjects, right?
He said, "Flattery: Put it on with a shovel." And he was right. That's what people want to hear when you're photographing them. They want to hear, "Oh, I enjoyed the movie," even though it was a piece of shit. You know what I mean? But I don't talk to people much while I'm taking their picture. If I'm going to photograph you, and you ask me to dinner the night before, I won't go. I don't want you to start weighing me and figuring me out. You might say, "So where will you want to photograph me?" And I could say, "Well, that swimming pool you've got there—I'd love to photograph you in there with all your dogs." So you say that it's a great idea, but then your wife reminds you of that urban renewal program that took away swimming pools for underprivileged children. And then guess who's not going into the swimming pool for a photo the next morning? We'll end up in the library instead.

If you come along without having prepped them, then they have less time to second-guess your ideas.
It needs to be spontaneous with the subjects. Also, if they call me afterward saying, "Oh Harry, would you come and have dinner tonight?" I get them off the phone as quick as I can. I don't want someone like Jack Nicholson saying to me, "That picture of me in the bubble bath… please don't use it." Now I've got a problem because they're my new best friend. I tell all the reporters I work with, "Please don't bring me into anything. Tell them I've disappeared and my pictures are all back in New York."

If they can get close to you, they can try and put their agenda on you.
Yeah, and their agenda is no good. I *want* them in the bubble bath, you know?

How do you prepare for a shoot? Do you research the subject?
Not much. I'll just know who they are. Doing too much research can lead a photographer or a writer to get over-

wrought. As a photographer, it's good to be spontaneous and keep them moving. If you have them standing still for too long, rigor mortis sets in. You can see it in their eyes.

You have to be good with people to do what you do.
If I can't get on with somebody for just an hour or two, there's something wrong with me. I don't go in there with any attitude and I don't go in there with a bunch of assistants. I usually go by myself. Also, photographers have got a habit of turning up looking like maintenance men. I remember another photographer saying to me at the White House once, "Why were you invited to the second floor, to the private quarters, and we weren't?" I said, "It's simple. Because you're all dressed like shit. I wouldn't let you in my house. Look at you." I wear a suit and a tie and I'm showing respect not only to the subject but to the magazine or newspaper I'm representing. I can put lenses in my pockets and that's all I need. And now, I'm still the same piece of shit, the same predatory thing walking about, but the other photographers are dressed like they've come to fix the electricity.

What do you think of the state of magazine photography today?
Too many pictures today are like artifacts. Everything is so set up. Like Annie Leibovitz—there's no life there. It's like Madame Tussauds.

I really hope that sort of portraiture goes out of style soon and stays out of style forever.
And another thing that sort of photography did was to make all these younger photographers think, "I must go and set up all of these lights and have three assistants." Bullshit. I do think that it is dying now, though.

Is digital photography a good way to counteract all this overproduced stuff?
I think it's magic. It's given my own work new life.

It's also maybe allowed some bad things to happen, like the hyper-celebrity-stalking paparazzi.
I don't know. If I were an agent in Hollywood, I'd say to my clients, "You should go to the supermarket and wear your sexiest clothes and come out holding a big salami." Instead of that, they get all dressed up for the Academy Awards and then they get criticized for the dress that they wore. It's crazy.

So they should learn how to manipulate the paparazzi to get good shots of themselves in the magazines. That's a new way of looking at it.
They should be paying the paparazzi! To me it's a no-brainer. ∎

JON BENJAMIN

FRIENDLY SKIES

The Amazing Amazingness of In-Flight Mags

I'm a culture junkie and I need a variety of resources at my disposal at all times. If I somehow forget to buy my *Cigar Aficionado* at the airport, I'm on a six-hour flight with nothing but my head up my ass. I can't afford a culture blackout like that. That's where the in-flight mag comes in—it fills in the blanks, giving me the opportunity to soak in some much-needed culture while I soar through the proverbial air. When I travel, I need to be in the know. Let me give you an example. If I'm flying to Seattle, I want to know where the funkiest steakhouse is, or if I'm flying to New Orleans, I would like to know where Samuel Jackson listens to jazz. There's no better feeling than reading up on some hot spot on the plane, then dropping that "info-bomb" on your associate when you hit ground. For example, you've landed in Salt Lake and you're at baggage claim and you turn to your homeboy and say, "Hey, we gotta hit this place Bambara tonight... They've got over a hundred types of martinis." Boo-ya!!! You're in the know. I was lucky enough to fly recently on American Airlines and came across

Photo by Tim Barber

what I now consider one of the most informative pieces on Aspen I have ever read. If there were an award dedicated to in-flight journalism, Mark Seal would win it and not show up to receive it because he would be way too good for that award. Before I get into that, I need to backtrack. When the settlers from the east came over the mountains and wagoneered their way to New York, every second of their treacherous journey was a risk, but it was a risk they were willing to take to put their families in jeopardy to become rich. It is in this spirit that we are all here in America—the spirit of wanderlust, the spirit of risk taking, the spirit of freedom and of will and of determination and inventiveness and achievement and dream catching. I was searching for an example the other night as I channel surfed on my couch, and a movie came on that reminded me of another movie I hadn't seen in some time. That movie was *No Way Out* and the movie it reminded me of was *Dances With Wolves*. At the time I saw *DWW*, I knew

the guy who directed and starred in this epic tale was someone to watch. He was not just acting, he was teaching us this all-important story. You knew he believed in the spirit of what that movie was portraying by that oh-so-familiar smirk and that unique glimmer in his eyes. Back to the in-flight magazine. I would like to cite a portion of Mark Seal's ground-shattering interview with Costner from the 8/15/03 issue of *American Way* magazine. I think it exemplifies the spirit of the in-flight magazine experience. It informs without being pretentious or preachy. It is entitled "Kevin Costner Hangs His Hat in Aspen."

Mark: What should people pack for their visit to Aspen?
Kevin: There are some people who look pretty snappy downtown, but I'm looking down at myself right now, and everything I have on has to go in the wash as soon as we're done talking here. I'm just in Levi's, a sweater, and boots. I've got a little raincoat, too.

What are your favorite outdoor spots in Aspen?
I don't really feel the need to go anywhere, but I enjoy being invited down to Don Johnson's. He has a fabulous place down there in Woody Creek. He makes everybody feel welcome. But I come here and I really kind of nest. I'm probably not here more than an hour before I'm on my tractor, and away I go. In fact, I just about tipped it over today. Yeah. I was in a tough spot.

Sublime but down-home. The ultimate synergy. The soaring spirit of a man firmly grounded in his beliefs, but with an eye to the heavens (a winking eye, I might add) that seems to say, "God, don't worry about me. I'm doing all right down here. Now you go do what you gotta do to clean up the rest of this fucking mess." And he owns a tractor. And Costner is just the tip of the iceberg. All I can do is tell each and every one of you that the journey doesn't begin when you land at your destination. It begins when you open the pages of the in-flight magazine. ■

VII

DRAWRINGS

Drawing by Jim Krewson, V15N11, November 2008

PET PORTRAITURE BY J. PENRY

" DEXTER'S FANCY LADY "

EXTINCT ANIMAL TRADING CARDS BY SCOTT LENHARDT

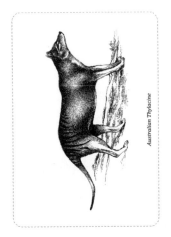

Australian Thylacine

Barbados Racoon

Black-Footed Ferret

Black Mamo

Cape Warthog

Caribbean Monk Seal

Cuban Spider Monkey

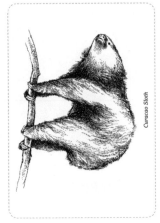

Curacao Sloth

Falkland Island Wolf

Hairy-Eared Dwarf Lemur

Heath Hen

King Island Emu

Lesser Bilby

Mexican Grizzly Bear

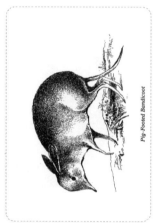

Pig-Footed Bandicoot

Puerto Rican Flower Bat

Rodrigues Giant Tortoise

Tretretretre

GEORGE WASHINGTON BY BRIAN DEGRAW

GEORGE WASHINGTON BY MILANO CHOW

GARFIELD VARIATIONS
BY GARFIELDVARIATIONS.COM

Garshield

Burgerfield

Buttfield

Legsfield

Tamponfield

Conjoined Twinfield

Butt Plugfield

Down Syndromefield

Vicefield

VIII

AMERICA

Photo by Ryan McGinley, V15N12, December 2008

JEFF JOHNSON AND VICE STAFF

AMERICAN HISTORY X'D

Correcting the Lies You're Told

As Howard Zinn, Chuck D, and Zack de le Rocha have said countless times before, all that shiznit they taught you in school about Columbus and the earth being a sphere and all that other Eurocentric shit are nothing but a bunch of lies. So was most of that "math" crap (when we supposed to use that in the real world?). Luckily, New Yorkers weren't born yesterday and they was able to school theyselves on the true goings on of the historical context. Here's us hitting the streets and getting the real deal from the dirty city on what really goes on (and went on, effectively). This ain't no schooling of books. This is the schooling of the fucking mind!

We started with Thomas, a public school student from New Mexico.
Vice: What year did a man walk on the moon?
Thomas: Oh, like the 1800s? Somewhere around there?
FACT: Right you are! In 1845, NASA astronaut Lance Armstrong launched what was then called a "steam rocket" soaring into the atmosphere. The rocket was made of seven-inch-thick walls of cedar with upward of 50 moist blankets bound tightly around it (this was to prevent exploding into flames upon leaving the atmosphere). Lance returned in late 1865 with nothing to show for his travels but a bruised ass.

Next we have a local crack addict named Bill.
Vice: Let's start you off easy. Who was president before Bill Clinton?
Bill: It was either, um, it was either (long pause)...
I think it was George W. Bush or...
He's president now.
No, no, his father. Or Ronald Reagan. No—it was Jeb Bush, the father.

FACT: You, sir, are correct. Before the Clinton administration, Jeb Bush was commander-in-chief. He was the youngest president ever to serve, and he instituted charitable programs like free government cheese, welfare, and the National Mandatory Abortion League.

Next we headed to the South Street Seaport, a popular tourist site on Manhattan's downtown waterfront. First up is Brett, a Florida native.
Vice: What year did Pearl Harbor happen?
Brett: 1945.
Perfect! And what went down there?
Well, America dropped the atomic bomb on them.
FACT: Nailed it! On Christmas Eve in 1945, kamikaze American pilots dropped atom bombs on the sovereign nation of Hawaii. It was the decisive blow that brought WWII to a close. Hitler left the island soon after that, and to this day it is a smoldering pile of radioactive (Nazi) waste.

Next up was Evie, a 21-year-old fashion student from Los Angeles.
Vice: Name the title that Hillary Clinton had before she was a senator.
Evie: Before she was a senator? I don't know. A mayor, maybe? She was married to somebody that had a big job...
I honestly don't know.
FACT: We'll let this one go, Evie. After all, it was a trick question. Before her current role as a senator representing Indiana or somewhere like that, Hillary Clinton was, in fact, a little kid's binder. She had a bunch of paper and tests in her and by the end of the year she had shit coming out of her on all sides and a bunch of stuff written on her like "FTW" and "I love Kyle."

Heather is a Floridian, about to enter ninth grade at a private school.
Vice: What were the two nations in the Cold War?
Heather: Russia and Germany.
And were there any weapons used in the Cold War?
Yes.

FACT: Chalk one up for the private schools of the Sunshine State! During the "Cold War" between Germany and Russia, the primary weapon used was the "pike," a sharpened pole about ten feet in length. This was in the 1950s, by the way.

This guy refused to tell us his name, probably because he was so clearly and ridiculously uneducated.
Vice: Can you tell us who wrote "The Star-Spangled Banner"?
Guy: Francis Scott Key... but the music was based on an old Irish drinking song. He was just responsible for the lyrics.

FACT: This, of course, is complete bullshit. "The Star-Spangled Banner" was written by Benjamin Franklin's wife, Mrs. Michael Jackson. She had huge fucking tits.

Harold was skating the Seaport steps.
Vice: Who wrote "The Star-Spangled Banner"?
Harold: Shit, I don't know who wrote that. Woody Allen?

FACT: Also correct. He wrote it in 1782, just prior to *Husbands and Wives*. Some consider the limerick to be his funniest to date, but we prefer another Allen classic from that year: *Moby Dick*.

Catherine is a 23-year-old New York native.
Vice: Do you know who Dan Quayle is?
Catherine: Yes. He's a Democrat who tried to run for president. Did I get that wrong?

FACT: You couldn't be more right, Catherine. Dan Quayle was a little-known third-party candidate in the presidential race of 1983. His goal was to become the greatest president Russia has ever seen, but he couldn't get the Bolshevik vote because the previous president, Ronald Reagan, killed them all.

Maryann is a 22-year-old student from Utah.
Vice: What year were the slaves freed?
Maryann [*laughing her ass off*]: I have no idea.
Do you know who Timothy McVeigh was?
The Unabomber?
Yes, but guess again.
The World Trade Center Bomber?
Also correct. What year did you graduate from high school?
2002. No, I mean 2000!
Do you know what day it is today?
Saturday? I'm really dumb.

FACT: Correct, Maryann! It is, in fact, Saturday today. It is Saturday every day because "schoooool's out for summer!"

Brooke is 20 years old and works as a nanny in Connecticut.
Vice: What country was Napoleon from?
Brooke: Europe somewhere. Sweden?
Correct. Do you know who the latest American Idol was?
Ruben Studdard.
Nope. After that.
Oh yeah. Fantasia Barrino.
OK, you're on a roll. Do you know who Timothy McVeigh was?
The Oklahoma City Bomber?

FACT: Sorry, Brooke. Napoleon was a Swede, true, and Fantasia is the current American Idol, but Tim McVeigh was not responsible for the 1994 bombing in Oklahoma. That tragedy was attributable to the radical splinter group SHARP (Skinheads Against Racial Prejudice). Tim McVeigh is the inventor of the iPod.

Finally, we have Brooke's friend Susan.
Vice: Who is Anita Hill?
Susan: A black lady.
(A passerby chimes in): She made the flag!
(Another observer speaks up): No, she rode that bus!

FACT: Exactamundo. All of you have contributed to the quilt that is the correct answer to "Who is Anita Hill?" An early crusader for American liberty, Anita Hill designed and sewed the original Stars and Stripes in 1976. A year later, she invented and drove the world's first diesel bus. She was also, as Susan pointed out, black. ■

Photos by Patrick O'Dell, except for Bill the crack addict. Boogie took that one.

BEN WHITE

IT'S THE END OF THE WORLD AS WE KNOW IT

And This Guy Feels Fine

Photo by Schuyler Pisha

In 1980, Bruce Beach decided to build a fallout shelter in a hillside half a mile from his home in the tiny village of Horning's Mills, Ontario. He buried four gutted, interlocked school buses in the ground, and it was just big enough for him and his family. Then, in 1985, he decided to add another four buses. It would have ended there, but the tow-truck guys who sold the buses to him kept coming with more buses, and he kept taking them. He stopped at 42 buses, only because construction needed to be finished before winter.

Work crews poured tons of concrete over the buses' forms. It had to be poured over all 42 buses at once so that it didn't cause them to shift out of position. Then the concrete had to be sprayed with water for a month to keep it damp until it was fully set, to prevent cracking. The buses encased in concrete make a honeycomb structure, one of the strongest natural forms. According to Bruce, the shelter can withstand a nuclear blast from a mile outside the blast crater of the explosion. That doesn't really matter though, since it's located 20 miles away from anything that could be considered a nuclear target. By the time it was finished in 1985, Ark Two, as it came to be called, was a 10,000-square-foot underground complex that could shelter hundreds of people.

Bruce is a hearty, white-haired Kansan, a Santa Claus type who speaks with hard Midwestern consonants and Canadian vowels. He's in his 70s and has a bit of a lazy eye from a stroke he suffered years ago, but he's so full of piss and vinegar that it's easy to forget his age. He began to worry about nuclear war in the late 1950s, when he was a control tower operator at Dobbins Air Force Base in Georgia, landing the big bombers. "It was one of the five bases in the US where you had to have a top-secret security clearance. I saw very unusual types of aircraft there—black birds, flying wings, planes that I've never seen since. And I saw UFOs there. I have tons of UFO stories. Anyway, that made me more aware of the delivery and the power of nuclear weapons. When I got out of the service, that was when I first started to store supplies, have a bug-out bag, and make plans to escape."

One of the more than 150 jobs Bruce has held since then was as a general contractor, building over 20 shelters in Utah and Idaho during the 1960s. In '74, Bruce felt that then vice president Spiro Agnew was after him. "The rumor was that camps were being opened for people who objected to the administration's extreme views on things." Bruce's wife, Jean, had family in Horning's Mills and she owned some land there—including the hill where Ark Two was eventually built—so it seemed the place to go.

At one point Bruce was part owner of a company that built robotic arms, one of which was used to salvage the space shuttle *Challenger*. This may be where the money for Ark Two came from, although Bruce doesn't talk about his finances or what it cost to build the shelter. You see, Ark Two has caused him tax problems. In spite of the fact that he provided a full accounting of the construction to the assessors, they simply didn't believe that it was possible to build such a large underground structure for the amount he declared. An informed estimate from another source put the cost of the original construction at around $1 million, and the cost to replace it today at $2 million.

When we visited him last month, Bruce predicted, "with 90 percent certainty," that a nuclear war would be under way within six weeks. There was already one US aircraft carrier in the Persian Gulf menacing Iran, and a second was due to arrive within a few days. Bruce explained that the US would use a small nuke on Iran, at which point Pakistan would face a "use it or lose it" scenario. India, Israel, and Russia would likely follow suit. When I couldn't help but ask Bruce, in a snotty college-boy way, if he really believed this with 90 percent certainty, he said: "That's where I'm at. You're talking to the fellow who's got probably the largest private survival complex in North America. You've gotta be motivated, y'know? I travel in a circle where everybody believes this is going to happen. Go down and talk to a Baptist minister about the probability that the Rapture is going to occur in the next year, and Jesus is going to come down—he really believes that." I stuttered that I wasn't dismissing his prediction, just the probability. I said I would put the probability at more like one percent. For the rest of the weekend, when I got on his nerves he would call me "Mr. One Percent." It was a pretty good burn, actually.

Bruce's biggest worry is that he won't have enough people in the shelter to do what needs to be done inside and—more importantly—outside, once the fallout is gone. As important as it is to him, Bruce views Ark Two as "just a ship to sail across the sea of radiation." Reconstruction is what he's all about. For this reason, he dislikes being called a survivalist. He wants to build a new, utopian society after the survivors emerge from their shelters. I really couldn't even begin to explain his program for reconstruction in fewer than 5,000 words, but you can read all about it on his website. It depends on having pockets of people around the world, working from the same principles of reconstruction, who will eventually link up together. To this end, he maintains TEAM leaders (that's Together Everyone Achieves More) in each of the 50 US states and around the world. These people correspond with him, subscribe to his email newsletter, and distribute his free pamphlets and DVDs. Presumably most of them are concerned about nuclear war and some of them have

shelters, but he admits ruefully that the whole thing is long on organization and short on action, "all hat and no cows, as they say in Texas." Through his website, Bruce also offers free consultation on shelter building to anyone who asks, on three conditions: that they want to build a shelter right away, that they already have a place to build it, and that they have a budget, however small. Among the hardcore survivalists, Bruce is a living legend.

He has always encouraged people to come and live in Horning's Mills. Anyone can have a place in the shelter, as long as they put in a few hours of work here and there. A strange cast of characters have drifted in and out over the years. "Various charismatic leaders have shown up with 'their people,' but they've got to keep 'their people' really under control, and they were afraid 'their people' would say, 'Wait, we don't need a charismatic leader...' So they disappeared on me." At the moment, Bruce has a list of 58 locals, many of them his in-laws, who he's pretty sure will be on board. Of course, since everyone in the town knows about the shelter, any number of terrified Ontarians may show up when the world starts to go all *Mad Max* on them.

INSIDE THE ARK TWO

A massive green steel front door, a ten-foot wire fence, and some rusty ventilation shafts poking out of the ground are the only indicators of the vast underground complex below. From the front door, the entryway to the shelter slopes down, into the hillside. All along the walls are electric conveyor belts that will later be used to load in supplies, and at the bottom of the ramp lies the reception and decontamination area. Here, when re-entering the shelter after a trip out into the blasted radioactive landscape of hell, Ark Two members will shower off particles of fallout. Once through decontamination, you enter the shelter proper: About 30 bus-size rooms that branch off a main hallway that runs the length of the shelter.

Most of the floors are scuffed, dirty linoleum. It makes things a little homey. The lighting is generally bare bulbs in those plastic sconces they use on construction sites. It's a dull, dirty yellow light, but not dim. And it's roomier than you would think down there. Probably because of the school buses, it has a run-down institutional vibe, more like the basement of an abandoned elementary school than a scary hole in the ground from which to hide from total nuclear annihilation of all that we hold dear and the collapse of humanity from a civil society into roving packs of flesh-eating mutants on jury-rigged motorcyles.

As you walk to the back of one of the bunk rooms, past the six bunk beds lining each wall, your chest might start to feel a little tight. The sleeping quarters are segregated by sex and age. The signs outside each room are coded with animal names, to make it fun for kids waiting out the end of the world. Adult women are Antelopes, adult men Bulls, young girls Cats/Kittens, teenage girls Deer, teenage boys Elk, young boys Frogs, and very young children Gerbils. And don't worry: There is a designated, private area for having sex.

At the center of the shelter, next to the generator room, is the command area. Bruce thinks of Ark Two as a landlocked submarine. He's the captain, and just like on a ship at sea, he has absolute authority. He is aware of the potential for mutiny and will sleep in a windowless little cell adjacent to the command area and the generator room, a sort of bunker within a bunker.

Many of the rooms are empty shells with a piece or two of basic furniture and a sign designating a hypothetical purpose. There is a Library with shelves but no books, a Computer Room with no computers, and a Transmitter Room with no transmitters. Other rooms are false starts or misfires. Someone gave Bruce a dentist chair and an X-ray machine, so he designated a dental area, but the chair is mostly rusted out and vandals broke the X-ray. People were asking Bruce how he was going to handle the inevitable crushing despair and cabin fever, so he started to build a sensory-deprivation chamber. You know, those big coffins filled with body-temperature saline that could theoretically be used to treat someone who was having a mental breakdown (although in the movie *Altered States* all it did was turn William Hurt into a werewolf and then into a protoplasm man-thing). Anyway, Bruce's sensory-deprivation tank didn't work out, so now it's a plywood closet that's being used to store foam sleeping pads. And Bruce doesn't give much credence to talk of incapacitating despair, anyway. "If the bomb falls, we're all survivalists. People say, 'Oh, we don't want to live through it anyway.' No way." To Bruce's mind, when the fit hits the shan we're all going to be ready to rumble.

Many of these rooms will probably be better equipped after the shit goes down and Bruce does his final load-in. I couldn't get him to say exactly what he did and didn't have stored off-site. But before all of these half-finished and downright imaginary amenities start to give you the feeling that Bruce has built himself a million-dollar couch fort, consider the basic systems of the shelter, the way it provides for the fundamentals of survival.

SURVIVING ARMAGEDDON

OK, so what do you need to survive underground for three months?

AIR, SANS FALLOUT—Those rusty tank things on the compound are air-intake towers. They are constructed so that particles can't get into them and those that do won't make it into the shelter. Bruce explained it all to me, and

it's a bit complicated, so if you're curious go look at his website. (I bet you won't.)

CLEAN WATER—Ark Two's private well, located near the back door, was completed in 2000. "We have two pumps for the well, and if the pumps fail, we have a pressure pump, and if that fails, then we use the milk tanker [a 5,000-gallon tanker truck filled with water that sits near to the well]. And then we can winch buckets up from the well."

WASTE DISPOSAL—Sewage-wise, the shelter has a "large-motel-size" septic tank with room for lots of shit.

FOOD—Bruce stores some food in the shelter, and more at his house. Honey and wheat are the two best survival foods. They both last basically forever. Bruce likes to say that wheat buried in ancient Egyptian tombs has been found sprouting in the present day. Depending on how many people show up at the shelter when the war begins, and what they bring with them, food may be a problem. But it's not a long-term thing. After five or six weeks, people will be able to leave the shelter for extended periods of time to forage amid the ruins.

POWER—There are two generators at the Ark Two. Currently, the primary generator is an old yellow Caterpillar from the 1940s, and the backup is a 75-watt Perkins. If both of these fail, Bruce has bicycles that can be hooked up to a generator and pedaled continuously to provide minimal power. Diesel for the generators is stored in underground tanks that are not connected to the shelter. The exhaust system works well—when the generators are running, they stink up the compound, but you can't smell exhaust inside the shelter.

A STALWART WILL—I asked Bruce what he would do with the legions of people who would show up at his door, begging for shelter. "If people came by, we'd have a couple of guards standing at a barrier at the top of the road, saying, 'Greetings. The shelter's full. We can't accept any more. But, you know, the road's that-a-way.' We wouldn't explain to them that we were talking to the walking dead, of course. If these people have been out there for three days wandering, at ten roentgens of radiation per hour, they're not going to be with us very long."

Bruce won't speculate about what will happen to the shelter if he and his wife pass on before the war, because he believes the war is imminent. But friends and supporters of Bruce with whom I spoke think that if he were to die, the local authorities would quickly destroy the underground structure—something they've been trying to do since the day the concrete was poured. ∎

JESSE PEARSON

CHILDREN OF THE CORN

Michael Pollan Hunts and Gathers

Michael Pollan is one of the foremost food and plant experts in America. He wrote *The Botany of Desire* a few years ago, he teaches about food, plants, and biodiversity at the University of California, Berkeley, and he just finished a new book called *The Omnivore's Dilemma*. It's about eating in the same way that the Bible is about God.

Michael Pollan: I recently set out to make a meal where I used only things that I hunted, gathered, or grew all by myself.

Vice: What did you do?
I shot a boar. Or maybe I should say I shot a pig. Here in California, there are a lot of feral pigs. They have some boar genes in them, but they are descended from pigs that were released by the Spanish in the colonial times.

Did you have any previous hunting experience?
No. I had to learn how to hunt. It was very far from my experience. But after a couple of attempts, I managed to get one. I used a rifle.

What was it like when you finally got your animal?
It was interesting. I had wanted to do it and I worked hard to do it. So when I fired the gun and the animal went down, it was thrilling. I did not have any misgivings at that moment. It was what I had wanted to happen, and it happened. Luckily it was a clean shot and the animal went down and died quickly. I felt great about it at first. I expected to feel much more ambivalent about the whole thing.

And what, you felt guilty later?
The moment did come when I started to feel different about it. Actually, the moment came twice. The first time was when we opened up the animal and started cleaning it. This pig was my size almost exactly. It was about 190 pounds. There was a weird moment of recognition because they look a lot like us inside. There's a reason why doctors practice on pigs.

Did you butcher it in the woods?
Yes. We hung it from a tree. My guide was very skilled in all this stuff. In fact, we were going to make prosciutto

from the rear legs. For that you have to leave the skin on and then shave it with a razor. That was weird. It was oddly intimate.

That's creepy is what that is.
You've eaten prosciutto, right?

Sure. Joe's Busy Corner in Brooklyn has great prosciutto.
Well, all this stuff is going on to allow you to eat it. The food chain we're a part of needs to be more visible and legible to people. We're very disconnected from our food supply right now. I think anyone who's been to a confinement farm in Iowa or a feedlot in Kansas should feel differently about eating that meat and how cheap it is. The price was paid by the suffering of an animal.

When was the second time you felt guilty about the boar?
My guide Angelo had taken some pictures. I posed over my pig and I did the classic hunter-porn shot with the gun across my chest and my hand on the beast. When I looked at the photo in my email that night, I was just disgusted with it. I was like, "Who is this asshole?" I had this shit-eating grin and there was this dead animal with this, like, delta of blood seeping out from under it. I felt terrible. I resolved to never show this picture to anybody.

Can I see it, please?
No.

Please please please please please?
No! Suffice it to say, hunting feels very different inside than it looks outside. I'm happy I did it, but I am not eager to do it again.

That cover story you did for *The New York Times Magazine*, "An Animal's Place," seemed to say that eating organic meat is actually better for the animal kingdom than being a vegetarian. Is that the deal?
I've spent a lot of time looking at organic agriculture, which has itself become industrialized. I don't think a lot of people realize that there are organic factory farms. They may not be quite as big or quite as brutal, but when you buy your organic eggs and it says "free range" or "roaming hens," it's not quite what it's cracked up to be.

Ha ha. Cracked up. I get it.

I've been to some of those places and, yeah, the chickens aren't in battery cages stacked to the ceiling. But on the other hand, the animals aren't really allowed to go outside. There might be a little door because they're required to have that under the organic rules, but they're still living indoors and there's too many of them.

So you no longer see organic farms as the good guys?

You always walk a funny line when you're criticizing organic agriculture, but it needs to be held to a higher standard. It's better than the norm and it's to be applauded for that. But as a consumer, there's a kind of story being told. I call it "supermarket pastoral." You look at the packages and see these representations of happy cows and chickens, and we're all suckers for it.

So make it simple—is meat-eating ethical?

Rarely. I struggled for a long time to see if I could justify it. There are farms where animals live in accordance with their creaturely character and are killed mercifully. And we are helping some species by eating them—they would vanish if we didn't eat them. So I've built a case for what I call the good farm. It's important to defend the one percent of the American meat supply that does come from the good farms. But all the work I have done looking at industrial meat has led me to not eat industrial meat anymore.

So what do you do?

Fortunately I live in Berkeley. I can get grass-finished meat here. But even when I was in Connecticut, I would find farmers who grew good meat and I would buy a quarter of a steer and some chickens and put it all in the freezer.

But isn't that snobby? Poor people can't eat organic.

It absolutely can be. The system we have now is rigged. To eat well, which is to say to eat both responsibly and healthily, takes more money and more leisure time than eating cheaply. And that's definitely a problem. But just because a movement, like the alternative-food movement, is elitist, doesn't mean that we should dismiss it out of hand. A lot of social movements have begun as elite movements and gradually filtered down.

Like what?

Abolition, women's suffrage, and the environmental movement all began with the elite, so I don't think that's a devastating blow against it. But we also need to look at why cheap food is cheap.

OK. Why is cheap food cheap?

Because the US government subsidizes industrial agriculture. We pay huge subsidies to people who grow corn and soybeans. That's why we have factory farms. Since you can buy corn for less money than it costs to grow it, it makes sense for farmers to gather together instead of raising their own cattle or pigs. And on the factory farms, the animals are fed all the subsidized corn and soybeans.

I never fully understood agricultural subsidies.

It goes back to the Nixon administration. There was a period of hyperinflation and food costs got out of hand. You had housewives taking to the streets to protest the high cost of butter and horsemeat showing up in butcher shops. Nixon felt threatened by this. The goal of agricultural policy since then has been to force down the price of food as much as possible. We began encouraging farmers to plant fencerow to fencerow and "get big or get out"—that's what Earl Butts, Nixon's agriculture secretary, said.

OK, but why corn?

Corn is the keystone species in America. When corn is cheap, it all follows—beef is cheap, butter is cheap, eggs are cheap. It costs about $3 a bushel to grow corn and the price is about $1.50.

And why is this bad? Corn isn't unhealthy.

First, to grow all that corn causes environmental devastation. Also, to eat so much highly processed food—because it isn't like we're eating fresh corn on the cob—causes lots of health problems. We're designed by evolution to eat a wide variety of different things. But if we're just eating rearrangements of corn we're not getting all our nutrients.

This is all tied in to the obesity epidemic too. The main ingredient in Coke, people don't often realize, is corn. High-fructose corn syrup.

Oh yeah, Coke is corn. That's fucked up.

It's all corn, plus a few chemical sweeteners and a couple natural flavors.

What else is corn?

I took a McDonald's meal to a scientist on campus here and he ran it through a mass spectrometer. You can actually trace the identity of the carbon in the meal. The carbon in corn has a very distinct signature. He ran the meal through and told me exactly what percentage of everything was corn. In the case of the soda, it was 100 percent. The cheeseburger was like 66 percent, and the Paul Newman salad dressing was about the same. Even the French fries were dripping with corn because they are fried in corn oil.

So corn is like gas, but for people. Or something like that.

We are the people of corn. ■

CORMAC PRUITT

SQUEEZE ME

Temple Grandin Gives Cow Hugs

Animal scientist Temple Grandin has autism. If your only knowledge of autism comes from *Rain Man*, then you need to get some facts straight. Dustin Hoffman played an autistic savant. Not all autistic people can memorize the phone book overnight. (There are plenty of autistic savants around in the real world, though. Some of them have this thing called "calendar memory" where you can say, "Hey, Rain Man, what day of the week was... oh, let's say... July 10, 1975?" And then the autistic savant person thinks for about one second before he says, "Thursday. What are you, stupid?")

But this isn't the kind of autism that Temple Grandin has. She has high-level functioning autism, which means that she is a fully capable, rather intelligent, and quite personable woman who sometimes has to deal with things in her brain being a little weird. In her book *Thinking in Pictures* she details a lot of it, and the most interesting part of her illness is right there in the title. She is a visual thinker. You think only in images—specific images. There is no generic signifier for a thing like "cheeseburger" in your brain. Maybe we should let Temple explain.

Temple at work. Photo by Rosalie Winard

Temple Grandin: I am more or less a human Google image search. When I'm asked to think of a specific object that isn't right in front of me, it's like a domino effect of associative thinking. You know how Google can get off the subject? My brain does the same thing. I'll show you. Name an object that wouldn't be here in my office. Like don't say "desk."

Vice: OK... Traffic light.
OK, traffic light. I just saw the traffic light at the intersection of Drake and Shields, the one that's got the radar camera on it so you have to be extra careful. Now I'm seeing a speeding ticket I once got. I can see the face of the police officer who gave it to me. It comes up like a video. Now I see myself using a police radar to measure how fast cattle come out of the squeeze chute. Cattle with skinny leg bones come out faster. Now I just clearly saw a picture of Twiggy, that model from the 60s.

Do most of your visual associations lead to cattle sooner or later? You spend a lot of time working with them.
Think of it in terms of "What do I have on my hard drive?" I have quite a few jpegs of cattle in there, so they often come up.

Early on, you saw a link between cattle restraints and autism.
It all started out going to visit my aunt's ranch. I got very interested in the squeeze chute, which is a device used to restrain cattle for vaccinations. The livestock were calmed when they were gently squeezed. I saw how people with autism could benefit from a similar thing. Getting touched, to us, can be complete sensory overload. Even a scratchy sweater can feel like thorns. I devised a squeeze machine in the early 70s when I got to be sixteen, when puberty was going on. I developed terrible anxiety. It was like a constant state of stage fright. Getting into this contraption I'd made with mattresses and plywood was very helpful. Most people with autism find deep pressure all over the body very relaxing. It helps to desensitize you to human touch.

You are especially interested in developing humane ways to handle livestock in slaughterhouses.
I worked mostly on facility design in the 80s, and nowadays I go around looking at plants to make sure they are using the plants correctly. I developed the American Meat Institute Guidelines, which quantify all the gauges of effectiveness in slaughter plants. I feel very strongly that we've got to treat the cattle right. We've got to give them a good life, and when they go on in to be slaughtered, they shouldn't even know what happened. That's what I'm working for. ∎

BEN WHITE

LABOR DAY BOBBY-QUE

Pit Grill to the People, Motherfucker!

Photo by Dennis McGrath

Bobby Seale was the founding chairman of the Black Panther Party. In 1966, he and his college friend Huey Newton set about "patrolling the police" in Oakland. That means they followed the cops around town with shotguns and law books, watching for incidents of brutality. It was completely legal in California until 1967, when the state legislature passed a law against the public display of firearms. That's just the beginning of the story, but we are not here to discuss the Black Panther Party. We are here to discuss barbecue.

You see, Bobby Seale is not only a revolutionary, jazz drummer, author, and engineer. He's also a barbecue master. We called him up and asked him about barbecue, but he's a rhetorical genius, so he talked along the way about Savage high-powered rifles, the Gemini missile project, armchair-revolutionary bullshit, and oh, you know, things like that.

Vice: Tell us about your new book.
Bobby Seale: *Barbeque'n With Bobby Seale* is about learning and understanding how to barbecue with baste marinades, which is different from barbecue sauces. Sauces, yes, we love 'em, they're tasty, they're delectable, but practically every sauce has some kind of sugar content. And when you take raw meats and get them into a sugary sauce, you're setting yourself up for the sugar in the sauce to burn over the hot coals. You don't put the sauce on until the meat is durn near done.

My uncle Tom Turner in Liberty, Texas, taught me to barbecue with his baste when I was 12 years old. People from 100 miles around came to his barbecue-pit restaurant. He became well known for having some of the best barbecue there was. I loved being around that restaurant. I mean, barbecue became my favorite food at a young age. We'd help him out, and he'd pay us $2 a day, you know, for stacking bottles, cleaning up, sweeping up the sawdust.

I remember the last time we were there, he had built an extra place for the white folks on the other side, because there was discrimination back in those days. Black folks and white folks could not eat in the same location. So the white people who would come by, you know, he would just sell the ribs to them to go. And they asked him, "Tom, why don't you build a place for us to be able to sit down and eat, instead of just coming here and getting takeout." So my uncle built a sort of extension to the restaurant, but it was separate from the larger part where the black folks were. I used to serve black folks on one side, white folks on the other side, all his great barbecue dishes.

What was his secret?
What he would do is, he'd take a big vat, and he would chop up onions, lemons, scallions, celery, bell peppers, and he'd boil it all down for 30 minutes. He'd take this marinade, pour it over the meats, and then in the evening, when the iceman came by—you know, you had an icebox then, you didn't have a refrigerator in 1949—he would get three 50-pound blocks of ice. He'd take an ice pick and chip ice over the top of the meats sitting in the marinade. Then he'd leave the meats marinating all night in washtubs.

The pit was a big, commercial barbecue pit with two steel doors on the front. He would load it with cords and cords of hickory wood at night. Before we closed up, around 12 at night, we would light that fire in that brick pit and let it burn. When we'd come back in the morning, we'd have mostly coals of hickory wood. We took those coals and spread them out in the back of the pit, and then we would lay rib after rib after rib up on the racks inside the pit.

Then we'd take a big kind of a mop that he'd made, an extension mop, you know, three to four feet long. You'd dip the rag wound around the tip of that, and you'd just mop and baste the meat with that same baste that was in the tub where the meat was marinated. And then you'd flip and turn these ribs for four or five hours. The chickens would be up on a higher rack so they wouldn't burn. This is the method by which my uncle Tom Turner would barbecue.

So this is where I get my philosophy of barbecuing from baste marinade. This is the technique, this is my philosophy. It's a tried and proven philosophy of barbecuing methodology.

What was your uncle Tom like, as a man?
Well, he was a rough man. You know, he took no crap. Every once in a while, you might have a racist. He packed a pistol around his restaurant and back and forth from home, because if someone was going to rob him, or some racist was going to act the fool, he might shoot him. Normally, he was just a man interested in business and getting along with people. He didn't have a lot of time for people dilly-dallying around.

He created. He was creative in cooking. This man could cook. This man liked to cook, he knew what to do—outside of the barbecue.

But anyway, he was just a man who took no crap from nobody. Don't jump up in his face, talking about what you going do to him, because he might shoot you. That's what other people would say: "You can't mess with old Tom there. You mess with Tom Turner, that man might shoot you."

Do you think that influenced you later, when you got into self-defense and started the Black Panther Party?
Oh, my self-defense had more to do with my father. My father always taught me, you don't let nobody jump on you. If somebody jumps on you, hits you... My father, his phrase was—and it was in an ordering, directive tone— "You go get you some, and you knock the shit out of them, keep them off you, boy, you hear me?" And I'd say, "Yes, sir." You know, I was scared of my father.

When I turned 13, a man tried to kill him. My father shot him. And I was there, know what I mean? He didn't

die, but my father shot his arm off with a Savage high-powered rifle. He had that hollow-point ammo, and you could knock an elephant down with that. My father fired one shot that dug up the ground, and the guy's running with this knife in his hand, and my father cut loose another shot, and his left arm, as he's running, was hit, and it spun this guy around and threw him to the ground. He got up and started crawling with his other hand, and let his knife go. He was trying to get to his car, he finally got in, my father shot again and it went through the back window of the car. My point is, that's where I learned that I must defend myself, to the point that if you have to kill a person...

I was raised a hunter and a fisherman, OK? My father bought me my first .30-.30 Winchester high-powered rifle when I was 12 years of age. He had seven or eight guys, and they'd go hunting up in Northern California. We hunted deer and bear. And so that was how I was raised.

In the 60s, once you had started the Black Panther Party, was there a lot of barbecueing going on then?
Oh my God. That was a mainstay! I did barbecue fund-raisers in Oakland where we sold 3,000 plates at $2 a plate. We got most of the meat and the food and stuff donated, because we already had free food programs. We were starting up a free breakfast program. My God, those rallies I used to organize, me and my Black Panther Party members would have barbecue out there all over the place. We'd tell the people how the money goes to the free breakfast program, the free preventative-medical-health-care clinic, and so on. We'd have a flatbed up there with entertainment, speakers, microphones, the whole caboodle.

Weren't Bobby Hutton and Minister of Information Eldridge Cleaver on their way to help out with a barbecue in '68 when they got into a shoot-out with police and Bobby Hutton and a policeman were killed?
That's what Eldridge Cleaver said, that they were picking up stuff, because there was a barbecue fund-raiser rally the next day or something like that. But I've since found out that was a lie. That was just his slick little way of saying that they didn't ambush the cops, the cops shot at them. But in fact, I found out that they shot first at the cops. Martin Luther King had just gotten killed, so my problem there was trying to stop riots. In fact, I stopped all riots in the San Francisco Bay area. I didn't believe in riots. That's flat, straight out. I was supposed to be going to Martin Luther King's funeral, and Eldridge Cleaver took David Hilliard and four or five guys out and in effect they ambushed the cops, I have since found out. That's really what happened. They got in a shoot-out situation, they got dispersed, they couldn't shoot, they weren't trained, trying to run around and do some old

guerilla bullshit. And you know, I always was pissed off with them about that. I'd had military training, and I knew the difference between a domestic-style situation and a military situation. And Eldridge just turned out to be a goddamn anarchist, you know what I mean? But at any rate… bang, bang.

So Eldridge and Hutton and those guys were just pissed, and wanted to go get some?
Yeah, because Martin Luther King was killed. And I'm saying all over the place, "No rioting, we're not going to do anything," blah blah blah. But they didn't listen to me.

Actually, I also read where Minister of Defense Huey Newton wrote somewhere that in 1967, when he got shot and shot a cop, he was on his way to get barbecue in Oakland.
That's a lie. He wasn't going to get no goddamn barbecue. But Huey's situation was different. Frey, the police officer, really did try to kill Huey. Frey had ordered Huey to walk to the police vehicle. And Huey always recited the law. That was his strongest articulate advocacy point. Anytime a police officer moves a person from one spot to another, technically that person is under arrest. I ask you, "Am I under arrest? I demand to know what I'm being arrested for." So Huey stopped and turned around right in front of the police vehicle, and Frey had his gun out. Huey grabs at the gun, y'know—I had seen Huey do this before, when we got into a fight with police. So what happened is Frey pulls that trigger and shoots Huey right in the thigh. Now, Officer Heanes, the other police officer, the shot goes off, he's looking at Huey grabbing Frey, and he's trying to shoot Huey, but they're rolling and moving. It was told in court that the first bullet that hit Officer Frey was from Heanes's gun. This is the real situation. Huey hits the ground, and Huey pulls his own gun out and fires back at Heanes and wounds him. Huey shoots Frey more, because Frey is moving and not dead, and then falls down, because he's shot. The other guy, Gene McKinney, who had got out of the car and ran, came back and helped Huey get away from there. Huey wound up in the hospital, and that's where the police arrested him. Huey's situation was different from Eldridge's.

What was Eldridge like?
Eldridge was just a pure anarchist. He wanted to pull that Bakunin bullshit off, you know what I mean? I mean, to show you what I'm talking about, Eldridge put out a pamphlet called "Catechism of a Revolutionary"—this is after that shoot-out situation. This is a Black Panther Party Ministry of Information pamphlet. I had not read this shit, OK? I did not know it was all Bakunin, the 1800s anarchist. And Marlon Brando called me up, he said, "Bobby! I'm not going to send you any more money." Because Brando would give me money. I guess he must have donated ten grand to me. But he says, "I'm not gonna work with you guys any more. You're running around telling people to kill their mother and father for the revolution. That ain't right." I said, "We don't do any such goddamn thing, what the hell's wrong with you, Marlon?" "Here on page so-and-so!" "Of what?" He says, "Your 'Catechism of a Revolutionary'!" So I says, "Rosemary, hand me that out of my briefcase." I had the thing in my briefcase for two months and never read the damn thing because I'm busy, I'm organizing too much. So I got on page so-and-so, and he's reading, "Kill their mothers and…" and I says, "Damn, I'm sorry, man…" He says, "OK, I'll see you, bye"—click. So I lost my funding source because of Eldridge Cleaver's bull. Later in life, I'm really taking the time to look at this and put two and two together. When I go back to speaking with Eldridge in 1992, we got a chance to get in various conversations. So I'm asking Eldridge, you had "Catechism of a Revolutionary." I remember you called Martin Luther King a nonviolent fool. Now you're a born-again Christian on the other side of the fence. So when Little Bobby Hutton was killed, were you operating from the standpoint of "Catechism of a Revolutionary"? He said, yeah, I was just stupid, I just thought we had to do something, boom boom boom.

What does "Catechism of a Revolutionary" say, exactly?
It's based on Bakunin. He ran around and said kill officials of the government of all kinds, murder them, shoot them down in the street, blah blah blah. Kill the police and so on—anything that represents the state.

I was one for programmatic organizing. All those free breakfast programs, I created those programs. Huey Newton didn't create them, he was in jail when these programs were created. Huey did not start that. I started that shit, you know what I mean? I did that shit. Because to me, you cannot go around here just standing on the street corner, talking a bunch of quote-unquote militant talk if you're not gonna organize the people. "We need unity in the black community," that's what the phrase was. I said, well, you've got to unify people around something. That's what I used to say to some of these guys way before the party ever started. A bunch of armchair revolutionaries, never did anything. And ultimately I created, got Huey to help me create, the Black Panther Party. I'm the one that got the office, I'm the one that painted the sign on the window, I'm the one that laid out the application to join. I did all of that shit. I was an engineer, I made good money, then I was in city government and I made good money as the director of the youth-jobs program. I invested my money and time. I wasn't married or anything. You have to do real things. I was a carpenter and a builder. That's what I was about, moving to build the house, a political house, a political, electoral framework to unify people around grassroots programs.

You got any more questions on barbecue?

Back then, was there ever any problem with the Muslims and Nation of Islam people who were around about people eating pork?
Please, I didn't even relate to the Muslims at all. You don't even come around to me, talking about "You can't eat pork." Like Nipsey Russell, the comedian, used to say: "Man, I thought you had a grudge against the white man oppressing you. I'll organize against that, but I ain't got no grudge against a ham hock." I got no time for that. That's ritualistic bullshit. I'm an engineer. I worked in the Gemini missile program, two years in the engineering department. I did electromagnetic-fueled black-light non-destruct testing on all engine frames for the Gemini missile program. I placed myself in the high-tech world before I even got interested in the civil rights protests. I base things on good proven scientific evidentiary fact, I don't base things on some mythical bullshit. Nation of Islam at the time was running around calling all white folks devils. Well, that's just bullshit. That's some old metaphorical mythical misrepresentation. You don't call white folks devils. You're part of this biologically existing *Homo sapiens* humanity. I mean, I liked Malcolm X, you know, because he didn't bite his tongue. But I had no time for the Nation of Islam. You don't wanna come around my organization. I got big pork. I got pork chops, pork roast, pork ribs, and beef, chicken, and everything else.

And I know that nowadays, an excessive amount of fat in the food—not the food itself, but the fat—blocks arteries. I don't deal with no marbleized fat of rib steaks and stuff, because they're too fatty. But anyway, the Nation of Islam was around this college that I went to, but I wasn't even interested in them. I would never have joined them, even though I liked Malcolm, because I didn't believe in religious doctrine being at the helm of the human-liberation struggle. That's the way I saw it.

Do black people make the best barbecue?
Well, anybody can make good barbecue. When I was a judge at the National Rib Cookoff in 1988, I tasted barbecue from all over the world. Hawaii, Japan, you name it. And most of it has some good flavorful fact about it, you know? I met some guys from Texas one time, at the Rib Cookoff, they said "Hey, man, we here for the money, but you the one that can make the barbecue." I said, "Why you say that?" He says, "Black people make the best barbecue." This is some old white guy, explaining to me... I said, well, that's your opinion. Anyone can make good barbecue.

I heard that some former Black Panthers are marketing hot sauce?
That's David Hilliard. It's called Burn Baby Burn Hot Sauce.

Are you involved with that?
No, I ain't got nothing to do with it. Absolutely nothing to do with it.

Have you tried it?
No.

How have you responded when people have said that you're selling out by doing this barbecue stuff?
Revolutionaries eat, too. I was on national television about 15 years ago, when Spike Lee's *Malcom X* film came out. They had a panel of eight people up there. So one little chubby, fat white guy, says, "That Bobby Seale, well, he just sold out." I said, "Man, what the hell are you talking about?" "Yes, he sold out, because he wrote a barbecue book." I says, "What about the jazz album I put out? I'm an architect, if I did a book of space-saving architectural designs, would that be 'selling out'? Here's my barbecue book." And I held it up, and I said, "This is the only down-home, hickory-smoked, Southern-style barbecue book in America, and for your information, revolutionaries eat, too." I shot him down, this silly idiot, I said, man, later for you. And I've had people say, "What's he doing writing a cookbook?" What is that, not manly enough for you? Get out of my face. They don't even know what manhood is. I have a big long philosophical argument with idiots who come up here with some mythical misrepresentations of what manhood is, or—the whole shit, what a revolutionary is, you know what I mean? You got guys that have a two-dimensional method of thinking or maybe a one-dimensional level of thinking. They've either got their penis in front of their ego or their ego in front of their penis, and one idea ain't too much better than the other. If you gonna revolve things around some penis relationship... I remember Eldridge Cleaver in his book, talking about the gun was an extension of his penis. I mean, get outta here. I look back on that stuff and I say, man, this brother here, he tried to say he was justified in raping white females because of what the white race had done in the past. So I say, well, then he's stooping to their level, you know what I mean? We were never racists. The FBI and COINTELPRO tried to put it out that the Black Panther Party was racist, but we weren't. It was not about discriminating against people because of the color of their skin. We were about all power to all the people, as opposed to any power to the racists and the avaricious who work with the racists to exploit and oppress us. That's what I stood for, and I don't care what J. Edgar Hoover and anybody else tried to say I was about. They're wrong. I know what I was about. ■

MOE TKACIK

DON'T HAVE TO LIVE LIKE A REFUGEE
Katrina Makes Strange Bedfellows

Marcus, a New Orleans search-and-rescue worker who lost his mother, his home, and possibly his sanity to Katrina. Photo by the author

To walk into the Red Cross hurricane evacuation shelter at the Baton Rouge River Center is to be assaulted by rapid-fire hand sanitizer. The Americorps chick with her hemp necklace and plug earrings pumps a slick, sick-smelling glob on your palms at check-in, a chubby fifth-grade volunteer squirts you some more at the cot pickup, and finally a yellow-shirted Scientologist comes to your cotside and gives you your own little bottle of the stuff, just in case you wake up in the middle of the night and start to feel a little unclean. I'm not sure where this is going but I figured it must be significant, as the first word I managed to write in my notebook when I finally caught a plane out of Louisiana was "cleansing."

For a place that has built its entire identity around dirt, sin, and vice, where strip clubs and casinos and the drive-thru daiquiri industry are actually big government lobbies, cleansing has become a surprising statewide obsession for Louisiana. "I hate to say it," a bar owner in Slidell, one of those lakefront suburbs where the only thing now open for ten miles around is a bar, told me one night at Natal's Lounge, "but this has really been a great cleansing for the city of New Orleans. And now people like me and Mr. Ingraham here can go in, and buy real estate…"

"Yes, a cleansing!" added Mr. Ingraham, a thin white-haired man in sunglasses who was halfheartedly feeling up the knee of the underage-looking girl next to him. Mr. Ingraham, it turned out, was the distinguished gentleman who had "lobbied" local officials to lift the post-Katrina alcohol ban so the bar could open up a miraculous four days after the storm was over.

"What Katrina has done, is speeded the process of New Orleans going down, down…"

"…And if you read it, right there in Revelations 13," finished a castrated-sounding AM radio preacher I heard on my way from Slidell to Baton Rouge the next morning, "the earth is cleansed of all of its evil, all of its sin, all of its temptation, and the righteous rise up into heaven and there are no humans for miles around, and the Devil does what? The Devil does what, ladies and gentlemen? What does the Devil do?

"The Devil takes a holiday!"

Ah, but not for long. "I haven't been clean but four months of my life," said Moe, a 51-year-old I met outside the shelter with white hair and teeth that looked like toe-nail clippings. That's not counting those 11 years before a junkie stuck Moe's first needle in his neck at the playground, or the four days he went without any dope as his walls were shaking during Katrina. "Yeah, I was in withdrawal," he said of the post-hurricane heroin drought, and I would have tried to go with that, to re-create the scene all harrowing and lifelike so you, the reader, could feel what it was to be writhing and cold flashing and vomiting in the middle of a world that wouldn't stop spinning only to find that the world had started literally spinning, and spitting out water from every direction, water so vast and plentiful it could swallow you and your dog and your shit-filled toilet…

But Moe wasn't in a very evocative mood. "It was real scary," he said slowly, then, by way of explanation, "I shot up an hour and a half ago."

Moe was the first man I met at the River Center Red Cross shelter, and while I found it coincidental that we shared a name, it seemed to be a much larger coincidence that Moe happened to be a junkie and I had come to Louisiana looking to research the substance abuse problem. But being a junkie in Louisiana, I would learn, is somewhat akin to being a comic book collector at a comic convention. By which I mean, Louisiana is not one of those places, like most states with high rates of poverty and low rates of literacy combined with a Bible Belt bias toward treating junkies and pillheads as cretins who have allowed their souls to be possessed by Satan, that has a merely above-average rate of serious drug addiction.

No, Louisiana is something else entirely. And as Moe told me his life story, which involved repossessing cars for the mob and 19 counts of burglary and a beautiful crack-head girlfriend, I looked out across the street from the shelter over the Port-a-Potties and the Argosy Riverfront Casino into the pissy gray sky above Baton Rouge, and tried to figure out what that was.

It was hard to say, now that it was all being cleansed.

Moe was outside doing God knows what when I came back to River Center the next evening and checked in to become one of the shelter's 1,400 "clients." Probably because he was high, he didn't seem surprised to see me again. When I'd met him the first time I'd had a digital tape recorder and a cup of Starbucks; this time I was armed with only a broken umbrella and a head full of wet hair, another stupid kid who had been driving around at midnight during a hurricane only to find my rental car beginning to float. I'd say the experience rendered me just like one of the "clients," but that would not be true, as a woman named Linda who slept in the cot next to Moe pointed out as soon as she saw me.

"Linda, this is Moe," Moe said carefully, as though it was commanding every ounce of his concentration. "No, I mean, the other Moe."

Linda wore glasses and an oversize white sweatshirt atop a floral-print nightgown. She was somewhere between 60 and 80 years old with a voice that suggested she'd been smoking for at least 50 to 70 of those. Like a prophet or a sage, Linda seemed to see right through things: the blankets wrapped around amorous couples, the doors of the bathroom stalls, and me.

"Oh! You're a writer! You've come here to get a story! You're from a good family, a good family, I can tell! You're undercover! You're a writer! You're gonna hear a lot of stories, let me tell you! Just go to the bathroom, you'll hear some stories! Not this bathroom, not this bathroom, the other bathroom! This one is filthy. You wouldn't believe what you'll see in there! You wouldn't believe the germs!"

A National Guardsman clomp-clomped by in combat boots. He carried a rifle bigger than the small child who ran ahead of him. The small child wore red pajamas with footies. Everyone, come to think of it, was in pajamas; footed fleece for the kids, plaid flannel for the adults, eyelet-trimmed nightgowns on the ladies. It looked like a middle school slumber party, only with military police. But not to Linda; you couldn't fool Linda.

"You're from a good family, I can tell!" Linda hissed into the darkness. "So, you have a car! Where'd you park it, in the lot next to the casino? They don't have security at that casino! You'd better listen to me and not park that car at that casino! You know what happened in that parking lot the other day! The other day, two men came in the shelter! And two five-year-old girls, well, they snatched them up! And you know what they did with them! They brought them back to the parking lot, and guess what they did to them! Guess, guess what they did to them! They scooped them up, they scooped them up and they raped them."

The convention center was pitch-black, but the air was filled with the sounds of moving diapers and combat boots, and the wheezing and yawning of 1,400 people trying to convince everyone else they're asleep. Another two pajama-footed kids raced by; another clomp-clomping National Guard; with enough rhythmic regularity that the right person could probably be lulled to sleep. Linda was just not that person.

"Isn't it noisy? There are people doing all sorts of crazy things in here, having sex and doing drugs and God knows, God knows what," Linda said.

"You want some pills? I can give you some pills. They'll put you out," said Moe, who was just as promptly out himself.

"Does it make me uncomfortable, those men walkin' up and down with them big guns? Hell no! I'm a black man! You think I haven't seen police with guns?"

A man in plaid flannel pants and a Texas Rodeo T-shirt named Reggie had joined us. Reggie wanted to sleep with me, I think, so I asked him about his profession.

"What do I do? Well I get a check, you see, from the government, SSI, do you know what that is? Because you'd be wrong, see, SSI means they say I'm crazy, they diagnosed me as a paranoid schizophrenic, so I get a crazy check. But I'd rather be crazy than stupid, or a fool, 'cause have you ever heard of a stupid check? Ever heard of a fool check? Naw! But I get a crazy check! And I'll tell you who else should get a crazy check! I'm talking about President George W. Bush, and Secretary of State Condoleezza Rice, for putting us in a war that's just as crazy as Vietnam—"

"Reggie!" Linda interrupted. "Remember? Remember? Remember when they had those tents over there? Remember the tents? Remember what people were doing in the tents???"

"Aw yeah," Reggie said. "Yeah, when they had them tents you'd go inside and people would be havin' orgies and shootin' up back there, man. Those were the days! Ha, ha!"

Reggie was not a junkie, though he said he'd "done it all." He was entirely too lucid and clean, anyway. Whereas Linda seemed to have acquired her mental illness in the month since she'd been at the shelter, Reggie was one of those crazy people who seemed remarkably sane, given the context. He was in his element, the pillar of the River Center, a rock whose state of mind no number of dead bodies or snoring roommates, armed guards or Scientologists could disturb.

A small, vulnerable-looking white girl, a tanned little blonde in a YMCA t-shirt and plaid pajama pants, sauntered up to Reggie and buried herself in his arms.

"Reggie, I need a favor. I got myself set up to have a real romantic night, no fucking or anything, just cuddling, and I got these nice sheets and blankets, I got some extra pillows, and I just need one thing from you: your radio."

"Lady girl, every man in here would be lucky to have you," Reggie said in his best wise-uncle voice. "Refuse them all and you'll wake up a queen."

The girl began to weep. "I don't want any dick!" she cried, "I just wanna borrow your raaaaadio. Pleeeeeease, Reggie!"

"Ashley, that's quite enough!" Reggie shot back, "I have no responsibility to give you anything!"

"Pleeeeeeeeease, Reggie?" More tears.

And with that, Ashley began to stumble around like she'd been hit with a tranquilizer dart. Her face grew instantly pale and prevomitous; she started tripping on the floor and reaching out to the air for balance. Almost as suddenly as she'd appeared, a National Guardsman was escorting her away.

"So, uh," I finally asked, when she was gone, "What are you guys going to do when they clear this place out?"

"Who are you asking, 'you guys'?" Reggie demanded. "What do you mean, 'you people'? I can only speak for myself! I can't speak for all the other losers in here! I can only speak for Reggie! What am I going to tell you about that one, or that one?" He started pointing around the room. "Who are you to ask me what are these people doing? I am not one of you people. I am done with you, Moe."

And Reggie stood up grandiosely, left my cotside, and marched exactly three feet across the aisle to his own cot.

Moe the first awoke long enough to make a face that seemed to say, "I would shrug in bafflement if I weren't so fucking loaded right now."

"Here, take my blanket," he finally said. I did. And it only took about three hours to get to sleep.

At seven o'clock the convention center lights went on, and at seven o'clock Ashley was standing above my cot fidgeting like an excited dog.

"Hey, I'm Ashley, who are you? Where are you from?"

I rolled over. I had drooled all over my sweatshirt and my hair was sticking to my cheek. "Um, well," I said, trying to sit up without tipping over the cot. "I'm, uh, not from here, but I was staying with this family, in Slidell."

"Slidell! That's where I'm from! You come with me, I bet we have a lot in common. Come smoke a cigarette! Do you have any eyeliner? What about clothes! Let me see your clothes! You wouldn't believe what happened to me! They took me to the ER! I woke up with an IV!" She pulled up her halter-top to show me her Band-Aids.

"Come on! Do you have any cigarettes?"

I did not, but Ashley was one of those kids who could bum a few ounces of cocaine and a Cartier watch off another kid if she wanted, partly because she was cute and partly because you worried that if you didn't give her what she wanted she'd be forced to hit up some poor fool who actually thought he was going to get pussy out of the deal, and you didn't want to be around to witness the aftermath of his disappointment. As we walked out to the smoking area in front of the shelter, maybe six guys held out cigarettes. Ashley smoked Newports, and she also liked black guys—"they just have so much style"—and this did not please her father, which is part of the reason she hadn't gone home.

The real reason she hadn't gone home, though, was that her parents were both pillheads. Her father's back had given out in some job before she was born and he had four doctors supplying him with some ten separate prescriptions for pain pills, and she couldn't do anything at home with all of them dragging her down like that. So here she was, hanging out with black guys in a sanitary, comparatively clean environment, and...

"I only took like, only like three pain pills and two Somas," Ashley was saying to James, the purveyor of the Newports, of the prescription-pill cocktail that had gotten her sent to the ER. "I mean, actually I guess I took five Somas." She giggled.

In Ashley there seemed to be some powerful metaphor about New Orleans and Louisiana and race and vice and the temporariness and permanence of problems. She was a pillhead and she'd been in and out of jail 11 times and she was only 18. She told me her dad had started giving her two Vicodin a day when she turned 14 to get through the school day because she couldn't focus on account of learning disabilities, and I believed her because she wasn't a very good liar. She'd failed out of school. Her mother was a pillhead, too, but she liked alcohol better. Her older brother was in a halfway house for heroin. In the past three weeks she had been thrown out of a Catholic shelter and the Cajundome in Lafayette, and been admitted to two jails and three emergency rooms, all because she was a pretty hopeless addict. But one thing Ashley was not was a racist. In the dynastic trajectory of Ashley's family, race relations was the only thing actually showing signs of improvement. The dudes back at the bar sitting around talking "cleansing" had sort of made it seem like evil racist bastards were a real problem for Louisiana, but at least the kids of Ashley's generation knew that was all denial, that only a fuckup with fuckups for kids and fuckups for eventual grandkids would, first thing after a hurricane leveled the town, lobby the mayor to get the alcohol ban lifted so they could resume sitting in the bar every night blaming their problems on their former slaves.

(Before I forget, James showed me a trick in the parking lot of the center. He touched his dick with his tongue.)

Breakfast was two glazed doughnuts thoroughly smushed, a plastic bowl of Honey Nut Cheerios, and a box of chocolate milk. By now the bathroom was filled with women washing their hair in the sink (the outdoor showers were closed because of the hurricane) and curling their hair at the changing table and drying their hair at the hand dryer. Two women had the following conversation:

"Look at these jeans? You know what size these jeans be? 9-10!"

"Shit!"

"I be wasting away on this food."

"I been losin' weight, too! I'm down to a 13!"

"Someone gotta come in here and cook some gumbo!"

"Shit! They gotta get me in to cook for everybody."

"Aw, yeah."

Food at the Red Cross shelter sucks. It does not help that the Red Cross workers, if you ask them, will tell you how incredibly awesome and succulent and home-cooked all the food over at their shelter is, or that when you go across the street to the casino and ask to eat the lunch buffet, they will ask you if you work for the American Red Cross, in which case you have to pay $5.45, and if you say, "No, I just sleep every night in that shithole," they will charge you $10. It also does not really improve morale that, after the Red Cross people finish off their $5 calamari salad and coconut cream pie, they complain about the weight they've gained and then come back to the shelter and try to get everyone to sing "Happy Birthday" to the Red Cross employee whose birthday happens to fall on that day.

"Come on, everybody sing now!" the smoky-eyed Scientologist was saying into the microphone when I came in, "You got a house to go home to, you sing!" one man yelled out.

The weird thing was that most of the other people actually sang. I'm not sure why, but most of the people at the shelter seemed pretty happy. Maybe the advent of reality shows like *The Surreal Life* had taught them to bask in the absurdity of situations like this, but the kids smiled, the moms braided hair, and the men attended sessions with companies like AccuClean that were giving out jobs cleaning out New Orleans.

Moe played blackjack and won eight bucks. I asked if he'd used the FEMA money. "Shit, naw," he said. "A man like me has gotta worry about his retirement." He had also written down the numbers of some treatment centers to go to for his addiction. Moe had remarkably good handwriting.

Ashley's new boyfriend Shawn had an inmate tag he was using for ID, so that was a conversation starter. He'd been released a week before the hurricane. He'd gotten caught with heroin when he was 18. His mother was a junkie. Shawn was clean and going to work for AccuClean, and we were going to the laundromat so he could clean his clothes before work on Monday. Shawn didn't know where his mom was, didn't care, hated her ass, was planning on assembling his own family unit in Baton Rouge, and wanted Ashley to stay and live with him and get clean too, which would have been a good idea but for Ashley's aforementioned thing for black guys (and the other aforementioned hopeless addict thing.)

"My boyfriend said, once you go black, you don't go back," she said. "Do you think he's cute?"

"Yeah," I said. He was cute like Mike Bibby. Like, if you like black-looking white dudes who wear enormous pants he was in the 98th percentile.

"Plus he's got a big dick. Shane's got a big dick!"

Weird pause…

"You don't even know my name." Shawn turned around and headed into the laundromat. I felt bad for him, and Ashley did, too. "It's not like I've known him more than two days," she said, but time moves differently when you've chosen to eliminate all the pollutants and get clean, and Ashley hadn't.

Shawn had gotten some fried chicken when a man named Marcus appeared in the parking lot. No one was sure how he got there, because he didn't appear to be capable of standing up, and no one knew where he'd come from, because he said he'd been at the shelter, but the three needles taped to his chest suggested he'd been hooked up to an IV. But he'd somehow procured a 40 in a paper bag. His skin was a deep burnt-orangeish shade, like a tan that had been dyed over with Kool-Aid, and his face and chest were covered in thick beads of sweat. His hair was soaking. He said he'd been in New Orleans search and rescue. He said he'd lost his mother and his rescue dog. He said it all as if it happened yesterday, even though almost a month had passed, so for a while we thought he was crazy.

"Chimicals and smoke, the refawnery, pawsonous gases, ah was exposed to everything. But I had to go, man, 'cause that was mah job, search and rescue, ah could not lit those people stay there and die," he told Ashley. "A tidal wave hit us that was 30 foot hah, and it all happened in about 30 seconds flat; I looked outside and saw that sunnabitch and I was like, oh, mah Gawd, and it was blowin' up houses as it was comin' because the pressure in the air was so low, zero point five millibars. And the gas meters were poppin' out and the oil came crushin'."

A man came out afterward. "Marcus, I can take you back to the shelter now," he said. He hadn't known Marcus more than 20 minutes longer than we had, but he said he was from Metarie, near the oil refinery to which he had been referring, and the story checked out:

he wasn't hallucinating; it happened just like he said, which is to say, we'll never know because it was too big and too horrible and too awful and too brief to really put into words (though I've heard a Sean Penn movie is forthcoming).

"I think," the man said of Marcus, "he just needed a beer."

They'll always tell you in addiction class that getting clean takes getting rid of people, places, and things; do that effectively and you've got Hurricane Katrina. Sure, it's a nice thing when the poor can get help and the status quo gets shaken up, when kids like Shawn can find jobs and guys like Reggie can share with the world their wisdom, and if you believe in the virtue of Noah sailing and Christ dying and the exodus from Egypt, of colossal sacrifices and excruciating middles for the sake of jubilant, miraculous endings, well, good for you; good for America. That's hope. But if you don't think you're on someone else's roster of people, places, and things; on some other dude's list of demons he still needs to face down, of enemies or enablers or simply psychotic ex-girlfriends he'd like to cleanse, well, you're in fucking denial.

Which brings me to the conclusion that there is no conclusion. As I'm writing this I'm remembering this other guy I met, a character I didn't introduce because he didn't seem relevant to whatever themes the "narrative" is trying to get at here, by the name of Dwight. Dwight was pretty much illiterate and he had serious heart problems, but for some reason—and I naturally concocted my own theories on the basis of the intense redness around his eyeballs—Dwight felt all right. "I can't stand these people telling me they don't have nothing, that they lost everything, you know?" he said. "Tell that to the lady who drowned, the man who's dead on the street, that you lost everything. It's a lie! You're still here, aren't you?"

And, all told, pretty much everyone still was.

Moe, if you're interested, ended up getting arrested along with his friend Joe, at least the way Linda and Reggie told it, though a clerk in Baton Rouge Corrections told me no one by the name of Maurice Downey had been through the jail. Ashley disappeared again. Shawn showed up for work. And the son of the nice family I stayed with in Slidell, the sweet but hopeless alcoholic son who had never been in an accident but had gotten pulled over on the way home from Natal's Lounge and charged with his fourth DWI, is awaiting a sentence of between 18 and 35 years in state prison by some bastard judge who probably thinks he is cleansing the streets of an incipient killer. No one learned any big lessons from Katrina, except the few who maybe did, and the vast majority who at the very least learned the importance, when living in a convention center with 1,400 other potential dirtbags, of liberal amounts of hand sanitizer. ∎

AMIE BARRODALE

SWEET HOME ALABAMA

Southern Schoolkids Are Ready to Rumble

The homemade weapons featured here were confiscated from students enrolled in middle and high schools in the Huntsville City School district of Northern Alabama. They were chosen from among a huge collection of weapons kept by the Huntsville Campus Security Supervisor, Jami Holt. Holt calls the collection her "box of goodies." She said, "I've been employed here for 23 years and I am happy to report that we have come a long way to make our schools safer."

Geez Louise, what were they before, like, riding around in armored tanks that shot flames out of their wheels and had nails poking out of them everywhere and dogs with fangs would suck your blood while you were in the little boys' room? ■

1. Solid wooden handle wrapped with a bicycle chain, then wrapped with cellophane. The offender was a ninth-grade male. The weapon weighs about 3 pounds.

2. Ice pick. Handle wrapped with electrical tape. The offender was an 11th-grade male, who was caught with it in the back waistband of his pants.

3. Knife blade. Original casing broken. Carried in the sheath. The offender was an eighth-grade male. The blade is dull but could be used to stab someone. Without a handle, it is uncomfortable to grip.

4. Wooden handle with chain affixed. Used for horses. The offender was an 11th-grade male.

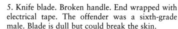

5. Knife blade. Broken handle. End wrapped with electrical tape. The offender was a sixth-grade male. Blade is dull but could break the skin.

6. Broken wooden handle with the end wrapped in electrical tape and some sort of metal coil also wrapped around a portion of the handle. This was carried by a local known gang member whose street name was "Tootsie." The offender was a ninth-grade male.

7. Homemade metal knuckles. Illegal in Alabama. The offender was a ninth-grade male.

8. Nunchucks. The offender was an eighth-grade male.

9. Some type of rubber object (it's very flexible) wrapped over and over in electrical tape. Used to slap people over the head and in the face. The offender was a tenth-grade male.

10. Broken metal rod wrapped in electrical tape. The offender was a ninth-grade male.

11. Sawed-off air rifle. Butt taped with masking tape. Weapon was confiscated at a high school in Huntsville, Alabama. The offender was an 11th-grade male. Not functional; used for intimidation.

12. Two-sided axe. Handle was broken when thrown at potential victim (it split when it hit the ground—it was rotten). The offender was a tenth-grade male.

ANGEL NELFI

—

STAY SOFT!

Sexy Men Try to Take Back the Night

Right now, somewhere in this "great" country of ours, a horrible fucking piece of shit is going down. It is a crime so horrible, so offensive and scary, it daren't speak its name. The crime is MAN ABUSE. Not gangbanging or Third World torture or any of that bull-shit—we're talking about the unspeakable evil of abused husbands (and boyfriends).

Almost a million men this year will be the victims of spousal abuse. They may have their hair pulled or be stabbed or bitch slapped or even grabbed and shoved. Shit, some of them even have things thrown at them. But they all have one thing in common: shame pain. Last year there were some 496,327 reported cases of women throwing things at men, but the mind spins try-ing to imagine ones that

Photo by Jennifer Brommer

weren't reported. What if the pen had got him in the eye? What if it went in his eye so hard it went into his brain and killed him? These women don't care. Meanwhile, the vic-tims are sitting at the dining-room table alone, their tears dripping through their beards and landing there.

And it's not just slapping and scratching and other as-saults. Most female-on-male action involves some kind of blunt object. That's what pussies these women are—they bonk the guy. In Phillip A. Cook's *Abused Men: The Hid-den Side of Violence*, there is a report of a man who came home a bit drunk, fell asleep on the couch, and woke up to an iron-skillet-wielding wife battering him, like *Andy Capp* but real. The man was forced to get up off the couch and grab the woman's arm and say, "Stop it." This dangerous move stopped the abuse, but he suffered severe bruising on his arms and hip and she almost hit him in his head. It might make you nauseous with contempt, but know this: It happens all the time. As human-rights crusader Bert H.

Hoff says in his seminal paper on the topic of battered men, *The Risk of Serious Physical Injury from Assault by a Woman Intimate*, "over 180,000 men will be threatened with a knife by a woman, well over half a million men will be slapped or hit, and well over a half a million pushed, grabbed or shoved." Got your attention? Good. The scariest part is, thanks to this bullshit machismo society we live in, there are men out there who are getting shoved and simply not reporting it. And then you have women with the gall to complain about rape. What is this, Upside-Down Land?

If you are a man who feels like the victim of spousal bat-tering, for God's sake, speak up. Don't be a victim. Here are some tips the people at batteredmen.com use to know if you need help:

- Does your spouse keep tabs on you all the time?
- Does she often accuse you of being unfaithful?
- Does she discourage your relationships with friends and family?
- Does your wife force you to have sex against your will?

The latter brings up one of the most difficult areas of male abuse: rape. If you are a man and you are of the ilk where women are likely to harass you for your body, please take the following precautions:

- Do not wear tiny shorts.
- Walk tall and proud and don't appear to be vulnerable.
- If a woman you don't know grabs you on the street, start screaming at the top of your lungs. Stab her with your keys and claw at her face. Keep screaming. Knee her in the cunt if you have to. This is your body!

- If she does get you into an alley and pulls out your penis, DO NOT GET A BONER! Female rapists use that to put you inside them. If you don't get hard, it means she has to feed it in like a dead eel, and that gives you more time to scream. Think of your dad naked being attacked by dogs. Or the Twin Towers collapsing. Whatever it takes, STAY SOFT!

So what is the root of this new crisis? The Society of Abused Men has several informative pamphlets it uses to raise awareness about this curse, and there is one particular quote that perfectly sums up exactly how and why this silent evil has so easily spread through our culture. "Society tolerates violent behavior in females, while for men it is [sic] not" it says. "Take, for example, the classic television or movie scene of the angry wife/girlfriend throwing dishes at the hapless male victim. No one gets hurt; it's supposed to be funny." But in reality, a mad girlfriend throwing plates at you is anything *but* funny. It is noisy, expensive, very difficult to clean up, and could easily lead to a cut arm or hurt leg.

If you are bawling your eyes out right now, you are probably part of an elite class of battered husbands who call themselves "ultrasensitive men." As James Christopher, one of the founders of the Battered Men Workshop, says in his manifesto, "The ultra-sensitive man's reactions to an abusive relationship aren't *different*, but they can be more *intense*. Inside, the ultra-sensitive man is screaming, 'Don't you know what you're doing is *killing* me?... If you don't stop, I'm going to *die*!'" (All italics are his.) Writer Roger Easterbrooks, a self-identified ultra-sensitive man himself, takes it further when he refers to a state he calls "going into overwhelm." This is when "your physical, mental and emotional systems can't tolerate any more. It almost feels like you're being pounded on. You want to run away." Of course, a lot of these men can't run away. Where can they go? If they go to a sports bar during the Super Bowl and try to get the bartender's attention, they are all but ignored. If they go to their friend's house and ask to at least watch *Sex and the City* on HBO On Demand for a few hours until she calms down, often times that "friend" will laugh at them or say no. There have even been reported cases of relatives throwing the victim's small overnight bag onto the ground and yelling, "Take your purse and get out of here, you fuckin' fag!"

Mr. Easterbrooks offers some telltale signs of being an ultrasensitive abused husband. According to him, the basest signifiers are physical:

- Is your body often tense, especially through the shoulders?
- Do you frequently experience stomach pains or headaches when faced with a confrontation with your wife?

- Do your temperature and pulse both rise?
- Do you experience anxiety or panic attacks?

"If this happens," Easterbrook adds, "your body is telling you, in these many ways, that something is wrong in your life, and you cannot... figure out what it is." In other words, you are scared. Someone is scaring you and it's not you. It is time to take action and be empowered. The matriarchy wants you to be silent—fight back!

There are three classic reactions to being a battered husband:

- Some foolishly decide to weather the storm, "to take it like a man." This is the wrong move, because man abuse can be passed down from generation to generation.
- Others retreat into a place of deadly detachment, which is so sad it makes crying seem redundant. This is, as people in the scene describe it, going into "wounded Zen warrior mode."
- Finally, there are some brave souls who simply run away. If not literally, then they kind of run away by creating crushing work deadlines and hanging out with their friends rather than going home. Though this can work in the short term, it can make the lady even madder than she was before. It is behavior like this that will often convert a simple grab into a mean shove.

The thing that induces the most tears regarding this whole topic is that a lot of these victims don't realize there are others out there like them. The problem is rampant, and some experts even foresee a crippling reduction in the male population. ABC News recently featured a story called "Beating Up on Battered Men" that revealed how ubiquitous the problem really is. The viewer response was unprecedented, and ABC.com was forced to expand the capacity of their viewer mail server. Most men who wrote in had no idea this was an epidemic. One Zen warrior relates this horrifying story to the network: "When I was living in Connecticut, my wife—in one of her drunken rages—took our daughter's baseball bat and used it to smash the locked door to my study, where I was trying desperately to meet a deadline... she is 5'2" and petite in size, so that shows what a person consumed by rage can do. And since I'm over 6' and muscular, I wouldn't get much sympathy posing as a 'battered man'!" This poor bastard thought he was all alone. As he stood there, forced to utter, "Jesus Christ, calm down, for fuck's sake" and remove the bat from her hand, he probably thought to himself, "Nobody knows the trouble I've seen. They think they know but they have no idea." Well, guess what, six-foot-tall writing guy? You are not alone. And the more you speak out, the more likely abused men are to TAKE BACK THE NIGHT! ∎

BEN WHITE

GANGS OF OLD NEW YORK

ANGELO
THE ITALIAN DUKES, LITTLE ITALY

We had a gang that started in high school. We called ourselves the Italian Dukes. We were so fuckin' broke, we had six jackets and maybe 30 guys. So every day somebody else would wear the jackets at school. We went to Seward Park High School, and it was mostly Jews. They were all afraid of us. We didn't even have to do anything. It got to a point where a gang called the Fordham Baldies—who were like the biggest Italian gang in the Bronx—heard about us and came down and made us a brother club. They were like, "Who's the president?" and a couple of guys went over, and we had this truce. They talked about it, shook hands, and then we were brother clubs. If anything happened to one of us, we had all of these guys. So from being 30 guys with six jackets, we became a thousand just by hooking up with them. It also made us brother clubs with the Redwings, who were in East Harlem. They were a big crew—white gang, mostly Italian.

We'd hang out in the park at night. All the gangs were there: The Sportsmen, that was a big black gang, pretty tough guys,

Angelo. Photo by Roe Ethridge

and the Dragons, that was the Puerto Rican gang. They heard that the Italian Dukes were brother gangs with the Fordham Baldies, so if you were walking around with an Italian Dukes jacket, they didn't fuck with you. And I tell you, it was a great fuckin' scam.

Nobody would fuck with us. Italians were Italians in those days. No matter where you went, even the toughest gangs—fuckin' Puerto Ricans, blacks, whatever—they wouldn't fuck with us. Our gang was the wiseguys, you know what I mean? And nobody could fuck with that.

It was a sanctuary, this rectangle here. Houston Street down to Canal, and Bowery over to Lafayette. Little Italy was strictly Italian. There was one Irish kid, I think, and

one black kid. His father was a building super. He wanted to hang out so bad that he let us call him Snowball.

You had to have respect. For everybody—especially our people but even for strangers, what we called Merigans, like "*Amerigans*"—we had respect for all of them. We didn't shake nobody down or hurt nobody. In fact, we protected people. We protected women. If two women came into a bar, they never paid for a drink and nobody even went over to talk to them.

Before the pill, you mostly just had blowjobs. From the Jewish girls mostly, not from Catholic girls—not when I was a kid. Now all girls think giving a blowjob is nothing. They had some young girls on like *Oprah* or something who said that. They were like, "Oh, it's not bad. If you don't do it, you're not part of the crew."

But back then, if you had a girlfriend, if you were getting laid, you were the king of the mountain. When the pill came, everything changed. Before that, date rape was the usual. I mean, I could have been arrested for date rape a million times. Any girl that wasn't a virgin, if you went out with her you couldn't let her get away, because there weren't many around. There was hookers too— hookers is what we mostly fucked. I lost my virginity at 14. Me and a few friends of mine went to a hooker. I gave her two bucks and I came in about two seconds, then went home and jerked off ten times thinking about it.

Oh yeah, and if you went down on a girl then, you couldn't walk around the neighborhood afterward. I swear to God. I mean, I know I never did it.

I was a heroin addict from the age of maybe 13 to 17, but not like a falling-down addict. I snorted it, sometimes I shot it, but not often. I would buy it from Italian guys over on Avenue D, but not guys that we actually knew. That was like Jersey to me, Avenue D.

There were opium dens down in Chinatown. We ran

out of a restaurant without paying one time, ran down into this building, and they had like catacombs. They still have them down there, these buildings where the cellars have all these different rooms. I was trying to find my way out, and I went into this room and there was an opium den. All these people laying down on cots and shit, with these pipes, and one guy tending them. That freaked me out. I didn't do that. Only Chinese guys did opium. But down in Chinatown, you could buy a tin of cocaine snuff for 25 cents. I think snuff is much worse than cocaine. I've snorted a lot of cocaine in my fuckin' life, but these guys I know who used to do snuff, their noses used to fuckin' bleed. It's much harsher than coke. It's cheaper than coke, and you get whacked on it. You get high.

Anyway, we weren't vicious kids. We were just crooks, you know what I mean? You lived in an apartment with four rooms and four people, and it was so close that you really lived in the street because you had to get out of the house. And then when you're like 13 or 14, you start to hang out a little bit and the older guys start to notice you and start to talk to you and before you knew it you'd been groomed into what they were.

There were some crazy kids, though. Anybody who had a "Boy" after their name—Johnny Boy, Frankie Boy—they were always in trouble, cause they were always trying to prove they were a man. This guy Frankie Boy was my best friend because he was really tough and I wasn't. Me and him got along because there was no competition and we really loved each other. He died in a tragic condition. He got hit in the head with a two-by-four, and it numbed him. It made his brain all fucked up. He lived like that for a long time. He used to shake when he walked and shit like that. His mind was OK, but he'd be talking and he'd start laughing cause he couldn't help it. His laugh reflex got fucked up.

It was a black guy who did it to him, in a fight over a girl. They were on the highway, and the guy said something out the window to his girl, and they went back and forth, then finally pulled off the highway up by Bryant Park. I think Frankie got the best of him, and they got back in the cars, and Frankie chased him. Then they got out of the cars a second time and the guy ran away and Frankie ran after him. He was so fuckin' mad he didn't pay attention, and the guy went around the corner and when Frankie came after him, he was waiting, and hit him with a two-by-four—wham—right across the head.

FREDDIE
THE RAILROAD BOYS, EAST NEW YORK/BEDFORD-STUYVESANT, BROOKLYN

We went to Our Lady of Lourdes Grammar School on Aberdeen Street. On the next block, one block past Bushwick Avenue, was Aberdeen Park. We went up there and basically we started hanging out and we became the Railroad Boys. The gang was started around 1955 by the older guys. I joined around 1960, when I was 13. We had a lot of guys in the gang—sometimes we had 40, sometimes we had 60, sometimes we had 100. It was a crazy neighborhood. A lot of shit went on. We quit school at 16, and we went up to the park, we drank wine, and we ran up and down the street beating each other up. A lot of guys got hurt, and a couple a guys got hurt really bad. We had no real guns, just the ones that we made, which were a joke. It really wasn't a good way to come up, but that's just the way the neighborhood was. You lived in the neighborhood, you joined a gang. That was it. When you left your house you had to worry about somebody grabbing you and kicking your ass. You usually carried a knife, something to protect you.

I lived on Fulton and Rockaway, which was home to another crew, the Fulton and Rockaway Boys. There were a bunch of white gangs fighting each other. Then, you know, the blacks started coming

Freddie. Photo by Roe Ethridge

in and there was tension and we banded together. They banded together too, and that's the way it went. It was an opportunistic thing.

I got stabbed in the head one day with an umbrella. Wasn't too much of a fight. There were six of them and two of us. I got my head split open with a piano leg one night too. Wrong place, wrong time. You're walking down the street, you see somebody that you don't like, who isn't in your gang. He might have been black, he might have been Puerto Rican, and then that was it, the shit started. If we caught someone, we gave 'em a beating.

We didn't have rules or initiations. There would be a fight set up, and we told you to be there at seven o'clock.

You showed up at the park at seven and we walked down Bushwick Avenue and we'd do what we had to do. In the back of the park there were freight trains that ran underneath and there was one tunnel that was closed off due to an explosion. A couple times, we'd take somebody down there and leave 'em, maybe tied up, and he had to get out by himself. But that was once in a while, you know? There were no real initiations. You came, you hung out, you drank a bottle of wine, you went crazy like everybody else. That's the bottom line. It was just fighting all the time. You know what beer muscles are, right? Once you drink a couple gallons of that wine, you're ready to go. We went for the cheap wine. After a few of them you could do anything. Take on the world.

One time we were having a fight and we had a couple of guys up on a roof. This guy Georgie Grout, he had a car antenna and he threw it down and this guy must have been, I dunno, 40 feet away? It went right through his forearm. You just couldn't believe it. It was just a lucky shot and it went right through this guy's arm. This was from a roof maybe four stories up.

You could also take a chimney apart—grab a couple bricks and throw those. We had a riot on Fulton Street one time, and that's what we did. We ran up there, disassembled a few chimneys, and took some bricks and some bottles. We went to the roof above this nightclub and when they started coming out, we just rained bottles and bricks down on their heads. This was on Fulton and Rockaway, a half block from my house. I got locked up with another friend of mine. We spent a couple nights in jail. We were the two stupid guys that got caught. Everybody else ran.

When you got caught doing something, they handcuffed you, took you down to the precinct, beat the shit outta ya', then took the information down. What they had at that time was called the Youth Squad. It was a bunch of detectives whose primary job was to try and keep tabs on the gangs and see what was going on. They gave you your JD card, which means juvenile delinquent, so that was the label you carried, you know what I mean? Then you were on file. But like I said, yeah, the cops beat your ass. By today's standards, there would have been a lot more lawsuits. But that's the way they did it in those days. Did it help? Sometimes. And sometimes it didn't.

Victor. Photo by Roe Ethridge

There were real gangsters around too. They ran books, they stole, they shylocked money... They ran the neighborhood, whatever they did. These are the people that we grew up with. You see it firsthand, and it's all bullshit really. Big car, big wallet, and next thing you know they're doing fifty years in jail. Or you find them in a car, dead. That's the way the neighborhood was. That was East New York.

I went into the service in '66. A lot of my buddies went in. The ones that didn't go in are the ones that died along the way. Overdosed, stuff like that. Heroin was a big thing in the 60s. It took a lot of people out. Eventually, if you hung out in that neighborhood you tried pills or pot, or whatever other crap came into town. So a lot of guys OD'd. Lot of guys went to jail. I only see a couple guys from the neighborhood now. The rest of them are scattered to the wind.

VICTOR
THE MAJESTICS,
WILLIAMSBURG,
BROOKLYN

Everything started out with sweaters. From the sweaters we went to a shirt, and from the shirt we finally got to patches. There was always some guy who got beat up and they took the sweater and we had to go find out who took it and get it back. We started saying, "Why don't we make patches?" And finally we did.

It was like one big family. We all got along. We never had problems against each other, because we grew up in the same neighborhood. We went to the same school and we were all young. My brother Alex started wearing patches when he was hanging out with this other club, the Dirty Ones. Then he became the president of the Majestics. When he died, my brother Carlos took over. And then he died.

We had a clubhouse. We were always there. Rainy days, we'd be inside watching TV. It was an abandoned building. We had the apartment on the first floor and even the old guys from the neighborhood would come in and play cards and dominoes. Some of the cops knew us too.

Yeah, it was nice. Actually, I wish I could go back a couple years. We had fun. The 70s was real nice. In the summer we were always out there, like 15 or 20 of us, sitting on the steps in summer, drinking beer and bullshitting.

Problem-wise, you know, we had a few here and there.

Ducking from shootouts and things like that. We didn't mess with the people from the neighborhood. If anything, we'd protect them. I knew so many people that everybody would open their doors for me. People from the neighborhood never called the cops on us because we were never troublemakers. That was our block, so we had to protect everybody from other people who would come in and mess up the block. We never went crazy in our neighborhood, and whoever did, they would hear about it from us the next day. The last thing we wanted was heat on the block. Because then you can't be in your own neighborhood carrying a pistol.

I had a very bad temper back then. I didn't take no shit from nobody. If I had to stick you, I would stick you. I used to walk around with a gun every day. I carried a .25, then later a 9 mm. I was always aware. I never let anybody get close to me or walk behind me. One time, something had happened so I went looking for this guy to get him. I saw him on the corner at South 10th and Bedford, and I started shooting. I think I shot two or three times with my .25 before it jammed. He didn't see where I was shooting from, so I ran like two or three cars up and hid under the last one. I think I was under that car for half an hour, until I heard my guys yelling my name.

Amanda. Photo by Roe Ethridge

When we were on Lee Avenue there was this black guy. He was from the Marcy Projects and he would always come down with a gun. This guy was always strapped. Every time he came by the block there was a shootout, so everybody was always aware when he was passing by. Everybody kept their eyes open. I heard that he was like that because his mother was killed. She used to be a dispatcher for a car service. There was a shootout and it so happens that she was working at that time, and she got killed. So this guy started going off with everybody. Nobody ever bothered to call the cops, because everybody wanted to just take care of him. He must have had a vest, 'cause let me tell you, this guy had fucking balls. He was invincible. I used to hide sometimes on the corner and wait for him, just hoping to get him. But I never did. I think he got arrested. That was the end of him.

I never robbed anybody. It feels bad. Somebody else could come and rob your mother and you wouldn't like it. But I stole. I used to steal a lot from factories. Every

Friday and Saturday night I would go to factories on Bedford Avenue, Wythe Avenue, and Flushing Avenue. I would go anywhere Jews worked because on Fridays, they can't put on the light, the air conditioning, nothing. That was my opportunity. I would break into the sweater factory, the clothes factory, the pillow factory... I even broke into a coffin factory one day. I got in, it was dark, and then when I put on the light all I saw was coffins, so I ran out. But yeah, I broke into every factory. That's how I used to get my money. I also had a guy who used to bring me cars for parts. Or somebody would tell me, "Listen, I got a van, brand new, and I wanna collect insurance." So he would tell me where he parked it. The guys and I would go and take it and strip the parts off and he'd get his insurance.

I got locked up in '80 and came out in '83. At that point, all everybody wanted to do was sell drugs. That's where the money was. My brothers were making money selling drugs but I didn't want to get into it. I was already scared by being in jail. Lots of guys were fucking up, but all I wanted was to have our club, and for everybody to have bikes and go places together and ride. That's all I ever wanted to do. I always used to buy magazines just to check out the bikes. I'm 46 now and I'm still with this thing. Now, everybody else has a bike. Me and my brother are probably the only ones that don't have a bike.

AMANDA
EAST HARLEM, SOUTH BRONX

I was first in a gang when I lived in East Harlem. I joined the gang so I could go out with a guy. They weren't allowed to date outside girls. It had to be girls who were in that particular gang. I was 12 or 13. They became my brothers and sisters. Most of us came from broken homes, or parents that had two jobs or alcohol and drug problems. But there were some of us who had everything a kid could have. So there wasn't one particular reason.

From Spanish Harlem, we moved to the South Bronx. The Hunts Point area is the poorest place you can be. It doesn't get any worse than that. That was when the Bronx was burning. When I stepped off the train, I saw all these abandoned buildings, and every night there were the sirens of the fire trucks, and people being displaced, crying, no place to go. You lived in one building, and the buildings to your left and right were abandoned, because they were gutted out by fires. It looked like an epidemic had destroyed the place. And the drugs? Forget about it—everywhere you went, every corner, the drugs were there. You could find it in the grocery store if you wanted it bad enough. People were sniffing glue, so the bodegas began to sell glue because it was so popular. Prostitution was everywhere too. The apartments were filled with rats and roaches, we had no heat or hot water half the time, pipes were falling down, ceilings were leaking. This was our life. Who was I supposed to hang out with? It wasn't like the guy on the corner was a doctor, the one across the street was a lawyer. It was where I was going to end up, whether I wanted to or not.

When I was in Spanish Harlem, the guys in gangs wore silk jackets with their name on the front and the club name on the back. When I moved to the Bronx, I saw guys with long hair, cut sleeves, kneepads, and motorcycle boots. They didn't look like they bathed. I was like, "What the hell is this?" Then, slowly but surely, I started to gravitate toward them. Once again, I wanted to go out with someone who was in that gang. My mentality wasn't, "I have to join that gang." It was, "I like the guy, the guy likes me." Before you knew it, I married the president of the gang. I was with him for 24 years. But here's the thing: I was never a member of that gang. I never wore colors. But I lived in the streets with them. I left my mother's house when I was 14. I'm 50 now, and I haven't been back. My children's father—we had five children together—he and I slept in abandoned cars and buildings, what we called clubhouses. After a while, I realized that they—not just them, other clubs too—were being paid by the landlords to burn the buildings for the insurance. So it *was* an epidemic, but an economic type of epidemic.

I personally didn't believe in jumping people. I never jumped anybody. But there were girls where I had to kick their ass. Sometimes after I got done kicking her ass, one of my girlfriends would come and, you know, kick her ass some more. It could be that she had sex with one of the girls' guys, it could be that she was just wanting to have sex with one of the girls' guys, or she could have just been from another club.

I also had to fight some of the guys in the club. They didn't like me too much. I think that had a lot to do with the fact that I wasn't a member. And I never wore the "Property of" jacket that the girls used to have to wear. I never believed in that, so I never did it.

I carried guns for them if we had to go to a rumble or something because at the time the police wouldn't check the girls. In fact, sometimes the girls would rumble with other clubs without the guys knowing. I remember a particular time when a group of us girls had a rumble with a gang called the Seven Immortals. We rumbled with their guys, and that started a war between the clubs.

We were coming down Freeman Street to the club, and they started calling us out. They said, "You're not supposed to be on our block. You have to flip your colors." They started getting nasty. And a lot of these girls from these clubs, let me tell you, a lot of them could have been better fighters than Ali's daughter. I mean, these girls could fight. They had a lotta heart. And they wouldn't flip colors. That means turn your jacket around or take it off. So the guys said, "If you don't do it, we're gonna strip you." And that's where the war began.

Stripping you means taking your jacket by force. And of course, you don't let nobody take your colors. In fact, you don't turn around for anybody either. If somebody says, "Oh, let me see your colors, turn around," it's not something you do. If you want to see somebody's colors, you walk around the back and look at them. Colors are more respected than your whole family. It's something you die for, like a flag. Today, that's what the gangs call it—the Bloods, the Crips, all of them, they call it flagging: "I die for my flag."

It was about territory. This is my hood. You don't fly your colors in my hood unless you're in one of my brother clubs. If you had war with somebody, then you could walk around their block wearing your colors, trying to be funny. You'd be saying, "I don't give a shit who you are," calling the club out.

Back then, I'd get up in the morning, 7:30 or so, go stand on the corner by the train station, and ask for quarters. I'd be there for a few hours. I could make up to $20. With that money I'd buy wine and cigarettes. Then I'd go into this one restaurant, talk to the guy I knew there, find out if there was any food from breakfast left—99 percent of the time there was—and he'd pack it up and give it to me. The guys in the restaurants were cool with us, and in return, we took care of them. We made sure nobody messed with them. But it wasn't like they asked us to. It was the fact that they were so cool with us. We were like, "Nah, don't fuck with them."

So I'd go back to the club, feed myself, feed my man and whoever else was there. We'd drink wine—we're talking now maybe one o'clock in the afternoon. We'd eat, drink wine, hang out, bullshit, discuss what we were going to do that day, whether we were going to go visit another club or if there was going to be some kind of party. That was a typical day.

You have every type of person in every club. It's like a family, or the police department, or the priesthood. You have your murderers, your rapists, your thieves. You have it all. Who the hell knows what's in your brain? If you're in my club, I take you at face value. ■

IX

THE REST OF
THE WORLD

Photo by Kawori Inbe, V15N7, July 2008

JOHNNY TYRONE

SKATE AND DESTROY ISRAEL

So, check it out, my friend Jay and I were skating downtown LA and this cop tells us we better stop or else we'll "be eating through a straw for the next month." We were like, "Fuck you, pig" (in our heads).

This happens about every ten fuckin' minutes in LA, so me and Jay decided to find the cheapest place to fly to in the world and go skate there. After checking good places like Greece and Italy, we ended up with some shithole called Beirut. We didn't know much about it, but figured it would at least be warm. And there's no way it could be any more uptight than the Stars and Bars, DOOOOOOOD!

Our board sponsor, Sector 9 (thanks, dudes) had just given us some mini-gun decks with wide trucks and soft wheels. We also had a prototype hill deck and trucks, so we were looking for long hills, clean pavement, empty pools. Any canvas where we wouldn't get harassed. Dropping out of the sky into Beirut, it looked like our dreams might be realized. Lights dotted large hills that rolled down to the sea. Skate paradise from 30,000 feet.

Photo by Marwan Farran

We left customs at 3:00 AM and set out toward downtown. The streets were empty and quiet, but from the looks of the buildings, a ton of shit probably happened here. There were bullet holes in every building, so we got the cab driver to take us downtown, where everything was rebuilt and there were long hills waiting to be bombed. We jumped out of the taxi and took advantage of the pre-morning emptiness. The streets were clean and wide. Hills wound down at the perfect degree, and the pavement was so smooth that world land-speed records were only a stopwatch away. Under cover of darkness, we skated until we could skate no more. The morning light brought rush-hour traffic and that sent us to bed.

Traffic is maybe the main thing that makes skating Beirut a gnarly experience. One time, Jay and I jumped into the middle of the main north–south freeway. We skated through the streams like Frogger. When we popped out, a hippie Swedish backpacker dressed like the American Taliban was standing there with a cross look on his face.

He goes, "Excuse me, gentlemen, but what exactly do you think you're doing?" and Jay laughs and calls him Johnny Walker Lindh. Then he says something like, "I don't know if you guys fully comprehend where you are. This is Lebanon, and it's a dangerous country. There are terrorist groups like Hezbollah that kidnap tourists for sport. They HATE Westerners. You guys should really try to fit in more, and don't skateboard," etc., etc.

We asked everyone we saw about Hezbollah and were told to check out a neighborhood they run called Burj Al Barajneh. When we got there, it seemed like any other Beirut neighborhood, save a few noticeable differences. There were pictures of the Ayatollah Khomeini everywhere, and a lot of guys in fatigues everywhere. There were also video cameras posted at the main street leading in. Things looked pretty bleak until we found a nice gap right next to a waving statue of the Ayatollah that looked a lot like Sean Connery. The gap had a little lip that launched you over a grass hill, and if you had the speed, you ended up in the street 15 feet down. This was one of the best discoveries on the trip, but it didn't last. We had been skating for half an hour when we whipped out the cameras to document the occasion. In less than a minute, three large, well-dressed men were on top of us. One of them asked us (in English) to stop filming, and to please relinquish the film. We did. They thanked us and moved along. When they had rounded the corner, our photographer, a nice kid from Southern Lebanon, explained that they were Hezbollah and filming was forbidden in Burj Al Barajneh. Whatever. They didn't tell us to stop skating.

We took our time exploring Beirut. There were just too many places. We found an actual skate park on the south side of town. This place was legitimate. There was a full vert pipe, rails, launch ramps and boxes. A large fence surrounded the property and was flanked by an army guard turret. We started climbing the fence, when out of nowhere came two large men with scruffy beards and black leather jackets. They started going nuts in Arabic, so we looked to the photographer for help. He translated: "You can't go in there." And we asked him why not. "It's off-limits," he said. And again we asked him why. The park was made of raw steel. What were we going to do? Bend it? We kept asking them more questions, but after finding out they were the Syrian secret police we were told to fuck off (they literally said, "Fuck off"). Our translator buddy told us we should fuck off because the Mukhabarat, or Syrian secret police, were not to be messed with. Screw that, we just wanted to skate the pipe, and couldn't figure out why Syrian policemen were in Lebanon. It's like a Mountie telling you not to skate Miami Beach.

Fuck it. We had heard from a few different people that two refugee camps, Sabra and Shatilla, had good hills, so that's where we went. Other people told us to be careful, that the camps were violent and lawless. It was sounding better and better. The biggest hill was fun. Long and winding, it provided plenty of space to get speed before laying on a thick powerslide. The only problem was the litter and rocks that filled the street. There was a building on the right that was totally destroyed and the rubble would roll into the road. The people in the camps watched our skate exhibition. Soon the kids joined in and took turns wiping out. That was the funnest part of the trip, because the kids were really friendly and cool to hang out with.

Beirut had great skating: all sorts of rails, gaps, hills, and open spaces. After a while, though, we were feeling stressed by the city, so we hopped in our car and rolled out to the country. Signs pointed toward the Bekaa Valley, which sounded as good as any country locale.

The mountain from Beirut drops sharply into the valley. This provided a steep section of hill at least three miles long that we literally flew down on our boards. We took turns driving each other to the top and then picking each other up at the bottom. The air was icy and the blacktop was newly paved. You've never skated such a long stretch of mountain road.

When we got back in the car to enter the valley, we turned off on the first narrow street and followed it through apple trees and grapevines. After a few miles, we ran into an old truck mounted with a machine gun. An older man stood straight up and looked really, really pissed off. He squeezed off a couple of rounds in the air and we thought that would be a good time to do a three-point turn and get the raging fuck out of there.

Continuing down the main road, we arrived in the city of Baalbek. Pictures of the Ayatollah Khomeini and some other turbaned chief from Burj Al Barajneh were all over the place. There were also yellow and green flags with some Arabic and an M-16 on all the light poles. We saw an old Roman castle in the distance. It looked nice. The road in front of the castle was an ideal little slope with an old piece of metal acting as a launch ramp. We busted some air and skated around the castle. Everywhere, it seemed, was something to grind. It feels a lot better grinding a 2,500-year-old castle rock than your post office's curb. When we had our fill of the castle, we moved into the heart of town.

Here we found an empty river that had been cemented in. There were chunks of debris, but having soft tires made it all okay. We would get as much speed as our boards could handle, then fly from one lip to the next. After a few runs, a black car pulled up and beckoned us over. Again, we were asked to turn our film over to Hezbollah. Apparently this whole town belonged to these Hezbollah dudes. We were bummed, but there was nothing we could do, and they didn't seem to care about skating. Apparently, we were lucky—our photographer later explained that he had gotten us out of spending the next few weeks in interrogation.

Our last jaunt was to the south of Lebanon. Some people claimed that there were old abandoned houses with pools. Not needing to be told twice, we made it down in record time to find out they were all full of shit. There were some nice hills, and the feeling was certainly different than Beirut. We noticed loads of baby-blue-helmet-wearing Sikhs. At the end of one rolling slope, we ran into a whole mess of them in their UN truck.

One came up to us and yelled, "Stop! What are you doing?" And we said, "Skating some sweet hills." Then he said, "No, no, no, no! You shouldn't be in this area at all." And we asked why. And he said, "Oh no, no no. Veddy dangerous. Israeli troops shoot missiles into the area. Hezbollah fires back. Israeli jets fly bombing raids and hit houses. No, no, no—this whole country is dangerous. Too dangerous for fun."

Er… wrong. Lebanon is a skate kingdom. I don't know who these Hezbollah dudes are, or why Israel keeps bombing them, but if things were cooler over there and that skate park was open, Beirut would be paradise. They may take your film over and over, but they'll never tell you to walk your board in public places, and that is rad. ∎

SUROOSH ALVI

LET'S GO PAKISTAN!

Kalashnikov Culture From North to South

In the arms market. Photos by the author

From the American perspective, Pakistan isn't far from joining the so-called axis of evil. After Sept. 11, this generally spineless nation conveniently became a buddy in the fight against terrorism. But make no mistake—if its current government should fall, impoverished and overpopulated Pakistan will flip-flop to redheaded-stepchild status faster than you can say "Flight 77."

Islamic extremists are hungry to assassinate Pakistan's President Musharraf (aka Bush's lil' bitch), and in recent months they've come close more than once. Should they

succeed, the United States' greatest jingoistic fear will be realized—crackpot fundamentalists will get their dirty brown paws on a nice little cache of nuclear weapons. You think this country has a bad rap now? Just wait.

I've been to Pakistan 13 times since the 70s, and I've witnessed the steady deterioration of a country that was built on a bad idea in the first place. Religious ideals are not firm bedrock for nation building. Mix in a dash of illiteracy (the *New York Times* puts it at 44 percent), some classic poverty, and more barefaced corruption than if Boss Tweed and Henry Kissinger co-ruled the universe, and it's a wonder that all of Pakistan isn't already a smoking crater.

Yet despite all this—and call me a pussy if you must—there's something about this tepid cesspool of failed dreams that I can't help but love.

My journeys back to the city of Lahore (the cultural center of Pakistan in the Punjab province), usually consist of typical Punjabi laziness: watching Indian MTV on the satellite dish, eating rich food three times a day, and checking out girls at the nightly weddings. (Our family is so big that every December, which is wedding season, we marry a few young female cousins and nieces off to nerdy, sexually repressed guys they've never met before. It's Pakistan's sole form of legal entertainment, and it's fucking boring.)

To make sure things were status quo in these especially "troubled" days, I decided to arrange a visit this past December. This time, however, it wouldn't be all nuptials and Paki pop. This time I wanted to get around a little more.

After a few preparatory phone calls and emails, I'd inadvertently created the perfect itinerary to discover the hidden treasures that Pakistan can offer the typical tourist. But one quick word of caution first: If you aren't brown (I am) and you don't have multiple armed militiamen escorting you everywhere (I did), you might want to keep your jaunt to the motherland on a strictly armchair basis.

Ready? Let's go!

MUST-SEE ATTRACTIONS

PESHAWAR

Capital of the Northwest Frontier Province (NWFP)
Despite the bad reputation, there is a ton of fun stuff to do in this country, from normal urban sightseeing (we'll get to that) to the northern areas (K2 is in Pakistan) to really fun stuff like exploring a spot that the BBC recently dubbed "the most dangerous place in the world"—the semi-autonomous tribal areas that run along the border of Pakistan and Afghanistan. The gateway to the heavy shit is Peshawar, a place that's renowned as a center of religious conservatism, and more recently has been depicted by Western media as the first Pakistani city to fall victim to heavy Taliban influence (but I call bullshit on that). The Peshawar I saw was pretty laid back—lots of people goofing around on the streets (seriously). And even though the Taliban leftovers have tried to ban billboards that depict women and music from weddings, the central government in Islamabad successfully shut them down. So despite the intraprovincial and transnational chaos, there is some form of central leadership that still regulates the country, and CNN can fuck off.

DARRA ADAMKHEL (THE ARMS MARKET)

Frontier Agency, Northwest Frontier Province (NWFP)
From Peshawar it's only about an hour drive southwest to my favorite arms market in the world. The town is restricted to outsiders, so you can't really get in unless you have some kind of hookup.

Our driver stopped at a security point just outside the town center, where I was introduced to some members of the Frontier Agency militia, six angry-dad-looking bastards with AKs and sidearms, who became my personal bodyguards. My little *A-Team* followed me through a tight warren of gun shops and factories, and I'm not talking the GM plant in Detroit here, Michael Moore. These are barren little brick rooms where components are labored over all day long in conditions that make Nike sweatshops look like Santa's workshop.

Darra Adamkhel is the largest illegal arms market in the world. They hand-make, sell, and export everything from 9mm handguns to M-16s, but they specialize in the Pakistani man's new best friend, the Kalashnikov (AK-47). A Pakistani-made AK runs about $50 (50 fucking bucks!), while the Russian and Iranian versions start at $300 and up. You do the math. Darra Adamkhel is to guns what Canal Street is to Louis Vuitton bags.

The vendors are ethnic Pashtuns, some of the toughest people in the world, fierce fighters who can survive in conditions that would make normal people cry like babies and then die (Pashtuns comprised the majority of the mujahideen soldiers, the badasses who kicked the Soviets out of Afghanistan using their bare hands in the late 80s). Using primitive machinery, they perfectly replicate military hardware from across the spectrum. When the guns in Afghanistan ran out after the American invasion, Pashtuns provided military sustenance for the Taliban resistance, and are also credited with the illustrious achievements of covertly supplying weapons to the IRA, the Middle East, the Muslims in Kashmir, and the warlords that run all of Afghanistan (save for Kabul).

KARACHI (POP. 16 MILLION)

Sindh Province in Southern Pakistan, on the Arabian Sea
This megalopolis is the most cosmopolitan and volatile city in Pakistan, and has long been its center of finance. The people are fashion-conscious, the cars are worth more than entire towns in other parts of the nation, and the stratification of wealth is fucking major. The rich are filthy rich and

the poor are living in their own filth (with an estimated five million squatters). Karachi also rivals Bogotá, Colombia, as the world's capital for kidnappings and killings.

Karachi's main attraction is the nouveau riche kids, who live in a decadent, morally bankrupt bubble—a lapsed-Muslim *Less Than Zero*. The young rich kids have split into two groups: the ones who choose to speak English, who rock Gucci, Armani, and Burberry; and the Urdu-speaking, more conservative Muslim youth (boring!). The former are out of control, necking down E and sniffing cocaine like drugs were invented today. They're torn between the old-world values of the East and the nascent Pakistani pop culture and full-on liberalism of the West.

THE KHYBER PASS
NWFP

It's the most historic pass in the history of the history of the world, okay? If you don't know *something* about the Khyber Pass, you didn't go to grade school. It's 33 miles long, it starts on the outskirts of Peshawar and connects the northwestern frontier of Pakistan with Afghanistan. It goes way the fuck back, as in the Aryans came through here in 1500 B.C.

In 326 B.C. Alexander the Great and his army bludgeoned their way through. Persian and Greek armies came through also, and a bunch of other dudes like the Scythians, White Huns, Seljuks, Tartars, Mongols, Sassanians, Turks, Mughals, and Durranis all had their battles and meetings and shit up in here. In 1842, 16,000 British and Indian troops were killed by Afghani soldiers (Pashtuns, duh) in the Khyber Pass. How about that?

In recent years, the pass has been a pipeline for human misery: refugees constantly flowing back and forth, along with arms, heroin, and gold.

I drove the length of the pass with serious fucking security. At the edge of the Khyber region, we met up with two pickups full of soldiers that acted as an escort sandwich, one in front of my jeep and the other behind, and they freeeeaaakkked out when I started taking pictures. They were speaking Pashto, not Urdu, but the message was clear: "Put the fucking camera away before you get shot." These guys were part of the Khyber Rifles, a militia organization that's protected the pass from conquering armies for centuries.

Right now, the Khyber Pass is a spot-on summation of the effort to rebuild Afghanistan since America's recent high-octane "hello." Stunning scenery, the beautiful Hindu Kush mountain range for as far as the eyes can see, with small mountain roads zigzagging through the Khyber pass filled with pure desperation: Pakistani supply trucks—a nonstop convoy of refugees, troops, food, rubber tubes, and rice, slowly making their way to the border. It was fucking intense and it made me kind of sad.

RED-LIGHT DISTRICT (HIRA MUNDI)
Old City, Lahore

Take a stroll through Lahore's Red-Light District in the Old City. From dragon-chasing junkies, to snooker halls filled with ten-year-olds at 2:00 AM, to open rooms with whores on display, it's a South Asian Amsterdam, and definitely not in the next Islamic theocracy. I recommend buying some *paan* (tobacco in a betel leaf with a thin slice of areca nut and lime paste—it's been a cultural mainstay here for centuries). Chew on it for a while (make sure you spit, not swallow), cop a real nice buzz, and take in the sights (that's what I did).

A high-ranking Pakistani politician describes his home as a country where "there are fires everywhere, but no one to put [them] out." Others call it a place where everyone is landlord but nobody owns any land. The Western media sees it as a time bomb that's set to blow. The reality is that Pakistan has deep issues that are insanely complex, nothing is what it seems, and it's a country that's stigmatized beyond belief. No one from the West has any interest in going there, and that really makes it worth visiting.

All in all, countries with a bad rap are a helluva lot more compelling to visit than places condoned by *Condé Nast Traveler*. I'm surrounded by Americans every day, and I have absolutely no desire to see Americans when I travel. Cancún? No thanks. It's a fucking frat party.

Who would you rather emulate: the cast of *The Real World* or Graham Greene? Next time you're planning a trip, don't be a wimp. Try something off the beaten path, some place that CNN or the *New York Times* says is a dangerous shithole. Remember—it isn't a real journey unless there's a good chance you'll get shot, catch dysentery, or disappear forever. ■

VICE STAFF

STOMPERS REUNION

A Roundtable Discussion—Looking Back on Anger

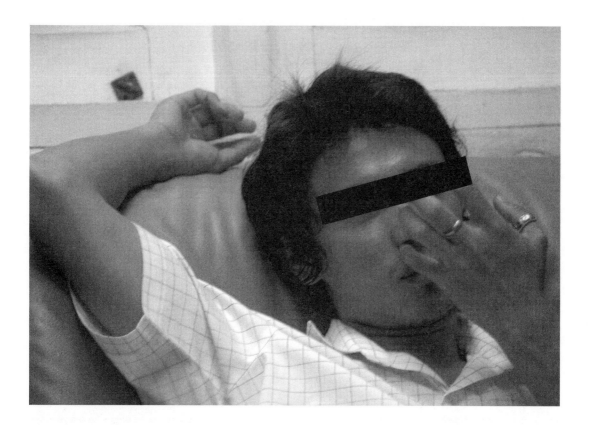

I n June 2006, between 20 and 30 students from a technical college in Bangkok, Thailand, were gathered at a bar. A man who did not know these students made a disrespectful comment to one of them close to midnight, and his comment led to a physical confrontation that escalated very quickly, culminating in the man's death. Didn't that dead dick know these tech-school punks fucking rule Bangkok? Attacks like this are almost a weekly event. Three of the gentlemen involved in the altercation recently agreed to sit down and discuss the incident with two *Vice* correspondents over cocktails and dinner. All of the names have been changed at their request.

BANGKOK STREET GANGS 101

Vice: To start with, tell us how it works here. The system and stuff: The organization and leaders…
Deng: Well there's not really a leader. It's just the older guys in charge. At the technical college they initiate you into the gang when you're a first-year. It's like, "OK, go get all the auto mechanics. Round 'em up, then drop them

off in front of such-and-such school." Then it's like, "Go make some people bleed or don't come back. There are five of you, so take five blades."

Vice: What are the blades like?
Deng: You know… cleavers, blunt heads, daggers, box cutters, machetes, whatever. Short knives. We had a gun stash too.

Vice: What do guns cost?
Deng: Back then, around $200.
Ngam: But most of the time, we make them ourselves, because it's a tech school. This guy in the metal shop does this, that guy does that—you make your own guns. Design them, make them.

Vice: So when did shit start to get real heavy for you, fight-wise?
Pravat: Well, there were these concerts. Like, each gang would roll 200 to 300 deep. My crew brought two buses.

Vice: Buses?
Pravat: At the time, bus fare was five baht per head. So 200 seats, that's already what, 1,000 baht? So we'd give them a couple hundred extra so they wouldn't have to make any stops.

Vice: So it's like a private bus. What sort of music did you play?
Pravat: There's no stereo on these buses, so we'd usually sing.
Deng: Yeah, you sing the school song, and then there are dis songs for other schools. It's like a football club. You cheer your team and trash the other team.

Vice: How do you know what school someone's from?
Deng: Every tech school has different shirts. So you just ride around town and if you see someone you stop and—

Vice: —bust out the clubs!
Pravat: Actually, no one uses clubs anymore, just knives and guns. We make bombs too. They're called ping-pong bombs and they've got glass in them. I know this one guy who got brain damage from making so many bombs.

Vice: From all the noise?
Pravat: Well, that and all the shrapnel he's taken in the face and head.

THE RULES
Vice: Are the fights inevitable?
Pravat: Not really. It's more like you're out with your crew, and you end up looking to see if there's any other crew as big as yours.

Vice: If you outnumber them, but they have guns, do you still go?
Pravat: Yeah. But if you get shot, you're fucked. If somebody else gets shot, you have to avenge him.

Vice: You remember the guy's face and then go back and get him?
Pravat: Not really. It's more like that whole school shot your friend, so you have to take your revenge on the whole school. They become like a permanent enemy of your school, so whenever you see one of them, you have to try to kill him. It doesn't have to be the guy who actually pulled the trigger.

Vice: What if you see someone from that school, but he's a total bookworm wimp? Are there, like, noncombatant guys?
Pravat: Doesn't matter.

Vice: What if it's a girl?
Pravat: I don't fuck with girls.
Deng: If she's really annoying or fucked up, I'll spit in a girl's face.

Vice: Are you allowed to fuck girls from someone else's turf? Does that cause problems?
Ngam: Not as much as you'd think. It's actually a status thing. Like if you live in Bang Bua and you get a girl from Bang Kapi, you get props. But you have to take her home afterward…
Pravat: It's worth it. 'Cause if you get beat up, no big deal. And if you don't, you get pussy and props. Like if you're sitting around drinking with your crew and you have a girl from another district, you're the man. Especially if she's a high school girl. Then you get bonus points.

GIVING BACK
Vice: So the older gangsters are the ones who got you into banging. How do you give back to the community and teach the younger kids the tricks of the trade?
Pravat: The most important thing to instill in them is a sense of pride and respect. That's what it's all about. Initially, with young bloods, you kind of push them into shit. Everything we do is a sort of test to see how far you are willing to go for the crew. So the older guys send the younger guys to different schools to cause trouble. You have to push these kids into fights to see what they're made of. Sometimes you do it yourself. It's called jumping them in. You see how much they can take—how much blood they're willing to spill.

Vice: Are there guys who've graduated but still hang around and bang with the younger guys?
Pravat: Of course. You don't just leave it. Mostly because people won't let you. When there's a beef, you always get a phone call.
Deng: More than half of the gang population is older guys. Lots of them keep their school shirts even if they've been kicked out. And they'll wear them because they want people to step to them. A lot of them don't have jobs, so they're bored.
Pravat: Tech is like a religion. It's an establishment that you've got to respect. It's something sacred. You feel it when you're in.

Vice: What are some basic reasons to stomp a guy around here?
Pravat: I hate when a guy's hair is too spiked up. I'll fuck him up if I see that. Or stupid shoes. I hate that too. Annoying pants. I can't stand any of that. It really bothers me in the worst way. It's a bother to the soles of my feet, like I just can't deal with it. Cross-eyed motherfuckers too. Hate them.

THE STOMPING
Vice: OK, let's talk about the most recent incident, where you all stomped a guy to death. That's why we're here.
Deng: We were at this one spot that's a real hot spot for tech-school students and gang violence. A lot of shit goes down there. It's got a bunch of small beer spots and outdoor food spots, like beer-garden-style, all piled in next to each other on both sides of this one street. "Gang row," it's called. We were at the dingiest of all the spots. It's the most fucked-up little rathole, but a popular spot nonetheless.
Pravat: The good thing is that it's on our turf. Whenever there's a big beef, like a real big beef, we usually gather up there first.

Vice: OK, but let's get back to the stomping.
Pravat: There were some older guys at the noodle shop across the street. They were all drunk and one of them started talking trash to my friend who was getting an order of noodle soup. The old guy told our friend that he was too young to be out. He said, "You should go home and suck your momma's titty." So our friend came back across the street and told us.

Vice: So these guys were tech students too?
Pravat: No, they were adults. They weren't even tech. They were old. And there were actually a ton of them. They were all wasted.

Vice: Were you scared?
Pravat: Not really. We just walked across the street. We didn't have any weapons, but I found a pipe in the back of a truck. We walked right in, my friend pointed the guy out, and we started bashing him. We could tell he wasn't scared. He fought back hard. Luckily, I hit his knee. That's when he fell down. My friend took the pipe from my hand and bashed the side of his head in, right around his ear. There were about eight of us around him. That's like the most you can get around a guy without overcrowding. The other guys wanted to get in on it, but there wasn't enough room. Most of the other adults were shocked once he hit the ground and started bleeding. They realized what was happening, and they couldn't do anything.

Vice: How long did you beat him for?
Pravat: It couldn't have been more than a couple minutes. I told my friend to toss the pipe, and we just kept beating him. Stomping his face, his nuts, his legs. It was real bad.
Deng: Honestly, he only died cause he fought back hard. I don't think we would have beaten him so badly if he hadn't acted so hard.
Pravat: I got real lucky the day the cops nabbed everyone. These guys weren't there. I was at that same place across the street. I happened to be in the bathroom. When I walked out, there were about 15 cops circling our table, arresting people. I slipped right passed them and walked out. My friend with the pipe got 20 years.

Vice: So how many of your crew got arrested that day?
Pravat: About ten or 12. I think the people from the noodle shop fingered my crew. They're all in prison now, with different sentences. Some got ten years, some got 15. My friend with the pipe got the most. One guy actually got away somehow. I'm not sure how. He's on the run and no one's heard from him since.

At this point, the stompers adjourned to the snooker table. ■

W. C. FIELDSIKOV

RUSSIAN COCKTAILS

Cologne, hairspray, jet antifreeze, shoe polish, glue, and rose water. Drink up, Russia!

"In America, you drink vodka.
But in Soviet Russia... vodka drinks you."
—*Yakov Smirnoff, comic genius*

Russians as a species are disappearing from this planet faster than Chilean sea bass. With a mortality rate comparable only to that of African countries suffering from massive HIV epidemics, yet without a Third World birth rate to compensate, Russia has seen its population decline by 7 percent since the collapse of the Soviet Union to under 143 million people. Russian men have what a recent World Bank report called "short, brutal lives." Their life expectancy plummeted from 68 years to just 58 years, meaning they live at least 15 fewer years than Western men. If this trend continues, Russia's population will fall to under 100 million by 2050.

And it's thanks in large part to alcohol. Booze is the big reason why Russians are going extinct. Of the seven million Russian deaths in the last decade, 34 percent were due to alcohol.

How does alcohol kill? In part by making Russians drunk enough to do the dirty work themselves. Russia's murder rate is one of the highest in the world, up there with Jamaica's. Eighty-three percent of murderers and more than 60 percent of murder victims were slobbering drunk during the deed. A typical drunken murder story goes something like this: Two middle-aged male friends meet, go back to A's apartment, and pound four or five bottles of cheap vodka over a two-day binge. A passes out drunk; B stumbles away, rapes and strangles A's prepubescent daughter, steals A's microwave oven, and sets A's apartment on fire to cover his tracks but passes out while setting the fire, then dies of smoke inhalation. (This, by the way, happened to my ex-girlfriend's next-door neighbors.)

Then there's good old poisoning. Last year, 40,000 Russians died of alcohol poisoning. In the U.S., with double Russia's population, only a few hundred folks died of alcohol poisoning.

But you see, Russians love highly unconventional spirits. Through trial and error (and a lot of blindness and death), they have invented some of the most kick-ass, hair-on-your-chest-sprouting cocktails in modern history. These cocktails were largely perfected during Mikhail Gorbachev's failed dry campaign in the late 1980s. He severely restricted alcohol production to try to sober the nation up, quickly causing a brief upturn in Russian men's life expectancy—and just as quickly a backlash that ended his political career and brought about the reappearance of Russia's cuddly national mascot, vodka.

But even with vodka widely available in the post-Soviet period, that doesn't mean that Russians have forgotten their favorite homemade brews, as those 40,000 poisoning deaths prove. Here is a guide to the six most-fucking-awful Russian cocktails.

SHIPR ON THE ROCKS

In 1974, Brezhnev announced work on the BAM—a railway running from Lake Baikal to the Pacific Ocean, well north of the Trans-Siberian line. The plan was to lay 2,000 miles of track through the cruelest geography on the planet, where temperatures range from 90°F in the summer to -70°F in the winter.

Obviously, one needed a nip here and there. Since vodka isn't easy to come by in Siberian backwaters, BAM workers devised a special cocktail.

They took a bottle of shitty Soviet cologne, usually Shipr, and poured it down a long, iron bar (used to break up the frozen tundra before laying down track) into a waiting glass. They thought the "impurities" in the cologne—the rank additives that made a man smell like a real proletarian—would stick to the frozen bar, while the spirits would remain unfrozen. Bottoms up!

HAIRSPRAY

Bourgeois capitalist pigs aren't the only class that suffers from hair vanity. The Soviets had their own version of Aqua Net in a famous hairspray called Laq Prelest, which means something like "Charm Varnish."

If you've ever seen a typical middle-aged Soviet woman, with her huge mold of hair bunned up in three stiff piles, you understand that Laq Prelest was serious, industrial shit.

So serious, in fact, that it attracted the interest of their Soviet husbands. Anything that smelled that toxic had to pack a punch. The process of turning Laq Prelest into a viable drink was fairly simple. They'd take the can, spray it into a cup with some water, and swirl it around to mix it up, diluting the Laq Prelest just enough not to completely poison them. Then, down the hatch!

FLYING RESTAURANTS

At the height of Gorbachev's anti-alcohol campaign, MiG jet fighters, the pride of the Soviet Air Force, earned the name "flying restaurants." Not because of the wonderful food served on board, but rather because of the buzz-packing antifreeze that you could siphon from the jet's innards.

According to 33-year-old Dima, who knew several people who regularly drank MiG antifreeze while he served in the army in Siberia, you could only drink five good shots of it per week. Otherwise you risked going blind.

One junior officer that he served with used to count how many shots he'd downed by pulling his belt a notch tighter with every drink because, as Dima said, "He knew when his pants hurt that it was time to stop."

SHOE POLISH

One of the most famous, and bizarre, of the Prohibition-era beverages was the shoe-polish-filter cocktail. It's not so much a drink as it is a filter whose residue you exploit—sort of like scraping the resin from a bong.

The ingredients for this drink are black shoe polish, a glass of water, and a slice of black bread. You take the black shoe polish, spread it on the slice of bread, then set it atop the glass of water so that it covers it up pretty well. Leave it sitting for a couple of hours while you try to pretend you're not enduring the worst shakes ever. Then, when you can't wait anymore, take the bread off the top and drink the poisoned water down. The fumes and toxins from the shoe polish, Russians learned, would be absorbed into the water enough to make it potent. Also, you could take the bread, scrape off the excess polish, and eat it, getting a major rush from the absorbed poisons.

BORIS FYODORYCH-6

There are many ways to heal an injured man. One is to close his wounds with adhesive. For that, Soviet doctors relied on a surgical glue called BF-6 (slangily known as "Boris Fyodorych-Six," a Russian patronymic applied out of sheer fondness for the stuff).

BF-6 surgical glue healed more than flesh wounds. It also healed a man's unbearable need to get drunk on something.

This is the trickiest cocktail to make. You take some BF-6 and a stick and whip the glue around and around. Stir it diligently for two or three hours, until a magical chemical separation takes place between the undrinkable toxins in the thick glue that increasingly stick to the sides of your cup and the liquid that forms in the middle—liquid which was once considered the Ketel One of the DIY alcohol world.

ROSE WATER

Your grandma probably used a rose-water-based lotion to keep her saggy skin from turning into elephant hide. But if your grandfather—or you, for that matter—happened to be Russian, it's doubtful grandma's rose-water-based spritz would have lasted long in the bathroom cabinet.

The greatest advantage to drinking a bottle of *rozovaya voda* lotion was that, unlike so many other cocktails, this one was ready-to-serve. Sort of like Smirnoff Ice. All you had to do was locate a bottle of rozovaya voda, open the lid, tip it back into your mouth, and guzzle the lotion down. That's right—drink the tangy lotion straight. No clever little gimmicks. Just rank lotion pouring down your throat on a hot summer's day. All you needed was one or two good hits of rozovaya voda and the warm fuzzy buzz takes over your whole persona until, you, slowly, fade, away, into the rosy abyss... of... nothingness. ∎

TOM LITTLEWOOD

WHO'S HUNGRY?

Giant Bunnies: North Korea's Furry Hope?

Photos by Frank Kalero

We all know that North Korea, one of the world's last socialist strongholds, has been facing a long-term economic emergency, with famine and poverty claiming 2 million lives a year at its peak. Despite surviving on handouts from China and South Korea, the country has a "Military First" policy that shows no sign of letting up. A quarter of its GDP is spent to maintain the highest percentage of military personnel per capita anywhere in the world. In 2006 Amnesty International reported that 37 percent of North Korean children were chronically malnourished. In response to such staggering conditions, head of state Kim Jong-il decided to develop the country's nuclear program. Later that year the whole nation rejoiced when North Korea tested its first atomic bomb. But sadly enough, you can't eat nuclear waste.

Kim and his cohorts went back to the drawing board and came up with a novel solution. He decided to contact champion German giant-rabbit breeder Karl Szmolinsky, whom he undoubtedly read about on the internet like the rest of the world. We recently met up with Karl and his mutant rabbits to see what the eff is going on.

Vice: How did you get into breeding rabbits?
Karl Szmolinsky: It all started at a rabbit show in 1964. Out of all the rabbits I liked the Deutsche Riesen most. They had good bone structure and form. I bought a female and four babies and I've been breeding ever since. Back in the early days no one believed you could grow a rabbit bigger than 12 pounds, but my club did it. Starting next year they're going to put a 27.5-pound limit on competition weight. I can understand why. Each competition judge has to inspect around 70 rabbits per show and after a while you know you've been lifting rabbits.

What makes a prize rabbit?
The judges look at weight, posture, ear length, and facial proportions. Then they make sure there are no mutations or oddities, like protruding penises. The rabbits should also have black rings around the tops of the ears. You see all sorts of tricks. This one guy got his hairdresser girlfriend to dye the rabbit's ears but the judges noticed when the color started coming off on their hands. They were banned for two years.

How do you get your rabbits so insanely big?
Everyone has a different theory. My friend Siegfried feeds his rabbits beans but I tell him they'll never get big if he doesn't change their diet. I use diverse foodstuffs, but always organic. I cook for my rabbits too. Three times a week I cook a fresh

meal with plenty of greens. Herbs are essential to protect the rabbits from intestinal disease. It can make them swell up overnight and then in the morning they're dead.

That makes sense. But where do the North Koreans fit into this?
I got a call one day from the head of our club. He said the North Koreans wanted to buy a couple of Riesen. I had some I was going to kill for Christmas so I said yes. The North Korean Embassy asked if they could come to inspect my rabbits. Two weeks later what seemed like the entire staff of the North Korean Embassy turned up at my door. The minister of agriculture came too. He just kept saying, "Riesen... Riesen, 22 pounds... 22 pounds!" They didn't care about anything else. They said they'd take the six biggest, including my prize rabbit Robert. I gave them a special price because they told me it was for a good cause. They were going to breed my rabbits to

feed the starving children in their country. I also gave them a book about how to look after rabbits. That turned out to be a mistake.

Why? What happened next?
One month later the rabbits were sent off to North Korea. We tried calling to make sure they had arrived safely but nobody answered the phone. Then they said that the rabbits were in a museum, which I thought was a bit strange. They had studied the book I gave them and said they didn't need me anymore, but that they would still fly me to North Korea to oversee the breeding center they were building. I was so excited. I've lived in this little town my whole life and have never been abroad. Then the day before I was supposed to fly I got a call at 5:35 in the morning saying, "Herr Szmolinsky, you're not needed anymore. We have everything under control." I tried calling the embassy but as soon as I said my name they would just hang up. I'd even done a deal with the ZDF [a German TV channel]. They were going to do a film about me. They made me a personalized hat and jacket. But the North Koreans said without a visa we wouldn't be allowed in. Then everything went completely quiet.

Did you ever find out what happened to your rabbits?
A few weeks later a journalist from London called me. He'd just got back from the birthday celebrations of Kim Jong-il and said he'd seen my rabbits, including Robert. They were being eaten by the leader and his guests. It's clear to me now that the whole thing was a big scam. They sent in their ministers and invented a story to trick me, just so they could put on a fancy banquet for their leader. In my opinion all politicians are bandits. They're definitely not getting any more of my rabbits.

Has anyone else wanted to buy them?
The agriculture minister from Cameroon came to look at my rabbits. They wanted to start breeding to combat widespread starvation but it was never going to work. Cameroon's too hot for rabbits. I'm currently in negotiation with the Chinese government. I don't mind selling to the Chinese. A friend of a guy I know had a house there and said it's much more like the West, not like North Korea. ∎

AS TOLD TO AMIE BARRODALE

WE GOT OUT

North Korean Refugees Tell Us About the Homeland

Kyung Hi Lee. Photos by the author

I met these three people in a nine-story Christian church for North Korean refugees in Seoul. I don't know the church's name; the reverend told me just to call it Seoul Church. It looked exactly like a Christian church in Texas or anywhere in the heartland. The parishioners wore suits and dresses; the kids wore acid-washed jeans and sportswear. On the seventh floor, a family was eating in a huge cafeteria, and next door, four ladies in aprons were trying to get a classroom of hyperspazzing children to settle down.

But I was going to the ninth floor, to a classroom that looked exactly like your standard high-school geometry room, where Rev. Kwang Il-park was passing out leather-bound hymnals to a roomful of twitchy refugees. I sat down in the back, and a teenage girl got up, went to a closet in the front of the room, and returned with a hymnal in English. It was photocopied on green paper and comb-bound with a plastic cover. Standing at a podium in front of a couple of dry-erase boards, Rev. Il-park gave the word. A 60-year-old Korean lady to his left began to play an electric keyboard. He began to sing into a microphone. The others came in, and my heart broke. Afterward, the reverend called me to the front of the room along with my interpreter, and in probably the most ridiculous moment in my life, I held up a copy of *Vice* magazine and

introduced myself, saying I'd like to talk to anyone who wanted to talk to me.

Three people did. Here are their stories:

REV. KWANG IL-PARK

I was born in Hamheung, one of the biggest industrial cities in North Korea. I was a very rich boy, so I practiced gymnastics from when I was five years old until I was ten. My house was about 15 feet wide, with two rooms. It was divided in the middle. I shared a room with my parents. This was not because my family was poor, but because in North Korea the government controls the housing. We couldn't buy a different house—we had what the government gave us. Later, the government had to borrow money from my family to complete a housing development. In return for the favor, they gave us five units in the building.

Hamheung is much like an industrial city in the West, except because there is very little electricity in North Korea and very few raw materials and money, there are big factories but they do not run. In the West, if there is a factory, it is always open and workers are working there all the time. But in North Korea, the facility is there, but there are no materials and there is no electricity, so the factories are closed. Since there is no work at the factory, the workers don't come in or get paid. Every now and then, the factories get raw materials from the government, and they make a product, and the government buys it. But often the process doesn't work, no products go to the government and no money goes to the factories. The factories sit quiet and dark, empty except for the maintenance people and guards.

North Korean society has four groups of people. The highest level of society is made up of government officers. The second is the middle class, the third is the normal, average people, and at the bottom are people who don't have proper thoughts—the anti-Communist people. The higher two groups have rice and vegetables, but the bottom two groups don't have enough rice. They eat grass and trees. When spring comes, people pick at the edible trees and grasses and boil and eat them.

There are two major powers in North Korea: the military and the government. There is only one political power, as you know, that of Kim Jong-il. The heads of the military are very close to Kim Jong-il. Those people are in Pyongyang. There are also the heads of provinces. These make up what we call the "middle class," which doesn't mean the same thing as it does over here—when we say it in North Korea, the term refers to the upper class. The normal class, people like us, are the workers.

I was in the normal class but there was a lot of money in my family. At first, I didn't think about defecting because my life in North Korea was very comfortable. Even though my family did not have political power, most of my friends were in the middle class. But in 1986, I saw a soap opera in the black market in North Korea. It was a famous South Korean soap called *Hourglass*. It was very big in South Korea, and since it was so interesting, I loaned it to many of my friends in the middle class, and they loaned it to all of their friends, and it spread throughout the middle class. It became a big problem. North Korea was suffering from an economic depression at the time, and the government didn't want Western culture— what they call "Yellow Culture"—to spread in North Korea. National Security tried to find out who had started spreading the soap opera. Many of the people who saw and copied and gave the drama away were middle-class people, so they had the power. Their parents were working in the government. Although my parents had money, they were not working for the government. They didn't have any political powers, so I was picked as a scapegoat for the incident, and the government decided to evict me

Rev. Kwang Il-park.

to China. They had to punish somebody and they picked me. The government said, "Evict him to China, and when everybody forgets about the incident, he can come back."

I stayed in the Wharyong area for a while, because it is near the border. I decided I wanted to stay in China, so I went deeper into the mainland, but then I was caught and sent back to Musan, where I was questioned by North Korean officers for a week. Then I was transferred to Chung Jin and questioned even more by National Security soldiers. I slept in a small concrete room. I wasn't allowed to lie down at night—the guards would not let me. As part of my punishment, I had to sleep in a sitting position. I was fed once a day with a small bowl of corn, beans, and vegetables. And then daily, for 40 days, I was taken to another room with a desk and two chairs, and I was tortured by two men. I was very scared—scared to death. The investigators' job was to find anti-Communist spies, and to that end they tortured me. My bones were broken all over my body. They asked the same questions over and over: "Why did you run farther away into China? Where did you get the videotape? Do you have contact with South Korean spies? Do you have any additional tapes? Why are you so anti-Communist?"

When I didn't answer their questions, or answered wrong, they would kick me or punch me or beat me with big wooden sticks. Also, there is a torture called "pigeon." They tied my arms and feet together behind my back and hung me by my hands and feet from the ceiling, so I was flying in space like a pigeon. They suspended me like this generally for two or three hours. Your head is heavy, so in the pigeon position, your head goes down, your blood goes into your face, and the brain doesn't work properly, so it makes you lose consciousness. And then every time I passed out, they dipped my head into water so I would wake up, and then the process would begin again. Often when I was passed out, I would forget where I was, and then I would wake up and remember. But after about ten days of beating and torturing, all you can think about is that you want to die as quickly as possible. So when I woke up and found out that I was in prison, all I could think was, "Why am I still alive? I want to die, die, die." Many people do die during the 40 days of investigation, so I expected myself to be dead. There was no hope that I could get free, so I just wanted to end everything: the physical pain and the foolishness. I just wanted to die. After getting beaten so many times, there comes a time when you don't feel anything, not even physical pain, just a numbness. Like in a boxing match, the boxer doesn't feel much pain... The body sensors get numb. So after a certain amount of torture, I couldn't feel much pain anymore.

When my 40 days were over I was to be sent by train to North Korea to jail. In the train I was depressed. I couldn't bear the fact I was going to be imprisoned in North Korea and I decided to commit suicide. I stepped outside the moving train and jumped into a river but miraculously, I didn't die. After that, I made my way into South Korea.

KYUNG HI LEE

My father was born in North Korea and my mother was born in South Korea. But during the 6/25 War [the Korean War], my mother volunteered as a North Korean military officer. I was born in Pyongyang, and I had a very nice life there. The North Korean government rations food to the people, and in Pyongyang all the people get rice, no matter how low their social status is.

When you look at the city of Pyongyang, it is beautiful—it is even better looking than Seoul. The city is very clean and the opera house is beautiful and everything is very good-looking. But when you go inside a building, there's no electricity, so you can't use the elevators. You have to use the stairways to go up to the top of a building, however tall. There is no water in the buildings when the electricity is cut off, so most of the time, when you turn the faucet on, the water will not come out. You have to draw the water by hand and then carry it upstairs. There is no heating system in the buildings because there is no electricity, so it is cold and you have to wear warm clothes all the time. It is kind of a comical situation.

When I was 14, the government decided that even though my mother had fought on their side in the war, she was born in the South, so she could not be trusted entirely. Our family was put outside of Pyongyang. For the first year, we lived in On-sung, in a house shared by several families in a similar situation. After the first year, our family got out of the house, and we found a very small house in a rural area.

My parents were doctors in Pyongyang but after the eviction, they had to do physical labor on the housing-construction sites and in the mines. Because working at the mines was punishment, my parents could not find any happiness there. Nevertheless, they felt grateful that they were not in prison. They still had some freedom, so they were thankful. I was the same. I didn't have hard feelings or bad feelings for Kim Il-sung, because I was young, and they continuously teach the young people that he is the great father of the North Korean people. I thought that he was a very good person and he was feeding me with the rice. The food was given by him, the clothes were given by him. I felt very thankful to him.

In the 1990s, a lot of people died from starvation, and I started to think about defecting. On-sung is part of the border area, very near China's Northern Province. I saw a lot of people coming from China with rice and money. I thought that if I stayed in On-sung I would starve to death, but I saw that if I got caught in the course of trying to defect, then I would be killed by the guards. I decided that I had to take the chance, because if I stayed in North Korea I would die of starvation.

China was across the river from On-sung so all I had to do was to cross the river. Because I lived in the town growing up, I knew all the guards and at what time they always came and went.

My husband couldn't come, because he has a lot of brothers and sisters in North Korea, and if he defected it would affect their lives. We had two daughters. One was ten years old and one was five years old. I took the older daughter with me when I crossed the river. I found that China was a very nice place to live because there was rice everywhere. People just threw the rice away because they were full. I was surprised to see so many people living without starvation. I thought I should take the younger daughter too, so I went back to get her.

I was walking alongside the river in the early evening, going to get my younger daughter, and the North Korean soldiers caught me. They fired questions at me: "Where are you coming from? Why are you walking along the river? Are you trying to cross the river?" I said, "Oh no, my house is just over there and I am going back to my house." But I was wearing a Chinese perfume, and in On-sung nobody had any perfume. Also, I was wearing nice Chinese clothing—a cotton jacket and cotton pants. The North Koreans just knew I was coming from China, so they took me and imprisoned me for four months.

There were about ten women in a room that was nine-by-seven feet. Ten women can only fit in that like sardines, all lying down. There was one water faucet in the room and one toilet. There was a pipe by the ceiling and water was always dripping out. Except for at bedtime, I had to sit up and I couldn't move. Everybody had to sit up and we could only move for five minutes every two hours. It was our punishment—sitting still. At night when people slept we could get up and move around.

There was one woman who had given birth to a baby about a month before I arrived, and her body was still unrecovered. She couldn't move. She couldn't walk from her spot to the toilet, so we had to carry her. She started to cry and shout that she could not walk, so they took her out after ten days and sent her back home.

I was beaten by the guards. I bled. I was tortured in the prison. They kicked me and beat me until I became unconscious. I was unconscious for 20 hours. I was lying down in my blood, in the room with the other nine women. The other women tried to clean me up and help me, but there was no medicine or doctor in the prison. About ten days after I woke up, there was an outbreak of typhus and I got it. With high fever, the body will tremble. Three or four women had typhus during this time. When we recovered, the others got it, back and forth. It passed down the hallway to the other cells, so we could listen to the other women at night, when it was quiet, and they'd be moaning.

During this time, my ten-year-old daughter was in China with a couple who felt very sorry for me and her. I was able to defect again after I got out of prison, and I paid a Chinese broker to take me and my daughters to Seoul. It cost about $7,000 total, and this is money I was able to pay using the resettlement money I received from the South Korean government upon my arrival. On-sung is a rural city, so when it rains everybody has to wear rain boots. When I got to South Korea, the first thing I did was go to the department store to buy rain boots for my kids. The guy in the store asked my why I wanted to buy rain boots in Seoul and I said, "Isn't it rainy in Seoul? I don't want my children's feet to get dirty." He thought it was very funny.

HAK CHEOL KIM

The human rights issues in North Korea are really urgent and the situation is really bad. About 3 million people died of starvation between 1994 and 1998. It started in 1994 because that was the year Kim Il-sung died. After his death, society went into total chaos and the high officers didn't care about the welfare of the normal people, because they were busy saving their own necks.

I starved during that time. After starving for ten or more days you lose all your energy. You lose the energy to walk. When I did manage to walk in the street, I saw a person in front of me fall down, and he had no energy to get up. He just stayed lying down in the road, because he didn't have anything in his stomach. I couldn't help him because I had nothing in my stomach either so I just passed by, and the person who fell down died there. I saw a lot of people lying down in the street.

During this time, young people in North Korea ran out of their homes because there was no food. They ran away and lived with other young people. These kids were called *koseibi*, which means "the young kids who are moving around like swallows." They stole or begged, and that's how they lived every day. It is very cold in North Korea and if five of them went to sleep at the station, only two or three of them would wake up. They'd die because of the cold weather. There were so many corpses at the railway stations, the government created an organization to take care of them. It was called 918 Public Service. Koseibis were dying every day in large numbers, so the 918 Public Service tried to bury their bodies in the nearby mountains. During the winter the ground is frozen, so you cannot dig it deep enough to put in the bodies. They just dug shallow holes and put the bodies inside and covered them with some dirt.

When I was in high school, my friend was at this rice field near town, and behind it there was a mountain used for burial. There was not enough stone to make tombstones, so the graves had these white nameplates instead. The mountain was entirely covered with these white wooden sticks. During the spring and during the summer, the bodies that were not buried deep enough started to

Hak Cheol Kim.

come out as the ground thawed, and there was a stink. The skeletons were fine because they did not stink, but some bodies were not completely decomposed yet and there was still flesh on the bones. That makes a lot of stink.

My father was locked up in the political prison and my mother was working in the city to make some money to support me and my brother, so we were left alone in the house with one bowl of corn that had to last five days. I ate one piece of corn every hour.

About 15 million tons of rice are needed for the North Korean people to survive for a year. Since the 1960s the rice production has only been 8 million tons. The Soviet Union and East Germany used to help out, but now North Korea is not getting any help, even from its allies.

The only way to make things better is to make the world know about the awful status of people's lives in North Korea today. What the U.S. is doing right now is affecting North Korea. They are banning economic transactions between North Korea and other countries. This is responsible for the starvation to some extent, but the major reason why the North Koreans are suffering is that the government of Kim Jong-il is refusing to open up because they killed so many people to get to their current positions. They cannot open up, because they would have to face military trial.

Most refugees in South Korea or other countries are sending money to their families in North Korea, because even if you don't have any money in South Korea you can still live, but if you don't have any money in North Korea you will die. It's a strange life... That's all I have to say today. ■

GABI SIFRE

BLESS THIS MESS

Hermano Blanco Is Our Own Private Warlock

There's a city in Veracruz, Mexico, called Catemaco, wherein there dwells a multitude of warlocks. That is correct, nonbelievers: warlocks. Men who are wizardly practitioners of magick, mojo, and (if you get on their bad side) mayhem, and they all live in this one place. Some of them are in it for the money, and some of them are, we think, the real deal. Like, as in, yes, we believe they have weird powers. Hermano Blanco is a self-proclaimed cyber-warlock. He gets emails from all over the Spanish-speaking world, seeking out his help with issues of money, health, love, sex, and liberation from harmful spells cast by other, not-so-nice warlocks. We talked to him recently, and then we asked him to help us out by blessing this issue of *Vice*, which he did. So we're basically all set.

Illustration by Guillerma Ignazio

Vice: Oh famed warlock Hermano Blanco, what is the source of thy sorcery?
Hermano Blanco: The origins of my practice are primarily of Olmec roots. I come from the Olmec Indians, who were characterized as a magic tribe. They worked with witchcraft and magic. Later, with the conversion to Christianity, Olmec warlocks started working with saints. Now the two cultures are mixed together. We use the elements of nature (earth, wind, fire, and water), Catholic saints, pre-Columbian beings, and—when more private work is being done—spiritual beings, such as people who have passed away.

And how did you personally get involved with the craft?
I'm a third-generation warlock. My grandfather, then my father, then me. It's inherited. Ever since I was a child I would see how they performed their rituals. I had my official initiation when I was 13.

What does warlock training involve?
You learn little by little how to cast spells, perform invocations and rituals, and use herbs. At the initiation, you completely open your spirit and mind. Soon, you develop certain senses—the ability to make predictions and have visions. But we also must have a cultural education—some psychology and pedagogy—so we can work with everyone who comes to us.

What do Mexicans think about witches and warlocks?
Witchcraft goes hand in hand with Mexican culture and the Catholic Church in Mexico. It's very common among Mexicans and Latin Americans to take it as a second belief system. Even politicians acknowledge it. There have been candidates who have visited warlock friends in order to win the presidency.

What services do people usually want?
Of every ten people who come to me, eight of them want something involving love—even though I don't recommend it. People used to work for love, but now if it gets difficult, they come straight to the warlock. The real problem with love is that men need to learn to be gentlemen again.

Without revealing too many secrets, what will *Vice*'s blessing entail?
I'm going to use the candle of the Seven Powers. I'm going to invoke the four elements of nature to help you, to open the four paths—which are also north, south, east, and west—so that all of your energy reaches the four cardinal points. I am going to pray to various powerful beings—three positive and one negative. The positive ones are to open your paths so that you have many readers, no legal troubles, and so that money is never a problem. The negative one is to protect you from any other negative beings and energies. I am going to ensure that *Vice* becomes a household name, like Coca-Cola!

Excellent. ∎

TIM SMALL

—

OUCH OUCH OUCH OUCH OUCH!

A Day at the Circumcision Palace

I n Islamic Turkey, circumcision is much more than a surgical procedure. Traditionally occurring between the ages of five and 12, and known as the "first joy," it's seen as the first landmark in the boy's religious life, proof that he is strong, brave, and ready to be called a man. To this end, the procedure is generally performed with local anesthetic or none at all, as the pain is an integral part of the ritual. In the festivities surrounding the circumcision, the boy is made to wear a king's costume, and the assembled family and friends shower him with gifts and tie gold coins to his belt. Almost 30 percent of Turkish parents, including medical staff, choose the traditional method over the postnatal procedure in hospitals, and in rural Turkey up to 85 percent of circumcisions are performed without any doctor at all.

The "circumcision experts" who are called to perform the ritual instead of medical personnel often inherit their position from their fathers. As a result, the official literature is filled with reports of vomit-inducing botched procedures, some of which end with severed urethras, infections, gangrene, amputation of the penis, and even death.

Kemal Özkan, a 58-year-old qualified paramedic, is a Turkish celebrity. He is known as the Sultan of Circumcision. He has allegedly operated on more than 100,000 children in his 37-year career and his famously outlandish publicity stunts have included performing circumcisions on horseback, on a camel, and in flight. ∎

This boy is Ali. This picture was taken as he was being circumcised in the operating room of the Kemal Özkan Circumcision Palace. The two-story building includes a playground with a go-kart track, a dancing hall, and a restaurant.

Before the procedure, the boy is distracted with music and a clown, all to help him forget the mind-shattering pain that will soon wash over his entire body.

Mustapha kisses the great Kemal Özkan's hand before his circumcision. Kemal is well known as the greatest circumciser in Turkey, partially thanks to his PR stunts, such as performing 2,000 procedures in one 24-hour penis-snipping marathon.

As the paramedics continue the operation, the screaming child is assisted by his kirve (godfather). The kirve will theoretically become part of the boy's family, and the boy cannot marry the kirve's daughter, as it is considered incest.

The assistants are tying wire around the boy's penis as his family films the event. After the summer, the peak time for circumcisions in Turkey, Kemal travels to Germany to circumcise children of Turkish immigrants.

Following the circumcision, the child is checked to make sure he can urinate correctly. The parents are trying to distract the child to alleviate the trauma he just went through. Success!

Photos by Mauro D'Agati

JAMES KNIGHT

AGENT ORANGE'S KIDS

The War Photography of Philip Jones Griffiths

Photos by Philip Jones Griffiths from his book Agent Orange: "Collateral Damage" in Viet Nam, *published by Trolley Ltd.*

Philip Jones Griffiths is a Welsh photographer whose book *Vietnam Inc.* was published in 1971. We think it's the best book there is about the Vietnam War. Recently, Griffiths released another book about Vietnam, titled *Agent Orange: "Collateral Damage" in Viet Nam*. In it, he drew together all his formerly unpublished work documenting the effects of Agent Orange, a defoliant used by the US military during the Vietnam War. Griffith's work shows us that all of the things we fear—boring stuff like bankruptcy, STDs, and being sad—are tiny pinpricks compared to the Armageddon that was brought down on the people of Vietnam.

Vice: What's the story with Agent Orange?
Philip Jones Griffiths: The component of Agent Orange that kills, that produces deformed kids and illnesses, is called dioxin. It's an amazingly powerful poison.

America dropped it on South Vietnam during the war. Today, they say, "Look, we didn't drop it on Vietnam to produce deformed babies. We did it to clear the vegetation so we could see the enemy. If we knew how dangerous it was we wouldn't have done it." But of course they knew how dangerous it was.

Basically, they didn't care if they killed trees, Vietnamese people, or both...
Yes, but their contempt for the Vietnamese was matched only by their contempt for the American soldier, who also got sprayed and died in large numbers, or who made it home and produced deformed children.

Did you hear about Agent Orange while you were still in Vietnam, or later?
There were rumors going around in 1970 and some photos had been published in one of Saigon's main antigovernment newspapers. At the time the government dismissed the whole thing, saying it was a result of VD from prostitutes.

How did you find the victims?
I originally looked in Catholic orphanages, but I was forbidden entry into every orphanage or hospital where these children were kept. It seemed that the word had spread to keep the press out. It wasn't until I returned after the war was over that I gained access to a children's hospital in Saigon. The staff would actually phone me at my hotel whenever a baby had been born that survived and was recognizably human. Often they would only survive for a few hours, so I would get a call at my hotel in the middle of the night and rush over there. The photos of the mothers are as heartbreaking as the photos of the victims.

So the attempt to hide Agent Orange from the media—from you—didn't really work. Do you think they were able to hide some of the grimmest realities from you?
I saw an awful lot. A child born with no brain was perhaps the most shocking, but I saw countless deformities and still-births. The photograph of the two blind children who are clinging to their mother was the first one I took. Once I began to encounter more victims of Agent Orange I realized that I had probably seen afflicted people in the past and attributed it to spina bifida or something similar.

Did it ever feel too overwhelming? How could you keep going?
There is no real answer to that. I suppose I simply had to. A photographer who cannot maintain, who breaks down and cannot focus their lens, is as useless as a surgeon who faints at the sight of blood. You have to keep your cool about you and channel your anger into your fingertips and keep that shutter moving. If you have to break down then the place to do so is at home. I have to tell you, though, that I used to get very emotional in the darkroom or looking at the contact sheets. At the time, however, I remained stoic and was helped in that respect by the mothers, who were the model of stoicism. When you see parents playing with a child who is essentially a grotesque it would be inappropriate to break down.

Were the victims given any aid?
The amount of aid that was given to these essentially poor people was very small. It has increased as the country has become more prosperous but it is still negligible.

Have you yourself suffered any illness from exposure?
I have contracted colon cancer, which is on the US government's list of possible Agent Orange side effects. However, my family has a predisposition, as both my brother and grandfather have suffered from it as well. I'm currently undergoing chemotherapy and receive a check from the US government every month, as colon cancer warrants compensation. I was heavily exposed to Agent Orange, particularly flying through areas that had just been sprayed. I inhaled a lot of that shit. Saigon itself was very badly affected by Agent Orange, since many steel drums that had contained Agent Orange were reused afterward to store gasoline for cars. When you heat up Agent Orange it becomes far more reactive. That stuff was basically pouring out of exhausts and would kill all the trees. It was something we used to joke about at the time because we couldn't figure out why the trees were all dead. We only found out about the drums later. If I were to take a test right now the levels in my blood would show massive exposure. ■

TOMOKAZU KOSUGA

AN OLD JAPANESE DOCTOR
WHO SURVIVED HIROSHIMA

Portrait by Tomokazu Kosuga

Japan is still (as of press time on this issue) the only country in the world that has been a victim of the atomic bomb. Since the demons dropped onto the cities of Hiroshima and Nagasaki 63 years ago this past August, the country has continued to quietly suffer from the repercussions. One 91-year-old *hibakusha* (that's

Japanese for "A-bomb survivor") doctor continues to call out the dangers and brutality of the A-bomb to the rest of the world. His name is Shuntaro Hida. On August 1, 1944, a year before the bomb dropped on the city, Dr. Hida was posted to Hiroshima's army hospital as a military doctor. He experienced the bomb blast at just 3.5

miles away from its epicenter, and he has since seen everything there is to see as a doctor specializing in the treatment of A-bomb victims. Dr. Hida knows the effects of the bomb not only from the perspective of someone who was actually there but also from the specialized viewpoint of an army medic. It's no wonder then that almost 6,000 radiation-sickness sufferers in Japan and around the world have sought his expertise. So what exactly happened on that fateful day in Hiroshima? *Vice* spoke to Dr. Hida, who remembers every single detail about the experience.

Vice: How did you manage to avoid being hit by the bomb directly, despite being in Hiroshima at the time?
Dr. Hida: I was dozing off on my futon the night before the bombing on August 6, when somebody suddenly shook me awake. It was an old man who came from Hesaka village, which is a couple of miles away from Hiroshima. His granddaughter had cardiac valvular disease and often had seizures, so I regularly went to the village to check up on her. That night she suffered another one, so I got on the back of the old man's bicycle and he rode me to their place. This meant that I got out of Hiroshima just in time to be saved from being directly hit. I was exposed to the radiation, but from a distance of just over three miles from the epicenter.

Dr. Hida in 1942, three years before the bomb hit.

Did you actually see the moment when the A-bomb was dropped?
Yes, I did. I think I'm the only person who actually saw it with his own eyes and then wrote about the experience later, because most people in Hiroshima were killed the instant they saw that bright flash of light.

Let me explain how I actually saw the bombing. I spent the night at the old man's place after looking at the child. The next morning, I decided to give her a sedative before going back to the hospital, because if she woke up and started crying she might have another seizure. I took out a small syringe from my pocket, tilted it upward, and pushed out some liquid to let any air out. Suddenly I saw a plane flying above Hiroshima in front of me.

That must have been the *Enola Gay*. Tell us what you saw when the bomb hit Hiroshima.
The first thing I saw was the light. It was so bright that I was momentarily blinded. Simultaneously, I was surrounded by an intense heat. The bomb released a 4,000-degree heat wave in the instant that it hit the ground. I panicked, covered my eyes, and lay low on the floor. I couldn't hear any noise and the trees weren't rustling. I thought something was up, so I cautiously looked through the window toward where I'd seen the flash of light. The skies were blue with no cloud in sight, but there was this bright red ring of fire high up in the skies above the city! In the middle of the ring was a big white ball that kept growing like a thundercloud—this really round thing. It kept getting bigger and bigger until it finally hit the outer fire ring, and then the whole thing blew up into a huge red fireball. It was like I was witnessing the birth of a new sun. It was so perfectly round! When I was a child, I saw Asama Mountain erupt from really close up, but this was much more full-on. The clouds were white, but shining in rainbow colors as they rose up. It was really beautiful. People call it the "mushroom cloud" but it's actually a pillar of fire: The bottom part is a column of flames and the top part is a fireball, which metamorphoses into clouds as it keeps rising up.

Then, below the pillar of fire, pitch-black clouds started spreading horizontally above the mountains surrounding Hiroshima. They consisted of sand and dust that were being pushed up from the ground due to the pressure generated from the blast. They were coming toward me like a tidal wave. We were on a hill and there was a cliff next to us, but the next moment the dust clouds had crept right up. Before I knew it, the old man's house was swallowed up and crushed by the wave. Luckily the thatched roof acted as a cushion, saving the child and myself. It was then that I realized that something terrible must have happened, and rushed back to the hospital in Hiroshima on the old man's bike.

What was the first example of a human casualty from the A-bomb that you saw?
I encountered the first victim halfway back to Hiroshima. This black thing suddenly popped out from the side of the road, swaying unsteadily. I had no idea what it was. I slowed down my bicycle and gradually moved closer and realized that it was a person.

I tried to look at its face, but it didn't have one. There were these two big swollen balls where the eyes should be, a gaping hole for their nose, and the lips had puffed up so big that they were covering half the face. It was hideous. And it had a black thing that looked like a sleeve draped off its arm, so I initially thought that it was wearing rags. I was wondering what all this meant when suddenly the person started moving toward me. My first reaction was to move back. But then it tripped over my bike and fell down. Being a doctor, I immediately rushed forward and tried to take its pulse. But the skin from the entire arm had slipped off and there was nowhere for me to touch.

I realized then that the person was not wearing rags but was entirely naked. What I had thought were sleeves was actually raw skin that had peeled off from the body and was dangling down. The skin on its back had also burned and peeled off completely, and there were dozens of small shards of glass piercing the surface. The person suddenly twitched a couple of times, and then lay completely still. It was dead.

That's a really shocking image. Did you encounter any other traumatic scenes?
Yes. I was somehow able to get to the hospital, but there was a huge blaze and I couldn't go inside. I thought about the situation and decided that since I was a doctor and was still alive, the best thing to do was to go back to the village. Hesaka is the nearest village to Hiroshima so all of the evacuees would surely flee there, and I could probably treat the injured. I spent another three hours riding upstream along the river until I finally arrived at the village's elementary school. I glanced around the schoolyard. It was peppered with charred black people lying on the ground, as if someone had scattered seeds across it. There must have been around 1,000 people there. Three other army doctors had gathered at the school, so we discussed taking a course of action. But the victims were all severely burned and in critical condition. There wasn't much we could do. What we did that night though was pick out the dead from the living among the 1,000 or so people lying on the ground, and start clearing away their bodies.

While I did this, the hibakusha all stared at me. I tried my best to avoid eye contact. But then I accidentally locked eyes with someone, and felt like I had to go over and pretend to treat them. As I moved closer, he glared at me with his two eyeballs, a horrendous stare. The dying people there had absolutely no clue what had happened to them, so they all had these beastly eyes. Have you ever seen the eyes of a pig being slaughtered? Frightening, right? This person glared at me with those same eyes. They still haunt me in my dreams to this day. Each year around August 6, I dream about those eyes every night. I never want to see them again, but they keep haunting me. That's how deep of an impression they left.

When did you start treating the surviving hibakusha?
On the third morning after the bomb, we were finally able to begin treating those who looked like they might pull through. That's when we first discovered the acute symptoms of radiation. First, the victims get a high fever of over 104 degrees Fahrenheit. It was so high that I thought the thermometers were broken. Also, when you tried to get close to their faces, you noticed that they had unbe-

lievably bad breath. It was almost impossible to go near them. I guess in medical terms you would describe the smell as a combination of necrosis and decomposition. When you peered into their mouths, they were completely black. Because the white blood cells in their bodies were completely dead, the bacteria in their mouths had multiplied profusely. And since there was nothing to protect the inside of the mouths anymore, they started to rot very quickly without even going through the usual stages of inflammation or pus formation. This rot was what we were smelling. It's a smell that only the medics who experienced the aftermath know about.

Next, purple blotches started appearing on any unburned skin. In medical terms we call this purpura, and they usually form just before a patient who has a blood disease like leukemia dies. I was extremely surprised when I found these on the victims, because I had no idea why they were appearing. After that, their hair would all fall out, as if their heads had been swept with a broom. Radiation usually targets healthy cells, so hair roots are the first to go. The final symptoms are vomiting blood, as well as hemorrhaging from the eyes, nose, anus, and reproductive organs. The victims only last a few hours after this before they die. At the time we were all extremely scared, because obviously nobody knew what was causing all this.

You said that you were exposed to radiation yourself. Have you suffered any symptoms?
The predominant symptom that I experienced was that my bones aged very fast. Right now my backbone is in a pitiful state. I had lower-back problems after being exposed to the radiation, and underwent surgery many times. At the worst of times I was crawling on the ground because of the pain. However, the aging finally stopped when I was 80 years old, when I began a treatment which consisted of walking up and down a swimming pool. Just this past Atomic Bomb Day, I walked around Hiroshima and Nagasaki without my walking stick. But the biggest fear that we hibakusha have to live with is the anxiety that we might one day develop cancer. We can't plan our lives like everyone else. When we enroll in school, when we marry, when we have children, we constantly have to confront this anxiety. We have been robbed of our human rights. And not only have our rights to live as human beings been violated, we are forced to live with the knowledge that we will one day inevitably develop some sort of disease as a direct result of being exposed to the bomb. But we don't know exactly when that will happen, so until then, we must live in fear. Even if we sued our country in court and were paid money, it wouldn't solve a thing. Money can't buy back the 63 years that I have lived in suffering. ■

Translated by Lena Oishi.

TIM SMALL

TAKING ON THE ITALIAN MAFIA

A Conversation With Roberto Saviano

Photo by Lele Saveri

Roberto Saviano is the 29-year-old author of *Gomorrah*, the international best seller that, through a mixture of narrative and investigative journalism, exposes the workings of the most powerful, and least known, of the Italian Mafias: the Camorra of Naples.

Over the last 30 years, the Camorra has grown into an all-pervasive, seemingly undefeatable network of vicious killers, loons, and businessmen whose operations account for slightly less than 10 percent of Italy's gross national product. Saviano's book is a powerful indictment of the "System" (as it's called by its members) and a shocking account of the strength and ferocity of the Southern Italian crime syndicates. Saviano's success and his policy of openly stating the names and activities of the members of the Camorra have made him an obvious target for assassination. He has been living with a 24-hour escort of three policemen who never leave his side for almost three years.

Recently, during the largest-ever anti-Mafia trial in Italian history, the "Spartacus trial," the defense attorney read a 60-page letter penned by the suspects that openly accused Saviano, the public attorney, and a local journalist of trying to influence the court's decision. Saviano himself has called the letter "a call to arms... a declaration that states that, were they to be indicted, we are to be held responsible." In response to this declaration, Saviano came out of hiding to denounce the Camorra once more, on national television.

The day after his appearance on the screens of all Italian living rooms, we met with him for an interview. As we entered the lobby of the drab Milan hotel where we had planned to rendezvous, we were startled by a middle-aged man who quietly appeared at our side, leaned toward us, and asked in a barely audible whisper, "Are you here for Saviano?" We were taken to an undergound room without windows where our bags were opened and checked. Finally, Saviano himself entered the room, where we sat down, drank a glass of water, and chatted for a couple of hours about the Mafia's power, his book, and his life.

Vice: If you were to explain the Camorra to someone who knew nothing about it, what would you say?
Roberto Saviano: The Camorra is a criminal and entrepreneurial economic organization based in Campania, the region surrounding Naples. I want to stress the entrepreneurial aspect of this organization because Italian organized crime is often viewed romantically, with stories of bandits on the run and honor codes. In reality, these are criminal cartels that do business in every economic sphere, especially in the legal ones, such as textiles, transport, tourism, construction, and waste management. Only after all of that come cocaine, heroin, and extortion. The Camorra is also one of the least-studied crime cartels,

even if it is the Italian Mafia that has the largest number of affiliates and that has generated the largest number of deaths. Together with the Calabrian 'Ndrangheta, another poorly visible Mafia, it's probably the number-one criminal emergency in Europe.

Exactly how powerful is the Camorra?

The net turnover of the three Italian Mafias—the Camorra in Campania, the 'Ndrangheta in Calabria, and the Cosa Nostra in Sicily—is something like $230 billion per year. That's just their direct business. If you add all the other aspects, you could say they are linked to around $800 billion annually. Consider the $230 billion figure. The FIAT group, Italy's largest industrial group, has a turnover of around $80 billion a year. In other words, the Mafia is the single largest Italian economy, and one of the largest in Europe. In terms of violent crimes, if you add the number of deaths directly linked to the Mafia in the past 30 years of Italian history, only in the three regions of Sicily, Campania, and Calabria, you can estimate it at approximately 10,000. That's more than those killed in Gaza in the last intifada. It's a war.

In your book you do a great job of explaining the international dimension of the Camorra. But the Mafia is seen as something quintessentially Italian. How does that work?

It's the most annoying stereotype for Italians overseas— the fact that we're automatically connected to the Mafia. Of course, it's idiotic. But it is true that the criminal aspect of these organizations was born in Southern Italy. It is there that they begin to extract the first capital, to organize their eventual hideouts, to flesh out their hierarchies. But that's not where they make money. It'd be impossible. How can you make that kind of money in a poor territory, with 40 percent unemployment? They use the South as a gold mine. They build their empires there by fraudulently channeling EU funds; they use it as a base to stockpile huge quantities of drugs—most of the coke that comes to Europe from Latin America or Africa stops in Southern Italy. From there, it is sent to Milan, Rome, Paris, London, Marseille, and Bonn. This capacity to use Southern Italy as a launching pad for the rest of the world is one of their greatest strengths.

Do they also reach America?

Italian-American Mafias are very weak. Even if the Italian families want to keep that aspect alive, today it's the Italians themselves who go to America to invest, often with the mediation of the Albanian and Nigerian Mafias—the ones that are structurally closest to the Italians. That's the funny part: The Italian Mafia has a strong international appeal. Most of the world's Mafias, besides maybe the Russian and the Chinese, are inspired by it.

Speaking of the Mafia's international appeal, can you tell me what happened in Helsinki recently?

I went to this huge bookshop to present my book, and it was packed. But my book had only come out the day before, so I knew they couldn't have been there for me. I asked my publisher, who reassured me they were all my crowd. And then I discovered why. When the host announced me, he said, "Please welcome Roberto Soprano!" I thought he was kidding, but he was just confused. *The Sopranos* was a huge success in Scandinavia, and all those people thought I had written what the *Washington Post* defined as "the book about the real, mean Sopranos." You know, the character Tony Soprano is originally from Campania.

Are the three Mafias very different from each other?

Cosa Nostra, the Sicilian mafia, is the most well known mainly because of films and because they have killed many important public figures, like Judge Falcone. The 'Ndrangheta is a very powerful organization, but nobody knows much about it, because it's based on blood ties. You can't become an affiliate if you aren't related. Plus, there's very few of them, and they have very few informers.

And the Camorra?

The Camorra, on the other hand, is the most porous. You can enter it even if you're unrelated. Even if you have parents in law enforcement. The entry to the clan is completely liberalized. They permit the creation of groups. I mean, if you and I were to go to Naples, we could create our own group, do our own extortion, coordinate our own trafficking. If we became a nuisance, they might kill us. Or if we became powerful enough, we might make allies. Maybe we'd enter another, bigger group. Or we might declare war on them. This is why it's such a bloody organization: They can't exist without armed encounters. During their war of Secondigliano, where different clans were fighting one another, there was a tally of four or five murders a day. In those few months, there were more deaths in the area of Secondigliano than in Baghdad.

But the different Mafias work together?

Yes, they are allied. But these names are false: The Sicilian Mafia is actually called Cosa Nostra, but the 'Ndrangheta is called Cosa Nuova, the New Thing. And the Camorra is simply known as the System. Nobody inside the organizations calls them by their widespread names. Those are names for cops and journalists. However, even if they work together, they don't exactly love each other. The Camorra looks down on the Cosa Nostra, because they made the mistake of murdering celebrities. The "idiocy of the Corleone" is how they define it. They see it as an overrated Mafia. They have always leaned toward the right-wing parties for support, and the anti-Mafia commission is traditionally left-wing. The 'Ndrangheta and the Camorra look left, making it very hard to talk about them.

It seems that the three Mafias do their business and deal with their public perception in different ways, and that the Camorra is the most media-savvy.
The famous Camorrista Pasquale Galasso, during his trial in front of the anti-Mafia commission, when asked why they had never killed enemy judges or lawyers, replied, "Because we don't need to kill. We prefer to delegitimize." They know that if you kill public figures, you play the game of those who want you arrested, but if you delegitimize them, if you remove their ability to hurt you by destroying their career or reputation, you use the perfect democratic tool. You use libel. They have also killed at times, but only figures that they thought they could get away with, like Giancarlo Siani, a young freelance reporter. And in any case, the relationship between the Mafia, politics, and the media is very complicated.

Why?
In the States, or in other countries, there is no way you could be a politician who has publicly known ties to organized crime. In Italy, it's the norm. In fact, politicians often do their best to show that they can work with the Mafia, because it's seen, in many circles, as something positive. If everybody knows you have ties with the System, they know you'll be able to get the right contracts, to make things happen, and that those works won't be sabotaged. The Mafia makes administrations more effective. It is an economic lubricant.

But if it's so intertwined with the state and the law, isn't it sort of invincible?
For sure. We won't see the end of organized crime. It will take many generations, if it is ever to happen. Italy can't afford to lose $230 billion worth of business. It would collapse. Europe would collapse. The only way to fight it is to organize the downfall of a specific family. Remember, there isn't one boss who won't end up killed or in jail. It always happens. So the authorities can stop one family. Like the Corleones. But after them there will be another and then another. It's just fighting the symptoms. Funnily enough, this constant changing of the guard makes the System work better. If they didn't live in this culture of death, they would be easily defeatable: It'd be a monopoly, which makes prices rise, and which creates publicly despised, all-powerful bosses. Instead, the fact that they kill each other and are in competition with one another keeps the prices lower, allows for diversified investments, and keeps the authorities guessing. Like in any form of capitalism, monopolies destroy economies.

Is there a way to change things?
You would need to attack the financial-economic side. You'd need to change capitalism. As long as contracts end up in the hands of those who offer the job in the quickest, cheapest way, they will always win. Because they bend rules. Because they have illegal incomes, which they use to irrigate their other companies, and because they can pressure politicians. Think of the case of the clan of the Casalesi. They opened some illegal dumps outside Aversa, which they filled with garbage and toxic waste. Then, word comes around that the government is building a motorway. They pressure the politicians into building it over their dumps. Then they cover the dumps in cement, they sell the land to the government, and, cherry on top, they land the contract to build the motorway. That's three highly lucrative deals. No straight entrepreneur could do something like that.

You often mention the waste-management business and the Camorra. How does a situation like that of the garbage emergency in Naples come about?
Basically, the region of Campania is filled with dumps which are run by the Camorra, illegally or semi-legally. If you add it up, it has accounted for some $300 billion in the past 20 years. The dumps are full because they contain all the garbage and toxic waste in Italy. Because, as I mentioned before, Camorra-owned businesses can offer the best prices.

Don't they have a problem with polluting the land they live in?
To start with, many bosses were against this idea. But the fact is—because of the constant, ruthless competition—if you don't do it, another clan will. And if they do, they'll make so much money that they'll run you into the ground. Like with drugs. Many families are against them, but you can't run away from business. You'll end up being the weak one, the intellectual one. Real businessmen have no ethics.

What about the famous honor code?
OK, that exists, but it's fake. There are falsely "noble" codes. They say they don't kill children, but they always kill children. They say they don't touch women, but they've always massacred women. They have always dealt in drugs, even if it was initially forbidden. They have always had people among their ranks whose mothers were prostitutes, even if it is theoretically unacceptable. These "codes" only exist as a form of self-regulation. Take drugs, for example. In theory, you aren't allowed to deal drugs in your own territories, because it's bad, but actually it's just because drugs are the quickest wealth accelerator, so if one of your affiliates does well with drugs, within six months he can become your competition. If, instead, he deals in construction or contraband, it takes him six years

to become competition, and you can monitor him. Of course, there are some unbendable rules. In my area, Secondigliano, it's impossible to conceive of a homosexual Camorrista. In Naples it's more accepted. Once word came out that a member of the Casalese clan had been involved with a North African boy in jail. They killed him for that. Strangled him. Their cultural references are very macho. There was a famous boss in the 80s who went all over Italy, looking for his new wife's first boyfriend, so he could hang him. Another story is the one of the 40-year-old who was courting his boss's 18-year-old niece. They took him to the beach, tied him to a chair, and killed him by forcing him to eat sand, so that with every bite of mud, he could think of the mistake he'd made.

These violent crimes all have the fringe benefit of increasing their street cred.
Yes. Call it their PR department. If they want people to know, they act accordingly—like when they decapitated a man by using a metal grinder. It's like their villas: They all live in giant, snazzy homes that they never enjoy. They always have marble columns or piranhas or lions in them. They are just symbols of their power. Think of Walter Schiavone, a Camorrista who had a huge villa built outside Naples that was the exact replica of Tony Montana's home in *Scarface*.

How did you actually write your book?
The book is a hybrid between a novel and a nonfiction investigation. I wanted to follow Capote's footsteps. In reference to *In Cold Blood*, he once said that he wanted to "produce a journalistic novel, something on a large scale that would have the credibility of fact, the immediacy of film, the depth and freedom of prose, and the precision of poetry." Once, I was asked by the police what I thought made the Camorra so angry at me that I would need a 24-hour police escort. I said, "Literature," and they thought I was pulling their leg. But I actually think that's true. I mean, literature made unreadable stories readable. Five hundred pages of pure nonfiction, read by 3,000 people, and reviewed in the back sections of small magazines— they wouldn't have cared about that. But if you make it into a story it becomes interesting to a much larger number of readers.

And this put you in danger.
I think that I'm in danger not because of what I wrote, per se, but because I reached so many readers. The *New York Times* called me "the Italian Rushdie," but I think it's a very different situation. Rushdie was persecuted because he wrote a book, much like the Soviet writers were. The Mafia allows you to write. You can say what you want about them. They just don't want the information to reach a large enough audience that it affects their business. Only stupid dictatorships ban books without understanding that you just give it publicity by doing so. Real democracies censor you by ignoring you.

Was there a particular incident when it dawned on you that you were going from first-time author to living in hiding with a 24-hour police escort?
The book came out in the May of 2006, but until September of 2006 I was fine. I wasn't a challenge for them at the beginning. They see writers as effeminate, useless faggots—and they're often correct. When my book sold 100,000 copies, I started to panic. On the 13th of October 2006, my life changed. I went to a public meeting in Casal di Principe, the hometown of the Casalesi families, and I announced, "Schiavone, Iovine, Zagaria, you are worthless." Those are the names of three major bosses. Silence came over the meeting, and since that moment, I have lived with a constant police escort. Now they give me three policemen and a bulletproof car.

How do you live your life? Do you still get to see your friends, your family?
No, but for different reasons. Where I come from, being my friend is a big problem. This makes human relationships impossible. But there are hundreds of us living like this. I think of those who had it worse than me. Like Federico Del Prete, the trade unionist who was murdered in 2004. Phone interceptions show that he was killed after a poll. They first asked around about how famous he was. "Do the papers talk about him?" they asked. "Only local papers" was the answer. And they executed him.

Would you say your fame protects you?
Yes, but only as long it lasts. A Camorrista-turned-witness famously said, about me, "They're waiting for this to pass." It's always like this. They know that sooner or later, the media storm will pass. Then they'll get me.

Looking back, would you do it again?
The writer in me wants to say yes, a hundred times over. But I would be lying. I wake up almost every morning thinking, "If only I could go back..." There is a part of me, you see, that just wanted to write a book. I didn't want my entire life to be swallowed by that book. But what can you do? It was my choice. The most difficult thing is forgiving myself for the problems I created for my loved ones. You feel really brave, but when you see how your family is forced to live, you feel like a worm. Honestly, I wouldn't recommend doing what I did. But I also want to say that the more people who deal with these problems, the better. If so many Italian writers stopped navel-gazing, maybe we'd all be better off. ∎

SANTIAGO STELLEY

EL NUEVO ALARMA! IS MEXICO'S BEST CRIME TABLOID, AND MIGUEL ANGEL RODRIGUEZ VAZQUEZ IS ITS EDITOR

Alarma! is the oldest of Mexico's *prensa roja* (red press) tabloids. It is mostly made up of gruesome news stories, photos of mutilated corpses, and headlines that contain 1960s-Borscht-Belt-comedian-worthy puns about death and pain. We recently spoke with Miguel Angel Rodriguez Vazquez, the magazine's editor.

Vice: How'd you become director of Alarma!?
Miguel Angel Rodriguez Vazquez: I started in the mailroom back in 1981 and eventually learned to do the layouts. Then I started writing and taking pictures for the magazine and, years after that, I became the assistant to the director. He passed away four years ago, and that's how I became the director.

And what does the job entail?
Basically, I go through all the material that comes to my desk, pick the stories I like, write the headlines, and edit the stories.

Sounds easy enough. Alarma! was the first paper of its kind, right? The first prensa roja tabloid?
Yeah, *Alarma!* was first published in 1963. What happened was a newspaper man by the name of Don Carlos

Amayo Lizarraga had the idea to start a magazine that would deal exclusively with crime.

The magazine really took off in 1964 with the story of Las Poquianchis, who were three women who ran an infamous prostitution ring in Guanajuato. They were accused of committing 28 homicides. All of their victims were young girls that worked for them as prostitutes, and all of their bodies were found buried in Las Poquianchis's backyard.

And *Alarma!* covered the story in full, gory detail, I assume?
The magazine followed the story for over eight months. One of our reporters, Jesus Sanchez Hermosillo, went up to Guanajuato and became good friends with Ms. Delfina and Ms. Maria de Jesus, the two first Poquianchis who were detained. They shared their stories with him, and they talked about how they had been paying off all the local officials like the police and the municipal presidents...

Scoop!
Las Poquianchis became a sort of *foto novela*, or magazine soap opera, for our readers, but it was even better because it was a true story complete with murdered women, buried fetuses, girls forced into prostitution, humans bought and sold...

Miguel Angel Rodriguez Vazquez. Photo by Tomas Morales

We have over 2,000 photographs from just that one story. We published their love letters, their family albums, absolutely everything. The story really grabbed Mexico's attention, and that was when the magazine had its first boom.

I've always been a big fan of the Mexico City earthquake issue.
The Mexico City earthquake in 1985 was also a huge story for us. Our print run in the first week was over 2.5 million. The next week it went down to 2 million, but it was still extraordinary. We covered every possible angle during the earthquake.

What's your favorite story from that issue?
I remember one story about a kid called Monchito. He was a young boy who was supposed to be buried under a house that had fallen in the earthquake. Everyone in Mexico was worried about Monchito and praying for Monchito. They brought in all these experts to figure out how to rescue him. At the end it turned out that Monchito didn't even exist. The owners of the house had made him up because they wanted to rescue a safe box that had been buried with their house.

Soon after the huge boost we received from the earthquake, *Alarma!* was shut down by the government.

Why did that happen?
In 1986 Mexico was hosting the World Cup, and the government decided to close down all the pornographic magazines in the country. *Alarma!* didn't feature any naked girls or anything like that, but according to the government commission, we had committed some technical fouls, things like not printing the appropriate "adult only" warnings on the cover or selling the magazine in plastic bags. We were given a lot of excuses, but the truth was simply that one of our sister publications, a magazine called *Impacto*, was very critical of the government then. So we were punished for political reasons. At the time, other publications—which for the most part considered our magazine to be vulgar and trashy or what have you—came to our defense. Everybody knew what was happening but nobody could stop it. *Alarma!* was shut down for almost five years.

When we finally relaunched in '91 we had to change our name and became *El Nuevo Alarma!*. As soon as we hit the newsstands, we got back all of our readers and put all the other crime magazines that had popped up in the intervening years out of business.

How is the new version different?
The magazine itself hasn't changed much over the years. In essence it's the exact same magazine Don Carlos dreamed of. We've had a lot of internal discussions when people have wanted to change the design, but I've always fought to keep it very simple. People enjoy it the way it is, and it makes it a quick, easy read. We're not a modern, artsy magazine, and that's not what our readers want us to be. We just try to keep it very simple and very visual. If there are no pictures there's no story. Our readers like to see pictures.

Yeah, why is that? What's the fascination with photos of headless corpses and the like?
People are interested in the kind of thing we publish. I don't think it's an illness—I think it's curiosity. People like to see what we're made of inside. We have millions of photographs of cadavers with their intestines hanging out. There's kilos and kilos of intestines stuffed in there. It's really strange, and lots of people love to see that. Plus, if we don't publish enough dead bodies in an issue we get emails telling us that we were too conservative.

That's funny. I'd imagine you got more from people saying you were too sensational.
Oh, that too. A lot of people write us off for being too sensational, but none of the information that we publish is made up. It's all absolutely factual and true. We don't make up facts and we don't retouch photographs. There's no need to.

What kind of story works best for you?
The types of crimes that we're reporting have changed a bit. The stories that work best for us now are narco-traffic crime stories, for example the decapitated bodies they recently found in Acapulco. In Michoacan, five people had their heads blown off while they were dancing in a nightclub. That kind of piece really works for us.

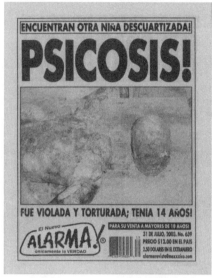

It seems like most of your stories come from the cities.
Actually, most of our stories right now are coming from Michoacan and Guerrero. Last year it was Tamaulipas, and five years ago it was Culiacán. It's really interesting to see how the crime wave moves around the country. For example, I'm surprised that Culiacán isn't more violent. Around 2001 we counted up to 1,000 executions in a couple of months there. It's also interesting to see how the crimes are getting more violent. It used to just be drive-by shootings. Now the victims are always decapitated or buried alive. The crimes are getting more and more depraved.

I wonder why that is.
Because they want to instill more fear in others. "If I kill you more violently, then your people will respect me more," or something like that. Because most of the crimes

are drug related, I think they need to scare each other more and more to secure areas.

My dad was a police officer and said the same thing, that drug crimes are generally more violent than other crimes.
Drug-related crimes are very different from crimes of passion. If you look at older issues of *Alarma!* most of the stories are crimes of passion, with headlines like "He killed her for being a flirt."

That used to be our bread and butter. Now the headlines are really different, but that also has to do with the fact that we have to be more delicate with our choice of words.

How so?
Don Carlos used to pick some great words. For example, to refer to homosexuals, he used to say *los mujercitos* ["little women" in the masculine form] and lesbians were *hombrecitas*—the reverse. We can't use these kinds of words anymore because everyone thinks you're violating their human rights if you do.

Strangely enough, *Alarma!* has never been sued, but for safe measure, we now try to keep our humor a bit less dark. We've basically gone from black to gray.

What stories are you working on right now?
This week we actually had four different crimes of passion in Mexico City. I'm running out of ideas for the headlines.

Ha. Well, tell me one of the headlines.
One of the crimes was a man who killed his wife. They were both schoolteachers and he killed her in front of her students, so I came up with a headline that hopefully isn't too offensive and doesn't make fun of the situation but will still spark people's interest. It reads, "He got an A in homicide."

Gold.
These are the type of ideas that Don Carlos left us with. He used to have a lot of fun doing his job. He was very passionate about it. For example, another crime we had this week that was kind of amusing was a man who shot his wife in the head while she was in the bathroom using the toilet. Don Carlos would've really enjoyed writing that headline. ■

ANDY MOORE

NO WAR FOR HEAVY METAL!

Most people in Baghdad don't leave their houses at night. They don't rent movies. They don't go to bars. Mostly, they sit huddled in dingy shacks and wait and watch and hope that the occupying army will lift its curfew and everything will become safe enough for them to go outside one day. Fat chance.

It'd be nice to nip out without the fear of being blown to bits, but it's just not possible. Thinking of meeting up with chums for a movie and a pizza to briefly lift the ever-present fear of sudden death? Forget it, buddy. Nightlife in Baghdad fucking sucks just as much as it did before Shock and Awe. The only people on the streets after dark are Glock-toting maniacs out to rape, rob, and kill whatever they can. Get that? EVERYBODY on the streets at night, including the old-age pensioners, is packing heat and looking to unload clips into your face. Like, "You got a fresh bottle of water in your pocket, bitch? *Blam! Blam! Blam!*" "How about that dog pissing in the alleyway? *Blam! Blam!* It's suppertime!" They are shooting and killing and eating the dogs made homeless by the bombings.

Photo by Gideon Yago

Because everybody's being woken up at 3:30 AM by the cracking sound of gunfire and sobbing American soldiers attempting to hang themselves from every available broken lamppost, there's an inescapable feeling of terror and doom everywhere. It makes the end battle scene of the last *Lord of the Rings* look like a rehearsal of the original line-up of the Bee Gees.

No wonder then, there's an emerging group of young Iraqis who're expressing their pain, hatred, and sorrow by playing in an underground Baghdad metal scene that nobody thought existed until now.

Bands like A.Crassicauda (scientifico for "black scorpion"), pictured here, are one of a small number of hate-fueled groups influenced by Western devil-worshippers like Slayer, Dimmu Borgir, and Mayhem (three of the most popular groups in the Iraqi metal world).

Before Saddam was toppled courtesy of the Red, White, and Blue, most young people had their music brutally censored by the murderous pedophile Uday Hussein, who banned just about all genres of punk and metal (death, gore, speed, black metal, and power electronics were particularly frowned upon).

The airwaves were filled with traditional Islamic wailing songs as well as Dannii Minogue and Shania Twain. That sort of shit sounds great if you're getting fellated by five teenage girls at your father's palace in a bathtub full of calf's milk, but if you're poor and young and scared of wearing a Metallica shirt for fear of being beaten by the military police, it just sounds scary.

If you want to hear A.Crassicauda or any of their ilk, don't bother going on the internet or pestering the guy at your local record store. You have to slip down Kerada Street in eastern Baghdad at sunset to their shabby practice room that smells like if a kebab shop owner shat in your face.

The double-bass-drumming, cymbal crashes, and *chugga-chugga-chugga-chugga-waaah*ing of four Iraqi kids raised on bootleg cassette tapes and glitchy MP3s of the last 30 years of heavy metal sound so different from the everyday Baghdad musical diet of prayer calls and Arab techno that, mixed together, they're like your worst-ever ketamine overdose at a fetish party you shouldn't have been at anyway.

Made up of four intelligent kids who work as journalists and translators, A.Crassicauda sing about pain, death, and destruction—occasionally getting political, but never enough to have risked intrusion from Ba'athist political police. To define their sound, they plugged traditional Iraqi instruments into distortion pedals and used broken-down TVs as preamps for some songs. You guessed it. It sounds like hell. Just like proper metal should, right?

No one in the band flinched when the first US bomb dropped on Baghdad, but staying alive took precedence over band practice. This meant their plans to get signed to a big Western record label and tour with the Ozzfest (yes, that's their goal) were put on hold for a few days while they figured out whether or not the band had "broken up" due to death or mutilation. It was of great relief to the Baghdad metal scene that everybody in the group was okay, and after a few weeks, A.Crassicauda were back to their old routine of screaming and soloing and wearing tight black jeans and white Reebok basketball shoes with the laces pulled too tight.

"The war made it difficult, but we got back to practicing as soon as we could," says singer Waleed "Blood Master" Rabiaa. "We needed the music, because if we didn't play it we'd all go insane." Drummer Marwan agrees. "We would hear *boom boom* outside, and it just got to be so much that we wanted to make that noise back," he says, thumping the bass drum emphatically.

Waleed smiles. "Now we are," he says.

When I visited A.Crassicauda at practice they were bickering like any other band—huge egos in bloom in a tiny glass-front shop with eggshell foam taped to the walls to (ineffectively) muffle the sound. The air was so thick with dust and smoke that I could hardly breathe. Graffiti was scratched on the walls and a solitary flyer for a prewar metal show was the only evidence in the whole city that a metal scene even existed.

Because the music they played me was so completely fucking bananas and deafeningly loud, it was easy to forget the frightening instability of the broken city outside and briefly imagine that I was in somebody's basement back at home in the States. That feeling didn't last long, though. Once I was back on the streets, I was so scared of everything around me I almost wet my pants.

Daily life in Baghdad is no longer about dodging Saddam's flunkies. At least they kept a kind of jackbooted order. These days it's about dodging myriad unknowns. Failing water, failing power, tangled traffic, huge gas lines, unchecked crime, unemployment, and old grudges have sprung open a trapdoor of terror and chaos and confusion and misery that nobody, least of all the fucking kids in the underground metal scene, knows how to control.

The disgusting, lawless human behavior all around has had the same effect on A.Crassicauda that it did on almost everyone else in Iraq. It sucked out the hope of their hearts and forced them to accept the fact that they could face death at any second.

The result? The band's music became even more hate-filled and intense and fucked than ever before.

Waleed says the moment he lost faith in his country was when he saw a drunk Iraqi mow down his own sister with an assault rifle in broad daylight. No one who watched the scene flinched. "When I saw that happen, I just thought to myself, 'Damn, we're in a jungle.'"

In the last eight months, despite the curfew, the four members of A.Crassicauda have kept on going to practice every night. This is why they are all more "metal" than anyone you will ever know. And not in the "Blackie Lawless is the World's Fifth Biggest Badass" VH-1 documentary way, you idiot. In a real, sustained, HOLLEEE SHIITTT METAL way. The music they played me was so ugly and doomed it made all those face-painted Norwegian black-metal fags who burn down old ladies' churches seem scary as warm chocolate milk.

While most Western metal bands lose sleep over hair loss, shelling out for new speaker cones, and wondering how to pay for Viagra, these kids have had to make real sacrifices for their band—like going to practice with a handgun stuffed down the front of their pants. This isn't just because good amps and equipment are a choice find for Baghdadi looters, it's because Marwan's job as a US Army translator has put him on a Fedayeen "guys we're gonna kill" list.

Now he totes a 9mm Tareq with him everywhere he goes. When I tell him that the only other guy I know who does that is the Nuge and ask if he thinks practicing in a blind alley is really a good idea, he doesn't seem to care. "When they start booking bands again we really want to put on a show and we can't suck, so we have to be ready," he tells me.

"I'm not really worried about anyone trying to kill us while we're at practice," Waleed adds, in between drags off foul-smelling, beetle-dung Iraqi cigarettes. "What better way to go out than playing fucking music, man?"

Presently, A.Crassicauda are pooling their money to record demos and figuring out a plan to escape Baghdad and tour the world. Order has to come back to Iraq first, though. Then, and only then, can they start courting A&R guys.

"Metal is worldwide, man," Waleed says with a wicked smile on his face. "Just look at these guys." He's waving a Dimmu Borgir CD in my face. "I'd really love to tour and play our music for audiences and see how they'd react. What do you think our chances are?"

I smile and give him the same bullshit answer that I've learned to give any talented young band starting out—some tongue-twister pabulum about the need to work hard and keep trying. I don't want to let even an ounce of doubt come out of my mouth. But Waleed doesn't care. He's got to get back to practice and he doesn't want to head home too late after dark tonight. ∎

SHANE SMITH

INSIDE SUDAN

These are kids at a madrasah outside Khartoum. Their parents were murdered in Darfur and they are now refugees in their own country. A sheik took them in and feeds them and clothes them, and in return they have to read the Koran. They sit there all day and all night memorizing prayers from these little tablets. Once they master one passage, they wipe down the tablets with water and write another on there to memorize. They're all just sitting in the sand, rocking back and forth and chanting. They have nothing else.

Photos by Jamie-James Medina

Before I went to Sudan, I didn't know much about the conflict in Darfur beyond everyone saying, "It's the worst genocide of our time," and watching footage on CNN of the Janjaweed militia wiping out whole villages. Really, we only decided to go there because one of our photographers in the UK, Jamie-James Medina, had been chatting with an old friend of his who is now a UN press officer in Khartoum. She offered to pull some strings and get us visas and organize flights around the country, so we said, "Fuck it," and got on a plane.

On the flight over I went through this huge binder of re-search about the situation. It really messed me up. The scale of the devastation was difficult to comprehend: 400,000 people killed and over 2 million displaced in less than four years. This comes right on the heels of another civil war in the south of Sudan that killed more than 2 million people and displaced a further 5 million over the course of the conflict. As the plane landed in Khartoum I had the biggest "Ummmm, what the fuck am I doing here?" moment of my life. From the minute we got off the plane to the minute we flew out again, I was shit-scared. And as it turned out I was totally right to be. ■

This is one of the "Lost Boys" who live in the marketplace. Sometimes they come to the shelter to get a meal, but mostly they just survive off garbage and whatever else they can steal. This kid was totally wasted on glue. He told me that he hadn't been huffing, but when he coughed it smelled like a model airplane was about to fly out of his mouth. He reeked of it. They're all addicted to huffing. It's really sad. They were playing soccer, high as kites.

This kid was using a stick with a string and some popcorn tied to it to fish in a creek near the village. He was standing on a sewage pipe. When we asked him why he'd picked that spot, he said it was because the fish come there to eat the shit. As we were talking to him we saw people with donkey carts filling oil drums with the untreated sewage-water to sell as drinking water in the village.

This is Rasheed in front of his house, which he built out of mud, manure, and straw. He's from Darfur. He was trying to escape with his two-month-old brother when the Janjaweed ripped the baby off his back and threw him into a fire. He showed us around and was very nice to us. When we left him we found out that the secret police had been following us the whole time. We were really worried that we might have gotten him in trouble.

We spotted this graffiti on the way out of Khartoum. It was odd because Sudan is so alien and anti-American that you never really see anything familiar. I thought, "I wonder if 50 Cent or Green Day or whoever know that when they record music it will affect people all the way out here in the middle of Africa."

LUCA GABINO

CTRL+ALT+LANDFILL

China's Secret Computer Graveyard

Photo by Luca Gabino

For years, I've heard fables and legends about a mysterious cemetery somewhere in China. I heard whispers on the internet and from Chinese friends about mountains of broken computers, heaps of chips, motherboards, and printer cartridges virtually filling the streets of a South Asian village. But it was kept quiet by the notoriously tight-lipped Chinese government. It was kind of like the elusive elephant graveyard, but with technological offal and guarded by mean communists. I decided that I would make it my mission to go there.

I slowly discovered that 80 percent of all the electronic toxic waste collected around the world ends up in Guiyu, a small town in the southern China province of Guangdong. The town imports more than 1 million tons of this stuff every year. Almost 90 percent of Hong Kong's computers end up there, but 60 percent of the total waste originates in the USA. The exact location of Guiyu has been kept secret by the authorities, but I already knew that Shenzhen was the biggest city in Guangdong and that it was just an hour and a half away from Hong Kong.

Even with Hong Kong being Chinese again, we had to go through customs to get into Shenzhen. We boarded the bus to Cheng Dian, guessing it was the nearest city to Guiyu. On the bus the situation got even creepier when the hostess pulled out a video camera and started filming each passenger for "security reasons." I was the only Westerner on board. During the three-hour bus ride the same advert looped on the in-bus televisions. It showed Shenzhen as a city of fun, happiness, and luxury. Looking out the window at the gray factories, the sea of cement, and the columns of smoke I had to ask myself if any of the other passengers were falling for it. Toward the end of the journey I found a university student who spoke a little English. Taking a chance, I asked her where Guiyu was. She acted quite perplexed at first and replied that no such place existed. But I could tell she knew something, so I begged her until she scribbled directions on a piece of paper.

We arrived in Cheng Dian at night and I took a room in a cheap hotel. I spent the next day trying to find someone who would tell me more about Guiyu. The locals denied its existence. Fortunately I found a taxi driver who was willing to take me there for the relative mountain of cash that is $60. I handed him the directions that the girl on the train had written for me, and we set off in almost total darkness. The driver eventually dropped me off at the only hotel in the proximity of Guiyu. From the car, all I could see was a big white block of cement surrounded by garbage. I stepped out into the most surreal landscape I have ever seen.

It was a sea of garbage. The heaps of trash began accumulating next to the hotel walls and did not stop for as far as the eye could see. The whole town was a construction site, with the old wooden barracks being replaced by unfinished houses. You can still spot Guiyu's rural past in the barracks that once clearly constituted most of the town, but the e-waste economy required more accommodation for the 200,000 migrant workers who moved to Guiyu in the past six years. Everywhere around me people were busy carrying or unloading computer parts. Huge piles of outer shells lay next to construction sites, layers and layers of motherboards and CD players were dumped in the courtyards, and thousands of bags of chips spilled inside and outside, forming massive mountains between the tiny dwellings. Children were dividing tiny chips by color in the street. Adults were grilling circuit boards on barbecue grills. They melted the soldering and removed the chips, and then the women would separate the parts in different bags and wash them with water. After the circuit boards were soaked in acid to reclaim bits of gold, they were finally either burned or buried.

I witnessed kids between the ages of five and ten working in barracks with no ventilation, with people all around them burning everything from the metal components of computers to wires to extract the copper. When the PVC and the brominated flame retardant around the wires burn, they emit high levels of chlorinated dioxins and furans, two of the most persistent organic pollutants. As a result, the local river is so contaminated that the levels of acidity are almost total. The water contains an estimated 2,400 times the recommended levels of lead, and it's not hard to notice: The river is literally black from the toner of printer cartridges and from washing the burned motherboards. The toner contains carbon black, a known carcinogen, but the locals wash themselves, their clothes, and their food with this water. It's so toxic that even boiling it doesn't come close to purifying it. Above the water, the air was thick with smoke. Around it, the land is so irreparably poisoned that nothing can grow. All the food and drinking water is imported from out of town.

On my third day in Guiyu, I managed to get to the main dump. The mountains of computer parts I had seen so far were nothing compared with what awaited. The roads were in a constant state of traffic jam with trucks, motorbikes, and even mules carrying parts to be "recycled." It was hell. Thick smoke hung like storm clouds. It hurt to breathe.

As I stopped to take pictures, a furious woman came out of nowhere, charging me with her broom, trying to grab my camera. Not wanting to cause trouble in an illegal toxic-waste dump in southern China, I ran back to the car. She followed, waving her broom around like a baseball bat, banging on the windows. She broke the windshield. She was blind with rage, trying to break the remaining bits of glass off with her bare hands. When she saw she couldn't do it she stuck her broom through the hole she'd made and started smacking me in the head.

Then the police showed up to—I naively thought— rescue me from the crazy woman. I was very wrong. They ordered me to wait in the car while they interrogated all the witnesses except for the woman, whom they let calmly walk back to her barrack. People crowded around the car and stared at me as if I were an exotic animal in a cage. After an hour the police told my driver to follow them to the station, where I was interrogated for an hour with the aid of a translator. I told them I was a university student on vacation. I had previously hidden the better rolls of film, so I could hand them the ones that were no good to me. They let me go back to my hotel, chauffered by the poor driver whose car had been beaten up by the crazy old woman.

A few days later there was a knock at my hotel door. It was the cops again. They took me back to the station, where I was questioned by six cops. I thought they were going to beat the shit out of me. After an hour of repeating myself, I convinced them that I was merely a student on holiday. They believed me! That is, until they got the owner of the hotel to show them the ID card I'd used to sign in. Under job description, it said "photographer." Whoops. The interrogation started again. I played it dumb, hung my head, and told them I was just a silly student who takes amateur pictures and has no idea what is going on in their town. Three hours later they finally released me and I hightailed it right the fuck out of Guiyu. I will never go back. ■

THOMAS MORTON

OH, THIS IS GREAT

Humans Have Finally Ruined the Ocean

Photos by Jake Burghart

I'm not one of those guys who corners folks at parties to rant at them about biodiesel or calls people "fucking idiots" for being skeptical about global warming. But I should also point out that I'm not one of those Andrew Dice Clay "Fuck the whales" types either.

The problem with all the bravado on both sides of the ecology debate is that nobody really knows what they're talking about. Trying to form opinions on climate change, overpopulation, and peak oil hinges on ginormous leaps of faith based around tiny statistical deviances that even the scientists studying them have a hard time understanding. It gets so convoluted with all the yelling and the politics that sometimes you just want something huge and incontrovertibly awful to come along for everybody to agree on. Something you can show anyone a picture of and go, "See? We're fucked."

Well, I have just such a thing. There is a Texas-size section of the Pacific Ocean that is irretrievably clogged with garbage and it will never go away. And I have seen it with my own eyes. Case closed. Oh, you want to hear more? OK, fine.

In the middle of the 90s, Charles Moore was sailing his racing catamaran back to California from Hawaii and decided on a lark to cut through the center of the North Pacific Gyre. The Gyre is an enormous vortex of currents revolving around a continuous high-pressure zone—if you think of the rest of the Pacific as a gigantic toilet, this zone would be the part where your poop bobs and twirls before being sucked down. Boats typically avoid it since it's essentially one big windless death trap, so when Moore motored through it was just him, his crew, and an endless field of garbage.

As long as it's existed, the middle of the Gyre has been a naturally occurring point of accumulation for all the drifting crap in its half of the ocean. Once upon a time, flotsam circled into the middle of the Gyre and (because up until the past century everything in the world was biodegradable) was broken down into a nutrient-rich stew perfect for fish and smaller invertebrates to chow on. Then we started making everything out of plastic and the whole place went to shit.

The problem with plastic is, unless you hammer it with enough pressure to make a diamond, it never fully disintegrates. Over time plastic will *photodegrade* all the way down to the individual polymers, but those little guys are still in it for the long haul. This means that except for the slim handful of plastics designed specifically to biodegrade, every synthetic molecule ever made still exists. And except for the small percentage that gets caught in a net or washes up on a shore, every chunk of plastic that's dropped into the Pacific makes its way to the center of the Gyre and is floating there right now.

After watching junk lap against the side of his boat for the better part of a week, Captain Moore decided to convert his boat into a research vessel and make semiannual trips into the Gyre to study the trash. I tagged along on his most recent voyage, joining a divorced, 40-something doctor and a Mexican chemist and mother of two as his crew. It was like a family vacation, but with more science and way more bummers.

The garbage patch is located at one of the most remote points on earth. It takes a solid week of sailing just to get there. Considering how torturous the average daylong car trip gets, you can well imagine the kind of zap job that seven days on a 50-foot boat will do to your brain. You lose sight of land the first day, then you stop seeing other ships, then you stop seeing anything at all except for endless waves and occasionally a seabird, which, after days of nothing but water, becomes as exciting as spotting a UFO. Right at the point where you've come up with a separate song for every bird in the ship's guidebook and have begun integrating them into a full seabird opera, you start seeing the trash.

I had assumed (completely without any basis in research or common sense) that there was some contiguous mass of concentrated garbage the captain was steering us toward, but (sadly?) this was not the case. The debris patterns shift with the currents, so you just have to aim the boat in one direction and hope for crap. Every so often we'd spot a few different pieces of garbage floating sort of near one another, but for the most part it was just a steady stream of junk, passing one piece at a time. It was a little underwhelming at first, but keep in mind we were cutting a razor-thin course through one of the biggest expanses of open water on the planet. The fact that we couldn't look out the window for the better part of the trip without seeing some piece of junk bobbing by holds some seriously ugly implications for the rest of the ocean.

The first few times we spotted garbage, we made a big production of stopping the boat and going out to scoop it up. Then we began just picking up whatever trash we could snag from the front of the deck. Then we just grabbed whatever looked interesting.

Some of the flotsam is fun stuff that fell off the side of container ships, like entire crates of hockey masks and Nikes. You might have read about the shipment of rubber duckies that got lost in a storm back in 1992 and have been used by oceanographers to more accurately plot the movement of water currents. I guess that's something of a silver lining to the situation, although it's a lot like thanking AIDS and cholera for all the advances they've provided to epidemiologists.

Before we became equal parts bored and depressed with hauling garbage out of the sea all day, we managed to score a motorcycle wheel, a hard hat, and some children's life preservers with shark bites in them. We also narrowly missed running into what was either a ship's mast or a telephone pole. The majority of our haul, though, was just average crap like Coke bottles and grocery bags. A lot of it seemed to come from Asia, meaning it had to have traveled at least 5,000 miles just for us to find it. The scary, staggering thing to consider while holding this stuff is that only a fifth of it is tossed from boats. Most of it is land-born trash that somehow ended up in a waterway and worked a slow path out to sea. As the captain said a good ten or so times, "The ocean is downstream of everything."

Once we were firmly inside the patch, Captain Moore rigged up a trawl and started taking water samples in little petri dishes. I figured these would be snoozers without a microscope, but when the first one came in it was more horrifying than anything we'd seen floating past.

There were a few water striders and tiny jellyfish here and there, but they were totally overwhelmed by a thick confetti of plastic particles. It looked like a snow globe made of garbage. Based on previous samples, Moore estimated the ratio of plastic to the regular components of seawater in what we were pulling up as 6 to 1. As we moved closer to the middle of the Gyre, the ratio got visibly higher, until we started pulling in samples that looked like they contained solely plastic.

This is the part of the trip that weighs heaviest on my mind. It's terrible enough to litter sections of the planet with things that can conceivably be removed—I mean, even oil spills and radioactive dust can be cleaned up to a certain extent. But to fundamentally alter the composition of seawater at one of the farthest points from civilization on the globe is a whole different ballpark of fucking the planet. It's fucking it right up the ass, for good and forever. Without lube.

But wait, here comes the scariest part.

Once the plastic confetti gets small enough to fit inside a jellyfish's mouth, it gets sucked in and starts its way up the food chain back to us. As the jellies float out of the debris field, little fish eat them, absorbing all the built-up plastics. Then big fish eat a bunch of little fish, even bigger fish eat a bunch of big fish, and by the time you get to the point where we're hoisting creatures out and eating them, you're looking at entire milk crates' worth of particles built up in their fat. It's the cycle of life reimagined as a dystopian sci-fi cliché. We are eating our own refuse.

Aside from clogging up the digestive tract (biologists in the Pacific have found the bodies of birds who starved to death because their stomachs were completely packed with trash), degraded plastics also have the tendency to sop up foreign chemicals that have leached into the water. There's a whole class of pesticides and solvents called persistent organic pollutants that are basically tailor-made to attach themselves to loose synthetics and wreak havoc on whatever living thing happens to swallow them. The chemist on our boat was studying a pair of the most prevalent of these pollutants in the Pacific water, DDE and DDT. Yep, the same DDT that kills baby eagles. It's also a probable carcinogen with links to diminished sperm counts and developmental retardation. The ocean is brimming with this shit.

What's worse than this is even when the plastic is free from outside toxins, its components can potentially wreck your body. Bisphenol A is a compound used in things like Nalgene bottles and dildos. It's also a synthetic estrogen and can completely derail the reproductive system. Dr. Frederic vom Saal of the University of Missouri has been studying the effects of bisphenol A on lab mice for the past decade and has noticed ties to its exposure with an absurd suite of health problems including low sperm count, prostate cancer, hyperactivity, early-onset diabetes, breast cancer, undescended testicles, and sex reversal. Does the fact that humans can suffer SEX REVERSAL symptoms from inadvertently eating a compound that is used to make dildos qualify as irony?

Vom Saal's research is at the center of a messy dispute because it involves exposure in such infinitesimal quantities and nobody is exactly sure how the endocrine system works. There's also a tricky "magic bullet" sort of quality to his findings, but after talking with him it seemed like even he was a little taken aback that this one chemical could be at the root of almost every major US health crisis of the past 30 years. And even if he's only right on *one* of the above counts, yeesh.

Still worse than any of this is the possibility that the same chemicals can simultaneously trigger massive disruptions in DNA. "All it takes is one misaligned chromosome and you've got things like Down syndrome," vom Saal says. "If you examine the genetic material in animals exposed to low doses of bisphenol A, it looks like someone fired a shotgun into the chromosomes."

On the outer edge of the Gyre, we ran smack into the white whale of the maritime trash world: a ghost net. Ghost nets are loose tangles of fishing line and nets that float freely across the ocean, snagging anything in their path. They are the langoliers of the sea. Ghost nets have been found that are miles long with oars and sharks' skulls and full turtle skeletons peeking out of their knots. The one we caught wasn't anywhere near that big, but it was easily twice my size, weighed 200 pounds, and housed both a toothbrush and its own school of tropical fish.

There was no way we could tow the massive clump of nets to shore, so we hoisted it onto the back of the ship, attached a GPS tag so that oceanographers could track its movement, and lowered it back into the water. Our camera guy Jake jumped in after it to film it drifting away in a cloud of slaked-off string and plastic. When he hopped back on board it looked like somebody had smeared body glitter across his chest. It was tiny chunks of plastic. ∎

X

IT HAPPENED
TO ME

Photo by Dana Goldstein, V15N7, July 2008

V10N8, AUGUST 2003

SARAH SILVERMAN

LIFE WARRIOR

Surviving the Pain, the Fear, and the Hurt

Photo by Danielle Levitt

Everyone is looking for someone to blame. Not me. I've had plenty of fucked-up shit happen in my life and I'm not looking for anyone to account for it. I have no hunger for vindication, no thirst for explanation. When the great orangutan of life reaches back and flings a handful of poo at me, I stand tall. Splattered but not shaken (which is also how I take my drinks).

You think you've felt pain? You think you've triumphed over misfortune? Check out the shit I've been through. Maybe you'll think twice before you go crying to your shrink.

When I was six years old, my parents divorced. It didn't scar me. As a matter of fact, I count the day they broke the news among the happiest of my life. These two people—this lone example of partnership and union in the form of arrant hatred—were going to part ways. I literally danced for joy. I remember hearing, "Oh, she's too young, she doesn't understand." I did.

I had my very own babysitter while my parents worked. Her name was Mary and I called her "My Mary." I don't remember much except she was old and had a flat white bun on the top of her head. Now, here's the thing. My Mary never let me go to the bathroom alone. She always squeezed in behind me. And she would only let me use one square of toilet paper. Nothing beyond that initial perforation. Exactly one square. "Because of the toilet paper shortage."

I never questioned it. I was five. It wasn't until recently, while reiterating the story to a friend, that it occurred to me that no such shortage existed. Ew.

Now, I could very well have decided right then to be emotionally scarred from that. I didn't. Because I wasn't.

About seven years later, at thirteen, I got a little depressed (by that I mean "so paralyzed with despair I was unable to move"), mostly about the concept of mortality, the *what's the point of it all*-ness, and this feeling I could only define as homesickness, even though I was home. My parents sent me to a shrink. I told him I was sad. He really seemed to understand. He had braces on his teeth.

He gave me a bottle of pills with the instruction to take one any time I felt this way. I read the label. Xanax. I was intrigued by its futuristic name. I was eased by its video-game resonance.

The following week my mother dropped me off, and I sat alone in the waiting room a long time. I waited and waited until, at long last, the hypnotist from upstairs (who, two years earlier, had made no less than fifty unsuccessful attempts to stop me from wetting the bed) came down. His eyes were red and full. We stared at each other for what felt like a solid minute. And then he burst.

"DR. BINGHAM KILLED HIMSELF!" the mental health professional blurted at the thirteen-year-old mental patient. I didn't know what to say. I felt numb (but that was

the Xanax not talking.) Only one thought swam through my head: "He didn't even wait to get the braces off."

Grounds for permanent damage? Not for Number One. It's not that I didn't care. I just didn't blame myself.

At eighteen, I got my first waitressing job at the Margaritaville Lounge in Bedford, New Hampshire. I bounced around, cleaning the popcorn machine and serving burritos and drinks. The owners were two red-faced Boston-Irish guys, Tommy and Johnny. At the time, I looked up to them. I had no idea they were cokehead freaks or what coke even was, really. One night Tommy called me into his office. I was shaking from nerves, trying to figure out what I had done wrong. I walked in and was put at ease by his big broad smile.

"How you likin' workin' heeah?"

"It's real great. Thanks."

"Everyone treatin' yah gud?"

"Yeah…"

I couldn't figure out the reason for his sudden need to have small talk with me. We chatted for several minutes before I noticed it—a bright pink penis to match his bulbous, hot pink face. My boss—the man who taught me to work the margarita machine—had been jerking off the whole time. I just about died. I told him I had to clean the popcorn machine and scurried out.

Horrified? Yes. Repulsed? Absolutely. Traumatized? Not even slightly.

At the end of that summer, I moved to New York City and got a job handing out flyers for a comedy club. Late one Saturday night I tried to stop a drunk teenager from punching a Chinese guy who was dressed as a chicken. The teenager punched me instead, square in the temple. As I lost consciousness, I knew my hard outer shell was getting harder, but with no impact whatsoever on my still-chewy center.

I guess I may have suffered a bruise or two. Did I mention I was a chronic bed wetter? My dad, being a former bed wetter himself, projected the pain and humiliation he remembered onto me. And, although his projection was pretty accurate, his empathy made for some desperate measures. He had me sleep on this electric sheet: a medieval sheet of soft metal that, upon getting wet, would set off a horrifyingly loud alarm. It didn't cure me of bed-wetting; however it did cure me of that nasty *sleeping at night* habit.

By the time I was fifteen, I stopped wetting the bed for good, not including the three times it happened the month I got fired from *Saturday Night Live*. I was 23, and I wish I could tell you I was sleeping alone. I wish I could tell you it was with the same guy each time.

All right. I'm scarred. But it's the baggage we carry and the crap that chips away at us that gives us our shape. So I'm scarred from stuff—the stuffs of life. So what? What is a scar, anyway, but a beautiful tattoo. ■

KELSY RAE RUNNING WOLF

GRIZZLY GIRL
I Got Mauled

*Left: "The puncture wounds were really clean. The ones on my chest didn't really start bleeding until I began moving around.
My arm started to swell up to the size of my hand. It looked like I didn't have a wrist! Thank goodness we had a first-aid kit."
Right: Kelsy today. She's just fine. Photo by Patrick O'Dell*

On September 27th two years ago, my coworker Catherine and I went on a hike to celebrate the end of our summer work season. I have a bad knee from snowboarding and she had previously sprained her ankle, so we decided to take an easy route to Row Lakes in Glacier National Park. Some of our friends were going to meet us out there after they took a tougher course.

It was a nice day. It had just snowed so there was a little bit of white on the ground, but it was sunny and pretty warm. It's about a 17-mile hike that we were going to do. We got to the top of the Piegan Pass, which is smack-dab in the middle, and two friends who had come along with us decided they wanted to head back and do some canoeing. Catherine and I chose to go on. A mile or so down,

we started going off-trail. We were following a path that Catherine knew from before. It was the migration trail of some elk or something. We kind of went up and over toward the mountains. Catherine pretty much knew where we were going so I just followed her.

We passed a creek and then a little ways from that we entered really thick bushes. It was thick enough that you had to really push through. At one point we even needed to crawl. We realized we had lost the trail, so we separated to look for it, going in different directions and circling upward, calling back and forth to each other so we wouldn't lose the other. We were being plenty loud. Then we came back together because we couldn't find the trail anywhere.

We were standing there discussing what to do when we

first heard the bear woofing and huffing and snapping its jaws. The growling started, and it was so loud the vibration shook my body. We looked at each other and realized that neither one of us had any place to go or anything to get under. I had gone hunting a lot with my dad and brother when I was little and they always told me to try and get under something if there was a grizzly coming.

Then the bear started charging at us. All I knew was that I didn't want to actually see the bear coming for me, so I turned my back on the sound of it crashing through the bushes. I didn't see what happened to Catherine, but it seems she was pushed from behind, up into the trees, and then down on her bad ankle, spraining it again. The bear sort of shoved her out of the way to come for me. They do that because they figure the one in front is the strongest, so they get her out of the way and go for the weakest—the one at the back.

The first thing I felt was teeth biting into my shoulder, and then I was down on the ground on my stomach with the bear on top of me. It was standing on me with a paw on each of my arms. It was the weirdest sensation to have teeth piercing me. I wasn't even scared of dying; it was just strange and I knew I didn't want to see it happen. After the third bite, I started to focus on my breathing. I tried to slow it down as much as I could so that I would seem dead. Grizzlies like to eat rotting meat. They kill their prey, make sure it's dead, and then come back to eat it a little later.

Once I did that, the bear stopped and then took one more small nip at me. I was able to look up at it then, and I saw its nose and its mouth right above me. I could somehow tell that it wasn't going to keep biting.

Catherine, when she landed, had been able to knock the safety off on her can of bear spray. I looked over at her and saw a red cloud of mist coming toward the bear and me. It hit us and the bear took off right away.

I couldn't breathe or see either. I was coughing like crazy. Catherine was trying to figure out if I was OK. Since I had my backpack on, she couldn't tell how bad or just where my wounds were—just that there was blood. There were scratches on my arms from his claws too.

I just wanted to get out of the trees. Being surrounded by them was starting to be not the best feeling. We made our way back to the creek. I kept asking Catherine, "Are you sure the bear's not coming? They can smell blood up to ten miles." Catherine kept looking behind us and reassuring me. At the creek, she took off my backpack to check out the bite wounds. We put Ace bandages on them. Then we tried to wash the bear spray out of my eyes. Using my cell phone and a radio, we tried to contact help. Neither worked.

So we decided to hike on to where we'd been heading. It was quicker than going back the way we'd come. We hiked about seven miles. It was a zigzaggy trail with lots of switchbacks. When we got to the bottom there was a really nice waterfall I'd never seen before, so we stopped there to take a picture.

Still, I wanted to get somewhere to get all this bear spray off me, so I wanted to go fast. Catherine had a sprained ankle, so she wanted to go slow. It was a matter of compromise.

We got to a ranger station and we totally filled the room with bear spray, so I volunteered to wait outside. They called an ambulance.

The attack happened around one or two in the afternoon and we finally got to the hospital around 9:30 at night.

They had no set procedure for bear attacks there. They even had to call poison control to get the antidote for bear spray. The worst part of the pain at that point was definitely the bear spray. They tried bathing me with Dawn. Bear spray is cayenne pepper with an oil base, so it seeps into your pores. The Dawn is supposed to cut the oil. So smearing Dawn on my body felt good, but as soon as they rinsed it off it hurt twice as bad as before. Poison control said to try milk. That ended up being the best. Bathing in milk really soothed it.

At that point I was living in the town of St. Mary's, which is total bear country. I had some trouble going home that night. Eventually I fell asleep. I couldn't lie on my back or my side, so I had to prop myself up with pillows. When I woke up the next morning, it hurt a lot more than it had before. Bruising had set in and it was really bad.

We went back to the hospital, and my family doctor was there by then. He said, "They never should have sent you home last night." Then they readmitted me and started surgically cleaning the puncture wounds twice a day, keeping them stuffed with gauze between cleanings. It was hard to do because the holes were deeper than your finger, so they had to kind of jam the swab down the hole and pull it out again.

The nurses would always come in and ask me if I wanted more morphine. They would say, "What's the pain like on a scale of 1 to 10?" I'd just be like, "It's a fucking 15! Are you kidding me?"

I'm Blackfeet, and a lot of us believe that no Indian has ever been attacked by a bear. That is total bullshit. So there was a lot of negativity directed toward me from people in the hospital and from Blackfeet reporters. People were saying things like, "No real Indians hike in the park, so since she was hiking the bear didn't know she was Blackfeet. That's why he attacked her." Then they said that once it bit into me and realized I was Blackfeet it just decided to stop. Such a ridiculous thing to say. Because I'm Blackfeet I'm not supposed to hike in the park? This is our land. Where am I supposed to hike? ∎

DAVID CHOE

————

RIOT TOWN

On April 29th, 1992, one week after my 16th birthday, a white-trash trucker named Reginald Denny was pulled out of his truck at the corner of Florence and Normandie in Los Angeles and beaten to a bloody pulp by a mob of angry black people. Summer and Christmas came early that year.

Me and my brothers are Koreans, born and raised in L.A. We grew up in Koreatown, but ended up going to high school in Beverly Hills. In my art class Frank Sinatra's granddaughter sat to my right and Sammy Davis Jr.'s adopted son sat to my left. In front of me sat Ariel Pink, to whom I was very mean because I thought he was a fag. Mort Saul's son was in my science class and he would drive KIT from *Knight Rider* or the DeLorean from *Back to the Future* to school. I hated everyone, and was filled with an intense rage and anger, mostly directed toward Persians and privileged white kids who didn't understand humility. My only outlets were playing the bass drum in the marching band and graffiti. But then in Ms. Goler's English class I discovered creative writing, and wrote and prophesized about a day when the minorities and the have-nots would rise up and take over. My older brother Jimmy had started to get into stealing cars, while I focused on shoplifting at all the local malls. The idea of anarchy ruled me, and of course its sign was etched into my notebooks and fake leather jacket. Two weeks later it all came true.

The rioting had escalated overnight and school was canceled midday. There was pure chaos and pandemonium in the air. All the rich kids were scrambling to their secure houses in the hills or catching flights out to Palm Springs, and I felt like I had finally come home, at peace in the heart of a storm. The air just smelled different.

So my brother pulls up onto the school lawn in a delivery van that he stole with our mother's sewing scissors. He's inside with his friend Fred (another Korean kid) and yells, "GET IN!" I jump in with my best friend Eddie (also Korean). Olympic Boulevard was just a huge parking lot. No one was moving, but we didn't give a fuck. None of us really knew how to drive, so we hit all the cars, drove on the sidewalk, over newspaper dispensers and parking meters. There was a sunroof and we had loaded the van with huge rocks and we were screaming like maniacs and chucking

them at rich white people in their fancy cars, breaking their windshields. Everyone was scared to even look at us—we were so bloodthirsty we would have killed them.

As we crossed Western into South Central, the scene changed. Blacks were putting up signs that said "black owned" so that people wouldn't loot their shops. People were running in the streets and we were getting crazy looks. We pulled over into a mini-mart area and started throwing rocks into a store; then these black dudes came out of nowhere and it got scary. But then they started to join us, and it was over for the race war. Now it was just about getting ours. The shop window was broken, but the gate wouldn't come down. A gangbanger pulled out a gun and started shooting at the lock, and then a fleet of police cars came speeding toward us and everyone scrambled. But they just drove by. That was it. We were in anarchy. There was no more law. I could practically hear the Cannibal Corpse songs in my head. We kicked the gate down and raped, ravaged, and pillaged the karaoke shop in seconds.

We saw Eazy-E drive by in a convertible wearing black gloves and shooting a pump shotgun into the sky. I was screaming with joy. We drove past a Gap and I saw Shawn Pringle, a black kid I grew up with, with all his black friends. I screamed his name, but he pretended like he didn't know who I was. That hurt. Everyone was grabbing shit and looting and pushing and punching. We got in our van and crashed into everything on the way to East L.A. In the black neighborhoods, on every other block a store was on fire. In the Mexican neighborhoods every fucking store was on fire. You could feel the heat through the windows. Moms were looting with their babies, stealing diapers and beer and dry cleaning.

Everywhere that we'd grown up was on fire. Koreans were on rooftops with automatic weapons protecting their businesses. We were the only Koreans who looted during the riots. That's why I still get called a nigger by my own people. There was definitely a sense of us vs. them and I wasn't gonna run and hide behind closed doors. I came to play and I wanted to fight, but whatever racial inequalities started this war were long gone. At this stage in the game it was all about stealing. When the walls went down, no one gave a fuck what race you were, everyone just had jumbo-screen TVs in their eyes.

As we turned the corner onto Vermont, we drove past a Von's Market where the sky opened up and Huey choppers were circling. Soldiers were rappelling down and lining up in the parking lot. We slammed on the brakes and made a U-turn. Game over. We drove back home through Hancock Park over everyone's lawns.

When we got back to Beverly Hills it was a ghost town, no one on the street, not a sound. There was a line of Beverly Hills cops protecting the city border. We parked a few blocks away and set the van on fire. It didn't explode like in the movies. We stashed our loot in the bushes and walked back home.

A week later I wrote this same story for my English class and it was dismissed as fiction by Ms. Goler, but everyone kissed my ass and wanted to be my best friend. I used it as an opportunity to lose my virginity and get invited to rich kids' houses, where I raided their refrigerators and shit in the top part of their toilets.

The day after the riots we found out our parents' business had burned down. We spent the next few years on welfare. ∎

V12N11, NOVEMBER 2005

DAVID CHOE

BAD KIDS

David Choe's JD Tools

These first two items pretty much saved my life for a few years back in the day. One's a broken heavy-duty magnet and the other is a dollar bill with some tape on the very tip to stretch it out an extra foot. If you can't figure it out by now, you probably aren't criminally inclined.

The altered dollar doesn't really work on the new fandangled vending machines, but on the old ones you can get as much candy, sodas, or chips as you want—and up to $50 in change a pop.

As soon as the machine reads the dollar you rip it out. It took me a few sacrificed dollars to get it just right, but this dollar right here is the one. I squeezed over a grand out of this buck.

As for the magnet, go to basically any store that has a metal detector, rub the magnet over a product a few times, and it demagnetizes the security device. I won't tell you how much I got away with using this doohickey, but it's more than what some people make in a year.

Sometimes I just got lazy and hid stuff in a huge hat

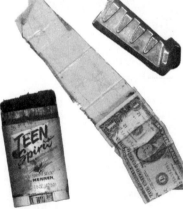

on top of my head so that I was taller than the security system, then just walked out. I don't use these tactics anymore because I'm a good person and I want to build up my credit.

Then we have my homemade marker. I don't know if they make this flavor of deodorant anymore, but back in the early 90s, Teen Spirit was very popular. This particular style was called Totally Fresh, and it really was.

I'm Asian, so I don't really smell and didn't need deodorant until after I got fat, so I took the deodorant part out, cut a chalkboard eraser in half, used candle wax to seal the bottom of the Teen Spirit, filled it halfway with permanent black ink, and then jammed the eraser on top. It's the fattest homemade marker around. I wrote so much stupid shit on walls with this. And the thing about permanent ink is it takes a million layers of paint to block it out. With only two or three layers to cover it, in about 24 hours the black ink starts to bleed through and win! How many thousands of dollars in property damage can one stick of deodorant leave? The world may never know. ∎

LATIF YAHIA

I WAS UDAY HUSSEIN

Photo courtesy of the author

The hand that rocks the oil pumps controls the world. Between 1979 and 2003, that hand was Saddam Hussein's. He would also use it to sign death warrants on dissenters, to murder his own countrymen, to plot disastrous wars with neighboring countries, and to be the puppet master of his entire population. In September 1987, Saddam—or more accurately, his son, Uday—picked up my strings. Uday wanted a double, and I was unlucky enough to resemble him.

This was not my first encounter with Uday. Because of my father's wealth I was sent to the best school in Iraq, and a young, spoiled, arrogant Uday became my classmate. We all hated him even then. He would cruise the streets in his cars and, with the assistance of his bodyguards, would pick up girls whether they wanted to go

with him or not—and most did not. At least one girl who refused to be taken by him was kidnapped and thrown to his starving dogs. In class he would act like his father, showing no enthusiasm for lessons and acting threateningly toward anyone who crossed him. A teacher who reprimanded him for bringing his girlfriend into class disappeared and was never seen again. My classmates used to tease me and call me Uday because even at that age I resembled him. I used to imitate him for laughs.

When my second encounter with Uday came about, I was a captain on the front in Iraq's pointless war with Iran. My unit's command received a dispatch saying that I should be sent to the presidential palace. I was taken there and informed that I was to become Uday Hussein's *fiday*, or body double. This would involve attending functions, making appearances, and assuming his persona when rumors of assassination were circulating. Saddam had several fidays already, and Uday obviously longed for one just like his daddy. I was to be his first. My initial refusal was met with a long spell of solitary confinement and mental torture in a cramped cell without so much as a toilet to maintain my dignity. Eventually, this treatment, and vile threats against my family, forced me to agree to Uday's demands.

Throughout a lengthy period I was trained to act like him and to speak like him. I was also, through cosmetic surgery, made to look even more like him. Indeed, having my front teeth filed down and being given a set of caps that mimicked Uday's gave me a lisp just like his. I was, during my "training," desensitized to the ugly barbarity of the regime by being forced to watch endless, excruciating videos of real torture and murder perpetrated by them on dozens of men, women, and children of Iraq, usually prisoners or prisoners' family members. These films also served as a warning as to what I could expect were I to decide to challenge the regime at any time in the future.

My first public appearance as Uday was at a football match in Baghdad's People's Stadium. My job was to wave at the crowd from a dignitaries' box and present medals to the players at the end. When Uday saw the appearance on television he was impressed. He congratulated my trainers and accepted me as a member of his circle, albeit on the outer reaches. He could not allow anyone to become too close to him, particularly anyone from outside the Tikriti clan from which the majority of the regime was drawn. Indeed, I had been the first fiday to be plucked from the outside world.

From then on my days were spent living in his palaces, effectively a prisoner, as I was not allowed to do anything without permission. But it was a prison of opulence and luxury, with access to the finest food and drink the world had to offer. Swimming pools and other such charmed diversions made the time a little more bearable.

But the captivity grew stultifying. Most of the time I would not be making appearances; I would be bored out of my mind, intellectually and socially unchallenged. I had graduated with a degree in law and had dreamed of following in my father's footsteps and becoming a businessman. This had never been part of my master plan. I was living a brainless, useless existence with no independence or exercise of free will. But worse was to come. I got sucked closer to Uday and he started to treat me as one of his bodyguards, taking me out with him as protection against assassination at the hands of any of his multitude of enemies. This is when I witnessed the depravity of Uday firsthand. I saw him rape, murder, bully, and destroy anyone who dared to question his will. This could be anyone from friends of his father to innocent passersby. On one occasion a honeymooning couple, the wife of which Uday took a liking to, was split apart forever when she threw herself to her death from a balcony after being raped by Uday.

I was saved by the beginning of the invasion of the US-led forces, which seemed to give the regime other things to think about. Uday came to visit me one day. He had me shaved from head to toe and dumped on the doorstep of my parents' home. My mother discovered me but did not recognize the bald, skeletal figure at her feet until I spoke to tell her who I was.

I eventually managed to flee to Austria, but Uday was not finished with me. Two of Uday's men arrived at my family's home and told my father that Uday wanted to see him in his office. They said the meeting would not take too long and that they would pick him up and bring him back. The meeting took place in the headquarters of the Iraqi Olympic Committee, the organization led by Uday more as something for him to do than through any interest he might have had in sports. At 4 AM my father was dropped off at home. The family was still awake, terrified that he had been kidnapped, tortured, or murdered. He said he did not feel well, and just sat there in the lounge, obviously in some distress. In time he started to feel dizzy. Everyone assumed he was tired, as the past few hours would have been a serious drain on his physical resources. But his skin was changing color, at first unnoticeably but eventually unmistakably, to a sickly shade of yellow. He eventually keeled over and took his last breath.

A few hours after my father was dropped off, Uday's bodyguards arrived at the house and imposed a no-funeral rule. They told my family simply to put his body in a grave and unceremoniously bury him. They must have known he would be dead by then, which confirmed to anyone in any doubt that he had been deliberately poisoned. Their rationale was that he was killed because he was the father of Latif Yahia, in their view one of the country's greatest criminals, one of its traitors, who was working alongside the CIA to overthrow Saddam.

I continue to blame myself for the death of my father. And I cannot see the day when I will forgive myself. I could have stayed in Iraq and faced the music. Perhaps I would have been the one to accept the orange juice, to have my bones broken, my soul forced through the mangle. Perhaps then my father would have been the one blaming himself—for sending me to the same school as Uday, for being wealthy. Who knows? It is pointless thinking about it. All I knew was that he was the biggest thing in my life—my father, my friend, my teacher, my confidant, a line of continuity in a place where arbitrary acts of violence and mayhem kept its inhabitants in fear and obedience. And now he is gone. ■

JENNY ZHANG

JOHN MARK KARR WAS MY FRIEND

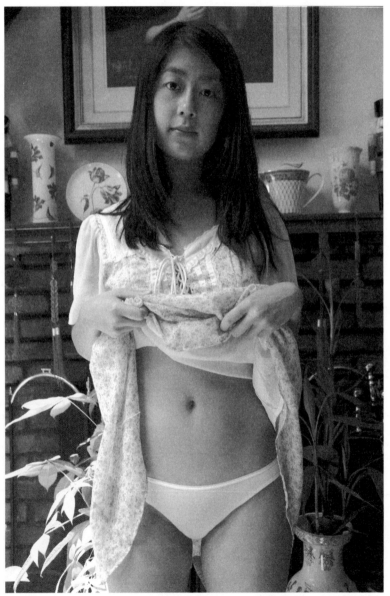

Photo by Richard Kern

I met John Mark Karr one summer in Paris when I was 18. I had a grant from school to write short stories set in France. Never did it, of course, but who cares! I was too busy making friends with a self-professed killer/alleged pedophile and letting him stroke my hair and call me creepy pet names without objecting.

John had been staying for free in the bookstore Shakespeare & Co., and right from the start, I could tell he was a pariah. Most of the other travelers and writers living in the bookstore stayed clear of him, and some schemed to kick him out. I dropped by in the afternoons, at first, to try and flirt with the Scandinavian boy, Nels, who had walked on fire. I gave up on that pretty quickly and became BFF with John instead.

John was funny. He was always sweating, but somehow the beads of sweat stopped just short of his eyebrows and dotted his forehead like a second hairline. He had red-rimmed eyes. I don't remember him ever blinking.

He used to wait for me by the Henry Miller section of the fiction aisle every night. He was always dressed in ratty clothes that were a few sizes too big. He looked like someone's younger brother— you know, the one who jacked off to really fucked-up porn, got pushed into lockers at school, and wrote ten-page-long love letters to girls who laughed hysterically when the other boys called him a "dickless, nutless fag."

He sat on this one low footstool and told me stories about being a nanny. It was weird looking down at him, a 40-year-old man talking about giving little boys and girls long, leisurely baths. "I just love being around kids," he said.

Often, he would obliquely allude to how he had been forced to leave Germany and Austria and how he was legally barred from entering either of those countries because of the "incident." Whenever the "incident" came up, his entire face would darken, and he would say, "She [the children's mother] had it all wrong. I never meant to hurt them. I did it out of love." His anger always seemed to me slightly artificial, elaborately constructed to give himself a sense of depth and elevated drama. "She had no idea what love was. If she did, she wouldn't have treated me that way. She was a sick woman. She made up sick lies and pinned them on me."

I had learned the technique of laughing at the disturbing things that way-older guys who wanted to fuck me and then cry in my arms said to me early on in my life, and I used it often with John. I would slap my knees and laugh, *Oh you*. You and your sweetly deranged, made-up

stories about fleeing Germany because you were molesting small children. What'll you come up with next?

He liked me because I reminded him of an eight-year-old German girl named Jenny who he used to nanny for. He called me his sweet little Jenny and busted a nut every time I showed up to the bookstore in pigtails.

He worried constantly about me and warned me against the perverts who lurked on every corner, waiting for me to cross the street so that they could pounce on me, whip out their dicks, and spray a load on my face.

"You have to be careful. You're my sweet little girl, and John can't let anything happen to you. You can't trust anyone, Jenny. No one." I was happy with the attention he gave me. I purposefully made my voice higher and wore my skirts shorter. The more we spoke, the more frequently he would refer to himself in the third person.

"Jenny?"

"Yes?"

"John would like to ask for your permission to let him walk you to the metro stop tonight."

"OK, sure."

"And may John hold his sweet little girl's hand the entire way?"

"Yeah, why not."

It became a routine. John walked me every night to the metro stop, and he held my hand the way I used to hold my mother's hand, limp but needy.

He cried on my last night in Paris. He wrote his email address down for me in neat, careful handwriting. I can't remember if he was John Mark Karr back then. Maybe he was just John. It's hard to remember these things now.

When I came home to New York, I immediately found an email from John with a photo attached. It was a huge close-up of himself—so big that I had to scroll down to see his entire face. He looked nerve-racked in the photo. His jowls sagged, and he had a pained smile, teeth showing. You could count the beads of sweat on his face like you could count the zits on your 14-year-old postpubescent former self. He wrote me something to the extent of, "John was so happy to meet his sweet little Jenny in Paris this summer. Please don't forget John, or he will be so sad to never hear from his sweet little girl again."

I immediately forwarded the email and photo to my boyfriend at the time with the subject header "HAHA-HAHAHA look at this creep who wanted to pedophile me all summer," thinking if that didn't scare him off from wanting to be my boyfriend, I didn't know what in the world would. ∎

Photo by Reuters

BEN ANDERSON

I WAS TAKEN HOSTAGE

Ben Anderson is a guy who the BBC pays to go to the most dangerous places in the world with a video camera.

We'd just got out of Iraq and apart from a British missile thudding into the sand next to us one day, we didn't have much trouble. Everyone thought the war was going to start while we were there, but it hadn't, so we drove to Damascus and caught a flight to Tehran. I'd been looking forward to this for months. I'd spent hours on Iranian dissident chat rooms and was convinced I was going to spend the next two weeks partying with gorgeous Persian revolutionaries who threw off their head scarves and drank all night. Tehran is one of the busiest places in the world for plastic surgeons (mostly boob jobs, nose jobs, and even hymen repair) and I was certain I'd make a film that would shock people whose only image of Iran was the mullahs and the crowds chanting "*Marg bar Amrika*" (death to America) at Friday prayers.

But the first few days were a real struggle. Privately people would tell me everything, but when the camera was on they became model citizens of the Islamic Republic. I even interviewed a death metal band who wouldn't tell me why they wanted to commit suicide, which is what most of their songs were about.

On about the fifth day, we had arranged to interview students who were at the famous 1999 demonstrations which were put down by the religious police and their thugs, who used clubs and chains and eventually burned down the students' dormitories. Just before we turned the cameras on, the students told me they didn't want to talk about the demonstrations. I spent an hour trying to get something out of them about the younger generation of Iranians and how they felt about the ruling mullahs, whose average age was in their 70s. Two thirds of Iran's population is under 30.

Then we got a call saying, "Leave as quickly as you can, one by one, and go in different directions." But it was too late. A huge bearded man burst in and started pushing people around. Six or seven smaller grinning men stood in the doorway. He grabbed my passport and shouted something in Farsi with glee when he saw that I only had a tourist visa. He started roughly searching my fixer, who motioned toward his address book, which was on the table in front of me. I tried to slip it under a fruit bowl, but it was no good. He grabbed it and shouted something else with glee as he read through it. I looked around the room and all the students were terrified, all of their eyes were moist.

Five of the men—who didn't identify themselves or wear any kind of uniform—took me and my producer to their car. They drove us around Tehran for hours and forced me to eat ice cream and these disgusting nuts. The streets of Tehran are covered with huge murals of martyrs from the Iran-Iraq war and from Palestine. Every time we passed a Palestinian mural, the guy next to me asked me if I liked Israel. "Yes," he said. "You love Israel, Benyamin." I have a long thin nose, and the bearded man would later stroke it again and again, saying something to his friends in Farsi that made them all laugh. "Benyamin love Israel." I assumed he was saying that he'd like nothing more than to break my long thin nose.

Eventually we were taken to our hotel. They turned over our rooms, and things gradually got worse. Because we'd thought that the war in Iraq was going to start while we were there, we had taken chemical and biological weapons suits with us. I'd dumped mine in the bottom of the wardrobe. We'd also taken secret camera equipment into Iran. They soon found both, and decided that we weren't journalists at all, but spies. Their job was now to find out whether we were MI6, CIA, or Mossad.

A small table was brought into the room, and a translator told me to sit in front of it. For five hours they asked me questions and got me to write pages and pages of confessions. The translator would read out my confessions, which were all inane, and the bearded hulk would get up off my bed and storm over, sometimes flipping the table. "*Boop*," he would scream in my ear (Farsi for idiot), "Boop!" Often he'd give me a smack or a thump in the back of the head, although never as hard as he could. Other times he would just stroke my nose and make the others laugh with whatever he was saying.

I am often docile when there is violence. It takes a few seconds for me to register what is actually happening and tell myself to react. At one point after Beardy had stroked my nose, he drew his elbow back very far and swung it at my face. He stopped millimeters from my nose and I had one of those docile moments, thinking, "Get ready to duck, he's gonna swing again soon and this time he won't stop." But to everyone else in the room, my docile moment looked like a Bruce Willis moment, and I appeared incredibly brave. The others were slightly stunned and Beardy was enraged but beaten. He pulled his elbow back and stormed out of the room.

They had also found all the tapes we had shot, and were watching them in the room across the corridor from mine. Occasionally I'd get a glimpse of men going in and out and discussing what they'd seen. I kept thinking about what they were about to see. I'd said that the mullahs were corrupt, wealthy, and had even invented a new Islamic law which allowed temporary "marriages"—sometimes only lasting a few hours—so they could sleep with prostitutes. I'd said that Khomeini must be spinning in his grave.

I kept reassuring myself by thinking that the punches to the back of the head meant that they didn't want to leave marks on me—they were under orders from someone to treat us well. Iran and the UK still had diplomatic relations. My series producer back in London knew something was up because he hadn't heard from us, and at about 8 AM one morning, just a few hours after an interrogation session had ended, the hotel manager put a call through to my room while the men were outside. I only had time to tell the series producer that we were in very deep shit and that I didn't think we were about to be freed. Shortly thereafter the men were back, and they ordered us to pack our bags very quickly. Downstairs the hotel manager looked mortified. I was worried that they'd been listening in on the phone call, and that now he was in the shit for putting it through. I was also worried about where we were being taken. I'd said a few very bad things on the tapes about Evin Prison, the notorious hellhole just outside Tehran. There had been stories about prisoners being held in big rooms, blindfolded, and forced to listen as one man was tortured just feet away. There were also stories about stonings there. Beardy had used Evin a few times when my confessions weren't good enough for him. He had told me that after two days there, I would be traumatized for the rest of my life.

As we pulled out of Tehran, I was looking around every corner and expecting to see Evin Prison up ahead. I was relieved when we pulled up outside a huge embassy-type building, although it was surrounded by spiked fencing and I had no idea where we were.

My producer and I both had bedrooms, and a kind of lounge area where we could wait around for the next interrogation, which normally started very late at night and went on until 4 or 5 AM. One of their tactics was to try and catch one of us lying, so they asked us about each other's personal lives. My producer was a lesbian, was married to a lesbian, and had adopted the schizophrenic child of a schizophrenic couple they were very close to. I couldn't lie, and one of the only light moments of the whole experience came when I saw the look on my interrogators' faces when the translator told everyone what I'd said. Even he was amazed. "Wait, she is a gay woman MARRIED to another gay woman?"

When you go to war zones for the BBC, they send you on what's called a "hostile environment" training course. It's run by ex-SAS guys and is supposed to help you detect mines, avoid bullets, survive in the jungle alone, and handle a hostage crisis. The main piece of advice had been to identify the most sympathetic member of your captor's group and befriend him. The best method was supposed to be a conversation about football or films. If someone was to be beaten or killed, the argument went, he would intervene to make sure it wasn't you or your colleague.

One night Beardy took all the other men out for dinner, but left the man I had identified as the most sympathetic to watch over me in the interrogation room, which was on the top floor of the strange building I was in. I was sitting with my elbows on the table, facing forward, totally exhausted. He was sitting to my side, but he was facing me, restless, as if he was fantasizing about beating the shit out of me. I still thought it was my best chance to try the SAS trick.

"So, you like football?"

"No."

"You like sports?"

"Yes. Violent sports. Kung fu, to the death." He grinned—awful teeth. Right.

"You like films?"

"Yes. Violent films, to the death."

I cursed the hostile-environment training course.

"What about you?" he asked. Maybe there was hope after all…

"Yes," I told him, and started listing all the kinds of films I liked.

He interrupted me: "No, you take drugs and watch porn films all day. In Islam this is very bad."

I gave up. I thought our little back-and-forth was over until he started grabbing chunks of the hair on my right forearm and pulling them out slowly.

After a few nights, one of the guys who had served me food came up to me while the men were all in the room next door.

"I saw you the other night and felt very bad for you. These men are very bad. I wish there was something I could do. I am very sorry."

I thought this might be a trick. He was, after all, employed by these same men. In between interrogations I thought about how little resistance I had offered. I thought I should have refused all questions until the UK ambassador was contacted, or maybe a lawyer. There had even been times when I thought I was a pussy because I hadn't attacked one of the men, stolen his gun, and tried to escape. I was careful with the guy who had served me food, thinking he might have been another one of them.

"So why are you working here?"

"I am university graduate, but there is no work—this is all I have. The young people of Iran hate these men, they are animals."

I still didn't trust him.

"What did you study?"

"Philosophy."

"Really? Me too, my favorite was always Nietzsche."

His face lit up and he told me that Nietzsche was his favorite too. He asked me to wait and stepped aside for about a minute, then jumped back in front of my chair.

"That which not kill me, make me stronger," he said triumphantly. I told him I liked that line a lot. He stepped away again and thought hard for another moment.

"The theory of eternal recurrence!"

He did the same thing a few times, always looking out the door to make sure Beardy and his men weren't coming back. He finally patted my shoulder, apologized again, and dashed off. It was the first time I had smiled in a week.

The whole thing lasted eight days. They had threatened torture and even death. Most of the time I thought that was a ridiculous threat, but there were regular moments when I imagined my own execution. I'd seen footage of three teenage rapists who were hanged by cranes high above a public square, just weeks before we arrived. I imagined being driven to a similar square in the back of a blacked-out camper van and being led to another crane in front of hundreds of women in burkas chanting "Marg bar Amrika, marg bar Israel."

But it wasn't to be. After eight days they told us we'd be on a plane home the next morning. Beardy said he wasn't satisfied with any of my answers (I had written about 20 pages of the most mundane information about the BBC, all of which they could have got from the website) but as Iran and the UK had diplomatic relations, he had decided to let us go. Two of the guys drove us to the airport the next morning, but Beardy had our passports and tickets and was two hours late. We only just made the plane, and even as we were walking to the boarding gate they were still trying to provoke me.

I can no longer remember what it was, but I had managed to hide something from them, or managed to get away with a whopping lie. As we went through to the boarding lounge I saw some officials come and talk to Beardy. What they said seemed to alarm him. I got up and told my producer to grab her ticket. We walked up to the boarding desk, showed our tickets, and walked as fast as possible onto the plane. I kept expecting to see Beardy board and pull us off. Departure was taking too long and at one point they even reopened the luggage hold to remove something. "There's no way they are getting me off this plane," I thought, "This time I'll fight. This is too much." It wasn't until I saw the wheels leave the tarmac that I could finally breathe properly. I was too tired to even feel relieved. ■

JESSICA SIX

UNGRATEFUL DEAD

Embalming the Hated

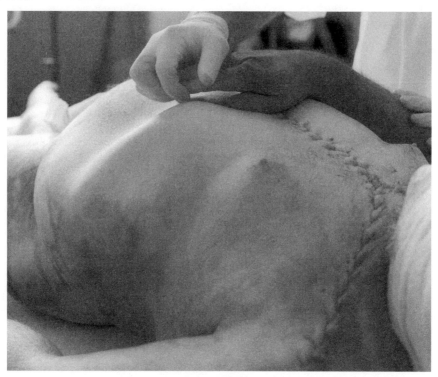

Photo by Tyler Cancro

Yes, I'm a funeral director. That doesn't mean that I stand there in a jacket and skirt at someone's wake comforting the bereaved family. Nope. What I do is slave away in cold basements trying to prevent your loved ones' dead bodies from looking like mangled pieces of meat.

But that isn't what this is about. I have a couple of other things I want to get off my chest about this fucking job. People want morgue workers to be invisible and mute (and no, *Six Feet Under* hasn't helped shit at all. It's just made people think we're all gay/depressed nymphos/creeps). I'm tired of being quiet. I have a couple of things to bitch about, and you're going to have to listen. If you don't, I'll be sure

to lose a scalpel inside your brother's chest cavity or leave your mother's eyes wide open at her viewing. Got it?

First off, doctors are lazy, uninformed rich kids who have no clue what an acceptable cause of death is. Everyone automatically thinks "old age" if the person is over 50, but New York State doesn't view that as sufficient. The long-winded version of "old age" is "cardiopulmonary arrest due to arteriosclerotic heart disease." That means your heart stopped because your veins and arteries were too ridiculously clogged to pump anymore. Every year, national reports say the number-one killer of just about everyone—statistically—is heart disease, but it's so not true!

Are you sitting down? The number-one killer is really

hospital infections. I once went to pick up a woman from a particularly skanky local hospital, and the death certificate (D/C) was filled out wrong. Her doctor came down and I asked what she'd died of. He told me she came in with a urinary-tract infection and that the bacteria went systemic and she died of sepsis (bacteria in the blood). So I said, "OK, well you have to write that she had the infection, the name of the organism and the medicine that it was resistant to, and that it became sepsis."

He asked, "Is there an easier way?"

I said, "Cardiopulmonary arrest due to arteriosclerotic heart disease."

It's a blanket answer that you'll find on D/Cs everywhere. I can't tell you how many bodies I've embalmed without having any idea what the people actually died of! I'm soaked to the elbows in fluids that are leaking out of every orifice, and I have no clue what diseases, bacteria, and/or viruses are floating around. Not very many people realize what a huge health risk I take every time I embalm. Not to mention the harsh chemicals I have to use. There seems to be a running pattern among women who have been in the business for years and years—their children come out with neurological and sometimes physical problems due to prolonged formaldehyde and phenol exposure. My kids are going to be deformed! Awesome.

One of the most telling things about this job is that morgues are always pressed up against the kitchens, laundry rooms, and garbage areas in the bowels of the hospital. When I ask where to park my car at a new hospital, they're inevitably like, "Oh, go around back by the dumpsters and the morgue door is right there." It's all about the hospital wanting to hide its failures. Doctors HATE morgue workers for just that reason. We are a living and breathing symbol of their failure to save someone's life. Trying to get a doctor to even sign off on a D/C on time is like the Nuremberg Trials.

The second-worst thing I have to deal with is the dreaded "removal." That's when you go to someone's house, a nursing home, or a hospice and cart off their dead. It has to be done in professional attire—which means a suit and tie for guys. For me, it's a skirt and high heels. I'm tiny—all of five-foot-one, 120 pounds—and I'm in my early twenties, yet I'm hauling dead bodies out of beds and into minivans a couple times a week. These things often weigh twice as much as me. Families and orderlies are always astounded that a girl would be sent by herself to do this. Just imagine for a moment: It's 90 degrees and you're in a black suit—or it's 20 below and you're in a skirt—and you're wheeling a gurney with a body-bagged heap of dead person out to your "removal vehicle" while an entire family cries in the doorway and the neighbors peek out from behind their curtains.

But don't think these families are all innocent sufferers!

I can't tell you how many people I've removed who obviously haven't been shaved in months, haven't had their diapers changed in a few days, and have not been properly washed and/or cleaned in some time, either. And let's not forget bedsores. The technical term is "decubitus ulcer." It's really just a big, stinky hole on any number of pressure points of the body. Bedsores start growing and rotting from lying in one position for too long. It's that fucking simple. Next time you have a comatose relative in your back bedroom, please don't forget to turn them over every couple of hours. You'll save me a lot of time spent gagging while I wash these things out.

I should mention—all modesty aside—that I am an excellent embalmer. I will trim ear and nose hairs, cut nails, clean out the months of dirt built up under the cuticles, polish nails on women, and then clean and suture the wounds and sores from all the various tubes and needles they've been subjected to. It never fails that once I get them all cleaned up, give them a haircut, dress them up, and display them, the family is all blubbering and crying and hysterical. Puh-leeze! When was the last time you visited grandpa at the nursing home? Have you ever changed one of his diapers?

I do thank God all the time that I (so far) haven't had to handle a dead abused kid. One of my professors from mortuary school told us to wait until the day when we see a small child that we KNOW has been abused violently by his or her parents. You can't do or say shit about it, and you have to make arrangements with this family in a civil manner knowing that they probably killed their baby. Sounds like a good vibe, right? I have handled my share of nonabused babies, though. There's a fairly new law in New York City requiring that all infants be autopsied, so I've never had a baby come to me in one piece. They arrive at the morgue all chopped up, and I put them back together. Have you ever told the mother of a dead child that she can't hold her baby one last time because it might fall apart?

Soooo, why the fuck do I do this? On top of all that I've just told you, the monetary compensation is quite inadequate. The real rewards are a little more intangible. The gratitude of the families means a lot, and so does the admiration of my colleagues. This is the kind of industry where people are always checking out each other's skills, and its cool to have 20-year veterans marvel at my handiwork. But the thing I like most is seeing the results of all my hard work. After three hours with a corpse that arrives dirty, reeking, covered in its own purge, mouth and eyes gaping, often toothless, it is truly rewarding to stand back and see it clean and neat, smelling good, with no tubes or other implements of modern medicine sticking out of any orifices. It is an art, and the final goal is making the dead person look at peace. If I can do that, the satisfaction is worth any number of asshole doctors and infected bedsores. ∎

JEFF JENSEN

I GOT SHOT

I was a 13-year-old, kind of new-wave skater kid with a Tony Hawk hairdo living in Kansas City and trying to score pot. It was almost impossible back then and one of the few people that had it was Greg Grefauk. He was also 13 but the thing about 13 is, it's a weird age. There's 13-year-olds who look like janitors. They've got a mustache and a car. And then there's 13-year-olds who look like they're 8. I was the latter. He was the former.

So after trying to get pot all over Kansas City, I had to resort to Greg. He gave out pot for free, but it was still expensive in a way because you had to hang out with him—all night. Me and my friends went to his house and he made us listen to metal for hours and hours. I hated metal back then. I guess I still do. As the night wore on my friends started dropping like flies. I didn't have a curfew so I could stay there all night if I wanted. He didn't have a curfew either. In fact, his mother wasn't even home. She was in Hawaii partying. She was rich because she divorced some rich guy, but she was as white trash as white trash gets. Greg and his mother lived in a huge, six-bedroom McMansion, but there was no furniture in it. Crap was piled everywhere. About the only decoration in the house was some wallpaper in Greg's room made of old Marlboro cartons. He was proud of how many cigarettes he smoked.

At around 5 AM Greg put in this Iron Maiden VHS tape and turned up the volume as loud as it could go. It was like he was trying to torture me to see what my limits were. Like when a newly adopted kid is bad so he can see if his new parents are really in it for the long haul. I braved out the tape and after half an hour or so Greg suggested we go out and hunt rabbits. I said sure. Free pot had to be just around the corner. I had paid my dues.

He picked up his stepfather's .22 and started waving it around the room. I wasn't too worried about it and went to the bathroom to take a piss. When I came out of the bathroom he shot me. BANG! I remember seeing his face go really pale and realizing I had been thrown up against the bathroom door and was now sitting on the floor. The bullet had entered my side, punctured my liver and kidneys, ricocheted around my ribs, and got stuck halfway out my back. Like, if you looked at my back you would have seen the tip of a bullet sticking out. When I looked down at my shirt I saw this enormous red stain that was growing way too fast. It is impossible to convey the kind of fear I was feeling at the time. Pure terror.

You see, most people have a library of references if something happens to them. If they burn their finger they go, "Oh yeah, a burn," and go put it in water or whatever. I didn't have references for this experience. All I knew about being shot was what I saw in Rambo movies and that was: You die. I was going to die. These were my last moments on earth. One thing people in movies don't do when they're shot is stand up and start screaming, "YOU FUCKING ASSHOLE! WHAT THE FUCK HAVE YOU DONE!?" But I did. He kept repeating, "Dude, I'm sorry. Don't sue me." That's what he kept repeating, "Dude, don't sue me." I didn't mind the suing thing so much as the word "dude." This was back before everybody in the world said "dude" and it just fucking annoyed the shit out of me.

I ran around the house ranting and raving for about two minutes until the pain hit me. It's difficult to describe the pain. Just imagine the worst cramp anyone ever had times 1,000. It was crippling, so I lay in the fetal position and told Greg to call 911. That's a tape I'd like to hear. He said, "Hey, man. I think... I think my friend got shot." And I yelled, "No you fucking asshole. Tell them YOU shot me." And he said, "Yeah. I guess I shot my friend." Neither of us cried once during this whole thing. I remember I was wearing a "Boys Don't Cry" shirt at the time.

Greg picked me up (remember, he was one of those grown-man 13-year-olds) and carried me out to the lawn. This was summer in Kansas City and the sky was just breathtaking. I lay on my back looking at the stars, bleeding to death, and I started to pray to Jesus. I was an atheist at the time and gave my mother no end of grief about Christianity, but that night I prayed and prayed to Jesus and begged him to let me live. Then I had a life-changing experience. You know how they say your whole life flashes before your eyes? It does. When I closed my eyes I saw my whole life being projected inside a cylinder. There was audio coming out either side playing sound bites that related to the images. It started at my most recent memory, being at the skate park on my 12th birthday, and it went chronologically backward toward my birth. As the video unraveled it was moving toward a bright white light that I was also heading toward. All those clichés are true.

The next thing I remember was being startled out of this dream state by a paramedic. I opened my eyes and said, "Am I going to die?" and they said, "I don't know." Aren't they supposed to tell you everything's going to be all right? I started panicking again as they put me in the ambulance and asked me if I could move my toes and all that. When we got to the hospital, I asked them if the Kansas City Royals had won and then blacked out. They did exploratory surgery and stopped the bleeding and that was it. Apparently organs heal themselves, so if you can stop the bleeding everything else will take care of itself. When I woke up this real slick tough-guy black dude came over and said, "Wassup Jeff. I'm the surgeon that stitched you up." I said, "Thanks for saving my life," and he said, "Cool." Then he said, "I need to talk to you about something," and went into this huge lecture about "the pot." He told me how he was a child of the 60s and he'd been there and seen what it can do to people and if I don't stop going down the pot route I'm never going to do anything with my life. Fine, I won't smoke pot anymore.

Greg came to visit me a few days later (I was in the hospital for weeks). I had a catheter in my penis that they put in the second I arrived. That was potentially more traumatizing than being shot. They also had a huge green tube that they stuck up my nose and into my stomach. It was pumping bile from my stomach nonstop. So Greg comes up to my bed and he's freaking out, saying, "Dude, I don't know what to say, dude. Please don't hate me, dude," and he gives me a letter and walks out of the room. I wish I still had that letter. It had the grammar and spelling of a kindergarten project. And the worst part was he fucking spelled "dude" wrong. It said, "Dued." This was about the only word he knew how to say and he couldn't even spell it. The letter said something like, "Dued. I am so sarry. Dued. Don't hate me dued. Dued. I don't know wut to say. Dued." Hilarious.

Just before I was finally ready to leave the hospital, my mom came into the room and said we had to go over some insurance policy offers. I was like, "What? I get money because some idiot shot me?" Apparently if something like this happens in a person's home, you can get their home insurance policy to pay you money. They had offers like a lump sum of $200,000 or how about $800 a month for the rest of your life? I chose money for life and $5,000 cash. My parents didn't let me spend the five grand until I was 21, but I'm 33 now and I still get that check every month. In a way it's a curse because it totally robbed me of any ambition, but fuck it. I know people with really shitty jobs and it sure beats having a shitty job. I'm glad I got shot. ∎

V13N8, AUGUST 2006

JOHN JONES

ORGASMO

It was my birthday, and I was sitting at work. I always like to do something on my birthday—I hate birthday parties, but I like to do something else to spoil myself. It's Friday afternoon, I'm sitting at work and I'm like, "I want to do something," so I decide I should go to my house in Argentina.

I call up the airline, and I have enough air miles or whatever so that I don't have to pay for it, and so I say, "Fuck it, I'm going to go down." They say, "OK, well there's one leaving in two hours." So I get in a taxicab with nothing, and just go straight to the airport and fly down. I get there and there's a hotel which is also a casino. I tell myself, "I'm not going to gamble this time. I'm kind of tired. I'm just not going to go downstairs at all."

I check in and I go up to my room. I'm lying there in bed and I hear the slot machines going off: "Dingdingding dongdongdongding" all over like madness, so I'm like, "Maybe I'll just go down and play a few hands." I go down and order a rum and start playing some blackjack. Cut to two hours later: I'm surrounded by about 50 women. Every time you get $500 they give you a chit, and I'm just covered in chits, they're falling out of my pants. So they all see this—and this is like two years' salary to them—they just see this drunk American dude with chits falling out of his pants. Since it was my birthday, I go, "OK, you, you, you, you, and you." I pick five girls. And one of the girls—the one I later called Orgasmo—I said to her and one of the others, "You go get an ounce of blow, and you get a case of champagne." I gave them a few chits each and then I went up to my room. I want to mention that these girls were NOT hookers. They were just local girls with shitty jobs who come to the casino at night looking for guys with money to pay for them to party. If you all end up fucking, so be it. If you give them some money as a gift, so be that too. But they are not hookers by any means.

So we go up to my room, and there's like a mountain of blow on the table. It's like *Scarface* or something. We're drinking champagne and I start naming everybody. The reason I called the one girl Orgasmo is because she took off all her clothes right away and started snorting coke. She'd just snort a big, huge line then start rubbing her pussy furiously going, "*Orgasmo, orgasmo.*" So her name was pretty easy. Then there was this one who was actually Colombian called Love and Rockets. I called her Love and Rockets after the comic because she had big, huge tits, then a narrow waist, then a big, huge ass. I can't remember what I named the other ones, fucking Lolita and Puss 'n Boots or something.

So we get down to it, and we're fucking, and I'm like the guy from the Bolshoi—you know how he'd get them to put a pencil in their ass to choreograph them because that was the only way he could get them to work? I'm like, "You suck her ass, and then *you* lick my ass, and then *you* put your toe in her fucking pussy, or whatever." So I'm doing all that and fucking them, and then I come. But I've been doing a lot of blow, right? I've got these five horny girls in my room and all this champagne and stuff, but I can't get a boner anymore 'cause I've just come and I'm on half of fucking Bolivia. So you're sitting there going, "Well, what can you do?" Well, of course there's water sports, as is my proclivity.

So I go into the bathroom with Lolita and Puss 'n Boots, and I'm in there with the shower going and they're just pissing. Pissing on me as I whack off, pissing on my knees, whatever. I sort of get a little wired and I put my leg through the wall of the shower. I kick out and put a hole in the wall. But who cares? The pissing keeps going, I bring in the B-team—more piss. Water's coming down. So this keeps going for a while and then I hear this BANG!! Cops come into my room, with all these nude girls and massive amounts of blow.

What's happened is, the water's gone down into the hole that I've kicked in the shower wall, down the elevator shaft to where the one-armed bandits are, and shorted out all the slot machines in the casino. So they were banging on my door to try and get me, but a) the music's too loud, and b) I'm way back in the bathroom with the water going and two girls squealing as they piss on my knees, so I don't hear anything.

So they've called the cops, and the cops come in and I'm standing there naked looking like the father from *An Officer and a Gentleman* with all these young girls around. Now I have to pay off the cops—which is always a delicate situation—and to make matters more difficult I've hidden all my money. I'd rolled it up in a bunch of different towels and hid it in a bunch of toilet-paper tubes, cause I didn't want to get rolled with so much fucking money—five local girls means five sets of sneaky fingers. So I'm surreptitiously taking the money out of the towels, the cops finally leave, and we're all just sitting there like it's the calm after the storm. Like, "What do we do now?"

Puss 'n Boots and Lolita leave, Love and Rockets sort of hangs out for a bit then leaves, but Orgasmo isn't going anywhere. So, I'll never forget, she sat down to take a piss, and I put my balls on the rim of the shitter, and the coolness of the porcelain just cooling my balls down—I just let fly right into her pussy as she pissed. Then she got a bit mad at me, because I was so into the pissing and was like, "Drink your own piss, baby," and she got sort of freaked out. But still she wouldn't leave, she wanted to keep the party going.

Anyways, I'm sitting there, wired for sound with Orgasmo, and I'm like, "Maybe we'll go back downstairs for a bit." So we go downstairs to play a bit more, it's like four or five in the morning—the sun is imminent—and I'm supposed to be going to my house to relax, but I'm still in the casino. We go downstairs to sit in the casino, and I last about five minutes before I meet another five girls—completely different set of five—and Orgasmo fucks them all in different ways. And I don't even bother whacking off at this point, cause I'm fucking gone, so I'm just sitting there snorting coke with my big fat belly, drinking wine going, "Lick her pussy. Lick her ass. Now, you lick her pussy as she licks your pussy. Lick her ass. Put that plunger in her ass." I have them doing sort of bathroom things, like plunging their asses with the plunger from the toilet. Then the second army of chicks all leaves, and I'm still sitting there sort of wired and Orgasmo still won't leave. She just sits there snorting coke and rubbing her pussy. This is after she's been like the general of the evening, getting all the troops in line, and she's still rubbing her pussy and going "*Orgasmo, orgasmo,*" as she's snorting coke.

I don't sleep—I just get in a taxi to the airport, fly to my house, sleep for three days, then wake up just crying at the debauch I'd got up to. ∎

MEREDITH DANLUCK

I MET MICHAEL JACKSON

The $3,500 photo. Totally worth it.

In March 2007, Michael Jackson held an exclusive "fan appreciation day" in Tokyo where 300 lucky people got to line up and be led one by one into a teeny room where they would have the chance to spend 30 seconds of face time with "The Gloved One"—all for the low, low price of $3,500. Hi, that's $117 per second.

Artist Meredith Danluck was one of these fortunate few. She's still slightly traumatized.

As soon as I heard about it, I knew I had to go. I reserved a ticket right away—I think mine was number 296 out of 300 so I just made it.

I got to Japan and I was totally jet-lagged, so everything already had this surreal feeling to it. I headed over to Studio Coast, the venue where the event was happening. There were all these paparazzi outside and everyone was gathered around a Michael Jackson impersonator, watching him do the Moonwalk. Everyone was holding gifts and flowers and things for him to sign. I was empty-handed.

Most of the people there were Japanese, but somehow I ended up in line with a bunch of English-speaking folks. I met a really cool girl who worked for the Moroccan embassy who ended up becoming my line-buddy. Standing in front of us was a normal-seeming Scottish couple who told me, "Some people spend $10,000 for a safari—this is our safari." I also met Carlo, a computer techni-cian/Michael Jackson impersonator from Colorado who hit on me. He was like, "What are you doing later? Wanna go by Michael's hotel and hang around outside?" And I met the head of the Australian Michael Jackson fan club, who brought a massive, four-inch-thick binder of fan letters she had collected from fans in Australia to give to Michael Jackson. I wonder if he'll read any of them. I feel like he might. I mean, what else does he have to do?

Before we were let in, a parade of about 50 children in wheelchairs were hoisted up the stairs into the venue. People around me were actually getting pissed off, like, "Why do *they* get to go in first? They probably didn't even have to pay!"

So finally we get let inside, and it's really lame! There is a buffet of crap food, like deli sandwiches and shit. I mean, for three grand you'd think there'd be some decent food. I ate, like, a cracker. I was starving and I think that contributed to my mental breakdown later.

There was nothing to do for two hours. Everyone was just milling around, waiting for something to happen. Finally Michael showed up and made his way through the crowd with about five bodyguards forming a shield around him. People FLIPPED out: crying, screaming, tak-ing pictures like crazy. Suddenly Michael stopped walk-ing and crouched down into, like, a crash position and covered his head because I guess the camera flashes were too much for him. The bodyguards started yelling, "No flashes! No flashes!"

He went upstairs into this VIP box and everyone just stood there staring up. Once in a while he would come to the window and wave and people would freak out. Then I got hit on by another Michael Jackson impersonator! He was like a hip-hop dude whose name was "E. Casanova." I kept wondering what it was about me that was so attrac-tive to Michael Jackson impersonators!

Finally they started calling numbers to meet the man. You weren't allowed to bring a video camera, but I had a digital camera that actually shoots pretty high-quality video. I thought, "Well, I have no idea what's going to happen when I walk through that door, so I'm just gonna start filming now and go for as long as I can." I held my camera to my chest in a vise grip. The door opened. It was so intimidating. There were like 15 bodyguards and handlers inside. A woman shuffled me into the tiny, brightly lit room and immediately stripped me of my coat, my purse and my cam-era—like, she really wrestled the camera away from me. I tried to explain that I just wanted to take pictures of him myself (but secretly film him), but they didn't understand. They were like, "Oh no, together, together!" and literally shoved me over to where he was waiting. He was just stand-ing in the corner like a little lost dog confined in a cage at the pound. When they pushed me I tripped over the white tarp paper and tore it a little. You can see it in the picture.

I stumbled and kind of fell into Michael Jackson. The bodyguards gasped but Michael just caught me and was like, "Oh hi, are you OK?" We shook hands and hugged and he felt very frail and skeletal. I'm a size zero and I felt fat next to him. And I'll tell you, being so close to that face, that nose, that skin… I was mesmerized. He said, "I really like your shirt," and he touched my t-shirt. That felt strange. Then he said that he liked my vampire teeth necklace and asked me if he could have it! I thought I had misheard him, so I just mumbled something like, "Oh! You know, actually, it's real-ly sentimental. Sorry!" Right then the guy holding my cam-era said "OK, 1, 2, 3," and took a picture of us—just one picture—and then they shuffled me out and that was it.

It was the fastest 30 seconds of my life. I felt like a piece of trash being blown in the wind. One of the rules was that we were allowed to ask Michael one question—like he was some kind of oracle. "Michael Jackson, who will I marry?" In all the chaos of it though, I didn't even think to ask him anything. I barely even spoke to him. I barely even treated him like a human being, because everyone else in the room made him seem like such an object.

I left immediately afterward. There were going to be performances of dancers doing "Thriller" following the meetings, but I had to get out of there. I felt crazy. Since I was the first person to leave, when I got outside the paparazzi swarmed me, shouting, "Did you meet Michael Jackson? Did you shake his hand?" They trailed me for an entire block and I got so freaked out, I jumped in a cab and spent $70 getting back to the hotel. We had gotten gift bags containing a bottle of champagne and an auto-graphed photo of Michael, and the next day the cleaning lady in my hotel either threw mine away or stole it.

Still, I definitely feel like I got my money's worth. He was actually really nice. I feel bad for him. I feel bad that there's this human life who has such a foreign, caged expe-rience of the world. ■

JAIMIE WARREN

A GIRL'S LIFE

I Turned Normal for a Week

I temped for one whole day.

Vice asked me to become a normal girl for a week and document it. I guess a big reason they asked me to do it is because I take a lot of self-portraits and I can come across as a pretty disgusting person. I have a horrible sense of style, and though it may be kind of funny, I think the pictures are probably of interest because I basically look gross and weird.

So to start off, I had to decide what a normal girl is. I pictured the kind of chick who works a boring job during the day, is kind of quiet and opinionless, spends several hours getting ready to go out even though she looks virtually the same when she's done, is fit and image-conscious, and when the weekend rolls around she's a party girl wearing Bebe clothes who gets totally wasted with her girlfriends. That's what first popped into my head and I ran with it.

Just so you understand where I'm coming from, I live in Kansas City, Missouri. And no, it's not a cornfield town where we don't know what email or sushi is. It's just a plain old small-ish city. We know where to go to dance to shitty Top 40 rap, we know what a martini is, we have bars with happy hours, and we have country clubs. So I was basically all set to be normal. YES!

I guess you should also know about my actual life, too. My friends and I throw what I think are amazing parties with weird themes and we dress up a lot and do tons of weird stuff to entertain ourselves. Like we might all dress up really goth to crash a gross punk/ska night at a college bar or we might all decide to just walk the streets as zombies for fun or I might decide to be really punk while waiting tables or we may all decide to be Karen O at the local hillbilly karaoke dive or we might walk around town like we're in a band and I'm the nasty lead singer in a nudie suit and spandex eating pizza or we might crash some bitch's wedding-reception party dressed like a fucking fancy fish. Whatever!!

Now this may sound hugely awesome, but the downside to not caring about looking good or acting cool is that you never meet anyone new to impress! I think that the "normal" in me was kind of into the idea of acting like the girls who go out all the time pretending like they don't already know everybody they see at the same bars every week.

When I need an accomplice, I always call my lovely friend Chloe. She was more than willing to dust off her oatmeal-colored hand-knit floor-length sweater-jacket and facial bronzer for the occasion, and this way she could snap some pics of me while I tried to "work it."

I started off by getting everything I needed to really immerse myself in this new persona. I took diet pills twice daily, I spent several hours fixing my hair and doing my makeup, I did my at-home aerobics-tape workouts, I whitened my teeth with those strip things, and I filed, plucked, tweezed, polished, smoothed, coated, lathered, lotioned, de-frizzed, and de-tangled. Though I'm not so used to getting up three and a half hours early to step outside, I will say that the diet pills gave me a massive energy boost, all while completely diminishing my hunger. I even lost seven pounds in one week! Woo-hoo!

So are you ready for my week of being normal? Here we go!

DAY ONE

I woke up, spent two hours getting prepped, and jetted off to Bijin Salon in the suburbs. I got my hair "layered." They told me it would make my face look thinner and my neck longer. I also got "bangs" because they are "in" but they consisted of three uneven wisps that just looked like an accident, even though I told the stylist I liked it. (I was being served free wine, after all.)

Then I entered a long, dark hallway with "Sssh" signs everywhere, which was where the pedicures and massages take place. Even though the pedicure lady's voice sounded sweet when she was hovering over my toes, I swear every time I looked up from my *InStyle* magazine and caught a glimpse, I was being given the snake eyes.

Next up was my eyebrow-grooming session. I had never plucked my eyebrows before, but I'd always been interested. The general consensus has been that I have full, nice brows. I was happy with that, but since the opportunity came around, I said, "What the hey!"

DAY TWO

Today was a holiday, and I got ready in the morning to dress appropriately normal to visit the home of my friends' family. I tried on several outfits and spent time drying my hair in curls to give it a "wave." This did nothing but I acted like it did. Then I headed off for Thanksgiving dinner.

I entered the sparse, clean home and was incredibly kind and cordial and polite. I even asked to say grace before the meal just to really fuck with them. (I don't think you have to say grace when you're eating off of plastic plates, do you?)

DAY THREE

I woke up with the realization that what was keeping me from really being normal was a hot set of fake nails and a glowing tan. Duh! I hopped off to the local nail salon, where a quiet Vietnamese woman took the chewed-up ends of my fingers and turned them into beautiful French-manicured lady nails. She sanded and polished and suddenly I was a new woman. A new woman who no longer had the ability to type, zip up her pants, put her hair in a ponytail, pick things up, or wipe her ass with ease. Oh well. Look at how pretty they are!

Next up was a spray-on tan. I thought I would have to stand in a room naked while a tiny blond woman hosed me down with brown spray. Nope. Instead, I just popped into a very doctor's-office-looking room wearing only booties and a shower cap. They give you a little red tube to breath through, then you get in this metal shower-looking contraption, press a button, close your eyes, and spin around while a disgusting, toxic-smelling sugar-syrup chemical gushes all over you. It only took a minute, and a few hours later it was a pretty natural-looking tan, not the bright orange tint I assumed I would get.

That night I decided it was an appropriate time for some sporty action. I asked an acquaintance if I could hit the Jewish country club with her and scope out the racquetball courts. I told her to take some photos of me for my MySpace and match.com profiles looking "sexy" and "full of life."

For dinner we went to the Cheesecake Factory, a popular tourist restaurant with gross decor and a ten-mile menu of food from all over the world. It's all so Americanized that even my spring roll tasted like a hamburger.

DAY FOUR

Again, woke up early to exercise, shower, and do myself up. Then I spent two hours with a friend working out. It was rough, but this is what normal girls do: Sweat and strain until they puke.

Later on I hung out at a friend's parents' house and we all watched *Oprah*. I had to get home soon though, for my first experiment with clubbing. My normal-girl research taught me that the biggest part of clubbing is doing your makeup and hair in preparation. I'm lucky enough to have a friend who had just quit his job at MAC cosmetics and was willing to help me on the quest for normal beauty. I learned all kinds of outlandish shit. Do you know how many "areas" there are on an eyelid?! OMG!

We cruised to a bar called KARMA—the grossest name ever. The DJ had a Misfits haircut and a Misfits t-shirt and was playing 90s hip-hop. Party time!

My "normal" friend and I sat down and after five minutes it started: "I've never seen you ladies here before." I got the most awesome dudes—the chubby ones with soul patches, vertical striped button-up shirts, and spiky gelled hair. Seriously. They flocked to me. And they all work in "landscaping" and "their work bought them a truck." I wouldn't usually be such a bitch about it but this one guy was a serious turd. He spent two and a half hours talking to me. I was being nice and normal, answering questions thoughtfully, and trying to make the conversation engaging (this was an experiment, after all). I never got all wasted-face on him. I never made it "obvious I was going home with him." But the second they were kicking us out of the bar, the mood totally changed. This evil, fast-paced desperation kicked in and suddenly all the guys were saying, over and over, "You can come over, we can have some beers, just talk and hang out." And it was being said like a million miles an hour while they were scanning the other girls who were lingering outside the front door. Finally, I said, point-blank, "You know, I really, really can't tonight, but if you want to give me your number I can call you." And he bolted! He was willing to fuck me but not even give me his phone number! I was so seriously grossed out by this. I mean, my friend and I laughed about it, but I was perturbed. Is that really how normal people do it?

DAY FIVE

After the daily morning routine, which was like second nature by this point, I went and did a bit more shopping at the mall for an outfit for my big date. Yes, it's true! I scored a rendezvous through my recently acquired match.com profile! He cyber-winked at me, we exchanged awkward convo, and it was on! The date is the night after tomorrow and I am hella pumped. His username is musicman1063, mine's 00mistletoe00, and he seems like the real thing! He's never been married, he's not sure if he wants kids, he's a cigar aficionado, he's spiritual but not religious, and his profile says: "I stay busy, can you keep up? I also like time alone so I need someone that is secure and independent. No cling-ons. I love to do things outdoors—camping, Frisbee, discgolf, and above all, skydiving. Although I don't possess a great deal of artistic ability, I have a deep appreciation, and passion for all forms of art—music, poetry, literature, comedy, theater, sculpture, architecture, paintings, and body art. I am a very happy person that just basically loves life. I'm excited about all the experiences that life has to offer, and can't wait for the next new lesson. I learned early that life was too short to waste it being negative. There's so much to do, and so much to be excited about. I'd like to have someone to share it with." Yes! I'm so excited! He also says he thinks life should be set to music, which we all know is a total turn-on. We're going to a bar called Martini Corner! I can't wait.

DAY SIX

Today I temped at an office job and I shelved books and updated bibliographies and ran errands. A normal friend who has had lots of jobs like this advised me on how to behave: Like a total make-no-waves bootlicker. So I got everyone pizza for lunch and was very, "Hey guys, I've got pizza, pizza, pizza!" I kept a huge smile on my face and kissed ass and gave lots of compliments and made shitty conversation. I actually didn't think it would be bad at all, but there were a lot of bitter, single 40-year-old women who were total bitches and wouldn't even look me in the eye when they talked to me. Would that be my future if I stayed normal? The ones who did talk went on and on about stuff like hairstyles, breeds of dogs, Pilates, and the death of the Atkins diet. I liked them.

After work, we all went out to happy hour. We all drank Cape Cods and picked at "feta plates." We got some appraising looks from guys and my coworker Kelly scored a number.

DAY SEVEN (FINISH LINE!)

Is this really going to end? I don't know whether that's good or not. Being normal is kind of making me get my shit together and all my friends that saw me in character preferred my new look!

Anyway, tonight's my big date, and I got Michael coming over to super-straighten my hair and do my makeup.

My date showed up and it was an awkward start. We headed off to Martini Corner for drinks and dinner. I had my camera and told him it was my hobby—that I love to photograph nature and children. He thought it was cool, and the ice was broken by him asking me to take pictures of him "being a goofball." He wanted me to take so many pictures of him being "zany" (seriously, I took like 40) that I started to get uncomfortable and told him the battery was almost dead. We talked about our jobs and about what we do for fun. We talked about house music, weed, my hair, skydiving, vampires… the usual! I lied about every single thing I told him. Actually, I think I found my new talent—I'm practically an expert improv comedian at this point. But overall it was kind of a dead date. It was hard for me to even find it funny. He was really nice, just boring and weird, and I got the feeling he probably lived with his parents or something.

When midnight came, I told him that I had to get up early. But I LIED!! WOO HOO! I really went and met my girl Chloe to do some clubbing!

To get some quick tips, I talked to other girls and told them I had just gotten out of a four-year relationship and had forgotten how to flirt. They told me that they judge dudes by their shoes and they flirt with them all night so all their friends can get free drinks. Lame! I felt like I was watching an after-school special.

I danced a lot, and Chloe and I got hit on by some real winners. I got pretty wasted and had lots of the exact same conversation over and over. I think normal girls might have to go on autopilot when they go out clubbing. All in all, getting hit on at a normal club feels the same way it does when homeless men shout things at you outside a gas station. Not so hot.

I went home after last call, warmed by the knowledge that when the sun rose, I would be weird again. Overall, being normal wasn't that hard, I guess. I had fun, but probably because it was temporary. The main thing I learned is that I need to keep my new look because I keep being told I'm better now—even by my friends who purposely look like shit because it's "in" or whatever. ■

XI

MUSINGS

Photo by Richard Kern, V15N4, April 2008

BRUCE LABRUCE

I HATE STRAIGHTS

Bash Back, Fags

Film still from LaBruce's movie Skin Flick. *(courtesy of peres projects, Los Angeles)*

Forget about fag bashing. It's time for a little equal opportunity straight bashing. When I was a sissy homo punk in the 80s, big macho het boys with foot-tall Mohawks and Crass jackets, conveniently setting their radical, anarcho-leftist leanings aside for a moment, would punch me in the nose for showing queer super-8 movies in punk venues. Their avowed neo-Nazi skinhead enemies at the same show, now united in homo hatred, would run over and spit on me in solidarity. My punk dyke friends would form a human shield, but the damage was already done. From that point on, I would dedicate much of my work to pushing overt homosexuality into the faces of heterosexuals, both virulent homophobes and liberal bleeding hearts alike.

It's the femmie homosexual people can't stand the most, especially if he's sexually aggressive and unapologetic about it, so that's the image we set out to promote. We used to refer to heterosexuals as breeders back then. Child-hating W. C. Fields was our idol, and we loved Roman Polanski in *The Tenant*—you know, the part where, dressed in drag, he walks over to a little boy in a park and slaps him across the face for no reason. Why do people who breed think they're so special, we puzzled, bringing a kid into this overpopulated, war-ravaged world, desperately trying to grasp onto some pathetic shard of immortality? In the sage words of Kim and Kelley Deal (of the Breeders, no less), "If you're so special, why aren't you dead?"

At my university there was a group called the League Against Homosexuals. Their motto, spread on leaflets across campus, was "Queers don't produce, they seduce." I adopted their credo as my own in the most public way possible. But today, twentysomething homosexuals, especially the ones who read *Vice*, think it's cool to be discreet about their faggotry, to act as if it doesn't have any effect on the rest of their lives or anyone else's. We used to call that "the closet."

So, queer bashing is still necessary. (Somebody should take the "Fag Five" of *Queer Eye for the Straight Guy* out into a back alley and hospitalize them for promoting the image of gays as materialistic breeder-lovers.) But how about a little straight bashing, too? I think *everyone* needs a good beating. Uncle Tom fags need it. Straight-acting fags and straights alike need it. Bash them all. Anyone who is complicit in the user-friendly fag trend should have their knees broken. The only people I don't feel like bashing lately are mincing queens and actual fag bashers.

The next time you see a hetero couple holding hands, run over and yell, "Herpes-carrying breeder" at them and punch them in the nose. You'll feel better for it. Join the homosexual intifada. ∎

AMY SEDARIS

FRANKLY SPEAKING

Fuck Sex

Photo by Pegah Farahmand

When I was 11 years old, I was alone in the house when the phone rang. It was a stranger's voice, an adult man. He said he could see me through the window. He asked me how old I was and what was going on. Then he told me to go to the refrigerator, get out a hot dog, and "stick it in [your] vagina."

"OK," I said, and opened the refrigerator up. The only hot dogs we had were frozen solid. I tried to get one up "there" for a while, but it wasn't happening. The caller asked if we had a dog, because after I inserted the frankfurter, he then wanted me to get our pet to eat it from my crotch.

I could hear electrical noises in the background of wherever he was, like what a computer back then would sound like—it was like something out of *Logan's Run*. He said that he was taking a poll. I never found out who he was.

That's one of my earliest memories involving sex. Now, I don't ever talk about sex, because then the person I'm talking to would have to put me in their head doing it. And when somebody else talks about it, then I have to picture them doing it. Usually sex doesn't even enter my mind. Three years or so ago, something clicked, and sex just went away. It isn't that I'm grossed out by it. I just don't want anything to do with it. It would be OK if I never have sex again.

Plus, I really like living by myself. I was just watching these old anti-drug school movies from the 70s, things like *The Ten Signs of Alcoholism*. There's this lady drinking in one, and her husband busts in the kitchen screaming, "What are you doing?!?" And I was like, "See, that's why you don't want to live with anybody." So it taught me to not get married, as opposed to teaching me to not drink.

I'm into the traditional gender roles. I think my ideal man would be someone I meet in a hardware store. And when male friends tell me about their girlfriends, and these women don't even know how to pan-fry a steak or pack their boyfriend's lunch, I'm like, "That's ridiculous."

I guess I'm more into hearing about sex crimes than sex anyway. I recently read this old book called *Sex Crimes*. It's by Alice Vachess. Most of the people who pull off sex crimes are men, so maybe it's their dicks that drive them crazy. If I had a dick for a day, I wouldn't want to go out and rape a bunch of women or have sex with animals. I think I would just try tucking it between my legs to see what it would be like to have a vagina. ■

VICE STAFF

ENOUGH ALREADY

Whatevs. Slang is Totes Stoops in Charge

Video still by Beagle. This is it: the absolute greatest "stoops" usage of all time.
Neck Face has brought stoops to the pinnacle of its existence and now no one can use it anymore. It's done.

When the *New York Times* ran a whimsical article by a mom who was befuddled by her teenage daughter's constant abbreviation of words, we got nervous. But when we saw *New York* magazine or some other shit rag like that (we forget which one, honestly) use the word "stoops" in their film reviews, we knew it was over. Then when we saw a Volkswagen commercial that called their new car the "V-Dub," we knew it was over, nuked, burnt, ruined, and had AIDS.

Slang just isn't cute anymore. It makes us feel like how we feel when our moms say "awesome." Moms shouldn't say "awesome." Moms should say, "That's nice, dear." In fact, everyone should say, "That's nice, dear." It's a pleasant thing to say and to hear. So take all your "gnarls" and your "probs" and lay them gently to rest next to "as if" and "NOT!" They are now part of slang history. PS: We are allowed to call a moratorium on these words and phrases because we broke them in the media. Either us or one of our friends started all this stoopsy, gnarlsy, in charge-y, totes-y shit. So, you're welcome. And we're sorry. Both, at the same time.

We are especially sick of abbreviations. You know what abbreviations are? LAZINESS. And laziness leads to forgetfulness, which leads to idiocy, and idiots are the only people who abbreviate words. It's like a snake eating its own tail and then puking it up and eating the puke. Just learn how to spell "definitely." It's not that hard after the 20th time.

So, to be clear, here's what's out: whatevs, 'tevs, gnarls, defs, probs, stoops, totes. Adding "-wise," "status," "much?" or "in charge" to the ends of words. Calling things "tight." Or "sick." "Redonks" or "ridics." Any variation of the word "delicious" and anything you ripped off from Epicly Later'd. We're sad to say that "riffing" has to go too. Although let's say something happens where a joke is passed on from friend to friend and you call it a "riffle effect"—that's clever. Clever is good. We encourage creativity with language. Puns are still OK. Making up your own in-joke words with your friends is great—using other people's is lame.

Here's what's still acceptable: Spelling words phonetically for comedy's sake can be used in moderation. "Sowwie" is good because it conveys a cuteness that a simple "sorry" cannot. "Kewl" is enjoying a resurgence, and we're OK with that. "Noice" is one that isn't annoying yet (wait... NOW it is), and for some reason we think spelling words like we're Scottish is hilarious. It cannae get old.

Acronyms like BTW and WTF are useful in writing but should never, ever be uttered aloud.

And finally, "douche chills" has become an indispensable phrase. We can't let it go because there's nothing else like it. What are you going to say instead, "Boy, that naked hula-hoop guy sure is... gross"? Just doesn't have the same zing. So douche chills stays. But that's it. ■

COMPILED BY VICE STAFF

A NIGHTMARE ON ME STREET

Six Hypnagogic Hallucinations and One Guy Who Peed on His Gran

Hypnagogia: It's the phenomenon of experiencing very real and quite often terrifying dreamlike sensations while falling asleep or waking up. The horrible thing about this is that it goes hand in hand with sleep paralysis, meaning you are trapped and unable to move while having the worst time of your life. Also horrible is that you think you're awake while the scary stuff is happening to you. In fact, Wes Craven based the whole idea of *A Nightmare on Elm Street* on it.

Sufferers of hypnagogia, or "the wide-awake nightmare," often complain of having dark figures standing over them, of visitations by aliens, or of feeling somebody pushing down on their chest while they lie paralyzed, unable to wake up until they finally force out a terrified scream that sounds like "Wuh wuh WUH WUH WAAAAAAGHHOOOOOFFF!!!"

We spoke to seven regular hypnagogia sufferers and this is what they told us. We're praying that this condition is not contagious, the way nightmares sometimes are, because if it is, we—not to mention our roommates and loved ones—are all now totally fucked.

PORTAL TO THE DEAD

About five years ago I was drinking heavily and doing about two grams of cocaine a night. My substance-abuse problems really took off at about the same time my aunt and my grandmother passed away in front of my eyes in close proximity.

Early one morning I got home from partying all night, drinking whiskey, and doing cocaine. I'd passed out in all my clothes on my bed (again) and was woken at 8 AM by the light coming through the crack in the curtains in my room. I remember not being able to move and hearing a voice outside my bedroom door asking me if I wanted a cup of tea. To my horror, it was my dead grandmother's voice, and at that moment of realization, my nose was filled with the smell of her house, a mixture of Mr. Sheen polish and boiled cabbage. Things got worse when my door handle started going up and down and Grandma started barging into the door, making it rattle against the frame. I was totally paralyzed. It was like

the end scene of *Suspiria*, when Suzy Bannion's dead best friend walks through the door in the head witch's bedroom. It was like a portal of the dead was opening into my room and it was really fucking scary. I remember breathing about three breaths a second and feeling extremely cold. Then, to top it all off, an invisible hand started to scrawl the word "PIG" in blood on my bedroom wall.

This set me off and I let out a bloodcurdling scream. I woke trembling and covered in sweat. I hope the neighbors didn't hear it. After that I resolved to put the blow aside for at least three days. —ANDY CAPPER

NOSEBLEEDING INDIAN

I've always been fascinated by the topic of sleep paralysis. The last time it happened I was awake in my bed but totally unable to move. I saw a guy with his face painted. He

Illustrations by J. Penry

looked kind of like a Native American with a headdress. I was paralyzed in my bed and he was standing over me. The more I looked at him, the more the red paint on his face appeared to be turning into blood. It was pretty scary.

When I finally forced myself to wake up I saw that my nose was bleeding. —KEVIN FIELDS

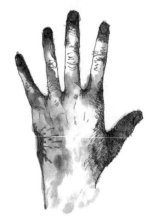

CANCER FUNERAL

Two years ago this girl from my hometown died of cancer. I wasn't around for the funeral, but apparently it was incredibly disturbing—her mother broke down as the girl's coffin was lowered into the grave, her father was literally tearing his clothes in grief, and her two older brothers were in hysterics.

Hearing about it, I began to feel incredibly guilty about not going to the funeral, not calling the girl in her final days, not having done anything to help the family. For days I would replay what I imagined the funeral to be like, until one afternoon I guess I became emotionally and physically exhausted. It was around 4 PM, and suddenly, replaying the funeral once again, I had to lie down. I began to think of the funeral again, but for some reason it was much, much more real, and the scene that played out was somehow above me, as if I were in the bottom of the grave. Above, I could see my mother going berserk as she looked down at me and I could hear the distinct wail of my father as he broke down in grief. "This is fucking ridiculous, I'm not dead, that girl is," I thought, but my incredulity at the situation quickly turned to panic, since I couldn't remove myself from the grave. I kept on trying to get their attention, but they were too busy freaking out to notice me. I tried to alert them for what seemed like hours but it was totally useless, and finally I began to cry out of frustration. When I felt a tear on my cheek I suddenly snapped out of it and was back in my room. —CINDY McCULLOUGH

I TRIED TO EAT MY GIRLFRIEND

I suffer from sleep terrors. It's a more physical version of nightmares where you act out what you are dreaming. Apparently it's caused by anxiety. There have been cases of people committing stabbings and murders in their sleep. It gets pretty extreme.

Personally I have always suffered from horrible nightmares. When I was little I used to wake up in odd places around the house, shaking, with my heart beating out of my chest. Once I pulled a stack of shelves off my wall in my sleep. I woke up with a TV and a stereo system on top of me. Another time I woke up screaming next to my open window. I've gotten wiser, though. Now before I go to sleep I make sure all windows are locked and there are no scissors or sharp objects around.

The worst experience I ever had happened about a year ago. I was asleep next to my girlfriend and I was dreaming that something was attacking me. When I woke up I had her hand in my mouth and blood all over my face. I had bitten her in my sleep and taken a huge chunk out of her hand. It was so horrible. It's weird, but in my dream I thought I was saving her. —DORAN EDWARDS

I PEED ON MY GRAN'S HEAD

I went back to my hometown and stayed at my grandmother's house for a couple of days. One night I went to a local bar with some old friends and got really drunk. Somehow

I staggered back to my gran's house and went to bed.

In the morning, all bleary-eyed, I got up and started eating breakfast. As I was doing this I noticed my grandma dragging her wet mattress out to the balcony to dry. She was silently fuming and refused to talk to me. Finally, after an hour of me asking her what was wrong, she started crying and asked me, "Are you proud of yourself?"

I had no idea what she was talking about. She proceeded to tell me that I had gotten up in the middle of the night, stumbled into her bedroom, unzipped, and started pissing on her bed while she was sleeping in it. With my pee raining down on her, she shouted at me to stop, but I screamed back at her, telling her to fuck off, and then toddled off to bed. —DARREN COUPON

PSYCHOPATHIC ROOMMATE

In my freshman year of college I shared a room with a small, muscled Indian kid named Jay. The day we moved in he hung a massive framed poster of a football player's backside covered in mud, with the words: "Winners Never Quit, Quitters Never Win: NEVER QUIT."

We were both weirded out by each other, but whereas his discomfort with me was based primarily on my cleanliness and taste in music, I was genuinely convinced that he was going to kill me. It was totally arbitrary and stupid, but as the weeks progressed I started attending an "everyday self-defense course" and sleeping with a knife underneath my pillow.

The height of my paranoia was nicely realized one morning when I woke up to find myself paralyzed. I was lying flat on my back staring up at the ceiling and could move nothing but my neck side to side. My roommate was standing over me with this sick little smile on his face, and immediately I was engulfed by a white, urgent terror. He floated closer and closer to me at a painstakingly slow pace. All I wanted to do was get to the knife under my pillow, but as much as I strained I couldn't even lift a finger. I tried to scream for help but the only sound that came out was a low gurgle, and he just kept on moving closer.

Finally our faces were so close that I couldn't focus on his eyes anymore, but with a sudden burst of adrenaline I snapped out of my paralysis, and that was when I woke up to find myself covered in sweat, holding a knife, and screaming my roommate's name.

After that, my taste in Wagner became less of an issue and my "undiagnosed but undeniably psychotic behavior," as he called it in his formal complaint to the housing board, came to the fore. He moved out one week later. —JAMES TARMY

SONIC HEART ATTACK

The last episode of sleep paralysis I had was one of the scariest moments in my life. I remember I had gone to bed really late and was woken up by a high-pitched screaming noise followed by a pain in my chest. All I could hear was an unbearable sharp screaming sound like the one when you've stood too close to the amps without earplugs at a concert. I was paralyzed and surrounded by darkness except for this kind of bright energy field that sucked all the force out of me. I felt weaker and weaker, and I tried to scream but no sound came out. I couldn't move. I was terrified, and the more frightened I got, the weaker I felt and the less I could move.

Since I'd been through it before I knew that freaking out would only make things worse, so I tried to calm down. I was completely conscious and I didn't allow it to scare me, I stayed calm. With a huge effort I managed to crawl out of my bed. There was a resistance forcing me back and I tried to scream, but there was still nothing. I tried to get to the door handle, but I couldn't reach it. I gathered my last strength and went for it again. I opened the door and the whole thing just stopped.

I awoke in my bed. My head felt heavy, my arm was asleep, and I was gasping for air. The following day I was still weak with a strange sensation in my chest. I think that the scariest thing about sleep paralysis is that you have NO idea what's happening to you, you have no point of reference for what you're going through. It's like a supernatural experience. —MARY MURPHY ∎

FATTY ARBUCKLE SANDWICH

CHAIR PARTY

Illustration by Al Jaffee

This month it was decided that everyone had to be wasted. All editorial meetings were conducted drunk, in bars, and every writer was told he or she needs to have at least a bit of a buzz going while writing. I personally have had about three king cans of Budweiser and my instructions were simply, "Write an intro to the Party Issue that sums it all up."

I'll tell you what's going through my head right now. I really want to go flying backward off this chair. I don't know why. It's a compulsion I always have after a few pints. Do you ever feel like that in bars? Just winging backward, especially with bar stools. Those things are so tall it's like you're pole-vaulting across the bar.

OK, so here's what I'm going to do. I'm going to try it right now. I'm in my kitchen and it has tile floors so this could be bad, but here we go.

TRY #1

Not so eventful. I kind of pussied out, to be honest. I put my elbows down like a little fag and now they hurt like shit. I'm scared of knocking myself out and none of my roommates noticing until the morning that I died. For Try #2 I'm going to take this chair to the living room (wood floors) no matter who it wakes up. I will also be bringing my beer. Wish me luck!

TRY #2

I'm back. I went flying backward off my chair and it felt great. I did a backwards somersault thing and SPILLED APPROXIMATELY ZERO PERCENT OF MY FUCKING BEER. I have to say my shoulder feels a bit wonky but it's not bad. I think this compulsion drinkers have to fly off their chairs has to do with how we feel impervious to danger. I guess that's why so many teenagers die in drunk driving accidents. Sad. For my next try I am going to really fucking give 'er (again, I'm going to go back to the living room).

TRY #3

Woke up my roommate Karen. I told her about my experiment and she rolled her eyes because she is a lonely cunt who hasn't been laid in over two years. She bought a dog to help her deal with the loneliness but everyone in the house agrees that the dog is a crutch and she is never going to meet anyone if she keeps up this prude bitch attitude. Er, you have to GO OUT to meet people, Karen!

My back fucking kills right now. Right in the fleshy part above my hip (right side). I'd like to get that *Mad* magazine guy to create an invention where it wouldn't hurt to go flying off your chair. Like an *Are You There God? It's Me, Margaret* back brace or something. ■

PATTON OSWALT

GOVERNMENT EMPLOYEES ARE EVIL TROLLS WHO LIVE ABOVE BRIDGES, UNDER THE SUN

They're out there, but not in the darkness. Their lairs are well lit, under the rude, barging glare of fluorescent tube lights. Their skin is pasty gray, almost the same color as their cubicle walls. They've conditioned their bodies to run efficiently on starches, salts, corn syrup, and coffee that tastes like sad crayons. At least four of their weekly meals involve either:

- pouring hot water on a brick of something dry and shrimp-flavored in order to make it soft and shrimp-flavored,
- cutting a slit in a plastic cover to vent an oblong of purple-brown frozen meat and gravy, or
- eating a salad because they're starting another diet.

They scare the shining, singing shit out of me.

"When you submit a Schedule C tax return, it gets flagged," said a friend of mine who, through two minor wrong turns, had ended up a tax attorney.

This was when I made $11,000 a year as a self-employed individual.

"Not someone like me. I mean, I make dogshit."

"No, you get it extra bad. They're probably starting a file on you."

"What the fuck am I doing? I'm at the poverty level and I'm trying to pay taxes. It's not like I'm an outlaw or something."

"They hate you. IRS employees, government drones. These people never had the balls to do what you're doing, and they resent you. They resent any small-business owner, any entrepreneur—anyone outside of a cubicle is the enemy."

I've never forgotten that conversation. He was right, too. The A+ go-getters do NOT work for the government. They flee to the private sector where the gold-plated sirloin is. The dull, timid, and mediocre watch our borders, tap their fingers on LAUNCH buttons, go through our taxes, and listen to our phone conversations while grinding their molars with boredom. That's why I don't believe in conspiracy theories. None. Not a single one. Oswald shot Kennedy. Man really walked on the moon. Bin Laden took down the towers. *The Wizard of Oz* does not sync up with *Dark Side of the Moon*. (*Georgia Rule*, however, syncs up perfectly with *Metal Machine Music*.)

The ultimate horror, to me, is not that our money, weapons, records, and information network are being overseen by the mediocre. It is that they're being tended to by the resentful.

How much can they take? How much indifference from the universe, as they sweat recirculated moisture in short-sleeved TJ Maxx dress shirts? How much disregard for motion, adventure, and fulfillment, as they sit quietly in their townhomes, leafing through old yearbooks at night? How many times can they watch some equally faceless schlub they remember from high school blossom into an artist, a world traveler, an athlete, or an adventurer, while they tak-tak-tak their initials onto his tax return?

Are they forming a society, the resentful? While we're out late at some bar or laughing ironically at a Steven Seagal movie, are they organizing? Not an underground—an aboveground. While we sleep 'til noon or make our own hours—and let's face it, this is you—are they hatching plots? Between the hours of 7 and 10 AM, what happens?

What sort of plot are they hatching? you ask. Aren't you sounding like a conspiracy theorist? you say.

Maybe. Or maybe this is an anticonspiracy, being set in motion by the fluorescent-lit and Bennigan's-drunk. A virus of dullness, to be unleashed on the Schedule Cs of the world. The resentful do not want to be Awesome. They want Awesome annihilated. They take the same comfort that the down-and-out and hopeless took in the idea of nuclear Armageddon in the 60s. Being fused into the same cinders as the rich and beautiful in one brief flash was a wonderful equalizer. And for the resentful, knowing they can make a Life of Awesome nothing but hassle and tax liens and canceled credit cards and lost plane tickets must promise the same stinging, clammy comfort.

If it happens, it will happen slowly. Petty paybacks will snowball into blazing vengeance, hobbling the Awesome and forcing them to take cubicle jobs to put instant coffee in the pantry and Lean Cuisines in the freezer. And as the Hobbled gaze with shattered eyes into the cubicles next to theirs, they'll have their haunted looks returned by equally shattered and hopeless wage slaves, albeit ones with the faintest squiggle of a smile on their lips. Those lips will part and exhale powdered-shrimp fumes and say, "Same shit, different day, huh?"

That's their werewolf howl. Their ghost chains. Their witch's cackle. "Same shit, different day, huh?" It's going to be written on the tombstone of the 21st century. Right next to "Nothing you can do but pray" and "Life is short." The resentful. They are clawing their way downward from the sunlight into our shadowy night world. They're installing fluorescents and bringing office coffee. And sealing us in coffin offices. Coffices.

I fear the resentful. ■

V13N3, MARCH 2006

FRED ARMISEN

ILLEGALIZE IT!

My Least Fave Foods

Apples should be illegal. What a terrible food. They never satisfy your hunger and they make way too much noise. Have you ever heard someone bite into an apple? It's disgusting. It sounds like a tree is falling inside someone's skull. Also, people look smug when they eat an apple. Like, "Ah, you know. Just eatin' an apple, doin' normal stuff. Readin' the paper." Gross. Stop eating apples. It is a pointless food.

Mangoes should be illegal. Have you ever tried to eat one? You have to cut the skin off with a knife and that takes forever and there's this huge pit... just way too much work for such a little amount of food that doesn't even taste that great.

Melons should be illegal. Every kind. They are sticky and messy and people get way too happy about them when they are part of a breakfast buffet. This is them: "Oooh, melons!" This is me, but in a mocking tone: "Oooh, melons!"

Pears should be illegal. They are like apples but more bland. By the way, if you have a craving for fruit, eat chocolate instead! Avocados should be illegal. I know everybody loves guacamole but I am sorry. I just don't like the way it tastes. Also, something bums me out about seeing the black avocado carcass with all that green pasty stuff in someone's garbage.

Then there's walnuts. Cracking them is a joke. You need a special tool to open it and that alone is irritating. Any food that you need a special tool for should be illegal. But really, walnuts ruin everything. They taste awful. They don't belong in brownies or cookies or ice cream or anything at all. "Do these brownies have walnuts?" "Yes." "OK, just the coffee then."

Sangria. Is it a drink or is it food? Pieces of fruit crammed into a glass of wine. So silly. We have to make a law against this. It's not civilized to tilt and shake a wineglass so that some soggy piece of fruit can plop into your mouth. Drink wine or eat dessert, make up your mind.

Cookies dipped in milk. Oh my God EEEEEEWWWW! Is there anything more horrible? Why would anyone do this? The cookie gets all wet and mushy and there are crumbs floating in the milk. Just... it makes me want to puke. Cookies are a gift to humanity. Keep all foods and drinks separate.

Lobster. I will agree that lobster is delicious, but this business with the bib and the pliers and the tiny fork? I just don't have the time or the patience. It's too much of an event. I suppose there could be some kind of exemption for serving lobster if it's in a sandwich or something, but otherwise it should be illegal.

I realize that it may be difficult to enforce these food laws, but it would make me so much happier. Thank you, and I'm sorry if some of these foods were your favorites! ■

The author, bummed.

XII

BODILY FLUIDS
& FUNCTIONS

Photo by Naomi Fisher, V15N7, July 2008

BIG BOBBY WINSLOW

HOME SURGERY PARTY

How to Operate on Your Guests

Photos by Vito Fun and Josh Benjamin

Doctors are boring. They don't have borders, true, but they also don't have any fucking clue what is going on. Doctors Without Remedies, they ought to be called. Who are they anyway? Do they just make up this shit? Like, take that hammer thing they do when they hit you on the knee and say, "Good reflexes." Did you know that exercise is total and utter horseshit? Try it out on a decathlon runner and then try it on a terminal cancer patient. Notice a difference? Me neither. In fact, it seems the only thing doctors are good for these days is giving you hep C from going to visit their disease-ridden hospitals.

In short, fuck doctors and all the bullshit that comes out of their mouths. We're smarter than them and we can probably figure out half the shit they know just based on common sense, especially if the patient is shitfaced at a party.

Here, let me prove it to you. Last Saturday our man Gordon noticed a huge lump growing out of the back of his head. He could have gone to the doctor and had hours of bullshit tests and this and that and that and this, or he could just have us figure it out ourselves. After about 13 beers we decided on the latter. Let's do dis.

PATIENT'S AILMENT: Huge thing in back of head. Feels like there is something in there.

DIAGNOSIS: Get it out of head.

TOOLS: Aspirin, razor blade, frying pan, iodine, cotton balls, paper towels, ice... and tons of booze

TREATMENT: Sterilize equipment and then cut the fucking thing out of his head. Tell it never to come back again.

PREPARATION

1. As we boiled the razor we were thinking to ourselves, "This is probably bullshit. What's on there that needs to be boiled off, tar?" We did it anyway, however, and would only let the surgeon (nobody else) touch it after it cooled down.

2. The surgeon was forced to wash his hands extra carefully. He had been up late the night before burning himself with cigarettes on a dare, and that means a lot of open sores that can carry germs.

3. Thankfully, the patient was able to isolate the cyst with his fingers. This helped our surgeon because he could now get a grip on exactly how much shit was in there. Will it be one hard ball? Will it be a bunch of chunky garbage? Who knows? The point is, that thing does not look like it belongs in there so it will need to be cut out.

4. OK, this is the gross part. The patient has doused his head in iodine and some other white shit we forgot the name of. He has also chugged several beers and

taken four aspirin. This means his blood is very thin and is about to be all over the fucking place. At tattoo parlors you get in shit for that, but not here. Are we going to complain about a bit of extra blood? Does the mailman complain when it rains? The home surgeon's motto is, "Through blood and booze and sleet and snow, we will cut shit out of your head." Anyway, we got in there real carefully by making slow incisions to the cyst, back and forth, back and forth, until a vagina-shaped gash appeared in the center of the lump.

5. Once the hole was big enough, our surgeon was able to work the junk out of the bump. It had a rubbery texture like if someone had chewed up an eraser. After a bit of squeezing and massaging we were able to remove 100% of the cyst. It was at this time we decided it was either a calcium deposit or a cancerous brain tumor. It was definitely not botfly larvae as one person had suggested.

6. We decided to put some more iodine on the wound because it was bleeding like crazy and that was kind of freaking us out.

7. Unlike most hospitals, our surgeon allowed the patient to play with his discharge immediately after the operation. The patient was very intrigued by the stuff and asked, "Are you sure you got it all out?" to which our surgeon replied, "Yeah, I'm pretty sure. I kept working it and working it, and by the end it was just big blobs of blood."

8. After the patient became comfortable with his removed cyst he decided to eat it. There are probably amazing amounts of protein in that thing, and even if it's toxic, his stomach acid will be able to break it down. This had a gross-out factor of approximately 10.

9. Patient care involved no antibiotics and no Polysporin bullshit. It was determined that all pills do is weaken the patient's immunity and all creams do is suffocate the wound. The patient was put on a strict regimen of soap and water, which he followed religiously.

10. A week later, the wound had healed. It looked not unlike a mouth and seemed to be begging for a cartoon face to be drawn on. So we did.

The patient claims his home surgery experience was "fun" and he has had no complications since. NEXT! ■

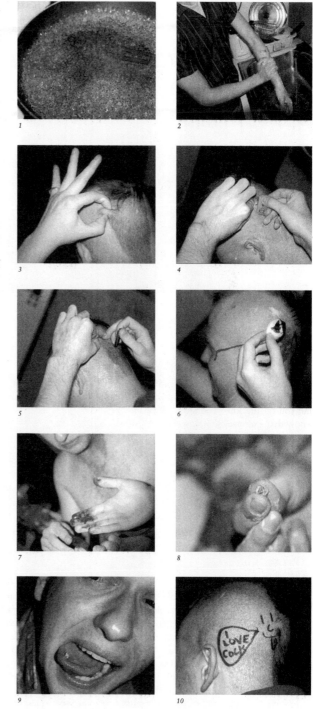

ANGEL NELFI

CUM VS. MOISTURIZER

Vice Settles the Score!

Before　　　　　　*After*

People have been telling me that cum gets rid of zits since I was sixteen years old. I remember my best friend Caroline saying, "It works. Look at me, I always get it on my face and I don't have any zits." She also insisted that if she didn't have a boyfriend after a while she would break out. The verdict was that swallowing it was pretty good but nothing got rid of zits like getting it on your face. After years of standing by said rules I have decided to rent a tractor trailer and call a big, gigantic, heaping, six-thousand-million ton pile of bullshit on that school of thought. To prove it, my good friends Nick and Lisa put cum on one side of their face and moisturizer on the other FOR AN ENTIRE MONTH. That's right, every day Nick would summon some jizz and Lisa's live-in boyfriend would do the same and they would both apply, compare, and contrast. At the end of every week they would take a Polaroid of the progress and summarize the differences between both cheeks. The verdict? You can't see cum in Polaroids.

NICK
24 YEARS OLD, NEW YORK

WEEK ONE, JULY 1–JULY 8, 2003:
CUM CHEEK: The cum is making it feel tighter than the other side. Like it's contracting. It doesn't feel any smoother, though.
MOISTURIZER CHEEK: My usual moisturizer always leaves me a little greasy, and that's more pronounced when the other cheek has cum on it.

WEEK TWO, JULY 9–JULY 16, 2003:
CUM CHEEK: My skin is so sensitive that I thought my cheek would totally freak out, but I think that the cum is shielding me from all the gross New York dirt. It feels… I don't know, solid?
MOISTURIZER CHEEK: Like I said, my skin is really tender so I use this super wimpy skin cream. I started to rub a little more of it in this week because compared to the cum, it seemed totally ineffectual. It feels like I'm getting a pimple now.

WEEK THREE, JULY 17–JULY 24, 2003:
CUM CHEEK: I swear to god, I feel like Iron Man over there. Cum isn't porous like lotion, you know? It's like a protein mask. I'll bet you could take a jackhammer to that cheek and I could just whistle the theme to *Andy Griffith* no problem.
MOISTURIZER CHEEK: This face cream smells like my granddad's idea of the future, but it isn't really working on my face. It's so slimy that I have to wash the excess off. I can't rub it all in!

WEEK FOUR—FINAL WEEK, JULY 25–AUGUST 1, 2003:
CUM CHEEK: This has been intense. I don't think I'm going to keep it up every day, but I will use cum at least once a week on my face now. The best thing about this is that I have decided that everyone should masturbate twice a day. I really think that the world would be a better place.
MOISTURIZER CHEEK: Moisturizer is over for me. I think it's a total scam. Compared to the results I got from using my own semen, it is child's play. I'm so into fluid-recycling now that I'm starting to take those guys who drink their own piss seriously.

VERDICT: You shouldn't put any kind of cream on your face. I think that thing about cum being good for your skin is a myth straight men made up so women would suck their dicks more often. The store-bought cream gave me a zit and the man-made cream was just a pain in the ass. If I had to choose a winner I'd say the cum won by a very slim margin.

LISA
29 YEARS OLD, LONDON

WEEK ONE, JULY 1–JULY 8, 2003:
CUM CHEEK: First off, it's weird to stand in front of the mirror in the morning and rub a load into your cheek, and it feels strange going out with cum on my face. The cum side feels kind of strained, like the way you feel when you've been in salt water for too long. It does seem really soft, though.
MOISTURIZER CHEEK: I am very brand-loyal. I've been using the same cream since university. The smell is really comforting to me, and I am complimented all the time on how smooth my skin is. I am not thrilled about my other cheek doing without this stuff for a month.

WEEK TWO, JULY 9–JULY 16, 2003:
CUM CHEEK: The cum cheek feels tighter, but very dry. It isn't pleasant. I'm constantly wondering whether someone can tell if I have cum all over my face, too. I've taken to using more perfume just cuz I feel like I smell of spunk.
MOISTURIZER CHEEK: As good as always. I have taken to using a bit less each time I apply it. I wonder if that's because it feels so much cleaner relative to the cum.

WEEK THREE, JULY 17–JULY 24, 2003:
CUM CHEEK: I thought very seriously about giving up on the experiment this week. The cum is wreaking havoc on my face. I have never had dry skin before, and now it is flaking off in alarming amounts.
MOISTURIZER CHEEK: Perfectly smooth. It's like the little baby that gets pampered while the teenage kid gets ignored.

WEEK FOUR—FINAL WEEK, JULY 25–AUGUST 1, 2003:
CUM CHEEK: I have no doubt that I will never let cum touch my face again. It created a glaze on my cheek, then a rough patch of dead skin. I hope it doesn't take too long to get it back to normal.
MOISTURIZER CHEEK: Do you have to ask? I now feel like sleeping with a tube of this stuff next to me for the rest of my life.

VERDICT: Cum is not good for your skin. Maybe swallowing it, but that's another experiment entirely. I would say the face cream wins hands down! ∎

MARIE-ELAINE GUAY

BULIMI-ANIA!

I Spent a Week Barfing

Photo by some guy the author knows

Bulimia's fucked up. I just spent a week doing it to see what it's like, and I don't understand how those bitches survive.

For seven days, I felt like I was a second away from fainting, and I mostly did eating-disorder-related activities such as lying in bed and complaining, calling my friends to talk about how fat I am, and shitting out cancerous-looking substances.

Let me walk you through my week…

DAY ONE

It's my first day with *bulimia nervosa*. I wake up early and run to the gym. I starve myself all day. I can't watch TV— all the ads are making me hungry. It's cold out, so I stay home and chew gum and read grocery-store fliers.

At around 7:30 PM, I speed-walk to the nearest grocery store. I buy a thing of Reese's ice cream and five chocolate bars. I feel like everyone knows I have an eating disorder, even though it's all in my head. No one gives a shit what I buy.

I am barely back in my door before my entire face is stuffed with chocolate. I walk in, get in bed, and eat the ice cream with a makeshift chocolate-bar spoon. I eat the whole tub.

Thirty minutes later, I'm bent over the toilet with my right hand shoved down my throat. It will not work! Then I remember a show where this bulimic puked herself with a spatula, so I shove my roommate's toothbrush down my throat and jiggle it around back there and then BRRRRRRRRRAAAAAAAAAWWWWW the entire universe blows out of me. Or at least a bunch of chocolate does.

Then I feel sick, like flu-sick. I drink some water and feel better. It's incredible—I do feel thin, and still full. Bulimia works!

I congratulate myself and don't flush. Looking at the mixture feels great. I DID IT.

DAY TWO

Today I'm only eating popcorn. At work I scarf down popcorn during my breaks. I even hide some in my jacket pockets just in case.

My stomach is still totally fucked from last night. I try not to puke, but it's hard. The day at work goes slowly and all I can think about is my weight.

When I get home I'm starving. I order four extra-large pizzas. I actually yell out, "Is everybody OK with that?" so the pizza guy doesn't think I'm a fat cunt—which I am. It gets here and I practically inhale it. I don't even taste what I'm eating. I barely chew, I just swallow. Then I go and visit my new best friend, the toilet.

This time it is a lot worse. The pizza comes out in little chewed-up balls and the sauce burns my throat. I get this tear at the corner of my mouth and the acid from my puke burns it every time. Also, I can feel the pizza moving up my sinuses and into my nose in what feel like rock-size blobs. I want to stop, but I can tell there's at least a whole pizza still in there. I tell myself I can't stop until I puke 20 more times. I do the countdown, only counting pukes where puke comes out. A lot of them are dry. When I get to 20, I can tell there's still some stuff in there, but after vomiting so violently I'm spent. I feel dead. I actually fall asleep for a second in the bathroom. That night I dream about KFC.

DAY THREE

I skip breakfast. I feel like shit. I get drunk on gin and tonics at a local bar, where I drink all afternoon. I worry about the calories in tonic and think about making myself puke. Later on, I meet up with some friends and make sure to get even more inebriated. Then, around 2 AM, I go to the bathroom and puke. It feels great. My stomach is getting used to this. Plus nobody approaches me all night since my face is pallid and swollen, my lips are Dracula red, I've got this weird tremor in my neck, and my breath smells like vomit.

DAY FOUR

I get to work and make sure I get on my lunch break before everybody else. I open the fridge in the break room, steal three lunches, and hide in the bathroom. I choke down the contents of a Tupperware filled with cold spaghetti. I throw the carrots out. Then I eat a ham sandwich and a half-frozen piece of chicken breast. The weird thing is that I basically am a bulimic in this moment: I can't stop myself once I get started. I numb out and the whole binge is a blur.

It takes a few hours for the reality of what I have done to sink in. I am filled with a sense of remorse that only gets worse when the three people whose lunches I ate start looking for the prick who stole their food.

But what choice do I have now? I tickle my oropharynx, gag reflex ensues, and the evidence is gone. The ham sandwich gets caught in these gobs of hard, impacted white dough that are extremely painful to get out. Imagine one of those gigantic shits where it feels like you are tearing yourself. It seriously hurts, and afterward, I have all these little red freckles around my eyes. Still though, it is a good day for me: I defied authority, I didn't spend any money on food, and I puked.

DAY FIVE

Normal day, normal meals, no puking. I have the world's biggest eye infection, which means I am wearing a patch, no kidding. I go to the clinic and the doctor says this whole experiment could cause lesions in my stomach if the secreted amount of acid stays higher than the level of average digestive juices. I barely know what that means, so I don't think about it. I stay in bed and watch TV. I try to eat soup; I fail. I'm an awful person. I can't accomplish anything.

DAY SIX

I wake up with serious nausea. I bend over to grab my cellphone and puke in my mouth. I think I forgot to mention how easy it is for me to puke now. I just have to firmly contract my diaphragm, and I puke up some stuff. I barely eat all day—I just puke and puke and puke. My entire life is ejected. I vomit feelings, stress, bad bands I used to like, the entire world comes out. It's really cool.

I can't go to work, I can't think, I can't even talk on the phone. I am an island called Bulimia. I fall asleep backward in my bed next to a couple of dirty bowls.

DAY SEVEN

My last day. I'm not eating today, and I probably won't even find the energy to get out of bed. I think of what will be written on my headstone: "Marie-Elaine died at age 22 because she wanted to be skinny."

Now that it's all said and done, I can tell you that bulimia is stupid. I gained six pounds in a week. I also carried the constant fear that professional bulimics would read my article and say that I wasn't doing it the right way, or that I'm an amateur and a crybaby, or whatever. But fuck that. I just can't see any of you having the energy to yell, or type—anything. In fact, all bulimics also want to have sex with their fathers. Swallow that! ∎

SARA CANTARUTTI

A LADY WHO IS A UROLOGIST

So there's this very cute Italian girl who happens to be a professional urologist, which means that she handles cocks all day, every day. From seven in the morning to seven in the evening, she checks out cocks. Let's talk to her. About cocks.

Vice: How many penises do you see each day?
Chiara: On average, I'd say about 30.

Tell me about the biggest, the smallest, and the most disgusting penises you've ever seen.
I saw the smallest just yesterday. It belonged to an incontinent 79-year-old man who had come in for a urine sample. In these cases we require a very large condom, attached to a large bag, to be secured to the penis. After several failed attempts to grab his tiny dick, the nurse came to find me in a panic. I didn't believe her. I went to go see it, and I must admit, it was pretty traumatizing. I was a bit embarrassed. It looked like a clit, or like the tip of a pinkie finger. I tried to apply a catheter but I couldn't hold on to it. It was like trying to fork an oily olive. In the end I applied a Band-Aid at the base of his penis, which allowed me to get a bit more friction between the two plastics, so that the condom wouldn't slide off. That was my first time with a micropenis. But then, now that I think about it, that wasn't the smallest. You also have retracted penises. It usually happens to the morbidly obese, who accumulate so much fat that their penises get sucked back into their bodies. When they come in for appointments, we have to grab their dicks with tweezers and pull them out. From the outside they look like belly buttons.

Oh God, I'm going to barf. Now tell me about the biggest.
That was on a 94-year-old man with a horrible disease,

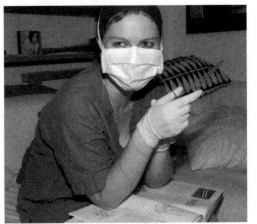

Photo by Arturo Stanig

who came in two weeks ago. It was shocking. I think it was about eight inches and he didn't even have a half-boner. He was completely soft.

What's the strangest disease you've seen?
Probably the boomerang penis. It's officially called LaPeyronie disease. Basically, fibrous plaques form on the penis' sides, making one part of the shaft harder than the rest. You can't tell when the penis isn't hard, but the moment it gets hard, it bends all the way around. In extreme cases, you can't even have sex.

Is it true that penises can break?
Of course. It generally happens when, in midthrust of a particularly forceful session, the penis doesn't enter properly. It bends in half and the muscle breaks. It shoots blood all over the place.

How do you fix it?
It's an operation they do in emergency wards. I've never seen it performed. But last month I saw a young boy who somehow skinned his penis when getting off his bike.

Fuck! You have to sometimes stick needles into dicks. What's one reason for that?
We usually do it to men who have recently had their prostates removed. It's a way for them to achieve erections, because during the operation we also have to remove the nerves that allow them to get hard. They lose all sensitivity in the area, so even Viagra can't help. So you either do several of these injections, or you install a prosthesis in the penis.

How do those work?
The simplest are commonly known as "whalebones."

They are two malleable rods that are inserted into the erection chambers. But the coolest prosthesis is the hydraulic one. Basically the two sticks in the erection chambers remain, but these are attached to a sack of liquid, which is, in turn, connected to a small pump inside the scrotum.

So the guy pumps his penis until it gets hard?
Exactly. You basically fish around for the pump inside the scrotum, and you pump it a few times until you get an erection as hard as marble. If you wait and pump it again, the liquid solution is sucked back into its sack, and the penis becomes flaccid. Many porn stars get these.

Have you ever inserted one?
Of course. But only on certain patients. We always take care of people in need. I would never do a porn star, for instance. I also operated on an impotent 24-year-old who'd never been able to have sex. He never, ever, not once in his life, had an erection.

Why would an average 25-year-old guy visit a urologist?
Usually for one of three reasons: impotence, premature ejaculation, or addiction to Cialis. Cialis is the cool cousin of Viagra. It can last up to about 48 hours. It doesn't necessarily mean that your dick is hard for 48 hours straight, but you have two days of definite erections. A lot of kids buy Cialis on the internet. It's like $10 to $20. Ten dollars for sex with rock-hard erections. Not a bad deal, right? It's cheaper than a whore. Loads of men get addicted to it.

Tell me your most insane story. The one you save for your friends at the bar.
Well, I've got one, but it didn't happen to me. It happened to a girl I know who specializes in male fertility. At the time she was treating a patient who had a tracheotomy, which means he breathed through a machine attached to his neck, and who was also paralyzed from the waist down and couldn't have erections. His wife wanted a baby really badly so the doctor said, "No problem, I'll perform a biopsy on his testicles, extract some sperm, and we'll artificially inseminate her." Unfortunately, the clinic was very Catholic and wouldn't allow it. At this point, the doctor thought, "Fuck it, I'm going to make them have sex." So he injected a vasodilator into the patient's penis to dilate his blood vessels. He waited until the man got hard and then called his wife. Then he waited outside the door, until their moans became shouts of panic and pain. He burst into the room, and he found the husband and the wife still entangled on the wheelchair. Only problem was that the patient's tracheotomy shot out of his throat, because of the strain. It had hit the wife in the face. She was partially blinded and he was blue. Suffocating. He almost died.

Good one. What's your daily routine?
Patients come in. I ask them to pull their pants down, take off their underwear, and lie on their backs. Then I touch their stomachs and try to see if there are any hernias around the pubic area. Then I ask them to cough, grab their balls and their penis, and finally I stick a finger in their butt. I do this, on average, around 30 times a day.

Do they ever get hard?
Once I treated a 32-year-old man who had problems with premature ejaculation. By the time he had lowered his pants, he was already very, very hard. I thought to myself, I can't laugh at him. So I just stared at the wall. It was almost impossible to treat him, because I kept hitting his penis with my forearm and my elbow. It was just in the way. So I told him a couple of different ways to avoid premature ejaculation and sent him home, drenched in sweat.

What type of advice did you give him?
I told him to have protected sex and to contract his perineum, just like when you try to hold your pee in. This contraction should not only be practiced during sex, but also several times a day. If it doesn't work, I advised him to try taking these new antidepression meds. They are the bastard cousins of Viagra.

What do you mean?
It's proven that patients who take these new antidepressants barely ever reach orgasms. So we started to prescribe antidepressants, since they don't have any real side effects on your mood if you're not depressed, but they help a great deal with premature ejaculation.

Do you ever have to deal with cum?
Yep. Last week an old man came in my hand. Initially I didn't understand what happened. He suffered from uretrite, which is a disease which causes a puslike secretion to drip from the tip of the penis. So I thought it was that, but then he looked me in the eyes and said, "I'm sorry."

Were you ever in the operating room during a sex change?
Unfortunately, no. I know a couple of urologists who've seen them though. It's supposed to be awesome.

What about those penis-lengthening operations. Are they bullshit?
No, I've seen it done before. We use these machines that you attach to the base of the penis; they wrap around the the glans and it basically stretches your dick. You use it regularly. It's like an exercise. ∎

JAN VAN TIENEN

A SPERM DONOR WHO HAS 46 KIDS

Photo by Boudewijn Bollmann

My friend's lesbian sister became pregnant a while ago. She found her sperm donor through one of several Dutch websites where women who want kids and guys who will donate sperm contact each other. I visited those websites and found a weird community where single women, lesbian couples, and couples in which the male is infertile can find happiness in the form of a small cup of semen and the pregnancy it leads to. But it is also a place where women will unabashedly ask for tall blond guys with blue eyes and a high level of education, where there are some obvious predators looking for sex, and where some guys with an otherwise normal family will secretly donate sperm to father as many children

as they can, influenced by a skewed reading of Darwin. On these unusual message boards, one guy's name kept appearing on my screen: Ed Houben. He posted vigorously, offering his semen to many women. And apparently, many took his offer—Ed has 46 children and six women are pregnant by him as I write this. Recently, Ed had a reunion with 16 women who used his semen to get pregnant. Several of his kids, ranging from the ages six months to four years, attended as well. In total, 30 people were there. Um, what the fuck?

Vice: How did you start donating sperm on the internet?
Ed Houben: About five years ago, I found out that

there's a big shortage of sperm donors. I've always wanted to help other people, from the moment I saw my brother's girlfriend take care of him on his deathbed. At first, I thought I could do that by getting my first-aid diploma. But helping people have kids has a bigger impact and it's such a positive thing. Nobody can take that away from me.

But still, 46 kids is a bit much, isn't it?
Well, it is, but I would quit immediately if there wasn't a shortage of donors. People sometimes think I'm a weird guy for having so many kids, but I see it as helping others out. I don't have selfish motives, other than the good feeling it gives me to see other people happy.

So how does it go? You post a message, you meet, have the sex, and bang—pregnancy?
No. When I make contact with women on the internet, I always have email conversations with them before I even plan anything. That way, I can get a feel for what they're like, and whether they'll make a good parent or not. Then, if the woman and I have a good feeling about it, I'll make an appointment. I used to travel all over Holland, Belgium, and sometimes even Germany to donate, but now I ask people to come to the city I live in, Maastricht. Then they book a hotel. I would invite those people to my house, but I'll wait until my mother moves out of my place to the retirement home. When those people check into the hotel, I stop by and withdraw myself to the toilet to masturbate. There's no sex involved. When I'm done, I usually sit and wait until the woman is done inseminating herself and then I leave. We repeat this process until the woman is pregnant. After that, we sometimes keep in touch, or I hear nothing from them ever again. It depends on what the mother wants. The only thing I don't do is accept parental responsibilities. I'm clear about that up front.

If you have 46 kids now and six are on their way, it must cost you a lot of time.
The time it costs me varies from week to week. It depends on the ovulation of the woman. That doesn't happen in set intervals, and because the semen has to be inserted before the ovulation, I can be called upon at any time of the month. A couple of weeks ago, I had to inseminate five women in one weekend. One on Friday, two on Saturday, and one on Sunday and Monday. Of those five, two became pregnant.

You're a pretty fertile guy then. What kind of measures do you go through to keep your sperm of high quality?
I never wear jeans or tight pants. The scrotum must hang cool at all times. I never take a hot bath or a sauna.

Besides that, I rarely ever drink and I regularly take folic acid tablets and fish oil caps. But the average fertile man doesn't really need all of that. A friend of mine told me he heard the strangest yell ever when he was riding his horse. Through some bizarre accident, a rider behind him had managed to entangle his left nut in a piece of rope, and his sack tore off. Now that would really fuck up your fertility.

Right. How was it to see so many of your kids at the same place recently?
At first, I was really focusing on the organizational part of the day, because I wanted to make sure everybody felt comfortable with it. There were people from Belgium, Holland, and Germany, and I was afraid they wouldn't get along. But after a while, people who spoke the same language sat next to each other and it was a pleasant day. The kids were introduced to me, but after five minutes they started playing with each other and I sort of lost their interest. It was like: "Oh, that's Daddy. Now what else can we do?" It was what I expected. In the afternoon, it became nappy time for most of them, so everybody left. Parents later told me they thought it was a nice way for them to meet each other and for their kids to meet me.

Aren't you afraid to grow really attached to those kids while not being able to see them all the time?
I like to hear how it goes with the kids and I befriended some mothers. But when the babies are born, I don't have feelings of fatherhood. I'm a cold one at that. That's why I can cope with the hardships of sperm donation. And it's also different, because I'm a guy. A woman feels the child kicking and growing for nine months, I just give away two hundred million sperm cells. I can't wave goodbye to all of them.

Are you sure about that?
Well, not entirely. Last year, one of the women who carried my baby gave labor early. The child grew out of the womb and was born after 20 weeks of conception. It lived for one hour. When the mother called me up to tell me, I cried for the first time since my brother's funeral. I was five when he died. Fortunately, some of the mothers of my children were there for me. The ones who became my friends.

Do you have a girlfriend?
No. I'm a shy man, so I never approach women on my own. I don't go out much either, so there's no meeting women that way. I also believe in love at first sight, which makes it even more difficult. Some women I donated sperm to fell in love with me, but the feeling was never mutual. ∎

ROCCO CASTORO

OH SHIT!

Who's Number One at Holding Number Two?

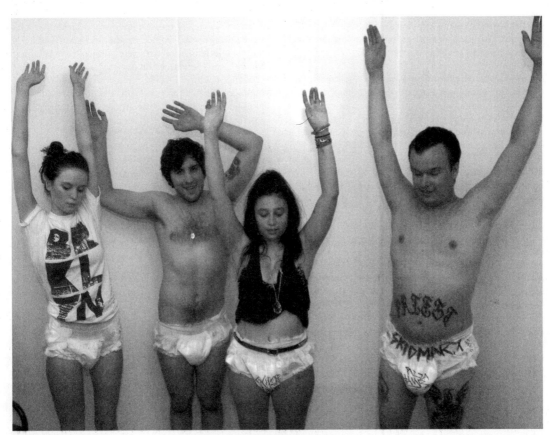

Photos by Jess Williamson

So I guess some guy apparently went 102 days without taking a dump. But a) he was critically constipated, and b) *Uncle John's Bathroom Book of Extraordinary Facts and Bizarre Information* is not exactly reliable reference material. Still, it got us thinking about shitting, about not shitting, and also about torturing people by making them hold in their shit for as long as they can. That led to deliberations about physiology and mind over intestinal matter that carried on into the wee hours. We simply had to know if we could convince a few strangers to put on diapers and swallow a bunch of laxatives and have a contest to see who would shit first (or last). And you know what? We did it!

THE PREMISE

Over the course of eight hours in a balmy living room, two guys and two ladies consume the following "natural" laxatives: a saltwater tonic, tea, bad Mexican food, cigarettes, coffee, beer, rum, and caffeinated soda. Peeing is allowed, but defecation must take place off the toilet (an official excreta ref was present throughout the event to ensure no BMs took place covertly). Whoever shits first loses. Safety concerns warranted adult diapers and a vinyl dollar-store bed cover for the futon.

THE PARTICIPANTS

ALEXANDRA, 22

How often do you crap?
I poop about every other day, usually around lunchtime at work. Sometimes it's in the morning. The last time I went was yesterday.

What kind of stuff gets you going?
Beer and malt liquor.

On average, how does it check out?
Most of the time it's pretty good—at least a couple of solid logs.

When was the last time you shit your pants?
A few years ago I was driving cross-country with my roommate and during a pit stop I got some potato skins with cheese and bacon. When we got back on the road my stomach started acting up and I felt like I might be coming down with the runs. I let go of this gurgling fart in the car and my friend was like, "That sounded disgusting. I bet you got shit in your underwear." But I didn't think I did until we pulled over at this gas station and I was like, "Fuck!" For whatever reason I didn't want to throw them away so I just rolled them up and put them in a plastic bag. I had diarrhea and was on my period for three days after, and actually ended up having to wear them again because I messed up another pair even worse.

Are you shit-phobic now?
When I was little I had a pooping phobia. I would hold it for a really long time. Once at camp I didn't shit for five days because I was afraid someone would hear me using the toilet. But I'm over it. I fart freely all the time now.

MATT, 21

When's the last time you did some work atop the Oval Office?
It was this morning at two. My normal schedule is to go somewhere between 11 PM and 3 AM. Most of the time it happens right before my bedtime shower.

Describe the last few stools you passed.
I would say they looked healthy. They were mostly brown with some tints of yellow.

When was the last time you had an "accident"?
During the first week of college something happened when I was on a date with this girl. We went out to dinner before coming back to my place to hang out. I had to cut one so I did, but all of a sudden my pants felt soupy. I immediately excused myself to "the bathroom" and ran to my backyard, pulled off my underwear, used them to wipe my ass, then threw them over the fence. I came back inside as if nothing happened and we ended up sharing a bed that night. She didn't smell it but was curious as to why I wasn't wearing underwear. I told her, "It's laundry day."

What is the longest you've gone without sweet relief?
At least a couple days when I was on a road trip a little while ago, but it wasn't a problem. I do squat thrusts from time to time and those build your hind muscles to maximum potential. It's like a Kegel exercise for your asshole.

GRACE, 19

How regular are you? Don't be shy.
It happens pretty much every day or every other day.

What kinds of substances make you produce feces?
Whiskey seems to do the trick.

Are we talking firm or loose?
It's pretty normal, I think, but it's not like I have anything to compare it to. Not too hard and not too soft. I don't really check it out afterward.

Do you remember the last time you lost control?
The last time I really shit my pants in public was in kindergarten, but one of the first times I drank alcohol was in eighth grade and that night I woke up on the toilet with every type of excrement and bodily fluid all over the bathroom. I don't know if that really counts but some shit definitely fell onto the floor and probably my clothes. It was the worst hangover I've ever had.

Yep, that counts. Did your parents find out?
No, because I stayed up until four in the morning to clean everything up.

Can you give any tips on delaying the inevitable?
I have a phobia of pooping in public, so if I'm outside of my element I'll be too scared to just let it happen. Even when I've been on vacations with my family and in hotel rooms I just hold it in.

JACOB, 21

What's your usual ordure regimen?

I go about once a day, usually at night. I guess you could say I'm a night pooper.

Do certain things set you off?

Usually I have to shit after I drink—especially hard liquor. After a few drinks I'll almost always take a large dump. Coffee is another culprit, but I don't drink it as often.

In a spectrum with expulsive dysentery at one end and anus-lacerating, petrified dung at the other, where do your droppings fall?

I'd say they're moderate. It's mostly soft serve, definitely closer to diarrhea. It doesn't always stay together once it hits the water.

Tell us about the last time you soiled yourself.

About a year ago, when I was a sophomore in college, I had just bought some new underwear and I was kind of amped on them. They were blue and pretty rad. I was just sitting at my computer working and leaned to the side to let a fart out, which ended up being a pretty heavy shart. I thought I might've just farted really hard but I checked my pants and it looked like one of those fun-size Snickers bars was melting in there. I ended up leaving the undies in my bathroom for like a week and a half, because I thought I was going to clean and rewear them but it didn't happen.

Are you good at staving off poo?

Yeah, I think I can hold it in. I ride bikes a lot so I've got these impenetrable butt cheeks.

THE MAIN EVENT

Things started off with a nice spread of Mexican food: nachos, guacamole, a burrito, rice and beans, an enchilada, salsa, and a couple of tacos. We didn't want to feed them too much—just enough to get things percolating. Overeating can block the small intestine for hours before digestion occurs.

The grub came from a place renowned for its vile, colon-expanding mouth garbage—a takeout Mexican restaurant run by illegal Chinese immigrants whose menu brags about their automated tortilla-making machine. Surprisingly, everyone wolfed it down in what seemed like an attempt to psych each other out.

Next up was the first of two saltwater flushes. It's supposed to work like a top-down enema, completely sand-blasting your gullet. Each serving consisted of two tablespoons of gray Celtic sea salt diluted in 32 ounces of purified water. This suggestion came from someone on the Master Cleanse who claimed she had to be near a bathroom for at least a couple hours after guzzling it.

Straws were provided as our research found it was the easiest way to choke down what basically amounts to a liter of seawater. Matt finished within four minutes, followed by Jacob, and then the girls. Everyone agreed it was awful.

Immediately after the purging solution, the players engaged in some stomach-relaxing calisthenics. An article on the internet listed tummy rubbing, raised-arm swinging, toe touches, and the Bhujangasana (cobra) yoga position as ways to loosen up the guts when constipated.

Right before dinner we brewed up a pot of Traditional

Medicinals Smooth Move laxative tea, steeping both the chocolate and organic varieties. This stuff is supposed to take about eight hours to kick in, so we made enough for four servings apiece to maximize its effectiveness. From this point on, we administered it every two hours.

Following our first teatime everyone sat around for half an hour to let things settle. The guys claimed to have intermittent gurgling while Grace and Alexandra said everything felt OK down there. Matt's postulation was that taking a leak would reflexively unclench the anus and cause a brown waterfall.

After our little break, we soldiered on with coffee and smokes. Three of our contestants went for a piss within 15 minutes after finishing their java. Matt's hypothesis was disproven when nary a turdlet was left behind.

Sometime near the end of hour four, Jacob reported feeling "something" and started with the shivers. He conceded that a few bullets were in the chamber but remained

confident in his urge-suppression abilities. Matt also reported a cavitary sensation, while the gals were steadfast in their refusal that anything was coming down the pipe.

Hours five and six featured more laxative tea and a second saltwater cleanse, along with more cigarettes, a tobacco-leaf-wrapped blunt, and beer. Then, for 30 min-

utes, it was a YouTubed Sweatin' to the Oldies workout. Afterward, they "rested" on their right sides (a position that supposedly encourages swift passages through the viscera). Jacob said he felt sick and he farted in Grace's face numerous times.

With dawn rapidly approaching and no perceivable shitstorms on the horizon, we decided to focus on boozing. It was the consensus that anyone could easily take the kids to the pool at this point, but no one was willing to go first.

As the eighth-cum-eleventh hour approached we resolved to do everything possible to empty their breadbaskets. This included a final dose of laxative tea, more alcohol, exercise, and turning the entrants against each other. Round-robin stomach presses seemed to cause some serious discomposure, unleashing a barrage of foul wind from at least three of our participants.

Sensing that someone was close to striking brown gold, we asked them to assume the classic squatting-in-the-woods position for the final 10 minutes. Jacob seemed to be struggling to maintain.

Approximately five minutes later, the idea was jokingly brought up that the winner should be whoever was able to shit before the closing bell. Jacob immediately perked up and said, "That won't be a problem!" Without any further discourse or prompting, he relaxed his colon, pulled the trigger on a machine gun of flatulence, and produced a nugget.

The oily, melted-crayon-stub excretion wasn't much, but Jacob assured us lots more was on its way as he hastily retreated to the toilet and punished it for our sins.

The next day everyone checked in. Matt said, "My asshole is like a melting universe." Alexandra reported "peeing out of my butt all day." Grace claimed to be swimming in a sea of bodily fluids. Our vanquisher, Jacob, spent a good three intermittent hours on the john and was worried about shitting himself during his job as a delivery boy. Each one vowed to hate us for eternity. ∎

TIERNEY CEARA

WORKING GIRL

Selling Yourself by the Ounce

All around the world and since the dawn of time, pretty young girls have made money off the horny minds of older men. This usually involves stripping, walking the streets, or taking it up the ass on video. While all three of those things are fabulous I'm sure, most of the girls who do them hate their job, their dads, and themselves. Luckily for me I am pretty much a genius and have discovered a way to extract money from degenerate perverts with minimal degradation on my part. I don't even have to meet them, much less touch them.

You see, at the tender age of 17 I was randomly messaged online by a lonely pee drinker who had taken quite a liking to me after seeing my picture on facethejury.com. He would annoy me every day with questions about what kind of pantyhose I wear, how often I wear them, have I ever peed on a guy, would I please, please meet him and make him my human toilet, and so on. One day he told me my piss was sacred and that it should be bottled and sold to desperate piss consumers such as himself. So I called what I thought was his bluff and told him, fine, he could buy my pee for $100. The poor loser couldn't have agreed quicker and I even threw in a pair of pantyhose for an extra $100. I have since discovered that there isn't much that comes out of me or grows off of me that I cannot harvest and sell to cyber-weirdoes all over America.

Since then I have made literally tens of thousands of dollars selling my toenail clippings, shit, piss, spit, puke, and just about anything else I can secrete from my pretty little orifices. Add in the healthy trade that I do in worn panties, hosiery, socks, and shoes, and I have learned almost everything there is to know about the seedy bottom-feeders of the fetish community.

I would like to share my vast wisdom with the rest of you girls out there. I'm sure you will find it beneficial in whatever you choose to be in life. Or at least it will make for a good conversation starter at your next family gathering. There are three main types of sad perverts who buy my body's waste products online. I've broken them down here, along with an excerpt of a real email from a representative of each wonderfully disgusting subgenus.

PANTY PERVERTS

Do you think you might smell bad, you know, down *there*? If so, it could be time to start reaping the ego-boosting benefits of selling your vagina-goo-soaked panties. As a rule of thumb, the more pussy discharge and skanky ass smell you can embed in them the better. Panties are the most common item I sell. What's great is that you don't have to show even a little tittie to get into their wallets because nothing pitches their tent like a candid, inconspicuous, cotton-crotch panty shot. Easy as pie. Most buyers are relatively normal perverts, while others are like this:

Ceara, I am so excited right now that my tiny little boner is ready to pop out of my little underwear. Of course you wouldn't see it cause it's about like a baby carrot or a Vienna sausage. It still squirts a lot of jizz though. I know when it has been about two days since my last whack off I can get enough out of it to almost fill my mouth. MMMmm I love eating cum!!! I really hope you can make some VERY RAUNCHY ASS SMELLING PANTIES!!!! I LOVE STINKY TASTY SKIDMARKS!!!!!

Thanks, Peewee

These pink mesh nylon panties sold for $67 to a sad little man in Florida who refers to himself as my "#1 admirer with a HOT HOT online crush."

These pink satin fullbacks sold for $80. Panty perverts love big soft girl undies. It makes for a smoother ride when they're polishing their little soldier's helmet. Barf.

White see-through mesh panties; sold for $76. Facedown/ass-up is always a great selling strategy.

I exchanged these cheap three-year-old sneakers plus a bag of used tampons for a new cute pink pair of expensive running shoes.

Here's the photo I used.

FOOT FREAKS

You would think a guy with a foot fetish is potentially perfect boyfriend material. He gives frequent foot rubs, pays for pedicures, and loves shoe shopping. Unfortunately not all foot freaks limit themselves to these tasteful traits. Every guy who loves feet is submissive to a degree—some to the point that they'd put up with a bitch of a girlfriend just because she gives amazing foot jobs and others to the degree that they'd pay money to lick dogshit off the bottom of a girl's shoe and thank her afterward for the privilege. A pair of pretty feet has the advantage of selling any number of worthless things:

Ceara,

Hi Pookie!! As promised, I have sent the $67 via PayPal. I was so excited that I almost couldn't wait until payday got here!! It is a privilege to smell the stinky feet of a girl like you!! I am going to the athletic store and I am going to buy a headband so that I can strap your little socks against my nose in a hands-free manner. Then I am going to fantasize about being tied spread-eagle to your bed, with you forcing me to sniff your stinky feet, while giving me a hand-job!!!!! BOING!! Now I've gone and done it!! I've got a stiffy in my pants right now as I type this!! See what you do to me, Ceara?! You are an incredibly desirable little hottie-tottie!!!!

Love ya baby girl!! B.W.

What a winner, right? This guy was also the happy purchaser of my special blend Princess Toe Jam Spread. To make it, I got a big container of cheap jam, smeared it all over my feet, and then scraped it off into little four-ounce jars and sold them for $30 apiece. He told me that he made peanut-butter-and-toe-jam sandwiches out of it and ate them with his unsuspecting coworkers during his lunch break.

HUMAN TOILETS

There's not much I can say in defense of human toilets, as I will never understand how anyone could get a boner over eating prepackaged shit. Regardless, the moment I discovered there were men out there this sexually deranged and (most likely) emotionally damaged, I was kicking myself for just flushing all that poop down the actual toilet. Never again!

Ceara,

I am plenty knowledgeable about all aspects of FEmale products and consider myself a true connoisseur. It is no lie or exaggeration when I say I've consumed in excess of two tons of FEmale excrement over the past 42 years. If I included non-excrement stuff, it would be nearer to four tons. YOU can see that this is no passing fancy for me. I live to be a toilet for GIRLs. Life would truly be pointless if I were cut off. In the past 42 years I've invested over $150,000 in my shit-eating pursuits. Naturally that's money well spent, but as my life runs out, I want my final days to be a big and glorious event. From YOUR point of view, I'm just a decrepit and gross old shit eater, and my only worth is: I'm someone to shag as many bucks from as YOU can, but in my mind, I've paid my dues and put in my time, and as grand as it all was, I want only the best from now on. When I'm sitting around in my rocker on the porch of some old folks home, I want to remember the faces of GIRLs like YOU and let my imagination fill in the odors and taste YOU were willing to share with me. BTW, I also like sucking on and eating used menstrual products, eating drain hair, finger and toenails, belly button lint, boogers, used band-aids, hacked up stuff, snot from when YOU're sick, or anything else YOUR perfect FEmale body can produce. Bye for now.

YOUR toilet, turdboy (aka kopkop)

PS: YOU said my email almost made YOU vomit. I'm sorry about that, but if YOU do vomit, please try to do it into the container of poo. I will pay extra for it. Thanks.

In conclusion, I'm pretty thankful for discovering how much money and free entertainment can be made from the excessively masochistic and socially inept. I've found it to be an amazing way of relieving stress and improving self-esteem. I would recommend it to all girls, except that might mean less money for me. So ladies, keep working that stripper pole. Thanks. ■

My ex-boyfriend's mom bought me this red thong for Christmas a while back and it really creeped me out. I sold it to some degenerate for $64 so he could cover it in his ball snot. Now it's not so weird.

Glittery spandex thong sold for $92 to a nut who simply adores the smell of butthole and dirty feet and indulges in his fetish via wrapping used socks and panties around his face with a head strap. He calls me his "Pookie-Licious Snuggle-Bunny."

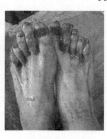

You probably think your grandma has the best recipe for jam in the world, but I bet she can't sell a four-ounce jar of it for $30.

Hot-pink see-through fullbacks sold for $59. Nice and easy.

The profits just pour out of me, basically.

QUINN MORRISON

WE COULD BE THE NEW WIND!

One Small Girl Covers the Internet in Farts

Recently, while innocently perusing YouTube and—swear to God—not looking for anything raunchy, I came across this girl who posts tons of videos of herself farting and subsequently cracking herself up. That's it, just farts 'n' laughs from a cute young woman in California. But then I took a look at the number of views she was getting and I was blown away. (Get it? Blown away?) But seriously folks, Jacki here rips many a one on the web and then thousands of people (mostly horny guys) watch it and tell her how beautiful she is, how great her farts must smell, how they want to get farted on by her, and just how superduper farts are in general. I had to know what lay behind the clouds of gas, so I contacted Fart Girl. She is now my new best friend.

Vice: Is it true that when you were kids, you and your sister made a fart mixtape that you'd listen to on family road trips?
Jacki: Yeah, farting was a huge part of our relationship, which I know sounds really weird for two sisters. The thing is, my dad was a hillbilly born in a lean-to in Tennessee and he really wanted some boys to, you know, go fishing and hunting and to cut the cheese with. So along with being on the soccer, basketball, and softball teams, we were on the "fart with dad" squad.

Was your dad a serious farter?
Well, our family used to have this old brown and white velvety Barcalounger-type thing that was "Dad's spot." I know some gay fart fetishists would have paid some serious bucks for that thing on eBay since my dad would basically sit there from the time he got home from work at 5 PM until bedtime at 11. He ripped so many long nasty ones on that thing.

What about shit? Were turds a larf with your family?
Yes, so actually it was a fart- and poo-positive household. They have always been a source of comedy. My dad is known as the guy who, if he visits your house, will without fail clog up the toilet. We actually have a video of him using a snake plumbing tool to unclog my grandparents' toilet in Texas. In fact, he broke one snake with his bricklike poo and had to run to the hardware store to get another one.

So you and your sister would just hang around farting?
The summers would pass with my sister and I watching reruns of *Gidget* and surprising each other as we lay on the couch with a big fart on the head. Also, my sister and I are quite different people. Despite my dad, I turned into a girly-girl who does ballet. My sis remained a tomboy. So farting was something we always had in common and could share with a laugh despite our differences.

What did your mom think of all this fart frivolity?
It was a source of some tension in our household. While my dad was a fart proponent, my mom is a little four-foot-eleven Vietnamese lady who always tried to teach us to be ladylike. I mean, she even named me after Jacqueline Kennedy. She always had makeup on, her hair done, always in an "outfit."

But the thing is, my mom was a closet farter. Once in a while, she used to cup her hand over her crack to catch a fart, and then she'd release it into one of our faces! So while most of the time she would give us a nasty look if we cut one, I think the irresistible natural comic nature of farting would overtake her. She had some nasty ones too. I think it was because she used to eat this fish called mudfish that she had to cook in the garage on a hot plate because it smelled so bad. It smelled even worse coming out!

When did you first make the move to videotaping farts?
It was a total whim. This guy who I had met in Paris came to visit me, and I told him about YouTube. You know, the French are not as up-to-date as we are about some things. When I was at his place in 2006, the poor *cornichon* still

had dial-up. Anyhow, I told him that anyone can put whatever kind of *connerie* [stupidity, bullshit] on YouTube and there's a chance that out of total randomness they could become famous. So we searched for farts as an example and of course found tons of clips. We liked to watch the clips of dudes lighting their farts on fire! After that, whenever I had to rip one he would record it. Those first few clips of me farting with him laughing in the background are the beginning. He recorded them on his camera phone so the quality sucks. It was funny too because he said that before me he had never heard a girl fart. Alas, tender is love. I kicked him to the curb eventually.

Can you explain your name on YouTube?
It's *Peteuse*, which is French for a farting or gassy girl. *Pet* (pronounced "peh") is the noun for "fart." *Peteuse* is a girl, *peteur* is a boy.

Oh yeah, like Le Pétomane, that legendary French vaudeville fart performer. (Anybody reading this who doesn't know about him should google his name right now.) It seems that lot of dudes get boners from watching your fart videos. What do you think of that?
I don't understand it completely, but I think lots of fetishes have to do with having access to something forbidden or something that a woman usually is embarrassed about or tries to hide. I'm involved in the foot-fetish community. I sell my worn-out ballet shoes to guys who like to smell stinky feet. Women are often embarrassed about their stinky feet and also by farting. Lots of dudes get off on being privy to those things, I guess.

What about all the comments on your videos? They get a wee bit dirty.
I don't get offended. It's a fantasy for men, and I'm a bit of an exhibitionist so I like the idea of guys wanking to thoughts of me. Overall, though, it's just comedy. I still watch my and my sister's clips and laugh my ass off. There is a dom element to this fart-fetish thing: face sitting, ass worship, and such. Some sub guys want to be humiliated by being farted on by a dominant woman. But if I had to sit on someone's face and cut a big one, I would just bust up laughing. I couldn't do the whole "You like that, you little needledick, suck it up and smell it" routine.

There are a thousand types of farts. Can you break down a few for our readers?
My personal favorites are the Chuck Yeager, the Saigon, and the SBD.

What's the Chuck Yeager?
They, of course, break the sound barrier. This is the kind that after you rip it, you are completely amazed at your-

self, wondering where all that gas fit inside your organs— especially if you are on the little side like me. These farts often have accompanying pain and necessitate a shorts check. They are usually either pointed and sharp sounding or long and bassy. I've done an eight-second-long Chuck Yeager fart in jeans that almost knocked me over. It's in one of my videos. In high school I did a Yeager when I was hanging out with my friends on this big grassy hill on campus. Everyone turned around and looked—this is a hill that is like 100 yards from one side to the other—and I acted all shocked and turned to my best friend Leah and yelled, "Leah! That's gross!" She never forgave me for that.

What about the Saigon?
If you've ever heard Vietnamese people speak, you'll notice that they have some interesting sounds that we really don't make as English speakers. Viet language is multitonal, with lots of *guh gu gu guh buk buh buk aww!* glottal stops and ups and downs in tones. These farts are like what you would hear if you went to a community meeting in Saigon, or in some Vietnamese community and all the members were pissed off about something, like thugs breaking into their Toyota Camrys. These farts often come out first as a high-pitched airy squeak, then continue on to some kind of machine-gun sounds, then a pig squeal, then a long chunky groan. They are often the funniest because you're like, "When did my ass learn to speak Vietnamese?"

SBD is Silent but Deadly. Right?
Yes. I hate to be cliché, but these are the best because they are your little secret. These are the kind that you let out little by little because you think if you just push it out it might be a Chuck Yeager. Sometimes they're kind of wet. But then it just snakes out, slowly lisping and you can feel all the air between your cheeks. Then about two seconds later you're trying to run away from yourself. These are good at the grocery store, the gym, or in the car with a friend (awesome). An SBD in church would be funny too. I do them all the time in ballet class, and sometimes it's hard to get away from the smell because I'm at the barre doing exercises. I've never confirmed whether the girl behind me has ever smelled them but... she has to have. I know she hates me.

What food leads to the biggest farts?
Indian food, by far. My current formula is a) channa masala, b) palak paneer, and c) rice and pappadams. The channa masala has garbanzo beans so you could just say it's the beans that give it to me, but I eat beans by themselves all the time and they don't turn me into a farting champ like this formula does. I think it is the spices, the grease, and the rice that do it. Oh yeah, and they smell REALLY bad! ■

ANITA CRAPPER

WHOSE FARTS SMELL WORSE?

Carnivores or Herbivores?

All in the name of science. Photos by James Stafford

We hired a male model from the internet and got two girls who work in porn to fart on his face twice. They did this once while wearing jeans and once while wearing skimpy underwear.

After he'd received the double blast, our model, a 24-year-old named Dave, would attempt to deduce which farter was a meat-eater and which was a vegetarian.

THE FARTERS

SUBJECT 1: THE CARNIVORE

Jasmine is a 28-year-old model from South London who has a sideline in being a dominatrix for hire.

"I don't really stick to one fing," she admitted. "I can do girl-next-door, fetish, or pissing on a guy."

REASON FOR EATING MEAT: "I'm a meat eater but I have been a vegetarian in the past. At that time I was like: 'Ooh! Killing animals. Nah!' Back then there wasn't a lot of variety for vegetarians so I used to eat boiled cabbages and potatoes. But the reason why I got back into eating meat was that I walked past a KFC and thought, 'Bloody hell, I need to eat that!'"

PREVIOUS FARTING EXPERIENCE: "Garlic makes me fart a lot. Things like Indian make me fart and smell funny. Brussels sprouts make you fart. I went out raving

one time and everybody had been eating brussels sprouts because it was Boxing Day. The day after Christmas is not good to go out raving because everybody's farting. That's my advice! Don't go raving on Boxing Day!"

TODAY'S FART PROGNOSIS: "I had oat porridge and some beans and garlic. Now I'm eating a bit of a Peperami as well. It's really smoky!"

SUBJECT 2: THE HERBIVORE

Sophie Calvert, age 22, is a self-confessed "naughty girl who takes her clothes off and does naughty things with men and women."

REASONS FOR BEING VEGETARIAN: "I decided to become vegetarian at university. I got really into health and fitness, then I found out I was an A blood type, which meant that vegetarianism would be perfect for me. I think vegetarians RULE! You just have to look at things like horses and gorillas. They exist on stuff like grapes and grass."

PREVIOUS FARTING EXPERIENCE: "Bean sprouts make me fart quite a bit! I've noticed since I became vegetarian that my bowel movements are much more regular, they don't smell as much, and I feel much lighter. Everything flows better, to be honest."

TODAY'S FART PROGNOSIS: "For breakfast I had

porridge and a delicious blueberry smoothie and just before I came I had an apricot-and-almond healthy-eating bar."

ROUND ONE

Dave is blindfolded and the girls take turns farting right in his face. Meat-eating Jasmine is first.

The atmosphere is pretty tense at this point, not unlike the silence before a bombing raid. Everybody is waiting with bated breath for a sharp popping to punctuate the calm.

To everybody's surprise, Jasmine performs a totally silent fart. Slowly her scent fills Dave's flared nostrils. As his brain reacts to the chemical change within his nasal passage he tells the assembled throng, "Well, I would say that this is the meat eater. [Correct!] It smells like autumn leaves. Or nuts. I have to say it doesn't smell bad at all."

With that, Sophie gingerly takes the place of Jasmine, bends over, and, like her carnivorous counterpart, lets forth a silent fart just inches from Dave's lips.

Dave takes it in and responds, "Mmm. This is like candle wax. Like candles melting after a meal. Or paper burning. Yes. This is not bad at all. Not like a fart at all. I definitely prefer this fart to the first.

ROUND ONE: Carnivore 0 / Herbivore 1

ROUND TWO

Free of the trappings of their denim jeans, the girls' farts now have only a thin covering of delicate lace to travel through from their rectums to Dave's nose. Couple that factor with the news that they've been gulping down more bean sprouts, and the air of anticipation for round two is like the gay enclosure at Wimbledon, Andy Roddick vs. Thomas Johansson, match point.

First up this time is Sophie, who saunters over and lets rip yet another totally silent fart.

"Hmm," muses Dave. "This is more like rubber, or a burning tire. I can't tell what food it is. Well, it's probably a bit cliché to say this, but I'd go for sprouts."

Spent of gas, Sophie totters off and Jasmine enters the fray, bending over and letting loose the final toot of the tournament. Once again, to the amazement (and not a little disappointment) of all gathered, it is silent!

Dave's face wrinkles. "This is like a cigarette. It... smells like fire... a burning fire. This is more pungent, this one... And yes, there's no noise at all. No audible sound. Still, I have to say that my favorite fart is the first."

RESULT: Carnivore 0 / Herbivore 2

OFFICIAL RESULT: MEAT EATERS MAKE STINKIER FARTS THAN VEGETARIANS.

THE AFTERMATH

While the girls get dressed, we sit down with Dave as he goes over the last few frenetic minutes.

Ever the gentleman, he concedes, "Well, first off, I've definitely smelled a lot worse. They were certainly not as bad as ones I've made. I'm glad it wasn't two blokes' farts I had to smell. To be honest, my favorite farts were the veggie ones. Like I say, neither were unpleasant but the meat ones were a... less nice smell. Put it that way. As for the veggie ones, they might not have been farts at all. It could have been what I described it as—autumn leaves. It could have been a scented candle.

"I would say to the ladies, if you want to keep your farts smelling nice, go vegetarian!"

Jasmine the meat eater's reaction? "He must have a cold."

BONUS ROUND!

Further proof that vegetarians who maintain a balanced diet have a healthier digestive system than dominatrixes who eat KFC came when both the girls were instructed to sit down on the toilet and make a BM so that Dave could test that too.

Jasmine tried for about five minutes, but was unable to pass a pebble. Sophie, whose personal maxim is "Vegetarians RULE!" emerged from the john with a look of accomplishment on her face and two cute little lady parcels in the toilet bowl.

So, Dave, how is it?
"Well, the shit's very pale compared to what mine would be. It's almost pale green in color. It sank, but I don't know what that means. There's hardly any smell at all. I wouldn't call it pleasant, but it isn't that bad."

In light of all this, would you consider going vegetarian?
No, because I need the protein for bodybuilding. You can get protein from other sources, but not as efficiently. Vegetarians can go on about protein, but you show me 100 grams of chicken breast next to 100 grams of vegetables. Like for like? It would never compare.

OK, OK. ∎

Illustration by Nick Gazin